D0168729

STEVE FALLON
CHRIS PITTS
NICOLA WILLIAMS

PARIS
CITY GUIDE

INTRODUCING PARIS

As iconic as an icon can get, the much-snapped Eiffel Tower (p116)

JAN STROMME

Well informed, eloquent and oh-so-romantic, the Ville-Lumière (City of Light) is a philosopher, a poet, a crooner. As it always has been, Paris is a million different things to a million different people.

Paris has all but exhausted the superlatives that can reasonably be applied to any city. Notre Dame and the Eiffel Tower – at sunrise, at sunset, at night – have been described countless times, as have the Seine and the subtle (and not-so-subtle) differences between the Left and Right Banks. But what writers have been unable to capture is the grandness and even the magic of this incomparable city.

Paris probably has more familiar landmarks than any other city in the world. As a result, first-time visitors often arrive in the French capital with all sorts of expectations: of grand vistas, of intellectuals discussing weighty matters in cafés, of romance along the Seine, of naughty nightclub revues, of rude people who won't speak English. If you look hard enough, you can probably find all of those. But another approach is to set aside the preconceptions of Paris and explore the city's avenues and backstreets as if the tip of the Eiffel Tower or the spire of Notre Dame wasn't about to pop into view at any moment.

You'll soon discover (as so many others have before you) that Paris is enchanting almost everywhere, at any time, even 'in the winter, when it drizzles' and 'in the summer, when it sizzles', as Cole Porter put it. And you'll be back. Trust us.

PARIS LIFE

Problem is, if you postpone your next trip to the City of Light for too long you might end up not recognising the place. While the Paris of Haussmann and Hugo and Toulouse-Lautrec is not – for better or worse – going to disappear overnight, the city is on the verge of redefining itself big time. President Nicolas

> 'The city is on the verge of redefining itself big time.'

Sarkozy's 10 able-bodied architects, whom he asked several years ago to help create *Le Grand Paris* (Greater Paris), have unveiled their plans. Predictably the ideas run the gamut from the sublime to the ridiculous, but all involve expansion beyond the bd Périphérique, the ring road 'moat' that separates Fortress Paris and its two million mostly well-heeled residents from the six million living in the usually unspeakable *banlieues* (suburbs), which gave then Interior Minister Sarkozy such a *mal de tête* (headache) back in 2005. The plans are, well, grand, with light-rail systems looping around the city's periphery, and eyesore train tracks submerged below parkland. It's not something those living *entre les murs* (within the walls, ie in central Paris) are looking upon kindly.

But the most ambitious scheme of all would involve the creation of a 'maritime metropolis' (unlike most other successful world-class cities, Paris does not have easy access to a port) by linking Paris by one-hour high-speed train with a newly constructed port called Paris Normandy at Le Havre. Sarkozy's own trip to the city 200km northwest of the capital proved to be his very own road to Damascus. Recalling a phrase attributed to his idol, Napoleon Bonaparte, the president gushed: 'Paris, Rouen, Le Havre – a single city with the Seine as the main street.' Pardon? But who knows? Before long we may all be singing 'I love Paris–Rouen–Le Havre in the springtime, I love Paris–Rouen–Le Havre in the fall...'

The café still plays a pivotal role in Parisian life

HIGHLIGHTS

①

ART PORTFOLIO

With more than 100 museums in Paris, there's something here for every interest, however obscure. And art is not just 'bullion' stashed away in safe houses. It can also be found out on the streets and down in the metro.

②

③

❶ Musée de l'Orangerie
Monet's sublime *Décorations des Nymphéas* (Water Lilies) are housed in two purpose-built rooms (p77).

❷ Palais de Tokyo
This fine art-deco 'palace' exhibits ephemeral artwork and installations meant to engage the viewer (p120).

❸ Artists in Montmartre
Art takes to the streets – literally – throughout Paris, but especially up in Montmartre (p132).

❹ Musée d'Orsay
This erstwhile train station contains some of the world's most important works by impressionists and postimpressionists (p107).

❺ Louvre Pyramid
Lambasted when it opened in 1989, IM Pei's Grande Pyramide (Great Pyramid) welcomes all and sundry to the Louvre (p70).

❻ Musée Rodin
The work of France's greatest sculptor is as fresh and modern as it was in the 19th century (p111).

WILL SALTER

IZZET KERIBAR

NEIL SETCHFIELD

5

JEAN-BERNARD CARILLET

FOOD & WINE

It is said that the French think mainly about two things: what they eat and what they drink. And an inordinate amount of time is spent thinking about, talking about and consuming lunch and dinner – matched with a suitable wine, of course.

TRAVEL DIVISION IMAGES / ALAMY

MARTIN MOOS

KATHRYN KLEINMAN / GETTY

❶ Classic Eating
Parisians are faithful rather than fickle when it comes to things comestible, and old favourites never die (p239).

❷ Contemporary Eating
The latest buzz word on the Paris dining scene is the *néo-bistro* (new bistro): small, informal, outstanding (p214).

❸ Boulangeries
They say that a Parisian will eat bread with bread, and there's no shortage of choices at most bakeries (p215).

❹ Wine
Beef with Bordeaux, shellfish with Champagne, foie gras with Sauternes – Parisians are always in search of the perfect match (p241).

❺ Cheese
The choice on offer at a *fromagerie* (cheese shop) in Paris can be overwhelming (p215).

❻ Pâtisseries
Parisians love *sucreries* (sweet things) and neon-coloured macaroons are the nibble of the moment (p235).

❼ Markets
Neighbourhood markets are very much a part of life in Paris (p222).

❽ Chalkboard Menu
A restaurant *carte* (menu) outside on *l'ardoise* (a chalkboard) will help you to decide before going in whether the place is to your taste and budget (p217).

❾ Steak-Frites
A standard feature of tourist menus in Paris, *steak-frites* is a deceptively simple but deliciously satisfying dish (p216).

WILL SALTER

WILL SALTER

OLIVER STREWE

BRUCE YUAN-YUE BI

DOMINIQUE CHARRIAU / GETTY

PARIS À LA MODE

Parisians always seem to look good – at work, at play, at rest. It has a lot to do with their inherent sense of style. When you see what's on offer in the boutiques, on the catwalk and after dark, you'll begin to feel a lot like them too.

WILL SALTER

❶ Les Grands Magasins
The big department stores, such as Le Bon Marché (p199) and Galeries Lafayette (p202), have excellent couture collections.

❷ Classic Labels
Chanel, Louis Vuitton, Agnès B, Jean-Paul Gaultier – Paris is awash with world-famous and coveted *étiquettes* (labels) (p203).

❸ Boutique Streets
The rue des Francs Bourgeois in the Marais is lined with fashionable boutiques selling clothing, hats, home furnishings and stationery (p205).

❹ Chic Shelter
Stylish boutique hotels can be found through-out Paris, but tried-and-true luxurious ones like the Hôtel Meurice (p328) are concentrated around the Louvre.

❺ Fashion under Glass
'Fashion is in the sky, in the street,' said Coco Chanel, and it's also in plenty of Parisian museums such as the Musée Galliera de la Mode de la Ville de Paris (p121).

JEAN-BERNARD CARILLET

BRUCE YUAN-YUE BI

WILL SALTER

SELECTA / ALAMY

PARIS MARAIS / ALAMY

6 'See & Be Seen' Scene
A choice seat on the terrace of a fashionable café along the bd St-Germain (p105) or the place des Vosges (p146) is like gold dust in fine weather.

7 Nights Out
A night at the opera (p306) – or theatre or ballet – followed by a late-night brasserie meal or cocktail is a classic night out in Paris.

8 Vintage Paris
The backstreets of Paris and the incomparable *passages couverts* (covered shopping arcades) (p182) offer a wealth of items for sale.

ANGELS IN THE ARCHITECTURE

The French capital is a treasure trove of architectural styles: from Roman arenas and Gothic cathedrals to postmodernist cubes and glass pyramids that not only look great but serve a function. You'll find interesting examples scattered throughout the city.

GLENN BEANLAND

❶ Cathédrale de Notre Dame de Paris
The most beautiful and complex Gothic sight in Paris, Notre Dame (p81) is one of the first ports of call for many visitors.

❷ Centre Pompidou
The 'bad boy' of exhibition spaces when it opened in 1977, this centre of art and culture (p78) and its 'insides-out' approach to architecture now has imitators worldwide.

❸ Musée du Quai Branly
The architectural 'accessory' of the moment, the 'vertical garden' puts new meaning to the phrase 'growing up in Paris' (p57).

❹ La Défense
This futuristic business and residential district (p175) to the west of the city centre is a happy hunting ground for both modern architecture and public art.

BRUCE YUAN-YUE BI

OLIVER STREWE

OLIVER STREWE

RACHEL LEWIS

JEAN-BERNARD CARILLET

NEIL SETCHFIELD

BRUCE YUAN-YUE BI

⑤ Guimard Metro Entrance
The noodle-like pale-green metalwork and glass canopy designed by art-nouveau architect Hector Guimard (1867–1942) still grace dozens of metro entrances (p103).

⑥ Basilique du Sacré Coeur
The view from the steps of this basilica (p132) on top of Butte de Montmartre (Montmartre Hill) is among the best in Paris.

⑦ Versailles
The sculpted and gilded château at Versailles (p354), southwest of Paris, is a monument to opulence and royal extravagance.

⑧ Panthéon
The world's largest secular 'church', this enormous mausoleum (p99) contains the mortal remains of the great and the good in French history.

❶ Couple in Park
Paris, Je t'aime (Paris, I Love You) – it's a phrase, a film and a lifetime commitment in the city for lovers (p53).

❷ Paris Plages
The Seine is at its most amusing when some of its banks are transformed into the 'beaches' of Paris Plages (p19).

❸ Dustless Highway
A tour boat glides quietly past the quays on the Seine (p401).

❹ Cycling in Town
The Vélib' scheme (p384) has put tens of thousands of bicycles within easy reach of most people, creating a city *à deux roues* (on two wheels).

WILL SALTER   WILL SALTER

EN PLEIN AIR

Paris loves the great outdoors, be it watching the world go by from the terrace of a café or horsing around in one of the city's many parks and gardens. A favourite playground is the Seine, especially in summer when some of its banks are transformed into the world's greatest 'urban beach'.

JOHN ELK III

CONTENTS

INTRODUCING PARIS 2

HIGHLIGHTS 4

THE AUTHORS 15

GETTING STARTED 16

BACKGROUND 23
History 23
Environment & Planning 38
Government & Politics 39
Media 40
Fashion 41
Language 43

THE ARTS &
ARCHITECTURE 45
The Arts 45
Architecture 55

NEIGHBOURHOODS 63
Itinerary Builder 66
Louvre & Les Halles 70
The Islands 81
Les Quartiers 85
The Latin Quarter 98
St-Germain & Invalides 105
Eiffel Tower & 16e 116
Champs-Élysées &
Grands Boulevards 124
Montmartre, Pigalle & 17e 132
Gare du Nord &
Canal St-Martin 139
Marais & Ménilmontant 145
Bastille & Gare de Lyon 156
Place d'Italie & Chinatown 163
Montparnasse & 15e 167
Beyond Central Paris 173
Walking Tours 178

SHOPPING 191
Louvre & Les Halles 192
The Islands 196
The Latin Quarter 197
St-Germain &
Invalides 198
Champs-Élysées &
Grands Boulevards 201
Montmartre,
Pigalle & 17e 203
Gare du Nord &
Canal St-Martin 204
Marais &
Ménilmontant 205
Bastille &
Gare de Lyon 210
Montparnasse & 15e 212
Beyond Central Paris 212

EATING 213
Louvre & Les Halles 221
The Islands 226
The Latin Quarter 227
St-Germain &
Invalides 231
Eiffel Tower & 16e 238
Champs-Élysées &
Grands Boulevards 240
Montmartre,
Pigalle & 17e 244
Gare du Nord &
Canal St-Martin 248
Marais &
Ménilmontant 252
Bastille &
Gare de Lyon 261
Place d'Italie &
Chinatown 268
Montparnasse & 15e 270
Beyond Central Paris 272

DRINKING	**275**		**SLEEPING**	**323**
Louvre & Les Halles	276		Louvre & Les Halles	328
The Islands	279		The Islands	330
The Latin Quarter	279		The Latin Quarter	330
St-Germain & Invalides	281		St-Germain & Invalides	333
Champs-Élysées & Grands Boulevards	283		Eiffel Tower & 16e	338
Montmartre, Pigalle & 17e	284		Champs-Élysées & Grands Boulevards	338
Gare du Nord & Canal St-Martin	285		Montmartre, Pigalle & 17e	340
Marais & Ménilmontant	286		Gare du Nord & Canal St-Martin	342
Bastille & Gare de Lyon	289		Marais & Ménilmontant	343
Place d'Italie & Chinatown	290		Bastille & Gare de Lyon	347
Montparnasse & 15e	291		Place d'Italie & Chinatown	349
Beyond Central Paris	292		Montparnasse & 15e	349

NIGHTLIFE & THE ARTS	**293**		**EXCURSIONS**	**353**
Cabaret	295		Versailles	354
Clubbing	296		Fontainebleau	362
Comedy	299		Vaux-le-Vicomte	366
Music	299		Chantilly	366
Dance	305		Senlis	370
Film	305		Chartres	370
Opera	306		Beauvais	375
Theatre	307		Giverny	376
			Auvers-sur-Oise	377
SPORTS & ACTIVITIES	**309**		Disneyland Resort Paris	380
Health & Fitness	310		Parc Astérix	381
Activities	311			
Spectator Sport	315		**TRANSPORT**	**383**
			DIRECTORY	**391**
GAY & LESBIAN PARIS	**317**		**LANGUAGE**	**411**
Shopping	318		**BEHIND THE SCENES**	**417**
Eating	318			
Drinking & Nightlife	318		**INDEX**	**421**
Sleeping	320			
Further Resources	320		**MAP LEGEND**	**432**

THE AUTHORS

Steve Fallon

Steve, who has worked on every edition of *Paris* and *France* except the first, was surrounded by things French from a very early age when his best friend's mother thought it would be a 'bunny day' (or was that a bonne idée?) to rock them in the same cradle. Convinced that Parisians were seriously devoid of a sense of humour after he and said best friend dropped water-filled balloons on the heads of passers-by from a 5e arrondissement hotel balcony at age 16, he nevertheless went back to the 'City of Light' five years later to complete a degree in French at the Sorbonne. Based in East London, Steve will be just one Underground stop away from Paris when Eurostar trains *finally* begin departing from Stratford. Steve was the coordinating author and wrote the Introducing Paris, Highlights, Getting Started, Background, Arts & Architecture, Gay & Lesbian Paris, Excursions and Transport chapters. He co-wrote the Neighbourhoods, Shopping, Eating, Drinking, Nightlife & the Arts, Sports & Activities and Sleeping chapters.

Chris Pitts

Christopher Pitts has lived in Paris since 2001. He first started writing about the city as a means to buy baguettes – and to impress a certain Parisian (it worked; they're now married with two kids). Over the past decade he has written for various publications, in addition to working as a translator and editor. Visit his website at www.christopherpitts.net. Chris wrote the Directory and co-wrote the Neighbourhoods, Shopping, Eating, Drinking, Nightlife & the Arts, Sports & Activities and Sleeping chapters.

Nicola Williams

Lonely Planet author, independent travel writer and editorial consultant Nicola Williams has lived in France and written about it for more than a decade. From her hillside house on the southern shore of Lake Geneva, it's a quick and easy hop to Paris, where she has spent endless years eating her way around and revelling in its extraordinary art and architecture – solo and *en famille*. Nicola has worked on numerous other titles for Lonely Planet, including *France, Discover France, Provence & the Côte d'Azur* and *The Loire*. She blogs at tripalong.wordpress.com and tweets @Trip along. Nicola wrote the Les Quartiers chapter and co-wrote the Neighbourhoods, Shopping, Eating, Drinking, Nightlife & the Arts, Sports & Activities and Sleeping chapters.

GETTING STARTED

Paris is a dream destination for countless reasons, but among the most obvious is that it requires so very little advance planning. Tourist literature abounds, maps are excellent and readily available, and the staff at tourist offices are often helpful and efficient. Paris is so well developed and organised that you don't have to plan extensively before your trip.

But this is fine only if your budget is unlimited, you don't have an interest in any particular period of architecture or type of music, and you'll eat or drink anything set down in front of you. This is Paris, one of the most-visited cities of the world, and depending on the time of year you'll find yourself in competition with either everybody or everybody and their brother. First and foremost, book your accommodation well ahead. And if you have specific interests – live big-name jazz, blockbuster art exhibitions, top-end restaurants – you'll certainly want to make sure that the things you expect to see and do will be available or open to you when you arrive. The key here is advance planning.

While Paris is a wonderful place to splurge on once-in-a-lifetime treats and adventures (p22), you'll be surprised at how much you can see for free (p96) or for a lot less than you'd expected. To plan a dream getaway to match your budget, see p22 for average costs and money-saving tips.

WHEN TO GO

As the old song says, Paris is lovely in springtime – however, winterlike relapses and heavy rains are not uncommon in the usually beautiful month of April. Though 'April in Paris' is the stuff of which dreams are made, the best months to visit are probably May and June – but early, before the hordes of tourists descend. Autumn is also pleasant – some people say the best months of the year to visit are September and October – but, of course, the days are getting shorter and in October hotel rooms are booked solid by businesspeople attending conferences and trade shows.

During winter Paris has all sorts of cultural events going on, while in summer the weather is warm – sometimes sizzling. In any case, in August Parisians flee for the beaches to the west and south, and many restaurateurs and café owners lock up and leave town too. It's true that you will find more places open in summer than even a decade ago, but it can still feel like a ghost town in certain districts. For further information on Paris' climate, see p392.

To ensure that your trip does (or perhaps does *not*) coincide with a public holiday, see p396. For a list of festivals and other events to plan around, see the following section.

ADVANCE PLANNING

Well ahead Try to book your accommodation months ahead, especially if it's high season and you want to stay in a boutique hotel like Mama Shelter (p348), a quirky little number like the Hôtel du 7e Art (p345), a 'find' such as the Hôtel Jeanne d'Arc (p345), or some place offering exceptional value for money such as the Hôtel Henri IV (p330). Take a look at some of the 'what's on' websites (p21) or the entertainment magazines *Pariscope* and *L'Officiel des Spectacles* (p294).

A month before you go If you're interested in serious fine dining at places like Le Grand Véfour (p221) or crowd-pleasers like Les Ombres (p238), book a table. Now is also the time to visit the Fnac and/or Virgin Megastore websites (p294) to get seats for a big-ticket concert, musical or play.

Two weeks before you go Blockbuster exhibitions at such venues as the Grand Palais (p129) or Centre Pompidou (p78) – or even a visit to the Louvre (p70) – can be booked in advance online via Fnac or Virgin Megastore for a modest fee. Sign up for an email newsletter via Expatica (p21) and check out some of those excellent tweets and blogs (p406). If you're interested in Paris' new crop of supper clubs (p262), think about booking now.

A day or two before you go Make sure your bookings are in order and you've followed all the instructions outlined in this chapter.

FESTIVALS & EVENTS

Innumerable festivals, cultural and sporting events and trade shows take place in Paris throughout the year; weekly details appear in *Pariscope* and *L'Officiel des Spectacles* (p294). You can also find them listed under 'What's On' on the website of the Paris Convention & Visitors Bureau (www.parisinfo.com). The following abbreviated list gives you a taste of what to expect throughout the year.

January & February

GRANDE PARADE DE PARIS
www.parisparade.com
The Great Paris Parade is relatively subdued after the previous night's shenanigans (p21). It takes place on the afternoon of New Year's Day, with marching and carnival bands, dance acts and so on. It used to be held in the small backstreets of Montmartre but has become so popular that it has spread to the Grand Boulevards, from rue du Faubourg St-Denis at bd Bonne Nouvelle in the 10e to place de la Madeleine in the 8e.

LOUIS XVI COMMEMORATIVE MASS
www.monuments-nationaux.fr
On the Sunday closest to 21 January, royalists and right-wingers attend a mass at the Chapelle Expiatoire (p130) marking the execution by guillotine of King Louis XVI in 1793.

FASHION WEEK
www.pretparis.com, in French
Prêt-à-porter, the ready-to-wear fashion salon held twice a year (in late January and in September), is a must for fashion buffs and takes place at the Parc des Expositions at Porte de Versailles in the 15e (metro Porte de Versailles), southwest of the city centre. For *haute couture* (high fashion)

and other collections, see Mode à Paris (www.modeaparis.com).

CHINESE NEW YEAR
www.paris.fr
Dragon parades and other festivities are held in late January or early February in two distinct Chinatowns: the smaller, more authentic one in the 3e, taking in rue du Temple, rue au Maire and rue de Turbigo (metro Temple or Arts et Métiers); and the larger, flashier one in the 13e in between porte de Choisy, porte d'Ivry and bd Masséna (metro Porte de Choisy, Port d'Ivry or Tolbiac).

SALON INTERNATIONAL DE L'AGRICULTURE
www.salon-agriculture.com
A 10-day international agricultural fair with produce and animals turned into starter and main-course dishes from all over France, held at the Parc des Expositions at Porte de Versailles in the 15e (metro Porte de Versailles) from late February to early March.

March–May

BANLIEUES BLEUES
www.banlieuesbleues.org, in French
The 'Suburban Blues' jazz, blues and R&B festival is held over five weeks in March and April in the northern suburbs of Paris, including St-Denis (p173), and attracts some big-name talent.

SALON DU LIVRE
www.salondulivreparis.com
The largest international book fair in France takes place over six days (usually Friday to Wednesday) in mid-March at the Parc des Expositions at Porte de Versailles in the 15e (metro Porte de Versailles).

DON'T LEAVE HOME WITHOUT...

- an adaptor plug for electrical appliances (if not from Europe)
- binoculars for viewing detail on churches and other buildings
- an immersion water heater or small kettle for an impromptu cup of tea or coffee
- tea bags if you need that cuppa since the French drink buckets of the herbal variety but not much of the black stuff
- premoistened towelettes or a large cotton handkerchief to soak in fountains and use to cool off in the hot weather
- sunglasses and sunblock, even in the cooler months
- swimsuit and thongs (flip-flops) for Paris Plage or swimming pool
- a Swiss Army knife, with such essentials as a bottle opener and strong corkscrew

PRINTEMPS DU CINÉMA
www.printempsducinema.com, in French
Selected cinemas across Paris offer film-goers a unique entry fee of €3.50 over three days (usually Sunday, Monday and Tuesday) sometime around 21 March.

FOIRE DU TRÔNE
www.foiredutrone.com, in French
This huge funfair, with 350 attractions spread over 10 hectares, is held on the pelouse de Reuilly of the Bois de Vincennes (metro Porte Dorée) for eight weeks from early April to late May.

MARATHON INTERNATIONAL DE PARIS
www.parismarathon.com, in French
The Paris International Marathon, usually held on the first or second Sunday of April, starts on the av des Champs-Élysées, 8e, and finishes on av Foch, in the 16e, attracting some 40,000 runners from around the world. The Semi-Marathon de Paris (www.semideparis.com) is a half-marathon held in early March; see the website for map and registration details.

FOIRE DE PARIS
www.foiredeparis.fr, in French
This huge modern-living fair, including crafts, gadgets and widgets as well as food and wine, is held from late April to early May at the Parc des Expositions at Porte de Versailles in the 15e (metro Porte de Versailles).

LA NUIT DES MUSÉES EUROPÉENNE
www.nuitdesmusees.culture.fr
Key museums across Paris throw open their doors at 6pm for one Saturday night in mid-May – the European Museums Night – and don't close till late. Some also organise special events.

ART DT-GERMAIN DES PRÉS
www.artsaintgermaindespres.com, in French
Some 70 galleries in the 6e come together in mid-May to showcase their top artists.

ATELIERS D'ARTISTES DE BELLEVILLE
www.ateliers-artistes-belleville.org, in French
More than 200 painters, sculptors and other artists in Belleville (metro Belleville) in the 10e open their studio doors to visitors over four days (Friday to Monday) in late May in

an event that has now been going for two decades.

FRENCH TENNIS OPEN
www.rolandgarros.com
The glitzy Internationaux de France de Tennis – the Grand Slam – takes place over two weeks from late May to early June at Stade Roland Garros (metro Porte d'Auteuil) at the southern edge of the Bois de Boulogne in the 16e.

June–August
FOIRE ST-GERMAIN
www.foiresaintgermain.org, in French
This six-week-long festival of concerts and theatre from early June to mid-July takes place on the place St-Sulpice, 6e (metro St-Sulpice) and various other venues in the quartier St-Germain.

FESTIVAL DE SAINT DENIS
www.festival-saint-denis.com, in French
This prestigious cycle of classical music concerts takes place in the Basilique de St-Denis (p173) and various other venues in St-Denis just north of Paris throughout the month of June. Book tickets well ahead.

FÊTE DE LA MUSIQUE
www.fetedelamusique.fr, in French
This national music festival, now in its third decade, welcomes in summer on summer solstice (21 June), caters to a great diversity of tastes (jazz, reggae and even classical)

top picks

JUST FOR KIDS

- CinéAqua (p120) The ultimate in high-tech aquariums as only defined by the 21st century.
- Cité des Sciences et de l'Industrie (p142) For kids of all ages, from the didactic to pure pleasure (Géode, Cinaxe etc).
- Eiffel Tower (p116) What kid doesn't want to climb a giant Mechano/Erector Set?
- Jardin d'Acclimatation (p122) A funfair to fill a day.
- Ménagerie du Jardin des Plantes (p98) The only place to observe wildlife in Paris at the time of research.

and features staged and impromptu live performances all over the city.

GAY PRIDE MARCH
www.gaypride.fr, in French
This colourful Saturday-afternoon parade (called Marche des Fiertés in French) in late June through the Marais to Bastille celebrates Gay Pride Day, with various bars and clubs sponsoring floats, and participants in some pretty outrageous costumes.

PARIS JAZZ FESTIVAL
www.paris.fr
There are free jazz concerts every Saturday and Sunday afternoon in June and July in the Parc Floral de Paris (metro Château de Vincennes).

LA GOUTTE D'OR EN FÊTE
www.gouttedorenfete.org, in French
This week-long world-music festival (featuring rai, reggae and rap) is held at square Léon, 18e (metro Barbès Rochechouart or Château Rouge) in late June.

PARIS CINÉMA
www.pariscinema.org
This 12-day festival in the first half of July sees rare and restored films screened in selected cinemas across Paris.

BASTILLE DAY (14 JULY)
www.paris.fr
Paris is *the* place to be on France's national day. Late on the night of the 13th, *bals des sapeurs-pompiers* (dances sponsored by Paris' firefighters, who are considered sex symbols in France) are held at fire stations around the city. At 10am on the 14th, there's a military and fire-brigade parade along av des Champs-Élysées, accompanied by a fly-past of fighter aircraft and helicopters. In the evening, a huge display of *feux d'artifice* (fireworks) is held at around 11pm on the Champ de Mars in the 7e.

PARIS PLAGES
www.paris.fr
Initiated in 2002, 'Paris Beach' is one of the most inspired and successful city recreational events in the world. Across four weeks, from mid-July to mid-August, two waterfront areas with different themes are transformed into sand and pebble

top picks

FOR FIRST-TIMERS

- Eiffel Tower (p116) Come on, already. You can't say you've been to Paris until you have at least gazed at *la madame*. But – oooh la la! – let's try a new position: from the bottom looking upward. *C'est si bon.*
- Av des Champs-Élysées (p125) It's not our favourite Parisian boulevard by any stretch of the imagination but it's another must-see. Again, be different. Stand in front of the eternal flame below the arch as night falls and watch the traffic rush past. Surreal.
- Notre Dame (p81) Christendom's most beautiful house of worship can be a mob-scene of picture-snapping infidels a lot of the time. Avoid the maddening crowds and attend Mass; you can see a lot from the pews. Failing that, there are usually organ concerts on Sunday afternoon around 5pm.
- Monet's Water Lilies (p77) Even we refuse to brave the crowds blocking da Vinci's (quite small) *Mona Lisa* in the Louvre. Head instead to the nearby Musée de l'Orangerie and Monet's sublime (and much larger) *Decorations des Nymphéas.*
- Food market (p222) Any one on our list will do but for a good overview of what's on offer in spades, check out our favourite Marché Bastille (Map p158).

'beaches', complete with sun beds, beach umbrellas, atomisers, lounge chairs and palm trees. They make up the 1.5km-long stretch along the Right Bank embankment (Voie Georges Pompidou) from the Pont Neuf (metro Pont Neuf) in the 1er to the Pont de Sully (metro Sully Morland) in the 4e, with a tropical feel to it; and a kilometre or so along the Bassin de la Villette in the 19e from the Rotonde de la Villette (metro Jaurès) to Rue de Crimée (metro Crimée), devoted to boating and other water sports. The beaches are open from 8am to midnight daily.

TOUR DE FRANCE
www.letour.fr
The last of 21 stages of this prestigious, 3500km-long cycling event finishes with a race up av des Champs-Élysées on the third or fourth Sunday of July, as it has done since 1975.

September & October

JAZZ À LA VILLETTE
www.jazzalavillette.com, in French
This super two-week jazz festival in the first half of September has sessions in Parc de la Villette, at the Cité de la Musique and in surrounding bars.

FESTIVAL D'AUTOMNE
www.festival-automne.com
The Autumn Festival of arts, now around for almost three decades, has painting, music, dance and theatre at venues throughout the city from mid-September to late December.

JOURNÉES EUROPÉENNES DU PATRIMOINE
www.journeesdupatrimoine.culture.fr, in French
As elsewhere in Europe on the third weekend in September – known as European Heritage Days in English – Paris opens the doors of buildings (eg embassies, government ministries, corporate offices – even the Palais de l'Élysée) normally off-limits to outsiders.

TECHNO PARADE
www.technoparade.fr, in French
Part of the annual festival called Rendez-vous Électroniques (Electronic Meeting), this parade involving some 20 floats and carrying 150 musicians and DJs wends its way on the periphery of the Marais on the third Saturday of September, starting and ending at place de la Bastille, 12e.

NUIT BLANCHE
www.paris.fr
'White Night' (or more accurately translated as 'All Nighter') is when Paris 'does' New York and becomes 'the city that doesn't sleep'. It's a cultural festival that lasts from sundown until sunrise – from 7pm to 7am – on the first Saturday and Sunday of October, with museums and recreational facilities such as swimming pools joining bars and clubs and staying open till the very wee hours.

FÊTE DES VENDANGES DE MONTMARTRE
www.fetedesvendangesdemontmartre.com, in French
This festival is held over five days from Wednesday to Sunday on the second weekend in October following the harvesting of grapes from the Clos Montmartre (p179), with costumes, speeches and a parade.

FOIRE INTERNATIONALE D'ART CONTEMPORAIN
www.fiac.com
Better known as FIAC, this huge contemporary art fair is held over four days in late October, with some 160 galleries represented at the Louvre and the Grand Palais.

November & December

AFRICOLOR
www.africolor.com, in French
This six-week-long African music festival is held for the most part in venues in the suburbs surrounding Paris (eg St-Denis, St-Ouen, Montreuil) from mid-November to late December.

JUMPING INTERNATIONAL DE PARIS
www.salon-cheval.com, in French
This annual showjumping tournament features the world's most celebrated jumpers at the Palais Omnisports de Paris-Bercy in the 12e (metro Bercy) over nine days in the first half of December. The annual International Showjumping Competition forms part of the Salon du Cheval at the Parc des Expositions at Porte de Versailles in the 15e (metro Porte de Versailles).

top picks

UNUSUAL EVENTS

- Paris Plages The next best thing after the seaside along France's smallest urban beaches.
- Gay Pride March Feathers and beads and participants in and out of the same make this Paris' most outrageous annual event.
- Fête des Vendanges de Montmartre Lots of noise for a bunch of old (and, some say, sour) grapes, but the street party is fun.
- Louis XVI Commemorative Mass Right-wing sob-fest for aristocrats, pretenders and their hangers-on – did 1789 even happen?
- Salon Internationale de l'Agriculture Lots to smell (cowpats), hear (braying donkeys), see (lambs gambolling), eat and drink at Europe's largest agricultural fair.

CHRISTMAS EVE MASS

Mass is celebrated at midnight on Christmas Eve at many Paris churches, including Notre Dame, but get there by 11pm to find a place.

NEW YEAR'S EVE

Bd St-Michel (5e), place de la Bastille (11e), the Eiffel Tower (7e) and, above all, av des Champs-Élysées (8e) are the places to be to welcome in the New Year in the City of Light.

COSTS & MONEY

If you stay in a hostel, or in a room without a shower or a toilet in a bottom-end hotel, and have picnics rather than dining out, it is possible to stay in Paris for €50 a day per person. A couple staying in a two-star hotel and eating one cheap restaurant meal each day should count on spending at least €80 a day per person. Eating out frequently, ordering wine and treating yourself to any of the many luxuries on offer in Paris will increase these figures considerably.

INTERNET RESOURCES

In terms of websites to consult before you go, Lonely Planet (www.lonelyplanet.com) is a good start for many of the city's more useful links. The following English-language websites are useful for learning more about Paris (and France) before setting out. For much more on what's going on in the city, check out some of the local blogs (p406).

Expatica (www.expatica.com) Lifestyle website for expats living in countries worldwide, including France, with regularly updated news, features and blogs.

French Government Tourism Office (www.francetourism. com) Official tourism site with all manner of information about travel in France, with lots and lots on Paris too.

Go Go Paris! Culture! (www.gogoparis.com) Clubs, hangouts, art gigs, dance around town, eating and drinking – everything a culture vulture living in Paris needs.

Mairie de Paris (www.paris.fr) Your primary source of information about Paris, with everything from opening times and what's on to the latest statistics direct from the Hôtel de Ville.

Paris Convention & Visitors Bureau (www.parisinfo.com) The official site of the Office de Tourisme et de Congrès – the city's tourist office – is super, with more links than you'll ever need.

HOW MUCH?

An hour's car parking from €1.50 (street), €2 (garage)

Average/fair/good seat at the opera €25/55/75

Cinema ticket €6 to €10.50 (adult)

Copy of Le Monde newspaper €1.40

Coffee at a café bar from €1.20

Grand crème at Champs-Élysées café terrace €5.50

Metro/bus ticket €1.60 (€11.60 for 10)

Entry to the Louvre €9.50 (adult)

Litre of bottled mineral water from €0.70 (supermarket), €1 (corner shop)

Pint of local beer from €6.50 (€5 at happy hour)

Pop music CD €10 to €18

Street snack from €2.50 (basic crêpe or galette)

Paris Digest (www.parisdigest.com) Useful site for making pretravel arrangements, with a forum.

SUSTAINABLE PARIS

For a densely populated urban centre inhabited for more than two millennia, Paris is a surprisingly healthy and clean city. Thanks mainly to Baron Haussmann (p35), who radically reshaped the city in the second half of the 19th century, a small army of street sweepers brush litter into the gutters from where it is hosed into sewers, and a city ordinance requires residents to have the facades of their buildings cleaned every 10 years.

These days, despite the city's excellent (and cheap) public transport system, Haussmann's wide boulevards are usually choked with traffic, and air pollution is undoubtedly the city's major environmental hazard. But things have improved tremendously on that score: the current (at the time of research) city leadership, which came to power in 2001 in coalition with the Green Party, first restricted traffic on some roads at certain times and created lanes only for buses, taxis and bicycles. Then, in 2007, in an unprecedented move for a city its size, Paris launched the Vélib' communal bicycle rental programme (p384). It has fundamentally changed the way Parisians (and footsore Lonely Planet authors) live and work. In April 2010 the government announced plans to turn a 3.5km section of highway on the Left

SIGNATURE SPLURGES

- Sip a cocktail – ideally a Bloody Mary, the bar's own invention – at Harry's New York Bar (p277).
- Tuck into *le baiser Ladurée* (layered almond cake with strawberries and cream) at Ladurée (p235), the most famous *pâtisserie* (cake shop) on the Champs-Élysées.
- Splash out on an evening *menu* at Les Ombres (p238) in the shadows (literally and by name) of the Eiffel Tower.
- Be queen of the night (regardless of sex and preferences) at Hôtel Caron de Beaumarchais (p344), about as over the top as you can get in hotel decoration.
- Pamper yourself at the overindulgent hammam of Les Bains du Marais (p310).
- Have your own personal scent mixed at the renowned *parfumerie* Fragonard (p205).
- Enjoy a night at the opera (or ballet), preferably at the Palais Garnier (p125), the more ornate of the two opera houses.
- Choose your open CD compilations at the musically renowned Buddha Bar (p283).
- Select a fine vintage wine or an excellent *eau-de-vie* (fruit brandy) from Lavinia (p195), one of the finest (and poshest) wine shops in town.
- Spin your wheels in pastel-coloured luxury on a vintage Vespa from Left Bank Scooters (p387).

Bank between the Musée d'Orsay and Pont d'Alma into a pedestrian- and bike-only zone.

If you want to keep Paris clean, leave your car at home and resist the temptation to rent one unless you're touring around the Île de France (p354). Instead, bring or rent a bike (p384), but remember that the Vélib' rental system is more of a way of getting from A to B than a recreational facility; enjoy the city on foot – Paris is an eminently walkable city (see p178); or use the public transport system, which is cheap and extremely efficient.

For further tips on how you can reduce your impact on the environment, contact Les Amis de la Nature (☎ 01 42 85 29 84; www.amisnature -pariscentre.org, in French; 30 quai des Célestins, 75004) or the World Wildlife Fund France (☎ 01 55 25 84 84; www.

wwf.fr, in French; 1 carrefour de Longchamp, 75116). Anyone who would like to help in the 'reforestation' of the capital and doesn't mind parting with €5 should visit 1 Parisien, 1 Arbre (1 Parisian, 1 Tree; www.1parisien1arbre.com, in French).

In theory, Parisians can be fined up to €183 for littering (that includes cigarette butts), but we've never heard of anyone having to pay. Smoking has been prohibited in all closed public areas – from train and metro stations to restaurants, bar and cafés – since 2008.

Don't be annoyed if you see locals drop paper wrappings or other detritus along the side of the pavement, however; it will be swept away by those ubiquitous street sweepers. In fact, Parisians are encouraged to use the gutters for litter if bins are not available.

HISTORY

With just under 12 million inhabitants, the greater metropolitan area of Paris is home to almost 19% of France's total population (central Paris counts just under 2.2 million people). Since before the Revolution, Paris has been what urban planners like to call a 'hypertrophic city' – the enlarged 'head' of a nation-state's 'body'. The urban area of the next biggest city – Marseilles – is just over a third the size of central Paris.

As the capital city, Paris is the administrative, business and cultural centre; virtually everything of importance in the republic starts, finishes or is currently taking place here. The French have always said *'Quand Paris éternue, la France s'en rhume'* (When Paris sneezes, France catches cold) but there have been conscious efforts – going back at least four decades – by governments to decentralise Paris' role, and during that time the population, and thus to a certain extent the city's authority, has actually shrunk. It dropped by 2% between 2004 and 2010 alone.

Paris has a timeless quality, a condition that can often be deceiving. While the cobbled backstreets of Montmartre, the terraced cafés of Montparnasse, the iconic structure of the Eiffel Tower and the placid waters of the Seine may all appear to have been in place since time immemorial, that's hardly the case.

EARLY SETTLEMENT

The early history of the Celts is murky, but it is thought that they originated somewhere in the eastern part of central Europe around the 2nd millennium BC and began to migrate across the continent, arriving in France some time in the 7th century BC. In the 3rd century a group of Celtic Gauls called the Parisii settled on the site of present-day Paris.

Centuries of conflict between the Gauls and Romans ended in 52 BC, with the latter taking control of the territory. The settlement on the Seine prospered as the Roman town of Lutetia (from the Latin for 'midwater dwelling'; in French, Lutèce), counting some 10,000 inhabitants by the 3rd century AD.

The so-called Great Migrations, beginning around the middle of the 3rd century AD with raids by the Franks and then by the Alemanii from the east, left the settlement on the south bank scorched and pillaged, and its inhabitants fled to the Île de la Cité, which was subsequently fortified with stone walls. Christianity had been introduced early in the previous century, and the first church, probably made of wood, was built on the western part of the island.

INVASIONS & DYNASTIES

The Romans occupied what would become known as Paris (after its first settlers) from AD 212 to the late 5th century. It was at this time that a second wave of Franks and other Germanic tribes under Merovius from the north and northeast overran the territory. Merovius' grandson, Clovis I, converted to Christianity and made Paris his seat in 508. Childeric II, Clovis' son and

TIMELINE

3rd century BC	52 BC	AD 845–86
Celtic Gauls called Parisii – believed to mean 'boat men' – arrive in the Paris area and set up a few wattle-and-daub huts on what is now the Île de la Cité, where they engage in fishing and trading.	Roman legions under Julius Caesar crush a Celtic revolt led by Vercingétorix on the Mons Lutetius (now the site of the Panthéon) and establish the town of Lutetia.	Paris is repeatedly raided by Vikings for more than four decades, including the siege of 885–86 by Siegfried the Saxon, which lasts 10 months but ends in victory for the French.

successor, founded the Abbey of St-Germain des Prés half a century later, and the dynasty's most productive ruler, Dagobert, established an abbey at St-Denis. The latter soon became the richest, most important monastery in France and the final resting place of its kings.

The militaristic rulers of the Carolingian dynasty, beginning with Charles 'the Hammer' Martel (688–741), were almost permanently away fighting wars in the east, and Paris languished, controlled mostly by its counts. When Charles Martel's grandson, Charlemagne (768–814), moved his capital to Aix-la-Chapelle (today's Aachen in Germany), Paris' fate was sealed. Basically a group of separate villages with its centre on the Ile de la Cité, Paris was badly defended throughout the second half of the 9th century and suffered a succession of raids by 'Norsemen' (Vikings).

CONSOLIDATION OF POWER

The counts of Paris, whose powers had increased as the Carolingians feuded among themselves, elected one of their own, Hugh Capet, as king at Senlis in 987. He made Paris the royal seat and lived in the renovated palace of the Roman governor on the Île de la Cité (site of the present Palais de Justice). Under Capetian rule, which would last for the next 800 years, Paris prospered as a centre of politics, commerce, trade, religion and culture. By the time Hugh Capet had assumed the throne, the Norsemen (or Normans, Gallicised descendants of the Vikings) were in control of northern and western French territory. In 1066 they mounted a successful invasion of England from their base in Normandy.

Paris' strategic riverside position ensured its importance throughout the Middle Ages, although settlement remained centred on the Île de la Cité, with the *rive gauche* (left bank) to the south given over to fields and vineyards; the Marais area on the *rive droite* (right bank) to the north was a waterlogged marsh. The first guilds were established in the 11th century, and rapidly grew in importance; in the mid-12th century the ship merchants' guild bought the principal river port, by today's Hôtel de Ville (city hall), from the crown. The boat, in fact, is now the symbol of Paris.

The 12th and 13th centuries were a time of frenetic building activity in Paris. Abbot Suger, both confessor and minister to several Capetian kings, was one of the powerhouses of this period; in 1136 he commissioned the Basilique de St-Denis. Less than three decades later, work started on the cathedral of Notre Dame, the greatest creation of medieval Paris. At the same time Philippe-Auguste (r 1180–1223) expanded the city wall, adding 25 gates and hundreds of protective towers.

The Marais, whose name means 'swamp', was drained for agricultural use and settlement moved to the Right Bank of the Seine. This would soon become the mercantile centre, especially around place de Grève (today's place de l'Hôtel de Ville). The food markets at Les Halles first came into existence in 1183 and the Louvre began its existence as a riverside fortress in the 13th century. In a bid to do something about the city's horrible traffic congestion and stinking excrement (the population numbered about 200,000 by the year 1200), Philippe-Auguste paved four of Paris' main streets for the first time since the Roman occupation, using metre-square sandstone blocks. By 1292 Paris counted 352 streets, 10 squares and 11 crossroads.

Meanwhile the Left Bank began developing not as a trade centre but as the centre of European learning and erudition, particularly in the so-called Latin Quarter. The ill-fated lovers Pierre Abélard and Héloïse (see the boxed text, p27) wrote the finest poetry of the age and their treatises

1066	1163	1253
The so-called Norman Conquest (and subsequent occupation) of England ignites almost 300 years of conflict between the Normans in western and northern France and the Capetians in Paris.	Two centuries of nonstop building reaches its zenith with the start of Notre Dame Cathedral under Maurice de Sully, the bishop of Paris; construction will continue for more than a century and a half.	La Sorbonne is founded by Robert de Sorbon, confessor to Louis IX, as a theological college for impoverished students in the area of the Left Bank known as the Latin Quarter, where students and their teachers communicated in that language exclusively.

on philosophy, and Thomas Aquinas taught at the new university. About 30 other colleges were established, including the Sorbonne.

In 1337 some three centuries of hostility between the Capetians and the Anglo-Normans degenerated into the Hundred Years' War, which would be fought on and off until the middle of the 15th century. The Black Death (1348–49) killed more than a third (an estimated 80,000 souls) of Paris' population but only briefly interrupted the fighting. Paris would not see its population reach 200,000 again until the beginning of the 16th century.

The Hundred Years' War and the plague, along with the development of free, independent cities elsewhere in Europe, brought political tension and open insurrection to Paris. In 1358 the provost of the merchants, a wealthy draper named Étienne Marcel, allied himself with peasants revolting against the dauphin (the future Charles V) in a bid to limit the power of the throne and secure a city charter. He and his supporters seized Paris but the dauphin's men recaptured it within two years, and Marcel and his followers were executed at place de Grève. Charles then completed the right-bank city wall and turned the Louvre into a sumptuous palace for himself.

After the French forces were defeated by the English at Agincourt in 1415, Paris was once again embroiled in revolt. The dukes of Burgundy, allied with the English, occupied the capital in 1420. Two years later John Plantagenet, duke of Bedford, was installed as regent of France for the English king, Henry VI, who was then an infant. Henry was crowned king of France at Notre Dame less than 10 years later, but Paris was almost continuously under siege from the French.

Around that time a 17-year-old peasant girl known to history as Jeanne d'Arc (Joan of Arc) persuaded the French pretender to the throne that she'd received a divine mission from God to expel the English from France and bring about his coronation as Charles VII. She rallied French troops and defeated the English at Patay, north of Orléans, and Charles was crowned at Reims. But Joan of Arc failed to take Paris. In 1430 she was captured, convicted of witchcraft and heresy by a tribunal of French ecclesiastics and burned at the stake. Charles VII returned to Paris in 1436, ending more than 16 years of occupation, but the English were not entirely driven from French territory (with the exception of Calais) for another 17 years.

The occupation had left Paris a disaster zone. Conditions improved while the restored monarchy moved to consolidate its power under Louis XI (r 1461–83), the first Renaissance king under whose reign the city's first printing press was installed at the Sorbonne. Churches were rehabilitated or built in the Flamboyant Gothic style (see p 57) and a number of *hôtels particuliers* (private mansions) such as the Hôtel de Cluny (now the Musée National du Moyen Age and the Hôtel de Sens (now the Bibliothèque Forney) were erected.

A CULTURAL 'REBIRTH'

The culture of the Italian Renaissance (French for 'rebirth') arrived in full swing in France during the reign of François I in the early 16th century partly because of a series of indecisive French military operations in Italy. For the first time, the French aristocracy was exposed to Renaissance ideas of scientific and geographical scholarship and discovery as well as the value of secular over religious life. The population of Paris at the start of François' reign in 1515 was 170,000 – still almost 20% less than it had been some three centuries before, when the Black Death had decimated the population.

Such writers as François Rabelais, Clément Marot and Pierre de Ronsard of La Pléiade (see p45) were influential at this time, as were the architectural disciples of Michelangelo and

1358	1429	1532–64
The Hundred Years' War (1337–1453) between France and England and the devastation and poverty caused by the plague lead to the ill-fated peasants' revolt led by Étienne Marcel.	French forces under Joan of Arc defeat the English near Orléans but three years later Joan is captured by the Burgundians, allies of the English, and burned at the stake in Rouen.	The 16th century is a period of heightened literary activity that sees the publication of Rabelais' five-part satirical work *Gargantua and Panagruel* over more than three decades.

Raphael. Evidence of this architectural influence can be seen in François I's château at Fontainebleau (p362) and the Petit Château at Chantilly (p366). In the city itself, a prime example of the period is the Pont Neuf, the 'New Bridge' that is, in fact, the oldest span in Paris. This new architecture was meant to reflect the splendour of the monarchy, which was fast moving towards absolutism, and of Paris as the capital of a powerful centralised state. But all this grandeur and show of strength was not enough to stem the tide of Protestantism that was flowing into France.

REFORM & REACTION

The position of the Protestant Reformation sweeping across Europe in the 1530s had been strengthened in France by the ideas of John Calvin, a Frenchman born in Picardy and exiled to Geneva. The edict of January 1562, which afforded the Protestants certain rights, was met by violent opposition from ultra-Catholic nobles whose fidelity to their faith was mixed with a desire to strengthen their power bases in the provinces. Paris remained very much a Catholic stronghold, and executions continued apace up to the outbreak of religious civil war.

The Wars of Religion (1562–98) involved three groups: the Huguenots (French Protestants supported by the English), the Catholic League and the Catholic king. The fighting severely weakened the position of the monarchy and brought the kingdom of France close to disintegration. On 7 May 1588, on the 'Day of the Barricades', Henri III, who had granted many concessions to the Huguenots, was forced to flee from the Louvre when the Catholic League rose up against him. He was assassinated the following year.

Henri III was succeeded by Henri IV, who inaugurated the Bourbon dynasty and was a Huguenot when he ascended the throne. Catholic Paris refused to allow its new Protestant king entry into the city, and a siege of the capital continued for almost five years. Only when Henri embraced Catholicism at St-Denis – *'Paris vaut bien une messe'* (Paris is well worth a Mass), he is reputed to have said upon taking Communion there – did the capital welcome him. In 1598 he promulgated the Edict of Nantes, which guaranteed the Huguenots religious freedom as well as many civil and political rights, but this was not universally accepted.

Henri consolidated the monarchy's power and began to rebuild Paris (the city's population was now about 450,000) after more than 30 years of fighting. The magnificent place Royale (today's place des Vosges) in the Marais and place Dauphine at the western end of the Île de la Cité are prime examples of the new era of town planning. But Henri's rule ended as abruptly and violently as that of his predecessor. In 1610 he was assassinated by a Catholic fanatic named François Ravaillac when his coach became stuck in traffic along rue de la Ferronnerie south of Les Halles. Ravaillac was executed by an irate mob of Parisians (who were mightily sick of religious turmoil by this time) by being quartered – after a thorough scalding.

Henri IV's son, the future Louis XIII, was too young to assume the throne, so his mother, Marie de Médici, was named regent. She set about building the magnificent Palais du Luxembourg and its enormous gardens for herself just outside the city wall. Louis XIII ascended the throne at age 16 but throughout most of his undistinguished reign he remained under the control of Cardinal Richelieu, his ruthless chief minister. Richelieu is best known for his untiring efforts to establish an all-powerful monarchy in France, opening the door to the absolutism of Louis XIV, and French supremacy in Europe. Under Louis XIII's reign two uninhabited islets in the Seine – Île Notre Dame and Île aux Vaches – were joined to form the Île de St-Louis, and

1572	1589	1635
Some 3000 Huguenots in Paris to celebrate the wedding of the Protestant Henri of Navarre (the future Henri IV) are slaughtered on 23–24 August, in what is now called the St Bartholomew's Day Massacre.	Henry IV, the first Bourbon king, ascends the throne after renouncing Protestantism; *'Paris vaut bien une messe'* (Paris is well worth a Mass), he is reputed to have said upon taking communion at the basilica in St-Denis.	Cardinal Richelieu, de facto ruler during the undistinguished reign of Louis XIII (1617–43), founds the Académie Française, the first and best known of France's five institutes of arts and sciences.

STAR-CROSSED LOVERS

He was a brilliant 39-year-old philosopher and logician who had gained a reputation for his controversial ideas. She was the beautiful niece of a canon at Notre Dame. And like Bogart and Bergman in Casablanca and Romeo and Juliet in Verona, they had to fall in love in medieval Paris of all damned times and places.

In 1118, the wandering scholar Pierre Abélard (1079–1142) found his way to Paris, having clashed with yet another theologian in the provinces. There he was employed by Canon Fulbert of Notre Dame to tutor his niece Héloïse (1101–64). One thing led to another and a son, Astrolabe, was born. Abélard did the gentlemanly thing and married his sweetheart. But they wed in secret and when Fulbert learned of it he was outraged. The canon had Abélard castrated and sent Héloïse packing to a nunnery. Abélard took monastic vows at the abbey in St-Denis and continued his studies and controversial writings. Héloïse, meanwhile, was made abbess of a convent.

All the while, however, the star-crossed lovers continued to correspond: he sending tender advice on how to run the convent and she writing passionate, poetic letters to her lost lover. The two were reunited only in death; in 1817 their remains were disinterred and brought to Père Lachaise cemetery (p155) in the 20e, where they lie together beneath a neo-Gothic tombstone in Division 7.

Richelieu commissioned a number of palaces and churches, including the Palais Royal and the Église Notre Dame du Val-de-Grâce.

ANCIEN RÉGIME & ENLIGHTENMENT

Le Roi Soleil (the Sun King) – Louis XIV – ascended the throne in 1643 at the age of five. His mother, Anne of Austria, was appointed regent, and Cardinal Mazarin, a protégé of Richelieu, was named chief minister. One of the decisive events of Louis XIV's early reign was the War of the Fronde (1648–53), a rebellion by the bourgeoisie and some of the nobility opposed to taxation and the increasing power of the monarchy. The revolt forced the royal court to flee Paris for a time.

When Mazarin died in 1661, Louis XIV assumed absolute power until his own death in 1715. Throughout his long reign, characterised by 'glitter and gloom' as one historian has put it, Louis sought to project the power of the French monarchy – bolstered by claims of divine right – both at home and abroad. He involved France in a long series of costly, almost continuous wars with Holland, Austria and England, which gained France territory but nearly bankrupted the treasury. State taxation to fill the coffers caused widespread poverty and vagrancy in Paris, which was by then a city of almost 600,000 people.

But Louis was able to quash the ambitious, feuding aristocracy and create the first truly centralised French state, elements of which can still be seen in France today. While he did pour huge sums of money into building his extravagant palace at Versailles, by doing so he was able to turn his nobles into courtiers, forcing them to compete with one another for royal favour and reducing them to ineffectual sycophants.

Louis mercilessly persecuted his Protestant subjects, whom he considered a threat to the unity of the state and thus his power. In 1685 he revoked the Edict of Nantes, which had guaranteed the Huguenots freedom of conscience.

It was Louis XIV who said '*Après moi, le déluge*' (After me, the flood); in hindsight his words were more than prophetic. His grandson and successor, Louis XV, was an oafish, incompetent

1682	14 July 1789	1793
Louis XIV, the 'Sun King', moves his court from the Palais des Tuileries in Paris to Versailles in a bid to sidestep the endless intrigues of the capital; his cunning plan works.	The French Revolution begins when a mob arms itself with weapons taken from the Hôtel des Invalides and storms the prison at Bastille, freeing a total of just seven prisoners.	Louis XVI is tried and convicted as citizen 'Louis Capet' (as all kings since Hugh Capet were declared to have ruled illegally) and executed; Marie-Antoinette's turn comes nine months later.

buffoon, and grew to be universally despised. However, Louis XV's regent, Philippe of Orléans, did move the court from Versailles back to Paris; in the Age of Enlightenment, the French capital had become, in effect, the centre of Europe.

As the 18th century progressed, new economic and social circumstances rendered the *ancien régime* (old order) dangerously out of step with the needs of the country and its capital. The regime was further weakened by the antiestablishment and anticlerical ideas of the Enlightenment, whose leading lights included Voltaire (François-Marie Arouet), Jean-Jacques Rousseau and Denis Diderot. But entrenched vested interests, a cumbersome power structure and royal lassitude prevented change from starting until the 1770s, by which time the monarchy's moment had passed.

The Seven Years' War (1756–63), known as the French and Indian War in the USA, was one of a series of ruinous military engagements pursued by Louis XV. It led to the loss of France's flourishing colonies in Canada, the West Indies and India. It was in part to avenge these losses that Louis XVI sided with the colonists in the American War of Independence (1775–83). But the Seven Years' War cost France a fortune and, more disastrously for the monarchy, it helped to disseminate at home the radical democratic ideas that were thrust upon the world stage by the American Revolution.

COME THE REVOLUTION

By the late 1780s, the indecisive Louis XVI and his dominating Vienna-born queen, Marie-Antoinette, known to her subjects disparagingly as *l'Autrichienne* (the Austrian), had managed to alienate virtually every segment of society – from the enlightened bourgeoisie to the conservatives – and the king became increasingly isolated as unrest and dissatisfaction reached boiling point. When he tried to neutralise the power of the more reform-minded delegates at a meeting of the États-Généraux (States-General) at the Jeu de Paume in Versailles (p354) from May to June 1789, the masses – spurred on by the oratory and inflammatory tracts circulating at places like the Café de Foy (p182) at Palais Royal – took to the streets of Paris. On 14 July, a mob raided the armoury at the Hôtel des Invalides for rifles, seizing 32,000 muskets, and then stormed the prison at Bastille – the ultimate symbol of the despotic *ancien régime*. The French Revolution had begun.

At first, the Revolution was in the hands of moderate republicans called the Girondins. France was declared a constitutional monarchy and various reforms were introduced, including the adoption of the *Déclaration des Droits de l'Homme and du Citoyen* (Declaration of the Rights of Man and of the Citizen). This document set forth the principles of the Revolution in a preamble and 17 articles, and was modelled on the American Declaration of Independence. A forward-thinking document called *Les Droits des Femmes* (The Rights of Women) was also published. But as the masses armed themselves against the external threat to the new government – posed by Austria, Prussia and the exiled French nobles – patriotism and nationalism mixed with extreme fervour and then popularised and radicalised the Revolution. It was not long before the Girondins lost out to the extremist Jacobins, led by Maximilien Robespierre, Georges-Jacques Danton and Jean-Paul Marat. The Jacobins abolished the monarchy and declared the First Republic in September 1792 after Louis XVI proved unreliable as a constitutional monarch. The Assemblée Nationale (National Assembly) was replaced by an elected Revolutionary Convention.

1799	1815	1848
Napoleon Bonaparte overthrows the Directory and seizes control of the government in a *coup d'état*, opening the doors to 16 years of despotic rule, victory and then defeat on the battlefield.	British and Prussian forces under the Duke of Wellington defeat Napoleon at Waterloo; he is sent into exile for the second time, this time to a remote island in the South Atlantic where he dies six years later.	After more than three decades of monarchy, King Louis-Philippe is ousted and the short-lived Second Republic is established with Napoleon's incompetent nephew at the helm.

ITALIAN TAKEAWAY

The 16th century was something of a watershed for French cuisine. When Catherine de Médeci, the future consort to François I's son, Henri II, arrived in Paris in 1533, she brought with her a team of Florentine *maître queux* (master chefs) and pastry cooks adept in the subtleties of Italian Renaissance cooking. They introduced such delicacies as aspics, truffles, *quenelles* (a form of dumpling), artichokes, macaroons and puddings to the French court. Catherine's cousin, Marie de Médeci, imported even more chefs into France when she married Henry IV in 1600. The French cooks, increasingly aware of their rising social status, took the Italians' recipes and sophisticated cooking styles on board, and the rest – to the eternal gratitude of epicures everywhere – is history.

In January 1793 Louis XVI, who had tried to flee the country with his family but only got as far as Varennes in Lorraine, was convicted as Louis Capet of 'conspiring against the liberty of the nation' and guillotined at place de la Révolution, today's place de la Concorde. His consort, Marie-Antoinette, was executed in October of the same year.

In March 1793 the Jacobins set up the notorious Committee of Public Safety to deal with national defence and to apprehend and try 'traitors'. This body had dictatorial control over the city and the country during the so-called Reign of Terror (September 1793 to July 1794), which saw most religious freedoms revoked and churches closed to worship and desecrated. Paris during the Reign of Terror was not unlike Moscow under Joseph Stalin.

Jacobin propagandist Marat was assassinated in his bathtub by the Girondin Charlotte Corday in July 1793 and by autumn the Reign of Terror was in full swing; by mid-1794 some 2500 people had been beheaded in Paris and more than 14,500 executed elsewhere in France. In the end, the Revolution turned on itself, 'devouring its own children' in the words of an intimate of Robespierre, Jacobin Louis Antoine Léon de Saint-Just. Robespierre sent Danton to the guillotine; Saint-Just and Robespierre eventually met the same fate. Paris celebrated for days afterwards.

After the Reign of Terror faded, a five-man delegation of moderate republicans led by Paul Barras, who had ordered the arrests of Robespierre and Saint-Just, set itself up to rule the republic as the Directoire (Directory). On 5 October 1795, a group of royalist *jeunesse dorée* (gilded youth) bent on overthrowing the Directory was intercepted in front of the Église St-Roch on rue St-Honoré. They were met by loyalist forces led by a young Corsican general named Napoleon Bonaparte, who fired into the crowd. For this 'whiff of grapeshot' Napoleon was put in command of the French forces in Italy, where he was particularly successful in the campaign against Austria. His victories would soon turn him into an independent political force.

LITTLE BIG MAN & EMPIRE

The post-Revolutionary government led by the five-man Directory was far from stable, and when Napoleon returned to Paris in 1799 he found a chaotic republic in which few citizens had any faith. In November, when it appeared that the Jacobins were again on the ascendancy in the legislature, Napoleon tricked the delegates into leaving Paris for St-Cloud to the southwest ('for their own protection'), overthrew the discredited Directory and assumed power himself.

At first, Napoleon took the post of First Consul, chosen by popular vote. In a referendum three years later he was named 'Consul for Life' and his birthday became a national holiday. By December 1804, when he crowned himself 'Emperor of the French' in the presence of Pope

1852–70	1870–1	1889
Paris enjoys significant economic growth during the Second Empire of Napoleon III and much of the city is redesigned or rebuilt by Baron Haussmann as the Paris we know today.	Harsh terms inflicted on France by victor Prussia in the Franco-Prussian War leads to open revolt and the establishment of the insurrectional Paris Commune.	The Eiffel Tower is completed in time for the opening of the Exposition Universelle (World Exhibition) but is vilified in the press and on the street as the 'metal asparagus' – or worse.

Pius VII at Notre Dame, the scope and nature of Napoleon's ambitions were obvious to all. But to consolidate and legitimise his authority Napoleon needed more victories on the battlefield. So began a seemingly endless series of wars and victories by which France would come to control most of Europe.

In 1812 Napoleon invaded Russia in an attempt to do away with his last major rival on the continent, Tsar Alexander I. Although his Grande Armée managed to capture Moscow, it was wiped out by the brutal Russian winter; of the 600,000 soldiers mobilised, only 90,000 – a mere 15% – returned. Prussia and Napoleon's other adversaries quickly recovered from their earlier defeats, and less than two years after the fiasco in Russia the Prussians, backed by Russia, Austria and Britain, entered Paris. Napoleon abdicated and was exiled to the island of Elba off the Tuscan coast of Italy. The Senate then formally deposed him as emperor.

At the Congress of Vienna (1814–15), the victorious allies restored the House of Bourbon to the French throne, installing Louis XVI's brother as Louis XVIII (Louis XVI's second son, Charles, had been declared Louis XVII by monarchists in exile but he died while under arrest by the Revolutionary government). But in February 1815 Napoleon escaped from Elba, landed in southern France and gathered a large army as he marched towards Paris. On 1 June he reclaimed the throne at celebrations held at the Champs de Mars. But his reign came to an end just three weeks later when his forces were defeated at Waterloo in Belgium. Napoleon was exiled again, this time to St Helena in the South Atlantic, where he died in 1821.

Although reactionary in some ways – he re-established slavery in France's colonies in 1802, for example – Napoleon instituted a number of important reforms, including a reorganisation of the judicial system; the promulgation of a new legal code, the Code Napoléon (or civil code), which forms the basis of the French legal system to this day; and the establishment of a new educational system. More importantly, he preserved the essence of the changes brought about by the Revolution. Napoleon is therefore remembered by many French people as the nation's greatest hero.

Few of Napoleon's grand architectural plans for Paris were completed, but the Arc de Triomphe, Arc de Triomphe du Carrousel, La Madeleine, Pont des Arts, rue de Rivoli and some buildings within the Louvre complex as well as the Canal St-Martin all date from this period.

RETURN OF THE MONARCHY

The reign of 'the gouty old gentleman' Louis XVIII (1814–24) was dominated by the struggle between extreme monarchists who wanted a return to the *ancien régime*, liberals who saw the changes wrought by the Revolution as irreversible, and the radicals of the working-class neighbourhoods of Paris (by 1817 the population of Paris stood at 715,000). Louis' successor, the reactionary Charles X (r 1824–30), handled this struggle with great incompetence and was overthrown in the so-called July Revolution of 1830 when a motley group of revolutionaries seized the Hôtel de Ville. The Colonne de Juillet in the centre of the place de la Bastille honours those killed in the street battles that accompanied this revolution; they are buried in vaults under the column.

Louis-Philippe (r 1830–48), an ostensibly constitutional monarch of bourgeois sympathies and tastes, was then chosen by parliament to head what became known as the July Monarchy. His tenure was marked by inflation, corruption and rising unemployment and was overthrown in the February Revolution of 1848, in whose wake the Second Republic was established. The population of Paris had reached one million by 1844.

1894	1905	1918
Army captain Alfred Dreyfus is convicted and sentenced to life imprisonment on trumped-up charges of spying for Germany but is later exonerated despite widespread conservative opposition.	The emotions aroused by the Dreyfus affair and the interference of the Catholic Church leads to the promulgation of *läcité* (secularism), the legal separation of church and state.	Armistice ending WWI signed at Fôret de Compiègne near Paris sees the return of lost territories (Alsace and Lorraine); the war, however, brought about the loss of over a million French soldiers.

FROM PRESIDENT TO EMPEROR

In presidential elections held in 1848, Napoleon's inept nephew, the German-reared (and accented) Louis Napoleon Bonaparte, was overwhelmingly elected. Legislative deadlock caused Louis Napoleon to lead a *coup d'état* in 1851, after which he was proclaimed Emperor Napoleon III. (Bonaparte had conferred the title Napoleon II on his son upon his abdication in 1814, but the latter never ruled.) A plebiscite overwhelmingly approved the motion (7.8 million in favour and 250,000 against), and Napoleon III moved into the Palais des Tuileries.

The Second Empire lasted from 1852 until 1870. During this period France enjoyed significant economic growth, and Paris was transformed by town planner Haussmann (see the boxed text, p35) into the modern city it is today. The city's first department stores were also built at this time – the now defunct La Ville de Paris in 1834 followed by Le Bon Marché in 1852 – as were the *passages couverts,* Paris' delightful covered shopping arcades (p182).

Like his uncle before him, Napoleon III embroiled France in a number of costly conflicts, including the disastrous Crimean War (1854–56). In 1870 Otto von Bismarck goaded Napoleon III into declaring war on Prussia. Within months the thoroughly unprepared French army was defeated and the emperor taken prisoner. When news of the debacle reached Paris the masses took to the streets and demanded that a republic be declared.

THE COMMUNE & THE 'BEAUTIFUL AGE'

The Third Republic began as a provisional government of national defence in September 1870. The Prussians were, at the time, advancing on Paris and would subsequently lay siege to the capital, forcing starving Parisians to bake bread partially with sawdust and consume most of the animals on display in the Ménagerie at the Jardin des Plantes. In January 1871 the government negotiated an armistice with the Prussians, who demanded that National Assembly elections be held immediately. The republicans, who had called on the nation to continue to resist the Prussians and were overwhelmingly supported by Parisians, lost to the monarchists, who had campaigned on a peace platform.

As expected, the monarchist-controlled assembly ratified the Treaty of Frankfurt. However, when ordinary Parisians heard of its harsh terms – a huge war indemnity, cession of the provinces of Alsace and Lorraine to the victors, and the occupation of Paris by 30,000 Prussian troops – they revolted against the government.

Following the withdrawal of Prussian troops on 18 March 1871, an insurrectionary government, known to history as the Paris Commune, was established and its supporters, the Communards, seized control of the capital (the legitimate government had fled to Versailles). In late May, after the Communards had tried to burn the centre of the city, the Versailles government launched an offensive on the Commune known as La Semaine Sanglante (Bloody Week), in which several thousand rebels were killed. After a mop-up of the Parc des Buttes-Chaumont, the last of the Communard insurgents, cornered by government forces in the Cimetière du Père Lachaise, fought a hopeless, all-night battle among the tombstones. In the morning, the 147 survivors were lined up against what is now known as the Mur des Fédérés (Wall of the Federalists). They were then shot, and buried in a mass grave. A further 20,000 or so Communards, mostly from the working class, were rounded up throughout the city and executed. As many as 13,000 people were jailed or transported to Devil's Island penal colony off French Guyana in South America.

1922	1940	25 August 1944
The doyenne at the centre of expatriate literary activity in Paris, Sylvia Beach of the Shakespeare & Company bookshop in rue de l'Odéon, publishes James Joyce's *Ulysses*.	After more than 10 months of *le drôle de guerre* (phoney war) Germany launches the battle for France, and the four-year occupation of Paris under direct German rule begins.	Spearheaded by Free French units, Allied forces liberate Paris and the city escapes destruction, despite Hitler's orders that it be torched; the war in Europe will end nine months later.

Karl Marx, in *The Civil War in France,* interpreted the Communard insurrection as the first great proletarian uprising against the bourgeoisie, and socialists came to see its victims as martyrs of the class struggle. Buildings destroyed in the fighting included the original Hôtel de Ville, the Palais des Tuileries and the Cours des Comptes (site of the present-day Musée d'Orsay). Both Ste-Chapelle and Notre Dame were slated to be torched but those in charge apparently had a change of heart at the last minute.

Despite this disastrous start, the Third Republic ushered in the glittering *belle époque* (beautiful age), with art nouveau architecture, a whole field of artistic 'isms' from impressionism onwards and advances in science and engineering, including the construction of the first metro line (1900). *Expositions universelles* (world exhibitions) were held in Paris in 1889 – showcasing the then maligned Eiffel Tower – and again in 1900 in the purpose-built Petit Palais. The Paris of nightclubs and artistic cafés made its first appearance around this time, and Montmartre became a magnet for artists, writers, pimps and prostitutes (see p178).

But France was consumed with a desire for revenge after its defeat by Germany, and jingoistic nationalism, scandals and accusations were the order of the day. The most serious crisis – morally and politically – of the Third Republic, however, was the infamous Dreyfus Affair. This began in 1894 when a Jewish army captain named Alfred Dreyfus was accused of betraying military secrets to Germany; he was then court-martialled and sentenced to life imprisonment on Devil's Island. Liberal politicians, artists and writers, including the novelist Émile Zola, who penned his celebrated open letter 'J'accuse!' (I Accuse!) in support of the captain, succeeded in having the case reopened – despite bitter opposition from the army command, right-wing politicians and many Catholic groups – and Dreyfus was vindicated in 1900. When he died in 1935 Dreyfus was laid to rest in the Cimetière de Montparnasse. The Dreyfus affair discredited the army and the Catholic Church in France. This resulted in more rigorous civilian control of the military and, in 1905, the legal separation of the Catholic Church and the French state.

THE GREAT WAR & ITS AFTERMATH

Central to France's entry into WWI was the desire to regain the provinces of Alsace and Lorraine, lost to Germany in the Franco-Prussian War. Indeed, Raymond Poincaré, president of the Third Republic from 1913 to 1920 and later prime minister, was a native of Lorraine and a firm supporter of war with Germany. But when the heir to the Austrian throne, Archduke Franz Ferdinand, was assassinated by a Bosnian Serb in Sarajevo on 28 June 1914, Germany and Austria–Hungary – precipitating what would erupt into the first-ever global war – jumped the gun. Within a month, they had declared war on Russia *and* France.

By early September German troops had reached the River Marne, just 15km east of Paris, and the central government moved to Bordeaux. But Marshal Joffre's troops, transported to the front by Parisian taxicabs, brought about the 'Miracle of the Marne', and Paris was safe within a month. In November 1918 the armistice was finally signed in a railway carriage in a clearing of the Forêt de Compiègne, 82km northeast of Paris.

The defeat of Austria–Hungary and Germany in WWI, which regained Alsace and Lorraine for France, was achieved at an unimaginable human cost. Of the eight million French men who were called to arms, 1.3 million were killed and almost a million crippled. In other words, 20% of all Frenchmen aged between 20 and 45 years of age were killed in WWI. At the Battle of

1949	1954	1958
Simone de Beauvoir publishes her ground-breaking and very influential study *Le Deuxième Sexe* (The Second Sex) just four years after French women win the right to vote.	As a portent of what is to happen to the rest of its overseas empire, France loses its bid to reassert colonial control over Indochina when its forces are soundly defeated at Dien Bien Phu in Vietnam.	De Gaulle returns to power after more than a dozen years in the opposition to form the Fifth Republic, in which power is weighted in the presidency at the expense of the National Assembly.

Verdun (1916) alone, the French, led by General Philippe Pétain, and the Germans each lost about 400,000 men.

The 1920s and '30s saw Paris become a centre of the avant-garde, with painters pushing into new fields of art like cubism and surrealism, Le Corbusier rewriting the textbook for architecture, foreign writers such as Ernest Hemingway and James Joyce drawn by the city's liberal atmosphere (p187) and nightlife establishing a cutting-edge reputation for everything from jazz clubs to striptease.

France's efforts to promote a separatist movement in the Rhineland, and its occupation of the Ruhr in 1923 to enforce German reparations payments, proved disastrous. But it did lead to almost a decade of accommodation and compromise with Germany over border guarantees, and to Germany's admission to the League of Nations. The naming of Adolf Hitler as German chancellor in 1933, however, would put an end to all that.

WWII & OCCUPATION

During most of the 1930s, the French, like the British, had done their best to appease Hitler. However, two days after the German invasion of Poland on 1 September 1939, Britain and France declared war on Germany. For the first nine months Parisians joked about *le drôle de guerre* – what Britons called 'the phoney war' – in which nothing happened. But the battle for France began in earnest in May 1940 and by 14 June France had capitulated. Paris was occupied, and almost half the population fled the city by car, by bicycle or on foot. The British expeditionary force sent to help the French barely managed to avoid capture by retreating to Dunkirk, described so vividly in Ian McEwan's *Atonement* (2001) and crossing the English Channel in small boats. The Maginot Line, a supposedly impregnable wall of fortifications along the Franco-German border, had proved useless – the German armoured divisions simply outflanked it by going through Belgium.

The Germans divided France into a zone under direct German rule (along the western coast and the north, including Paris), and into a puppet-state based in the spa town of Vichy and led by General Philippe Pétain, the ageing WWI hero of the Battle of Verdun. Pétain's collaborationist government, whose leaders and supporters assumed that the Nazis were Europe's new masters and had to be accommodated, as well as French police forces in German-occupied areas (including Paris), helped the Nazis round up 160,000 French Jews and others for deportation to concentration and extermination camps in Germany and Poland. (In 2006 the state railway SNCF was found guilty of colluding in the deportation of Jews during WWII and was ordered to pay compensation to the families of two victims.)

After the fall of Paris, General Charles de Gaulle, France's undersecretary of war, fled to London. In a radio broadcast on 18 June 1940, he appealed to French patriots to continue resisting the Germans. He set up a French government-in-exile and established the Forces Françaises Libres (Free French Forces), a military force dedicated to fighting the Germans alongside the Allies.

The underground movement known as the Résistance (Resistance), or Maquis, whose active members never amounted to more than about 5% of the French population, engaged in such activities as sabotaging railways, collecting intelligence for the Allies, helping Allied airmen who had been shot down, and publishing anti-German leaflets. The vast majority of the rest of the population did little or nothing to resist the occupiers or assist their victims or collaborated; a backlash immediately after the war led to the execution of an estimated 9000

BACKGROUND HISTORY

1962	1968	1977
War in Algeria is brought to an end after claiming the lives of more than 12,000 people; three-quarters of a million Algeria-born French citizens arrive in France and many taken up residency in Paris.	Paris is rocked by student-led riots that bring the nation and the city to the brink of civil war; as a result de Gaulle is forced to resign the following year.	The Centre Pompidou, the first of a string of *grands projets*, huge public edifices through which French leaders seek to immortalise themselves, opens to great controversy near Les Halles.

people, the majority without trial. Most historians and military experts now agree that the overall military effectiveness of the Resistance was limited. But it did serve as an enormous boost to French morale and has had an enormous impact on French literature and cinema right up till today.

The liberation of France started with the Allied landings in Normandy on D-day (Jour-J in French): 6 June 1944. On 15 August that same year, Allied forces also landed in southern France. After a brief insurrection by the Résistance and general strikes by the metro and police, Paris was liberated on 25 August by an Allied force spearheaded by Free French units – these units were sent in ahead of the Americans so that the French would have the honour of liberating the capital the following day. Hitler, who visited Paris in June 1940 and loved it, demanded that the city be burned towards the end of the war. It was an order that, thankfully, had not been obeyed.

POSTWAR INSTABILITY

De Gaulle returned to Paris and set up a provisional government, but in January 1946 he resigned as president, wrongly believing that the move would provoke a popular outcry for his return. A few months later, a new constitution was approved by referendum. De Gaulle formed his own party (Rassemblement du Peuple Français) and would spend the next 13 years in opposition.

The Fourth Republic was a period that saw unstable coalition cabinets follow one another with bewildering speed (on average, one every six months), and economic recovery that was helped immeasurably by massive American aid. France's disastrous defeat at Dien Bien Phu in Vietnam in 1954 ended its colonial supremacy in Indochina. France also tried to suppress an uprising by Arab nationalists in Algeria, where over a million French settlers lived.

The Fourth Republic finally came to an end in 1958, when extreme right-wingers, furious at what they saw as defeatism as opposed to tough action in dealing with the uprising in Algeria, began conspiring in an effort to overthrow the government. De Gaulle was brought back to power to prevent a military coup and even possible civil war. He soon drafted a new constitution that handed considerable powers to the president at the expense of the National Assembly.

CHARLES DE GAULLE & THE FIFTH REPUBLIC

The Fifth Republic was rocked in 1961 by an attempted coup staged in Algiers by a group of right-wing military officers. When it failed, the Organisation de l'Armée Secrète (OAS) – a group of French *colons* (colonists) and sympathisers opposed to Algerian independence – turned to terrorism, trying several times to assassinate de Gaulle and nearly succeeding in August 1962 in town of Clamart just southwest of Paris. The book and film *The Day of the Jackal* portrayed a fictional OAS attempt on de Gaulle's life.

In 1962, after more than 12,000 had died as a result of this 'civil war', de Gaulle negotiated an end to the war in Algeria. Some 750,000 *pied-noir* (black feet), as Algerian-born French people are known in France, flooded into France and the capital. Meanwhile, almost all of the other French colonies and protectorates in Africa had demanded and achieved independence. Shrewdly, the French government began a programme of economic and military aid to its former colonies to bolster France's waning importance internationally and to create a bloc of French-speaking nations – *la francophonie* – in the developing world.

1986	1989	1994
Victory for the opposition in the National Assembly elections forces President Mitterrand to work with a prime minister and cabinet from the right wing.	President Mitterrand's *grand projet*, Opéra de Paris Bastille, opens to mark the bicentennial of the French Revolution; IM Pei's Grande Pyramide is unveiled at the Louvre.	Eurostar trains link Waterloo station in London with the Gare du Nord in Paris in just over three hours.

HAUSSMANN'S HOUSING

Few town planners anywhere in the world have had as great an impact on the city of their birth as did Baron Georges-Eugène Haussmann (1809–91) on Paris. As prefect of the Seine *département* under Napoleon III between 1853 and 1870, Haussmann and his staff of engineers and architects completely rebuilt huge swaths of Paris. He is best known (and most bitterly attacked) for having demolished much of medieval Paris, replacing the chaotic narrow streets – easy to barricade in an uprising – with the handsome, arrow-straight and wide thoroughfares for which the city is now celebrated. He also revolutionised Paris' water-supply and sewerage systems and laid out many of the city's loveliest parks, including large areas of the Bois de Boulogne (p122) and Bois de Vincennes (p161) as well as the Parc des Buttes-Chaumont (p143) and Parc Montsouris. The 12 avenues leading out from the Arc de Triomphe were also his work.

Paris retained its position as a creative and intellectual centre, particularly in philosophy and film-making, and the 1960s saw large parts of the Marais beautifully restored. But the loss of the colonies, the surge in immigration, economic difficulties and an increase in unemployment weakened de Gaulle's government.

A PIVOTAL YEAR

The year 1968 was a watershed not just in France but throughout Western Europe. In March a large demonstration in Paris against the war in Vietnam was led by student Daniel 'Danny the Red' Cohn-Bendit, who is today copresident of the Green/Free European Alliance Group in the European Parliament and known as 'Danny the Green'. This gave impetus to the student movement, and protests were staged throughout the spring. A seemingly insignificant incident in May 1968, in which police broke up yet another in a long series of demonstrations by students of the University of Paris, sparked a violent reaction on the streets of the capital; students occupied the Sorbonne and barricades were erected in the Latin Quarter. Workers joined in the protests and six million people across France participated in a general strike that virtually paralysed the country and the city. It was a period of much creativity and new ideas with slogans appearing everywhere, such as *'L'Imagination au Pouvoir'* (Put Imagination in Power) and *'Sous les Pavés, la Plage'* (Under the Cobblestones, the Beach), a reference to Parisians' favoured material for building barricades and what they could expect to find beneath them.

The alliance between workers and students couldn't last long. While the former wanted to reap greater benefits from the consumer market, the latter wanted (or at least said they wanted) to destroy it – and were called 'fascist *provocateurs*' and 'mindless anarchists' by the French Communist leadership. De Gaulle took advantage of this division and appealed to people's fear of anarchy. Just as Paris and the rest of France seemed on the brink of revolution, 100,000 Gaullists demonstrated on the av des Champs-Élysées in support of the government and stability was restored.

POMPIDOU TO CHIRAC

There is no underestimating the effect the student riots of 1968 had on France and the French people, and on the way they govern themselves today. After stability was restored the government

1998	2001	2002
France beats Brazil to win the World Cup at the spanking-new Stade de France (Stadium of France) in St-Denis north of central Paris.	Socialist Bertrand Delanoë becomes the first openly gay mayor of Paris (and of any European capital) but is wounded in a knife attack by a homophobic assailant the following year.	President Jacques Chirac overwhelmingly defeats Front National leader Jean-Marie Le Pen to win second term.

made a number of immediate changes, including the decentralisation of the higher education system, and reforms (eg lowering the voting age to 18, enacting an abortion law and increasing workers' self-management) continued through the 1970s, creating, in effect, the modern society that is France today.

President Charles de Gaulle resigned in 1969 and was succeeded by the Gaullist leader Georges Pompidou, who was in turn replaced by Valéry Giscard d'Estaing in 1974. François Mitterrand, long-time head of the Partie Socialiste (PS), was elected president in 1981 and, as the business community had feared, immediately set out to nationalise privately owned banks, large industrial groups and various other parts of the economy. However, during the mid-1980s Mitterrand followed a generally moderate economic policy and in 1988, aged 69, he was re-elected for a second seven-year term.

In the 1986 parliamentary elections the right-wing opposition led by Jacques Chirac, mayor of Paris since 1977, received a majority in the National Assembly; for the next two years Mitterrand was forced to work with a prime minister and cabinet from the opposition, an unprecedented arrangement in French governance known as *cohabitation*.

In the May 1995 presidential elections Chirac enjoyed a comfortable victory. (Mitterrand, who would die in January 1996, decided not to run again because of failing health.) In his first few months in office Chirac received high marks for his direct words and actions in matters relating to the EU and the war in Bosnia. His cabinet choices, including the selection of 'whiz kid' foreign minister Alain Juppé as prime minister, were well received. But Chirac's decision to resume nuclear testing on the French Polynesian island of Mururoa and a nearby atoll was met with outrage in France and abroad. On the home front, Chirac's moves to restrict welfare payments (designed to bring France closer to meeting the criteria for the European Monetary Union) led to the largest protests since 1968. For three weeks in late 1995 Paris was crippled by public-sector strikes, battering the economy.

In 1997 Chirac took a big gamble and called an early parliamentary election for June. The move backfired. Chirac remained president but his party, the Rassemblement Pour la République (RPR; Rally for the Republic), lost support, and a coalition of Socialists, Communists and Greens came to power. Socialist Lionel Jospin, a former minister of education in the Mitterrand government (who, most notably, promised the French people a shorter working week for the same pay), became prime minister. France had once again entered into a period of *cohabitation* – with Chirac on the other side of the table this time around.

For the most part Jospin and his government continued to enjoy the electorate's approval, thanks largely to a recovery in economic growth and the introduction of a 35-hour working week, which created thousands of (primarily part-time) jobs. But this period of *cohabitation*, the longest-lasting government in the history of the Fifth Republic, ended in May 2002 when Chirac was returned to the presidency for a second five-year term with 82% of the vote. This reflected less Chirac's popularity than the fear of Jean-Marie Le Pen, leader of the right-wing Front National, who had garnered nearly 17% of the first round of voting against Chirac's 20%.

Chirac appointed Jean-Pierre Raffarin, a popular regional politician, as prime minister and pledged to lower taxes with declining revenues from a sluggish economy. But in May 2005 the electorate handed Chirac an embarrassing defeat when it overwhelmingly rejected, by referendum, the international treaty that was to create a constitution for the EU.

In the autumn of the same year riots broke out in Paris' *cités*, the enormous housing estates or projects encircling the capital, home to a dispossessed population of mostly blacks and North

2003	2004	2005
Hundreds of mostly elderly and housebound Parisians die from complications arising from an unusually hot summer; a review of the health and emergency-response systems gets under way.	France bans the wearing of Muslim headscarves and other religious symbols in schools.	The French electorate overwhelmingly rejects EU Constitution; the suburbs surrounding Paris are wracked by rioting by Arab and African youths.

Africans. In some of the worst violence seen in Paris since WWII, thankfully there were no deaths but 3000 arrests and millions of euros in property damage. Parisians began to talk about and debate ethnic origin and affirmative action, but these remained essentially problems 'out there' in the *banlieues* (suburbs).

The trouble became more central – both literally and figuratively – in March 2006 after parliament passed the controversial Contrat de Première Embauche (CPE; First Employment Contract). Supporters argued that the plan would reduce unemployment by 20% while detractors said it would encourage a regular turnover of cut-rate staff and not allow young people to build careers. The majority of the nation's universities went on strike, workers and students mobilised and 1.5 million protesters took to the streets nationwide. In Paris, demonstrators torched cars and clashed with police, who responded with tear gas and water cannons. The government decided to withdraw the CPE altogether later in 2006.

PARIS TODAY

Against this backdrop it came as no surprise that Prime Minister Dominique de Villepin, President Chirac's loyal henchman and heir apparent who had never been elected to public office, did not even make it to the first post in the national elections of spring 2007. Instead, the get-tough Interior Minister Nicolas 'Sarko' Sarkozy, who famously fanned the flames during the 2005 race riots by calling the rioters *'racaille'* (rabble or riffraff) and whose loyalty to Chirac seemed to blow with the prevailing wind, stood as the UMP (Union for a Popular Movement) candidate against Socialist Ségolène 'Ségo' Royal, who appeared to be the left's only hope of ending a dozen years of right-wing incumbency. Neither candidate received an absolute majority in the first round of voting but in the second Sarkozy took 53% of the popular vote.

In his first year as president, Sarkozy succeeded where his predecessors failed in getting unions and employee groups to compromise on benefits and saw the national unemployment rate fall to 7.5%, the lowest level in more than two decades. But many of even his staunchest supporters were less than impressed with his performance and his popularity in the polls one year dropped down to less than 40% (against 67% just after the May 2007 election). That's partly due to what the French now calling *peopolisation*, another Anglo-French neologism, this one meaning excessive media interest in and coverage of politicians' private lives. Mind you, Sarkozy's divorcing his wife of 18 years just three months after taking office and his subsequent marriage to Italian–French model and pop singer Carla Bruni would have tongues wagging in even the most taciturn of societies. Indeed, his well-publicised holidays with the rich and famous and what some French people see as his extravagance have earned him the sobriquet 'President Bling-Bling', a reference to an American hip-hop term meaning showy, often crass jewellery. Waiting in the wings are the Socialists and their coalition partners, encouraged by their successes – including the power base of Paris – in the March 2010 local elections, where they garnered 54% or the vote against the UMP's 35%, claiming victory in 21 of the nation's 22 regions.

According to the polls published just before publication, Sarkozy's approval rating had shrunk to 27% and – worse – the nation's love affair with the Premier Couple (First Couple) appeared to be ending. Was theirs too? In early 2010 tabloids were full of reports of both the president's and his wife's alleged infidelities. *Sacré bleu, alors!*

2007	2008	2010
Pro-American pragmatist Nicolas Sarkozy, Interior Minister under Chirac, beats Socialist candidate Ségolène Royal to become France's new president.	Mayor Bertrand Delanoë wins re-election to a second term of office.	President Sarkozy's power base is substantially weakened in nationwide local elections that see his party, the UMP, receiving just 35% of the vote against the Socialist coalitions' 55%.

ENVIRONMENT & PLANNING

THE LAND

The city of Paris – the capital of both France and the historic Île de France region – covers an area of just under 87 sq km (or 105 sq km if you include the Bois de Boulogne and the Bois de Vincennes). Within central Paris – which Parisians call *intra-muros* (Latin for 'within the walls') – the Right Bank is north of the Seine, while the Left Bank is south of the river.

Paris is a relatively easy city to negotiate. The ring road, known as the Périphérique, makes an irregularly shaped oval containing the entire central area. The Seine cuts an arc across the oval, and the terrain is so flat that the 130m-high Butte de Montmartre (Montmartre Hill) to the north is clearly visible for some distance.

Paris is divided neatly into two by the Seine and into 20 arrondissements, which spiral clockwise from the centre in a logical progression. City addresses *always* include the number of the arrondissement, as streets with the same name exist in different districts. In this book, arrondissement numbers are given after the street address using the notation generally used by the French: 1er for *premier* (1st), 2e for *deuxième* (2nd), 3e for *troisième* (3rd) and so on. On some signs or commercial maps, you will see the variations 2ème, 3ème etc and sometimes IIe, IIIe etc.

There is almost always a metro station within 500m of wherever you are in Paris so all offices, museums, hotels, restaurants and so on included in this book have the nearest metro or RER (a network of suburban lines) station given immediately after the contact details. Metro stations generally have a *plan du quartier* (map of the neighbourhood) on the wall near the exit(s).

GREEN PARIS

Though more than 100,300 trees (mostly plane trees and horse chestnuts) line the avenues and boulevards of Paris, the city can often feel excessively built-up. Yet there are 465 parks, gardens and promenades to choose from. Over the past 15 years, the city government has spent a small fortune transforming vacant lots and derelict industrial land into new parks. Some of the better ones are Parc de Bercy (p160) and the unique Promenade Plantée (p157), the 'planted walkway' above the Viaduc des Arts, both in the 12e; the Jardin de l'Atlantique (p170), behind the Gare Montparnasse, and Parc André Citroën (Map p168) on the banks of the Seine, both in the 15e; Parc de la Villette (p139) and Parc des Buttes-Chaumont (p143), both in the 19e; and Parc de Belleville (p145), 20e. Parks under construction include the football-pitch-sized Jardin Serge Gainsbourg at Porte des Lilas (Map p140) in the 20e and the enormous Parc Martin Luther King at Clichy Batignolles (Map p134) in the 17e, where the 2012 Olympiad would have taken place had Paris won the bid.

In just about every park in Paris, regardless of the size, you'll see a signboard illustrating and explaining the trees, flowers and other plants of the city. Most are rich in birdlife, including magpies, jays, great and blue tits, and even woodpeckers, owls and kestrels. In winter, seagulls are sometimes seen on the Seine, and a few hardy ducks also brave the river's often swift-flowing waters. Believe it or not, 32 mammals live in the parks of Paris, there are crayfish in the city's canals, and the Seine is teeming with roach, carp, bleak, pike and pike-perch.

top picks

PARKS & GARDENS

- **Parc de La Villette** (p139) Central Paris' largest open space, with shaded walkways, themed gardens, follies and two show-stopping museums.
- **Jardin du Luxembourg** (p106) Paris as it once was, this is where locals relax on folding sage-green chairs, sail model boats and visit a historical marionette theatre.
- **Parc des Buttes-Chaumont** (p143) Created by Haussman, this is Paris' own central park, with grottoes, waterfalls and lake with an island.
- **Parc Floral de Paris** (p161) Part of the enormous Bois de Vincennes, this delightful park is a kiddie magnet by day and a concert venue by night.
- **Bois de Boulogne** (p122) Paris' green lung, this 'anything goes' (especially after dark) woodland boasts gardens, an amusement park and its very own château.

URBAN PLANNING & DEVELOPMENT

In 1967 stringent town-planning regulations in Paris, which had been on the books since Haussmann's time, were relaxed and buildings were allowed to 'soar' to 37m. However, they had to be set back from the road so as not to block the light. But this change allowed the erection of high-rise buildings, which broke up the continuity of many streets. A decade later new restrictions required that buildings again be aligned along the road and that their height be in proportion to the width of the street. In some central areas that means buildings cannot go higher than 18m.

In 2007 Mayor Bertrand Delanoë challenged the law – and Parisians' way of thinking – when he invited a dozen architectural firms from around the world to submit drawings for towers exceeding 100m in three different areas of the city, including Porte de la Chapelle in the 18e and the Masséna-Bruneseau district of the 13e but not the traditional skyscraper district of La Défense. Delanoë's pet project is the so-called Triangle, a 200m-tall glass structure to be built in the Parc des Expositions at the Porte de Versailles in the 15e. It's by Herzog & de Meuron, the same firm who did London's Tate Modern in 1999.

GOVERNMENT & POLITICS

LOCAL GOVERNMENT

Paris is run by the *maire* (mayor), who is elected by the 163 members of the Conseil de Paris (Council of Paris). They serve terms of six years. The mayor has around 18 *adjoints* (deputy mayors), whose offices are in the Hôtel de Ville (City Hall).

The first mayor of Paris to be elected with real powers was Jacques Chirac in 1977; from 1871 until that year, the mayor was nominated by the national government as the capital was considered a dangerous and revolutionary hotbed. After the 1995 election of Chirac as national president, the Council of Paris elected Jean Tiberi as mayor, a man who was very close to the president and from the same party. In May 2001, Bertrand Delanoë, a Socialist with support from the Green Party, became the first openly gay mayor of Paris (and of any European capital). The next election, which should have taken place in 2007, was deferred until March 2008 in deference to the national elections that year. Delanoë handily won re-election to a second term in the second round of voting.

The mayor has many powers, but they do not include control of the police, which is instead handled by the Préfet de Police (Chief of Police), part of the Ministère de l'Intérieur (Ministry of the Interior). Delanoë continues to enjoy widespread popularity, particularly for his efforts to make Paris a more liveable city by promoting the use of bicycles and buses, reducing the number of cars on the road and creating a more approachable and responsible city administration.

Paris is a *département* – Ville de Paris (No 75), part of the Île de France region – as well as a city and the mayor is the head of both. The city is divided into 20 arrondissements and each has its own *maire d'arrondissement* (mayor of the arrondissement) and *conseil d'arrondissement* (council of the arrondissement), who are also elected for six-year terms. They have very limited powers, principally administering local cultural activities and sporting events.

NATIONAL GOVERNMENT

France is a republic with a written constitution adopted by referendum in September 1958 (the so-called Constitution of the Fifth Republic) and adapted 18 times since, most notably in 1962 when a referendum was organised calling for the election of the president by direct universal suffrage; in 1993 when immigration laws were tightened; in 2000 when the president's term was reduced from seven to five years; in 2003 when parliament approved amendments allowing for the devolution of wide powers to the regions and departments; and in 2007 when it banned the death penalty.

As the capital city, Paris is home to almost all the national offices of state, including, of course, the Parlement (Parliament), which is divided into two houses: the Assemblée Nationale (National Assembly) and the Sénat (Senate). The 577 deputies of the National Assembly are directly elected in single-member constituencies in a two-rounds system for terms lasting five years (next election: 2012). Until September 2004 the rather powerless Senate counted 321 senators, each elected to a nine-year term. Now the term is six years and the number of senators has been increased to 346 to reflect changes in France's demographics. Senators are indirectly elected by one half every three years. The president of the republic is directly elected for a term lasting five years and can stand for re-election.

Executive power is shared by the president and the Conseil des Ministres (Council of Ministers), whose members – including the prime minister – are appointed by the president but are responsible to parliament. The president serves as commander-in-chief of the armed forces and theoretically makes all major policy decisions.

MEDIA

The main national daily newspapers are *Le Figaro* (centre-right; aimed at professionals, businesspeople and the bourgeoisie; www.lefigaro.fr), *Le Monde* (centre-left; popular with professionals and intellectuals; www.lemonde.fr), *France Soir* (right-wing; working and middle class; www.francesoir.fr), *Libération* (left-wing; popular with students and intellectuals; www.liberation.fr) and *L'Humanité* (erstwhile mouthpiece of the French Communist Party; working class and intellectuals; www.humanite.fr). The capital's own daily is *Le Parisien* (centre; working class; www.leparisien.fr) and is easy to read if you have basic French. *L'Équipe* (www.lequipe.fr) is a daily devoted exclusively to sport and *Paris Turf* (www.paris-turf.com) to horse racing.

News weeklies with commentary include the comprehensive, left-leaning *Le Nouvel Observateur* (centre-left; http://tempsreel.nouvelobs.com) and the more conservative *L'Express* (www.lexpress.fr).

For some investigative journalism blended with satire, pick up a copy of *Le Canard Enchaîné* (www.lecanardenchaine.fr) – assuming your French is of a certain level, of course. *Paris Match* (www.parismatch.com) is a gossipy, picture-heavy weekly with a penchant for royalty and film stars. No group of people in Europe blog as much as the French do and there is no better way to understand what the French are thinking at the moment than entering the French blogosphere (see p406).

Public radio is grouped under the umbrella of Radio France (www.radiofrance.fr), which broadcasts via a network of dozens of radio stations, of which seven are the most important. These include national stations France Inter (87.8 MHz FM in Paris), the flagship talk station specialising in music, news and entertainment; the very highbrow France Culture (93.5 MHz

top picks

HISTORICAL READS

- Paris: The Secret History, Andrew Hussey (2006) – a book not unlike Peter Ackroyd's *London: The Biography*, this colourful historical tour of Paris opens the door to many of the city's mysteries with the help of the so-called dangerous classes, a traditional term for the immigrants, activists, beggars, revolutionaries and criminals.
- The Seven Ages of Paris: Portrait of a City, Alistair Horne (2002) – this superb, very idiosyncratic 'biography' of Paris divides the city's history into seven ages – from the 13th-century reign of Philippe-Auguste to President Charles de Gaulle's retirement in 1969.
- Is Paris Burning? Larry Collins & Dominique Lapierre (1965) – this is a tense and very intelligent reportage of the last days of the Nazi occupation of Paris.
- The Flâneur: A Stroll Through the Paradoxes of Paris, Edmund White (2001) – doyen of American literature and long-term resident (and *flâneur* or 'stroller') of Paris, White notices things rarely noticed by others – veritable footnotes of footnotes – in this loving portrait of his adopted city.
- Parisians: An Adventure History of Paris, Graham Robb (2010) – from the author of 2008's award-winning *The Discovery of France: A Historical Geography* comes this inventive, highly entertaining 'history' recounted by selected characters as diverse as Zola and Hitler.
- Paris Changing, Christopher Rauschenberg (2007) – modern-day photographer follows in the footsteps of early 20th-century snapper Eugène Atget in this 'spot the difference' album of before-and-after photos.
- Paris: The Biography of a City, Colin Jones (2005) – although written by a University of Warwick professor, this one-volume history is not at all academic. Instead, it's rather chatty, and goes into much detail on the physical remains of history as the author walks the reader through the centuries and the city.

FM); France Musique (91.7 MHz FM), which broadcasts over 1000 classical-music and jazz concerts each year; Radio Bleu (107.1 MHz FM), a network of stations for over-50s listeners; and France Info, a 24-hour news station that broadcasts headlines in French every few minutes and can be heard at 105.5 MHz FM. FIP (105.1 MHz FM) has a wide range of music – from hip-hop and *chanson* to world and rock – while Le Mouv' (92.1 MHz FM) is bubblegum pop.

Radio France Internationale (RFI; www.rfi.fr), France's voice abroad since 1931 and independent of Radio France since 1986, broadcasts in over 20 languages, including English (www.english.rfi.fr) and can be reached in Paris at 738 kHz AM. Arte Radio (www.arteradio.com) is a multilingual Franco-German web radio station featuring news reports and music.

Among the private radio networks, RTL (104.3 MHz FM) is still the leading general-interest station, though its audience is ageing. The droves of FM pop-music stations include Hot Mix Radio, Nostalgie and Chérie FM, most of which follow the phone-in format with very loud wisecracking DJs. Hard-core clubbers in Paris turn the dial to Radio Nova at 101.5 MHz FM for the latest on the nightclub scene. FG DJ (98.2 MHz FM), formerly Radio FG, is the station for house, techno, dance and rhythm and blues. TSF Jazz (89.9 MHz FM) is the nation's only all-jazz station.

Radio broadcasters in France have to play at least 40% of their music in French at prime time – a law passed in 1994 to protect French pop from being swamped by English-language imports – and stations can be fined if they don't comply. This helps explain why so many English-language hits are re-recorded in French – not always very successfully.

More than half of France's seven major national terrestrial TV channels (www.francetelevisions.fr) are public: France 2 and France 3 are general-interest stations designed to complement each other: the former focuses on news, entertainment and education, while the latter broadcasts regional programmes and news. France 5 targets its audience with documentaries (eg a daily health programme) and cartoons for the kids. France 4 is for young adults while France Ô is a satellite channel. The French–German public channel Arte, which shares is analogue channel with France 5, is a highbrow cultural channel.

The major private stations are the Franco-German TF1, M6 and Canal+. TF1 focuses on sport and entertainment – *télé-réalité* (reality TV) is a big deal here, with *La Ferme Célébrités* (Celebrity Farm) a huge hit since 2004. With about a third of all French viewers, it is the most popular station in France. M6 lures a youngish audience with its menu of drama, music and news programmes. Canal+ is a mostly subscription-only channel that shows lots of films, both foreign and French.

FASHION

'Fashion is a way of life,' Yves St Laurent once pronounced, and most Parisians would agree. They live, breathe and consume fashion. After all, to their reckoning, fashion is French – like gastronomy – and the competition from Milan, Tokyo or New York simply doesn't cut the mustard.

But what few Parisians know (or want to admit) is that an Englishman created Parisian *haute couture* (literally 'high sewing') as it exists today. Known as 'the Napoleon of costumers', Charles Frederick Worth (1825–95) arrived in Paris at the age of 20 and revolutionised fashion by banishing the crinoline (stiffened petticoat), lifting hemlines up to the oh-so-shocking ankle length and presenting his creations on live models. The House of Worth stayed in the family for four generations until the 1950s.

THE SHOW OF SHOWS

The Paris fashion *haute-couture* shows are scheduled in late January for the spring/summer collections and early July for autumn/winter ones. However, most established couturiers present a more affordable *prêt-à-porter* (ready-to-wear) line, and many have abandoned *haute couture* altogether. Prêt-à-porter shows are usually in late January and September. All major shows are ultra-exclusive affairs – even eminent fashion journalists must fight tooth and nail to get a spot on the sidelines. For an overview of Parisian fashion, check out Le Bon Marché (p199), which has an excellent collection of all the big labels and couture designs. For some catwalk action, there's a weekly fashion show at 3pm on Friday (excluding January, February and August) on the 7th floor of Galeries Lafayette (p202). Bookings are essential. In some stores you can join mailing lists to receive fashion-show invitations, but you need to be in Paris at the right time to attend.

THE BEAUTIFUL & THE DAMNED: REAL PARISIANS IN HISTORY

Virtually everyone French is 'Parisian' – at least the ones you meet outside the country. The vast majority of the ambitious make their way to the capital ('if I can make it there, I'll make it *n'importe où*'), don the gay apparel of Gay Paree and never go home. But we're not talking about *parisiens en plastique* (plastic Parisians) who don't know their Left from their Right Bank. Who were the born-and-bred Parisians who changed the course of history?

Voltaire (1694–1778)

Claim to fame: The writer and philosopher François-Marie Arouet – better know by his penname Voltaire – was a key figure of the Enlightenment, and his political writings advocating social reform and civil liberties and criticising the Catholic Church helped bring about the French Revolution. Who knew? When a priest asked him on his deathbed to renounce Satan and his works, Voltaire reportedly said, 'For God's sake, let me die in peace' and turned away. He was buried in consecrated ground. Find him at the Pantheon (p99), where he was interred in 1791 with a million mourners in attendance.

Marcel Proust (1871–1922)

Claim to fame: Arguably the greatest novelist France has yet produced, Proust published a seven-volume *roman fleuve* (epic novel) between 1909 and his death that explores the meaning of experiences recovered from the subconscious that is a microcosm of France and Europe at the start of the last century. Who knew? Although the 'official' translation of his opus is now *In Search of Lost Time,* most people and references use the more poetic title *À la Recherche du Temps Perdu* (Rememberance of Things Past). Seek him in spirit at the Musée Carnavalet (p146), where his cork-lined bedroom from his flat on the blvd Haussmann – he was very noise sensitive – is on display in room 147, but find him 2m down in lot 85 at the Cimetière du Père Lachaise (p155).

Édith Piaf (1915-63)

Claim to fame: The 'Urchin Sparrow', who rose from the backstreets of Belleville singing in a husky voice devoid of self-pity about street life, unrequited love, violence and death, is generally considered France's greatest singer and is as iconic to Paris as the Eiffel Tower. Who knew? Piaf, whose middle name was Giovanna, was part Italian and part Kabyle (North African Berber). Seek her spirit at La Java (p303), the dance hall where she got her first break, or the Musée Édith Piaf (p155), but find her at the Cimetière du Père Lachaise (p155), where she is buried in lot 97.

Indeed, the British are still key players on the Paris fashion scene today, notably in the form of erstwhile *enfant terrible* and now chief designer for Dior, John Galliano. But Galliano is hardly the only 'wild child' couturier in Paris; Jean-Paul Gaultier draws his influence from the punk movement, dresses men in skirts and is famous for fitting Madonna into her signature conical bra.

But you probably won't encounter women clad in Gaultier (or even Galliano) rubbing shoulders in the metro. Paris style remains quintessentially classic, with Parisian women preferring to play it safe (and sometimes slightly sexy) in monotones. It could be said that today's *parisiennes* are the legitimate daughters of the great Coco Chanel, celebrated creator of the 'little black dress'.

Indeed, nostalgia for Chanel as well as Givenchy, Féraud and other designers from the heyday of Paris fashion in the 1950s has contributed to the big demand for vintage clothing. Twice a year the big auction house Hôtel Drouot (p201) hosts *haute-couture* auctions.

But it's not all about yesterday and looking backward. There are, in fact, several contemporary 'Paris styles' that often relate to certain geographical areas and social classes. The funky streetwear style, heavily inspired by London, can be associated with the trendy shops around rue Étienne Marcel in the Louvre & Les Halles neighbourhood and the Marais. The 3e is particularly known for its up-and-coming young designers and their boutiques, including Galerie Thomas Nelson (Map p148; ☎ 01 42 71 12 51; www.galeriethomasnelson.com; 4 rue du Bourg l'Abbé, 3e; Ⓜ Étienne Marcel), which offers showcase space for young designers who can't afford their own boutiques; what's being called the 'Vélibre' of prêt-à-porter' Paperdolls (Map p148; ☎ 06 16 13 33 48; Espace des Créateurs, 7 rue Commines, 3e; Ⓜ Filles du Calvaire), the brainchild of Franco-British designer Candy Miller, where you can you can hire labels; and just south, Xuly Bët (Map p148; ☎ 0 899 651 379; 95 blvd Beaumarchais, 3e; Ⓜ St-Sébastien Froissart), Mali designer Lamine Badian Kouyaté's new boutique for his – and like-minded designers' – creations.

Meanwhile more upper-crust 'BCBG' *(bon chic bon genre)* shops at Le Bon Marché (p199), the renovated and extended Max Mara (Map p126; ☎ 01 47 20 61 13; 31 av Montaigne, 8e; Ⓜ George V) or Chanel

Jean-Paul Sartre (1905–80) & Simone de Beauvoir (1906–86)

Claims to fame: The 'wall-eyed little man who figured it all out', according to the American magazine *Life*, the 20th century's foremost French thinker developed the philosophy known as existentialism in which 'Existence precedes (or, more accurately in English, takes priority over) essence', meaning that man must create himself because there is no eternal 'natural self' or 'meaning of life'. Sartre's lifelong companion, the writer De Beauvoir, applied existentialist concepts to the predicament of women in French society, notably in her seminal work *Le Deuxième Sexe* (The Second Sex), published in 1949. Who knew? Sartre was the first Nobel Laureate (1964) to decline the prize (he had already refused the Légion d'Honneur, France's highest accolade, almost 20 years before). Look for their ghosts at the Café de Flore (p281), the couple's local of choice in the 1940s and '50s, but find them lying side by side in a shared plot in the Cimetière du Montparnasse (p170).

Auguste Rodin (1840–1917)

Claim to fame: Widely considered the progenitor of modern sculpture, Rodin was able to overcome the conflict between neoclassicism and romanticism, and his sumptuous bronze and marble figures of men and women helped to revitalise sculpture as an expressive medium. His work today looks as fresh and modern as it did in the 19th century. Who knew? Rodin's on-again-off-again mistress of almost two decades, the sculptor Camille Claudel, was the older sister of the French Catholic poet and diplomat Paul. When she and Rodin split, she had a nervous breakdown and Paul committed her to an asylum for the rest of her life. Find him walking the halls and gardens of his beloved residence in the 7e, now the Musée Rodin (p111).

Catherine Deneuve (1943–)

Claim to fame: Many people both home and abroad believe the actress is the most beautiful woman in the world. And we'd be inclined to agree. But La Deneuve is more than just a pretty face. In a career that spanned more than half a century and 100 films, she has won two Césars and been nominated for a BAFTA and an Oscar. Who knew? Deneuve's face was the model for Marianne, the national symbol of France, from 1985 to 1989. Find her shadow *en passant* anywhere underground – her greatest and most lasting film was *Le Dernier Métro* (The Last Metro; 1980) directed by François Truffaut and co-starring Gérard Depardieu.

(p203) and rarely ventures outside her preferred districts: the 7e, 8e and 16e. The chic Left Bank *intello* (intellectual) struts her agnès b (p193) and APC (p206).

The eastern districts of Oberkampf, Bastille, the area of the 10e around Canal St-Martin and the Batignolles section of Clichy in the 17e tend to be the stomping ground of the *bobo* (bourgeois bohemian), whose take on style is doused in nostalgia for her voyage to India, Tibet or Senegal and her avowed commitment to free trade and beads. Younger professional *bobos* frequent Colette (p194), Kabuki Femme (p194) and Isabel Marant (p210).

Despite the invasion of 'Made in China' clothes for clones, Parisians almost never look like fashion victims nor do they go in for anything remotely vulgar or brassy. They stick to a neutral palette: black, grey, beige, brown and white, adding good accessories and great haircuts. They may mix and match designer labels with H&M, making it look like it was all bought on the posh av Montaigne in the 8e. And it is this elegance that attracts visitors from around the globe.

This is a society that coined the expression *lèche-vitrine* (literally 'window-licker') for window-shopping; 'tasting' without buying is an art like any other so don't be shy about just having a look. The fancy couture houses on av Montaigne may seem daunting, but in most, no appointment is necessary and you can simply walk in. Don't expect overly friendly service but do expect courtesy; after all, how are they to know that behind your jeans and sneakers you're not hiding a significant trust fund and a penchant for Lagerfeld?

LANGUAGE

Respect for the French language is one of the most important aspects of claiming French nationality, and the concept of *la francophonie*, linking the common interests everywhere French is spoken, is supported by both the government and the people. Modern French developed

SPEAKA DA LINGO

Verlan, a kind of French Pig Latin, has been the lingua franca of choice among the *branché* (hip) street-smart of Paris for almost two decades now. It's really just a linguistic sleight of hand, and its very name is illustrative of how it works. *L'envers* means 'reverse' in French, right? Well, twist it around – take the 'vers' and have it precede the 'l'en' and you get *verlan* – more or less. Of course that's the easy bit; shorter words – 'meuf' for *femme* (woman), 'keum' for *mec* (guy), 'teuf' for *fête* (party), 'keuf' for *flic* (cop) and 'auch' for *chaud* (hot; as in cool) are a bit trickier to recognise for the uninitiated.

In recent years the language has started to go mainstream and a few words of verlan – for example *beur* (French-born Algerian and from the French *Arabe*) – have entered the lexicography (if not dictionary) of standard French. Of course, the whole idea of verlan was for it to be a secret language – a kind of Cockney rhyming slang – for youths to communicate freely in front of parents and criminals in front of the police, so most words have to do with sex or drugs. The next step was obvious: re-verlan words already in the lingo. So now *beur* is *reub* in hip-hop circles and *keuf* is *feuk*.

from the *langue d'oïl*, a group of dialects spoken north of the Loire River that grew out of the vernacular Latin used during the late Gallo-Roman period. The *langue d'oïl* – particularly the *francien* dialect spoken in the Île de France encircling Paris – eventually displaced the *langue d'oc*, the dialects spoken in the south of the country.

Standard French is taught in schools, but its various accents and subdialects are an important source of identity in certain regions. In addition, some languages belonging to peoples long since subjected to French rule have been preserved. These include Flemish in the far north; Alsatian on the German border; Breton, a Celtic tongue, in Brittany; Basque, a language unrelated to any other, in the Basque Country; Catalan, the official language of nearby Andorra and the autonomous Spanish republic of Catalonia, in Roussillon; Provençal in Provence; and Corsican, closely related to Tuscan Italian, on the island of Corsica.

French was *the* international language of culture and diplomacy until WWI, and the French are sensitive to its decline in importance and the hegemony of English, especially since the advent of the internet. It is virtually impossible to separate a French person from his or her language, and it is one of the things the French love most about their own culture. Your best bet is always to approach people politely in French, even if the only words you know are '*Pardon, parlez-vous anglais?*' (Excuse me, do you speak English?). Don't worry; they won't bite.

For more on what to say and how to say it *en français*, see p411. Lonely Planet also publishes the more comprehensive *French* phrasebook.

THE ARTS & ARCHITECTURE

THE ARTS

Paris is a bottomless well when it comes to the arts. There are philharmonic orchestras, ballet and opera troupes, theatre companies and copious cinemas from which to choose your art form. And its museums are among the richest in the world, with artwork representing the best of every historical period and school from the Romans to postmodernism. Government funding has been cut back but still allows local venues to attract top international performers, and the number of international arts festivals hosted here seems to grow each year.

LITERATURE

The written word is something that matters deeply to French people, and it is an important focus in their sense of identity. Problem is, nowadays there are no schools or clear literary trends emerging, some authors are impossible to read and, relatively speaking, little contemporary literature finds its way into English translation. Much French writing today tends to focus in a rather nihilistic way on what the nation has lost in recent decades (such as identity, international prestige etc), particularly in the work of Michel Houellebecq, who rose to national prominence in 1998 with his *Les Particules Élémentaires* (Atomised). And accessibility? In 2002 the winner of the Prix Goncourt (Goncourt Prize), the most prestigious Francophonie literary award – *Les Ombres Errantes* by Pascal Quignard – was denounced even by some of the prestigious prize's judges as 'over-erudite' and 'inaccessible' to the average reader.

Such novels do not help the traveller get into the head of Paris, to see and feel how the city thinks and works. For now perhaps it is better to stick with the classics of French literature or even those writers who are more descriptive and thus accessible. The *roman policier* (detective novel), for example, has always been a great favourite with the French, and among its greatest exponents has been Belgian-born Georges Simenon, author of the Inspector Maigret novels. *La Nuit du Carrefour* (Maigret at the Crossroads) portrays Montmartre at its 1930s sleaziest and seediest. And then there are the works of all those foreigners, such as Gertrude Stein and George Orwell (p47) and, more recently, Cara Black (p49).

Going back in time, in the history of early medieval French literature Paris does not figure largely, though the misadventures of Pierre Abélard and Héloïse (p27) took place in the capital as did their mutual correspondence, which ended only with their deaths.

François Villon, considered the finest poet of the late Middle Ages, received the equivalent of a Master of Arts degree from the Sorbonne before he turned 20. Involved in a series of brawls, robberies and generally illicit escapades, 'Master Villon' (as he became known) was sentenced to be hanged in 1462 supposedly for stabbing a lawyer. However, the sentence was commuted to banishment from Paris for 10 years, and he disappeared forever. As well as a long police record, Villon left behind a body of poems charged with a highly personal lyricism, among them the *Ballade des Pendus* (Ballad of the Hanged Men), in which he writes his own epitaph, and the *Ballade des Femmes du Temps Jadis,* which was translated by the English poet and painter Dante Gabriel Rossetti as the 'Ballad of Dead Ladies'.

The great landmarks of French Renaissance literature are the works of François Rabelais, Pierre de Ronsard (and other poets of the Renaissance group of poets known as La Pléiade) and Michel de Montaigne. The exuberant narratives of the erstwhile monk Rabelais blend coarse humour with erudition in a vast *œuvre* that seems to include every kind of person, occupation and jargon to be found in the France of the early 16th century. Rabelais had friends in high places in Paris, including Archbishop Jean du Bellay, whom he accompanied to Rome on two occasions. But some of Rabelais' friends and associates fell afoul of the clergy, including his publisher Étienne Dolet. After being convicted of heresy and blasphemy in 1546, Dolet was hanged and then burned at place Maubert in the 5e arrondissement.

During the 17th century, François de Malherbe, court poet under Henri IV, brought a new rigour to the treatment of rhythm in literature. One of his better-known works is his

top picks

BOOKS ABOUT PARISIANS & THE FRENCH

- An Englishman in Paris: L'Éducation Continentale, Michael Sadler (2003) – rollicking, *very* funny (mis)adventures of a self-proclaimed Francophile teacher in the City of Light.
- The Last Time I Saw Paris, Elliot Paul (2001) – a classic work by an American expat that looks back on the working-class Paris of the interwar years in a series of interwoven episodes.
- The French, Theodore Zeldin (1983) – dated but highly acclaimed survey of French passions, peculiarities and perspectives by this British scholar who was appointed to a committee advising the Sarkozy government on labour-market reforms in 2007.
- The Death of French Culture, Donald Morrison (2010) – the book that grew out of the (in)famous *Time* magazine article in 2007 has this American in Paris pondering on past glory and suggesting that France and its culture no longer speak to the world. Thought-provoking.
- Un Peu de Paris, Jean-Jacques Sempé (2001) – wordless, gentle portrait of Paris and Parisians in cartoons from a national institution whose work appears frequently in the *New Yorker*.
- Savoir Flair, Polly Platt (2000) – subtitled '211 Tips for Enjoying France and the French', this book by a 30-year expat Paris resident will help you understand what makes the French tick.
- The Secret Life of France, Lucy Wadham (2009) – a young Oxford grad marries an older Frenchman and goes native in rural France, learning about the real France.
- Paris in Mind, Jennifer Lee (2003) – an anthology of essays and excerpts by 29 American writers – from Edith Wharton and James Baldwin to David Sedaris and Dave Barry (who discusses how to pronounce the French 'r').
- The House in Paris, Elizabeth Bowen (1949) – Paris through the eyes and ears of an 11-year-old English girl sequestered for 24 hours in a Parisian townhouse. Dark, evocative, classic.
- Foreign Tongue: A Novel of Life and Love in Paris, Vanina Marsot (2009) – a fetching tale of an American gal who breaks up with her boyfriend, moves to Paris, devotes her time to translating an erotic French novel into English and, well, meets boy. Make that boys. Great descriptions of food and social life in Paris.

sycophantic *Ode* (1600) to Marie de Médici. Transported by the perfection of Malherbe's verses, Jean de La Fontaine went on to write his charming *Fables* in the manner of Aesop – though he fell afoul of the Académie Française (French Academy) in the process. The mood of classical tragedy permeates *La Princesse de Clèves* by Marie de La Fayette, which is widely regarded as the precursor of the modern character novel.

The literature of the 18th century is dominated by philosophers, among them Voltaire (François-Marie Arouet) and Jean-Jacques Rousseau. Voltaire's political writings, arguing that society is fundamentally opposed to nature, had a profound and lasting influence on the century, and he is buried in the Panthéon. Rousseau's sensitivity to landscape and its moods anticipate romanticism, and the insistence on his own singularity in *Les Confessions* made it the first modern autobiography. He, too, is buried in the Panthéon.

The 19th century produced Victor Hugo, as much acclaimed for his poetry as for his novels, who lived on the place des Vosges before fleeing to the Channel Islands during the Second Empire. *Les Misérables* (1862) describes life among the poor and marginalised of Paris during the first half of the 19th century; the 20-page flight of the central character, Jean Valjean, through the sewers of the capital is memorable. *Notre Dame de Paris* (The Hunchback of Notre Dame; 1831), a medieval romance and tragedy revolving around the life of the celebrated cathedral, made Hugo the key figure of French romanticism.

Other influential 19th-century novelists include Stendhal (Marie-Henri Beyle), Honoré de Balzac, Amandine Aurore Lucile Dupin (better known as George Sand) and, of course, Alexandre Dumas, who wrote the swashbuckling adventures *Le Compte de Monte Cristo* (The Count of Monte Cristo) and *Les Trois Mousquetaires* (The Three Musketeers). The latter tells the story of d'Artagnan, based on the historical personage Charles de Batz d'Artagnan (c1611–73), who arrives in Paris as a young Gascon determined to become one of the guardsmen of Louis XIII.

In 1857 two landmarks of French literature were published in book form: *Madame Bovary* by Gustave Flaubert and *Les Fleurs du Mal* by Charles Baudelaire. Both writers were tried for the supposed immorality of their works. Flaubert won his case, and his novel was distributed without censorship. Baudelaire, who moonlighted as a translator in Paris (he intro-

STRANGERS IN PARIS

Foreigners (*étrangers*, or strangers, to the French) have found inspiration in Paris since Charles Dickens used the city alongside London as the backdrop to his novel on the French Revolution, *A Tale of Two Cities*, in 1859. The glory days of Paris as a literary setting, however, were without a doubt the interwar years (p187).

Both Ernest Hemingway's *The Sun Also Rises* and the posthumous *A Moveable Feast* portray bohemian life in Paris between the wars; many of the vignettes in the latter – dissing Ford Maddox Ford in a café, 'sizing up' F Scott Fitzgerald in a toilet in the Latin Quarter and overhearing Gertrude Stein and her lover, Alice B Toklas, bitchin' at one another from the sitting room of their salon near the Jardin du Luxembourg – are classic and *très parisien*.

Language guru Stein, who could be so tiresome with her wordplays ('Pigeons on the grass, alas') and endless repetitions ('A rose is a rose is a rose is a rose') in books like *The Making of Americans*, was able to let her hair down by assuming her lover's identity in *The Autobiography of Alice B Toklas*. It's a fascinating account of the author's many years in Paris, her salon on the rue de Fleurus in the 6e and her friendships with Matisse, Picasso, Braque, Hemingway and others. It's also where you'll find that classic recipe for hashish brownies. Stein's *Wars I Have Seen* is a personal account of life in German-occupied Paris.

Down and Out in Paris and London is George Orwell's account of the time he spent working as a *plongeur* (dishwasher) in Paris and living with tramps in Paris and London in the early 1930s. Both *Tropic of Cancer* and *Quiet Days in Clichy* by Henry Miller are steamy novels set partly in the French capital. Mention should also be made of Anaïs Nin's voluminous diaries and fiction, especially her published correspondence with Miller, which is highly evocative of 1930s Paris.

For a taste of Paris in the 1950s try *Giovanni's Room*, James Baldwin's poignant account of a young American in Paris who falls in love with an Italian bartender, and his struggle with his sexuality. *Satori in Paris* by Jack Kerouac is the sometimes entertaining (eg the scene in the Montparnasse gangster bar) but often irritating account of the American Beat writer's last trip to France.

duced the works of the American writer Edgar Allan Poe to Europe in editions that have since become classics of English-to-French translation), was obliged to cut half a dozen poems from his work and was fined 300 francs. He died an early and painful death, practically unknown. Flaubert's second-most popular novel, *L'Éducation Sentimentale* (Sentimental Education), presents a vivid picture of life among Parisian dilettantes, intellectuals and revolutionaries during the decline and fall of Louis-Philippe's monarchy and the February Revolution of 1848.

The aim of Émile Zola, who came to Paris with his close friend, the artist Paul Cézanne, in 1858, was to transform novel-writing from an art to a science by the application of experimentation. His theory may now seem naive, but his work influenced most significant French writers of the late 19th century and is reflected in much 20th-century fiction as well. His novel *Nana* tells the decadent tale of a young woman who resorts to prostitution to survive the Paris of the Second Empire.

Paul Verlaine and Stéphane Mallarmé created the symbolist movement, which strove to express states of mind rather than simply detail daily reality. Arthur Rimbaud, apart from crowding an extraordinary amount of exotic travel into his 37 years and having a tempestuous sexual relationship with Verlaine, produced two enduring pieces of work: *Illuminations* and *Une Saison en Enfer* (A Season in Hell). Rimbaud stopped writing and deserted Europe for Africa in 1874, never to return. Verlaine died at 39 rue Descartes (5e) in 1896.

Marcel Proust dominated the early 20th century with his giant seven-volume novel *À la Recherche du Temps Perdu* (Remembrance of Things Past), which is largely autobiographical and explores in evocative detail the true meaning of past experience recovered from the unconscious by 'involuntary memory'. In 1907 Proust moved from the family home near av des Champs-Élysées to the apartment on blvd Haussmann that was famous for its cork-lined bedroom (now on display at the Musée Carnavalet in the Marais, p146) from which he almost never stirred. André Gide found his voice in the celebration of gay sensuality and, later, left-wing politics. *Les Faux-Monnayeurs* (The Counterfeiters) exposes the hypocrisy and self-deception to which people resort in order to fit in with others or deceive themselves.

André Breton led the group of French surrealists and wrote its three manifestos, although the first use of the word 'surrealist' is attributed to the poet Guillaume Apollinaire, a fellow traveller of surrealism who was killed in action in WWI. As a poet, Breton was overshadowed by Paul Éluard and Louis Aragon, whose most famous surrealist novel was *Le Paysan de Paris* (Nightwalker). Colette (Sidonie-Gabriel Colette) enjoyed tweaking the nose of conventionally moral readers with titillating novels that detailed the amorous exploits of such heroines as the schoolgirl Claudine. Her best-known work is *Gigi* but far more interesting is *Paris de Ma Fenêtre* (Paris from My Window), dealing with the German occupation of Paris. Her view, by the way, was from 9 rue de Beaujolais in the 1er, overlooking the Jardin du Palais Royal.

After WWII, existentialism developed as a significant literary movement around Jean-Paul Sartre, Simone de Beauvoir and Albert Camus, who worked and conversed in the cafés of blvd St-Germain in the 6e. All three stressed the importance of the writer's political engagement. *L'Âge de Raison* (The Age of Reason), the first volume of Sartre's trilogy *Les Chemins de la Liberté* (The Roads to Freedom), is a great Parisian novel; the subsequent volumes recall Paris immediately before and during WWII. De Beauvoir, author of *Le Deuxième Sexe* (The Second Sex), had a profound influence on feminist thinking. Camus' novel *L'Étranger* (The Stranger) reveals that the absurd is the condition of modern man, who feels himself a stranger – more accurately translated as 'outsider' in English – in his world.

In the late 1950s certain novelists began to look for new ways of organising narrative. The so-called *nouveau roman* (new novel) refers to the works of Nathalie Sarraute, Alain Robbe-Grillet, Boris Vian, Julien Gracq, Michel Butor and others. However, these writers never formed a close-knit group, and their experiments took them in divergent directions. Today the *nouveau roman* is very much out of favour in France, though the authors' names often appear in print and conversation.

Mention must also be made of *Histoire d'O* (Story of O), the highly erotic sadomasochistic novel written by Dominique Aury under a pseudonym in 1954. It sold more copies than any other contemporary French novel outside France.

In 1980 Marguerite Yourcenar, best known for her memorable historical novels such as *Mémoires d'Hadrien* (Hadrian's Memoirs), became the first woman to be elected to the Académie Française. Several years later Marguerite Duras came to the notice of a larger public when she won the Prix Goncourt for her novel *L'Amant* (The Lover) in 1984. It was turned into successful film in 1992.

Philippe Sollers was one of the editors of *Tel Quel*, a highbrow and left-wing Paris-based review that was very influential in the 1960s and early 1970s. His 1960s novels were highly experimental, but with *Femmes* (Women) he returned to a conventional narrative style.

Another editor of *Tel Quel* was Julia Kristeva, best known for her theoretical writings on literature and psychoanalysis. In recent years she has turned her hand to fiction, and *Les Samuraï* (The Samurai; 1990), a fictionalised account of the heady days of *Tel Quel*, is an interesting document on the life of the Paris intelligentsia. Roland Barthes and Michel Foucault are other authors and philosophers associated with the 1960s and '70s.

So-called accessible contemporary authors who enjoy a wide following include Patrick Modiano, Yann Queffélec, Pascal Quignard, Denis Tillinac and Nicole de Buron, a very popular mainstream humour writer whose books sell in the hundreds of thousands. Fred Vargas is a popular writer of crime fiction.

More serious authors whose careers and works are closely scrutinised by the literary establishment and the well-read include Jean Echenoz, Nina Bouraoui, Jean-Philippe Toussaint, Annie Ernaux and Erik Orsenna. Others are Christine Angot, '*la reine de l'autofiction*' famous for her autobiographical novels, the best-selling novelist Marc Levy, and Yasmina Khadra, a former colonel in the Algerian army who adopted his wife's name as a nom de plume.

Two recent winners of the Prix Goncourt have been controversial for rather less-than-literary reasons. Jonathan Littell, who took the prize in 2006 for *Les Bienveillantes*, is actually a New York–born American, though he was largely educated in France and writes in French. And it wasn't enough that the original title of Gilles Leroy's award-winning *Alabama Song* (2007) was in English, the theme – the story of the descent into madness of Zelda Fitzgerald, wife of novelist F Scott Fitzgerald and written in the first person – is centred squarely on the other side of the puddle. In 2009 the Franco-Senegalese writer Marie N'Diaye became the first women to win the Goncourt in over a decade with her *Trois Femmes Puissantes* (Three Powerful Women).

PAINTING

The philosopher Voltaire wrote that French painting began with Nicolas Poussin, the greatest representative of 17th-century classicism who frequently set scenes from ancient Rome, classical mythology and the Bible in ordered landscapes bathed in golden light. It's not a bad starting point.

In the 18th century Jean-Baptiste Chardin brought the humbler domesticity of the Dutch masters to French art. In 1785 the public reacted with enthusiasm to two large paintings with clear republican messages: *The Oath of the Horatii* and *Brutus Condemning His Son* by Jacques-Louis David. David became one of the leaders of the French Revolution, and a virtual dictator in matters of art, where he advocated a precise, severe classicism. He was made official state painter by Napoleon Bonaparte, glorifying him as general, first consul and then emperor, and is best remembered for his *Death of Marat,* depicting the Jacobin propagandist lying dead in his bath.

Jean-Auguste-Dominique Ingres, David's most gifted pupil in Paris, continued in the neoclassical tradition. The historical pictures to which he devoted most of his life (eg *Oedipus and the Sphinx*, the 1808 version of which is in the Louvre) are now generally regarded as inferior to his portraits. The name of Ingres, who played the violin for enjoyment, lives on in the phrase *violon d'Ingres*, which means 'hobby' in French.

The gripping *Raft of the Medusa* by Théodore Géricault is on the threshold of romanticism; if Géricault had not died early aged 33 he probably would have become a leader of the movement, along with his friend Eugène Delacroix. Delacroix's most famous, if not best, work is *Liberty Leading the People*, which commemorates the July Revolution of 1830 (p30).

The members of the Barbizon School brought about a parallel transformation of landscape painting. The school derived its name from a village near the Forêt de Fontainebleau (Forest of Fontainebleau; p362), where Camille Corot and Jean-François Millet, among others, gathered to paint *en plein air* (in the open air). Corot is best known for his landscapes (*The Bridge at Nantes, Chartres Cathedral*); Millet took many of his subjects from peasant life (*The Gleaners*) and had a great influence on Van Gogh.

LOCAL KNOWLEDGE: CARA BLACK

A Francophile from California... How does that work? Francophilia goes way back. I had French nuns in school, my uncle studied under Georges Braque on the GI Bill after the war and in 1971, while travelling through Paris, I went to rue du Bac and knocked on the door of my favourite writer, [two-times Prix Goncourt winner] Romain Gary. He invited me to his café for an espresso and a cigar. We both had both.

Ah, smoke – but fire? All this murder and darkness in the City of Light? That all came about much later, in 1993. I was walking around the place des Vosges and remembered a visit to Paris almost a decade before when I stayed with my friend Sarah. She had taken me on a tour of the pregentrified Marais and shown me the ancient abandoned building where her Jewish mother had hidden during the war and from where the rest of the family had been deported to Auschwitz. The idea for my first book *Murder in the Marais* came to me on the plane going home.

Do you get down and dirty in your research? I crawl under buildings, explore restrooms in old cafés, visit ghost metro stations, go down into the city sewers and even the tunnels under the Palais Royal. I interview private detectives and the police – I'm one of only two American women writers to have spent time in the Préfecture and recently got a tour of the special ops security unit out at Versailles and did some shooting at their firing range. Some of them have become friends and I take them to dinner.

Now we're cooking! What's on the menu? Murder most fowl? Steak saignant ('bleeding', or rare)? Anything but the *écrévisse* (freshwater crayfish) that come from the Seine. They feed on corpses. I discovered that while researching *Murder on the Île Saint-Louis*. One restaurant was still selling them.

Why are you almost always Right and not Left Bankwise? I don't write about the Paris of tourists, where people wear berets and carry baguettes. I'm not really comfortable on the Left Bank though I killed a few people on that side last year in *Murder in the Latin Quarter* and will be offing a few more next year in the 16e. I feel better where my friends live – the Marais, Belleville, Montmartre. I understand these places.

I wish I could... Tie a scarf the way French women do.

I wish I hadn't... Buried Baudelaire in Père Lachaise cemetery. He's actually in Montparnasse.

I'll always come back to Paris for... Felafel at L'As de Felafel (p260), hot chocolate at Ladurée (p235), bicycle rides along the Canal St-Martin, the old stones of the place des Vosges and the ghosts. Paris is full of ghosts and they communicate. You only need to listen.

Interviewed by Steve Fallon

Cara Black (www.carablack.com), who divides her time between Paris and San Francisco, is the author of a best-selling murder-by-arrondissement series set in Paris and featuring the intrepid, half-French-half-American sleuth Aimée Leduc. The latest is Murder in the Palais Royal, *the 10th in the series.*

Millet anticipated the realist program of Gustave Courbet, a prominent member of the Paris Commune (he was accused of, and imprisoned for, destroying the Vendôme Column), whose paintings show the drudgery of manual labour and dignity of ordinary life *(Funeral at Ornans, The Angelus)*.

Édouard Manet used realism to depict the life of the Parisian middle classes, yet he included in his pictures numerous references to the Old Masters. His *Déjeuner sur l'Herbe* and *Olympia* both were considered scandalous, largely because they broke with the traditional treatment of their subject matter. He was a pivotal figure in the transition from realism to Impressionism.

Impressionism, initially used as a term of derision, was taken from the title of an 1874 experimental painting by Claude Monet, *Impression: Soleil Levant* (Impression: Sunrise). Monet was the leading figure of the school, which counted among its members Alfred Sisley, Camille Pissarro, Pierre-Auguste Renoir and Berthe Morisot. The Impressionists' main aim was to capture the effects of fleeting light, painting almost universally in the open air – and light came to dominate the content of their painting.

Edgar Degas was a fellow traveller of the Impressionists, but he preferred painting café life *(Absinthe)* and in ballet studios *(The Dance Class)* than the great outdoors. Henri de Toulouse-Lautrec was a great admirer of Degas, but chose subjects one or two notches below: people in the bistros, brothels and music halls of Montmartre (eg *Au Moulin Rouge*). He is best known for his posters and lithographs, in which the distortion of the figures is both satirical and decorative.

Paul Cézanne is celebrated for his still lifes and landscapes depicting the south of France, though he spent many years in Paris after breaking with the Impressionists. The name of Paul Gauguin immediately conjures up studies of Tahitian and Breton women. Both painters are usually referred to as post-Impressionists, something of a catch-all term for the diverse styles that flowed from Impressionism.

In the late 19th century Gauguin worked for a time in Arles in Provence with the Dutch-born Vincent Van Gogh, who spent most of his painting life in France and died in the town of Auvers-sur-Oise (p377) north of Paris in 1890. A brilliant, innovative artist, Van Gogh produced haunting self-portraits and landscapes in which bold colour assumes an expressive and emotive quality.

Van Gogh's later technique paralleled pointillism, developed by Georges Seurat, who applied paint in small dots or uniform brush strokes of unmixed colour, producing fine 'mosaics' of warm and cool tones in such tableaux as *Une Baignade, Asnières* (Bathers at Asnières). Henri Rousseau was a contemporary of the post-Impressionists but his 'naive' art was totally unaffected by them. His dreamlike pictures of the Paris suburbs and of jungle and desert scenes (eg *The Snake Charmer*) have influenced art right up to this century.

Gustave Moreau was a member of the symbolist school. His eerie treatment of mythological subjects can be seen in his old studio, which is now the Musée National Gustave Moreau (p130) in the 9e. Fauvism took its name from the slight of a critic who compared the exhibitors at the 1905 Salon d'Automne (Autumn Salon) with *fauves* (beasts) because of their wild brushstrokes and radical use of intensely bright colours. Among these 'beastly' painters were Henri Matisse, André Derain and Maurice de Vlaminck.

Cubism was effectively launched in 1907 with *Les Demoiselles d'Avignon* by the Spanish prodigy Pablo Picasso. Cubism, as developed by Picasso, Georges Braque and Juan Gris, deconstructed the subject into a system of intersecting planes and presented various aspects simultaneously. Good examples are Braque's *Houses at l'Estaque* and *Woman Playing the Mandolin* by Picasso.

In the 1920s and '30s the so-called École de Paris (School of Paris) was formed by a group of expressionists, mostly foreign born, including Amedeo Modigliani from Italy, Foujita from Japan and Marc Chagall from Russia, whose works combined fantasy and folklore.

Dada, both a literary and artistic movement of revolt, started in Zürich in 1915. In Paris, one of the key Dadaists was Marcel Duchamp, whose *Mona Lisa* adorned with moustache and goatee epitomises the iconoclastic spirit of the movement. Surrealism, an offshoot of Dada, flourished between the wars. Drawing on the theories of Sigmund Freud, it attempted to reunite the conscious and unconscious realms, to permeate everyday life with fantasies and dreams. Among the most important proponents of this style in Paris were Chagall, as well as René Magritte, André Masson, Max Ernst, André Breton and Piet Mondrian. The most influential, however, was the Spanish-born artist Salvador Dalí, who arrived in the French capital in 1929 and painted some of his most seminal works (eg *Sleep, Paranoia*) while residing here. To see his work, visit the Dalí Espace Montmartre, p135).

WWII ended Paris' role as the world's artistic capital. Many artists left during the occupation, and though some returned after the war, the city never regained its old magnetism, with New York and then London picking up the baton. A few postwar Parisian artists worth noting have been Jean Fautrier, Nicolas de Staël, Bernard Buffet and Robert Combas, one of whose larger-than-life murals can be seen in rue des Haudriettes (4e) in the Marais (Map p152). This is just one of 120 commissioned murals commissioned in Paris. In addition check out the fine set of wall paintings by a group of four artists at 52 rue de Belleville, 20e (Map p148).

SCULPTURE

By the 14th century, sculpture was increasingly commissioned for the tombs of the nobility. In Renaissance Paris, Pierre Bontemps decorated the beautiful tomb of François I at the Basilique de St-Denis (p173), and Jean Goujon created the Fontaine des Innocents (p79). The baroque style is exemplified by Guillaume Coustou's *Horses of Marly* at the entrance to the av des Champs-Élysées.

In the mid-19th century, memorial statues in public places came to replace sculpted tombs. One of the best artists in the new mode was François Rude, who sculpted the Maréchal Ney statue (Map p108), *Maréchal under Napoleon,* outside La Closerie des Lilas, and the relief on the Arc de Triomphe. Another sculptor was Jean-Baptiste Carpeaux, who began as a romantic, but whose work – such as *The Dance* on the Palais Garnier and his fountain in the Jardin du Luxembourg – look back to the gaiety and flamboyance of the baroque era. At the end of the 19th century Auguste Rodin's work overcame the conflict between neoclassicism and romanticism. One of Rodin's most gifted pupils was his lover Camille Claudel, whose work can be seen along with that of Rodin in the Musée Rodin (p111).

Both Braque and Picasso experimented with sculpture, and in the spirit of Dada, Marcel Duchamp exhibited 'found objects', one of which was a urinal, which he mounted, signed and dubbed *Fountain* in 1917.

One of the most influential sculptors to emerge in Paris before WWII was the Romanian-born Constantin Brancusi, whose work can be seen in the Atelier Brancusi, which is part of the Centre Pompidou (p78). After the war César Baldaccini – known simply as César to the world – used iron and scrap metal to create his imaginary insects and animals, later graduating to pliable plastics. Among his best-known works are the *Centaur* statue (Map p112) in the 6e and the statuette handed to actors at the Césars (French cinema's equivalent to the Oscars). Two sculptors who lived and worked most of their adult lives in Paris and each have a museum devoted to their life and work are Ossip Zadkine (p107) and Antoine Bourdelle (p171).

In 1936 France put forward a bill providing for 'the creation of monumental decorations in public buildings' by allotting 1% of all building costs to public art, but this did not really get off the ground for another half-century when Daniel Buren's *Les Deux Plateaux* sculpture (p78) was commissioned at Palais Royal. The whole concept mushroomed, and artwork started to appear everywhere in Paris: in the Jardin des Tuileries (*The Welcoming Hands;* p75), throughout La Défense (p175), Parc de la Villette (eg *Bicylette Ensevelie,* 1990; p139) and even in the metro (see the boxed text, p103).

MUSIC

In the 17th and 18th centuries French baroque music influenced much of Europe's musical output. Composers François Couperin and Jean Philippe Rameau were two luminaries of this period.

top picks

ART & SCULPTURE MUSEUMS

- Musée du Louvre (p70) Many of the works of art mentioned in the Painting section, including Ingres' *Oedipus and the Sphinx* and *Raft of the Medusa* by Théodore Géricault, live here.
- Musée Rodin (p111) Without a doubt the best museum devoted to sculpture in Paris.
- Musée d'Orsay (p107) This is the Fort Knox of Impressionism and no one worth his/her palette is not represented here.
- Musée Atelier Zadkine (p107) Come here to view this sculptor's work carved from lovely and very tactile fruit woods.
- Musée d'Art Moderne de la Ville de Paris (p120) This is where you'll see examples of just about every major artistic movement of the last century.

top picks

CDS

- **Édith Piaf: Live at the Paris Olympia** – a collation of live recordings made in the 1950s and '60s, this album contains 20 of the belle of Belleville's classics, including 'Milord', 'Hymne à l'Amour' and, of course, 'Non, Je Ne Regrette Rien'.
- **Georges Brassens: Le Disque d'Or** – everything you need to know about one of France's greatest performers (and the inspiration for Jacques Brel) is in this 21-track double helping.
- **Anthologie Serge Gainsbourg** – this three-CD anthology includes the metro man's most famous tracks, including 'Le Poinçonneur des Lilas' and 'Je t'aime…Moi Non Plus' in duet with Brigitte Bardot.
- **La Nouvelle Chanson Française** – like it or not, this five-pack by various artists gives directions to the way vocals are heading in French music, with everything from traditional and cabaret to folk-electronic and Paris club sound.
- **Abd al Malik: Danté** – the award-winning third album from French rapper of Congolese origins who sings of 'La France Arc-en-Ciel' (Rainbow France) and lists Jacques Brel as one of his inspirations.
- **Arnaud Fleurent-Didier: La Réproduction** – hot on humorous nostalgia-driven existentialist lyrics, Fleurent-Didier might at first look like just another *nouvelle chanson* devotee but manages to seduce where others fail.
- **Camille: Music Hole** – the latest effort from massively popular bobo (bourgeois bohemian) icon Camille Dalmais

France produced and cultivated a number of brilliant composers in the 19th century, including Hector Berlioz, Charles Gounod, César Franck, Camille Saint-Saëns and Georges Bizet. Berlioz was the founder of modern orchestration, while Franck's organ compositions sparked a musical renaissance in France that would go on to produce such greats as Gabriel Fauré and the impressionists Maurice Ravel and Claude Debussy. The latter's adaptations of poems are among the greatest contributions to the world of music.

More recent classical composers include Olivier Messiaen, for decades the chief organist at the Église de la Trinité in the 9e. Until his death in 1992 at the age of 84 he combined modern, almost mystical music with natural sounds such as birdsong. His student, the radical Pierre Boulez, includes computer-generated sound in his compositions.

Jazz hit Paris with a bang in the 1920s and has remained popular ever since. France's contribution to the world of jazz has been great, including the violinist Stéphane Grapelli and the legendary three-fingered Roma guitarist Django Reinhardt, whose birth centenary was feted nationwide in 2010.

The most popular form of indigenous music is the *chanson française*, with a tradition going back to the troubadours of the Middle Ages. 'French songs' have always emphasised lyrics over music and rhythm, which may explain the enormous success of rap in France in the 1990s, especially of groups like MC Solaar, NTM and I Am. The *chanson* tradition, celebrated by street singers such as Lucienne Delisle and Dahlia, was revived from the 1930s onwards by the likes of Édith Piaf and Charles Trénet. In the 1950s singers like Georges Brassens, Léo Ferré, Claude Nougaro, Jacques Brel and Barbara became national stars; the music of balladeer/folk singer Serge Gainsbourg – very charming, very sexy and very French – remains enormously popular almost two decades after his death. Indeed, a biopic celebrating his life – *Serge Gainsbourg: Une Vie Héroïque* (Serge Gainsbourg: A Heroic Life) – was released in late 2009 to wide acclaim.

The turn of the new millennium saw a revival of this genre called *la nouvelle chanson française*. Among the most exciting performers of this old-fashioned, slightly wordy genre are Vincent Delerm, Bénabar, Jeanne Cherhal, Camille, Soha and a group called Les Têtes Raides. The latest crooner to arrive on the scene is Arnaud Fleurent-Didier.

France was among the first countries to 'discover' *sono mondiale* (though 'world music' is suffering of late as non-French musicians often can't get visas to perform here). You'll come across everything from Algerian rai and other North African popular music (Khaled, Cheb Mami, Rachid Taha) and Senegalese *mbalax* (Youssou N'Dour) to West Indian *zouk* (Kassav, Zouk Machine) and Cuban salsa. In the late 1980s, Mano Negra and Les Négresses Vertes were two bands that combined many of these elements – often with brilliant results. Magic System from Côte d'Ivoire has helped popularise *zouglou* (a kind of West African rap and dance music) with its album *Premier Gaou*, and Congolese Koffi Olomide still packs the halls.

Acts from Mali to keep an eye (and an ear) out for are the blind singing couple, Amadou and Mariam, and Rokia Traoré.

Two hugely popular, almost poetic French–African rapper-slammers are three-time Victoire de la Musique–award winner, Abd al Malik, and the jazzier Oxmo Puccino.

In recent years a distinctly urban and highly exportable Parisian sound has developed, often mixing computer-enhanced Chicago blues and Detroit techno with 1960s lounge music and vintage tracks from the likes of Gainsbourg and Brassens. Among those playing now are Parisian duo Daft Punk, who adapt first-wave acid house and techno to their younger roots in pop, indie rock and hip-hop, and erstwhile Mano Negra leader Manu Chao, whose music is simple guitar and lyrics – plain and straightforward.

One could be forgiven for thinking that popular music in France is becoming dynastic. The very distinctive M (for Mathieu) is the son of singer Louis Chédid; Arthur H is the progeny of pop-rock musician Jacques Higelin; and Thomas Dutronc is the offspring of 1960s idols *père* Jacques and Françoise Hardy. And the Gainsbourg dynasty doesn't look like ending any time soon. Serge's daughter with Jane Birkin, Charlotte, released her third album at the end of 2009.

Noir Désir was *the* sound of French rock until its lead singer, Bertrand Cantat, was imprisoned for the murder of his girlfriend and it disbanded. Worth noting are Louise Attack, Mickey 3D, Nosfell, who sings in his very own invented language. Even worse, the hottest group to emerge in France in recent years, the electronic trio Pony Pony Run Run, sing – shock horror – in English. It's a long way from the *yéyé* (imitative rock) of the 1960s as sung by Johnny Hallyday, otherwise known as 'Johnny National' (until he took Belgian nationality for tax reasons a few years back).

CINEMA

With more than 300 films being screened at any one time, Parisians go to the cinema on average once a week, and with monthly *à volonté* (at will) cards costing just €20, this makes for a cheap and entertaining night out. People here take films, especially French films – France is the leading film producer in Europe, making over 160 films a year – very seriously. Parisians always prefer to watch foreign films in their original language with French subtitles.

France's place in film history was firmly ensured when the Lumière brothers from Lyon invented 'moving pictures' and organised the world's first paying public film-screening – a series of two-minute reels – in Paris' Grand Café on the blvd des Capucines (9e) in December 1895.

In the 1920s and 1930s avant-garde directors, such as René Clair, Marcel Carné and the intensely productive Jean Renoir, son of Impressionist painter Pierre-Auguste, searched for new forms and subjects.

In the late 1950s a large group of young directors arrived on the scene with a new genre, the so-called *nouvelle vague* (new wave). This group included Jean-Luc Godard, François Truffaut, Claude Chabrol, Eric Rohmer, Jacques Rivette, Louis Malle and Alain Resnais. This disparate group of directors believed in the primacy of the film maker, giving rise to the term *film d'auteur* (literally, 'author's film' but meaning a film that reflects the director's personal creative vision).

Many films followed, among them Alain Resnais' *Hiroshima Mon Amour* (Hiroshima My Love) and *L'Année Dernière à Marienbad* (Last Year at Marienbad), and Luis Buñuel's *Belle de Jour*. François Truffaut's *Les Quatre Cents Coups* (The 400 Blows) was partly based on his own rebellious adolescence. Jean-Luc Godard made such films as *À Bout de Souffle* (Breathless), *Alphaville* and *Pierrot le Fou,* which showed even less concern for sequence and narrative. The 'new wave' continued until the 1970s, by which time it had lost its experimental edge and appeal.

Of the directors of the 1950s and 1960s who were not part of the new wave school, one of the most notable was Jacques Tati, who made many comic films based around the charming, bumbling figure of Monsieur Hulot and his struggles to adapt to the modern age. The best examples are *Les Vacances de M Hulot* (Mr Hulot's Holiday) and *Mon Oncle* (My Uncle).

The most successful directors of the 1980s and 1990s included Jean-Jacques Beineix, who made *Diva* and *Betty Blue,* Jean-Luc Besson, who shot *Subway* and *The Big Blue,* and Léos Carax *(Boy Meets Girl).*

Light social comedies *La Vie Est un Long Fleuve Tranquille* (Life is a Long Quiet River) by Étienne Chatiliez, *8 Femmes*, with its all-star cast (including Catherine Deneuve and Isabelle Huppert) by François Ozon and the Marseille comedy *Taxi* have been among the biggest hits in France in recent years.

top picks

PARIS FILMS

- À Bout de Souffle (Breathless; France, 1959) – Jean-Luc Goddard's first feature is a carefree, fast-paced B&W celebration of Paris – from av des Champs-Élysées to the cafés of the Left Bank.
- Last Tango in Paris (USA, 1972) – in Bernardo Bertolucci's classic, Marlon Brando gives the performance of his career portraying a grief-stricken American in Paris who tries to find salvation in anonymous, sadomasochistic sex.
- La Haine (Hate; France, 1995) – Matthieu Kassovitz's incendiary B&W film examines the racism, social repression and violence among Parisian *beurs* (young French-born Algerians).
- Les Quatre Cents Coups (The 400 Blows; France, 1959) – based on the French idiom *faire les quatre cents coups* (to raise hell), François Truffaut's first film is the semiautobiographical story of a downtrodden and neglected Parisian teenage boy who turns to outward rebellion.
- Le Fabuleux Destin d'Amélie Poulain (Amelie; France, 2001) – one of the most popular French films internationally in years, Jean-Pierre Jeunet's feel-good story of a winsome young Parisian do-gooder named Amélie takes viewers on a colourful tour of Pigalle, Notre Dame, train stations and, above all, Montmartre.
- Paris, Je t'aime (Paris, I Love You; France, 2006) – an ode to Paris in 18 short films shot in different arrondissements (the 11e and 15e were dropped at the last minute) by different directors, including the Coen Brothers and Gus Van Sant.
- La Môme (La Vie en Rose; 2007) – a biopic so faithful to the person and the time, that it's as if Édith Piaf – played by the highly honoured Marion Cotillard – had just woken up from a long sleep at Père Lachaise cemetery. *Incroyable.*

Matthieu Kassovitz's award-winning *La Haine* (Hate), apparently inspired by such American films as *Mean Streets, Taxi Driver* and *Do the Right Thing*, examined the prejudice and violence among young French-born Algerians. Alain Resnais' *On Connaît la Chanson* (Same Old Song), based on the life of the late British TV playwright Dennis Potter, received international acclaim and six Césars in 1997.

Other well-regarded directors active today include Bertrand Blier (*Trop Belle pour Toi;* Too Beautiful for You), Cédric Klapisch (*Un Air de Famille;* Family Relations), German-born Dominik Moll (*Harry, un Ami qui Vous Veut du Bien;* With a Friend like Harry), Agnès Jaoul (*Le Gout des Autres;* The Taste of Others), Yves Lavandier (*Oui, Mais…;* Yes, But…), Catherine Breillat (*À Ma Sœur;* Fat Girl) and Abdellatif Kechiche (*La Graine et le Mulet;* The Secret of the Grain), who won his second César in 2008.

Among the most popular and/or biggest-grossing French films at home and abroad in recent years have been Jean-Pierre Jeunet's feel-good *Le Fabuleux Destin d'Amélie Poulain* (Amélie); Christophe Barratier's *Les Choristes* (The Chorus), about a new teacher at a strict boarding school who affects the students' lives through music; *De Battre Mon Cœur s'est Arrêté* (The Beat My Heart Skipped) by Jacques Audiard, a film noir about a violent rent collector turned classical pianist confronting his own life and that of his criminal father; and *Paris, Je t'aime* (Paris, I Love You), a two-hour film made up of 18 short films each set in a different arrondissement. The runaway success story in terms of awards in recent years has been Olivier Dahan's *La Môme* (La Vie en Rose), starring Marion Cotillard as Édith Piaf. Not only did Cotillard pick up a César, Golden Globe and BAFTA for her efforts, she was also the first French woman to win an Oscar for best actress since Simone Signoret was so honoured for *Room at the Top* in 1959. But the biggest French money spinner was the 2008 *Bienvenue Chez les Ch'tis* (Welcome to the Ch'tis), a rural comedy about a postal worker from the south who moves to Picardy in the north and falls for the charm of the locals. It drew audiences of more than 20 million, the first French film to do so, and grossed $193 million, the most successful French film of all time.

Jacques Audiard's gripping prison thriller *Un Prophète* (A Prophet) won the 2009 César for best film (as well as in numerous other categories) and was nominated for an Academy Award as best foreign movie. The year also saw erstwhile *nouvelle vague* director Alain Resnais back on form with the critically acclaimed romantic (mis)adventure *Les Herbes Folles* (Wild Grass). A recent personal favourite was *Welcome* by Philippe Lioret, the story of a young Iraqi–Kurdish refugee's attempt to reach Britain with veteran Vincent Lindon as a swimming instructor at a Calais pool.

THEATRE

France's first important dramatist was Alexandre Hardy, who appeared in Paris in 1597 and published over a relatively short period hundreds of plays that were enormously popular in their day. Though few of his works (about three dozen of which have survived) have withstood the test of time, Hardy was an innovator who helped bridge the gap between the French theatre of the Middle Ages and Renaissance and that of the 17th century.

During the golden age of French drama in the 17th century the most popular playwright was Molière. Like William Shakespeare, he started his career as an actor; Laurent Tirard's 2007 biopic *Molière* is a credible (though fictionalised) account of his early years. Plays such as *Tartuffe,* a satire on the corruption of the aristocracy, won him the enmity of (and a ban from) both the state and the church but are now staples of the classical repertoire. Pierre Corneille and Jean Racine, in contrast, drew their subjects from history and classical mythology. Racine's *Phèdre,* taken from Euripides, is a story of incest and suicide among the descendants of the Greek gods, while Corneille's tragedy *Horace* is derived from the historian Livy.

Theatre in France didn't really come into its own again until the postwar period of the 20th century with the arrival of two foreigners, both proponents of the so-called Théâtre de l'Absurde (Theatre of the Absurd), who wrote in French. Works by Irish-born Samuel Beckett, such as *En Attendant Godot* (Waiting for Godot; 1952), are bleak and point to the existentialist meaninglessness of life but are also richly humorous. The plays of Eugène Ionesco – eg *La Cantatrice Chauve* (The Bald Soprano; 1948) – can be equally dark and satirical but ultimately compassionate.

Plays performed in Paris are – for obvious reasons – performed largely in French but more and more mainstream theatres are projecting English-language subtitles on screens. For information on theatres that host English-speaking troupes and/or stage plays in languages other than French, see p307.

DANCE

Ballet as we know it today originated in Italy but was brought to France in the late 16th century by Catherine de Médici. The first *ballet comique de la reine* (dramatic ballet) was performed at an aristocratic wedding at the Parisian court in 1581. It combined music, dance and poetic recitations (usually in praise of the monarch) and was performed by male courtiers with women of the court forming the corps de ballet. Louis XIV so enjoyed the spectacles that he danced many leading roles himself at Versailles. You can see Louis go through his paces in Ken Russell's 1971 film *The Devils* based on Aldous Huxley's *The Devils of Loudun* (1952). In 1661 he founded the Académie Royale de Danse (Royal Dance Academy), from which modern ballet developed.

By the end of the 18th century, choreographers such as Jean-Georges Noverre had become more important than the musicians, poets and the dancers themselves. In the early 19th century, romantic ballets, such as *Giselle* and *Les Sylphides,* were better attended than the opera. For 10 years from 1945 Roland Petit created such innovative ballets as *Turangalila,* with music by Olivier Messiaen, and *Le Jeune Homme et la Mort.* Maurice Béjart shocked his audiences with his *Symphonie pour un Homme Seul* (which was danced in black in 1955), *Le Sacre du Printemps* (The Rite of Spring) and *Le Marteau sans Maître,* with music by Pierre Boulez.

Today French dance seems to be moving in a new, more personal direction with such performers as Maguy Marin, Laurent Hilaire and Aurélie Dupont. Choreographers include the likes of Odile Duboc, Caroline Marcadé, Jean-Claude Gallotta, Jean-François Duroure, Boris Charmatz and, perhaps the most interesting and visible of modern French choreographers, Philippe Decouflé. Among the biggest names in contemporary dance are Angelin Preljocaj, Brahim Bouchelaghem and the godfather of French hip-hop dance, Gabin Nuissier.

ARCHITECTURE

Parisians have never been as intransigent as, say, Londoners in accepting changes to their cityscape, nor as unshocked by the new as New Yorkers appear to be. But then Paris never had as great a fire as London did in 1666, which offered architects a tabula rasa on which to redesign and build a modern city, or the green field that was New York in the late 18th century.

It took disease, clogged streets, an antiquated sewage system, a lack of open spaces and Baron Georges-Eugène Haussmann (p35) to drag Paris out of the Middle Ages into the modern world, and few town planners anywhere in the world have had as great an impact on the city of their birth as he did on his.

Haussmann's 19th-century transformation of Paris was a huge undertaking – Parisians endured years of 'flying dust, noise, and falling plaster and beams', as one contemporary observer wrote; entire areas of the city (eg the labyrinthine Île de la Cité) were razed and hundreds of thousands of (mostly poor) people displaced. Even worse – or better, depending on your outlook – it brought to a head the *vieux* (old) Paris versus *nouveau* (new) Paris, a debate in which writer Victor Hugo played a key role and which continues to this day.

GALLO-ROMAN

Traces of Roman Paris can be seen in the residential foundations and dwellings in the Crypte Archéologique (p83) under the square in front of Notre Dame; in the partially reconstructed Arènes de Lutèce (p104); and in the *frigidarium* (cooling room) and other remains of Roman baths dating from around AD 200 at the Musée National du Moyen Age (p104).

The Musée National du Moyen Age also contains the so-called Pillier des Nautes (Boatsmen's Pillar), one of the most valuable legacies of the Gallo-Roman period. It is a 2.5m-high monument dedicated to Jupiter and was erected by the boatmen's guild during the reign of Tiberius (AD 14–37) on the Île de la Cité. The boat has become the symbol of Paris, and the city's Latin motto is *'Fluctuat Nec Mergitur'* (Tosses but Does Not Sink).

MEROVINGIAN & CAROLINGIAN

Although quite a few churches were built in Paris during the Merovingian and Carolingian periods (6th to 10th centuries), very little of them remain.

When the Merovingian ruler Clovis I made Paris his seat in the early 6th century, he established an abbey dedicated to Sts Peter and Paul on the south bank of the Seine. All that remains of this once great abbey (later named in honour of Paris' patron, Ste Geneviève, and demolished in 1802) is the Tour Clovis (p187), a heavily restored Romanesque tower within the grounds of the prestigious Lycée Henri IV just east of the Panthéon.

Archaeological excavations in the crypt of the 12th-century Basilique de St-Denis (p173) have uncovered extensive tombs from both the Merovingian and Carolingian periods. The oldest of these dates from around AD 570.

ROMANESQUE

A religious revival in the 11th century led to the construction of a large number of *roman* (Romanesque) churches, so-called because their architects adopted many architectural elements (eg vaulting) from Gallo-Roman buildings still standing at the time. Romanesque buildings typically have round arches, heavy walls, few (and small) windows that let in very little light, and a lack of ornamentation that borders on the austere.

No civic buildings or churches in Paris are entirely Romanesque in style, but a few have important representative elements. The Église St-Germain des Prés (p105), built in the 11th century on the site of the Merovingian ruler Childeric's 6th-century abbey, has been altered many times over the centuries, but the Romanesque bell tower over the west entrance has changed little since AD 1000. There are also some decorated capitals (the upper part of the supporting columns) in the nave dating from this time. The choir, apse and truncated bell tower of the Église

FOR FURTHER INFORMATION

Those wanting to learn more about French architecture should visit the new Cité de l'Architecture et du Patrimoine (p117) in the Palais de Chaillot. Contemporary architecture in the capital is the focus of the permanent 800-sq-metre exhibition called 'Paris, Visite Guidée' (Paris, a Guided Tour) at the Pavillon de l'Arsenal (Map p148; ☎ 01 42 76 33 97; www.pavillon-arsenal.com; 21 blvd Morland, 4e; admission free; ⏰ 10.30am-6.30pm Tue-Sat, 11am-7pm Sun; Ⓜ Sully Morland), which is the city's town-planning and architectural centre. It also has rotating exhibits.

St-Nicholas des Champs (Map p148), now part of the Musée des Arts et Métiers, are Romanesque dating from about 1130. The Église St-Germain L'Auxerrois (p75) was built in a mixture of Gothic and Renaissance styles between the 13th and 16th centuries on a site used for Christian worship since about AD 500. But the square belfry that rises from next to the south transept arm is Romanesque.

GOTHIC

The Gothic style originated in the mid-12th century in northern France, where the region's great wealth attracted the finest architects, engineers and artisans. Gothic structures are characterised by ribbed vaults carved with great precision, pointed arches, slender verticals, chapels (often built or endowed by the wealthy or by guilds), galleries and arcades along the nave and chancel, refined decoration and large stained-glass windows. If you look closely at certain Gothic buildings, however, you'll notice minor asymmetrical elements introduced to avoid monotony.

The world's first Gothic building was the Basilique de St-Denis (p173), which combined various late-Romanesque elements to create a new kind of structural support in which each arch counteracted and complemented the next. Begun in around 1135, the basilica served as a model for many other 12th-century French cathedrals, including Notre Dame de Paris and the cathedral at Chartres.

In the 14th century, the Rayonnant – or Radiant – Gothic style, which was named after the radiating tracery of the rose windows, developed, with interiors becoming even lighter thanks to broader windows and more translucent stained glass. One of the most influential Rayonnant buildings was Ste-Chapelle (p97), whose stained glass forms a curtain of glazing on the 1st floor. The two transept façades of the Cathédrale de Notre Dame de Paris (p81) and the vaulted Salle des Gens d'Armes (Cavalrymen's Hall) in the Conciergerie (p83), the largest surviving medieval hall in Europe, are other fine examples of the Rayonnant Gothic style.

By the 15th century, decorative extravagance led to what is now called Flamboyant Gothic, so named because the wavy stone carving made the towers appear to be blazing or flaming (*flamboyant*). Beautifully lacy examples of Flamboyant architecture include the Clocher Neuf (New Bell Tower) at Chartres' Cathédrale Notre Dame (p370), the Église St-Séverin (Map p100) and the Tour St-Jacques (p80), a 52m tower which is all that remains of an early 16th-century church. Inside the Église St-Eustache (p79), there's some outstanding Flamboyant Gothic arch work holding up the ceiling of the chancel. Several *hôtels particuliers* (private mansions) were also built in this style, including the Hôtel de Cluny, now the Musée National du Moyen Age (p104), and the Hôtel de Sens (now the Bibliothèque Forney, p184).

RENAISSANCE

The Renaissance, which began in Italy in the early 15th century, set out to realise a 'rebirth' of classical Greek and Roman culture. It had its first impact on France at the end of that century, when Charles VIII began a series of invasions of Italy, returning with some new ideas.

GROWING UP IN PARIS

A signature architectural feature of Paris that is now being exported to cities like London is the vertical garden – called a *mur végétal* (vegetation wall) in French – especially that of Patrick Blanc (www.verticalgardenpatrickblanc.com). His works can be found in several locations around Paris but the most famous is the one facing the Seine at the Musée du Quai Branly (p117). Seeming to defy the very laws of gravity, the museum's vertical garden consists of some 15,000 low-light foliage plants from Central Europe, the USA, Japan and China planted on a surface of 800 sq metres. The reason they don't fall is that they are held in place by a frame of metal, PVC and non-biodegradable felt but no soil.

Other places to view M Blanc's handiwork:

- BHV Homme Men's department of the Bazar de l'Hôtel de Ville (p206) located nearby at 36 rue de la Verrerie, 4e.
- Centre Commercial des Quatre Temps, La Défense (p176)
- Fondation Cartier pour l'Art Contemporain, 14e (p171)
- Six Senses Spa, the Westin Paris (3 rue de Castiglione, 1er; Ⓜ Tuileries)

The Early Renaissance style, in which a variety of classical components and decorative motifs (columns, tunnel vaults, round arches, domes etc) were blended with the rich decoration of Flamboyant Gothic, is best exemplified in Paris by the Église St-Eustache (p79) on the Right Bank and Église St-Étienne du Mont (p104) on the Left Bank.

Mannerism, which followed Early Renaissance, was introduced by Italian architects and artists brought to France around 1530 by François I; over the following decades French architects who had studied in Italy took over from their Italian colleagues. In 1546 Pierre Lescot designed the richly decorated southwestern corner of the Cour Carrée of the Musée du Louvre (p70). The Petit Château at the Château de Chantilly (p366) was built about a decade later.

The Marais remains the best area for spotting reminders of the Renaissance in Paris proper, with some fine *hôtels particuliers* from this era such as Hôtel Carnavalet, housing part of the Musée Carnavalet (p146), and Hôtel Lamoignon (p185). The Mannerist style lasted until the early 17th century when it was subsumed by the baroque style.

BAROQUE

During the baroque period – which lasted from the tail end of the 16th to the late 18th centuries – painting, sculpture and classical architecture were integrated to create structures and interiors of great subtlety, refinement and elegance. With the advent of the baroque, architecture became more pictorial, with painted church ceilings illustrating the Passion of Christ to the faithful, and palaces invoking the power and order of the state.

Salomon de Brosse, who designed Paris' Palais du Luxembourg in the Jardin du Luxembourg (p106) in 1615, set the stage for two of France's most prominent early baroque architects: François Mansart, designer of the Église Notre Dame du Val-de-Grâce (Map p100), and his young rival Louis Le Vau, the architect of the Château de Vaux-le-Vicomte (p366), which served as a model for Louis XIV's palace at Versailles.

Other fine examples of French baroque are the Église St-Louis en l'Île (p97); the Chapelle de la Sorbonne (p104); the Palais Royal (p78); and the 17th-century Hôtel de Sully (p146), with its inner courtyard decorated with allegorical figures.

Rococo

Rococo, a derivation of late baroque, was popular during the Enlightenment (1700–80). The word comes from the French *rocaille* (loose pebbles), which, together with shells, were used to decorate inside walls and other surfaces. In Paris, rococo was confined almost exclusively to the interiors of private residences and had a minimal impact on churches and civic buildings, which continued to follow the conventional rules of baroque classicism. Rococo interiors, such as the oval rooms of the Hôtel de Rohan-Soubise now housing the Archives Nationales (National Archives; p147), were lighter, smoother and airier than their baroque predecessors, and tended to favour pastels over vivid colours.

NEOCLASSICISM

Neoclassical architecture, which emerged in about 1740 and remained popular in Paris until well into the 19th century, had its roots in the renewed interest in classical forms. Although it was, in part, a reaction against baroque and its adjunct, rococo, with their emphases on decoration and illusion, neoclassicism was more profoundly a search for order, reason and serenity through the adoption of the forms and conventions of Graeco-Roman antiquity: columns, simple geometric forms and traditional ornamentation.

Among the earliest examples of this style in Paris are the Italianate façade of the Église St-Sulpice (p106), designed in 1733 by Giovanni Servandoni, which took inspiration from Christopher Wren's Cathedral of St Paul in London; and the Petit Trianon at Versailles (p354), designed by Jacques-Ange Gabriel for Louis XV in 1761. The domed building housing the Institut de France (p114) is a masterpiece of early French neoclassical architecture, but France's greatest neoclassical architect of the 18th century was Jacques-Germain Soufflot, who designed the Panthéon (p99).

Neoclassicism really came into its own, however, under Napoleon, who used it extensively for monumental architecture intended to embody the grandeur of imperial France and its capital. Well-known Paris sights designed (though not necessarily completed) during the First

Empire (1804–14) include the Arc de Triomphe (p124); the Arc de Triomphe du Carrousel (p75); Église de Ste-Marie Madeleine (p129); the Bourse de Commerce (p80); and the Assemblée Nationale (p114) in the Palais Bourbon. The climax of 19th-century classicism in Paris, however, is the Palais Garnier (p125), designed by Charles Garnier to house the opera and to showcase the splendour of Napoleon III's France.

ART NOUVEAU

Art nouveau, which emerged in Europe and the USA in the second half of the 19th century under various names (Jugendstil, Sezessionstil, Stile Liberty) caught on quickly in Paris, and its influence lasted until about 1910. It was characterised by sinuous curves and flowing, asymmetrical forms reminiscent of creeping vines, water lilies, the patterns on insect wings and the flowering boughs of trees. Influenced by the arrival of exotic *objets d'art* from Japan, its French name came from a Paris gallery that featured works in the 'new art' style.

Paris is still graced by Hector Guimard's art nouveau metro entrances (see boxed text, p103). There are some fine art nouveau interiors in the Musée d'Orsay (p107); an art nouveau glass roof over the Grand Palais (p129); and, on rue Pavée in the Marais, a synagogue designed by Guimard (p145). The city's main department stores, including Le Bon Marché (p198) and Galeries Lafayette (p202), also have elements of this style throughout their interiors.

top picks

PARIS ARCHITECTURE BOOKS

- Guide de l'Architecture Moderne á Paris/Guide to Modern Architecture in Paris, Hervé Martin (2001) – an excellent and very complete guide to all types of architecture; includes walking tours of the city.
- Paris: Architecture & Design, edited by Christian van Uffelen (2004) – a well-illustrated and very useful introduction to Paris' contemporary architecture, inside and out.
- Paris 2000+: New Architecture, Sam Lubell & Axel Sowa (2007) – as new as tomorrow, this richly illustrated coffee-table book focuses on 30 buildings that have gone up since 2000.
- Paris, Grammaire de l'Architecture: XXe-XXIe Siècles, Simon Texier (2009) – contemporaneous with the preceding title, this is a new edition of a far more serious French-language tome examining late 20th- and early 21st-century structures.

MODERN

France's best-known 20th-century architect, Charles-Édouard Jeanneret (better known as Le Corbusier), was born in Switzerland but settled in Paris in 1917 at the age of 30. A radical modernist, he tried to adapt buildings to their functions in industrialised society without ignoring the human element. Not everyone thinks he was particularly successful in this endeavour, however.

Most of Le Corbusier's work was done outside Paris, though he did design several private residences and the Pavillon Suisse, a dormitory for Swiss students at the Cité Internationale Universitaire in the southeastern 14e bordering the blvd Périphérique. Perhaps most interesting – and frightening – are Le Corbusier's plans for Paris that never left the drawing board. Called Plan Voisin (Neighbour Project; 1925), it envisaged wide boulevards linking the Gare Montparnasse with the Seine and lined with skyscrapers. The project would have required bulldozing much of the Latin Quarter.

One of the best examples of modernist architecture in all of Paris is the Maison de Verre (Map p108; 31 rue St-Guillaume, 7e; M Sèvres Babylone), the exquisite 'Glass House' designed by Pierre Chareau and completed in 1932. Unfortunately only architects and architecture students get the green light to visit the interior.

Until 1968, French architects were still being trained almost exclusively at the conformist École de Beaux-Arts, which certainly shows in most of the early structures erected in the skyscraper district of La Défense (p175). It can also be seen in such structures as the UNESCO building (Map p108), erected in 1958 southwest of the École Militaire in the 7e, and the unspeakable, 210m-tall Tour Montparnasse (1973; p171), whose architects, in our opinion, should have been driven in tumbrels to the place de la Concorde and guillotined.

CONTEMPORARY

France owes a fair amount of its most attractive and successful contemporary buildings in its capital city to the narcissism of its presidents. For centuries France's leaders have sought to immortalise themselves by erecting huge public edifices – known as *grands projets* – in Paris, and the recent past has been no different. The late president Georges Pompidou commissioned the once reviled but now beloved Centre Beaubourg (Renzo Piano and Richard Rogers, 1977), later renamed the Centre Pompidou (p78), in which the architects – in order to attempt to keep the exhibition halls as spacious and uncluttered as possible – put the building's insides out.

Pompidou's successor, Valéry Giscard d'Estaing, was instrumental in transforming the derelict Gare d'Orsay train station into the glorious Musée d'Orsay (p107), a design carried out by the Italian architect Gaeltana Aulenti in 1986. François Mitterrand, with his decided preference for the modern and taste for the stage, surpassed all of the postwar presidents with a dozen or so monumental projects in Paris costing taxpayers a whopping €4.6 billion. By contrast Jacques Chirac's only *grand projet* of 12 years in office was the magnificent Musée du Quai Branly (p116), the first major art gallery to open in Paris since the Centre Pompidou.

President Nicolas Sarkozy, who witnessed firsthand the 2005 race riots in Paris' northern suburbs (p37), has turned his attentions to the *banlieues* (suburbs) in particular and the Parisian metropolis as a whole. In 2007, he set up a commission to select 10 architects to head up multidisciplinary teams. The remit: plans for transforming Paris into a model 'post-Kyoto metropolis of the 21st century'.

Paris Mayor Bertrand Delanoë's vision is rather more down to earth. His pet project is the so-called Triangle, a 200m-tall glass structure in the shape of a – well, guess – to be built in the Parc des Expositions at the Porte de Versailles in the 15e. It's by Herzog & de Meuron, the same firm who did London's Tate Modern in 1999.

BUILDING NEW INSPIRATION

For the most part, skyscrapers and other tall buildings are restricted to La Défense (p175), but that doesn't mean other parts of Paris are bereft of interesting and inspired new buildings. Some of our favourites:

Louvre & Les Halles

Immeuble des Bons Enfants (Map 76; 182 rue St-Honoré, 1er; M Palais Royal-Musée du Louvre) Home to the Ministère de la Culture et Communication (Ministry of Culture & Communication), this inspired structure (Francis Soler and Frédéric Druot, 2004) is actually two separate and disparate buildings 'linked' by a metallic web of 'tracery' that lets in light and allows the diversity of the existing buildings to be seen.

Marché de St-Honoré (Map 72; place du Marché St-Honoré, 1er; M Tuileries or Opéra) This monumental glass hall (Ricardo Bofill, 1996) of offices and shops replaces an unsightly parking garage (now underground) and evokes the wonderful *passages couverts* (covered shopping arcades) that begin a short distance to the northeast (p182).

St-Germain & Invalides

Musée du Quai Branly (p117) Jean Nouvel's structure of glass, wood and sod takes advantage of its three-hectare experimental garden designed by Gilles Clément. A wall of the block facing the Seine is a 'vertical garden' (p57).

Champs-Élysées & Grands Boulevards

Hôtel Drouot (p201) We like this zany structure (Jean-Jacques Fernier and André Biro, 1980), a rebuild of the mid-19th-century Hôtel Drouot, for its 1970s design.

Gare du Nord & Canal St-Martin

Crèche (Map p140; 8ter rue des Récollets, 10e; M Gare de l'Est) This day nursery (Marc Younan, 2002) of wood and resin in the garden of the Couvent des Récollets looks like a jumbled pile of gold- and mustard-coloured building blocks. A central glass atrium functions as a 'village square'.

Les Orgues de Flandre (Map p140; 67-107 av de Flandre & 14-24 rue Archereau, 19e; M Riquet) These two enormous housing estates are known as 'the Organs of Flanders' due to their resemblance to that musical instrument

Since the early 1980s, Paris has seen the construction of such structures as IM Pei's controversial Grande Pyramide at the Musée du Louvre (p70), a glass pyramid that serves as the main entrance to the hitherto sacrosanct – and untouchable – Louvre and an architectural *cause célèbre* when it opened in 1989; the city's second opera house, the tile-clad Opéra de Paris Bastille (p157) designed by Uruguayan architect Carlos Ott in 1989; the monumental Grande Arche de la Défense (p177) by Danish architect Johan-Otto von Sprekelsen, which opened the same year; the delightful Conservatoire National Supérieur de Musique et de Danse (1990; p301) and Cité de la Musique (1994; p143), designed by Christian de Portzamparc and serving as a sort of gateway from the city to the whimsical Parc de la Villette; the twinned Grandes Serres (Great Greenhouses) built by Patrick Berger in 1992 at the main entrance to the Parc André Citroën (Map p168); the Ministère de l'Économie, de l'Industrie et de l'Emploi (Map p158) designed by Paul Chemetov and Borja Huidobro in 1990, with its striking 'pier' overhanging the Seine in Bercy; and the four glass towers of the €2 billion Bibliothèque Nationale de France (BNF; p163), the National Library of France, which was designed by Dominique Perrault and opened in 1995.

On a much more human scale is the redeveloped warehouse district known as Masséna Nord (North Masséna; Map p164) just south of the BNF. Narrow streets and open blocks link such conversions as the Grands Moulins, an old mill now the hub of the new Paris Diderot University; Les Frigos, a former SNCF cold-storage warehouse and now a colourful artists' squat; and a new architecture school contained in an old factory complete with smokestack.

One of the most beautiful and successful of the late 20th-century modern buildings in Paris is the Institut du Monde Arabe (p99), a highly praised structure that opened in 1987 and successfully mixes modern and traditional Arab and Western elements. It was designed by Jean Nouvel, France's leading and arguably most talented architect. We can't wait to see his Philharmonie de Paris (p61).

and their street address. Storeys are stacked at oblique angles and the structures appear to be swaying, though they are firmly anchored at the end of a park south of the blvd Périphérique.

Philharmonie de Paris (Map p140; Parc de la Villette, 19e; M Porte de Pantin) The ambitious new home of the Orchestre de Paris has an auditorium of 2400 'terrace' seats surrounding the orchestra.

Bastille & Gare de Lyon

Cinémathèque Française (p156) The former American Centre (Frank Gehry, 1994), is a fascinating building of creamy stone that looks, from some angles, as though it is falling in on itself.

Direction de l'Action Sociale Building (Map p158; 94-96 quai de la Rapée; M Quai de la Rapée) The headquarters of Social Action (Aymeric Zublena, 1991) is unabashed in proclaiming the power of the state, with a huge square within and vast glass-and-metal gates.

Église Notre Dame de l'Espérance (Map p158; 47 rue de la Roquette, 11e; M Bastille) Startling both for its modern design and size (it stands 20m tall and is 11m wide), the interior of the Church of Our Lady of Hope (Bruno Legrand, 1997) is filled with interesting features, including Nicolas Alquin's Croix d'Espérance (Cross of Hope) made from an 18th-century oak beam and three gold squares representing the Trinity.

Place d'Italie & Chinatown

M2K Bibliothèque (p305) This pleasure palace (Wilmotte & Namur, 2003) flanking the Bibliothèque Nationale de France is contained in a glass shoebox that glimmers at night.

Passerelle Simone de Beauvoir (Map p164) This delightful 304m-long footbridge, built by Dietmar Feichtinger Architects in 2006, glides across the Seine, linking the 12e and 13e arrondissements, and at night looks like a blade of light.

Montparnasse & 15e

Fondation Cartier pour l'Art Contemporain (p167) Jean Nouvel set to 'conceal' the Cartier Foundation for Contemporary Arts when he designed it in 1993. In some ways the structure appears at once both incomplete and invisible.

However, not everything new, different and/or monumental that has appeared in the past two decades has been a government undertaking. The vast majority of the buildings in La Défense (p175), Paris' skyscraper district on the Seine to the west of the city centre, are privately owned and house some 1500 companies, including the head offices of 14 of France's top 20 corporations. Unfortunately, most of the skyscrapers here are impersonal and forgettable 'lipstick tubes' and 'upended shoeboxes', with a few notable exceptions including the Cœur Défense (Défense Heart; 2001), the Tour EDF (2001) and the Tour T1 (2008). But outranking them all in size, beauty and sustainability will be Tour Phare (Lighthouse Tower), a 300m-tall office and retail tower of 71 storeys that torques like a human torso and, through awnings that are raised and lowered when the sun hits them, uses light as a building material. It will now be completed in 2014.

NEIGHBOURHOODS

top picks

- Centre Pompidou (p78)
- Ste-Chapelle (p97)
- Musée du Louvre (p70)
- Cathédrale de Notre Dame de Paris (p81)
- Eiffel Tower (p116)
- Cimetière du Père Lachaise (p155)
- Musée Rodin (p111)
- Musée de l'Orangerie (p77)
- Cité de l'Architecture et du Patrimoine (p116)
- Jardin du Luxembourg (p106)

What's your recommendation? www.lonelyplanet.com/paris

NEIGHBOURHOODS

Paris is a compact, easily negotiated city. Twenty arrondissements (city districts) spiral clockwise from the centre and are important locators; their numbers are always included in addresses.

Each of Paris' arrondissements has a distinct personality. The 1er has plenty of sights but few residents, the 5e is studenty, the 7e full of ministries and embassies; the 10e was traditionally working-class but is now a trendy district in which to live, while the 16e is a bastion of the well-heeled. But the profiles are not always so cut and dried; the lay of the land becomes much clearer to visitors when they see the city as composed of named *quartiers* (quarters or neighbourhoods).

The mother of all museums is in the neighbourhood we call Louvre & Les Halles; if you are looking for Paris framed or under glass this is the district for you. Here you'll also find Les Arts Décoratifs devoted to applied arts, design and advertising; the Musée de Orangerie with its sublime impressionist collection; and the original bad boy of exhibition spaces, the Centre Pompidou.

For history and architecture on a grand scale, the Île de la Cité is your compass point, with Notre Dame, the Conciergerie and Ste-Chapelle all standing virtually side by side. For romance, though, cross the bridge east to Île de St-Louis or even south to the Latin Quarter. The students may be moving on to other quartiers and arrondissements, but intellectuals continue to pontificate in the cafés of the Quartier Latin and *les avante-gardistes* are still in control of the galleries and watering holes of the neighbouring St-Germain district.

There is no Paris without the Eiffel Tower, the most iconic of city icons, but the Champs-Élysées, with its landmark Arc de Triomphe at one end and the epic-proportioned place de la Concorde at the other, is a close second (though the offerings on the *boulevard* itself are now somewhat limited). Fans of *haute couture* should make the so-called Golden Triangle just south of the Champs-Élysées their prime destination. Those of more modest means but still with that urge to shop will head for the *grands magazines* (department stores) of the Grands Boulevards. And with its beautiful, Haussmann-era buildings, this district is for many visitors a reflection of the way they think Paris should look architecturally.

In search of the Paris of Central Casting, where everyone paints, wears a beret and sings to accordion music? Head up to Montmartre, the Paris of myth and films. Contiguous is Pigalle, the naughty red-light district that today looks pretty tame.

Party animals should set their sights on the Marais, Ménilmontant and/or Bastille; this is where Paris pulsates after dark. It's not a, err, hard-and-fast rule but to simplify, let's just say that the Marais is the playground of gays and lesbians, Ménilmontant offers what used to be called an alternative scene elsewhere (and still is here) and Bastille is today's *quartier* for some of the best music – be it live, canned or whistled in the metro – in town.

That's a claim to fame Montparnasse used to be able to make. But the brasseries and bistros where writers like Ernest Hemingway and F Scott Fitzgerald both worked and partied are now rather pricey eating establishments that attract foreigners and *les faubourgeois* (suburbanites) all in search of their own private Paris moment. For a taste – both sensual and metaphysical – of the Paris of today, head eastward to Chinatown. It's colourful, it's multiracial and it all tastes as good as it always did.

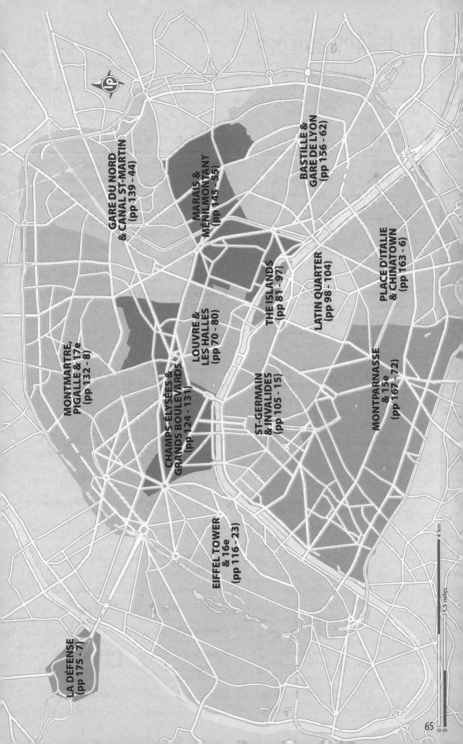

MONTMARTRE, PIGALLE & 17e
(pp 132 - 8)

GARE DU NORD
& CANAL ST-MARTIN
(pp 139 - 44)

MARAIS &
MÉNILMONTANT
(pp 145 - 55)

BASTILLE &
GARE DE LYON
(pp 156 - 62)

CHAMPS-ÉLYSÉES &
GRANDS BOULEVARDS
(pp 124 - 131)

LOUVRE &
LES HALLES
(pp 70 - 80)

THE ISLANDS
(pp 81 - 97)

LATIN QUARTER
(pp 98 - 104)

PLACE D'ITALIE
& CHINATOWN
(pp 163 - 6)

ST-GERMAIN
& INVALIDES
(pp 105 - 15)

MONTPARNASSE
& 15e
(pp 167 - 72)

EIFFEL TOWER
& 16e
(pp 116 - 23)

LA DÉFENSE
(pp 175 - 7)

4 km

1.5 miles

0

65

ITINERARY BUILDER

It's easy to see lots of Paris in a very short time; familiar sights and landmarks seem to leap out at you from every corner. But to really get under the skin of Paris you'll want to look beyond the obvious. This Itinerary Builder should help you find a range of both obvious and slightly more obscure places in eight featured neighbourhoods.

AREA	ACTIVITIES	Sights	Museums & Galleries	Activities
Louvre & Les Halles	Centre Pompidou (p78)	Musée du Louvre (p70)	Spa Nuxe (p311)
	Église St-Eustache (p79)	Les Arts Décoratifs (p74)	Jardin des Tuileries (p75)
	Passages Couverts (p182)	Musée de l'Orangerie (p77)	Vit'Halles Beaubourg (p311)
Latin Quarter	Panthéon (p99)	Institut du Monde Arabe (p99)	Jardin des Plantes (p98)
	Mosquée de Paris (p99)	Musée National d'Histoire Naturelle (p99)	Hammam de la Mosquée de Paris (p310)
	Sorbonne (p102)	Musée National du Moyen Age (p104)	Piscine Pontoise (p314)
St-Germain & Invalides	Église St-Sulpice (p106)	Fondation Dubuffet (p107)	Jardin du Luxembourg (p106)
	Église St-Germain des Prés (p105)	Musée National Eugène Delacroix (p111)	
	Institut de France (p114)	Pièce Unique Variations (p199)	
Eiffel Tower & 16e	Eiffel Tower (p116)	Musée du Quai Branly (p117)	Bike Tours (p400)
	Bois de Boulogne (p122)	Musée Marmottan-Monet (p117)	Bateaux-Mouches (p401)
	CinéAqua (p120)	Cité de l'Architecture et du Patrimoine (p117)	
Champs-Élysées & Grands Boulevards	Arc de Triomphe (p124)	Grand Palais (p129)	Espace Joïya (p310)
	Av des Champs-Élysées (p125)	Musée National Gustave Moreau (p130)	Paris Story (p400)
	Palais Garnier (p125)	La Pinacothèque (p129)	L'Open Tour (p401)
Montmartre, Pigalle & 17e	Basilique du Sacré Cœur (p132)	Musée de la Vie Romantique (p133)	Montmartre Walking Tour (p178)
	Place du Tertre (p133)	Musée Jacquemart-André (p133)	Cook'n with Class (p393)
	Cimetière de Montmartre (p133)	Musée Nissim de Camondo (p133)	
Marais & Ménilmontant	Place des Vosges (p146)	Musée Carnavalet (p146)	Les Bains du Marais (p310)
	Pletzl (p145)	Musée des Arts et Métiers (p147)	Nomades (p313)
	Cimetière du Père Lachaise (p155)	Maison de Victor Hugo (p146)	
Bastille & Gare de Lyon	Cinémathèque Française (p161)	Maison Rouge (p160)	Parc de Bercy (p160)
	Viaduc des Arts (p157)	Cité Nationale de l'Histoire de l'Immigration (p156)	Paris à Vélo, C'est Sympa (p312)
	Passerelle Simone de Beauvoir (p156)	Maison de Jardinage (p161)	Canal Cruises (p401)

HOW TO USE THIS TABLE

The table below allows you to plan a day's worth of activities in any area of the city. Simply select which area you wish to explore, and then mix and match from the corresponding listings to build your day. The first item in each cell represents a well-known highlight of the area, while the other items are more off-the-beaten-track gems.

Eating	Drinking	Shopping
Aux Lyonnais (p223)	Le Fumoir (p278)	L'Ecritoire (p196)
Chez la Vieille (p223)	Le Cochon a l'Oreille (p277)	E Dehillerin (p196)
Le Vaudeville (p224)	Angélina (p279)	Boîtes à Musique Anna Joliet (p195)
Bistrot Les Papilles (p227)	Le Verre à Pied (p280)	Shakespeare & Company (p197)
L'Agrume (p227)	Le Pub St-Hilaire (p280)	Magie (p197)
Le Pré Verre (p229)	Le Vieux Chêne (p280)	
Ze Kitchen Galerie (p232)	Café de Flore (p281)	Pâtisserie Sadaharu Aoki (p200)
Le Comptoir de Relais (p233)	Comptoir des Cannettes (p283)	Bonton Bazar (p201)
Les Cocottes (p234)	Le 10 (p282)	La Dernière Goutte (p200)
		Le Dépôt-Vente de Buci (p211)
L'Astrance (p238)		
Firmin Le Barbier (p239)		
58 Tour Eiffel (p239)		
Le Boudoir (p241)	Delaville Café (p285)	Galeries Lafayette (p202)
Le Roi du Pot au Feu (p242)	Au Limonaire (p283)	Place de la Madeleine (p203)
Makoto Aoki (p241)	Au Général La Fayette (p283)	Guerlain (p202)
Le Miroir (p244)	O P'tit Douai (p284)	Ets Lion (p204)
Cul de Poule (p246)	Le Progrès (p284)	La Citadelle (p204)
Chez Toinette (p244)	La Fourmi (p284)	
L'Ambassade d'Auvergne (p256)	La Perle (p287)	Sic Amor (p207)
Le Petit Marché (p254)	Le Pick-Clops (p287)	CSAO Boutique & Gallery (p209)
Chez Janou (p255)	Café Baroc (p287)	Red Wheelbarrow Bookstore (p205)
Sardegna a Tavola (p261)	La Liberté (p289)	Marché aux Puces d'Aligre (p210)
L'Écailler du Bistrot (p262)	Le Pur Café (p289)	La Maison du Cerf-Volant (p210)
Les Amis de Messina (p262)	Le Bistrot Peintre (p290)	Fermob (p212)

GREATER PARIS

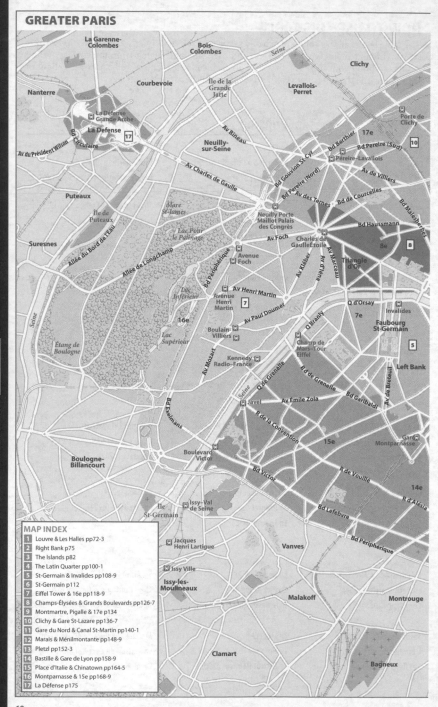

MAP INDEX

1 Louvre & Les Halles pp72-3
2 Right Bank p75
3 The Islands p82
4 The Latin Quarter pp100-1
5 St-Germain & Invalides pp108-9
6 St-Germain p112
7 Eiffel Tower & 16e pp118-9
8 Champs-Élysées & Grands Boulevards pp126-7
9 Montmartre, Pigalle & 17e p134
10 Clichy & Gare St-Lazare pp136-7
11 Gare du Nord & Canal St-Martin pp140-1
12 Marais & Ménilmontante pp148-9
13 Pletzl pp152-3
14 Bastille & Gare de Lyon pp158-9
15 Place d'Italie & Chinatown pp164-5
16 Montparnasse & 15e pp168-9
17 La Défense p175

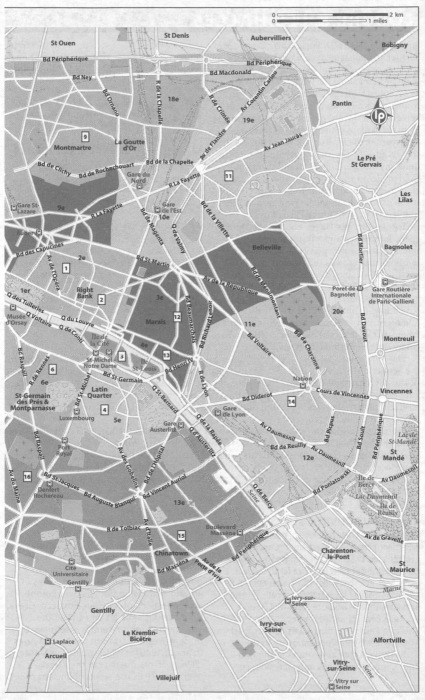

LOUVRE & LES HALLES

Drinking p276; Eating p221; Shopping p192; Sleeping p328

The 1er arrondissement contains some of the most important sights for visitors to Paris. Though it can boast a wild and exciting side, it remains essentially a place where history and culture meet head on along the banks of the Seine.

Sculptures merge with lawns, pools and fountains, while casual strollers lose themselves in the lovely promenade stretching from the gardens of the Tuileries to the square courtyard of the Louvre. To the north, under the arcades of the rue de Rivoli, the pace quickens with bustling shops and chaotic traffic. Parallel to rue de Rivoli, rue St-Honoré runs from place Vendôme to Les Halles, leaving in its wake the Comédie Française and the manicured gardens of the Palais Royal.

The Forum des Halles and rue St-Denis seem kilometres away but are already visible, soliciting unwary passers-by with bright lights, jostling crowds and painted ladies. The mostly pedestrianised zone between the Centre Pompidou and the Forum des Halles (with rue Étienne Marcel to the north and rue de Rivoli to the south) is filled with people day and night, just as it was for the 850-odd years when part of it served as Paris' main *halles* (marketplace) for foodstuffs.

top picks

LOUVRE & LES HALLES

- Musée du Louvre (p70) The mother of all museums under one seemingly endless roof.
- Musée de l'Orangerie (p77) An exquisite space in which to enjoy Monet's *Decorations des Nymphéas* (Water Lilies).
- Centre Pompidou (p78) A kind of Louvre for the 21st century, with a day of culture and fun for the whole family.
- Jardin des Tuileries (p75) A verdant oasis in which to recharge those batteries and a chance to enjoy Paris at its symmetrical best.
- Église St-Eustache (p79) One of the least known (and beautiful) churches in Paris.

The Bourse (Stock Exchange) is the financial heart of the 2e arrondissement to the north, the Sentier district (around the Sentier metro and rue d'Aboukir and rue de Cléry), the centre of the city's garment trade and the Opéra, its ode to music and dance. From rue de la Paix, where glittering jewellery shops display their wares, to blvd Poissonnière and blvd de Bonne Nouvelle, where stalls and fast-food outlets advertise with garish neon signs, this arrondissement is a real hotchpotch.

Useful metro/RER stops for this part of town include Châtelet, Châtelet–Les Halles, Concorde, Étienne Marcel, Les Halles, Louvre–Rivoli, Palais Royal–Musée du Louvre, Pont Neuf, Rambuteau and Tuileries. Major bus lines include the 27 (rue de Rivoli) for the blvd St-Michel and Place d'Italie; the 69 (near Louvre Rivoli metro) for Invalides and Champ de Mars (Eiffel Tower); the 72 for place de la Concorde, Grand Palais, Alma Marceau and Bois de Boulogne; and the 67 for Pigalle.

MUSÉE DU LOUVRE Map p76

☎ 01 40 20 53 17; www.louvre.fr; permanent collections/permanent collections & temporary exhibits adult €9.50/14, after 6pm Wed & Fri adult €6/12, permanent collections free for EU resident under 26yr, everyone under 18yr & after 6pm Fri for 18-25yr, 1st Sun of the month free for all; ⏰ 9am-6pm Mon, Thu, Sat & Sun, to 10pm Wed & Fri; Ⓜ Palais Royal–Musée du Louvre

The vast Palais du Louvre was constructed as a fortress by Philippe-Auguste in the early 13th century and rebuilt in the mid-16th century for use as a royal residence.

The Revolutionary Convention turned it into a national museum in 1793.

The paintings, sculptures and artefacts on display in the Louvre Museum have been amassed by subsequent French governments. Among them are works of art and artisanship from all over Europe and collections of Assyrian, Etruscan, Greek, Coptic and Islamic art and antiquities. The Louvre's *raison d'être* is essentially to present Western art from the Middle Ages to about 1848 (at which point the Musée d'Orsay across the river in the 7e takes over), as well as the works of ancient civilisations that formed the starting point for Western art.

When the museum opened in the late 18th century it contained 2500 paintings and *objets d'art;* today some 35,000 are on display. The 'Grand Louvre' project inaugurated by the late President Mitterrand in 1989 doubled the museum's exhibition space, and both new and renovated galleries have opened in recent years devoted to *objets d'art* such as the crown jewels of Louis XV (Room 66, 1st floor, Apollo Gallery, Denon Wing).

Daunted by the richness and sheer size of the place (the south side facing the Seine is 700m long and it is said that it would take nine months to look at every piece of art in the museum), locals and visitors alike often find the prospect of an afternoon at a smaller museum far more inviting, meaning the Louvre may be the most actively avoided museum in the world. Eventually, most people do their duty and visit, but many leave overwhelmed, unfulfilled, exhausted and frustrated at having got lost on their way to da Vinci's *La Joconde,* better known as *Mona Lisa* (Room 7, 1st floor, Salle de la Joconde, Denon Wing; see the boxed text, p75). Since it takes several serious visits to get anything more than a brief glimpse of the works on offer, your best bet – after checking out a few that you really want to see – is to choose a particular period or section of the Louvre and pretend that the rest is in another museum somewhere across town.

The most famous works from antiquity include the *Squatted Scribe* (Room 22, 1st floor, Sully Wing), the *Code of Hammurabi* (Room 3, ground floor, Richelieu Wing) and that armless duo, the *Venus de Milo* (Room 7, ground floor, Denon Wing) and the *Winged Victory of Samothrace* (opposite Room 1, 1st floor, Denon Wing). From the Renaissance, don't miss Michelangelo's *The Dying Slave* (Room 4, ground floor, Michelangelo Gallery, Denon Wing) and works by Raphael, Botticelli and Titian (1st floor, Denon Wing). French masterpieces of the 19th century include Ingres' *The Turkish Bath* (off Room 60, 2nd floor, Sully Wing), Géricault's *The Raft of the Medusa* (Room 77, 1st floor, Denon Wing) and works by Corot, Delacroix and Fragonard (2nd floor, Sully Wing).

The main entrance and ticket windows in the Cour Napoléon are covered by the 21m-high Grande Pyramide, a glass pyramid designed by the Chinese-born American architect IM Pei. You can avoid the queues outside the pyramid or at the Porte des Lions entrance by entering the Louvre complex via the Carrousel du Louvre entrance (Map p76), at 99 rue de Rivoli, or by following the 'Musée du Louvre' exit from the Palais Royal–Musée du Louvre metro station. Buy your tickets in advance online, from the ticket machines in the Carrousel du Louvre or by phoning ☎ 0 892 684 694 or ☎ 01 41 57 32 28, or from the *billeteries* (ticket offices) of Fnac or Virgin Megastores (p294) for an extra €1 to €1.60, and walk straight in without queuing. Tickets are valid for the whole day, so you can come and go as you please. They are also valid for the Musée National Eugène Delacroix (p111) on the same day.

The Louvre is divided into four sections: the Sully, Denon and Richelieu wings and Hall Napoléon. Sully creates the four sides of the Cour Carrée (literally 'square courtyard') at the eastern end of the complex. Denon stretches along the Seine to the south; Richelieu is the northern wing running along rue de Rivoli.

The split-level public area under the Grande Pyramide is known as the Hall Napoléon (☺ 9am-10pm Wed-Mon; temporary exhibition galleries ☺ 9am-6pm Mon, Thu & Sun, 9am-10pm Wed, 9am-8pm Sat). The hall has a temporary exhibition hall, a bookshop and souvenir store, a café and auditoriums for lectures and films. The centrepiece of the Carrousel du Louvre (p192), the shopping centre that runs underground from the pyramid to the Arc de Triomphe du Carrousel (p75), is the pyramide inversée (inverted glass pyramid), also by Pei.

Free English-language maps of the complex (entitled *Plan/Information Louvre*) can be obtained from the circular information desk in the centre of the Hall Napoléon. Excellent publications to guide you if you are doing the Louvre on your own are the *Louvre Visitors' Guide* (€8), *Louvre Masterpieces* (€10), *Louvre: The 300 Masterpieces* (€12) and the hefty, 485-page *A Guide to the Louvre* (€17). An attractive and useful memento is the DVD entitled *Louvre: The Visit* (€26). All are available from the museum bookshop.

English-language guided tours (☺ 01 40 20 52 63) lasting 1½ hours depart from the area under the Grande Pyramide, marked *Acceuil des Groupes* (Groups Reception), at 11am,

LOUVRE & LES HALLES

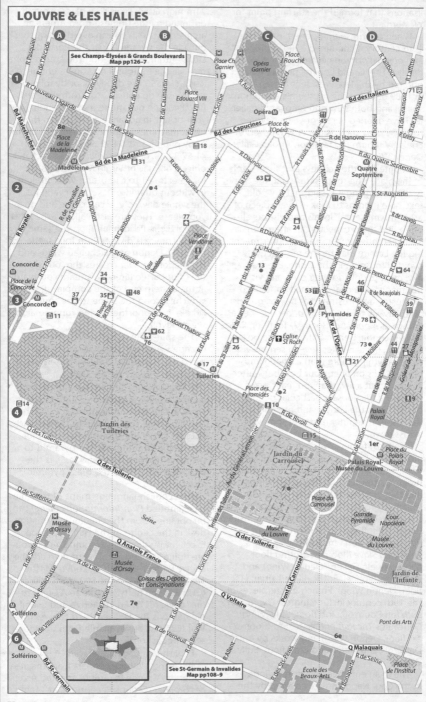

See Champs-Élysées & Grands Boulevards
Map pp126–7

See St-Germain & Invalides
Map pp108–9

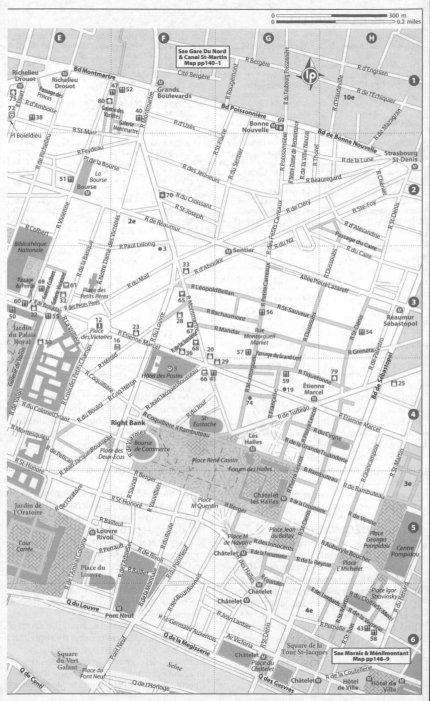

See Gare Du Nord
& Canal St-Martin
Map pp140–1

See Marais & Ménilmontant
Map pp148–9

LOUVRE & LES HALLES

INFORMATION
CCO Bureau de Change 1   C1
Cityrama 2   C4
Cours de Cuisine Olivier Berté 3   F3
École Ritz Escoffier 4   B2
Main Post Office 5   F4
Paris Convention & Visitors
   Bureau (Main Branch) 6   C3

SIGHTS   (pp70–80)
Arc de Triomphe du Carrousel 7   C5
Colonne Vendôme 8   B3
Daniel Buren Sculpture 9   D4
Galerie Colbert ....(see 49)
Galerie Nationale du Jeu de
   Paume ....(see 11)
Jeanne d'Arc Statue 10   C4
Jeu de Paume 11   A3
Louis XIV Memorial 12   E3
Marché de St-Honoré 13   C3
Musée de l'Orangerie 14   A4
Musée de la Mode et du
   Textile (Les Arts Décoratifs) .....(see 15)
Musée de la Publicité (Les Arts
   Décoratifs) 15   C4
Musée des Arts Décoratifs (Les
   Arts Décoratifs) ....(see 15)
Musée en Herbe 16   F3
Paris Vision 17   B4
Théâtre-Musée des Capucines 18   B2
Tour Jean Sans Peur 19   G4

SHOPPING   (pp191–212)
A Simon 20   F3
Antoine 21   D4
Boîtes à Musique Anna Joliet 22   E3

Bonpoint 23   F3
Brentano's 24   C2
Canicrèche 25   H4
Colette 26   C3
Didier Ludot 27   D3
Erotokritos 28   F3
Kiliwatch 29   G4
La Petite Robe Noire 30   E3
Lavinia 31   B2
Legrand Filles & Fils 32   E3
Librairie Gourmande 33   F3
Maria Luisa Accessories 34   A3
Maria Luisa Femme 35   A3
Marithé & François Girbaud 36   F3
WH Smith 37   A3

EATING   (pp213–74)
Aux Lyonnais 38   E1
Baan Boran 39   D3
Chez Papa Grands Boulevards
   Branch 40   F1
Comptoir de la Gastronomie 41   F4
Drouant 42   D2
Franprix 43   H6
Hidden Kitchen 44   D3
Hippopotamus Opéra Branch 45   D1
Kunitoraya 46   D3
L'Arbre à Cannelle 47   F1
L'Ardoise 48   B3
Le Grand Colbert 49   E3
Le Grand Véfour 50   E3
Le Vaudeville 51   E2
Les Troubadours 52   F1
Lina's ....(see 23)
Monoprix Opéra 53   C3
Porta da Selva 54   H3

Restaurant du Palais Royal 55   E3
Rue Montorgueil Market 56   G3
Stohrer 57   G3
Supermarché G20 58   H6
Villa Papillon 59   G4
Willi's Wine Bar 60   E3

DRINKING   (pp275–92)
À Priori Thé 61   E3
Angélina 62   B3
Harry's New York Bar 63   C2
La Champmeslé 64   D3
Le Café Noir 65   F3
Le Cochon à l'Oreille 66   F4
Le Cœur Fou 67   F3
Le Tambour 68   F3

NIGHTLIFE   (pp293–308)
Le Rex Club 69   G1
Social Club 70   F2

THE ARTS   (pp293–308)
Agence Marivaux 71   D1
Opéra Comique 72   E1

SPORTS & ACTIVITIES   (pp309–16)
Harnn & Thann 73   D3
Spa Nuxe 74   G4

SLEEPING   (pp323–51)
Hôtel Favart 75   E1
Hôtel Meurice 76   B3
Hôtel Ritz Paris 77   B2
Hôtel Thérèse 78   D3
Hôtel Tiquetonne 79   H4
Hôtel Vivienne 80   E1

2pm and (sometimes) 3.45pm Monday to Saturday, excluding of course Tuesday. Tickets cost €5 in addition to the cost of admission. Groups are limited to 30 people, so it's a good idea to sign up at least 30 minutes before departure time.

Self-paced audioguide tours in six languages, with 1½ hours of commentary, can be rented for €6 under the pyramid at the entrance to each wing.

LES ARTS DÉCORATIFS Map p72

☎ 01 44 55 57 50; www.lesartsdecoratifs.fr; 107 rue de Rivoli, 1er; permanent collections/permanent collections & temporary exhibits adult €9/13, 18-25yr €7.50/10.50, permanent collections free for EU resident under 26yr, everyone under 18yr; ☽ 11am-6pm Tue, Wed & Fri-Sun, to 9pm Thu; Ⓜ Palais Royal–Musée du Louvre

The Palais du Louvre contains three other privately administered museums collectively known as the Decorative Arts in its Rohan Wing. Admission includes entry to all three here as well as the Musée Nissim de Camondo (p133) in the 8e.

The Musée des Arts Décoratifs (Applied Arts Museum), which begins on the 3rd floor and continues over six more floors, displays furniture, jewellery and such objets d'art as ceramics and glassware from the Middle Ages and the Renaissance through the Art Nouveau and Art Deco periods to modern times.

The much smaller Musée de la Publicité (Advertising Museum), which shares the 3rd floor, has some 100,000 posters in its collection dating as far back as the 13th century, and innumerable promotional materials touting everything from 19th-century elixirs and early radio advertisements to Air France as well as electronic publicity. Only certain items are exhibited at any one time; most of the rest of the space is given over to special exhibitions.

The Musée de la Mode et du Textile (Museum of Fashion & Textiles) on ground through 2nd floors has some 16,000 costumes dating from the 16th century to today, including haute couture creations by the likes of Chanel and Jean-Paul Gaultier. Most of the outfits are warehoused, however, and displayed during regularly scheduled themed exhibitions.

ARC DE TRIOMPHE DU CARROUSEL
Map p72

place du Carrousel, 1er;
Ⓜ **Palais Royal–Musée du Louvre**

Erected by Napoleon to celebrate his battlefield successes of 1805, this triumphal arch, which is set in the Jardin du Carrousel at the eastern end of the Jardin des Tuileries, was once crowned by the ancient Greek sculpture called *The Horses of St Mark's*, 'borrowed' from the portico of St Mark's Basilica in Venice by Napoleon but returned after his defeat at Waterloo in 1815. The quadriga (the two-wheeled chariot drawn by four horses) that replaced it was added in 1828 and celebrates the return of the Bourbons to the French throne after Napoleon's downfall. The sides of the arch are adorned with depictions of Napoleonic victories and eight pink-marble columns, atop each of which stands a soldier of the emperor's Grande Armée.

ÉGLISE ST-GERMAIN L'AUXERROIS
Map p76

☎ **01 42 60 13 96; www.saintgermainauxerrois.cef. fr; 2 place du Louvre, 1er;** ◷ **9am-7pm Mon-Sat, to 8pm Sun;** Ⓜ **Louvre–Rivoli or Pont Neuf**

Built between the 13th and 16th centuries in a mixture of Gothic and Renaissance styles and with similar dimensions and ground plans to those of Notre Dame, this once royal parish church stands on a site at the eastern end of the Louvre that has been used for Christian worship since about AD 500. After being mutilated in the 18th century by clergy intent on 'modernisation', and damaged during the Revolu-

tion, the church was restored by the Gothic Revivalist architect Eugène Viollet-le-Duc in the mid-19th century. It contains some fine Renaissance stained glass.

LOUVRE DES ANTIQUAIRES Map p76

☎ **01 42 97 27 27; www.louvre-antiquaires.com; 2 place du Palais Royal;** ◷ **11am-7pm Tue-Sun Sep-Jun, to 7pm Tue-Sat Jul & Aug;**
Ⓜ **Palais Royal–Musée du Louvre**

A tourist attraction in itself, this extremely elegant 'mall' houses some 70 antique shops spread over three floors and is filled with *objets d'art*, furniture, clocks, classical antiquities and jewellery. Visit the place as you would the Louvre across the road, bearing in mind that all the stuff here is up for grabs.

JARDIN DES TUILERIES Map p72

☎ **01 40 20 90 43; 113 rue de Rivoli, 1er;**
◷ **7am-9pm Apr, May & Sep, 7am-11pm Jun-Aug, 7.30am-7.30pm Oct-Mar;** Ⓜ **Tuileries or Concorde**

The formal, 28-hectare Tuileries Garden, which begins just west of the Jardin du Carrousel, was laid out in its present form, more or less, in 1664 by André Le Nôtre, who also created the gardens at Vaux-le-Vicomte (p366) and at Versailles (p354). The Tuileries soon became the most fashionable spot in Paris for parading about in one's finery; today it is a favourite of joggers and forms part of the Banks of the Seine World Heritage Site listed by Unesco in 1991. There are some lovely sculptures within the gardens, including Louise Bourgeois' *The Welcoming Hands* (1996), which faces place de la Concorde.

The Voie Triomphale (Triumphal Way), also called the *Axe Historique* (Historic Axis), the western continuation of the Tuileries' east–west axis, follows the av des Champs-Élysées to the Arc de Triomphe

---

MONA LISA: THE TRUTH BEHIND THE SMILE

So much has been written about the painting the French call *La Joconde* and the Italians *La Gioconda*, yet so little has been known about the lady behind that enigmatic smile. For centuries admirers speculated on everything from the possibility that the subject was mourning the death of a loved one to that she might have been in love – or in bed – with her portraitist, Leonardo da Vinci.

Mona (actually *monna* in Italian) is a contraction of *madonna*, while Gioconda is the feminine form of the surname Giocondo. With the emergence of several clues in recent years, it has been established almost certainly that the subject was Lisa Gherardini (1479-1542?), the wife of Florentine merchant Franceso del Giocondo, and that the painting was done between 1503 and 1506 when she was around 25 years old. At the same time, tests done in 2005 with 'emotion recognition' computer software suggest that the smile on 'Madam Lisa' is at least 83% happy. And one other point remains unequivocally certain despite occasional suggestions to the contrary: she was not the lover of Leonardo, who preferred his *Vitruvian Man* to his *Mona*.

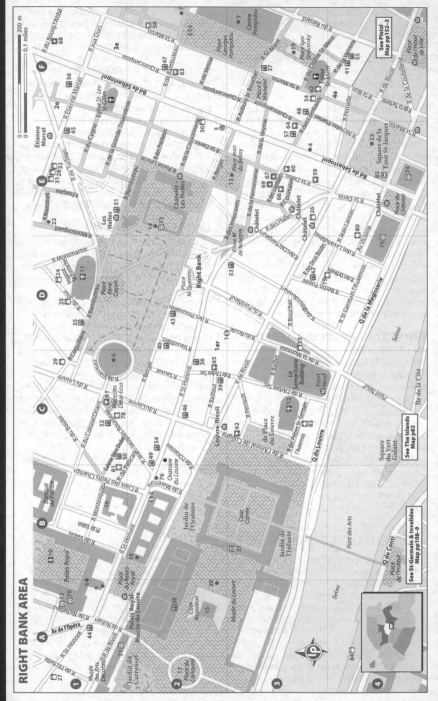

RIGHT BANK AREA

See Pletzl
Map pp152–3

See St-Germain & Invalides
Map pp108–9

See The Islands
Map p82

Right Bank

and, ultimately, to the Grande Arche in the skyscraper district of La Défense (p175).

JEU DE PAUME Map p72

☎ 01 47 03 12 50; www.jeudepaume.org; 1 place de la Concorde, 8e; adult/senior, student & 13-18yr €7/5, free for student & under 26yr 5-9pm last Tue of month; ⌚ noon-9pm Tue, to 7pm Wed-Fri, 10am-7pm Sat & Sun; Ⓜ Concorde

The Galerie du Jeu de Paume – Site Concorde (Jeu de Paume National Gallery at Concorde), which stages innovative exhibitions of contemporary art, is housed in an erstwhile *jeu de paume* (real, or royal, tennis court) in the northwestern corner of the Jardin des Tuileries.

MUSÉE DE L'ORANGERIE Map p72

☎ 01 44 77 80 07; www.musee-orangerie.fr, in French; Jardin des Tuileries, 1er; adult/student & 18-25yr €7.50/5.50, permanent collections free for EU resident under 26yr, everyone under 18yr & 1st Sun of the month; ⌚ 9am-6pm Wed-Mon; Ⓜ Concorde

This museum in the southwestern corner of the Jardin des Tuileries is, with the Jeu de Paume, all that remains of the once palatial Palais des Tuileries, which was razed during the Paris Commune (p31) in 1871. It exhibits important impressionist works, including an eight-panel series of Monet's *Decorations des Nymphéas* (Water Lilies) in two huge oval rooms purpose-built in 1927 to the artist's specifications, as well as paintings by Cézanne, Matisse, Renoir, Rousseau, Soutine and Utrillo. Add €2 for temporary exhibits. A 1½-hour guided tour in English at 2.30pm on Monday and Thursday costs €8/6; an audioguide is €5.

PLACE VENDÔME Map p72

Ⓜ Tuileries or Opéra

This octagonal square, and the arcaded and colonnaded buildings around it, was built

RIGHT BANK AREA

INFORMATION
Best Change	1	D2
Chambre de Commerce et d'Industrie de Paris	(see 6)	
Le Change du Louvre	2	B2
Milk	3	E2
Pharmacie des Halles	4	E3

SIGHTS (pp70–80)
Atelier Brancusi	5	F2
Bibliothèque Publique d'Information	(see 7)	
Bourse de Commerce	6	C1
Carrousel du Louvre Entrance	(see 71)	
Centre Pompidou	7	F3
Comédie Française	(see 70)	
Conseil d'État	8	A1
Crown-shaped Metro Entrance	9	A1
Daniel Buren Sculpture	10	B1
Église St-Eustache	11	D1
Église St-Germain l'Auxerrois	12	C3
Fontaine des Innocents	13	E3
Forum des Halles	14	E2
Grande Pyramide	15	A2
Immeuble des Bons Enfants	16	B1
Inverted Glass Pyramid	17	A2
Louvre des Antiquaires	18	B2
Mechanical Fountains	19	F3
Mini Pei Pyramids	20	A2
Musée du Louvre	21	B3
Musée National d'Art Moderne	(see 7)	
Palais Royal	(see 8)	
Spa Nuxe	22	E1
Tour St Jacques	23	E4

SHOPPING (pp191–212)
Agnès B Enfant	(see 24)	
Agnès B Femme	24	D1
Agnès B Homme	25	D1

André	26	E3
Astier de Villatte	27	A1
Barbara Bui	28	E1
Carrousel du Louvre Entrance	(see 71)	
E Dehillerin	29	C1
Ekivok	30	E2
Kabuki Femme	31	E1
Kabuki Homme	32	E1
Kenzo	33	D3
L' Écritoire	34	F3

EATING (pp213–76)
Au Pied de Cochon	35	D1
Baan Boran à Emporter	36	C2
Café Beaubourg	37	F3
Café Marly	38	A2
Chez La Vieille	39	C2
Djakarta Bali	40	D2
Franprix	41	F4
Franprix Châtelet	42	D3
Franprix Les Halles	43	D2
Higuma	44	A1
Joe Allen	45	E1
Kaï	46	C2
Khatag	47	F2
La Table des Gourmets	48	F3
Le Petit Mâchon	49	C2
Le Véro Dodat	50	C1
Léon de Bruxelles Les Halles Branch	51	E1
L'Épi d'Or	52	C1
Saveurs Végét'halles	53	D3
Scoop	54	C2
Supermarché G20	55	F4
Ta Sushi	56	F1
Thai Classic	57	E3

DRINKING (pp275–92)
Café La Fusée	58	F2

Café Oz	59	E3
Eagle Paris	60	E3
Le Café des Initiés	61	C1
Le Fumoir	62	C3
Le Troisième Lieu	63	F2
l'Imprévu	64	E3
Ô Chateau	65	C2
Wolf Bar	66	E3

NIGHTLIFE (pp293–308)
Le Baiser Salé	67	E3
Les Bains Douches	68	F1
Sunset/Sunside	69	E3

THE ARTS (pp293–308)
Comédie Française	70	A1
Comédie Française Studio Théâtre	71	A1
Discount Ticket Window	72	A1
Fnac Forum des Halles	73	E2
Théâtre de la Ville	74	E4
Théâtre du Châtelet	75	D4
Virgin Megastore	(see 71)	

SPORTS & ACTIVITIES (pp309–16)
Club Med Gym	76	B2
Vit'Halles Beaubourg	77	F2

SLEEPING (pp323–51)
BVJ Paris-Louvre	78	C1
Grand Hôtel de Champaigne	79	D3
Hôtel Britannique	80	E4
Hôtel de Lille Louvre	81	B1
Hôtel St-Merry	82	F3
Le Relais du Louvre	83	C3

TRANSPORT (pp383–90)
Batobus Stop	84	A4
Noctilien (Night Bus) Stops	85	E4

between 1687 and 1721. In March 1796, Napoleon married Josephine, Viscountess of Beauharnais, in the building that's at No 3 in the southwest corner. Today, the buildings around the square house the posh Hôtel Ritz Paris (p328) and some of the city's most fashionable boutiques, especially jewellery stores. Place Vendôme has been synonymous with the bauble trade since the Second Empire of the mid-19th century.

In the centre of the square stands the 43.5m-tall Colonne Vendôme (Vendôme Column; Map p72), which consists of a stone core wrapped in a 160m-long bronze spiral that's made from hundreds of Austrian and Russian cannons captured by Napoleon at the Battle of Austerlitz in 1805. The 425 bas-reliefs on the spiral celebrate Napoleon's victories between 1805 and 1807. The statue on top depicts Napoleon in classical Roman dress. The painter Gustave Courbet (p50) was jailed for trying to dismantle the column during the Paris Commune.

PALAIS ROYAL Map p76

01 42 96 13 32; www.monuments-nationaux.fr; 6 rue de Montpensier, 1er; M Palais Royal–Musée du Louvre

The Royal Palace, which accommodated a young Louis XIV for a time in the 1640s, lies to the north of place du Palais Royal and the Louvre. Construction was begun in 1624 by Cardinal Richelieu, though most of the present neoclassical complex dates from the latter part of the 18th century. Today it contains the governmental Conseil d'État (State Council; Map p76) and is closed to the public.

The colonnaded building facing place André Malraux is the Comédie Française (p307), founded in 1680 and the world's oldest national theatre.

Just north of the palace is the Jardin du Palais Royal (Map p72; ☎ 01 47 03 92 16; 2 place Colette, 1er; ⏰ 7.30am-10pm Apr & May, 7am-11pm Jun-Aug, 7am-9.30pm Sep, 7.30am-8.30pm Oct-Mar), a lovely, 21-hectare park surrounded by two arcades. On the eastern side, Galerie de Valois (Map p72) shelters designer fashion shops, art galleries and jewellers, while Galerie de Montpensier (Map p76) on the western side still has a few old shops remaining.

At the southern end there's a controversial sculpture (Map p72) of black-and-white striped columns of various heights by Daniel Buren. It was started in 1986, interrupted

by irate Parisians and finished – following the intervention of the Ministry of Culture and Communication – in 1995. The story (invented by Buren?) goes that if you toss a coin and it lands on one of the columns, your wish will come true.

CENTRE POMPIDOU Map p76

☎ 01 44 78 12 33; www.centrepompidou.fr; place Georges Pompidou, 4e; M Rambuteau

The Centre National d'Art et de Culture Georges Pompidou (Georges Pompidou National Centre of Art & Culture), also known as the Centre Beaubourg, has amazed and delighted visitors since it was inaugurated in 1977, not just for its outstanding collection of modern art but also for its radical architectural statement (p60).

The Forum du Centre Pompidou (admission free; ⏰ 11am-10pm Wed-Mon), the open space of the centre at ground level, has temporary exhibits and information desks to help you get your bearings. The 4th and 5th floors of the centre exhibit a fraction of the almost 65,000-plus works by 5700 artists of the Musée National d'Art Moderne (MNAM; National Museum of Modern Art; adult €10-12, 18-25yr €8-9, EU resident under 26yr & everyone under 18yr free & 1st Sun of the month free for all; ⏰ 11am-9pm Wed-Mon), France's national collection of art dating from 1905 onward, and including the work of the Surrealists and Cubists as well as Pop Art and contemporary works.

The huge Bibliothèque Publique d'Information (BPI; ☎ 01 44 78 12 33; www.bpi.fr; ⏰ noon-10pm Mon & Wed-Fri, 11am-10pm Sat & Sun), entered from rue du Renard, takes up part of the 1st as

MUSEUM CLOSING TIMES

The vast majority of museums in Paris close on Mondays, though more than a dozen, including the Louvre, the Centre Pompidou and the Musée National du Moyen Age, are closed on Tuesdays instead. It is also important to remember that all museums and monuments in Paris shut their doors or gates between 30 minutes and an hour before their actual closing times, which are the ones we list in this chapter. Therefore if we say a museum or monument closes at 6pm, for example, don't count on getting in much later than 5pm. That said, in early 2009 a blockbuster exhibition at the Grand Palais (p129) called Picasso et Ses Maîtres (Picasso and His Teachers) proved so popular that the galleries were kept open round the clock for the last three days.

THE INS & OUTS OF PARIS

In Paris, when a building is put up in a location where they've run out of consecutive street numbers, a new address is formed by fusing the number of an adjacent building with the notation *bis* (twice), *ter* (thrice) or even *quater* (four times). In essence, the street numbers 17bis and 89ter are the equivalent of 17a and 89b in English.

The *portes cochères* (street doors) of most apartment buildings in Paris can be opened only by a *digicode* (entry code), which is usually alphanumeric (eg 26A10) and changed periodically; the days of the concierges, who would vet every caller before allowing them entry, are well and truly over.

Once you do get inside, you'll find that the doors of many apartments are unmarked: the occupants' names are nowhere in sight and there isn't even an apartment number. To know which door to knock on, you'll usually be given cryptic instructions, such as *cinquième étage, premier à gauche* (5th floor, first on the left) or *troisième étage, droite droite* (3rd floor, turn right twice).

In France (and in this book), the 1st floor is the floor above the *rez-de-chaussée* (ground floor).

well as the entire 2nd and 3rd floors of the centre. The 6th floor has two galleries for temporary exhibitions (included in the higher entrance fee) and a trendy restaurant called Georges, with panoramic views of Paris. (If you want a view of the view without eating, a ticket costs €3 for adults and is free for those under 26.) There are cinemas (adult/senior & 18-25yr €6/4) and other entertainment venues on the 1st floor and in the basement.

Atelier Brancusi (Map p76; 55 rue Rambuteau, 4e; admission free; 2-6pm Wed-Mon), across place Georges Pompidou to the west of the main building, is a reconstruction of the studio of Romanian-born sculptor Constantin Brancusi (1876–1957) designed by Renzo Piano. It contains some 160 examples of his work, including hundreds of drawings, sketches, paintings and photographs.

West of the centre, Place Georges Pompidou and the nearby pedestrian streets attract buskers, musicians, jugglers and mime artists, and can be a lot of fun. South of the centre on place Igor Stravinsky, the fanciful mechanical fountains (Map p76) of skeletons, hearts, treble clefs and a big pair of ruby-red lips, created by Jean Tinguely and Niki de St-Phalle, are a positive delight.

FORUM DES HALLES Map p76

☎ 01 44 76 96 56; www.forum-des-halles.com; 1 rue Pierre Lescaut, 1er; shops 10am-8pm Mon-Sat; Les Halles or Châtelet les Halles
Les Halles, the city's main wholesale food market, occupied the area just south of the Église St-Eustache from the early 12th century until 1969, when it was moved lox, stock and cabbage head to the southern suburb of Rungis, near Orly. In its place, this unspeakably ugly, four-level, underground shopping centre with some 170 shops was

constructed in the glass-and-chrome style of the late 1970s; it's slated to be gutted and rebuilt by 2012, topped with La Canopée, an architecturally stunning 'canopy' above the shops as well as public spaces such as an auditorium and conservatory. Topping the complex at street level is a popular garden, also slated for a major facelift, with a rather stunning sculpture by Henri de Miller (1953–99) called *Listen*. In the warmer months, street musicians, fire-eaters and other performers display their talents here, especially at place Jean du Bellay, which is adorned by a multitiered Renaissance fountain, the Fontaine des Innocents (1549). It is named after the Cimetière des Innocents, a cemetery formerly on this site from which two million skeletons were disinterred after the Revolution and transferred to the Catacombes (p167).

ÉGLISE ST-EUSTACHE Map p76

☎ 01 42 36 31 05; www.saint-eustache.org, in French; place du Jour, 1er; 9.30am-7pm Mon-Fri, 10am-7pm Sat, 9am-7.15pm Sun; Les Halles
This majestic church, one of the most beautiful in Paris, is just north of the gardens next to the Forum des Halles. Constructed between 1532 and 1637, St-Eustache is primarily Gothic, though a neoclassical facade was added on the western side in the mid-18th century. Inside, there are some exceptional Flamboyant Gothic arches holding up the ceiling of the chancel, though most of the ornamentation is Renaissance and even classical. Above the western entrance, the gargantuan organ, with 101 stops and 8000 pipes dating from 1854, is used for concerts (long a tradition here) and at Sunday Mass at 11am and 6pm.

BOURSE DE COMMERCE Map p76

☎ 01 55 65 55 65; 2 rue de Viarmes, 1er; admission free; ☽ 9am-6pm Mon-Fri; Ⓜ Les Halles

At one time the city's grain market, the circular Trade Exchange was capped with a copper dome in 1811. The murals running along internal walls below the galleries were painted by five different artists in 1889 and restored in 1998. They represent French trade and industry through the ages.

TOUR JEAN SANS PEUR Map p72

☎ 01 40 26 20 04; www.tourjeansanspeur.com, in French; 20 rue Étienne Marcel, 2e; adult/student & 7-18yr €5/3; ☽ 1.30-6pm Wed-Sun Apr–early Nov, 1.30-6pm Wed, Sat & Sun early Nov–Mar; Ⓜ Étienne Marcel

The Gothic, 29m-high Tower of John the Fearless was built by the Duke of Bourgogne as part of a splendid mansion in the early 15th century, so he could take refuge from his enemies at the top. It is one of the very few examples of feudal military architecture extant in Paris. Visitors can ascend the 140 steps of the spiral staircase to the turret on top. A guided tour at 3pm costs €8 (including admission fee).

TOUR ST-JACQUES Map p76

square de la Tour St-Jacques, 4e; Ⓜ Châtelet

The Flamboyant Gothic, 52m-high St James Tower just north of place du Châtelet is all that remains of the Église St-Jacques la Boucherie, which was built by the powerful butchers guild in 1523 as a starting point for pilgrims setting out for the shrine of St James at Santiago de Compostela in Spain. The church was demolished by the revolutionary Directory in 1797, but the bell tower, recently cleaned and now a sparkling white and sand colour, was spared so that it could be used to drop globules of molten lead in the manufacture of shot.

Drinking p279; Eating p226; Shopping p196; Sleeping p330

Paris' pair of islands could not be more different. With its quaint car-free lanes, legendary ice-cream maker and bijou portfolio of street plaques celebrating famous residents of the past, Île St-Louis is a joy. Its boutiques lining the central street might not be worth the trip in itself, but browse and there's no saying what gem you might find.

At the island's western end, the area around Pont St-Louis and Pont Louis-Philippe is one of the city's most romantic spots. On summer days, lovers mingle with cello-playing buskers and teenaged skateboarders. After nightfall, the Seine dances with the watery reflections of streetlights, headlamps, stop signals and the dim glow of curtained windows. Occasionally, tourist boats with super-bright flood lamps cruise by. You really are in Paris.

Stand on the square in front of Notre Dame on big-brother Île de Cité and there is no doubt where you are: dodging snap-happy tourists, street sellers pushing Eiffel Tower key rings and backpackers guarding piles of packs while their mates check out the cathedral is a taste of the best and worst of Paris. Sensibly, not very many Parisians live on this island.

top picks

THE ISLANDS

- **Cathédrale de Notre Dame de Paris (p81)** The crowning glory of medieval Gothic architecture.
- **Ste-Chapelle (p97)** A masterpiece of delicacy, with a curtain of richly coloured stained glass.
- **La Conciergerie (p83)** Where Marie-Antoinette and thousands of others spent their final days before losing their heads.
- **Pont Neuf (p97)** The oldest 'New Bridge' in town and an architectural delight.

Metro stations convenient for the island include Cité, Pont Marie, Pont Neuf, St-Michel Notre Dame and Sully Morland. Useful buses on Île de la Cité are the 47 through the Marais to Gare de l'Est and the 21 to Opéra & Gare St-Lazare. On Île St Louis it's the 67 to Jardin des Plantes and Place d'Italie and the 87 through Latin Quarter to École Militaire and Champ de Mars.

ÎLE DE LA CITÉ

The site of the first settlement in Paris (c 3rd century BC) and later the centre of the Roman town of Lutetia, Île de la Cité remained the centre of royal and ecclesiastical power even after the city spread to both banks of the Seine during the Middle Ages. As the institutions on the island grew, so did the island. Buildings on the middle part were demolished and rebuilt during Baron Haussmann's urban renewal scheme of the late 19th century (see p35); the population – considered the poorest in the city – fell from 15,000 in 1860 to 5000 less than a decade later.

The Île de la Cité, mainly in the 4e arrondissement (its western tip is in the 1er) is home to two institutions devoted to maintaining public order: the judiciary (Palais de Justice) and the police (Préfecture de Police).

CATHÉDRALE DE NOTRE DAME DE PARIS Map p82

☎ 01 42 34 56 10; www.cathedraledeparis.com; 6 place du Parvis Notre Dame, 4e; audioguide €5;

⏲ 8am-6.45pm Mon-Fri, to 7.15pm Sat & Sun, information desk 9.30am-6pm Mon-Sat, 9am-6pm Sun; Ⓜ Cité

This is the heart of Paris – so much so that distances from Paris to every part of metropolitan France are measured from place du Parvis Notre Dame, the square in front of the Cathedral of Our Lady of Paris. A bronze star across the street from the cathedral's main entrance marks the exact location of *point zéro des routes de France*. To the west, Charlemagne (AD 742–814), emperor of the Franks, rides his steed under the trees.

Notre Dame, the most visited unticketed site in Paris with upwards of 14 million people crossing its threshold a year, is not just a masterpiece of French Gothic architecture but was also the focus of Catholic Paris for seven centuries.

Built on a site occupied by earlier churches and, a millennium before that, a Gallo-Roman temple, it was begun in 1163 according to the design of Bishop Maurice de Sully and largely completed by the early 14th century. The cathedral was badly

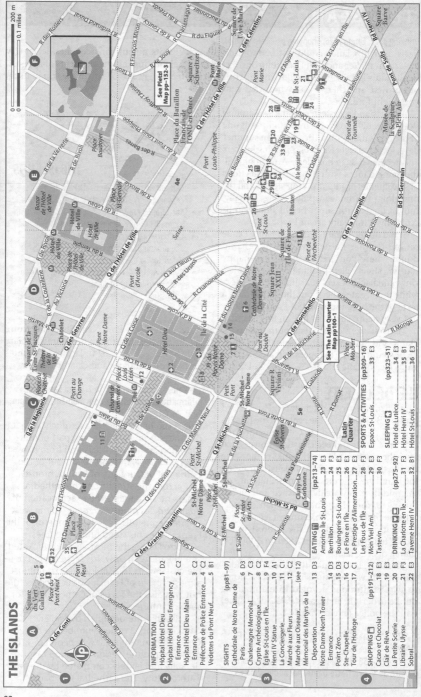

THE ISLANDS

See Pletzl Map pp152–3

See The Latin Quarter Map pp100–1

INFORMATION
Hôpital Hôtel Dieu......................1 D2
Hôpital Hôtel Dieu Emergency
　Entrance....................................2 C2
Hôpital Hôtel Dieu Main
　Entrance....................................3 C2
Préfecture de Police Entrance....4 C2
Vedettes du Pont Neuf...............5 B1

SIGHTS (pp81–97)
Cathédrale de Notre Dame de
　Paris..6 D3
Charlemagne Memorial..............7 C3
Crypte Archéologique................8 C2
Église St-Louis en l'Île................9 F4
Henri IV Statue.........................10 A1
La Conciergerie.........................11 C1
Marché aux Fleurs....................12 C2
Marché aux Oiseaux...............(see 12)
Mémorial des Martyrs de la
　Déportation.............................13 D3
Notre Dame North Tower
　Entrance...................................14 D3
Point Zéro.................................15 D3
Ste-Chapelle..............................16 C2
Tour de l'Horloge......................17 C1

SHOPPING (pp191–212)
Cacao et Chocolat.....................18 E3
Clair de Rêve............................19 E3
La Petite Scierie........................20 E3
Librairie Ulysse.........................21 F3
Sobral.......................................22 E3

EATING (pp213–74)
Amorino Île St-Louis.................23 E3
Berthillon.................................24 F3
Boulangerie St-Louis.................25 E3
Le Flore en l'Île........................26 E3
Le Prestige d'Alimentation........27 E3
Les Fous de l'Île.......................28 F3
Mon Vieil Ami..........................29 E3
Tastevin...................................30 F3

DRINKING (pp275–92)
La Charlotte en Île....................31 F3
Taverne Henri IV......................32 B1

SPORTS & ACTIVITIES (pp309–16)
Espace St-Louis.........................33 E3

SLEEPING (pp323–51)
Hôtel de Lutèce........................34 E3
Hôtel Henri IV..........................35 B1
Hôtel St-Louis...........................36 E3

damaged during the Revolution; architect Eugène Emmanuel Viollet-le-Duc carried out extensive renovations between 1845 and 1864. The cathedral is on a very grand scale; the interior alone is 130m long, 48m wide and 35m high and can accommodate more than 6000 worshippers.

Notre Dame is known for its sublime balance, though if you look closely you'll see all sorts of minor asymmetrical elements introduced to avoid monotony, in accordance with standard Gothic practice. These include the slightly different shapes of each of the three main portals, whose statues were once brightly coloured to make them more effective as a *Biblia pauperum* – a 'Bible of the poor' to help the illiterate faithful understand Old Testament stories, the Passion of the Christ and the lives of the saints. One of the best views of Notre Dame is from square Jean XXIII, the little park behind the cathedral, where you can appreciate better the forest of ornate flying buttresses that encircle the chancel and support its walls and roof.

Inside, exceptional features include three spectacular rose windows, the most renowned of which are the 10m-wide one over the western facade above the 7800-pipe organ, and the window on the northern side of the transept, which has remained virtually unchanged since the 13th century. The central choir, with its carved wooden stalls and statues representing the Passion of the Christ, is also noteworthy. There are free 1½-hour guided tours (2pm Wed & Thu, 2.30pm Sat) of the cathedral, given in English.

The trésor (treasury; adult/student/3-12yr €3/2/1; 9.30am-6pm Mon-Fri, 9.30am-6.30pm Sat, 1.30-6.30pm Sun) in the southeastern transept contains artwork, liturgical objects, church plate and first-class relics, some of them of questionable origin. Among these is the Ste-Couronne, the 'Holy Crown', which is purportedly the wreath of thorns placed on Jesus' head before he was crucified, and was brought here in the mid-13th century. It is exhibited between 3pm and 4pm on the first Friday of each month, 3pm to 4pm every Friday during Lent, and 10am to 5pm on Good Friday.

The entrance to the Tours de Notre Dame (Towers of Notre Dame; 01 53 10 07 00; www.monuments-nationaux.fr; rue du Cloître Notre Dame; adult/18-25yr €8/5, free for EU resident under 26yr & everyone under 18yr, 1st Sun of month Nov-Mar free for all; 10am-6.30pm Mon-Fri, 10am-11pm Sat &

Sun Jul & Aug, 10am-6.30pm daily Apr, May & Sep, to 5.30pm daily Jan-Mar & Oct-Dec) is from the North Tower. Climb the 422 spiralling steps to the top of the western facade, where you'll find yourself face-to-face with the cathedral's most frightening gargoyles, the 13-tonne bell Emmanuel (all of the cathedral's bells are named) in the South Tower, and, last but not least, a spectacular view of Paris from the Galerie des Chimères (Dreams Gallery).

LA CONCIERGERIE Map p82

 01 53 40 60 97; www.monuments-nationaux.fr; 2 blvd du Palais, 1er; adult/18-25yr €7/4.50, free for EU resident under 26yr & everyone under 18yr, 1st Sun of month Nov-Mar free for all; 9.30am-6pm Mar-Oct, 9am-5pm Nov-Feb; M Cité

The Conciergerie was built as a royal palace in the 14th century for the concierge of the Palais de la Cité, but later lost favour with the kings of France and became a prison and torture chamber. During the Reign of Terror (1793–94) it was used to incarcerate alleged enemies of the Revolution before they were brought before the Revolutionary Tribunal, which met next door in the Palais de Justice. Among the almost 2800 prisoners held in the dungeons here (in various 'classes' of cells, no less) before being sent in tumbrels to the guillotine were Queen Marie-Antoinette (see a reproduction of her cell) and, as the Revolution began to turn on its own, the radicals Danton, Robespierre and, finally, the judges of the Tribunal themselves.

The 14th-century Salle des Gens d'Armes (Cavalrymen's Hall) is a fine example of the Rayonnant Gothic style. It is the largest surviving medieval hall in Europe. The capitals on the central pillar of the adjoining Salles des Gardes (Guards' Room) represent Abélard and Héloïse (p27). The Tour de l'Horloge (Map p82; Clock Tower; cnr blvd du Palais & quai de l'Horloge, 1er), built in 1353, has held a public clock aloft since 1370.

A joint ticket with Ste-Chapelle (p97) costs adult/18-25yr/EU resident under 26yr & everyone under 18yr €11/7.50/free.

CRYPTE ARCHÉOLOGIQUE Map p82

 01 55 42 50 10; www.paris.fr; 1 place du Parvis Notre Dame, 4e; adult/14-26yr €4/3; 10am-6pm Tue-Sun; M Cité

The Archaeological Crypt is under the square in front of Notre Dame. The 117m-long and

(Continued on page 97)

IT'S FREE

The permanent collections at the majority of the *musées municipaux* (city museums), run by the Mairie de Paris (www. paris.fr), are free. Temporary exhibitions always incur a separate admission fee.

City museums taking part in this scheme include the following:

Maison de Balzac (p122)

Maison de Victor Hugo (p146)

Musée Bourdelle (p171)

Musée Carnavalet (p146)

Musée Cernuschi (p138)

Musée Cognacq-Jay (p147)

Musée d'Art Moderne de la Ville de Paris (p120)

Musée de la Vie Romantique (p133)

Musée des Beaux-Arts de la Ville de Paris (Petit Palais; p130)

Musée Jean Moulin & Mémorial du Maréchal Leclerc de Hauteclocque et de la Libération de Paris (p170)

Musée Atelier Zadkine (p107)

At the same time, the *musées nationaux* (national museums) in Paris have reduced rates for those aged over 60 and between 18 and 25, and sometimes for everyone else on one day or part of a day per week (eg Sunday morning). They are always free for EU residents under 26 years of age, all those under 18 years, and for everyone on the first Sunday of each month (although not always year-round – see the following list and notations). Again, you will have to pay separately for temporary exhibitions.

The museums and monuments in question (and their free-admission days) are:

Arc de Triomphe (p124) 1st Sunday of the month November to March only.

Basilique de St-Denis (p173) 1st Sunday of the month November to March only.

Cité de l'Architecture et du Patrimoine (p116)

Cité Nationale de l'Histoire de l'Immigration (p156)

Conciergerie (p83) 1st Sunday of the month November to March only.

Musée d'Art et d'Histoire (p174)

Musée de la Chasse et de la Nature (p147)

Musée de l'Assistance Publique-Hôpitaux de Paris (p104)

Musée de l'Orangerie (p77)

Musée d'Orsay (p107)

Musée du Louvre (p70)

Musée du Quai Branly (p117)

Musée Guimet des Arts Asiatiques (p120)

Musée Ernest Hébert (p110)

Musée National d'Art Moderne (Centre Pompidou; p78)

Musée National du Moyen Age (Musée de Cluny; p104)

Musée National Eugène Delacroix (p111)

Musée National Gustave Moreau (p132)

Musée Rodin (p111)

Panthéon (p99) 1st Sunday of the month November to March only.

Ste-Chapelle (p97) 1st Sunday of the month November to March only.

Tours de Notre Dame (p83) 1st Sunday of the month November to March only.

FRANK WING

LES QUARTIERS

It is not hyperbole to say that Paris is the world's most beautiful, most romantic city. But it's not an urban museum or a Gallic theme park. Do the sights and ogle at the icons; they're all part of the Paris package. Then jump on the metro or a bus and get off at a place you've never heard of, wander through a *quartier* (neighbourhood) where French mixes easily with Arabic, Bengali or Vietnamese. Poke your head into side-street boutiques or just lounge on a café terrace and watch Parisians pass by. More than anything else, theirs is a city to discover.

Walking on rue des Francs Bourgeois, the Marais

WILL SALTE

LOUVRE & LES HALLES

The very heart of Paris, this busy Right Bank quarter gets its charisma from the lion's share of sights and monuments it cradles. The mammoth Musée du Louvre can not be missed (in every sense), while marketplace-turned-transport-hub Les Halles remains as people-packed as it was a century ago.

CAROLE MARTIN

WILL SALTER

❶ Café Marly
Come here (p223) not so much for the food (which ain't half bad) but for the magnificent views of the Louvre and the Grande Pyramide as well as the tier 2 starlets nibbling on radicchio.

❷ Palais Royal
With its gardens and galleries, sculptures and history (the French Revolution effectively started at a café here), this former 'Royal Palace' (p78) is *the* spot to hang out on a warm day.

❸ Jardin des Tuileries
There is no lovelier spot in Paris to stroll, mooch or jog between sculptures and flowerbeds than this riverside garden (p75) safeguarded by the 'Banks of the Seine' Unesco World Heritage Site.

❹ Centre Pompidou
Paris' Musée National d'Art Moderne (National Museum of Modern Art), ensconced in this architecturally bold, 1970s cultural centre (p78), is the world's second most visited museum (after the Louvre). See why.

MARAIS & MÉNILMONTANT

Night-owl stomping-ground Marais, once Paris' most fashionable residential district, deals a perfect hand of historic hôtels particuliers (private mansions) and tomorrow's modish bars. Neighbouring Ménilmontant, plain-Jane working-class district until the 1990s, matches suit with a hip drinking scene.

WILL SALTER

WILL SALTER

❶ Rue Vieille du Temple
In the Marais district, this bar-lined party street (p279) is one big drinking fest over 1930s zinc and contemporary design.

❷ Village St-Paul
A stylish courtyard of antique galleries and designer boutiques fills this redeveloped and picturesque area (p184) in the southern Marais.

❸ Place des Vosges
This lovely city square (p146)– Paris' oldest – begs café lounging and a promenade beneath elegant 17th-century architecture.

❹ Cimetière du Père Lachaise
Gravestones in the world's most opulent cemetery (p155) read like a Who's Who of French history and the arts: 800,000 deceased call this enormous necropolis home.

❺ Marché Belleville
Among the city's most colourful markets, this multicultural street market (p222) is an easy trip to Africa and the Middle East.

CHRISTOPHER GROENHOUT

THE ISLANDS

Twins separated at birth, these islands are chalk and cheese: quaint Île St-Louis means chichi residents, gourmet shops and posh restaurants; Île de la Cité, 3rd-century BC spot where it all began, is packed with big sights of Notre Dame proportion.

HUW JONES

GREG ELM

GLENN BEANLAND

❶ Cathédrale de Notre Dame de Paris

Scale the towers of Paris' cathedral and rub shoulders with gargoyles to get the most out of this masterpiece of Gothic architecture (p81); 10 million souls cross its threshold each year.

❷ Berthillon

There is no ice-cream maker more legendary than Île St-Louis' Berthillon (p227). Pick from 70 flavours, then stroll along rue St-Louis en l'Île and grab a pew on Pont St-Louis to watch buskers perform, cone in hand.

❸ Ste-Chapelle

Visit on a sunny day to be dazzled by the piercing blue of Paris' oldest and finest stained glass (p97).

THE LATIN QUARTER

The stronghold of Paris' academia since the 13th century, this oh-so-literary neighbourhood on the Left Bank where Hemingway & co drank in the 1920s takes its name from the lingua franca – Latin – used by professors and students aeons ago. Turn east to spot green 'lung' Jardin des Plantes and the minaret of Paris' central mosque.

❶ Bouillon Racine
Built as a soup kitchen for workers a few years into the 20th century, this restaurant (p234) seduces with its breathtaking art-nouveau splendour.

❷ Rue Mouffetard
Here you'll find fishmongers, greengrocers, cheese makers, butchers and florists; with its early-morning market (p222), medley of stall-clad shop fronts, and fresh produce piled high, this foodie street begs a meander.

❸ Shakespeare & Company
A legend in its own time: browse the packed shelves of the city's most famous English-language bookshop (p197), just across the river from Notre Dame.

❹ Institut du Monde Arabe
Surely no Parisian facade is more extraordinary or clever than that of the Arab World Institute (p99), a motorised fusion of Arab and Western architectural styles.

❺ Place de la Sorbonne
Chapelle de la Sorbonne (p104), the university's gold-domed church where the mortal remains of Cardinal Richelieu lie buried, is the standout feature of this pretty 'village' square (p102).

WILL SALTER

GREG ELMS

JEAN-BERNARD CARILLET

WILL SALTER

ST-GERMAIN & INVALIDES

A part of Paris that lured artists and writers with its cheap rents and vibrant cafés in the interwar period, this Left Bank quartier today is uber-chichi with sky-high rents and café crème prices to match. Its forte: stylish boutiques and specialist shops selling all manner of goods make it a real shopping mecca.

❶ Carrefour de l'Odéon
A prime spot for lapping up the subtle buzz of chic St-Germain des Prés is this traffic- and people-busy crossing: grab a culinary pew at Le Comptoir du Relais (p233) or Les Éditeurs (p233) and enjoy.

❷ Les Deux Magots & Café de Flore
Sartre, Simone de Beauvoir, Hemingway and André Breton hung out at Paris' most famous literary cafés (p281 and p282). Do the same.

❸ Jardin du Luxembourg
Apple orchards and chestnut groves; chess, t'ai chi and 1920s toy sailboats: no city park paints a better portrait of Parisians at play than the pea-green lawns of Luxembourg (p106).

❹ Église St-Sulpice
Its role in Dan Brown's *The Da Vinci Code* made this mostly 18th-century church (p106), Italianate outside, neoclassical inside, a real bestseller.

❺ Église St-Germain des Prés
What a pedigree! The bell tower above the western entrance of Paris' oldest church still standing (p105), has hardly changed since AD 990.

❻ Le Petit Zinc
Feast on lavish seafood platters and an original art-nouveau interior to match at this time-less upmarket restaurant masquerading as a brasserie (p233).

GLENN BEANLAND

WILL SALTER

JEAN-BERNARD CARILLET

CHAMPS-ÉLYSÉES & GRANDS BOULEVARDS

Noisy, frenetic, traffic-packed: be it the faithful rushing to catch a performance at Paris' favourite opera house or shoppers letting rip in the great department stores of the Grands Boulevards, the pace here is urban-fast. The grandiose climax immortalised in song and romanticised the world over: the fabulous av des Champs-Élysées…

JEAN-BERNARD CARILLET

BRUCE YUAN-YUE

IZZET KERIBA

KARL BLACKWELL

❶ Palais Garnier

By day, take a tour, guided or DIY, of this classic example of opulent, Second Empire architecture (p125). By night it's all about ballet, theatre and dance (p306).

❷ Place de la Concorde

So that's where Louis XVI and thousands more were guillotined during the Reign of Terror in 1793–94. This square (p129), linked to place de l'Étoile by the Champs-Élysées, is quite simply enormous.

❸ Galeries Lafayette

There's more to Paris' best-known department store (p202) than shopping: its Friday-afternoon fashion shows and the panoramic views from its rooftop terrace will sweep you off your feet.

❹ Arc de Triomphe

Climb to the top of Paris' signature arch (p124) and gasp: what a breathtaking, bird's-eye view of the Axe Historique, from the Louvre to La Défense!

❺ Rue Montorgueil

This street market (p222) more or less took over from Les Halles when it moved lock, stock and pig's trotter out of the city in the late 1960s.

WILL SALTER

What a colourful neighbourhood to keep you on your toes. From hilltop Montmartre with its struggling artists, cancan and cabarets, to the red-light district of Pigalle and the stiffer, mixed-bag 17e arrondissement, it doesn't disappoint. This is the Paris of legend and romance, the cinematic hooker with the heart of gold.

GLENN VAN DER KNIJFF

❶ Basilique du Sacré Cœur
Spiral 234 steps to the top of this Parisian icon (p132) which took more than four decades to complete – on a clear day the view is spectacular.

❷ Moulin Rouge
How unfortunate: the 19th-century windmill of Paris' most famous cabaret (p295) burnt down. What you see is the 1925 replacement.

❸ Place du Tertre
Ground zero of touristy Paris, this crowded Montmartre square (p133) is a relentless fiesta of packed café terraces, street performers and overzealous portrait artists.

❹ Clos Montmartre
Quel surprise! The 2000 vines in this 1930s vineyard (p179), the only one extant in central Paris, produce an average 800 bottles of wine a year.

❺ Cimetière de Montmartre
Writers, composers, artists, film directors and dancers lay to rest in this lovely necropolis (p133), the most famous in Paris after Père Lachaise.

RUSSELL MOUNTFOR

BRUCE YUAN-YUE BI

WILL SALTER

OLIVIER CIRENDINI

95

JEAN-BERNARD CARILLET

OLIVIER CIRENDINI

BASTILLE & GARE DE LYON

The gentrification of the Bastille area continues apace – the buoyant profusion of restaurants speaks volumes. By the waterfront, the excitement continues with 19th-century chais (wine warehouses) morphing into happening bars and hip music clubs bedding down in old river barges.

JEAN-BERNARD CARILLET

❶ Maison Rouge & Viaduc des Arts
Two inspired art addresses: view seldom-seen pieces in contemporary gallery Maison Rouge (p160) and artisan art under the arches of a disused railway viaduct (p157).

❷ Parc de Bercy
A green ode to contemporary landscape design, this modern riverside park (p160) with ponds and islands is the bee's knees to caper footloose and fancy-free.

❸ Opéra Bastille
Never as popular as the Palais Garnier, this opera house (p157) has a 2700-seat auditorium with perfect acoustics and some of the most ambitious opera productions in the city.

❹ Marché Bastille
Shop till you drop at the best open-air market in Paris (p222).

(Continued from page 83)

28m-wide area displays *in situ* the remains of structures built on this site during the Gallo-Roman period, a 4th-century enclosure wall, the foundations of the medieval foundlings hospice and a few of the original sewers sunk by Haussman.

MARCHÉ AUX FLEURS Map p82
place Louis Lépin, 4e; ⊗ 8am-7.30pm Mon-Sat; Ⓜ Cité
The Île de la Cité's flower market has brightened up this square since 1808. On Sundays it becomes a Marché aux Oiseaux (bird market; ⊗ 9am-7pm).

MÉMORIAL DES MARTYRS DE LA DÉPORTATION Map p82
square de l'Île de France, 4e; ⊗ 10am-noon & 2-7pm Apr-Sep, to 5pm Oct-Mar; Ⓜ St-Michel Notre Dame
The Memorial to the Victims of the Deportation, erected in 1962, is a haunting monument to the 160,000 residents of France (including 76,000 Jews, of whom 11,000 were children) deported to and murdered in Nazi concentration camps during WWII. A single barred 'window' separates the bleak, rough concrete courtyard from the waters of the Seine. Inside, the Tomb of the Unknown Deportee is flanked by hundreds of thousands of bits of back-lit glass, and the walls are etched with inscriptions from celebrated writers and poets.

PONT NEUF Map p82
Ⓜ Pont Neuf
The sparkling white stone spans of Paris' oldest bridge, ironically called 'New Bridge', have linked the western end of the Île de la Cité with both river banks since 1607 when the king inaugurated it by crossing the bridge on a white stallion. The occasion is commemorated by an equestrian statue of Henri IV, who was known to his subjects as the Vert Galant ('jolly rogue' or 'dirty old man', depending on your perspective). View the bridge's seven arches, decorated with humorous and grotesque figures of barbers, dentists, pickpockets, loiterers etc, from a spot along the river or a boat.

Pont Neuf and nearby place Dauphine were used for public exhibitions in the 18th century. In the last century the bridge itself became an *objet d'art* on at least three occasions: in 1963, when School of Paris artist Nonda built, exhibited and lived in a huge Trojan horse of steel and wood on the bridge; in 1984 when the Japanese designer Kenzo covered it with flowers; and in 1985 when the Bulgarian-born 'environmental sculptor' Christo famously wrapped the bridge in beige fabric.

STE-CHAPELLE Map p82
☎ 01 53 40 60 97; www.monuments-nationaux.fr; 4 blvd du Palais, 1er; adult/18-25yr €8/5, free for EU resident under 26yr & everyone under 18yr, 1st Sun of the month Nov-Mar free for all; ⊗ 9.30am-6pm Mar-Oct, 9am-5pm Nov-Feb; Ⓜ Cité
This is the place to visit on a sunny day! Security checks make it long and snail-slow to get into this gemlike Holy Chapel, the most exquisite of Paris' Gothic monuments, tucked away within the walls of the Palais de Justice (Law Courts). But once in, be dazzled by Paris' oldest and finest stained glass.

Built in just under three years (compared with nearly 200 for Notre Dame), Ste-Chapelle was consecrated in 1248. The chapel was conceived by Louis IX to house his personal collection of holy relics (including the Holy Crown now kept in the treasury at Notre Dame). The chapel's exterior can be viewed from across the street from the law courts' magnificently gilded 18th-century gate, which faces rue de Lutèce.

A combined ticket with the Conciergerie costs adult/18-25yr/EU resident under 26yr & everyone under 18yr €11/7.50/free.

ÎLE ST-LOUIS

Downstream from Île de la Cité and entirely in the 4e arrondissement, St-Louis was actually two uninhabited islets called Île Notre Dame (Our Lady Isle) and Île aux Vaches (Cows Island) in the early 17th century. That was until a building contractor called Christophe Marie and two financiers worked out a deal with Louis XIII to create one island and build two stone bridges to the mainland. In exchange they could subdivide and sell the newly created real estate. This they did with great success, and by 1664 the entire island was covered with fine, airy, grey-stone houses facing the quays and water.

The only sight as such, French Baroque Église St-Louis en l'Île (Map p82; ☎ 01 46 34 11 60; 19bis rue St-Louis en l'Île, 4e; ⊗ 9am-1pm & 2-7.30pm Tue-Sat, to 7pm Sun; Ⓜ Pont Marie) was built between 1664 and 1726.

THE LATIN QUARTER

Drinking p279; Eating p227; Shopping p197; Sleeping p330

There is no better strip to see, smell and taste the Quartier Latin (Latin Quarter), 5e, than rue Mouffetard, a thriving market street that is something of a local mecca with its titillating line-up of patisseries, *fromageries* (cheese shops) and fishmongers, interspersed by the odd *droguerie-quincaillerie* (hardware store) – easily spotted by the jumble of laundry baskets, buckets etc piled on the pavement in front. Knowing what's happening is easy here: go into Le Verre à Pied (p280), order *un café* at the bar and the market-stall holders will soon start chatting to you. Or try Cave La Bourgogne (p280), where old ladies with pet lapdogs gather each day at 10.30am for a coffee and a chinwag.

The centre of Parisian higher education since the Middle Ages, the Latin Quarter is so called because conversation between students and professors was in Latin until the Revolution. Academia remains a focal point of life – the Sorbonne is here – though its near monopoly on Parisian academic life is not what it was. But bury your nose in one of the quarter's late-opening bookshops, linger in a café, eat cheap in its abundance of budget restaurants or clink drinks during a dozen different happy hours and there will almost certainly be a student or academic affiliated with the Sorbonne sitting next to you.

Come the warmer months, everyone spills over to place St-Michel, place de la Sorbonne and other pigeon-filled squares. Movie buffs watch classics on rue des Écoles, and activists and sympathisers join under the same banner at the Mutualité to chant slogans and fight the good fight. Fancy a *pied à terre* around the corner from the Sorbonne? A 40-sq-metre, contemporary loft-style apartment costs around €430,000.

top picks

THE LATIN QUARTER

- Panthéon (p99) Let your soul soar inside this domed church, one of Paris' most beautiful examples of 18th-century neoclassicism.
- Institut du Monde Arabe (p99) Allow as much time to savour the exterior as the interior of the Arab World Institute, a stunning example of 1980s architecture.
- Grande Galerie de l'Évolution (Musée Nationale d'Histoire Naturelle; p99) Play safari in Paris: this Natural History Museum gallery is a big must for kids.
- Musée National du Moyen Age (p104) Time travel back to the Middle Ages – the gardens at this museum are particularly enchanting.
- Mosquée de Paris (p99) Get a taste of multicultural Paris with the city's 1920s central mosque – feast afterwards on couscous in the fabulous North African restaurant within its ornate Moorish walls.

Arriving by metro, the handiest stops to jump off are St-Michel by the Seine; Cluny–La Sorbonne or Maubert Mutualité on blvd St-Germain; and Censier Daubenton or Gare d'Austerlitz by the Jardin des Plantes. Bus stops include the Panthéon for the 89 to Jardin des Plantes and 13e (Bibliothèque National de France François Mitterrand); blvd St-Michel for the 38 to Centre Pompidou, Gare de l'Est & Gare du Nord; and rue Gay Lussac for the 27 to Île de la Cité, Opéra & Gare St-Lazare. Boats dock at the Jardin des Plantes Batobus stop on quai St-Bernard.

JARDIN DES PLANTES Map p100

☎ 01 40 79 56 01, 01 40 79 54 79; rue Cuvier, 5e; ☯ 7.30am-7pm; Ⓜ Gare d'Austerlitz, Censier–Daubenton or Jussieu

Paris' 24-hectare botanical garden, founded in 1626 as a medicinal herb garden for Louis XIII, is idyllic to stroll or jog around. You'll find a rosary, iris garden, the Eden-like Jardin d'Hiver (Winter Garden) or Serres (Greenhouses), the Jardin Alpin (Alpine Garden; admission Mon-Fri free, Sat & Sun adult/4-15yr/under 4yr €1/0.50/free;

☯ 8-4.40pm Mon-Fri, 1.30-6pm Sat, 1.30-6.30pm Sun Apr-Oct), with 2000 mountainous plants; and the gardens of the École de Botanique, where students of the School of Botany 'practise' and green-fingered Parisians savvy up on horticultural techniques.

During the Prussian siege of Paris in 1870, most of the animals in the Ménagerie du Jardin des Plantes (adult/4-15yr/under 4yr €8/6/free; ☯ 9am-6pm Mon-Sat, 9am-6.30pm Sun) were eaten by starving Parisians. Though a recreational animal park, the medium-sized zoo dating to 1794 in the northern section of the garden does much research into the reproduction of rare and endangered species.

A two-day combined ticket covering all of the Jardin des Plantes sights, including the park's mightily impressive Grande Galerie de l'Évolution (p99), costs adult/child €20/15.

MUSÉE NATIONAL D'HISTOIRE NATURELLE Map p100

☎ 01 40 79 30 00; www.mnhn.fr; 57 rue Cuvier, 5e; Ⓜ Censier–Daubenton or Gare d'Austerlitz
Housed in three buildings on the southern edge of the Jardin des Plantes, the National Museum of Natural History was created in 1793 and became a site of significant scientific research in the 19th century.

A highlight for kids: life-sized elephants, tigers and rhinos play safari in the Grande Galerie de l'Évolution (Map p100; Great Gallery of Evolution; 36 rue Geoffroy St-Hilaire, 5e; adult/4-13yr €7/5, permanent collection free for EU residents under 26yr; ⊗ 10am-6pm Wed-Mon), where imaginative exhibits on evolution and humanity's effect on the global ecosystem, including global warming, fill 6000 sq metres. Rare specimens of endangered and extinct species dominate the Salle des Espèces Menacées et des Espèces Disparues (Hall of Threatened and Extinct Species) on level 2, while down on level 1 the Salle de Découverte (Room of Discovery) houses interactive exhibits for children.

Giant natural crystals dance with sunlight in the Galerie de Minéralogie et de Géologie (Mineralogy & Geology Gallery; Map p100; 36 rue Geoffroy St-Hilaire; adult/4-13yr €8/6; ⊗ 10am-6pm Wed-Mon).

Displays on comparative anatomy and palaeontology (the study of fossils) fill the Galerie d'Anatomie Comparée et de Paléontologie (Map p100; 2 rue Buffon; adult/4-13yr €7/5, free for EU residents under 26yr; ⊗ 10am-5pm Mon & Wed-Fri, 10am-6pm Sat & Sun).

MOSQUÉE DE PARIS Map p100

☎ 01 45 35 97 33; www.mosquee-de-paris.org, in French; 2bis place du Puits de l'Ermite, 5e; adult/7-25yr €3/2; ⊗ 9am-noon & 2-6pm Sat-Thu; Ⓜ Censier–Daubenton or Place Monge
Paris' central mosque, with its striking 26m-high minaret, was built in 1926 in the ornate Moorish style popular at the time. Visitors must be modestly dressed and remove their shoes at the entrance to the prayer hall.

The complex includes a North African-style restaurant (p228) and hammam (p310).

INSTITUT DU MONDE ARABE Map p100

☎ 01 40 51 38 38; www.imarabe.org; 1 place Mohammed V, 5e; Ⓜ Cardinal Lemoine or Jussieu
The Institute of the Arab World, set up by France and 20 Arab countries to promote cultural contacts between the Arab world and the West, is housed in a highly praised building (1987) that successfully mixes modern and traditional Arab and Western elements. Thousands of *mushrabiyah* (or *mouche-arabies*, photo-electrically sensitive apertures built into the glass walls), inspired by the traditional latticed-wood windows that let you see out without being seen, are opened and closed by electric motors in order to regulate the amount of light and heat that reach the interior of the building.

The institute hosts some fascinating temporary exhibitions (enter at 1 rue des Fossés Bernard; Map p100; adult/13-25yr/under 12yr €7/4/free, parent accompanying child €5; ⊗ 10am-6pm Tue-Sun). Its permanent museum, closed for renovation since April 2010, will focus on painting a global vision of the Arab world through 9th- to 19th-century art and artisanship, instruments from astronomy and other fields of scientific endeavour in which Arab technology once led the world, contemporary Arab art and so forth.

PANTHÉON Map p100

☎ 01 44 32 18 00; www.monum.fr; place du Panthéon, 5e; adult/18-25yr €8/5, free for EU residents under 26yr, 1st Sun of month Oct-Mar free; ⊗ 10am-6.30pm Apr-Sep, to 6pm Oct-Mar; Ⓜ Luxembourg
The domed landmark was commissioned by Louis XV around 1750 as an abbey church dedicated to Ste Geneviève in thanksgiving for his recovery from an illness, but due to financial and structural problems it wasn't completed until 1789 – not a good year for church openings in Paris. Two years later the Constituent Assembly turned it into a secular mausoleum and bricked up most of the windows.

The Panthéon is a superb example of 18th-century neoclassicism. It reverted to its religious duties two more times after the Revolution but has played a secular role ever since 1885, when God was evicted in favour of Victor Hugo. Among the crypt's

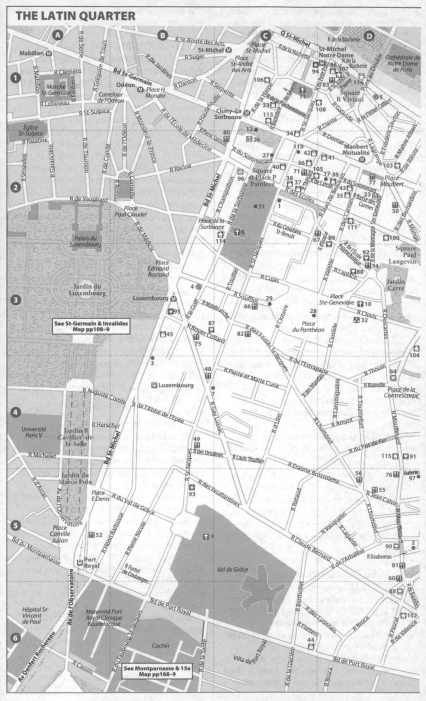

THE LATIN QUARTER

See St-Germain & Invalides
Map pp108–9

See Montparnasse & 15e
Map pp168–9

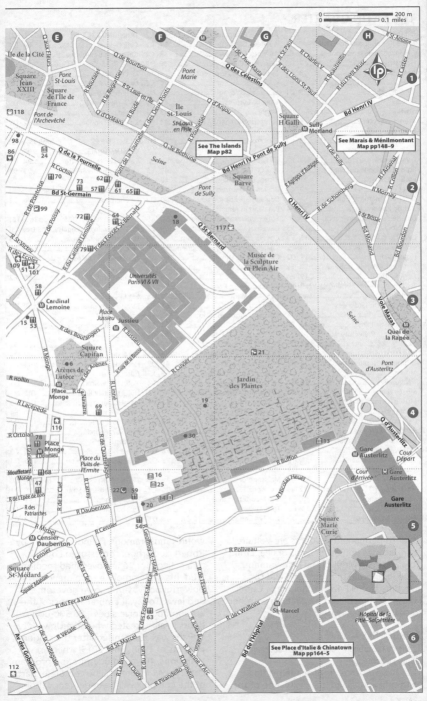

See The Islands
Map p82

See Marais & Ménilmontant
Map pp148–9

See Place d'Italie & Chinatown
Map pp164–5

THE LATIN QUARTER

INFORMATION
Cours de Langue et Civilisation
Françaises de la Sorbonne...........1 C2
Gepetto & Vélos..............................2 D5
La Cuisine Paris..............................3 B4
Milk..4 B3
Zeidnet..5 D1

SIGHTS   (pp98–104)
Arènes de Lutèce............................6 E4
Centre de la Mer.............................7 B4
Chapelle de la Sorbonne.................8 C2
Église Notre Dame du
  Val-de-Grâce................................9 B5
Église St-Étienne du Mont...........10 D3
Église St-Séverin..........................11 C1
Forêt de la Licorne.......................12 C1
Galerie d'Anatomie Comparée
  et de Paléontologie...................13 H4
Galerie de Minéralogie et de
  Géologie....................................14 F5
Gepetto & Vélos...........................15 D3
Grande Galerie de l'Évolution......16 F5
Hôtel Marignan.............................17 D2
Institut du Monde Arabe..............18 F2
Jardin Alpin..................................19 F4
Jardin des Plantes Entrance.........20 F5
Medieval Garden.....................(see 12)
Ménagerie du Jardin des
  Plantes......................................21 G3
Mosquée de Paris.........................22 F5
Musée de la Préfecture de
  Police...23 D2
Musée de l'Assistance
  Publique-Hôpitaux de Paris 24 E2
Musée National d'Histoire
  Naturelle...................................25 F5
Musée National du Moyen Age .. 26 C2
Musée National du Moyen Age
  Entrance....................................27 C2
Panthéon......................................28 C3
Panthéon Entrance.......................29 C3
Serres Tropicales (Jardin
  d'Hiver).....................................30 F4
Sorbonne......................................31 C2
Tour Clovis....................................32 D3

SHOPPING   (pp191–212)
Abbey Bookshop............................33 C1
Album..34 C2
Aspasie & Mathieu.........................35 D2

Au Vieux Campeur.........................36 C2
Au Vieux Campeur.........................37 C2
Au Vieux Campeur.........................38 C2
Aux Vieux Campeur.......................39 D2
La Boutique du Créateur de
  Jeux..40 C2
Librairie de Voyage........................41 D2
Librairie Eyrolles...........................42 C2
Magie...43 D2
Pâtisserie Sadaharu Aoki.............44 C6
Play Factory...................................45 B3
Shakespeare & Company...............46 D1

EATING   (pp213–74)
Aux Cérises de Lutèce....................47 E5
Bistrot Les Papilles........................48 B4
Boulangerie Bruno Solques...........49 B4
Boulangerie Eric Kayser................50 D2
Breakfast in America......................51 E3
Bullier University Restaurant........52 A5
Carrefour Market...........................53 E3
Censier University Restuarant......54 F5
Châtelet University Restaurant.....55 D5
Chez Léna et Mimille.....................56 D5
Chez René......................................57 E2
Kootchi..58 E3
La Mosquée de Paris......................59 F5
La Salle à Manger..........................60 D5
La Tour d'Argent............................61 F2
La Tour d'Argent Boutique............62 E2
L'Agrume.......................................63 F6
L'AOC...64 F2
Le Baba Bourgeois.........................65 F2
Le Comptoir du Panthéon.............66 C3
Le Coupe-Chou..............................67 D2
Le Foyer du Vietnam.....................68 E5
Le Jardin des Pâtes........................69 E4
Le Petit Pontoise...........................70 E2
Le Pré Verre...................................71 C2
Le Puits de Légumes......................72 E2
Les Pâtes Vivantes........................73 E2
Les Pipos..74 D3
Machu Picchu................................75 B3
Marché Franprix............................76 D5
Marché Maubert............................77 D2
Marché Monge..............................78 E4
Moissonnier...................................79 E3
Monoprix.......................................80 C2
Rue Mouffetard Market.................81 D5
Tashi Delek....................................82 C3
The Tea Caddy...............................83 D1

DRINKING   (pp275–92)
Café Delmas..................................84 D4
Cave de la Bourgogne...................85 D6
Curio Parlor Cocktail Club.............86 E2
Le Crocodile...................................87 B3
Le Piano Vache..............................88 D3
Le Pub St-Hilaire...........................89 D3
Le Verre à Pied..............................90 D5
Le Vieux Chêne.............................91 D4
Le Violon Dingue...........................92 D3

NIGHTLIFE   (pp293–308)
Café Universel...............................93 B5
Caveau de la Huchette..................94 C1
Le Petit Journal St-Michel.............95 B3

THE ARTS   (pp293–308)
Le Champo.....................................96 C2

SPORTS & ACTIVITIES   (pp309–16)
Au Point Vélo Hollandais ....(see 45)
Bowling Mouffetard......................97 D5
Free Scoot......................................98 E2
Hammam de la Mosquée de
  Paris.......................................(see 22)
Piscine Pontoise............................99 E2

SLEEPING   (pp323–51)
BVJ Paris-Quartier Latin..............100 D2
Familia Hôtel................................101 E3
Hôtel de l'Espérance....................102 D6
Hôtel de Notre Maître
  Albert..103 D2
Hôtel des Grandes Écoles............104 D3
Hôtel du Collège de France..........105 C2
Hôtel du Levant...........................106 C1
Hôtel Esmeralda..........................107 D1
Hôtel Henri IV Rive Gauche.........108 D1
Hôtel Minerve..............................109 E3
Hôtel St-Christophe.....................110 E4
Hôtel St-Jacques..........................111 D2
Port Royal Hôtel...........................112 E6
Résidence Le St-Germain.............113 C1
Select Hôtel.................................114 C2
Young & Happy Hostel.................115 D4

TRANSPORT   (pp383–90)
Bateaux Parisiens Stop................116 D1
Batobus Stop...............................117 G2
Batobus Stop...............................118 E1
Eurolines......................................119 C2

80 or so permanent residents are Voltaire, Jean-Jacques Rousseau, Louis Braille, Émile Zola and Jean Moulin. The first woman to be interred in the Panthéon was the two-time Nobel Prize-winner Marie Curie (1867–1934), reburied here (along with her husband, Pierre) in 1995.

SORBONNE Map p100

12 rue de la Sorbonne, 5e; Ⓜ Luxembourg or Cluny–La Sorbonne

The *crème de la crème* of academia flock to this distinguished university, one of the world's most famous. Founded in 1253 by Robert de Sorbon, confessor to Louis IX, as a college for 16 impoverished theology students, the Sorbonne soon grew into a powerful body with its own government and laws. Today, it embraces most of the 13 autonomous universities – 35,500-odd students in all – created when the University of Paris was reorganised after the student protests of 1968. Until 2015, when an ambitious, 10-year modernisation program costing €45 million will be complete, parts of the complex will be under renovation.

UNDERGROUND ART

Museums and galleries are not the sole repositories of art in Paris. Indeed, it is all around you – even underground. Almost half of the 300 metro stations were given a facelift to mark the centenary of the world-famous Métropolitain at the turn of the millennium, and many of them were assigned specific themes, usually relating to the *quartier* or the name of the station (eg Montparnasse Bienvenüe looks at the creation of the metro since it was an engineer named Fulgence Bienvenüe who oversaw the building of the first 91km from 1886 while Carrefour Pleyel, named in honour of the 18th-century composer and piano-maker Ignace Joseph Pleyel, focuses on classical music). Work has continued apace at even more stations over the past decade.

The following list is just a sample of the most interesting stations from an artistic perspective. The specific platform is mentioned for those stations served by more than one line.

Abbesses (Map p134; line 12) The noodle-like pale-green metalwork and glass canopy of the station entrance is one of the finest examples of the work of Hector Guimard (1867–1942), the celebrated French art nouveau architect whose signature style once graced most metro stations. For a complete list of the metro stations that retain *édicules* (shrine-like entranceways) designed by Guimard, see www.parisinconnu.com.

Arts et Métiers (Map p148; line 11 platform) The copper panelling, portholes and mechanisms of this station recall Jules Verne, Captain Nemo and collections of the nearby Musée des Arts et Métiers.

Assemblée Nationale (Map p108; line 12 platform) Gigantic posters of silhouettes in red, white and blue by artist Jean-Charles Blais represent the MPs currently sitting in parliament on the surface. And, yes, they are updated every five years.

Bastille (Map p158; line 5 platform) A 180-sq-metre ceramic fresco features scenes taken from newspaper engravings published during the Revolution, with illustrations of the destruction of the infamous prison.

Bibliothèque (Map p164; line 14) This enormous station – all screens, steel and glass – on the high-speed (and driverless) Météor resembles a hi-tech cathedral.

Champs-Élysées–Clemenceau (Map p126; transfer corridor btwn lines 1 & 13) The elegant frescoes in blue enamelled faïence recall Portuguese *azulejos* tiles and so they should: they were installed as part of a cultural exchange between Paris and Lisbon in 1995.

Chaussée d'Antin–Lafayette (Map p126; line 7 platform) Large allegorical painting on the vaulted ceiling recalls the Marquis de Lafayette (1757–1834) and his role as general in the American Revolution.

Cluny–La Sorbonne (Map p100; line 10 platform) A large ceramic mosaic replicates the signatures of intellectuals, artists and scientists from the Latin Quarter through history including Molière, Rabelais and Robespierre.

Concorde (Map p72; line 12 platform) What look like children's building blocks in white-and-blue ceramic on the walls of the station are 45,000 tiles that spell out the text of the *Déclaration des Droits de l'Homme et du Citoyen* (Declaration of the Rights of Man and of the Citizen), the document setting forth the principles of the French Revolution.

Javel–André Citroën (Map p118; line 10 platform) Photographs and display cases examine the life and work of inventor and automobile manufacturer André Citroën (1878–1935).

Louvre–Rivoli (Map p76; line 1 platform & corridor) Statues, bas-reliefs and photographs offer a small taste of what to expect at the Musée du Louvre above ground.

Palais Royal–Musée du Louvre (Map p76; line 1) The zany entrance on the place du Palais by Jean-Michel Othoniel is composed of two crown-shaped cupolas (one representing the day, the other night) consisting of 800 red, blue, amber and violet glass balls threaded on an aluminium structure. Sublime.

Parmentier (Map p158; line 3 platform) The theme in this station is agricultural crops, particularly the potato in honour of the station's namesake, Antoine-Auguste Parmentier (1737–1817), who brought the spud into fashion in France.

Pont Neuf (Map p82; line 7) With the former mint and the Musée de la Monnaie de Paris just above it, the focus here is on medals and coins.

Place de la Sorbonne links blvd St-Michel and the Chapelle de la Sorbonne, the university's gold-domed church, built between 1635 and 1642. The remains of Cardinal Richelieu (1585–1642) lie in a tomb with an effigy of a cardinal's hat suspended above it here.

MUSÉE NATIONAL DU MOYEN AGE
Map p100

☎ 01 53 73 78 00; www.musee-moyenage.fr; 6 place Paul Painlevé, 5e; adult/18-25yr €8.50/6.50, free for EU residents under 26yr, 1st Sun of the month free; ⏱ 9.15am-5.45pm Wed-Mon; Ⓜ Cluny–La Sorbonne or St-Michel

The National Museum of the Middle Ages occupies both a *frigidarium* (cooling room), which holds remains of Gallo-Roman *thermes* (baths) dating from around AD 200, and the 15th-century Hôtel des Abbés de Cluny, Paris' finest example of medieval civil architecture. Inside, spectacular displays include statuary, illuminated manuscripts, weapons, furnishings and *objets d'art* made of gold, ivory and enamel. But nothing compares with *La Dame à la Licorne* (The Lady with the Unicorn), a sublime series of late-15th-century tapestries from the southern Netherlands hung in circular room 13 on the 1st floor. Five of them are devoted to the senses while the sixth is the enigmatic *À Mon Seul Désir* (To My Sole Desire), a reflection on vanity.

Small gardens northeast of the museum, including the Jardin Céleste (Heavenly Garden) and the Jardin d'Amour (Garden of Love), are planted with flowers, herbs and shrubs that appear in masterpieces hanging throughout the museum. To the west the Forêt de la Licorne (Unicorn Forest) is based on the illustrations in the tapestries.

ARÈNES DE LUTÈCE Map p100

49 rue Monge, 5e; admission free; ⏱ 9am- 9.30pm Apr-Oct, 8am-5.30pm Nov-Mar; Ⓜ Place Monge

The 2nd-century Roman amphitheatre, Lutetia Arena, once sat around 10,000 people for gladiatorial combats and other events. Found by accident in 1869 when rue Monge was under construction, it's now used by neighbourhood youths for playing football, and by old men for *boules* and *pétanque* (a variant on the game of bowls).

CENTRE DE LA MER Map p100

☎ 01 44 32 10 90; www.oceano.org, in French; Institut Océanographique; 195 rue St-Jacques, 5e; adult/3-12yr €5/2.50; ⏱ 10.30am-12.30pm & 1.30-5.30pm Mon-Fri; Ⓜ Luxembourg

France has a long history of success in the field of oceanography (think Jacques Cousteau and, well, Jules Verne), and the Sea Centre cruises through that science, as well as marine biology, via temporary exhibitions, aquariums, scale models and audiovisuals. Kids will love the aquariums and the audiovisuals.

ÉGLISE ST-ÉTIENNE DU MONT Map p100

☎ 01 43 54 11 79; 1 place Ste-Geneviève, 5e; ⏱ 8am-noon & 2-7pm Tue-Sat, 9am-noon & 2.30-7pm Sun; Ⓜ Cardinal Lemoine

The Church of Mount St Stephen, built between 1492 and 1655, contains Paris' only surviving rood screen (1535), separating the chancel from the nave; the others were removed during the late Renaissance because they prevented the faithful assembled in the nave from seeing the priest celebrate Mass. In the nave's southeastern corner, a chapel contains the tomb of Ste Geneviève. A highly decorated reliquary nearby contains all that is left of her earthly remains – a finger bone. Ste Geneviève, patroness of Paris, was born at Nanterre in AD 422 and turned away Attila the Hun from Paris in AD 451.

MUSÉE DE L'ASSISTANCE PUBLIQUE-HÔPITAUX DE PARIS Map p100

☎ 01 40 27 50 05; www.aphp.fr/musee, in French; Hôtel de Miramion, 47 quai de la Tournelle, 5e; adult/13-18yr €4/2, 1st Sun of the month free; ⏱ 10am-6pm Tue-Sun Sep-Jul; Ⓜ Maubert–Mutualité

A museum devoted to the history of Parisian hospitals since the Middle Ages may not sound like a crowd-pleaser, but some of the paintings, sculptures, drawings and medical instruments are very evocative of their times.

Drinking p281; Eating p231; Shopping p198; Sleeping p333

From the packed pavement terraces of literary café greats Les Deux Magots (p282) and Café de Flore (p281), where Sartre, de Beauvoir and various other postwar Left Bank intellectuals drank, to the pocket-sized studios of lesser-known romantic and Russian cubist artists, this quarter (essentially the 6e arrondissement) oozes panache. Yet weave your way through the shopaholic crowds on blvd St-Germain, past flagship *prêt-à-porter* stores and vast white spaces showcasing interior design, and there's little hint of St-Germain des Prés' legendary bohemia. The arrival of the fashion industry changed all that jazz years ago.

Looking west towards the Eiffel Tower in the neighbouring 7e arrondissement is Faubourg St-Germain, an elegant if staid *quartier* that graces the streets between the Seine and rue de Babylone, 1km south, with beautiful 18th-century mansions. The smooth lawns of Esplanade des Invalides map its western fringe green.

Despite passing fashions, there remains a startling cinematic quality to this soulful part of the Left Bank where Pierre and Jean-Pierre restore antique ivory in their 1930s family shop; where gourmands talk bread and wine with local legends like Apolliana Poilâne (p215) and Juan Sánchez (p200); where well-dressed ladies take their 1960s cast-offs to vintage dealers on rue de Buci; where artists, writers, actors and musicians cross paths in the shadow of the École Nationale Supérieure des Beaux Arts, the Académie Française and the Odéon-Théâtre de l'Europe.

top picks

ST-GERMAIN & INVALIDES

- Musée d'Orsay (p107) Revel in magnificent art at Paris' next best museum after the Louvre.
- Jardin du Luxembourg (p106) See where Parisians play: the city's most legendary park is a particular must-stroll at weekends.
- Musée Rodin (p111) Indulge in one of those exquisitely Parisian moments with a meander around the Rodin Museum's beautiful sculpture-studded gardens.
- Église St-Germain (p105) Get to the heart of this chic neighbourhood, born out of a 6th-century abbey, with Paris' oldest standing church.
- Musée National Eugène Delacroix (p111) Pair a visit to this lovely art studio–museum with the Louvre or Musée d'Orsay.

Stroll past the portfolio of designer boutiques on rue du Cherche Midi, past Patrick Blanc's flamboyant vegetal wall growing inside No 7, past the constant crowd gathered at the foot of guillotined revolutionary leader Georges Danton on Carrefour de l'Odéon, past heaps of fresh produce at the Rue Raspail market and Rue Cler markets and watch it leap out at you. *La vie germanopratine* (St-Germain life) is *belle*.

This area is well served by the metro and RER: get off at St-Germain des Prés, Mabillon or Odéon for its busy blvd St-Germain heart. Buses stop on blvd St-Germain for the 86 to Odéon, Pont Sully (Île St-Louis) and Bastille; on rue de Rennes for the 96 to place Châtelet, Hôtel de Ville, St-Paul (Marais), rue Oberkampf and rue de Ménilmontant; and on Quai d'Orsay for the 63 to Gare d'Austerlitz and Gare de Lyon, and the 83 to Grand Palais, Rond Point des Champs-Élysées and rue du Faubourg St-Honoré. The 73 links the Musée d'Orsay with place de la Concorde, av des Champs-Élysées and La Défense.

On the Seine, Batobus boats dock by quai Malaquais for St-Germain des Prés and quai de Solférino for the Musée d'Orsay. Paris Canal Croisières uses the pier at quai Anatole France for canal boats to Bassin de la Villette (19–21 quai de la Loire).

ÉGLISE ST-GERMAIN DES PRÉS
Map p112

☎ 01 55 42 81 33; 3 place St-Germain des Prés, 6e;
🕑 8am-7pm Mon-Sat, 9am-8pm Sun;
Ⓜ St-Germain des Prés

Paris' oldest standing church, the Romanesque St Germanus of the Fields, was built in the 11th century on the site of a 6th-century abbey and was the dominant place of worship in Paris until the arrival of Notre Dame. It has been altered many times since, but the Chapelle de St-Symphorien (to the right as you enter) was part of the original abbey and is believed to be the resting place of St Germanus (AD 496–576), the first bishop of Paris. The Merovingian kings were buried here during the 6th and 7th centuries, but their tombs disappeared during the Revolution. The bell tower over the western entrance has changed little since 990, although the spire dates only from the 19th century. The vaulted ceiling is a starry sky that seems to float forever upward.

ÉGLISE ST-SULPICE Map p112

☎ 01 46 33 21 78; place St-Sulpice, 6e; ◷ 7.30am-7.30pm; Ⓜ St-Sulpice

In 1646 work started on the twin-towered Church of St Sulpicius, lined inside with 21 side chapels, and took six architects 150 years to finish. What draws most people to the church is not its lovely Italianate facade with two rows of superimposed columns, nor its neoclassical decor influenced by the Counter-Reformation; rather, the building was the setting for a crucial discovery in Dan Brown's *The Da Vinci Code*.

The frescoes in the Chapelle des Sts-Anges (Chapel of the Holy Angels), first to the right as you enter the chapel, depict Jacob wrestling with the angel (to the left) and Michael the Archangel doing battle with Satan (to the right) and were painted by Eugène Delacroix between 1855 and 1861. The monumental, 20m-tall organ loft dates back to 1781. Listen to the organ in its full glory during 10.30am Mass on Sunday or the occasional Sunday-afternoon organ concert.

CHAPELLE NOTRE DAME DE LA MEDAILLE MIRACULEUSE Map p108

☎ 01 49 54 78 88; www.chapellenotredamede lamedaillemiraculeuse.com, in French; 140 rue du Bac, 6e; ◷ 7.45am-1pm & 2.30-7pm Mon & Wed-Sun, 7.45am-7pm Tue; Ⓜ Rue du Bac or Vaneau

Situated across the street from Le Bon Marché department store, tucked away at the end of a courtyard, is this extraordinary chapel where, in 1830, the Virgin Mary spoke to a 24-year-old novice called Catherine Labouré. In a series of three miraculous apparitions that took place in the chapel the young nun was told to have a medal made that would protect and grace those who wore it. The first Miraculous Medals were made in 1832 – the same year a cholera epidemic plagued Paris – and its popularity spread like wild

fire as wearers of the medal found themselves miraculously cured or protected from the deadly disease. Devout Roman Catholics around the world still wear the medal today.

Catherine Labouré (1806–76), the eighth child of a Burgundy farmer, was beatified in 1933 and her body moved to a reliquary beneath the altar of Our Lady of the Globe (to the right as you face the main altar) inside the Chapel of Our Lady of the Miraculous Medal.

JARDIN DU LUXEMBOURG Map p108

Ⓜ Luxembourg

Keen to know what the city does during its time off? Then stroll around the formal terraces, chestnut groves and green lawns of this 23-hectare park, where Parisians of all ages flock in all weather. Be it jogging, practising t'ai chi, gossiping with girlfriends on one of the garden's signature sage-green chairs (fancy one to take home? See p212), reading or romancing, the Jardin du Luxembourg is *the* voyeur's spot to peek on Parisians. Opening hours vary seasonally, opening some time between 7.30am and 8.15am and closing sometime between 5pm and 10pm.

Urban orchards hang heavy with dozens of apple varieties in the southern part of the *jardin* (garden). Bees have produced honey in the nearby Rucher du Luxembourg since the 19th century; don't miss the annual Fête du Miel (Honey Festival), two days of tasting and buying the aviary's sweet harvest in late September in the Pavillon Davioud (55bis rue d'Assas). This ornate pavilion is also the spot where green-fingered Parisians partake of gardening courses with the École d'Horticulture (64 Blvd St-Michel, 6e). For sports-minded souls, there are six tennis courts.

The park is a backdrop to the Palais du Luxembourg, built in the 1620s for Marie de Médici, Henri IV's consort, to assuage her longing for the Pitti Palace in Florence, where she had spent her childhood. Since 1958 the palace has housed the Sénat (Senate, upper house of French parliament; reservations ☎ 01 44 54 19 49; www.senat.fr; rue de Vaugirard, 6e; adult/18-25yr €8/6), which can be visited via a guided tour at 10.30am every Saturday per month. Situated east of the palace is the Italianate Fontaine des Médici, an ornate fish pond (1630).

Top spot for sun-soaking – there's always loads of chairs here – is the southern side of the palace's 19th-century, 57m-long Orangery (1834) where lemon and orange trees, palms, grenadiers and oleanders shelter from the cold. Nearby the heavily guarded Hôtel du Petit Luxembourg (rue de Vaugirard, 6e) was the modest 16th-century pad where Marie de Médici lived while Palace du Luxembourg was being built. The president of the Senate has called it home since 1825.

Luxembourg Garden offers all the delights of a Parisian childhood a century ago. At the octagonal Grand Bassin, 1920s toy sailboats can be rented (per 30/60 minutes €2/3.20) to sail on the water, and nearby ponies take children for rides (€2.50). At the pint-sized Théâtre des Marionnettes du Jardin du Luxembourg (☎ 01 43 26 46 47; admission €4; ☯ 3.30pm Wed, 11am & 3.30pm Sat & Sun, daily during school holidays) marionette shows guarantee a giggle, whether you understand French or not. Complete the day with a romp around the kids' playground (adult/child/under 15 months €2.60/1.60/free; ☯ 10am–park close) – the green half is for kids aged seven to 12 years, the blue half for under-sevens – or a summertime waltz on the old-fashioned carousel (merry-go-round).

MUSÉE ATELIER ZADKINE Map p108

☎ 01 55 42 77 20; www.zadkine.paris.fr, in French; 100bis rue d'Assas, 6e; admission free; ☯ 10am-6pm Tue-Sun

The Musée Atelier Zadkine covers the life and work of Russian cubist sculptor Ossip Zadkine (1890–1967), who arrived in Paris in 1908, and lived and worked in this cottage for almost 40 years. Zadkine produced an enormous catalogue of sculptures made from clay, stone, bronze and wood: one room displays figures he sculpted in contrasting walnut, pear, ebony, acacia, elm and oak. The occasional temporary exhibition commands a token admission fee.

FONDATION DUBUFFET Map p108

☎ 01 47 34 12 63; www.dubuffetfondation.com, in French; 137 rue de Sèvres, 6e; adult/under 10yr €6/ free; ☯ 2-6pm Mon-Fri; Ⓜ Duroc

Situated in a lovely 19th-century hôtel particulier (private mansion) at the end of a courtyard, the foundation houses the collection of Jean Dubuffet (1901–85), chief of the Art Brut school (a term he himself coined to describe all works of artistic expression not officially recognised). Much of his work is incredibly modern and expressive.

MUSÉE DE LA MONNAIE DE PARIS
Map p112

☎ 01 40 46 55 35; www.monnaiedeparis.fr; 11 quai de Conti, 6e; admission free; ☯ 11am-5.30pm Tue-Fri, noon-5.30pm Sat & Sun; Ⓜ Pont Neuf

The Parisian Mint Museum traces the history of French coinage from antiquity to the present and displays presses and other minting equipment. There are some excellent audiovisual and other displays, which help to bring to life this otherwise niche subject.

The museum building, the Hôtel de la Monnaie, became the royal mint during the 18th century and is still used by the Ministry of Finance to produce commemorative medals and coins, as well as official weights and measures. One-hour guided tours of the ateliers (workshops; €3) must be reserved in advance.

MUSÉE D'ORSAY Map p108

☎ 01 40 49 48 14; www.musee-orsay.fr; 62 rue de Lille, 7e; adult/18-25yr €8/5.50, plus temporary exhibitions €9.50/7, permanent exhibitions free for EU residents under 26yr, 1st Sun of month free; ☯ 9.30am-6pm Tue, Wed & Fri-Sun, to 9.45pm Thu; Ⓜ Musée d'Orsay or Solférino

In a former train station (1900) facing the Seine, this museum displays France's national collection of paintings, sculptures, objets d'art and other works produced between the 1840s and 1914. The vast collection includes the fruits of the impressionist, postimpressionist and art nouveau movements.

Many visitors head straight to the upper skylight-lit level to see the impressionist paintings by Monet, Renoir, Pissarro, Sisley, Degas and Manet and the postimpressionist works by Van Gogh, Cézanne, Seurat and Matisse. But there's a great deal to see on the ground floor, too, including early works by Manet, Monet, Renoir and Pissarro. The middle level has some magnificent art nouveau rooms.

English-language guided tours (information ☎ 01 40 49 48 48; €6 plus admission fee) last 1½ hours and include 'Masterpieces of the Musée d'Orsay'. There are also tours and

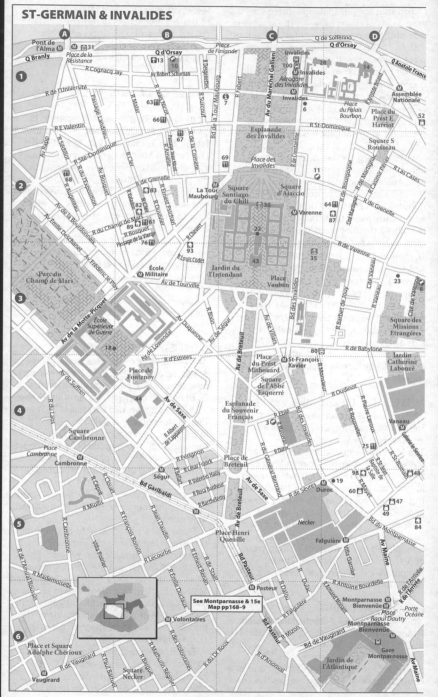

ST-GERMAIN & INVALIDES

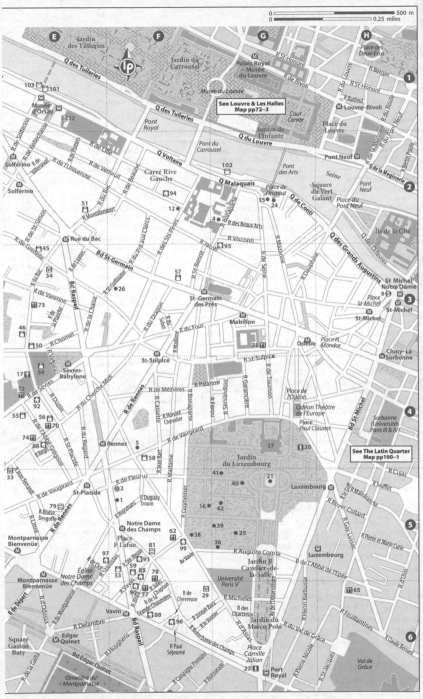

See Louvre & Les Halles
Map pp72–3

See The Latin Quarter
Map pp100–1

ST-GERMAIN & INVALIDES

INFORMATION
Alliance Française.................................1 F5
Children's Playground ....(see 16)
Cyber Latin...2 F5
Dutch Embassy...................................3 C4
École des Beaux-Arts 4 G2
Étudiants de L'Institut
  catholique de Paris...........................5 F4
France-Canada Chamber of
  Commerce.......................................6 C1
Inlingua...7 C1
Italian Embassy..................................8 D3
La Marina de Paris.....................(see 103)
Société Touristique de Services
  (STS) Exchange Office......................9 H3
South African Embassy.....................10 B1
Swiss Embassy..................................11 C2

SIGHTS   pp105–15
5bis Rue Verneuil (Serge
  Gainsbourg's Former Home)....12 F2
Académie Française.....................(see 15)
American Church in Paris 13 B1
Assemblée Nationale (Palais
  Bourbon)....................................14 D1
Bibliothèque Mazarine 15 G2
Carousel.......................................16 F5
Chapelle Notre Dame de la
  Medaille Miraculeuse................17 E4
École Militaire 18 A3
Église du Dôme....................(see 43)
Église St-Louis des Invalides.......(see 22)
Fondation Dubuffet 19 D5
Fontaine des Médicis....................20 G4
Grand Bassin................................21 G5
Hôtel des Invalides.......................22 C2
Hôtel Matignon............................23 D3
Institut de France.........................24 G2
Jardin du Luxembourg..................25 G5
Maison de Verre...........................26 F3
Maréchal Ney Statue....................27 G6
Ministère des Affaires
  Étrangères.................................28 C1
Musée Atelier Zadkine..................29 F6
Musée de l'Armée.........................30 C2
Musée des Égouts de Paris 31 A1
Musée des Plans-Reliefs ....(see 43)
Musée d'Orsay..............................32 E1

Musée Ernest Hébert.....................33 E5
Musée Maillol-Fondation Diana
  Vierny.......................................34 E3
Musée Rodin................................35 C3
Orchards.......................................36 G5
Palais du Luxembourg...................37 G4
Pavillon Davioud..........................38 F5
Rucher du Luxembourg (Apiary) 39 G5
Sénat....................................(see 37)
Shetland Ponies for Hire...............40 G5
Tennis Courts................................41 G5
Théatre de Marionettes du Jardin
  du Luxembourg.........................42 G5
Tombeau de Napoléon 1er............43 C3
Unesco Building............................44 B4

SHOPPING 🛍   pp191–212
Bébé Bonton...............................45 E3
Bonton Bazar...............................46 E3
Chercheminippes.........................47 D5
Chercheminippes.........................48 D5
Chercheminippes (Menswear).....49 D5
Conran Shop.................................50 E3
Deyrolle.......................................51 E2
Grenelle Bonton...................(see 45)
Knoll..52 D1
La Clef des Marques......................53 F5
La Grande Épicerie de Paris........(see 72)
Le Bon Marché..............................54 E4
Le Palais des Thés........................55 E4
Lin et Cie................................(see 90)
Mouton à Cinq Pattes.............(see 92)
Mouton à Cinq Pattes..................56 E4
Multi Change................................57 F3
Pâtisserie Sadaharu Aoki..............58 E4
Rouge et Noir................................59 F5
Tea & Tattered Pages....................60 D5

EATING 🍴   pp213–74
Amorino......................................61 B2
Amorino......................................62 F5
Bellota Bellota.............................63 B1
Besnier..64 D2
Boulangerie Bruno Solques.........65 H6
Boulangerie-Pâtisserie Stéphane
  Secco..66 B1
Brasserie Thoumieux....................67 B2
Café Constant...............................68 A2

Café de l'Esplanade.....................69 C2
Chez Les Filles.............................70 E4
Gérard Mulot................................71 G3
La Grande Épicerie.......................72 E4
La Pâtisserie des Rêves.................73 E3
Les Cocottes..........................(see 68)
Mamie Gâteaux............................74 E4
Quatrehommes.............................75 D4
Rue Cler Market............................76 B2
Sensing..77 F6
Toyo...78 F5

DRINKING   pp275–92
Café du Musée Rodin...............(see 35)
Café Thomieux.......................(see 67)

THE ARTS 🎭   pp293–308
Fnac Montparnasse.......................79 E5
La Pagode....................................80 C3
Lucinaire......................................81 F5

SLEEPING 🛏   pp323–51
Cadran Hôtel................................82 B2
Grand Hôtel Lévêque....................83 B2
Hôtel Aviatic................................84 D5
Hôtel Danemark............................85 F5
Hôtel de Sèvres............................86 E4
Hôtel de Varenne..........................87 D2
Hôtel des Académies et des Arts 88 F6
Hôtel du Champ-de-Mars.............89 B2
Hôtel Jardin Le Bréa.....................90 F6
Hôtel La Sainte-Beuve..................91 F5
Hôtel Le Placide...........................92 E4
Hôtel Muguet...............................93 B3
Hôtel Verneuil..............................94 F2
Ladurée..95 G3
L'Apostrophe................................96 F6
Le Six...97 E5
Mayet Hôtel.................................98 D5
Pension Les Marronniers..............99 F5
Résidence des Palais..............(see 99)

TRANSPORT   pp383–90
Aérogare des Invalides ....(see 100)
Air France Buses..........................100 C1
Batobus Stop................................101 E1
Batobus Stop................................102 G2
Paris Canal Croisières...................103 E1

workshops designed with kids and families in mind. Details and hours for all are listed on its website.

To cut the length of time spent queuing to get into the museum, buy tickets in advance online or at Kiosque du Musée d'Orsay (🕘 9am-5pm Tue-Fri school holidays, Tue only rest of year), in front of the museum. With an advance ticket purchase you get in via the less-busy entrance C. Those who prefer to go at their own pace can DIY with a 1½-hour audioguide tour (€5) covering 80 major works.

Museum tickets are valid all day, meaning you can leave and re-enter the museum as you please. The reduced entrance fee of €5.50 (€7 including temporary exhibition) applies to everyone after 4.15pm (6pm on Thursday). Those visiting the Musée Rodin (p111) on the same day save €2 with a combined ticket (€12).

MUSÉE ERNEST HÉBERT
Map p108

☎ 01 42 22 23 82; 85 rue du Cherche Midi, 6e;
🕘 12.30-6pm Mon & Wed-Fri, 2-6pm Sat & Sun;
Ⓜ St-Placide

Portrait painter Ernest Hébert (1817–1908) did likenesses of society people of the Second Empire and the *belle époque* and was therefore not short of a coin or two. The artist's wonderful 18th-century townhouse and its baubles – not his saccharine, almost cloying portraits – is the draw here, though. The museum was closed for renovations at the time of research.

MUSÉE MAILLOL-FONDATION DINA VIERNY Map p108

☎ 01 42 22 59 58; www.museemaillol.com; 61 rue de Grenelle, 7e; adult/11-25yr €11/9; ⏲ 10.30am-7pm Wed, Thu & Sat-Mon, to 9.30pm Fri; Ⓜ Rue du Bac

This splendid little museum focuses on the work of sculptor Aristide Maillol (1861–1944) who died in a car crash. It also includes works by Matisse, Gauguin, Kandinsky, Cézanne and Picasso, all from the private collection of Odessa-born Dina Vierny (b 1915–), Maillol's principal model for 10 years from the age of 15. The museum is located in the stunning 18th-century Hôtel Bouchardon.

MUSÉE NATIONAL EUGÈNE DELACROIX Map p112

☎ 01 44 41 86 50; www.musee-delacroix.fr; 6 rue de Furstemberg, 6e; adult/under 18yr €5/free, free for EU residents under 26yr, 1st Sun of month free; ⏲ 9.30am-5pm Wed-Mon, to 5.30pm Sat & Sun Jun-Aug; Ⓜ Mabillon or St-Germain des Prés

The Eugène Delacroix Museum, in a courtyard off a leafy 'square', was the romantic artist's home and studio at the time of his death in 1863, and contains a collection of his oil paintings, watercolours, pastels and drawings. If you want to see his major works, such as *Liberty Leading the People*, pay a visit to the Musée du Louvre (p70) or

the Musée d'Orsay (p107); here you'll find many of his more intimate works (eg *An Unmade Bed*, 1828) and his paintings of Morocco.

MUSÉE RODIN
Map p108

☎ 01 44 18 61 10; www.musee-rodin.fr; 79 rue de Varenne, 7e; adult/18-25yr permanent or temporary exhibition €7/5, both exhibitions plus garden €10/7, free for EU residents under 26yr, 1st Sun of month free, garden only €1; ⏲ 10am-5.45pm Tue-Sun; Ⓜ Varenne

The Rodin Museum is one of the most relaxing spots in the city, with its garden bespeckled with sculptures and trees in which to contemplate *The Thinker*. Rooms on two floors of the 18th-century Hôtel Biron display vital bronze and marble sculptures by Auguste Rodin, including casts of some of his most celebrated works: *The Hand of God, The Burghers of Calais, Cathedral*, that perennial crowd-pleaser *The Thinker* and the sublime, the incomparable, that romance-hewn-in-marble called *The Kiss*. There are also more than a dozen works by Camille Claudel (1864–1943), sister to the writer Paul and Rodin's mistress. The garden closes its gates later than the museum: at 6.45pm April to September and at 5pm October to March. Purchase tickets online to avoid queuing.

HÔTEL DES INVALIDES
Map p108

Ⓜ Invalides, Varenne or La Tour Maubourg

A 500m-long expanse of lawn known as the Esplanade des Invalides separates Faubourg

---

FAUBOURG STREET ELEGANCE

In the 18th century, Faubourg St-Germain – a formal world of exquisite ironwork, gold leaf, Seine-side art galleries and conventional manners – was Paris' most fashionable neighbourhood. Elegant *hôtels particuliers* (private mansions) ran riot on rue de Lille, rue de Grenelle and rue de Varenne, now an overdose of embassies, cultural centres and government ministries; Hôtel Matignon (57 rue de Varenne) has been the official residence of the French prime minister since the start of the Fifth Republic (1958), and it was to the stylish pad at No 53 that Edith Wharton moved in 1910 to write *Le Temps de l'Innocence* (The Age of Innocence).

Framing all this Parisian refinement is the Eiffel Tower in the skyline, the gracious curve of the Seine at eye level and, underfoot, the smooth lawns of Les Invalides where it always feels like Sunday. If you suddenly find yourself leaping on a bike and pedalling along the river to watch the kaleidoscope of the National Assembly, the cavernous railway-station shell of the Musée d'Orsay and Quai Voltaire's bijou art galleries flash by, don't be surprised. Just make sure you jump off at 5bis rue Verneuil to see the quarter's finest example of timeless extravagance – the house where Parisian singer, sexpot and *provocateur* Serge Gainsbourg lived from 1969 until his death in 1991. Neighbours have long since given up scrubbing off the reappearing graffiti and messages from fans.

ST-GERMAIN

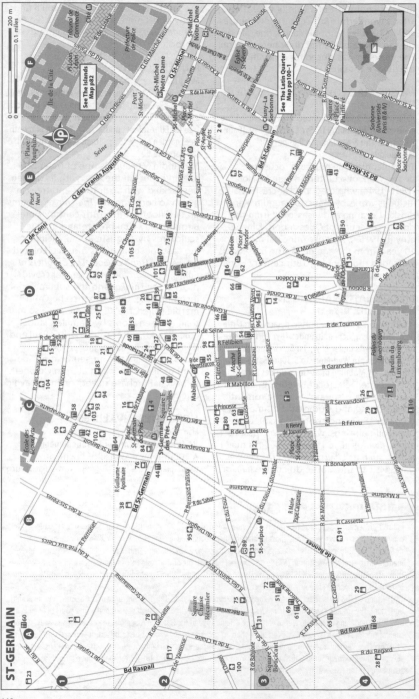

See The Islands
Map p82

See The Latin Quarter
Map pp100–1

ST-GERMAIN

INFORMATION
Eurocentres 1 D2
Pharmacie Bader 2 E3

SIGHTS   **pp105–15**
Centaur Statue 3 B3
Église St-Germain des Prés 4 C2
Église St-Sulpice 5 C3
Georges Danton Statue................. 6 D3
Hôtel du Petit Luxembourg.......... 7 C4
Musée de la Monnaie de Paris......8 D1
Musée National Eugène
   Delacroix 9 C2
Orangery 10 C4

SHOPPING   **pp191–212**
Alexandra Sojfer 11 A1
Au Plat d'Etain 12 C3
Cacao et Chocolat......................... 13 D2
Cave St-Sulpice 14 D3
Downtown...................................... 15 C1
Flamant Home Interiors............... 16 C2
Galerie François Rénier................. 17 A2
Galerie Loevenbruck..................... 18 D1
Galerie Loft 19 C1
Galerie Onega............................(see 88)
Hapart 20 D2
Huilerie J Leblanc et Fils............... 21 C1
Ivoire.. 22 C3
Kartell 23 A1
La Dernière Goutte........................ 24 C2
La Galerie Moderne....................... 25 D1
La Maison de Poupée.................... 26 C4
Le Dépôt-Vente de Buci 27 C2
L'Embellie...................................... 28 A4
Les Beaux Draps de Jeanine
   Cros.. 29 A4
Librairie Le Moniteur.................... 30 D4
Maison du Chocolat...................... 31 A3
Mariage Frères.............................. 32 E2
Marithé et François Girbaud........ 33 B3
Pièce Unique Variations 34 D1

Pièce Unique Variations................35 D1
Pierre Hermé..................................36 B3
Ragtime..37 C2
Shu Uemura 38 B2
Taschen...39 D2
Village Voice 40 C3

EATING   **pp213–74**
Amorino..41 D2
Au Pied de Fouet 42 C1
Bouillon Racine..............................43 E4
Brasserie Lipp.................................44 B2
Carrefour Market............................45 D2
Casa Bini 46 D3
Chez Allard.....................................47 E2
Chez Hanafousa 48 C2
Cosi...49 D2
Crèmerie Restaurant Polidor 50 E4
Cuisine de Bar 51 A3
Da Rosa 52 D1
Fish la Boissonnerie.......................53 D2
Gérard Mulot 54 D3
Huîterie Regis 55 C2
KGB...56 E2
La Jacobine.....................................57 D2
Ladurée...58 C1
l'Arbuci...59 D2
L'Atelier de Joël Robuchon..........60 A1
Le Cherche Midi 61 A3
Le Comptoir du Relais...................62 D3
Le Machon d'Henri.........................63 C3
Le Petit Zinc 64 C2
Le Salon d'Hélène 65 A4
Les Éditeurs....................................66 D3
Mabillon University Restaurant...67 D2
Marché Raspail...............................68 A4
Matteo & Paola 69 A4
Mazet University Restaurant........70 C2
Monoprix...71 E3
Poilâne..72 C1
Roger La Grenouille........................73 D2
Ze Kitchen Galerie 74 E1

DRINKING   **pp275–92**
Alcazar ....(see 88)
Au Sauvignon 75 A3
Café de Flore 76 B2
Café La Palette...............................77 D1
Café Le Basile 78 A2
Centre de Dégustation Jacques
   Vivet 79 C4
Comptoir des Canettes.................80 C3
Kilàli..81 D3
Le 10 ....82 D3
Le Zéro de Conduite......................83 C1
Les Deux Magots...........................84 C2
Les Etages St-Germain...................85 D2
L'Urgence Bar................................86 E4
Prescription Cocktail Club............87 D1

NIGHTLIFE   **pp293–308**
Le Wagg 88 D2

THE ARTS   **pp293–308**
Théâtre du Vieux Colombier 89 B3

SLEEPING   **pp323–51**
Hôtel d'Angleterre.........................90 C1
Hôtel de l'Abbaye Saint
   Germain.....................................91 B4
Hôtel de Nesle...............................92 D1
Hôtel des 2 Continents..................93 C1
Hôtel des Marronniers 94 C1
Hôtel du Dragon............................95 B2
Hôtel du Globe 96 D3
Hôtel du Lys...................................97 E3
Hôtel Le Clément...........................98 D2
Hôtel Le Clos Médicis 99 E4
Hôtel Lindbergh...........................100 A3
Hôtel Relais St-Germain ....(see 62)
Hôtel St-André des Arts...............101 D2
Hôtel St-Germain des Prés 102 C1
La Villa..103 C1
L'Hôtel..104 C1
Relais Christine............................105 D2

St-Germain from the Eiffel Tower area. At the southern end of the esplanade, laid out between 1704 and 1720, is the final resting place of Napoleon, the man many French people consider to be the nation's greatest hero.

Hôtel des Invalides was built in the 1670s by Louis XIV to provide housing for 4000 *invalides* (disabled war veterans). On 14 July 1789, a mob forced its way into the building and, after fierce fighting, seized 32,000 rifles before heading on to the prison at Bastille and the start of the French Revolution.

North of Hôtel des Invalides' main court-yard, in the so-called Cour d'Honneur, is the Musée de l'Armée (Army Museum; ☎ 01 44 42 38 77; www.invalides.org; 129 rue de Grenelle, 7e; adult/18-25yr €9/7; 🕑 10am-6pm Mon & Wed-Sat, 10am-9pm Tue, 10am-6.30pm Sun Apr-Sep, to 5pm Oct-Mar, closed 1st

Mon of month) – the nation's largest collection on French military history.

South is Église St-Louis des Invalides, once used by soldiers, and Église du Dôme (🕑 10am-7pm Jul & Aug, to 6pm Sep & Apr-Jun, to 5pm Oct-Mar) which, with its sparkling golden dome (1677–1735), is one of the finest religious edifices erected under Louis XIV. It received the remains of Napoleon in 1840. The very extravagant Tombeau de Napoléon 1er (Napoleon's Tomb; 🕑 10am-6pm Apr-Sep, to 5pm Oct-Mar, closed 1st Mon of month), in the centre of the church, comprises six coffins fitting into one another like a Russian *matryoshka* doll.

Admission to the Army Museum includes entry to all the sights in Hôtel des Invalides, including the Musée des Plans-Reliefs (☎ 01 45 51 95 05; http://plans-reliefs.monuments-nationaux.fr; 🕑 10am-6pm Apr-Sep, to 5pm Oct-Mar, closed 1st Mon of month), an esoteric museum full of scale models of towns, fortresses and chateaux across France.

ASSEMBLÉE NATIONALE
Map p108

☎ 01 40 63 60 00; www.assemblee-nat.fr; 33 quai d'Orsay & 126 rue de l'Université, 7e; Ⓜ Assemblée Nationale or Invalides

The lower house of the French parliament, known as the National Assembly, meets in the 18th-century Palais Bourbon, which fronts the Seine. Tours are available through local deputies, making citizens and residents the only ones eligible. Next door is the Second Empire-style Ministère des Affaires Étrangères (Ministry of Foreign Affairs; ☎ 01 43 17 53 53; 37 quai d'Orsay, 7e), built between 1845 and 1855.

INSTITUT DE FRANCE
Map p108

☎ 01 44 41 44 41; www.institut-de-france.fr; 23 quai de Conti, 6e; Ⓜ Mabillon or Pont Neuf

The French Institute, created in 1795, brought together five of France's academies of arts and sciences. The most famous of these is the Académie Française (French Academy), founded in 1635 by Cardinal Richelieu. Its 40 members, known as the Immortels (Immortals), have the Herculean (some say impossible) task of safeguarding the purity of the French language. The domed building housing the institute, across the Seine from the Louvre's eastern end, is a masterpiece of French neoclassical architecture.

France's oldest public library, the Bibliothèque Mazarine (Mazarine Library; ☎ 01 44 41 44 06; www.bibliotheque-mazarine.fr; ☉ 10am-6pm Mon-Fri, closed 2 weeks in Aug) founded in 1643, is in the same building. You can visit the bust-lined, late-17th century reading room or consult the library's collection of 500,000 volumes, using a free, two-day admission pass obtained by leaving your ID at the office to the left of the entrance. An annual membership/10-visit *carnet* to borrow

---

I SPY WITH MY LITTLE EYE

Paris has immortalised people from its past with statues and monuments since the mid-19th century. Père Lachaise, Montmartre and Montparnasse cemeteries burst with wonderfully evocative likenesses of heroes and villains, poets and philosophers, and revolutionaries and autocrats, and there's a resident stone or bronze celebrity in even the tiniest park or square. The following is a selection of the larger-than-life characters you should try to spot – not difficult – on your way around Paris.

St-Denis, patron saint of France (also known as Dionysius of Paris), introduced Christianity to Paris and was beheaded by the Romans for his pains. You can see him carrying his unfortunate head under his arm on the carved western portal of the Cathédrale de Notre Dame de Paris (Map p82).

Ste-Geneviève, the patroness of Paris, was born at Nanterre in AD 422 and turned Attila the Hun away from the city in 451. Now she stands, ghostly pale and turning her back on Paris, high above the Pont de la Tournelle (Map p82), just south of Île St Louis in the 5e. Plucky Jeanne d'Arc (Joan of Arc; Map p72) tried unsuccessfully to wrest Paris from the English almost a millennium later; her gilded likeness now stands in place des Pyramides, next to 192 rue de Rivoli, 1er.

Henri IV (Map p82), known as the Vert Galant ('jolly rogue' or 'dirty old man', depending on your perspective), sits astride his white stallion on the Pont Neuf in the 1er, exactly as he did when he inaugurated the 'New Bridge' in 1607. Charlemagne (Map p82), emperor of the Franks, rides his steed under the trees in front of Cathédrale de Notre Dame, while a poor imitation of the Sun King, Louis XIV (Map p72), prances in place des Victoires in the 2e. Georges Danton (Map p112), a leader of the Revolution and later one of its guillotined victims, stands with his head very much intact near the site of his house at Carrefour de l'Odéon in the 6e.

Napoleon, horseless and in Roman drag, stands atop the column in place Vendôme (Map p72) in the 1er. The latest addition is a 3.6m-tall bronze of General Charles de Gaulle (Map p126) in full military regalia at the bottom of av des Champs-Élysées, ready to march down to the Arc de Triomphe in a liberated Paris on 26 August 1944.

But it's not just people who are immortalised. An illuminated bronze replica of New York's Statue of Liberty (Map p168) faces the Big Apple from a long and narrow artificial island in the Seine. And have a look at the impressive Centaur statue (Map p112) in the centre of Carrefour de la Croix Rouge in the 6e, which was sculpted by César Baldaccini. Impossible to miss, the statue of the mythological half-horse, half-man has disproportionate gonads the size of grapefruits. Now that's what we call larger than life.

books costs €15/7.50 and requires two photos.

MUSÉE DES ÉGOUTS DE PARIS
Map p108

☎ 01 53 68 27 81; www.egouts.tenebres.eu, in French; place de la Résistance, 7e; adult/student & 6-16yr €4.20/3.40; ⏱ 11am-5pm Sat-Wed May-Sep, to 4pm Sat-Wed Oct-Dec & Feb-Apr; Ⓜ Pont de l'Alma

The Paris Sewers Museum is a working museum whose entrance, a rectangular maintenance hole topped with a kiosk, is across the street from 93 quai d'Orsay, 7e. Raw sewage flows beneath your feet as you walk through 480m of odoriferous tunnels, passing artefacts illustrating the development of Paris' waste-water disposal system. The sewers keep regular hours except – God forbid – when rain threatens to flood the tunnels, and in January, when it is closed. Not recommended for anyone afraid of rats.

Eating p238; Sleeping p338

With its hourly sparkles that illuminate the evening skyline, the Eiffel Tower needs no introduction. Ascending to its viewing platforms will offer you a panorama over the whole of Paris, with the prestigious neighbourhood of Passy (the 16e arrondissement) stretching out along the far banks of the Seine to the west. In the 18th and 19th centuries, Passy was home to luminaries such as Benjamin Franklin and Balzac. Defined by its sober, elegant buildings from the Haussmann era, it was annexed to the city only in 1860.

While most of the area today won't send the same frisson of excitement down your spine as taking the lift up to the top of the tower, Passy is nonetheless home to some fabulous museums, and culture vultures will certainly be busy. There's the Musée Marmottan-Monet, with the world's largest collection of Monet paintings; the hip Palais de Tokyo, with modern art installations; the Musée Guimet, France's standout Asian art museum; the underrated Cité de l'Architecture et du Patrimoine, with captivating sculptures, scale models and murals; and a host of smaller collections devoted to fashion, crystal, wine and even sub-Saharan art. On the Left Bank is the prominent Musée du Quai Branly, introducing indigenous art and culture from outside Europe, while at the city's western edge is the leafy refuge of the Bois de Boulogne.

The area is served by metro line 6 (running from Charles de Gaulle Étoile past the Eiffel Tower to Gare Montparnasse in the south), line 9 (running southwest from the Grands Boulevards) and RER line C (which runs east–west along the Seine, with a stop at the Eiffel Tower). There is also a Batobus (public ferry) stop at the Eiffel Tower.

top picks

EIFFEL TOWER & 16E

- Eiffel Tower (p116) Time your visit for dusk to get the best of both worlds.
- Musée du Quai Branly (p117) Like all good Paris museums, this collection of indigenous artwork is as controversial as it is innovative.
- Cité de l'Architecture et du Patrimoine (p117) From cathedral portals and gargoyles to stained glass and intricate scale models.
- Musée Guimet des Arts Asiatiques (p120) A transcendent collection of paintings and statuary, from Afghanistan to Japan.
- Musée Marmottan-Monet (p117) Can't get enough of Monet & Co? A must for admirers of Impressionism.
- Musée Dapper (p121) Unsung museum featuring African and Caribbean art and performances.

EIFFEL TOWER Map p118

☎ 08 92 70 12 39; www.tour-eiffel.fr; to 2nd fl adult/12-24yr/4-12yr €8.10/6.40/4, to 3rd fl €13.10/11.50/9, stairs to 2nd fl €4.50/3.50/3; ⏰ lifts & stairs 9am-midnight mid-Jun–Aug, lifts 9.30am-11pm, stairs 9.30am-6pm Sep–mid-Jun; Ⓜ Champ de Mars–Tour Eiffel or Bir Hakeim

There are many ways to experience the Eiffel Tower, from an evening ascent amid the lights to a meal in one of its two restaurants (p239), and even though some seven million people come annually, few would dispute the fact that each visit is unique. Like many Parisian icons (the Centre Pompidou or the Louvre's glass pyramid), it has gone from being roundly criticised by city residents to much loved – though the transformation didn't take place overnight.

Named after its designer, Gustave Eiffel, la Tour Eiffel was built for the 1889 Exposition Universelle (World Fair), marking the centenary of the French Revolution. At the time it faced massive opposition from Paris' artistic and literary elite, and the 'metal asparagus', as some Parisians snidely called it, was almost torn down in 1909 – spared because it proved an ideal platform for the transmitting antennas needed for the newfangled science of radiotelegraphy.

Today, the three levels are open to the public (entrance to the 1st level is included in all admission tickets), though the top level will close in heavy wind. You can either take the lifts (in the east, west and north pillars) or, if you're feeling fit, the stairs in the south pillar up to the 2nd platform. Highly recommended is the online booking system (www.tour-eiffel.fr) that allows you to buy your tickets in advance, thus avoiding the monumental queues at the ticket office. Note that you need to be able to print out your tickets to use this service or have your ticket on a smart-phone screen (eg Blackberry or iPhone) that can be read by the scanner at the entrance.

PARC DU CHAMP DE MARS Map p118
Ⓜ Champ de Mars–Tour Eiffel or École Militaire
Running southeast from the Eiffel Tower, the grassy Field of Mars (named after the Roman god of war) was originally used as a parade ground for the cadets of the 18th-century École Militaire (Military Academy; Map p108), the vast, French-classical building (1772) at the southeastern end of the park in the 7e, which counts none other than Napoleon Bonaparte among its graduates. The wonderful Wall for Peace memorial (2000; www.wallforpeace.com) of steel and etched glass facing the academy and the statue of Maréchal Joffre (1870–1931) are by Clara Halter.

On 14 July 1790 the Fête de la Fédération (Federation Festival) was held on the Champ de Mars to celebrate the first anniversary of the storming of the Bastille. Four years later it was the location of the Fête de l'Être-Suprême (Festival of the Supreme Being), at which Robespierre presided over a ceremony that established a revolutionary 'state religion'.

The Marionnettes du Champ de Mars (☎ 01 48 56 01 44; allée du Général Marguerite, 7e; Ⓜ École Militaire) stages puppet shows (€3) in a covered and heated *salle* (hall) in the park at 3.15pm and 4.15pm on Wednesday, Saturday and Sunday.

MUSÉE DU QUAI BRANLY Map p118
☎ 01 56 61 70 00; www.quaibranly.fr; 37 quai Branly, 7e; adult/18-25yr & student €8.50/6, EU resident under 26yr free, 1st Sun of month free; ⏱ 11am-7pm Tue, Wed & Sun, to 9pm Thu-Sat Ⓜ Pont de l'Alma or Alma–Marceau
Opened to great fanfare in mid-2006, the architecturally impressive but unimaginatively named Quai Branly Museum introduces the art and cultures of Africa, Oceania, Asia and the Americas through innovative displays, film and musical recordings. With *Là où dialoguent les cultures* (Where cultures communicate) as its motto, the museum is one of the most dynamic and forward-thinking in the world. The anthropological explanations are kept to a minimum; what is displayed here is meant

to be viewed as art. A day pass allowing entry to the temporary exhibits as well as the permanent collection costs €10/7 per adult/concession; an audioguide is €5. And don't miss the views from the 5th-floor restaurant Les Ombres (p238).

MUSÉE MARMOTTAN-MONET Map p118
☎ 01 44 96 50 33; www.marmottan.com; 2 rue Louis Boilly, 16e; adult/8-25yr €9/5; ⏱ 11am-9pm Tue, to 6pm Wed-Sun; Ⓜ La Muette
This museum, two blocks east of the Bois de Boulogne between Porte de la Muette and Porte de Passy, has the world's largest collection of works by impressionist painter Claude Monet (1840–1926) – about 100 – as well as paintings by Gauguin, Sisley, Pissarro, Renoir, Degas, Manet and Berthe Morisot. It also contains an important collection of French, English, Italian and Flemish miniatures from the 13th to the 16th centuries.

PALAIS DE CHAILLOT Map p118
place du Trocadéro et du 11 November, 16e; Ⓜ Trocadéro
The two curved, colonnaded wings of the Palais de Chaillot, built for the 1937 Exposition Universelle, and the terrace in between them afford an exceptional panorama of the Jardins du Trocadéro (named after a Spanish stronghold near Cádiz captured by the French in 1823), the Seine and the Eiffel Tower.

In the palace's eastern wing is the standout Cité de l'Architecture et du Patrimoine (☎ 01 58 51 52 00; www.citechaillot.fr; 1 place du Trocadéro et du 11 November, 16e; adult/18-25yr €8/5, EU resident

THE EIFFEL TOWER IN NUMBERS
- Height: 324m
- Distance seen from the 2nd level: 50 to 70km
- Number of steps: 1665
- Number of rivets: 2.5 million
- Number of 'sparkle' lights: 20,000
- Tonnes of iron: 7300
- Coats of paint since 1889: 19
- Length of time it takes a team of 25 to do one paint job: 18 months
- Distance tightrope-artist Philippe Petit traversed in 1989, from the Palais Chaillot (across the Seine) to the Tower's 2nd level: 700m

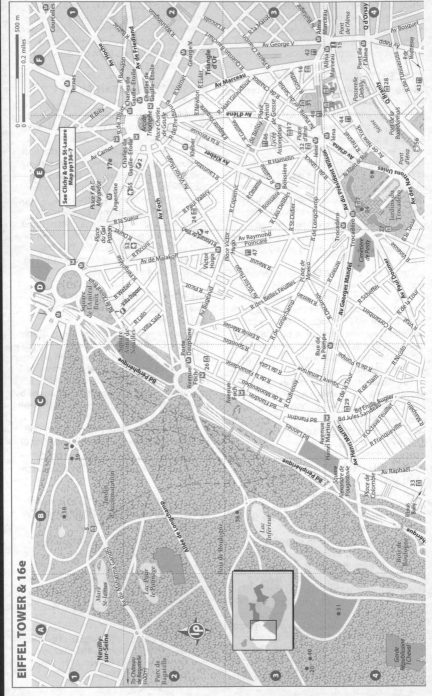

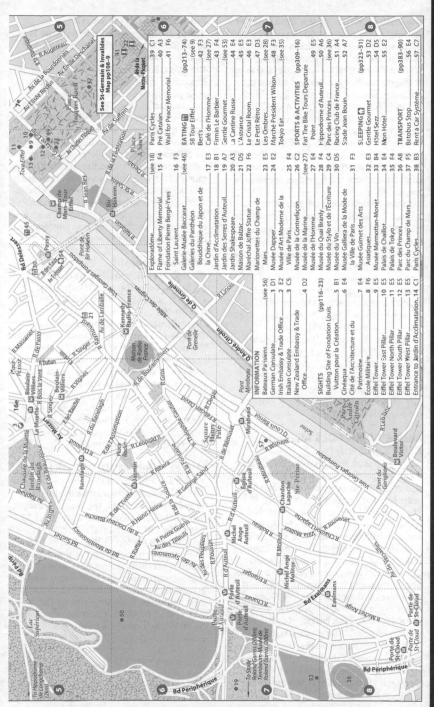

See St-Germain & Invalides
Map pp108–9

Paris Cycles............................(see 18)	
Flame of Liberty Memorial.............15	F4
Fondation Pierre Bergé-Yves	
Saint Laurent............................16	F3
Galeries du Panthéon.................(see 46)	
Bouddhique du Japon et de	
la Chine..................................17	E3
Jardin d'Acclimatation................18	B1
Jardin des Serres d'Auteuil..........19	A7
Jardin Shakespeare....................20	A3
Maison de Balzac.......................21	D5
Maréchal Joffre Statue................22	F6
Marionettes du Champ de	
Mars..23	E5
Musée Dapper...........................24	E2
Musée d'Art Moderne de la	
Ville de Paris.............................25	F4
Musée de la Contrefaçon............26	C2
Musée de la Marine...................(see 27)	
Musée de l'Homme....................27	E4
Musée du Quai Branly.................28	F4
Musée du Stylo et de l'Écriture.....29	C4
Musée du Vin.............................30	D5
Musée Galliera de la Mode de	
la Ville de Paris..........................31	F3
Musée Guimet des Arts	
Asiatiques..................................32	E3
Musée Marmottan-Monet............33	B4
Palais de Chaillot.......................34	E4
Palais de Tokyo..........................35	E4
Parc des Princes........................36	A8
Parc du Champ de Mars..............37	F5
Paris Cycles................................38	B3

	.39 C1
Pré Catalan...............................40	A3
Wall for Peace Memorial.............41	F6

EATING (pp213–74)
58 Tour Eiffel...........................(see 9)	
Bert's..42	F3
Café de l'Homme.....................(see 27)	
Firmin Le Barbier......................43	F4
Gentle Gourmet.......................(see 53)	
La Cantine Russe.......................44	E4
L'Astrance................................45	E5
Le Petit Rétro............................46	E3
Le Cristal Room.........................47	D3
Les Ombres.............................(see 28)	
Marché Président Wilson.............48	F3
Tokyo Eat................................(see 35)	

SPORTS & ACTIVITIES (pp309–16)
Fat Tire Bike Tours Departure	
Point...49	E5
Hippodrome d'Auteuil.................50	A6
Parc des Princes......................(see 36)	
Racing Club de France................51	A4
Stade Jean Bouin.......................52	A7

SLEEPING (pp323–51)
Gentle Gourmet.........................53	D2
H3tel Sezz................................54	D5
Mon Hotel.................................55	E2

TRANSPORT (pp383–90)
Bétobus Stop.............................56	E4
Rent a Car Système....................57	C7

INFORMATION
Bateaux Parisiens.....................(see 56)	
German Consulate.......................1	D1
Irish Embassy & Trade Office..........2	E2
Italian Consulate...........................3	C5
New Zealand Embassy & Trade	
Office...4	D2

SIGHTS (pp116–23)
Building Site of Fondation Louis	
Vuitton pour la Création...............5	B1
Cinéaqua.....................................6	E4
Cité de l'Architecture et du	
Patrimoine..................................7	E4
École Militaire..............................8	F6
Eiffel Tower..................................9	E5
Eiffel Tower East Pillar.................10	E5
Eiffel Tower North Pillar...............11	E5
Eiffel Tower South Pillar...............12	E5
Eiffel Tower West Pillar................13	E5
Entrance to Jardin d'Acclimatation.14	C1

under 26yr free; ⊙ 11am-7pm Mon, Wed & Fri-Sun, to 9pm Thu), a mammoth 23,000 sq metres of space spread over three floors and devoted to French architecture and heritage. While it may sound about as exciting as an academic textbook, it really is a fantastic museum. The highlight is the light-filled ground floor, which contains a beautiful collection of 350 plaster and wood casts *(moulages)* of cathedral portals, columns and gargoyles, and replicas of murals and stained glass originally created for the 1878 Exposition Universelle. The views of the Eiffel Tower from the windows are equally monumental.

In the western wing are two other museums. The Musée de la Marine (Maritime Museum; ☎ 01 53 65 69 69; www.musee-marine.fr; 17 place du Trocadéro et du 11 November, 16e; adult/18-25yr €7/5, EU resident under 26yr free; ⊙ 10am-6pm Wed-Mon), to the right of the main entrance, examines France's naval adventures from the 17th century until today and boasts one of the world's finest collections of model ships, as well as ancient figureheads, compasses, sextants, telescopes and paintings.

The Musée de l'Homme (Museum of Mankind; ☎ 01 44 05 72 72; www.mnhn.fr; 17 place du Trocadéro et du 11 November, 16e; adult/4-16yr & student €7/5; ⊙ 10am-5pm Mon, Wed-Fri, to 6pm Sat & Sun), focuses on human development, ethnology and population growth. It is closed for renovations until 2012.

MUSÉE GUIMET DES ARTS ASIATIQUES Map p118

☎ 01 56 52 53 00; www.museeguimet.fr; 6 place d'Iéna, 16e; permanent collection adult/senior & student €7.50/5.50, EU resident under 26yr & all under 18yr free; ⊙ 10am-6pm Wed-Mon; Ⓜ Iéna
The Guimet Museum of Asiatic Arts is France's foremost repository for Asian art and has sculptures, paintings, *objets d'art* and religious articles from Afghanistan, India, Nepal, Pakistan, Tibet, Cambodia, China, Japan and Korea. Part of the collection, comprising Buddhist paintings and sculptures brought to Paris in 1876 by collector Émile Guimet, is housed in the Galeries du Panthéon Bouddhique du Japon et de la Chine (Buddhist Pantheon Galleries of Japan & China; ☎ 01 40 73 88 00; 19 av d'Iéna; admission free; ⊙ 9.45am-5.45pm Wed-Mon; Ⓜ Iéna) in the scrumptious Hôtel Heidelbach a short distance to the north. Don't miss the wonderful Japanese garden (⊙ 1-5pm Wed-Mon) here.

PALAIS DE TOKYO Map p118

☎ 01 7 23 54 01; www.palaisdetokyo.com; 13 av du Président Wilson, 16e; adult/senior & 18-26yr €6/4.50; ⊙ noon-midnight Tue-Sun; Ⓜ Iéna
The Tokyo Palace, created for the 1937 Exposition Universelle and now a contemporary art space, has no permanent collection. Instead its shell-like interior of polished concrete and steel is the stark backdrop for rotating, interactive art installations (the rooftop, for example, has been the setting for attention-getting projects like the transient Hotel Everland and the see-through restaurant Nomiya). There's a great lunch deal called 'Formule Palais' (€16), which includes admission and lunch at Tokyo Eat (⊙ noon-11.30pm), the museum's trendy café. It's one of the better creative spaces in western Paris; DJs often hit the decks at night.

CINÉAQUA Map p118

☎ 01 40 69 23 23; www.cineaqua.com; 2 av des Nations Unies, 16e; adult/13-17yr/3-12yr €19.50/15.50/12.50; ⊙ 10am-7pm Apr-Sep, 10am-6pm Oct-Mar
On the eastern side of the Jardins du Trocadéro is Paris' largest aquarium. It's not the best you'll ever see, but it's a decent rainy-day destination for families, with a shark tank and some 500 species of fish on display. There are also, somewhat oddly, three cinemas inside (only one of which shows ocean-related films), though non-French-speaking kids will need to be old enough to read subtitles, as almost everything is dubbed into French.

MUSÉE D'ART MODERNE DE LA VILLE DE PARIS Map p118

☎ 01 53 67 40 00; www.mam.paris.fr in French; 11 av du Président Wilson, 16e; temporary exhibits from adult €5-9, 13-25yr, senior & student €2.50-5.50, under 13yr & permanent collections free; ⊙ 10am-6pm Tue-Sun, to 10pm Thu; Ⓜ Iéna
The permanent collection at the city's modern art museum displays works representative of just about every major artistic movement of the 20th and nascent 21st centuries: Fauvism, Cubism, Dadaism, and so on up through video installations. While it merits a peek – you'll find works by Modigliani, Matisse, Braque and Soutine here – the permanent collection is nowhere near the level of the Centre Pompidou. There is one jewel of a room though, containing several gorgeous canvases from Dufy and Bonnard.

GALERIE-MUSÉE BACCARAT

Map p118

☎ 01 40 22 11 00; www.baccarat.com; 11 place des États-Unis, 16e; adult/student & 18-25yr €5/3.50; ☺ 10am-6.30pm Mon & Wed-Sat; Ⓜ Boissière or Kléber

Showcasing 1000 stunning pieces of crystal, many of them custom-made for princes and dictators of desperately poor former colonies, this flashy museum is at home in its striking new rococo-style premises designed by Philippe Starck in the ritzy 16e. It is also home to a superb restaurant called – what else? – Le Cristal Room (p238).

MUSÉE DAPPER Map p118

☎ 01 44 00 91 75; www.dapper.com.fr; 35 rue Paul Valéry, 16e; adult/senior/under 26yr €6/4/free, last Wed of month free; ☺ 11am-7pm Wed-Mon; Ⓜ Victor Hugo

This fantastic museum of sub-Saharan African and Caribbean art collected and exhibited by the nonprofit Dapper Foundation (in a 16th-century *hôtel particulier* with wonderful 21st-century add-ons) stages a couple of major exhibitions each year. The collection consists mostly of carved wooden figurines and masks, which famously influenced the work of Picasso, Braque and Man Ray. The ever-active auditorium sponsors African and Caribbean cultural events year-round – from concerts and storytelling to films and marionette performances.

FONDATION PIERRE BERGÉ-YVES SAINT LAURENT Map p118

☎ 01 44 31 64 31; www.fondation-pb-ysl.net; 3 rue Léonce Reynaud, 16e; adult/10-25yr & senior €5/3; ☺ 11am-6pm Tue-Sun; Ⓜ Alma–Marceau

This foundation dedicated to preserving the work of the *haute couture* legend organises two to three temporary exhibits (not necessarily related to YSL) per year, with an emphasis on fashion and art.

MUSÉE GALLIERA DE LA MODE DE LA VILLE DE PARIS Map p118

☎ 01 56 52 86 00; www.galliera.paris.fr; 10 av Pierre 1er de Serbie, 16e; adult/14-26yr/student & senior €7/3.50/5.50; ☺ 10am-6pm Tue-Sun; Ⓜ Iéna

The Fashion Museum of the City of Paris, housed in the 19th-century Palais Galliera, warehouses some 90,000 outfits and acces-

top picks

FOR CHILDREN

- Centre Kapla (p392) Build an Eiffel Tower or Parisian church from thousands of miniature wooden planks.
- CinéAqua (p120) Two words: shark tank.
- Cité des Sciences (p142) Hands-on science exhibits for kids from ages two and up, plus two special-effects cinemas, a planetarium and a retired submarine. *And* there are great themed playgrounds in the park.
- Eiffel Tower (p116) You can't lose.
- Jardin d'Acclimatation (p122) Amusement park with puppet shows, boat rides and a small water park.
- Jardin du Luxembourg (p106) Sail toy boats, laugh with the puppets and take a ride on the antique carousel. And then sail the boats again.
- Musée National d'Histoire Naturelle (p99) Life-size stuffed elephants and giraffes in one building, dinosaur skeletons in the other.
- Musée en Herbe (p392) Art exhibits and workshops designed specially for children.
- Palais de la Découverte (p129) Hands-on science exhibits off the Champs-Élysées.

sories – from canes and umbrellas to fans and gloves – from the 18th century to the present day and exhibits them along with items borrowed from collections abroad offering tremendously successful temporary exhibitions. The sumptuous Italianate palace and gardens dating from the mid-19th century are worth a visit in themselves. The museum is closed for renovation until late 2011.

MUSÉE DU VIN Map p118

☎ 01 45 25 63 26; www.museeduvinparis.com; rue des Eaux, 5 square Charles Dickens, 16e; adult/senior & student €11.90/9.90; ☺ 10am-6pm Tue-Sun; Ⓜ Passy

The not-so-comprehensive Wine Museum, headquarters of the prestigious International Federation of Wine Brotherhoods, introduces visitors to the fine art of viticulture with various mock-ups and displays of tools. Admission includes a glass of wine at the end of the visit. Entry is free if you have lunch at the attached Restaurant Musée du Vin.

FLAME OF LIBERTY MEMORIAL
Map p118

Ⓜ **Alma–Marceau**

This bronze sculpture – a replica of the one topping New York's Statue of Liberty – was placed here in 1987 on the centenary of the launch of the *International Herald Tribune* newspaper, as a symbol of friendship between France and the USA. On 31 August 1997 in the place d'Alma underpass below, Diana, Princess of Wales, was killed in a devastating car accident along with her companion, Dodi Fayed, and their chauffeur, Henri Paul, and the Flame of Liberty became something of a memorial to her,
decorated with flowers, photographs, graffiti and personal notes. It was renovated and cleaned in 2002 and, this being the age of short (or no) memories, apart from a bit of sentimental graffiti on a wall nearby there are no longer any reminders of the tragedy that happened so close by and had so much of the Western world in grief at the time.

MAISON DE BALZAC Map p118
☎ 01 55 74 41 80; www.balzac.paris.fr, in French; 47 rue Raynouard, 16e; temporary exhibits adult/14-26yr/senior & student €4/2/3, permanent collections free; ☽ 10am-6pm Tue-Sun; Ⓜ Passy or Kennedy Radio France

---

WORTH THE TRIP: BOIS DE BOULOGNE

The 845-hectare Boulogne Wood owes its informal layout to Baron Haussmann, who, inspired by London's Hyde Park, planted 400,000 trees here. Along with various gardens and other sights, the wood has 15km of cycle paths and 28km of bridle paths through 125 hectares of forested land. The Bois de Boulogne is served by metro lines 1 (Porte Maillot, Les Sablons), 2 (Porte Dauphine), 9 (Michel-Ange–Auteuil), and 10 (Michel-Ange–Auteuil, Porte d'Auteuil) and the RER C (Av Foch, Av Henri Martin). Be warned that the area becomes a distinctly adult playground after dark, especially along the Allée de Longchamp running northeast from the Étang des Réservoirs (Reservoirs Pond), where all kinds of prostitutes cruise for clients.

Families will be most interested in the Jardin d'Acclimatation (☎ 01 40 67 90 82; www.jardindacclimatation.fr; av du Mahatma Gandhi; admission €2.90, under 3yr free; ☽ 10am-7pm Apr-Sep, to 6pm Oct-Mar; Ⓜ Les Sablons), a great amusement park for kids with puppet shows, boat rides, a small water park, art exhibits for kids and sometimes special movies. Some activities cost extra.

Just south of here is the planned site of the Fondation Louis Vuitton pour la Création (www.fondationlouisvuitton.fr), a fine arts centre designed by Frank Gehry, expected to open near the end of 2012.

The enclosed Parc de Bagatelle (☎ 01 40 67 97 00; adult/7-25yr €5/2.50 Jun-Oct, free Nov-May; ☽ 9.30am-8pm Jun-Oct, 9.30am-5pm Nov-May), in the northwestern corner, is renowned for its beautiful gardens surrounding the Château de Bagatelle (☎ 01 40 67 97 00; route de Sèvres à Neuilly, 16e; adult/7-25yr €6/3; ☽ tour at 3pm Sat & Sun Apr-Oct), built in 1775. There are areas dedicated to irises (which bloom in May), roses (June to October) and water lilies (August). The Pré Catalan (Catalan Meadow; ☽ 9.30am-8pm, to 5pm low season) to the southeast includes the Jardin Shakespeare, in which plants, flowers and trees mentioned in Shakespeare's plays are cultivated. Exhibitions, flower shows or other events in the park and gardens cost €3/1.50 per adult/concession.

Located at the southeastern end of the Bois de Boulogne is the Jardin des Serres d'Auteuil (☎ 01 40 71 74 60; av de la Porte d'Auteuil, 16e; ☽ 9am-8pm, to 6.30pm low season; Ⓜ Porte d'Auteuil), a garden with impressive conservatories that opened in 1898.

The southern part of the wood takes in two horse-racing tracks, the Hippodrome de Longchamp for flat races and, for steeplechases, the Hippodrome d'Auteuil, as well as the Stade Roland Garros, home of the French Open tennis tournament (p316). Also here is the Tenniseum-Musée de Roland Garros (☎ 01 47 43 48 48; 2 av Gordon Bennett, 16e; adult/under 18yr €7.5/4, with stadium visit €15/10; ☽ 10am-6pm Tue-Sun; Ⓜ Porte d'Auteuil), the world's most extravagant tennis museum, tracing the sport's 500-year history through paintings, sculptures and posters. Visitors to the museum can watch at least 200 hours of play from 1897 to today, including all of the French Open's men's singles matches since 1990 and interviews with all major players. Tours of the stadium take place at 11am and 3pm in English and at 2pm and 5pm in French; reservations are required.

Rowing boats (☎ 01 42 88 04 69; per hr €15; ☽ 10am-6pm mid-Mar–mid-Oct) can be hired at Lac Inférieur (Ⓜ Av Henri Martin), the largest of the wood's lakes and ponds. It sometimes opens at the weekend in winter. Paris Cycles (☎ 01 47 47 76 50; per hr €5; ☽ 10am-7pm mid-Apr–mid-Oct) hires out bicycles at two locations in the Bois de Boulogne: on av du Mahatma Gandhi (Ⓜ Les Sablons), across from the Porte Sablons entrance to the Jardin d'Acclimatation amusement park, and near the Pavillon Royal (Ⓜ Av Foch) at the northern end of Lac Inférieur.

This pretty, three-storey spa house in Passy, about 800m southwest of the Jardins du Trocadéro, is where the realist novelist Honoré de Balzac (1799–1850) lived and worked from 1840 to 1847, editing the entire *Comédie Humaine* and writing various books. There's lots of memorabilia, letters, prints and portraits and is probably for diehard Balzac fans only.

MUSÉE DE LA CONTREFAÇON Map p118

☎ 01 56 26 14 00; 16 rue de la Faisanderie, 16e; adult/12-16yr €4/3; ⏱ 2-5.30pm Tue-Sun; Ⓜ Porte Dauphine

This fascinating museum east of Porte Dauphine is the real thing, dedicated to the not-so-fine art of counterfeiting. Apparently nothing is sacred to the manufacturers of ersatz: banknotes, liqueurs, designer clothing, even Barbie and Ken dolls. What makes this museum, established by the Union des Fabricants (Manufacturers' Union), so interesting is that it displays the real against the fake and lets you spot the difference. Most of the time it's as plain as the nose (the real, not the plastic one) on your face.

MUSÉE DU STYLO ET DE L'ÉCRITURE

Map p118

☎ 06 07 94 13 21; 3 rue Guy de Maupassant, 16e; adult/senior & student €2/1; ⏱ 2-6pm Sun; Ⓜ Av Henri Martin or Rue de la Pompe

The Museum of the Pen and of Penmanship has the most important collection of writing utensils in the world – with pens dating back to the mid-18th century – as well as paper and calligraphy. It can be visited on other days if you phone and book in advance.

CHAMPS-ÉLYSÉES & GRANDS BOULEVARDS

Drinking p283; Eating p240; Shopping p201; Sleeping p338

The 8e arrondissement was born under a lucky star, it would seem. Its avenues radiate from the Arc de Triomphe – known as place de l'Étoile or place Charles de Gaulle – bathing in the glow of fame. First among them is the av des Champs-Élysées, the symbol of French grandeur and luxury, which extends to the enormous place de la Concorde in the southeast. A national rallying point, even Parisians who wouldn't set foot here under normal circumstances find themselves drawn to the avenue during parades, races (the Tour de France or Paris Marathon) and the celebrations that take place after major sporting victories or on New Year's Eve.

No less famous is Paris' magnificent opera house, the Palais Garnier, that abuts the eight contiguous Grands Boulevards that stretch from elegant place de la Madeleine in the 8e eastwards to the place de la République across town. The Grands Boulevards were laid out under Louis XIV in the 17th century on the site of obsolete city walls and served as a centre of café and theatre life through much of the 18th and 19th centuries, reaching the height of fashion during the *belle époque* (p31). North of the western end of the Grands Boulevards is blvd Haussmann (8e and 9e), known for some of Paris' most famous department stores, including Galeries Lafayette and Le Printemps.

For many, the area's top attraction is the luxury shopping (p201) – you'll stumble across designer brands and gourmet food shops at almost every turn – but there are quite a few sights to explore after you've strolled the Champs, huffed up the stairs to the top of the Arc de Triomphe and dropped in on the phantom at the Opéra. Of particular note are the standout art exhibits at the Grand Palais and La Pinacothèque, the science exhibits at the Palais de la Découverte (for children) and, for those who have been there and done that, the little-known Musée National Gustave Moreau.

Transport options are plentiful. Metro line 1 follows the Champs-Élysées, connecting the area to central and eastern Paris; line 8 links Invalides (on the Left Bank) with Madeleine, Opéra and the Grands Boulevards; line 9 cuts east-southwest from the Grands Boulevards to the Champs-Élysées; line 14 goes from Châtelet to Madeleine; and the express RER A stops at Auber (Opéra) and Charles de Gaulle Étoile. There's also a Batobus (public ferry) stop at the Champs-Élysées.

top picks

CHAMPS-ÉLYSÉES & GRANDS BOULEVARDS

- Arc de Triomphe (p124) Climb the arch to survey the Axe Historique, which extends from the Louvre to La Défense.
- Av des Champs-Élysées (p124) Over-the-top, grandiose and even kind of kitsch; you can't leave Paris without strolling the avenue.
- Triangle d'Or (p203) or a Parisian department store (p202) Go on a *haute couture* treasure hunt.
- Palais Garnier (p125) View a performance or take a tour of the opulent 19th-century opera house.
- Place de la Madeleine (p129) Gourmet food, fashion and art come together in the square surrounding the neoclassical Église de la Madeleine.
- Grand Palais (p129) Some of the best temporary art exhibits in Paris are on display beneath the huge glass dome.

ARC DE TRIOMPHE Map p126

☎ 01 55 37 73 77; www.monuments-nationaux. fr; viewing platform adult/18-26yr €9/5.50, EU resident under 26yr free, 1st Sun of month Nov-Mar free; ☉ 10am-11pm Apr-Sep, to 10.30pm Oct-Mar; Ⓜ Charles de Gaulle-Étoile

The Triumphal Arch is 2km northwest of place de la Concorde in the middle of place Charles de Gaulle (aka place de l'Étoile), the world's largest traffic roundabout and the meeting point of 12 avenues (and three arrondissements). It was commissioned in 1806 by Napoleon to commemorate his imperial victories but remained unfinished when he started losing – at first battles and then whole wars. It was finally completed under Louis-Philippe in 1836. Among the armies to march triumphantly through the Arc de Triomphe were the Germans in

1871, the Allies in 1919, the Germans again in 1940 and the Allies again in 1944.

The most famous of the four high-relief panels at the base is to the right, facing the arch from the av des Champs-Élysées side. Entitled *Départ des Volontaires de 1792* (Departure of the Volunteers of 1792) and also known as *La Marseillaise* (France's national anthem), it is the work of François Rude. Higher up, a frieze running around the whole monument depicts hundreds of figures, each one 2m high. A brand-new multimedia exhibit underneath the viewing platform allows you to examine the sculptures in greater detail.

From the viewing platform on top of the arch (50m up via 284 steps and well worth the climb) you can see the dozen broad avenues – many of them named after Napoleonic victories and illustrious generals – radiating towards every compass point. Av de la Grande Armée heads northwest to the skyscraper district of La Défense (p175), where the Grande Arche, a hollow cube measuring 110m on each side, defines the western end of the Grand Axe (the 'Great Axis' linking the Louvre and the Arc de Triomphe). Tickets to the viewing platform of the Arc de Triomphe are sold in the underground passageway that surfaces on the even numbered side of av des Champs-Élysées. It is the only *sane* way to get to the base of the arch and is *not* linked to nearby metro tunnels.

AVENUE DES CHAMPS-ÉLYSÉES
Map p126

Ⓜ Charles de Gaulle–Étoile, George V, Franklin D Roosevelt or Champs-Élysées–Clemenceau

Av des Champs-Élysées (the name refers to the 'Elysian Fields' where happy souls dwelt in the hereafter, according to Greek myth) links place de la Concorde with the Arc de Triomphe. The avenue has symbolised the style and *joie de vivre* of Paris since the mid-19th century and today is most popular with international brands looking to promote their prestige. While you can safely give Gap and Benetton a miss, some of the car showrooms are somewhat off-the-wall (with racing simulators, futuristic models, éclair bars and wi-fi zones) and can be a fun, if slightly bizarre, experience.

Some 400m north of av des Champs-Élysées is rue du Faubourg St-Honoré (8e), the western extension of rue St-Honoré. It has renowned couture houses, jewellers, antique shops and the 18th-century Palais de l'Élysée (cnr rue du Faubourg St-Honoré & av de Marigny, 8e; Ⓜ Champs-Élysées Clemenceau), which is the official residence of the French president.

At the bottom of av des Champs-Élysées, on place Clemenceau, is a 3.6m-tall bronze statue of General Charles de Gaulle in full military gear ready to march down the broad avenue to the Arc de Triomphe in a liberated Paris on 26 August 1944.

PALAIS GARNIER Map p126
www.operadeparis.fr, in French; place de l'Opéra, 9e; Ⓜ Opéra

This renowned opera house was designed in 1860 by Charles Garnier to showcase the splendour of Napoleon III's France. Unfortunately, by the time it was completed – 15 years later – the Second Empire was but a distant memory and Napoleon III had been dead for two years. Still, this is one of the most impressive monuments erected in Paris during the 19th century; today it stages ballets, classical music concerts and,

---

CHRIS' TOP PARIS DAY

I'd begin my day at the Marché d'Aligre (aka Marché Couvert Beauvau, p222), where, with the family in tow, we'd pick up organic pastries at Moisan (p215) and then stop for a coffee (or hot chocolate) at one of the street-side cafés. Settled in among the Tunisian pastry shops and traditional French cheese sellers, we'll watch the crowds go about their weekly food shopping as we eat breakfast. Then it's time for a walk down the Promenade Plantée (p157), which traverses the 12e arrondissement three storeys above street level. Descending back to earth at Place de la Bastille (p156), we'll take a detour through the Place des Vosges (p146), before hopping on a metro up to Canal St-Martin for a pizza picnic with Pink Flamingo (p251).

It'll be hard to tear the kids away from the water, but promises of a fun museum – the Cité des Enfants (p143) or Palais de la Découverte (p129) across town – should do the trick. After everyone's energy begins to wane, we'll drop off the kids at the grandparents for the evening, so Perrine and I can indulge in a romantic soirée: dinner at Makoto Aoki (p241), L'Office (p249) or Michelangelo (p245). Or maybe (yawn) we'll just catch one of the hundreds of movies showing instead!

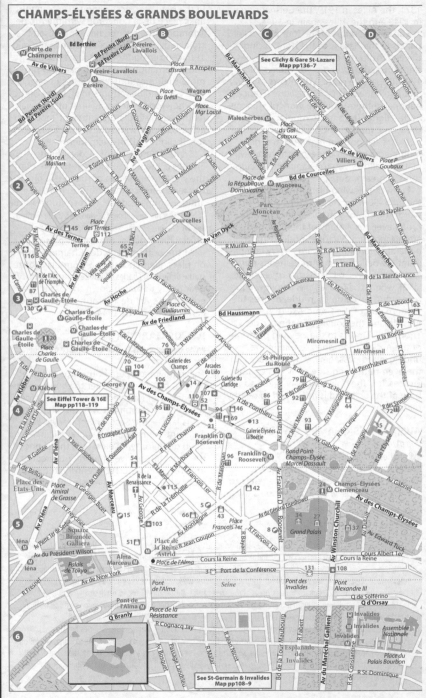

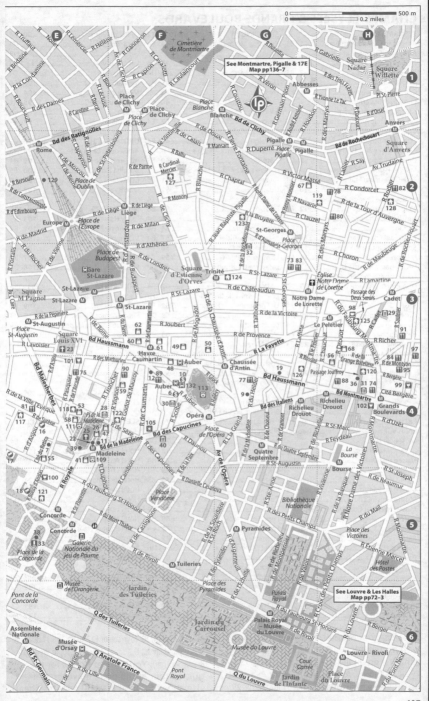

NEIGHBOURHOODS CHAMPS-ÉLYSÉES & GRANDS BOULEVARDS

See Montmartre, Pigalle & 17E
Map pp136–7

See Louvre & Les Halles
Map pp72–3

CHAMPS-ÉLYSÉES & GRANDS BOULEVARDS

INFORMATION
American Cathedral in Paris............ 1 B5
American Chamber of
  Commerce.. 2 C3
Bateaux Mouches................................ 3 B5
Belgian Embassy................................. 4 A3
Canadian Embassy.............................. 5 B5
Canadian Government
  Department of Commercial
  & Economic Affairs....................(see 5)
CCO Bureau de Change...................... 6 F4
Franco-British Chamber of
  Commerce & Industry.................... 7 F4
German Embassy.................................. 8 C5
Institut Parisien de Langue et
  de Civilisation Françaises............. 9 G4
Kanoo Bureau de Change.................10 F4
La Boutique Orange...........................11 E4
L'Open Tour...12 F4
NewWorks Champs-Élysées
  Branch..13 C4
Pharmacie des Champs.....................14 B4
Spainish Embassy...............................15 B5
UK Consulate.......................................16 E4
UK Embassy & Trade Office...............17 E4
USA Embassy & Trade Office.............18 E5
USA Embassy Trade Office.................19 G4

SIGHTS   pp124–31
Arc de Triomphe.................................20 A3
Av des Champs-Élysées......................21 B4
Belle Époque Toilets..........................22 E4
Chapelle Expiatoire............................23 E3
Charles de Gaulle Statue...................24 D5
Église de Ste-Marie
  Madeleine.......................................25 E4
Flower Market.....................................26 E4
Galeries Nationales du Grand
  Palais..(see 27)
Grand Palais..27 C5
La Pinocothèque.................................28 E4
Louis Vuitton Espace Culturel....(see 64)
Musée de la
  Franc-Maçonnerie..........................29 H3
Musée de l'Opéra.........................(see 113)
Musée des Beaux-Arts de la
  Ville de Paris.............................(see 37)
Musée du Parfum...............................30 F4
Musée Grévin......................................31 H4
Musée National Gustave
  Moreau..32 G3
Obelisk..33 E5
Palais de la Découverte.....................34 C5
Palais de l'Élysée................................35 D4
Palais Garnier...............................(see 113)
Passage Jouffroy................................36 H4
Petit Palais..37 D5
Place de la Concorde.........................38 E5
Place de la Madeleine........................39 E4
Théâtre-Musée des
  Capucines.......................................40 F4

SHOPPING 🛍   pp191–212
Boutique Maille..................................41 E4
Chanel...42 C5
Christian Dior.....................................43 C5
Christian Lacroix................................44 D4
Darty..45 A2
Eres..(see 28)
Espace IGN...46 C4
Fauchon...(see 28)
Fauchon..47 E4
Galeries Lafayette – Home
  Design..48 F4
Galeries Lafayette – Men's
  Store...49 F3
Galleries Lafayette – Main Store..50 F3
Givenchy...51 B5
Guerlain..52 B4
Hédiard..53 E4
Hédiard..54 B4
Hermès..55 E4
Hôtel Drouot.......................................56 H4
Jean-Paul Gaultier.............................57 B4
La Maison de la Truffe.......................58 E4
La Maison du Miel..............................59 F4
Lafayette Gourmet.......................(see 49)
Le Printemps de la Beauté et
  Maison..60 F3
Le Printemps de la Mode..................61 F3
Le Printemps de l'Homme..................62 F3
Les Caves Augé...................................63 D3
Louis Vuitton......................................64 B4
Mariage Frères 8e Branch..................65 B3
Max Mara..66 B5
Musical Instrument Shops.................67 G2
Postage Stamp Shops........................68 H3
Séphora..(see 110)
Virgin Megastore...............................69 C4

EATING 🍴   pp213–74
Bistro Romain Champs-Élysées
  Branch..70 B4
Bistrot du Sommelier.........................71 D3
Bugsy's..72 D4
Casa Olympe.......................................73 G3
Chartier...74 H4
Chez Papa 8e Branch.........................75 E4
Cojean...76 B3
Cojean...77 G2
Cul de Poule.......................................78 H2
Dalloyau...79 C4
Food Shops...80 H2
Franprix...81 E4
Franprix Rodier...................................82 H2
Hôtel l'Amour..............................(see 119)
Jean...83 G3
La Boule Rouge...................................84 H4
Ladurée...85 B4
Le Boudoir..86 C4
Le Hide..87 A3
Le J'Go..88 H4
Le Persil Fleur....................................89 F4

Le Roi du Pot au Feu.........................90 F4
L'Épicerie......................................(see 78)
Les Ailes...91 H3
Les Pâtes Vivantes.....................(see 125)
Makoto Aoki.......................................92 C4
Market...93 C4
Monoprix...94 C4
Nouveau Paris-Dakar.........................95 H4
Spoon..96 C4
Supernature..97 H4

DRINKING 🍷🍸   pp275–92
Au Général La Fayette........................98 H3
Au Limonaire.......................................99 H4
Buddha Bar.......................................100 E5
Cricketer..101 E4
O'Sullivan's.......................................102 H4

NIGHTLIFE ★   pp293–308
Crazy Horse.......................................103 B5
Le Lido de Paris................................104 B4
L'Olympia..105 F4
Queen..106 B4
Regine's...107 B4
Showcase...108 D5

THE ARTS 🎭   pp293–308
Agence Perrossier & SOS
  Théâtres.......................................109 E4
Fnac Champs-Élysées.......................110 B4
Kiosque Théâtre Madeleine.............111 E4
Kiosque Théâtre Ternes....................112 A2
Palais Garnier..............................(see 113)
Palais Garnier Box Office.................113 F4
Salle Pleyel.......................................114 B3
Virgin Megastore.........................(see 69)

SPORTS & ACTIVITIES pp309–16
Espace Joïya.....................................115 B5

SLEEPING 🛏   pp323–51
Hidden Hotel.....................................116 A3
Hôtel Alison......................................117 E4
Hôtel Amarante................................118 E4
Hôtel Amour......................................119 H2
Hôtel Chopin.....................................120 H4
Hôtel de Crillon................................121 E5
Hôtel de Sèze...................................122 F4
Hôtel Joyce.......................................123 G2
Hôtel Langlois...................................124 G3
Hôtel Monte Carlo............................125 H3
Hôtel Peletier Haussmann
  Opéra..126 G4
Résidence Cardinal...........................127 F2
Woodstock Hostel.............................128 H2

TRANSPORT   pp383–90
ADA Car Rental.................................129 E2
Air France Buses...............................130 A3
Batobus Stop.....................................131 C5
Roissybus...132 F4

of course, opera (p306). You can visit it along with a small museum (mostly temporary exhibits) on an unguided tour (adult/10-25yr €9/5; ⏰ 10am-4.30pm). Alternatively, reserve a spot on an English-language guided tour (☎ 08 25 05 44 05; adult/10-25yr/senior €12/6/10; ⏰ 11.30am & 2.30pm daily Jul & Aug, 11.30am & 2.30pm Wed, Sat & Sun Sep-Jun). You can get tickets for the guided tour at the door; however, staff advise showing up at least 30 minutes ahead of time. Note that the performance area cannot be visited when daytime rehearsals or matinees are scheduled; try to arrive before 1pm or check the website for the exact schedule.

PLACE DE LA CONCORDE Map p126
M Concorde

Place de la Concorde was laid out between 1755 and 1775. The 3300-year-old pink granite obelisk with the gilded top standing in the centre of the square was presented to France in 1831 by Muhammad Ali, viceroy and pasha of Egypt. Weighing 230 tonnes and towering 23m over the cobblestones, it once stood in the Temple of Ramses at Thebes (now Luxor). The eight female statues adorning the four corners of the square represent France's largest cities (at least in the second half of the 18th century).

In 1793, Louis XVI's head was lopped off by a guillotine set up in the northwest corner of the square near the statue representing the city of Brest. During the next two years, another guillotine – this one near the entrance to the Jardin des Tuileries – was used to behead 1343 more people, including Marie-Antoinette and, six months later, the Revolutionary leader Danton. Shortly thereafter, Robespierre lost his head here, too. The square was given its present name after the Reign of Terror in the hope that it would become a place of peace and harmony.

PLACE DE LA MADELEINE Map p126
M Madeleine

Ringed by fine-food shops, place de la Madeleine is 350m north of place de la Concorde, at the end of rue Royale. The square is named after the 19th-century neoclassical church in its centre, the Église de Ste-Marie Madeleine (Church of St Mary Magdalene; ☎ 01 44 51 69 00; www.eglise-lamadeleine.com, in French; place de la Madeleine, 8e; ⊙ 9.30am-7pm). Constructed in the style of a Greek temple, what is now simply called 'La Madeleine' was consecrated in 1842 after almost a century of design changes and construction delays. It is surrounded by 52 Corinthian columns standing 20m tall, and the marble-and-gilt interior is topped by three sky-lit cupolas. You can hear the massive organ being played at Mass at 11am and 7pm on Sunday.

The monumental staircase on the south side affords one of the city's most quintessential Parisian panoramas: down rue Royale to place de la Concorde and its obelisk and across the Seine to the Assemblée Nationale. The gold dome of the Invalides appears in the background.

Paris' cheapest belle époque attraction is the public toilet (⊙ 10am-6.15pm) on the east side of La Madeleine, which dates from 1905. There has been a flower market (⊙ 8am-8pm) on the east side of the church since 1832.

GRAND PALAIS Map p126
☎ Information 01 44 13 17 17, www.grandpalais. fr; bookings ☎ 08 92 700 840, www.rmn.fr; 3 av du Général Eisenhower, 8e; with/without booking adult €12/11, student & 13-25yr €9/8, under 13yr free; ⊙ 10am-10pm Fri-Mon & Wed, to 8pm Thu; M Champs-Élysées–Clemenceau

Erected for the 1900 Exposition Universelle, the Grand Palais now houses the Galeries Nationales beneath its huge 8.5-ton Art Nouveau glass roof. Some of Paris' biggest exhibitions (Renoir, Chagall) are held here, lasting three to four months. The Nave, in the same building, also stages special events (an impromptu Prince concert, holiday lightshows), which require a separate ticket. Booking in advance for either is strongly recommended. Ongoing renovations will expand the exhibit space.

LA PINACOTHÈQUE Map p126
☎ 01 42 68 02 01; www.pinacotheque.com; 28 place de la Madeleine, 8e; adult/12-25yr €10/8; ⊙ 10.30am-6pm, to 9pm Wed; M Madeleine

One of the best private museums in Paris, La Pinacothèque organises three to four major exhibits per year. The focus is primarily on 20th-century art (Pollock, Utrillo, Munch, Lichtenstein) but it has also hosted China's terracotta army and a Dutch Masters retrospective. Download the current mp3 audioguide or exhibit app (both in French) from the website.

PALAIS DE LA DÉCOUVERTE Map p126
☎ 01 56 43 20 20; www.palais-decouverte.fr, in French; av Franklin D Roosevelt, 8e; adult/senior, student & 5-18yr €7/4.50; ⊙ 9.30am-6pm Tue-Sat, 10am-7pm Sun; M Champs-Élysées–Clemenceau

This children's science museum has excellent temporary exhibits (eg moving life-like dinosaurs) as well as a hands-on, interactive permanent collection focusing on astronomy, biology, physics and the like. Some of the older exhibits have French explanations only, but in general this is a good family outing. The planetarium (admission €3.50) has four shows a day; there are also hourly science demonstrations (both in French).

PETIT PALAIS Map p126

☎ 01 53 43 40 00; www.petitpalais.paris.fr; av Winston Churchill, 8e; temporary exhibits adult/ 14-26yr/senior & student €9/4.50/6.50, permanent collections & under 14yr free; ☼ 10am-6pm Wed-Sun, to 8pm Thu (temporary exhibit only); Ⓜ Champs-Élysées–Clemenceau

Like the Grand Palais opposite, this architectural stunner was also built for the 1900 Exposition Universelle, and is home to the Paris municipality's Museum of Fine Arts. It specialises in medieval and Renaissance *objets d'art* such as porcelain and clocks, tapestries, drawings and 19th-century French painting and sculpture. There are also some standout paintings here by such artists as Rembrandt, Colbert and Cézanne.

CHAPELLE EXPIATOIRE Map p126

☎ 01 44 32 18 00; www.monuments-nationaux.fr; square Louis XVI, 8e; adult/18-25yr €5/3.50; ☼ 1-5pm Thu-Sat; Ⓜ St-Augustin

The austere, neoclassical Atonement Chapel, opposite 36 rue Pasquier, sits atop the section of a cemetery where Louis XVI, Marie-Antoinette and many other victims of the Reign of Terror were buried after their executions in 1793. It was erected by Louis' brother, the restored Bourbon king Louis XVIII, in 1815. Two years later the royal bones were removed to the Basilique de St-Denis (p173).

MUSÉE NATIONAL GUSTAVE MOREAU Map p126

☎ 01 48 74 38 50; www.musee-moreau.fr; 14 rue de La Rochefoucauld, 9e; adult/18-25yr €7.50/5.50, 1st Sun of month free, reduced admission with ticket from Palais Garnier or Musée d'Orsay; ☼ 10am-5.15pm Wed-Mon; Ⓜ Trinité

The Gustave Moreau Museum is dedicated to the eponymous symbolist painter's work. Housed in what was once Moreau's studio, the two-storey museum is crammed with 4800 of his paintings, drawings and sketches. Some of Moreau's paintings are fantastic – in both senses of the word. One particularly highlight is *La Licorne* (The Unicorn), inspired by *La Dame à la Licorne* (The Lady with the Unicorn) cycle of tapestries in the Musée National du Moyen Age (p104).

MUSÉE DU PARFUM Map p126

☎ 01 47 42 04 56; www.fragonard.com; 9 rue Scribe, 2e; admission free; ☼ 9am-6pm Mon-Sat; Ⓜ Opéra

If the art of perfume-making entices, stop by this collection of copper distillery vats and antique flacons and test your nose on a few basic scents (how many can you identify correctly?). It's run by the *perfumerie* Fragonard and located in a beautiful old *hôtel particulier*; free guided visits are available in multiple languages. Another branch is a short distance south, in the Théâtre-Musée des Capucines (Map p72; ☎ 01 42 60 37 14; 39 blvd des Capucines, 2e; ☼ 9am-6pm Mon-Sat; Ⓜ Opéra).

LOUIS VUITTON ESPACE CULTUREL Map p126

☎ 01 53 57 52 03; www.louisvuitton.com/espacecul turel; 60 rue de Bassano, 8e; admission free; ☼ noon-7pm Mon-Sat, 11am-7pm Sun; Ⓜ George V

SEINE-FUL PURSUITS

The Seine is more than just Paris' dustless highway or the line dividing the Right Bank from the Left. The river's award-winning role comes in July and August, when some 5km of its banks are transformed into Paris Plages (p19), 'beaches' with real sand, water fountains and sprays. But the riverbanks can be just as much fun at the weekend during the rest of the year when the Paris Respire (p312) scheme goes into effect. The banks between the Pont Alexandre III (Map p126) and the Pont d'Austerlitz (Map p158) have been listed as a Unesco World Heritage Site since 1991, but the choicest spots for sunning, picnicking and maybe even a little romancing are the delightful Square du Vert Gallant, 1er (Ⓜ Pont Neuf), the little park at the tip of the Île de la Cité named after that rake Henri IV (see p97), and the Quai St-Bernard, 5e, just opposite the Jardin des Plantes. Here you'll find the Musée de la Sculpture en Plein Air (Open-Air Sculpture Museum; Map p100; ☎ 01 43 26 91 90; square Tino Rossi, 5e; admission free; ☼ 24hr; Ⓜ Quai de la Rapée). A salad beneath a César or a baguette beside a Brancusi is a pretty classy way to see the Seine up close, short of actually getting on it by joining a cruise (see p401).

At the top of Louis Vuitton's flagship store is this modern art gallery with changing exhibits throughout the year. The main entrance is off a side street (at the time of research it was via an art-installation elevator that had no lights or buttons), but you can also reach it via the mammoth flagship store, which, of course, is something of a sight in itself.

MUSÉE GRÉVIN Map p126

☎ 01 47 70 85 05; www.grevin.com; 10 blvd Montmartre, 9e; adult/senior & student/6-14yr €20/17/12; ⏱ 10am-6.30pm Mon-Fri, to 7pm Sat & Sun; Ⓜ Grands Boulevards

This large waxworks museum inside the passage Jouffroy boasts an impressive 300 wax figures. They largely look more like caricatures than characters, but where else do you get to see Marilyn Monroe, Charles de Gaulle and Spiderman face to face, or

the original death masks of some of the French Revolution leaders? The recently renovated Palais des Mirages (Hall of Mirrors), created for the 1889 Exposition Universelle, dazzles, but the admission fee is positively outrageous and just won't stop a-growin' each year.

MUSÉE DE LA FRANC-MAÇONNERIE
Map p126

☎ 01 45 23 74 09; www.museedelafrancmaconnerie.org; 16 rue Cadet, 9e; adult/18-26yr €6/4; ⏱ 2-6pm Tue-Sat; Ⓜ Cadet or Peletier

This museum, housed in the colossal and rather impressive Grande Orient de France building, provides a brief introduction to the secretive world of Freemasonry, which grew out of medieval stonemasons' guilds of the 16th century. A visit to the museum including a guided tour of the building (in French) on Saturday afternoons costs €7.

MONTMARTRE, PIGALLE & 17E

Drinking p284; Eating p244; Shopping p203; Sleeping p340

One of the wellsprings of Parisian myth, Montmartre has always stood apart. From its days as a simple village on the hill where wheat was ground into flour to the bohemian lifestyle that Toulouse-Lautrec and other artists immortalised in the late 19th and early 20th centuries, the area has repeatedly woven itself into the city's collective imagination. Most recently, it has provided inspiration for the big screen, in such films as *Moulin Rouge* (2001) and *Le Fabuleux Destin du Amélie Poulain* (*Amelie* in English, 2002) and, in a much more realistic take, in the acclaimed French TV series *Pigalle, La Nuit* (2009), which featured the fictional owner of Folie's Pigalle (p296).

Today, of course, the area thrives on busloads of tourists, who have come to climb the cascading steps up to Sacré Cœur and wander through the narrow hillside lanes that give Montmartre so much of its allure. But even with all the souvenir kitsch and milling crowds, it's hard not to appreciate the views looking out over Paris, or find some romance relaxing in a backstreet café.

Back down at the foot of the hill is the rough-and-ready charm of the city's red-light district, a mix of erotica shops, striptease parlours, trendy nightspots, clubs and cabarets. It may be seem off-putting at first, but if you take the time to wander you'll find some unusual, less-touristy areas. The *quartier* to the south known as Nouvelles Athènes (in the 9e arrondissement), with its beautiful Graeco-Roman architecture and private gardens, is well worth exploring.

Further west is the 17e arrondissement, a veritable kaleidoscope of identities. Its southern neighbourhoods – with their beautiful, Haussmann-era buildings – are an extension of the *haut bourgeois* (upper middle class) 8e and 16e arrondissements, while its northern neighbourhoods assert their working-class, anarchistic roots. Of note in this area are three private art collections housed in opulent old residences (all actually in the 8e arrondissement), now on display to the public: the Musée Jacquemart-André, the Musée Nissim de Camondo and the Musée Cernuschi.

Metro lines 2 and 12 link Montmartre to the rest of Paris (with the main stops being Pigalle and Abbesses) while the 17e is served by lines 2, 3 and 13. A useful stop is Place de Clichy, an interchange for lines 2 and 13. A miniature train (www.promotrain.fr; adult/child 3-12yr €3.50/3, 🕙 10am-6pm, to midnight Jul & Aug) runs between place Blanche and place du Tertre.

top picks

MONTMARTRE, PIGALLE & 17E

- Basilique du Sacré Cœur (p132) Panoramic views from the outside, glittering mosaics within.
- Place du Tertre (p133) Montmartre's picturesque main square – but only if you go early (real early).
- Montmartre Walking Tour (p178) Discover the erstwhile village on an insider's tour.
- Le Divan du Monde (p297), La Fourmi (p284), Folie's Pigalle (p296), Hôtel Amour (p255) Get a taste of Pigalle nightlife.
- Musée de la Vie Romantique (p133) Small museum in the picturesque neighbourhood Nouvelle Athènes.
- Cimetière de Montmartre (p133) Seek out the graves of Zola, Stendhal and Degas.

BASILIQUE DU SACRÉ CŒUR Map p134

☎ 01 53 41 89 00; www.sacre-coeur-montmartre. com; 35 rue du Chevalier de la Barre, 18e; 🕙 6am-10.30pm; Ⓜ Anvers

Sacred Heart Basilica, perched at the very top of Butte de Montmartre, was built from contributions pledged by Parisian Catholics as an act of contrition after the humiliating Franco-Prussian War of 1870–71. Construction began in 1876, but the basilica was not consecrated until 1919. In a way, atonement here has never stopped; a perpetual prayer 'cycle' that began at the consecration of the basilica continues round the clock to this day.

Some 234 spiralling steps lead you to the basilica's dome (admission €5, cash only; 🕙 9am-7pm Apr-Sep, to 5.30pm Oct-Mar), which affords one of Paris' most spectacular panoramas; they say you can see for 30km on a clear day. Weighing in at 19 tonnes, the bell called La Savoyarde in the tower above is the largest in France. The chapel-lined crypt, visited in conjunction with the dome, is huge but not very interesting. If you don't want to walk the hill, you can use a regular metro ticket to take the funicular (6am-midnight).

PLACE DU TERTRE Map p134
Ⓜ Abbesses
Half a block west of Église St-Pierre de Montmartre, which once formed part of a 12th-century Benedictine abbey, is what was once the main square of the village of Montmartre. These days it's filled with cafés, restaurants, tourists and rather obstinate portrait artists and caricaturists, who will gladly do your likeness. Whether it looks even remotely like you is another matter.

MUSÉE DE LA VIE ROMANTIQUE
Map p134
☎ 01 55 31 95 67; www.vie-romantique.paris.fr, in French; 16 rue Chaptal, 9e; temporary exhibitions adult/14-26yr €7.50/5, permanent collection free; 10am-6pm Tue-Sun; Ⓜ Blanche or St-Georges
One of our favourite small museums in Paris, the Museum of the Romantic Life is in a splendid location at the lovely Hôtel Scheffer-Renan in the centre of the district once known as 'New Athens'. The museum, at the end of a film-worthy cobbled lane, is devoted to the life and work of Amandine Aurore Lucile Dupin Baronne (1804–76) – better known to the world as George Sand – and her intellectual circle of friends and is full of paintings, *objets d'art* and personal effects. Don't miss the tiny but delightful garden.

MUSÉE JACQUEMART-ANDRÉ
Map p136
☎ 01 45 62 11 59; www.musee-jacquemart-andre. com; 158 blvd Haussmann, 8e; adult/7-17yr & student incl audioguide €11/8.50; 10am-6pm; Ⓜ Miromesnil
The Jacquemart-André Museum, founded by collector Édouard André and his portraitist wife Nélie Jacquemart, is in an opulent mid-19th-century residence on one of Paris' posher avenues. It has furniture, tapestries and enamels, but is most noted for its paintings by Rembrandt and Van Dyck and Italian Renaissance works by Bernini, Botticelli, Carpaccio, Donatello, Mantegna, Tintoretto, Titian and Uccello. Don't miss the Jardin d'Hiver (Winter Garden), with its marble statuary, tropical plants and double-helix marble staircase. Just off it is the delightful *fumoir*

(the erstwhile smoking room) filled with exotic objects collected by Jacquemart during her travels. The salon de thé (tearoom; 11.45am-5.45pm) is one of the most beautiful in the city.

MUSÉE NISSIM DE CAMONDO
Map p136
☎ 01 53 89 06 50; www.lesartsdecoratifs.fr; 63 rue de Monceau, 8e; adult/18-25yr €7/5; 10am-5.30pm Wed-Sun; Ⓜ Monceau or Villiers
The Nissim de Camondo Museum, housed in a sumptuous mansion modelled on the Petit Trianon (p357) at Versailles, displays 18th-century furniture, wood panelling, tapestries, porcelain and other *objets d'art* collected by Count Moïse de Camondo, a Sephardic Jewish banker who settled in Paris from Constantinople in the late 19th century. He bequeathed the mansion and his collection to the state on the proviso that it would be a museum named in memory of his son Nissim (1892–1917), a pilot killed in action during WWI. The museum is run by the same group responsible for the trio of museums in the Rohan Wing of the Palais du Louvre called Les Arts Décoratifs (p74).

CIMETIÈRE DE MONTMARTRE
Map p134
8am-6pm Mon-Fri, 8.30am-6pm Sat, 9am-6pm Sun mid-Mar–early Nov, 8am-5.30pm Mon-Fri, 8.30am-5.30pm Sat, 9am-5.30pm Sun early Nov–mid-Mar; Ⓜ Place de Clichy
Established in 1798, this 11-hectare cemetery is perhaps the most celebrated necropolis in Paris after Père Lachaise. It contains the graves of writers Émile Zola (whose ashes are now in the Panthéon), Alexandre Dumas (fils) and Stendhal, composers Jacques Offenbach and Hector Berlioz, artist Edgar Degas, film director François Truffaut and dancer Vaslav Nijinsky – among others. The entrance closest to the Butte de Montmartre is at the end of av Rachel, just off blvd de Clichy, or down the stairs from 10 rue Caulaincourt.

Maps showing the location of the tombs are available free from the conservation office (☎ 01 53 42 36 30; 20 av Rachel, 18e) at the cemetery's entrance.

MUSÉE DE MONTMARTRE Map p134
☎ 01 49 25 89 39; www.museedemontmartre. fr, in French; 12 rue Cortot, 18e; adult/senior,

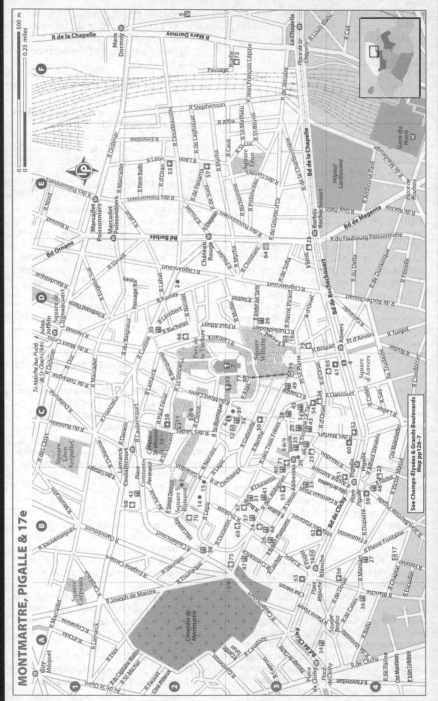

See Champs-Élysées & Grands Boulevards
Map pp126–7

MONTMARTRE, PIGALLE & 17e

INFORMATION		
Children's Playground	1	B2
Cook'n with Class	2	D2
European Exchange Office	3	C3
Internet Café	(see 35)	
Paris Convention & Visitors		
Bureau Kiosk	4	C4
Sri Manikar Vinayakar		
Alayam Temple	5	F2
Syndicate d'Initiative de		
Montmartre	6	C3
Taxiphone	(see 35)	

SIGHTS	(pp132–8)	
Basilique du Sacré Cœur	7	C3
Cimetière de Montmarte		
Entrance	8	A3
Cimetière de Montmarte	9	A2
Cimetière St-Vincent	10	C2
Clos Montmartre	11	C2
Dalí Espace Montmartre	12	C3
Église St-Pierre de		
Montmartre	13	C3
Moulin de la Galette	14	B2
Moulin Radet	15	B2
Musée de la Halle St-Pierre	16	D3
Musée de la Vie Romantique	17	B4
Musée de l'Érotisme	18	B3
Musée de Montmartre	19	C2
Place des Abbesses	20	C3
Place du Tertre	21	C3

SHOPPING	(pp191–212)	
Andrea Crews	22	B4
Ets Lion	23	C3

La Citadelle	24	C3
Tati	25	D3

EATING	(pp213–74)	
8 à Huit	26	B3
À La Cloche d'Or	27	B4
Au Grain de Folie	28	C3
Au Petit Budapest	29	C3
Aux Négociants	30	C3
Café Burq	31	B3
Chez Plumeau	32	C3
Chez Toinette	33	B3
Crêperie Pen-Ty	34	A3
Il Duca	35	C3
Isaan	36	A4
La Mascotte	37	B3
Le Café Qui Parle	38	B2
Le Chéri-Bibi	39	D3
Le Coquelicot	40	B3
Le Grenier à Pain	41	B3
Le Maquis	42	B2
Le MIroir	43	C3
Le Mono	44	B3
Le Refuge des Fondus	45	C3
Le Relais Gascon	46	C3
Le Relais Gascon	47	B3
Marché des Gastronomes	48	B4
Michelangelo	49	C3

DRINKING	(pp275–92)	
Au Rendez-Vous des Amis	50	C3
Chào Bà Café	51	B4
Ice Kube	(see 72)	
La Fourmi	52	C4
Lavoir Moderne Parisien	53	E2

Le Progrès	54	C3
Le Sancerre	55	B3
O P'tit Douai	56	B4
Olympic Café	57	E2

NIGHTLIFE	(pp293–308)	
Au Lapin Agile	58	C2
Folie's Pigalle	59	B4
La Cigale	(see 52)	
Le Divan du Monde	60	C4
L'Élysée-Montmartre	61	C4
Les Trois Baudets	62	B3
Moulin Rouge	63	B3

THE ARTS	(pp293–308)	
Virgin Megastore	64	D3

SLEEPING	(pp323–51)	
Adagio Montmartre City		
Aparthotel	65	C4
Ermitage Hôtel	66	D2
Hôtel Bonséjour Montmartre	67	B3
Hôtel Caulaincourt Square	68	B2
Hôtel des Arts	69	B3
Hôtel Particulier		
Montmartre	70	B2
Hôtel Regyn's Montmartre	71	C3
Kube Hôtel	72	F3
Le Village Hostel	73	D3
Plug-Inn Hostel	74	B3
Terrass Hôtel	75	B3

TRANSPORT	(pp383–90)	
Funicular to Sacré Cœur	76	C3
Funicular Upper Station	77	C3

student & 10-25yr €7/5.50; 🕑 11am-6pm Tue-Sun; Ⓜ Lamarck–Caulaincourt

The Montmartre Museum displays paintings, lithographs and documents mostly relating to the area's rebellious and bohemian/artistic past. It is located in a 17th-century manor house, which is the oldest structure in the *quartier*, and also stages exhibitions of artists who are still living in the *quartier*. There's an excellent bookshop here that also sells small bottles of the wine produced from grapes grown in the Clos Montmartre (p179).

DALÍ ESPACE MONTMARTRE Map p134
☎ 01 42 64 40 10; www.daliparis.com; 11 rue Poulbot, 18e; adult/student & 8-26yr/senior €10/6/7; 🕑 10am-6.30pm; Ⓜ Abbesses

More than 300 works by Salvador Dalí (1904–89), the flamboyant Catalan surrealist printmaker, painter, sculptor and self-promoter, are on display at this surrealist-style basement museum located just west of place du Tertre. The collection includes Dalí's strange sculptures (most

in reproduction), lithographs, many of his illustrations and furniture (including the famous 'lips' sofa).

MUSÉE DE LA HALLE ST-PIERRE
Map p134

☎ 01 42 58 72 89; www.hallesaintpierre.org, in French; 2 rue Ronsard, 18e; adult/student, senior & under 26yr €7.50/6; 🕑 10am-6pm daily Sep-Jul, noon-6pm Mon-Fri Aug; Ⓜ Anvers

Founded in 1986, this museum and gallery is in the lovely old covered St Peter's Market across from square Willette and the base of the funicular. It focuses on the primitive and Art Brut schools; there is no permanent collection as such but the museum stages some three temporary exhibitions a year. There's a decent café on site.

MUSÉE DE L'ÉROTISME Map p134
☎ 01 42 58 28 73; www.musee-erotisme.com; 72 blvd de Clichy, 18e; adult/senior & student €9/6; 🕑 10am-2am; Ⓜ Blanche

The Museum of Erotic Art attempts to raise around 2000 titillating statuary,

CLICHY & GARE ST-LAZARE

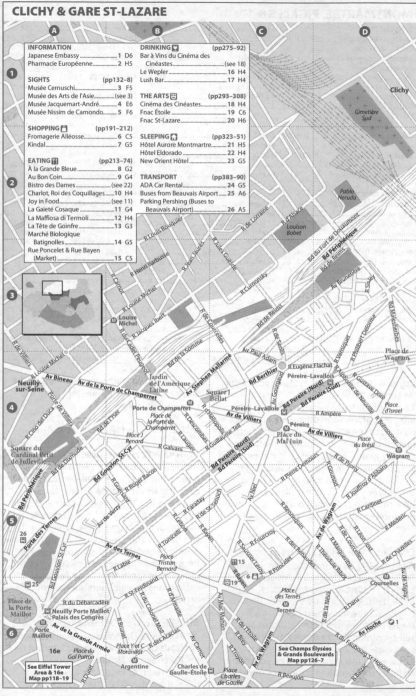

INFORMATION
Japanese Embassy................................1 D6
Pharmacie Européenne.........................2 H5

SIGHTS (pp132–8)
Musée Cernuschi.................................3 F5
Musée des Arts de l'Asie.................(see 3)
Musée Jacquemart-André.....................4 E6
Musée Nissim de Camondo....................5 F6

SHOPPING (pp191–212)
Fromagerie Alléosse............................6 C5
Kindal..7 G5

EATING (pp213–74)
À la Grande Bleue................................8 G2
Au Bon Coin......................................9 G4
Bistro des Dames...........................(see 22)
Charlot, Roi des Coquillages................10 H4
Joy in Food..................................(see 11)
La Gaieté Cosaque............................11 G4
La Maffiosa di Termoli.......................12 H4
La Tête de Goinfre............................13 G3
Marché Biologique
  Batignolles.................................14 G5
Rue Poncelet & Rue Bayen
  (Market).....................................15 C5

DRINKING (pp275–92)
Bar à Vins du Cinéma des
  Cinéastes.................................(see 18)
Le Wepler......................................16 H4
Lush Bar...17 H4

THE ARTS (pp293–308)
Cinéma des Cinéastes........................18 H4
Fnac Étoile.....................................19 C6
Fnac St-Lazare.................................20 H6

SLEEPING (pp323–51)
Hôtel Aurore Montmartre.....................21 H5
Hôtel Eldorado.................................22 H4
New Orient Hôtel..............................23 G5

TRANSPORT (pp383–90)
ADA Car Rental.................................24 G5
Buses from Beauvais Airport.................25 A6
Parking Pershing (Buses to
  Beauvais Airport)...........................26 A5

See Champs Élysées
& Grands Boulevards
Map pp126–7

See Eiffel Tower
Area & 16e
Map pp118–19

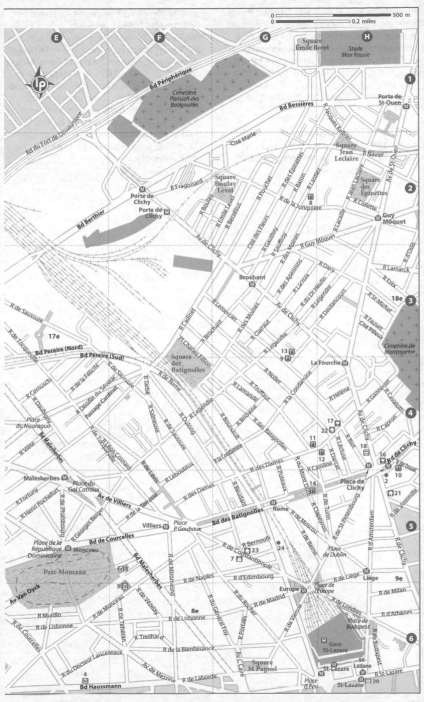

stimulating sexual aids and fetishist items from days gone by to a loftier plane, with antique and modern erotic art from four continents spread out across several floors and a large amount of descriptive information. But the majority of the punters know why they are here. Nevertheless, some of the exhibits are, well, breathtaking, to say the least.

MUSÉE CERNUSCHI Map p136

☎ 01 53 96 21 50; www.cernuschi.paris.fr, in French; 7 av Vélasquez, 8e; temporary exhibits adult/14-26yr €9/4.50, permanent collections free; ✆ 10am-6pm Tue-Sun; Ⓜ Villiers

The Cernuschi Museum, renovated and its exhibition space redefined and enlarged in recent years, houses the city of Paris' Musée des Arts de l'Asie (Asian Arts Museum). In essence it's a collection of ancient Chinese art (funerary statues, bronzes, ceramics) and some works from Japan assembled during an 1871–73 world tour by the Milan banker and philanthropist Henri Cernuschi (1821–96), who settled in Paris before the unification of Italy.

Drinking p285; Eating p248; Shopping p204; Sleeping p342

Close to the Gare du Nord is where the Grands Boulevards of bourgeois Paris begin to fray at the edges and merge into the multi-ethnic communities that make up parts of the 10e and 19e arrondissements. Large populations of Indians, Bangladeshis, Pakistanis, West Indians, Africans, Turks and Kurds live in the areas around blvd de Strasbourg and rue du Faubourg St-Denis, and walking north along the latter (east of the Gare du Nord) will bring you to Paris' new Little India.

The area's real drawcard, however, is the Canal St-Martin (inaugurated in 1825), which emerges here from beneath the streets of Paris to link waterways in the eastern suburbs with the Seine. Its banks have undergone an urban renaissance in the past decade, and the southern stretch is an ideal spot for café lounging, quay-side summer picnics and late-night drinks. Hip new bistros have moved in, and if you've come to Paris to indulge your tastebuds, you'll probably wind up in the area sooner rather than later.

top picks

GARE DU NORD & CANAL ST-MARTIN

- Canal St-Martin (p139) Find out what all the buzz is about along the canal.
- Parc de la Villette (p139) Catch a performance at the city's largest cultural playground.
- Cité des Sciences et de l'Industrie (p142) Kids of all ages love this mega science museum.
- Cité de la Musique (p143) For world music performances and an impressive instrument collection.

Following the canal to the northeast, where it becomes the Canal de l'Ourcq, takes you into the little-visited 19e arrondissement. It may not possess the beauty of central Paris, but it is nonetheless full of delightful surprises, like the Parc de la Villette, a vast park that hosts innumerable cultural events and the impressive science museum at the Cité des Sciences et de l'Industrie.

Metro lines 5 and 7 both run northeast along the upper part of the canal, while line 2 runs northwest, connecting Père Lachaise and Belleville with Montmartre (Pigalle) and Charles de Gaulle–Étoile. République, near the southern tip of the Canal St-Martin, is also a handy interchange. Trains arrive in the Gare du Nord and Gare de l'Est. Both airports are served by the RER B, which stops in Gare du Nord.

CANAL ST-MARTIN Map p140

Ⓜ République, Jaurès, Jacques Bonsergent

The tranquil, 4.5km-long St-Martin Canal links the 10e with Parc de la Villette (Map p140) in the 19e via the Bassin de la Villette and Canal de l'Ourcq, and the canal makes its famous dogleg turn in this arrondissement. Its shaded towpaths are a great place for a romantic stroll or cycle and take you past nine locks, metal bridges and ordinary Parisian neighbourhoods. Parts of the water-way – built to link the Seine with the 108km-long Canal de l'Ourcq – are higher than the surrounding land. You can take a tour on a canal boat (p401). Note that many neighbourhood shops/bistros close on Sunday and Monday.

PARC DE LA VILLETTE Map p140

☎ 01 40 03 75 75; www.villette.com, in French; Ⓜ Porte de la Villette or Porte de Pantin

The largest park in Paris, the Parc de la Villette is a cultural centre, kids' playground and landscaped urban space all rolled into one. The French love of geometric forms defines the futuristic layout – the colossal mirrorlike sphere of the Géode cinema, an undulating strip of corrugated steel stretching for hundreds of feet, the bright-red cubical pavilions known as *folies* – but it is intersection of two canals, the Ourcq and the St-Denis, that brings the most natural and popular element: water. Although it is a fair hike from central Paris, consider the trip here for one of the many events (world, rock and classical music concerts; art exhibits; cinema; circuses; modern dance) or if you have children.

Events are staged in the wonderful old Grande Halle (formerly a slaughterhouse – the Parisian cattle market was located here from 1867 to 1974), Le Zénith (p299), the Cabaret Sauvage (p302), the Cité de la Musique (p143), or the Conservatoire National Supérieur de Musique et de Danse (p301). Additionally, the new Paris

NEIGHBOURHOODS GARE DU NORD & CANAL ST-MARTIN

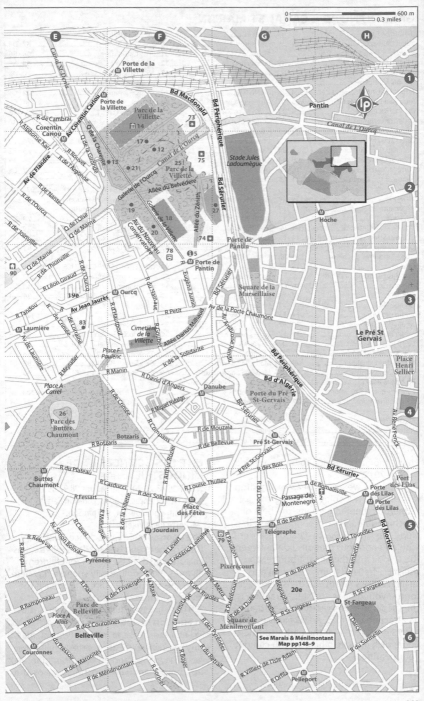

See Marais & Ménilmontant
Map pp148–9

GARE DU NORD & CANAL ST-MARTIN

INFORMATION
Canal Cruises Canauxrama 1 D3
Church of Jesus Christ of the
  Latter Day Saints 2 H5
Hitel Internet Café .... (see 87)
Hôpital Lariboisière 3 A4
Information & Ticket Office 5 F3
Paris Canal Croisières 6 D3
Paris Convention & Visitors
  Bureau Gare de l'Est 7 B5
Paris Convention & Visitors
  Bureau Gare du Nord 8 B4
Porte St Denis 9 A6
Porte St Martin 10 B6
Statue of the Republic 11 C6

SIGHTS   pp139–44
Argonaute 12 F2
Cinaxe 13 F2
Cité de la Musique .... (see 74)
Cité des Sciences et de l'Industrie... 14 F1
Conservatoire National Supérieur
  de Musique et de Danse .... (see 78)
Crèche 15 B5
Franprix Faubourg St Denis
  Branch 16 A6
Géode 17 F2
Grande Halle 18 F2
Jardin des Dunes 19 F2
Jardin des Miroirs 20 F2
Jardin du Dragon 21 F2
Le 104 .... 22 D2
Les Orgues de Flandre 23 D3
Musée de la Musique .... (see 74)
Musée de l'Éventail 24 B6
Parc de la Villette 25 F2
Parc des Buttes Chaumont 26 E4
Paris Philharmonic 27 G2

SHOPPING   pp191–212
Antoine et Lili 28 C5
APC 29 C6

Bazar Éthic .... (see 30)
Liza Korn 30 C6
Maje 31 C6
Rue de Paradis 32 A5
Rue Martel 33 A5

EATING   pp213–74
Aux Deux Canards 34 A6
Bob's Juice Bar 35 B5
Buffalo Grill Gare du Nord
  Branch 36 A4
Chez Casimir .... (see 37)
Chez Michel 37 A4
Chez Papa 38 C4
Dishny 39 B4
Du Pain et des Idées 40 C6
Food Shops 41 A6
Franprix Magenta Branch 42 B5
Fromagerie 43 A6
Hôtel du Nord 44 C5
Istanbul 45 B5
Jambo 46 D5
Jardin des Voluptés 47 A6
Krishna Bhavan 48 B4
La Cantine de Quentin 49 C5
La Marine 50 C6
La Paella 51 B5
Le Bastringue 52 D3
Le Cambodge 53 C6
Le Chansonnier 54 C4
Le Mauricien Filao 55 A6
Le Réveil du Xe 56 B6
Le Verre Volé 57 C5
L'Office 58 A5
Madame Shawn 59 C6
Madame Shawn (Ari) 60 C6
Marché Couvert St-Quentin 61 B5
Palais des Rajpout 62 B6
Passage Brady 63 B6
Passage de Pondicherry .... (see 62)
Pink Flamingo 64 C5
Pooja 65 A6
Terminus Nord 66 B4

DRINKING   pp275–92
Café Chéri(e) 67 D5
Chez Prune 68 C6
Delaville Café 69 A6
La Sardine 70 D5
L'Atmosphère 71 C5
Le Jemmapes 72 C6

NIGHTLIFE   pp293–308
Alhambra .... (see 40)
Cabaret Sauvage 73 F1
Cité de la Musique 74 F2
Le Zénith 75 F2
New Morning 76 A5
Point Éphémère 77 C4

THE ARTS   pp293–308
Conservatoire National
  Supérieur de Musique et
  de Danse 78 F3
Le Regard du Cygne 79 G5
MK2 Quai de la Loire 80 D3
MK2 Quai de Seine 81 D3

SPORTS & ACTIVITIES   pp309–16
Centre Sivananda 82 B5
Hammam Medina 83 E3
Patinoire Pailleron 84 D4

SLEEPING   pp323–51
Hôtel du Nord 85 B6
Hôtel Garden St-Martin 86 C6
Hôtel La Vieille France 87 B4
République Hôtel 88 C6
Sibour Hôtel 89 B5
St Christopher's Inn 90 E3

TRANSPORT   pp383–90
Bus Terminal 91 B4
RATP Bus 350 to Charles de
  Gaulle Airport 92 B5
RATP Bus 350 to Charles de
  Gaulle Airport 93 B4

Philharmonic hall is due to be completed here in 2012.

When the weather's pleasant, children (and adults) will enjoy exploring the numerous themed gardens, the best of which double as playgrounds. These include the Jardin du Dragon (Dragon Garden), with an enormous dragon slide between the Géode and the nearest bridge, and the Jardin des Dunes (Dunes Garden) and Jardin des Miroirs (Mirror Gardens). However, for the young ones, the star attraction is the Cité des Sciences et de l'Industrie (p142) and its attached cinemas. An information centre (☉ 9.30am-6.30pm) is at the park's southern edge; pick up a map here so you can get your bearings.

CITÉ DES SCIENCES ET DE L'INDUSTRIE Map p140

☎ 01 56 43 20 20, reservations 08 92 69 70 72; www.cite-sciences.fr; 30 av Corentin Cariou, 19e; ☉ 10am-6pm Tue-Sat, to 7pm Sun; Ⓜ Porte de la Villette

The enormous City of Science & Industry, at the northern end of Parc de la Villette, has all sorts of science exhibits for children of all ages. You could easily spend a day here with the kids in tow. (Bring a picnic if the weather is nice.)

There are two main exhibit areas inside, in addition to a planetarium (level 1; admission €3; ☉ 10am-6pm Tue-Sat, to 7pm Sun), two cinemas, a tiny aquarium (level 2; admission free; ☉ 10am-6pm Tue-Sat, to 7pm Sun) and an old submarine. Pick up English-language brochures, maps and schedules at the circular information counter by the main entrance.

On the ground floor is the brilliant Cité des Enfants (level 0; admission €6), with imaginative, hands-on demonstrations of basic scientific principles in two sections: for two- to seven-year-olds, and for five- to 12-year-olds. In the first, kids can explore, among other things, the conduct of water (waterproof ponchos provided), a building site and a maze. The second lets children build toy houses with industrial robots and stage news broadcasts in a TV studio. Visits to both last 1½ hours and are scheduled five times a day (seven at weekends), beginning at 10am. Each group of children must be accompanied by an adult. It can be a madhouse at weekends and during school holidays; reserving your timeslot several days in advance (and attaching tracking devices to your children) is highly recommended. An additional temporary exhibit (€6) is usually open on this floor as well.

The huge Explora (levels 1 & 2; adult/7-25yr/under 7yr €8/6/free), the heart of the exhibitions at the Cité des Sciences et de l'Industrie, looks at everything from space exploration and automobile technology to genetics and sound. Most exhibits are for ages seven and older. Tickets are valid for a full day and allow you to enter and exit at will. Access to some temporary exhibits costs an additional €2.

The giant mirrorlike sphere known as the Géode (☎ 08 92 68 45 40; www.lageode. fr, in French; adult/senior & 3-25yr €10.50/9, 3D films €12.50/11; ☼ 10.30am-8.30pm) shows hi-res 3D and Imax films (40 minutes each) projected onto a 180-degree screen to surround you with the action. Headsets for an English soundtrack are available for free. Reach the Géode via level 0.

The Cinaxe (admission €4.80; ☼ 10.30am-5pm), a cinema with hydraulic seating for 60 people, moves in synchronisation with the action on the screen. It's across the walkway from the southwestern side of the Cité des Sciences. Shows begin every 15 minutes.

The Argonaute (admission €3, under 7yr free; ☼ 10am-5.30pm Tue-Sat, to 7pm Sun), a French Navy submarine commissioned in 1957 and dry-docked in the park in 1989, is just southeast of the Géode.

CITÉ DE LA MUSIQUE Map p140

☎ 01 44 84 44 84; www.cite-musique.fr; 221 av Jean Jaurès, 19e; ☼ noon-6pm Tue-Sat, 10am-6pm Sun; Ⓜ Porte de Pantin

The City of Music, on the southern edge of Parc de la Villette, is a striking, triangular-shaped concert hall whose mission is to bring nonelitist music from around the world to Paris' multi-ethnic listeners. (For information on concerts and other musical events, see p302.) Next door is the new Paris Philharmonic hall (opening 2012) as well as the prestigious Conservatoire National Supérieur de Musique et de Danse (p301), a top school for classical musicians and dancers that also stages student performances.

The Musée de la Musique (Music Museum; ☎ 01 44 84 44 84; adult/senior, student & 18-25yr/under 18yr €8/5.60/4, free for EU resident under 26) in the Cité de la Musique displays some 900 rare musical instruments; you can hear many of them being played on the audioguide (free). There is also a music-related media library here, the Médiathèque.

PARC DES BUTTES-CHAUMONT
Map p140

rue Manin & rue Botzaris, 19e; ☼ 7.30am-11pm May-Sep, to 9pm Oct-Apr; Ⓜ Buttes–Chaumont or Botzaris

Encircled by tall apartment blocks, the 25-hectare Buttes-Chaumont Park is the

HÔTEL DU NORD

If you want a glimpse of life along the canal before it became cool, the movie to watch is Marcel Carné's *Hôtel du Nord* (1938). The story revolves around the residents of the hotel – including a canal worker, prostitute, drifting criminal and lovesick girl – and is hardly short on drama; it begins with a botched double suicide and ends with a murder. The highlight, though, is the dialogue, delivered with an old-fashioned Parisian accent that, let's face it, is a lot more fun than the French you hear today. One of the most unforgettable lines in all French cinema belongs to Arletty's character (the prostitute). Accused of being a 'suffocating atmosphere' in a lovers' spat, she responds, '*Atmosphère? Atmosphère?! Est-ce que j'ai une gueule d'atmosphère?!*' (Atmosphere? Atmosphere?! Do I look like an atmosphere?!) Today, the movie is referenced in the names of a local hotel (p343), restaurant (p249) and bar (p286).

closest thing in Paris to Manhattan's Central Park. The park's forested slopes hide grottoes and artificial waterfalls, and the lake is dominated by a temple-topped island linked to the mainland by two footbridges. Once a quarry and rubbish tip, the park was given its present form by Baron Haussmann in time for the opening of the 1867 Exposition Universelle.

LE 104 Map p140

☎ 01 53 35 50 00; www.le104.fr; 104 rue d'Aubervilliers or 5 rue Curial, 19e; ☯ 11am-8pm Tue-Thu & Sun, to 11pm Fri & Sat; Ⓜ Stalingrad or Crimée

A former funeral parlour turned city-funded art space, Le 104 has the potential to give a jolt of vitality to an otherwise neglected neighbourhood. Spread out over a massive 39,000 sq metres, the complex includes studios for resident artists, exhibition galleries, a second-hand store and café for coffee breaks. But mixing artists with government bureaucracy is not always for the best, and Le 104 went through some serious growing pains in its opening year. As this book went to print, things were still very low-key here – the best advice is to check acitivity on the website and time visits around scheduled events.

PORTE ST-DENIS & PORTE ST-MARTIN Map p140

cnr rue du Faubourg St-Denis & blvd St-Denis, 10e; Ⓜ Strasbourg–St-Denis

St-Denis Gate, a 24m-high triumphal arch, was built in 1673 to commemorate Louis XIV's campaign along the Rhine. On the northern side, carvings represent the fall of Maastricht in the same year (note the gilded fleur-de-lys).

Two blocks east is a similar arch, the less impressive, 17m-high Porte St-Martin (St Martin Gate). It was erected two years after Porte St-Denis to commemorate the capture of Besançon and the Franche-Comté region by Louis XIV's armies.

MUSÉE DE L'ÉVANTAIL Map p140

☎ 01 42 08 90 20; www.annehoguet.fr; 2 blvd de Strasbourg, 10e; adult/student & senior €6/4; ☯ 2-6pm Mon-Wed; Ⓜ Strasbourg–St-Denis

Big fans of this museum, we always find it almost impossible to walk by without checking on our favourite items – screen, folding and brisé (the kind with overlapping struts) fans. Around 900 of the breeze-makers are on display, dating as far back as the mid-18th century. The small museum is housed in what was once a well-known fan manufactory, and its original showroom, dating from 1893, is sublime. It closes during August.

MARAIS & MÉNILMONTANT

Drinking p286; Eating p252; Shopping p205; Sleeping p343

The Marais, the area of the Right Bank north of Île St-Louis, was exactly what its name in French implies – 'marsh' or 'swamp' – until the 13th century, when it was converted to farmland. In the early 17th century, Henri IV built the place Royale (today's place des Vosges), turning the area into Paris' most fashionable residential address and attracting wealthy aristocrats who then erected their own luxurious private mansions.

When the aristocracy moved out of Paris to Versailles and Faubourg St-Germain during the late 17th and the 18th centuries, the Marais and its townhouses passed into the hands of ordinary Parisians. The 110-hectare area was given a major facelift in the late 1960s and early '70s.

Though the Marais has become a coveted trendy address in recent years, it remains home to a long-established Jewish community. The historic Jewish quarter – the so-called Pletzl (from the Yiddish for 'little square') – starts in rue des Rosiers, then continues along rue Ste-Croix de la Bretonnerie to rue du Temple, where expensive boutiques sit side-by-side with Jewish bookshops and stores selling religious goods and *cacher* (kosher) grocery shops, butchers, restaurants and takeaway falafel joints. Don't miss the Art Nouveau synagogue (Map p152; 10 rue Pavée, 4e) designed in 1913 by Hector

top picks

MARAIS & MÉNILMONTANT

- Place des Vosges (p146) Paris' oldest planned square is a triumph of symmetry and understated *bon goût* (good taste).
- Cimetière du Père Lachaise (p155) Final resting place of the rich, the famous and the infamous.
- Musée Carnavalet (p146) Take an in-depth look at Paris from the Gallo-Roman period right up until today.
- Mémorial de la Shoah (p151) Learn the truth about the German occupation of Paris and the horrors of the Holocaust.
- Hôtel de Sully (p146) This 17th-century aristocratic mansion boasts two Renaissance courtyards festooned with allegorical reliefs.

Guimard, who was also responsible for the city's famous metro entrances (see the boxed text, p103). The Marais has also become the epicentre of gay and lesbian; you'll find a lot of bars and clubs (not to mention restaurants, a bookshop and a hotel) catering to both groups.

At the same time Ménilmontant, a solidly working-class *quartier* with little to recommend it until the 1990s, today boasts almost as many restaurants, bars and clubs as the Marais, especially along rue de Ménilmontant. Further on, the inner-city 'village' of Belleville, centred on blvd de Belleville in the 20e to the east, remains for the most part unpretentious and working class – though that too is changing – and is home to large numbers of immigrants, especially Muslims and Jews from North Africa and Vietnamese and ethnic Chinese from Indochina. The multicultural tone of rue de Belleville and rue de Ménilmontant is amplified by blvd de Belleville, where a colourful, abundant market spills out over the footpaths.

Metro stations useful for the Marais include Arts et Métiers, Chemin Vert, Hôtel de Ville, Pont Marie, Rambuteau and St-Paul. For Ménilmontant and Belleville they are Belleville, Couronnes, Ménilmontant, Oberkampf and Pyrénées. The Marais is well served by buses including the 29 from rue des Francs Bourgeois to Bastille and Gare de Lyon and the 76 from rue de Rivoli through the 11e via rue de Charonne to the 20e and Porte de Bagnolet. From rue de Ménilmontant the 96 goes to rue Oberkampf, through the Marais and over to the blvd St-Michel and Odéon. From the rue des Pyrénées the 26 heads up to the Parc des Buttes-Chaumont and over to Gare du Nord and Gare St-Lazare.

HÔTEL DE VILLE Map p152

☎ 39 75; www.paris.fr; place de l'Hôtel de Ville, 4e; Ⓜ Hôtel de Ville

After having been gutted during the Paris Commune of 1871, Paris' city hall was rebuilt in luxurious neo-Renaissance style from 1874 to 1882. The ornate facade is decorated with 108 statues of noteworthy Parisians. There's a Salon d'Accueil (Reception Hall; 29 rue de Rivoli, 4e; Ⓨ 10am-7pm Mon-Sat), which dispenses information and brochures and is used for temporary (and very popular) exhibitions, usually with a Paris theme. Some exhibitions take place in the Salle St-Jean (5 rue Lobau, 4e), which is entered from the eastern side of the building.

PLACE DES VOSGES Map p148
Ⓜ St-Paul or Bastille

Inaugurated in 1612 as place Royale and thus the oldest square in Paris, Place des Vosges (4e) is an ensemble of 36 symmetrical houses with ground-floor arcades, steep slate roofs and large dormer windows arranged around a large and leafy square. Only the earliest houses were built of brick; to save time, the rest were given timber frames and faced with plaster, which was later painted to resemble brick. The square received its present name in 1800 to honour the Vosges *département* (administrative division) for being the first in France to pay its taxes.

The author Victor Hugo lived in an apartment on the 3rd floor of the square's Hôtel de Rohan-Guéménée from 1832 to 1848. He moved here a year after the publication of *Notre Dame de Paris* (The Hunchback of Notre Dame) and completed *Ruy Blas* while living here. The Maison de Victor Hugo (Map p148; Victor Hugo House; ☎ 01 42 72 10 16; www.musee-hugo. paris.fr; 6 place des Vosges, 4e; permanent collections free, temporary exhibits adult/14-26yr/senior & student €7/3.50/5; Ⓨ 10am-6pm Tue-Sun) is now a municipal museum devoted to the life and times of the celebrated novelist and poet, with an impressive collection of his personal drawings and portraits.

HÔTEL DE SULLY Map p152
62 rue St-Antoine, 4e; Ⓜ St-Paul

This aristocratic mansion dating from the early 17th century today houses the headquarters of the Centre des Monuments Nationaux (☎ 01 44 61 20 00; www.monuments-nationaux.fr; Ⓨ 9am-12.45pm & 2-6pm Mon-Thu, 9am-12.45pm & 2-5pm Fri), the body responsible for many of France's historical monuments; there are brochures and lots of information available on sites nationwide. The Hôtel de Sully bookshop (p205) is excellent for 'Parisiana', and the two Renaissance-style courtyards (p184) are worth the trip alone.

MUSÉE CARNAVALET Map p152
☎ 01 44 59 58 58; www.carnavalet.paris.fr, in French; 23 rue de Sévigné, 3e; permanent collections free, temporary exhibits adult/14-26yr/senior

& student €7/3.50/5; Ⓨ 10am-6pm Tue-Sun; Ⓜ St-Paul or Chemin Vert

This enormous museum, subtitled Histoire de Paris (History of Paris), is housed in two *hôtels particuliers*: the mid-16th-century Renaissance-style Hôtel Carnavalet, home to the letter-writer Madame de Sévigné from 1677 to 1696, and the Hôtel Le Peletier de St-Fargeau, which dates from the late 17th century.

The artefacts on display in the museum's sublime rooms chart the history of Paris from the Gallo-Roman period in the former Orangerie to modern times on the 1st floor and fill more than 100 rooms. Some of the nation's most important documents, paintings and other objects from the French Revolution are here (rooms 101 to 113), as is Fouquet's stunning Art Nouveau jewellery shop from the rue Royale (room 142) and Marcel Proust's cork-lined bedroom from his apartment on blvd Haussmann (room 147), where he wrote most of the 7350-page literary cycle *À la Recherche du Temps Perdu* (Remembrance of Things Past).

MUSÉE PICASSO Map p152
☎ 01 42 71 25 21; www.musee-picasso.fr, in French; 5 rue de Thorigny, 3e; Ⓨ 9.30am-6pm Wed-Mon Apr-Sep, 9.30am-5.30pm Wed-Mon Oct-Mar; Ⓜ St-Paul or Chemin Vert

The Picasso Museum, housed in the stunning mid-17th-century Hôtel Salé, forms one of Paris' best-loved art collections. Unfortunately it was undergoing a massive renovation at the time of research and will not reopen until 2012. Its collection includes more than 3500 drawings, engravings, paintings, ceramic works and sculptures from the *grand maître* (great master), Pablo Picasso

IF WALLS COULD TALK

Centuries of history are inscribed on the facades and pediments of the 4e arrondissement and in the narrow streets, alleys, porches and courtyards; today the Marais is one of the few neighbourhoods of Paris that still has much of its pre-revolutionary architecture intact. These include the house at 3 rue Volta (Map p148) in the 3e arrondissement, parts of which date back to 1292; the one at 51 rue de Montmorency (Map p148), also in the 3e and dating back to 1407, which is now a restaurant called Auberge Nicolas Flamel (p254); and the half-timbered 16th-century building at 11 and 13 rue François Miron (Map p152) in the 4e.

(1881–1973), which his heirs donated to the French government in lieu of paying inheritance taxes. The museum also normally shows Picasso's personal art collection, which includes works by Braque, Cézanne, Matisse, Modigliani, Degas and Rousseau.

MUSÉE COGNACQ-JAY Map p152

☎ 01 40 27 07 21; www.cognacq-jay.paris.fr, in French; 8 rue Elzévir, 3e; permanent collections free; ⊙ 10am-6pm Tue-Sun; Ⓜ St-Paul or Chemin Vert
This museum in the Hôtel de Donon brings together oil paintings, pastels, sculpture, objets d'art, jewellery, porcelain and furniture from the 18th century assembled by Ernest Cognacq (1839–1928), founder of La Samaritaine department store (now undergoing a protracted overhaul) and his wife Louise Jay. Although Cognacq appreciated little of his collection, boasting to all who would listen that he had never visited the Louvre and was only acquiring collections for the status, the artwork and objets d'art give a pretty good idea of upper-class tastes during the Age of Enlightenment.

ARCHIVES NATIONALES Map p152

☎ 01 40 27 60 96; www.archivesnationales. culture.gouv.fr, in French; 60 rue des Francs Bourgeois, 3e; Ⓜ Rambuteau or St-Paul
France's National Archives are housed in the Soubise wing of the impressive, early 18th-century Hôtel de Rohan-Soubise, which also contains the Musée de l'Histoire de France (Museum of French History; ☎ 01 40 27 60 96; www.archivesnationales.culture.gouv.fr/chan, in French; adult/senior & 18-25yr €3/2.30; ⊙ 10am-12.30pm & 2-5.30pm Mon & Wed-Fri, 2-5.30pm Sat & Sun; Ⓜ Rambuteau or St-Paul). The museum contains antique furniture and 18th-century paintings but primarily documents – everything from medieval incunabula and letters written by Joan of Arc to the wills of Louis XIV and Napoleon. The ceiling and walls of the interior are extravagantly painted and gilded in the rococo style; look out for the Cabinet des Singes, a room filled with frescoes of playful, cheeky monkeys painted by Christophe Huet between 1749 and 1752.

MUSÉE DES ARTS ET MÉTIERS
Map p148

☎ 01 53 01 82 00; www.arts-et-metiers.net; 60 rue de Réaumur, 3e; permanent collections/ permanent collections & temporary exhibits adult

€6.50/7.50, 18-25yr €4.50/5.50; ⊙ 10am-6pm Tue, Wed & Fri-Sun, to 9.30pm Thu; Ⓜ Arts et Métiers
The Arts & Crafts Museum, the oldest museum of science and technology in Europe, is a must for anyone with an interest in how things work. Housed inside the 18th-century priory of St-Martin des Champs, some 3000 instruments, machines and working models from the 18th to 20th centuries are displayed according to theme (from Construction and Energy to Transportation) across three floors. Taking pride of place in the attached church of St-Martin des Champs is Foucault's original pendulum, which he introduced to the world in 1855, and Louis Blériot's monoplane from 1909. There are lots of workshops and other activities here for children. An audioguide costs €5. Permanent collections are free for EU residents under 26, everyone under 18 and for everybody on the first Sunday of the month and from 6pm to 9.30pm Thursday.

MUSÉE DE LA CHASSE ET DE LA NATURE Map p152

☎ 01 53 01 92 40; www.chassenature.org, in French; 62 rue des Archives, 3e; adult/student & 18-25yr €6/4.50; ⊙ 11am-6pm Tue-Sun; Ⓜ Rambuteau or Hôtel de Ville
The Hunting & Nature Museum may sound like an oxymoron to the politically correct, but in France, where hunting is a very big deal, to show your love for nature is to go out and shoot something – or so it would seem. The delightful Hôtel Guénégaud (1651), which reopened in 2007 after a two-year renovation, is positively crammed with weapons, paintings, sculpture and objets d'art related to hunting and, of course, lots and lots of trophies – horns, antlers, heads.

MUSÉE D'ART ET D'HISTOIRE DU JUDAÏSME Map p152

☎ 01 53 01 86 60; www.mahj.org; 71 rue du Temple, 3e; permanent collection adult/EU resident under 26yr & everyone under 18yr €6.80/free, temporary exhibit adult/18-25yr €7/4.50; ⊙ 11am-6pm Mon-Fri, 10am-6pm Sun; Ⓜ Rambuteau
The Museum of the Art & History of Judaism, housed in the sumptuous Hôtel de St-Aignan (1650), traces the evolution of Jewish communities from the Middle Ages to the present, with particular emphasis on the history of Jews in France but also that of communities in other parts of Europe

MARAIS & MÉNILMONTANT

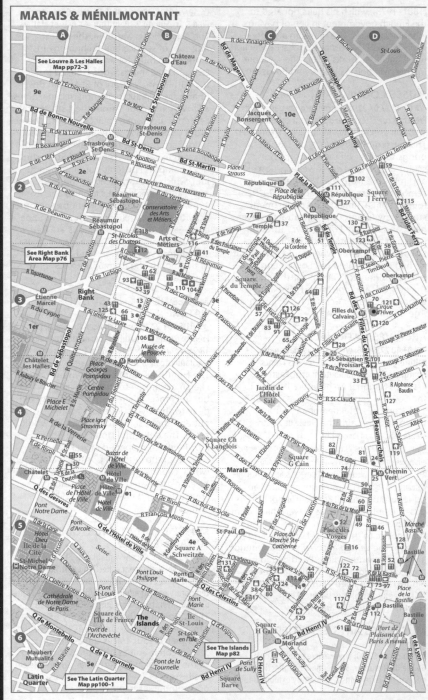

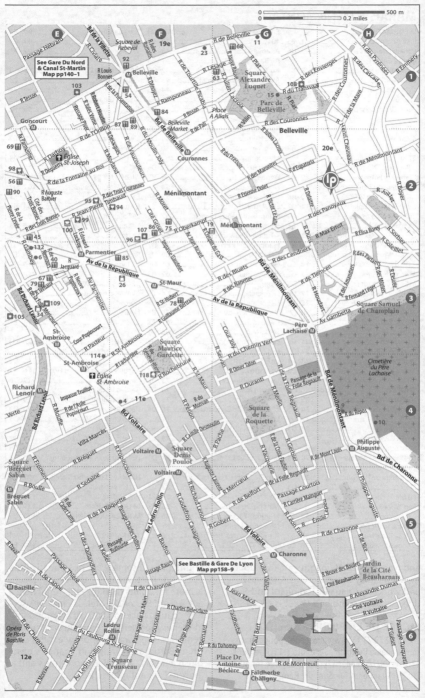

MARAIS & MÉNILMONTANT

INFORMATION
Bike About Tours.................................1 B5
Canauxrama Pier................................2 D6
Centre Gai et Lesbien de
  Paris Île de France..........................3 B3
Copy-Top..4 F4
Cyber Squ@re.....................................5 C2
Langue Onze.......................................6 E3
Paris à Vélo, C'est Sympa!..................7 D4

SIGHTS   (pp145–55)
3 Rue Volta (Medieval
  House)..8 B3
51 Rue de Montmorency
  (Medieval House)...................... (see 43)
Cemetery Entrance.............................9 H4
Cimetière du Père Lachaise
  Conservation Office.....................10 H4
Édith Piaf's Birthplace......................11 G1
Église St-Nicolas des
  Champs..12 B3
Galerie Thomas Nelson....................13 B3
Hôtel de Rohan-Guéménée........ (see 16)
House Where Jim Morrison
  Died...14 C6
Maison de l'Air.................................15 G1
Maison de Victor Hugo....................16 D5
Musée de la Magie............................17 C6
Musée des Arts et Métiers................18 B2
Musée des Automates.................. (see 17)
Musée Édith Piaf..............................19 F2
Paperdolls..20 D3
Pavillon de l'Arsenal........................21 C6
Places des Vosges............................22 D5
Wall Paintings..................................23 F1
Xuly Bët...24 D4

SHOPPING   (pp191–212)
Atelier d'Autrefois............................25 D5
Boutique Obut..................................26 F3
Darty...27 D2
Grand Bonton...................................28 D3
Julien Caviste....................................29 C3
La Boutique des Inventions........ (see 17)
La Maison de l'Astronomie...............30 A4
La Maison du Hamac........................31 D2
Le Repaire de Bacchus.....................32 C3
Merci..33 D4
Puzzle Michèle Wilson.....................34 E3
Red Wheelbarrow
  Bookstore.......................................35 C5
Surface to Air Branch.......................36 C3
Tati 3e Branch..................................37 C2
Village St-Paul..................................38 C6

EATING 🍴   (pp213–74)
404..39 B3
Asianwok...40 E3
Au Bascou...41 B3
Au Trou Normand.............................42 D3
Auberge Nicolas Flamel....................43 A3
Aux Vins des Pyrénées......................44 C5
Bistro Florentin...............................45 E2
Bistrot de l'Oulette...........................46 D5
Bob's Juice Bar.................................47 B3
Bofinger...48 D5
Café Hugo..49 D5
Chez Janou.......................................50 D5
Chez Jenny.......................................51 C2
Dalloyau..52 D5
Derrière..53 B3
Dong Huong.....................................54 F1
Ed l'Epicier Supermarket..................55 A4
El Paladar...56 E2
Franprix Bretagne Branch.................57 C3
Franprix Jean-Pierre
  Timbaud Branch............................58 D3
Franprix Jules Ferry Branch..............59 D2
Gérad Mulot....................................60 D5
Grand Apétit....................................61 D6
Happy Nouilles.................................62 B3
Krung Thep.......................................63 G1
La Briciola..64 C3
La Fougasse......................................65 C3
L'Ambassade d'Auvergne................66 B3
L'Ave Maria......................................67 E3
Le Baratin..68 G1
Le Chateaubriand............................69 E2
Le Clown Bar....................................70 D3
Le Dôme Bastille.............................71 D5
Le Nôtre..72 D5
Le Petit Bofinger.............................73 D5
Le Petit Marché...............................74 D5
Le Porokhane...................................75 F2
Le Repaire de Cartouche..................76 D4
Le Temple..77 C2
Le Tire Bouchon...............................78 F3
Le Villaret..79 E3
L'Enoteca...80 C6
Les Caves St-Gilles...........................81 D4
Mai Thai..82 D4
Marché Couvert des Enfants
  Rouges...83 C3
Marché Belleville.............................84 F1
Marche Ou Crêpe.............................85 F3
Merguez Factory..............................86 F2
New Nioullaville...............................87 F1
Noodle Shops & Restaurants...........88 B3
Reuan Thai.......................................89 F1

Soya Cantine Bio.............................90 E2
Taeko...91 C3
Tai Yien...92 F1

DRINKING 🍷🍺   (pp275–92)
Andy Wahloo...................................93 B3
Au Chat Noir....................................94 F2
Au P'tit Garage................................95 E2
Café Charbon...................................96 F2
Café des Phares...............................97 D5
La Caravane.....................................98 E2
L'Alimentation Générale..................99 E2
L'Autre Café...................................100 E2
Pop In...101 D4

NIGHTLIFE ⭐   (pp293–308)
La Favela Chic.................................102 D2
La Java...103 E1
L'Attirail...104 B3
Le Bataclan.....................................105 E3
Le Duplex.......................................106 B3
Le Nouveau Casino.........................107 F2
Le Vieux Belleville...........................108 G1
Satellite Café..................................109 E3
Le Tango...110 B3

SPORTS & ACTIVITIES   (pp309–16)
Club Med Gym................................111 D2
Nomades..112 D6
Neuve St-Pierre..............................113 C5
Vélo Cito...114 E4

SLEEPING 🛏   (pp323–51)
Auberge de Jeunesse Jules
  Ferry...115 D2
Austin's Arts et Métiers Hôtel.....116 B2
Castex Hôtel...................................117 D6
Garden Hôtel..................................118 F4
Hôtel Bastille de Launay.................119 D3
Hôtel Beaumarchais.......................120 D3
Hôtel Croix de Malte......................121 D3
Hôtel de la Herse d'Or....................122 D5
Hôtel de Nevers..............................123 D2
Hôtel du 7e Art..............................124 C5
Hôtel du Séjour Beaubourg............125 A3
Hôtel du Vieux Saule......................126 C3
Hôtel Les Jardins du Marais...........127 D4
Hôtel Lyon Mulhouse.....................128 D5
Hôtel St-Louis Marais.....................129 C6
Le Général Hôtel............................130 D2
MIJE Le Fauconnier.........................131 C5

TRANSPORT   (pp383–90)
ADA Car Rental..............................132 E3

and North Africa. Highlights include documents relating to the Dreyfus Affair (p31) and works by Chagall, Modigliani and Soutine. An adult combined ticket is €9.50.

MUSÉE DE LA POUPÉE Map p152

☎ 01 42 72 73 11; www.museedelapoupeeparis. com; impasse Berthaud, 3e; adult/3–11yr/senior & 12–25yr €8/3/5, under 12yr free Sun, free for all 2nd Fri; ⊙ 10am-6pm Tue-Sun; Ⓜ Rambuteau

Frightening to some – all those beady little eyes and silent screams – the Doll Museum is more for adults than for children. There are around 500 of the lifeless creatures here, dating back to 1800, all arranged in scenes representing Paris through the centuries. There are temporary exhibitions (think Barbie and Cindy and 'France's best plush animals') as well as workshops and a 'hospital' for antique dolls.

MÉMORIAL DE LA SHOAH Map p152

☎ 01 42 77 44 72; www.memorialdelashoah.org, in French; 17 rue Geoffroy-l'Asnier, 4e; admission free; ⊙ 10am-6pm Sun-Wed & Fri, to 10pm Thu; Ⓜ St-Paul

Established in 1956, the Memorial to the Unknown Jewish Martyr has metamorphosed into the Memorial of the Holocaust and an important documentation centre. The permanent collection and temporary exhibits relate to the Holocaust and the German occupation of parts of France and Paris during WWII; the film clips of contemporary footage and interviews are heart-rending and the displays instructive and easy to follow. The actual memorial to the victims of the Shoah, a Hebrew word meaning 'catastrophe' and synonymous in France with the Holocaust, stands at the entrance, where there is a wall (2006) inscribed with the names of 76,000 men, women and children deported from France to Nazi extermination camps. A guided tour (☎ 01 53 01 17 86) in English departs at 3pm on the second Sunday of each month.

MAISON EUROPÉENNE DE LA PHOTOGRAPHIE Map p152

☎ 01 44 78 75 00; www.mep-fr.org; 5-7 rue de Fourcy, 4e; adult/senior & 8-25yr €6.50/3.50, 5-8pm Wed free; ⊙ 11am-8pm Wed-Sun; Ⓜ St-Paul or Pont Marie

The European House of Photography, housed in the overly renovated Hôtel Hénault de Cantorbe (dating – believe it or not – from the early 18th century), has cutting-edge temporary exhibits (usually retrospectives on single photographers), as well as an enormous permanent collection on the history of photography and its connections with France. There are frequent showings of short films and documentaries on weekend afternoons. The Japanese garden at the entrance is a delight.

PARIS HISTORIQUE Map p152

☎ 01 48 87 74 31; www.paris-historique.org, in French; 44-46 rue François Miron, 4e; admission free; ⊙ 11am-8pm Mon-Sat, 2-7pm Sun; Ⓜ St-Paul

The information centre for the Association for the Conservation and Appreciation of Historic Paris should be on your tick list if you are interested in medieval Paris and, especially, the Marais. It provides information, has a research library and some displays, organises exhibitions and has lists of available guided tours (adult/student & child €10/4) of the area at 2pm or 2.30pm most days.

MUSÉE DE LA MAGIE Map p148

☎ 01 42 72 13 26; www.museedelamagie.com, in French; 11 rue St-Paul, 4e; adult/3-12yr €9/7; ⊙ 2-7pm Wed, Sat & Sun, daily Easter & Christmas school holidays; Ⓜ St-Paul

The Magic Museum in the 16th-century *caves* (cellars) of the house of the Marquis de Sade examines the ancient arts of magic, optical illusion and sleight of hand, with regular magic shows (last one usually at 6pm) included. Some visitors may feel that the displays and very basic magic tricks do not justify the high admission fee. In fact, a

TAKING ON PARIS' MUSEUMS

Warm-up exercises, half-hour breathers, a portable seat, bottled water and an energy-providing snack… It might sound as if you're preparing for a trek in the Alps, but these are some of the recommendations for tackling Paris' more than 100 museums. And with dozens of major ones free of charge on at least one day of the week, the temptation to see more is now greater than ever.

Take the Louvre, for example. Encompassing some 40 sq hectares, the museum has nine enormous departments spread over 60,600 sq metres of gallery space and some 8.5 million annual visitors (against the British Museum's 5.9 million), all elbowing each other to see what they want to see in a limited amount of time. It's hardly surprising that many people feel worn out almost by the time they've descended into the Cour Napoléon.

To avoid museum fatigue wear comfortable shoes and make use of the cloakrooms. Be aware that standing still and walking slowly promote tiredness; sit down as often as you can. Reflecting on the material and forming associations with it causes information to move from your short- to long-term memory; your experiences will thus amount to more than a series of visual 'bites'.

Tracking and timing studies suggest that museum-goers spend no more than 10 seconds viewing an exhibit and another 10 seconds reading the label as they try to take in as much as they can before succumbing to exhaustion. To avoid this, choose a particular period or section to focus on, or join a guided tour of the highlights. And use the catering facilities – the restaurant, café and/or snack bar – that every museum has for a bit of well-earned R&R and sustenance.

PLETZL

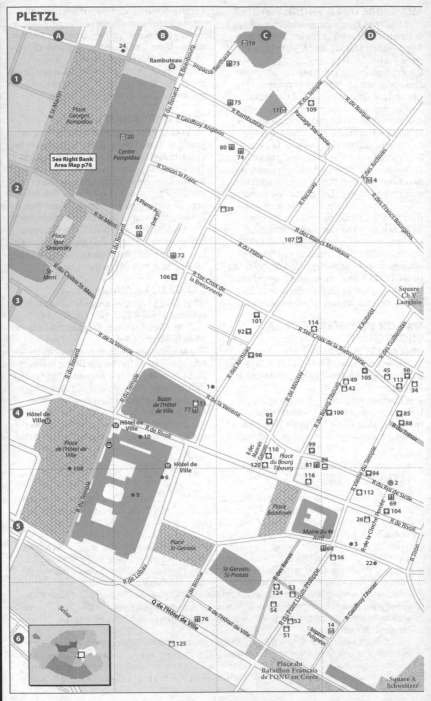

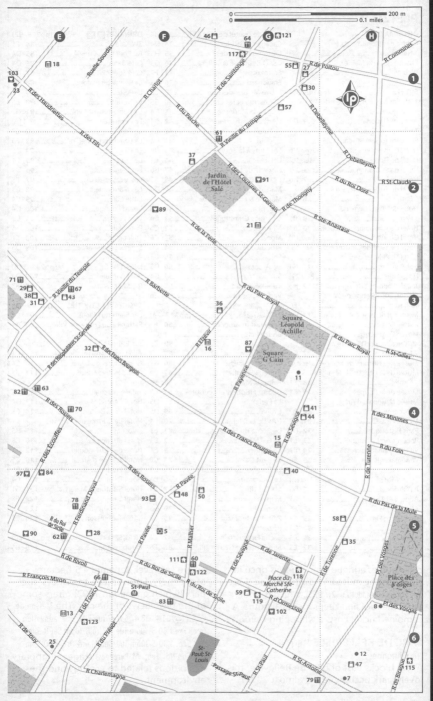

E   F   G   121   H

18
103
23
R des Haudriettes
Ruelle Sourds
R Charlot
R de Saintonge
R du Perche
46
64
117
55   27
30
R de Poitou
R Commines
R Debelleyme
R St-Claude
57
61
R Vieille du Temple
R des Coutures St-Gervais
37
Jardin de l'Hôtel Salé
91
R de Thorigny
R du Roi Doré
R Debelleyme
89
R de la Perle
21
R Ste-Anastase
R Ste-Anastase

71
29
38
31
R Vieille du Temple
67
43
R Barbette
R du Parc Royal
36
Square Léopold Achille
R du Parc Royal
R St-Gilles
32
R des Blancs Manteaux
R des Francs Bourgeois
R Elzévir
16
87
Square G Cain
R Payenne
11
82
63
70
R des Rosiers
R de Sévigné
41
44
R des Minimes
R des Écouffes
R des Francs Bourgeois
15
R du Foin
R de Turenne
97
84
R des Rosiers
R Pavée
40
R du Pas de la Mule
78
R Ferdinand Duval
93
48
50
58
R du Roi de Sicile
R Pavée
5
R Malher
R de Sévigné
R de Turenne
35
90
62
28
111
60
122
R de Tarente
Pl des Vosges
R de Rivoli
R du Roi de Sicile
118
Place du Marché Ste-Catherine
Place des Vosges
R François Miron
66
St-Paul
83
59
119
R d'Ormesson
8
Pl des Vosges
13
123
R de Foucy
102
R de Jouy
25
R du Prévôt
St-Paul-St-Louis
12
47
115
R Charlemagne
Passage St-Paul
R St-Paul
R St-Antoine
79
7
R de Birague

NEIGHBOURHOODS   MARAIS & MÉNILMONTANT

PLETZL

INFORMATION
Centre des Monuments
  Nationaux ....(see 7)
Pharmacie de la Mairie 1 B4
Web 46...2 D5

SIGHTS   (pp145–55)
16th-Century Half-Timbered
  Houses......................................3 D5
Archives Nationales 4 D2
Art Nouveau Synagogue 5 F5
Entrance to Sale St-Jean..................6 B5
Hôtel Carnavalet.......................(see 15)
Hôtel de Donon.........................(see 16)
Hôtel de St-Aignan ....(see 17)
Hôtel de Sully.............................7 H6
Hôtel de Sully (Courtyard
  Entrance)...................................8 H6
Hôtel de Ville (Mairie de
  Paris)...9 B5
Hotel de Ville Salon d'Accueil 10 B4
Hôtel Guénégaud ....(see 18)
Hôtel Hénault de Cantorbe .... (see 13)
Hôtel Le Peletier de
  St-Fargeau 11 G4
Hôtel Salé ....(see 21)
Jeu de Paume - Site Sully............ 12 H6
Maison Européenne de la
  Photographie 13 E6
Mémorial de la Shoah 14 D6
Musée Carnavalet..................... 15 G4
Musée Cognacq-Jay 16 F3
Musée d'Art et d'Histoire du
  Judaïsme 17 C1
Musée de l'Histoire de France ..... (see 4)
Musée de la Chasse et de la
  Nature................................... 18 E1
Musée de la Poupée 19 C1
Musée Nationale d'Art
  Moderne 20 B2
Musée Picasso 21 G2
Paris Historique 22 D5
Robert Combas Mural 23 E1
Vit'Halles Beaubourg 24 B1
Winemaker Relief 25 E6

SHOPPING   (pp191–212)
A l'Olivier................................. 26 D5
Abou d'Abi Bazar 27 G1
Alternatives 28 E5
Antoine et Lili.......................... 29 E3
APC 30 G1
Bains Plus................................. 31 E3
Barbara Bui............................... 32 E3

Bazar de l'Hôtel de Ville (BHV)......33 B4
Cacao et Chocolat......................34 D4
Clothing Boutiques....................35 H5
CSAO Boutique & Gallery...........36 G3
Erotokritos 37 F2
Fragonard 38 E3
I Love My Blender.......................39 C2
La Charrue et les Étoiles.............40 G5
L'Agenda Moderne 41 G4
L'Artisan Parfumeur 42 D4
Le Palais des Thés......................43 E3
L'Éclaireur................................44 G4
Les Mots à la Bouche.................45 D4
L'Habilleur................................46 F1
Librairie de l'Hôtel de Sully........47 H6
L'Ours du Marais.......................48 F5
Mariage Frères..........................49 D4
Marithé & François Girbaud
  Branch....................................50 F5
Mélodies Graphiques.................51 C6
Mi Amor...................................52 C6
Monastica.................................53 C6
Produits des Monastères............54 C6
Shine 55 G1
Sic Amor 56 D5
Surface to Air 57 G1
Tumbleweed 58 H5
Vert d'Absinthe.........................59 G6

EATING   (pp213–74)
Breakfast in America..................60 F5
Breizh Café................................61 G2
Caffé Boboli..............................62 E5
Chez Marianne 63 E4
Chez Nénesse............................64 G1
Curieux Spaghetti......................65 B2
Franprix Marais..........................66 E5
Georget (Robert et Louise)..........67 E3
La Perla.....................................68 D5
L'Alivi......................................69 D5
L'As de Felafel 70 E4
Le Dôme du Marais 71 E3
Le Gai Moulin 72 B3
Le Hangar 73 C1
Le Petit Dakar 74 C2
Le Potager du Marais 75 C1
Le Trumilou 76 B6
Ma Cantine 77 B4
Maison Marais...........................78 E5
Monoprix..................................79 G6
Pain, Vin, Fromage....................80 C2
Pozzetto...................................81 C4
Sacha Finkelsztajn.....................82 E4
Supermarché G20 Bastille..........83 F6

DRINKING   (pp275–92)
3W Kafé...................................84 E5
Au Petit Fer à Cheval.................85 D4
Café Baroc 86 D4
Café Suédois.............................87 G3
La Chaise au Plafond..................88 D4
La Perle 89 F2
La Tartine 90 E5
L'Apparement Café 91 G2
Le Central Bar ....(see 113)
Le Cox.....................................92 C3
Le Loir dans la Théière 93 F5
Le Pick Clops 94 D5
Le Quetzal 95 C4
Les Étages................................96 C4
Les Jacasses 97 E5
Les Marronniers 98 C3
Little Café.................................99 C4
Lizard Lounge........................100 D4
Open Café..............................101 C3
Pure Malt...............................102 G6
Quiet Man..............................103 E1
Stolly's Stone Bar....................104 D5

NIGHTLIFE   (pp293–308)
Point Virgule 105 D4
Raidd Bar................................106 B3

SPORTS & ACTIVITIES   (pp309–16)
Les Bains du Marais..................107 C2
Patinoire de l'Hôtel de Ville.......108 A4

SLEEPING   (pp323–51)
Allô Logement Temporaire........109 C1
Grand Hôtel du Loiret...............110 C4
Grand Hôtel Malher..................111 F5
Hôtel Caron de
  Beaumarchais........................112 D5
Hôtel Central Marais 113 D4
Hôtel de la Bretonnerie 114 C3
Hôtel de la Place des
  Vosges...................................115 H6
Hôtel de Nice 116 C5
Hôtel du Petit Moulin................117 G1
Hôtel Jeanne d'Arc 118 G5
Hôtel Pratic 119 G6
Hôtel Rivoli 120 C4
Hôtel Saintonge Marais 121 G1
Hôtel Sévigné 122 F5
MIJE Le Fourcy........................123 E6
MIJE Maubuisson 124 C6

TRANSPORT   (pp383–90)
Batobus Stop...........................125 B6

collection of antique wind-up toys once included in the museum now forms the Musée
des Automates (adult/3-12yr €6/5), which is under
the same roof and keeps identical hours. A
combined ticket costs a whopping €12/9.

PARC DE BELLEVILLE Map p148
Ⓜ **Couronnes**
A few blocks east of blvd de Belleville, this
lovely park occupies a hill almost 200m

above sea level, set amid 4.5 hectares
of greenery. Little known to visitors, the
park (which opened in 1992) offers some
of the best views of the city. The Maison de
l'Air (☎ 01 43 28 47 63; 27 rue Piat, 20e; admission
free; ⏱ 1.30-5.30pm Tue-Fri, to 6.30pm Sat & Sun
Apr-Sep, 1.30-5.30pm Tue-Sun Mar & Oct, 1.30-5pm
Tue-Sun Nov-Feb; Ⓜ Pyrénées) stages temporary
exhibitions related to ecology and the
environment.

GRAVE CONCERNS AT PÈRE LACHAISE

Camp as a row of tents and as fresh as tomorrow, Oscar Wilde (1854–1900) is apparently as flamboyant in death as he was on his deathbed in what is now L'Hôtel (p333), when he proclaimed: 'My wallpaper and I are fighting a duel to the death – one of us has *got* to go.' It seems that the Père Lachaise grave of the Irish playwright and humorist, who was sentenced to two years in prison in 1895 for gross indecency stemming from his homosexual relationship with Lord Alfred 'Bosie' Douglas (1870–1945), has been attracting admirers, who plaster the ornate tomb with indelible lipstick kisses.

But Wilde's tomb is not the only grave concern at Père Lachaise these days. A security guard had to be posted near the grave of rock singer Jim Morrison (1943–71) not long ago after fans began taking drugs and having sex on his tomb. The cemetery's conservation office has even issued a leaflet outlining the rules of conduct when visiting the grave. Meanwhile, up in division 92, a protest by women a few years back saw the removal of a metal fence placed around the grave of one Victor Noir, pseudonym of the journalist Yvan Salman (1848–70), who was shot and killed by Pierre Bonaparte, great-nephew of Napoleon, at the age of just 22. According to legend, a woman who strokes the amply filled crotch of Monsieur Noir's prostrate bronze effigy will enjoy a better sex life or even become pregnant. Apparently some would-be lovers and mothers were rubbing a bit too enthusiastically and the larger-than-life-size package was being worn down.

MUSÉE ÉDITH PIAF Map p148

☎ 01 43 55 52 72; 5 rue Crespin du Gast, 11e; admission free; ⏰ by appointment 1-6pm Mon-Wed, 10am-noon Thu; Ⓜ Ménilmontant

Some 1.5km from the birthplace of the iconic *chanteuse* (singer) Édith Piaf (see p304) and closer to her final resting place in the Cimetière du Père Lachaise, this museum follows the life and career of the 'urchin sparrow' through memorabilia, recordings, personal objects, letters and other documentation. Book at least a week in advance.

CIMETIÈRE DU PÈRE LACHAISE

Map p148

☎ 01 55 25 82 10; www.pere-lachaise.com; ⏰ 8am-6pm Mon-Fri, 8.30am-6pm Sat, 9am-6pm Sun mid-Mar–early Nov, 8am-5.30pm Mon-Fri, 8.30am-5.30pm Sat, 9am-5.30pm Sun early Nov–mid-Mar; Ⓜ Philippe Auguste, Gambetta or Père Lachaise

The world's most visited cemetery, Père Lachaise (named after a confessor of Louis XIV) opened its one-way doors in 1804. Its 69,000 ornate, even ostentatious, tombs of the rich and/or famous form a verdant, 44-hectare sculpture garden. Among the 800,000 people buried here are: the composer Chopin; the playwright Molière; the poet Apollinaire; writers Balzac, Proust, Gertrude Stein and Colette; the actors

Simone Signoret, Sarah Bernhardt and Yves Montand; the painters Pissarro, Seurat, Modigliani and Delacroix; the *chanteuse* Édith Piaf; the dancer Isadora Duncan; and even those immortal 12th-century lovers, Abélard and Héloïse (see p27), whose remains were disinterred and reburied here together in 1817 beneath a neo-Gothic tombstone.

Particularly visited graves are those of Oscar Wilde, interred in division 89 in 1900, and 1960s rock star Jim Morrison, who died in a flat at 17-19 rue Beautreillis (4e; Map p148) in the Marais in 1971 and is buried in division 6.

On 27 May 1871, the last of the Communard insurgents, cornered by government forces, fought a hopeless, all-night battle among the tombstones. In the morning, the 147 survivors were lined up against the Mur des Fédérés (Wall of the Federalists), shot and buried where they fell in a mass grave. It is in the southeastern section of the cemetery.

Père Lachaise has five entrances, two of which are on blvd de Ménilmontant. Maps indicating the location of noteworthy graves are available for free from the conservation office (☎ 01 55 25 82 10; 16 rue du Repos, 20e) in the southwestern corner of the cemetery. Organised tours (adult/concession €6/3; ⏰ 2.30pm Sat Mar-Nov) in French depart from here.

Drinking p289; Eating p261; Shopping p210; Sleeping p347

After years as a run-down immigrant neighbourhood notorious for its high crime rate, the Bastille area has undergone a fair degree of gentrification, which started with the advent of the Opéra de Paris Bastille more than two decades ago. The courtyards and alleyways of the 11e arrondissement used to belong to artisans and labourers; the areas around rue du Faubourg St-Antoine, rue de Charonne and rue de la Roquette buzzed with the sound of cabinet makers, joiners, gilders and the like at work. Today most of that's gone, replaced with artists and their lofts. But the old spirit lives on in some hidden parts of the 11e, and the areas to the east of place de la Bastille in particular retain their lively atmosphere and ethnicity.

The southern part of the 12e arrondissement is a fairly well-to-do *quartier*, and at the weekend hordes of cyclists and football players head for the woods of the Bois de Vincennes. Walkers can stroll along the Promenade Plantée, a path along the viaduct above av Daumesnil. Within the arches, there are upmarket shops, galleries and cafés. On the other side of the Gare de Lyon, there's the Parc de Bercy, where an orchard, vegetable patch and garden have replaced the old wine market.

Long cut off from the rest of the city but now joined to the Left Bank by the driverless Météor metro line (number 14), the vehicular Pont Charles de Gaulle and the stunning Passerelle Simone de Beauvoir footbridge linking Parc de Bercy with the Bibliothèque National de France, Bercy has some of Paris' most important contemporary buildings, including Palais Omnisports de Paris–Bercy, serving as both an indoor sports arena and a venue for concerts, ballet and theatre; the giant Ministère de l'Économie, des Finances et de l'Industrie; and the stunning Cinémathèque Française. Across the river is the new architecture of the redeveloped Masséna Nord warehouse district (p60). The development of Bercy Village, a row of former *chais* (wine warehouses) dating from 1877 that now houses bars and restaurants, and the arrival of river barges fitted out with music clubs have given the 12e a new lease of life after dark.

Metro stations useful for Bastille are, of course, Bastille as well as Charonne, Faidherbe Chaligny, Ledru Rollin and Voltaire. For the Gare de Lyon area and Bercy they are Bercy, Cour St-Émilion, Daumesnil, Gare de Lyon and Nation. Useful bus routes include the 86 from Bastille to Ledru Rollin, Nation and the Bois de Vincennes; the 65 from Gare de Lyon to Bastille, République, Gare de l'Est and Gare du Nord (via rue du Faubourg St-Denis); and the 24 from rue de Bercy for quai St Bernard, blvd St-Michel, Pont Neuf, quai du Louvre, place de la Madeleine and place de la Concorde.

top picks

BASTILLE & GARE DE LYON

- Opéra de Paris Bastille (p157) One of the late President François Mitterrand's grandest and most enduring *grands projects*.
- Cinémathèque Française (p161) A veritable temple to film in a land where the medium is considered to be the '7th art'.
- Cité Nationale de l'Histoire de L'Immigration (p156) Poignant look at the people who have built modern Paris and, by extension, France.
- Viaduc des Arts (p157) A wonderful place for a walk, a browse and maybe even a shop.

PLACE DE LA BASTILLE Map p158

Ⓜ **Bastille**

The Bastille, built during the 14th century as a fortified royal residence, is the most famous monument in Paris that no longer exists. The notorious prison – the quintessential symbol of royal despotism – was demolished shortly after a mob stormed it on 14 July 1789 and freed a total of just seven prisoners. The site where it once stood, place de la Bastille (11e and 12e),

is now a very large and very busy traffic roundabout.

In the centre of the square is the 52m-high Colonne de Juillet (July Column), whose shaft of greenish bronze is topped by a gilded and winged figure of Liberty. It was erected in 1833 as a memorial to those killed in the street battles that accompanied the July Revolution of 1830 (p30) – they are buried in vaults under the column – and was later consecrated as a memorial to the victims of the February Revolution of 1848.

OPÉRA DE PARIS BASTILLE Map p158

☎ 0 892 899 090; www.opera-de-paris.fr; 2-6 place de la Bastille, 12e; Ⓜ Bastille
Paris' giant 'second' opera house, but in fact its main one nowadays, was designed by the Uruguayan architect Carlos Ott and inaugurated on 14 July 1989, the 200th anniversary of the storming of the Bastille. It has three theatres, including the main auditorium with around 2700 seats, all of which have an unrestricted view of the stage. There are 1¼-hour guided tours (☎ 01 40 01 19 70; adult/under 10yr/senior, student & 10-25yr €11/6/9) of the building, which depart at wildly different times depending on the week and the season. Check the website or phone the box office for departure times. Tickets go on sale just 10 minutes before departure at the box office (☎ 0 892 899 090; 130 rue de Lyon, 12e; ☼ 10.30am-6.30pm Mon-Sat).

MUSÉE DU FUMEUR Map p158

☎ 01 46 59 05 51; www.museedufumeur.net; 7 rue Pache, 11e; adult/senior & student €5/3; ☼ 12.30-7pm Tue-Sat; Ⓜ Voltaire
The Smoker's Museum traces the history of one of mankind's greatest vices: the smoking of tobacco. Hard-core butt-fiends will feel vindicated, though the museum takes an impartial stance, providing (as it states on entry) 'a vantage point for the observation of changing behaviours'. Done up as an old tobacco warehouse, the museum

has a wonderful collection of portraits as well as a superb book- and gift shop.

ÉGLISE NOTRE DAME DE L'ESPÉRANCE Map p158

☎ 01 40 21 49 39; 47 rue de la Roquette, 11e; ☼ 9am-5pm; Ⓜ Bastille
If you're in the area (or feeling a bit guilty about that late night) head for the wonderful Church of Our Lady of Hope designed by Bruno Legrand in 1997. Startling both for its modern design and size (it stands 20m tall and is 11m wide), the interior is filled with all sorts of interesting elements and features, including Nicolas Alquin's *La Croix d'Espérance* (Cross of Hope) made of an 18th-century oak beam and three gold squares representing the Trinity, and calligrapher Franck Lalou's fragments of the Scriptures etched onto glass of the facade facing rue de la Roquette.

VIADUC DES ARTS Map p158

Ⓜ Gare de Lyon or Daumesnil
The arches beneath this disused railway viaduct running along av Daumesnil southeast of place de la Bastille are a showcase for both designers and artisans; if you need your Gobelins tapestry restored, porcelain repainted or the bottom of your antique saucepan re-coppered, this is the place to come. The top of the viaduct forms a leafy, 4.5km-long promenade called the Promenade Plantée (Map p158; ☼ 8am-sunset Mon-Fri, from 9am Sat & Sun), which offers excellent views of the surrounding area. Don't miss the spectacular Art Deco police station (Map p158; 78 av Daumesnil,

STEVE'S TOP PARIS DAY

If it's Sunday morning and this is Paris, I'm going to sacrifice my 'greasy morning' (*grasse matinée;* a lie-in) and get myself to the closest *marché découvert* (open-air market), which, seeing as I'm staying with my best *copine* at her *belle époque* flat near place de la République, is Marché Bastille (p222), a hop, skip and four metro stops south on the orange (No 5) or purple (No 8) line. I've just realised I'm fresh out of essentials like truffle oil and those huge Breton *tourteaux* (crabs) that taste of the very sea itself and I must stock up. Having made my purchases, I'll no longer be in such a hurry so I'll wend my way through medieval Marais, stopping for a *grand crème* (coffee with cream) and a *pain au chocolat* (chocolate brioche) at Café Hugo (p258) in the scrumptious place des Vosges. The landmark bridge Pont de Sully leads to my favourite island, Île St-Louis, but once I reach the Île de la Cité, I'll eschew Notre Dame in favour of the smaller, more delicate Ste-Chapelle (p97) and its stunning stained glass. Before lunch (somewhere on the rue Montorgueil) I'll window-shop at the boutiques of rue Étienne Marcel or have another look at the antique clothes for sale in the Galerie de Montpensier (p182). Though close by, the Louvre is just too daunting for a postprandial visit; instead I'll hop on a Vélib' and cruise along the car-free (it's Sunday!) banks of the Seine. If I feel culturally peckish, I'll make my way to the Musée Guimet (p157) and have a Zen-like kip in the annexe's peaceful Japanese garden. As far as I'm concerned, any corner café works for an *apéro* (sundowner), but since I'm in the neighbourhood, I'll walk down to the Palais de Chaillot for a pastis (aniseed-flavoured aperitif) at the incomparable Café de l'Homme (p238) and its views.

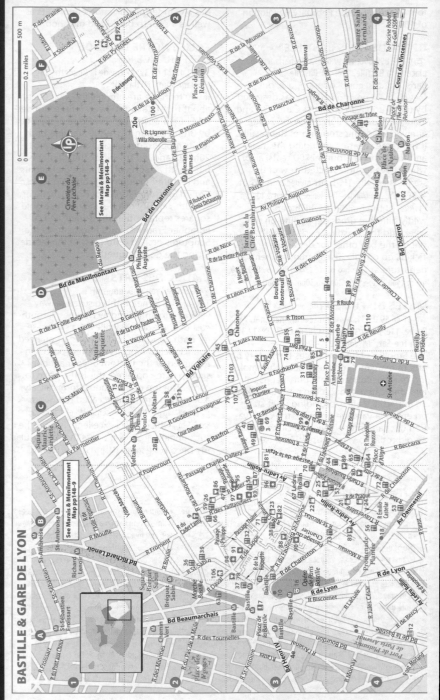

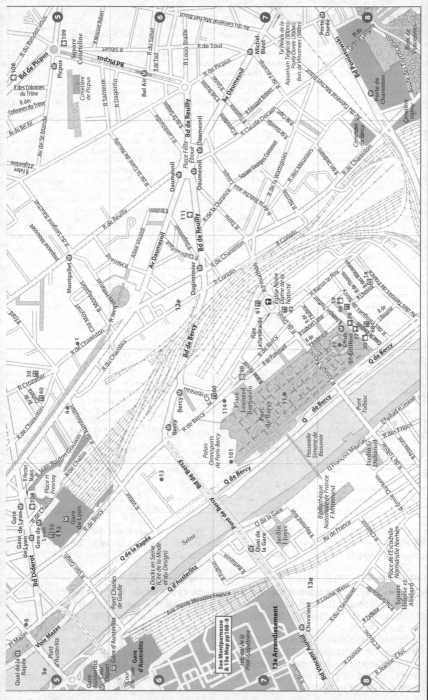

BASTILLE & GARE DE LYON

INFORMATION
La Maison des Femmes de Paris.... 1 D5
Paris Convention & Visitors
  Bureau........................... 2 B5
Phon'net............................ 3 C3

SIGHTS pp156–62
Art Deco Police Station............ 4 C5
Bibliothèque du Film...........(see 98)
Centre Kapla....................... 5 D4
Children's Playground.............. 6 A4
Cinémathèque Française..........(see 98)
Colonne de Juillet................. 7 A3
Direction de l'Action Sociale
  Building......................... 8 A5
Église Nore Dame de
  l'Espérance...................... 9 B2
Entrance to Opéra Bastille........10 A3
Maison du Jardinage...............11 C7
Maison Rouge......................12 A4
Ministère de l'Économie, de
  l'Industrie et de l'Emploi......13 B6
Musée des Arts Forains............14 D8
Musée du Fumeur...................15 C1
Opéra Bastille Box Office.........16 A3
Pavillon du Lac du Parc de
  Bercy............................17 D8
Promenade Plantée.................18 B4
Viaduc des Arts................(see 18)

SHOPPING pp191–212
Album.............................19 D8
Bercy Village.....................20 D8
Chemins de Bretagne...............21 B4
Fermob............................22 B3
Isabel Marant.....................23 B3
La Maison du Cerf-Volant..........24 B4
Marché aux Puces d'Aligre......(see 64)
Première Pression Provence........25 B3
Rue Keller........................26 B2
Viaduc des Arts................(see 18)

EATING pp213–74
À La Banane Ivoirienne............27 C3
À la Renaissance..................28 C2
Agua Limón........................29 B3
Athanor...........................30 C5
Au Vieux Chêne....................31 C3
Bistrot Les Sans Culottes.........32 B3
Bistrot Paul Bert.................33 D3

Boulangerie Bazin.................34 B3
Café de L'Industrie...............35 B2
Café de L'Industrie Annexe........36 B2
Chez Heang........................37 A3
Chez Paul.........................38 B3
Chez Ramulaud.....................39 D4
Comme Cochons.....................40 C5
Crêperie Bretonne Fleurie de
  l'Épouse du Marin...............41 C3
Franprix..........................42 B3
Khun Akorn........................43 E4
La Gazzetta.......................44 C4
La Muse Vin.......................45 D2
La Partie de Campagne.............46 D8
La Plancha........................47 B2
L'Autre Boulange..................48 D4
Le Mouton Noir....................49 C3
Le Souk...........................50 B3
Le Square Trousseau...............51 B4
Le Train Bleu.....................52 B4
Le Viaduc Café....................53 B4
L'Ébauchoir.......................54 C4
L'Écailler du Bistro..............55 D3
L'Encrier.........................56 B4
Les Amis de Messina...............57 D4
Les Domaines qui Montent..........58 C2
Les Galopins......................59 B2
Les Grandes Marches...........(see 10)
Lina's............................60 C7
L'Oulette.........................61 D7
Mansouria.........................62 C3
Marché Bastille...................63 A2
Marché Couvert Beauvau............64 C4
Moisan............................65 C4
Monop'............................66 B3
Monoprix Bastille.................67 B3
Nicolas...........................68 D8
Paris Hanoi.......................69 C3
Paris Main d'Or...................70 B3
Patati Patata.....................71 B3
Sardegna a Tavola.................72 B4
Swann et Vincent..................73 B4
Unico.............................74 D3
Waly Fay..........................75 C3

DRINKING pp275–92
Chai 33...........................76 D8
Frog at Bercy Village.............77 D8
Iguana Café.......................78 B3
La Liberté........................79 C4

Le Baron Rouge....................80 B4
Le Bistrot du Peintre.............81 C3
Le Café du Passage................82 B3
Le China..........................83 B4
Le Pure Café......................84 C3
Les Funambules....................85 C3
L'Interface.......................86 B2
Pause Café........................87 B3
Sanz Sans.........................88 B3
Troll Café........................89 B4

NIGHTLIFE pp293–308
Barrio Latino.....................90 B3
La Chapelle des Lombards..........91 B3
La Flèche d'Or....................92 F1
La Scène Bastille.................93 B3
Le Balajo.........................94 B3
Le Keller.........................95 B3
Le Motel..........................96 B3
Les Disquaires....................97 B3

THE ARTS pp293–308
Cinémathèque Française............98 C7

SPORTS & ACTIVITIES pp309–16
Candie............................99 C3
Club Med Gym.....................100 F2
Palais Omnisports de
  Paris-Bercy....................101 C7
Patinoire Sonja Henie.........(see 101)
Vit'halles Nation................102 E4

SLEEPING pp323–51
BLC Design Hotel.................103 C3
Hostel Blue Planet...............104 B3
Hôtel Candide....................105 C2
Hôtel Daval......................106 B2
Hôtel des Arts...................107 C3
Hôtel du Printemps...............108 F5
Hôtel Le Cosy....................109 F5
Hôtel Les Sans Culottes.......(see 32)
Le Quartier Bastille Le
  Faubourg.......................110 D4
Le Quartier Bercy Square.........111 E6
Les Sans Culottes.............(see 32)
Mama Shelter.....................112 F1

TRANSPORT pp383–90
Free Scoot.......................113 C2
Rent a Car Système...............114 C7

12e) at the start of rue de Rambouillet, which is topped with a dozen huge, identical marble caryatids.

MAISON ROUGE Map p158

☎ 01 40 01 08 81; www.lamaisonrouge.org; 10 blvd de la Bastille, 12e; adult/student, senior & 13-18yr €7/5; ☼ 11am-7pm Wed-Sun, to 9pm Thu; Ⓜ Quai de Rapée

Subtitled 'Fondation Antoine de Galbert' after the man who endowed it, this cutting-edge gallery shows contemporary artists and has good access to seldom-seen works from private collections. There's a decent restaurant here open during museum hours and for lunch on Tuesday. Sunday brunch costs €24.

PARC DE BERCY Map p158

rue Paul Belmondo, 12e; ☼ 8am-sunset Mon-Fri, from 9am Sat & Sun; Ⓜ Bercy or Cour St-Émilion

This park, which links the Palais Omnisports with Bercy Village, is a particularly attractive, 13.5-hectare public garden. On an island in the centre of one of its large ponds is the Pavillon du Lac du Parc de Bercy (☎ 01 71 28 50 56; 1 rue François Truffaut, 12e; ☼ 10am-6pm

WORTH THE TRIP: BOIS DE VINCENNES

Paris' green lung to the southeast, the Bois de Vincennes (Map p158; blvd Poniatowski, 12e; Porte de Charenton or Porte Dorée) encompasses 995 hectares of woods, parkland and important sites, most of them just outside the blvd Périphérique (ring road). On the wood's northern edge, Château de Vincennes (Palace of Vincennes; ☎ 01 48 08 31 20; www.chateau-vincennes.fr; av de Paris, 12e; ☼ 10am-6pm Apr-Oct, to 5pm Nov-Mar; M Château de Vincennes) is a bona fide royal chateau with massive fortifications and a moat. The chateau grounds can be strolled free of charge; the 52m-high dungeon (1369), a prison during the 17th and 18th centuries, and the Gothic Chapelle Royale (Royal Chapel), which has just emerged from a massive facelift, can be visited on a guided tour (adult/18-25yr/EU resident under 26 & everyone under 18yr €8/6/free; call ahead for tour times) or a self-paced audioguide tour (adult/2 sharing €4/6.50), available at the crypt ticket kiosk.

South of the Château de Vincennes is the Parc Floral de Paris (☎ 01 49 57 24 84; www.parcfloraldeparis.com; Esplanade du Chateau de Vincennes & rte de la Pyramide, 12e; adult/7-18yr €3/1.50; ☼ 9.30am-8pm, to 5pm winter; M Château de Vincennes), a vast green floral area with a butterfly garden, nature library and kids' play areas; it's host to some quite magical open-air concerts in summer.

The 15-hectare Parc Zoologique de Paris (☎ 01 44 75 20 10; www.mnhn.fr; 53 av de St-Maurice, 12e; ☼ 9am-6.30pm, to 5pm winter; M Porte Dorée), also known as the Zoo de Vincennes and home to some 600 animals, was undergoing a major renovation at the time of research.

Apr-Sep, 11am-5pm Oct-Mar), with temporary exhibitions and conferences. The Maison du Jardinage (☎ 01 53 46 19 19; 41 rue Paul Belmondo, 12e; admission free; ☼ 1.30-5.30pm Tue-Fri, to 6.30pm Sat & Sun Apr-Sep, 1.30-5.30pm Tue-Sun Mar & Oct, 1.30-5pm Tue-Sun Nov-Feb) in the centre of the park takes a close look at gardening and the environment.

CINÉMATHÈQUE FRANÇAISE
Map p158

☎ 01 71 19 33 33; www.cinemathequefrancaise.com; 51 rue de Bercy, 12e; permanent collection adult/under 12yr/senior & 12-26yr €5/2.50/4, temporary exhibitions €7/3.50/6; ☼ noon-7pm Mon, Wed, Fri & Sat, to 10pm Thu, 10am-10pm Sun; M Bercy
This national institution, better known for screening classic French and cutting-edge foreign films, is housed in stunning postmodern premises with plenty of exhibition space for its permanent collection and temporary exhibitions. It also houses screening rooms, the Bibliothèque du Film (Film Library; ☎ 01 71 19 32 32; ☼ 10am-7pm Mon-Fri, 1-6.30pm Sat) for researchers and an excellent specialist bookshop. Enter from place Leonard Bernstein.

MUSÉE DES ARTS FORAINS Map p158

☎ 01 43 40 16 15; www.pavillons-de-bercy.com; Les Pavillons de Bercy, 53 av des Terroirs de France, 12e; adult/child €12.50/4; ☼ by appointment; M Cour St-Émilion
The Museum of the Fairground Art, housed in three old wine warehouses in Bercy

Village, is a wonderful collection of old amusements from 19th-century funfairs including carousels, organs and stalls. Most of the items still function and are pure works of art. The place is usually rented only out for corporate events with minimum numbers but phone or visit the website and try your luck. The tour lasts 1½ hours.

PALAIS DE LA PORTE DORÉE
Off Map p158

☎ 01 53 59 58 60; 293 av Daumesnil, 12e; ☼ 10am-5.30pm Tue-Fri, to 7pm Sat & Sun; M Porte Dorée
Built as part of the Exposition Coloniale Internationale of 1931 when all seemed right with the world at home and abroad, the lavish 'Palace of the Golden Door', which retains some delightful Art Deco elements including frescoes of the peoples of the world, today houses two major attractions.

The Cité Nationale de l'Histoire de l'Immigration (www.histoire-immigration.fr, in French; adult/18-26yr/EU resident under 26 & everyone under 18yr during exhibitions periods €5/3.50/free, non-exhibition periods €3/2/free), on the building's mezzanine and 1st floors, is not a museum to visit for a spot of light relief. A heavyweight, it documents the hot-potato topic of immigration to France through a series of informative historical displays that cover groups as diverse as the Vietnamese, Portuguese, Jews and Russians. The multimedia permanent collection called Repères (Landmarks) and the gallery of personal items given by members of the public are emotive and informative. Fine temporary exhibitions look at such topics as the *maghrébin* (North African) experience in France and the strengths, weaknesses and life expectancy of mothers, languages of immigrants, and their descendants.

Fish and sea creatures from around the globe swim in circular tanks spread throughout the Aquarium Tropical (www.aquarium-portedoree. fr; adult/14-26yr/family €6.50/5/8) in the lower ground floor of the Palais de la Porte Dorée. It too was established in 1931 and is a venue for both teaching and recreation; watch out for those schools groups on Wednesdays.

PLACE D'ITALIE & CHINATOWN

Drinking p290; Eating p268; Sleeping p349

Serious change is afoot in the 13e arrondissement, a once nondescript area south of the Latin Quarter and Jardin des Plantes (5e) that spirals out from big busy traffic hub Place d'Italie. The area's renaissance was heralded in the 1990s by the controversial Bibliothèque Nationale de France and by the arrival of the high-speed Météor metro line, and is slated not to stop until 2015 (when the 26-year ZAC Paris Rive Gauche redevelopment project – see www.parisrive gauche.com – ends).

A glamorous strip of interior-design shops now fronts riverside Quai de la Gare immediately north of the National Library and MK2 entertainment complex (p306). Then there's the swimming pool on the Seine (p314) that floats not quite in the shade of the latest designer bridge to grace the river, the Passerelle Simone de Beauvoir (2006) – across which Right Bank night owls from Bercy hotfoot it to a trio of music venues moored in front of the library.

Cutting-edge architecture and design is one face of the 13e, a working-class district that will never lose its feisty spirit and down-to-earth grit. A place proud of its history, it has both a blvd Auguste Blanqui and place Nationale, a pairing propitious to the reconciliation between anarchism and patriotism.

Flit from Chinese restaurant to Vietnamese stall in the capital's Chinatown, the area between av d'Italie and av de Choisy, and you feel you've imperceptibly changed continents. Or trip past the graffiti-covered facade of Les Frigos and you could be in Berlin. In the Butte aux Cailles *quartier*, the jewel in this arrondissement's crown, people still sing revolutionary songs from the time of the Paris Commune over chichi cuisine.

Bibliothèque (for the library area) and Place d'Italie (for Butte auc Cailles) are the main stops on the metro line for this neck of the woods. Bus 62 from the Bibliothèque Nationale de France François Mitterrand crosses the 13e along rue Tolbiac to rue d'Alésia (14e) and rue de la Convention (15e). Pick up the 47 to place d'Italie, rue Monge, quai St Michel, Hôtel de Ville and Gare de l'Est from Port d'Italie; and the 67 to Mosquée de Paris, Jardin des Plantes, Île de St-Louis, Hôtel de Ville and Pigalle from place d'Italie. The 83 to Jardin de Luxembourg, St-Germain and Invalides also leaves place d'Italie.

BIBLIOTHÈQUE NATIONALE DE FRANCE Map p164

☎ 01 53 79 53 79, 01 53 79 40 41; www.bnf.fr; 11 quai François Mauriac, 13e; temporary exhibitions adult/18-26yr from €7/5; ☺ 10am-7pm Tue-Sat, 1-7pm Sun; Ⓜ Bibliothèque

The four glass towers of the €2 billion National Library of France – conceived as a 'wonder of the modern world' – opened in 1995. No expense was spared to carry out a plan that many said defied logic. While books and historical documents are shelved in the sunny, 23-storey and 79m-high towers (shaped like half-open books), patrons sit in artificially lit basement halls built around a 'forest courtyard' of 140 50-year-old pines, trucked in from the countryside. The towers have since been fitted with a complex (and expensive) shutter system and the basement is prone to flooding from the Seine. The national library contains around 12 million tomes stored on some 420km of shelves and can hold 2000 readers and 2000 researchers. Temporary exhibitions (entrance E) revolve around 'the word', focusing on everything from storytelling to bookbinding and French heroes.

MUSÉE NATIONAL DU SPORT
Map p164

☎ 01 45 83 15 80; www.museedusport.fr; 93 av du France, 13e; adult/18-26yr €4/2, 1st Sun of month free; ☺ 10am-6pm Tue-Fri, 2-6pm Sat & Sun; Ⓜ Bibliothèque

A 2010 addition to this increasingly happening arrondissement, Paris' National Museum of Sports covers just that: football, tennis, the Tour de France or polo ... you name it, there is sporting paraphernalia to match in this modern space with bags of kid appeal. Ogle at skis used by triple gold medallist and 1968 French skiing legend Jean-Claude Killy; see the prototype motorcycle with three wheels used by Jean Naud to bike from Paris to Timbuktu in 1986; or sign the kids up for a 'how to be a sports commentator' or Olympic Games workshop (€5).

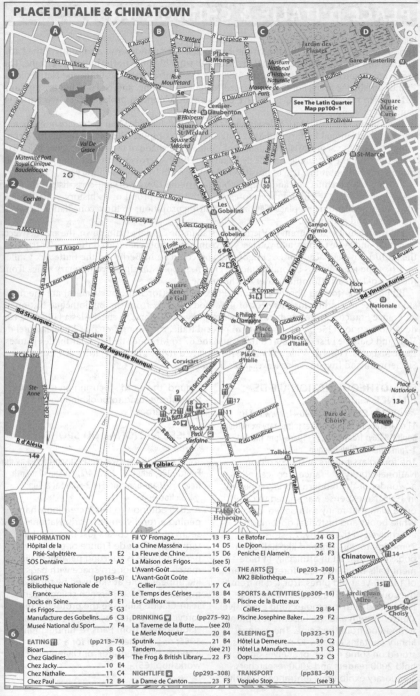

INFORMATION		
Hôpital de la		
Pitié-Salpêtrière	1	E2
SOS Dentaire	2	A2

SIGHTS	(pp163–6)	
Bibliothèque Nationale de		
France	3	F3
Docks en Seine	4	E1
Les Frigos	5	G3
Manufacture des Gobelins	6	C3
Musée National du Sport	7	F4

EATING	(pp213–74)	
Bioart	8	G3
Chez Gladines	9	B4
Chez Jacky	10	E4
Chez Nathalie	11	C4
Chez Paul	12	B4

Fil 'O' Fromage	13	F3
La Chine Masséna	14	D5
La Fleuve de Chine	15	D6
La Maison des Frigos	(see 5)	
L'Avant-Goût	16	C4
L'Avant-Goût Coûte		
Cellier	17	C4
Le Temps des Cerises	18	B4
Les Cailloux	19	B4

DRINKING	(pp275–92)	
La Taverne de la Butte	(see 20)	
Le Merle Moqueur	20	B4
Sputnik	21	B4
Tandem	(see 21)	
The Frog & British Library	22	F3

NIGHTLIFE	(pp293–308)	
La Dame de Canton	23	F3

Le Batofar	24	G3
Le Djoon	25	E2
Peniche El Alamein	26	F3

THE ARTS	(pp293–308)	
MK2 Bibliothèque	27	F3

SPORTS & ACTIVITIES	(pp309–16)	
Piscine de la Butte aux		
Cailles	28	B4
Piscine Josephine Baker	29	F2

SLEEPING	(pp323–51)	
Hôtel La Demeure	30	C2
Hôtel La Manufacture	31	C3
Oops	32	C3

TRANSPORT	(pp383–90)	
Voguéo Stop	(see 3)	

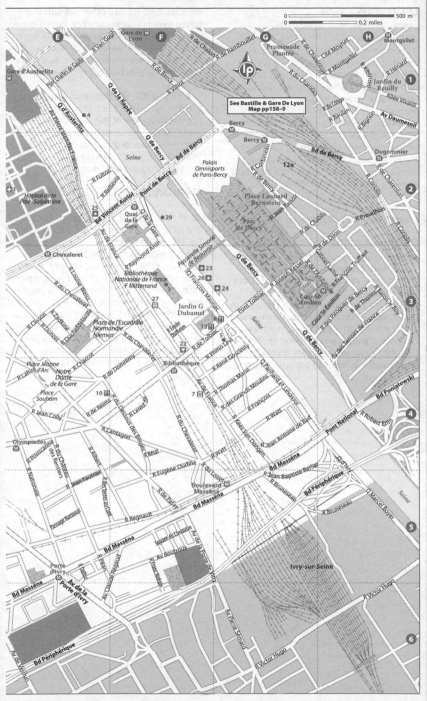

0   500 m
0   0.2 miles

Gare de Lyon

Gare d'Austerlitz

R Van Gogh

R de Chalon   R de Rambouillet

Promenade
Plantée

Cité Moynet

R de Chalons   R Montgallet

Montgallet

R Hénard

R Albinoni

Jardin du
Reuilly

Allée Vivaldi

Pont Charles de Gaulle

Q de la Rapée

R de Bercy

R Villiot

R du Charolais

R du Congo

R Baulan

Av Daumesnil

Q d'Austerlitz

Bd de Bercy

Seine

Bd de Bercy

Bercy

Bercy

R Corbineau

12e

Dugommier

Q Pierre Mendès France

Palais
Omnisports
de Paris-Bercy

R de Bercy

R de Charenton

R Coriolis

R Fulton

R Bellevue

Pont de Bercy

Place Leonard
Bernstein

R Jean Renoir

R de Chablis

R Proudhon

R Coriolis

Hôpital de la
Pitié-Salpêtrière

25 Bd Vincent Auriol

Quai
de la
Gare

Q de la Gare

29

Parc
de Bercy

R de Dijon

Gabriel Lamé

R de Pommard

R François Truffaut

R Baron-le-Roy

Av de France

R Raymond Aron

Passerelle Simone
de Beauvoir

Q de Bercy

R Joseph Kessel

Cour St-
Émilion

R de Thorins

Av des Terroirs de France

Chevaleret

R Louise Weiss

R du Chevaleret

Bibliothèque
Nationale de France
F Mitterrand

3

Q François Mauriac

Pont Tolbiac

Cour St-Émilion

R des Piroques de Bercy

Av du Terroirs de France

R Clisson

R Dunois

R Duchefdelaville

R Abel Gance

27

Jardin G
Duhamel

23

26

24

Seine

R du Chevaleret

Place de l'Escadrille
Normandie
Niemen

R Émile
Durkeim

13

22

R de Tolbiac

5

R Primo Levi

Q de Bercy

Place Jeanne
d'Arc

Notre
Dame
de la Gare

R L'Abbé d'Arc

R Charcot

R de Domrémy

Bibliothèque

R René Goscinny

R des Grands Moulins

R François

R Watt

Bd Poniatowski

Place
Soupam

R de Reims

10

7

Av de France

R Thomas Mann

Pont National

R Robert Estin

R Jean Colly

R de Reims

R du Dessous des Berges

R Léred

R du Chevaleret

Reese Van Dongen

R Jean Antoine de Baïf

Olympiades

R Cantagrel

R Watt

Bd Masséna

R Poncarme

R du Château
des Renters

R Albert

R Jean-Baptiste Berlier

R Bruneseau

Bd Périphérique

Q Marcel Boyer

Seine

Jean Faultrie

R Réal

Nationale

Boulevard
Masséna

R Bruneseau

Porte
d'Ivry

Av de la
Porte d'Ivry

Av de Choisy

R de Patay

R Régnault

Bd Masséna

Square du Limousin

Av de la Porte de Vitry

Ivry-sur-Seine

R Victor Hugo

Bd Masséna

Av d'Ivry

Bd Périphérique

R Victor Hugo

See Bastille & Gare De Lyon
Map pp158–9

1

2

3

4

5

6

E   F   G   H

LES FRIGOS Map p164

www.les-frigos.com; 19 rue des Frigos, 13e;
Ⓜ Bibliothèque

Its name translates as 'The Refrigerators' and that is precisely what this 1920s industrial building plastered from head to foot in graffiti used to be – a storage depot for refrigerated railway wagons. A cow lounges beneath a tree in front of it and inside some 200 artists use what is now an established artists' squat (artists pay rent to the city, which now owns the place) as gallery and studio space. Its many galleries have no fixed opening hours: hedge your bets and hope you bump into someone willing to show you around, or look out for one of the fabulous open days and other events Les Frigos hosts (click 'Agenda' on its website).

DOCKS EN SEINE Map p164

www.paris-docks-en-seine.fr; 36 quai d'Austerlitz, 13e; Ⓜ Gare d'Austerlitz

One of Paris' most exciting projects, Docks en Seine is a 20,000-sq-metre riverside warehouse – goods were once brought to it by barge – transformed post-millennium into a state-of-the-art cultural centre with boutiques, eating and drinking spaces, panoramic terrace, sun deck and waterside promenades aplenty across which concerts, markets, cinema and other delightful al fresco events spill in summer. Paris' fashion school, the Institut Français de la Mode (French Fashion Institute; www.ifm-paris.com), is also here, hence the complex's dual name, Cité de la Mode et du Design (City of Fashion & Design).

Built in 1907, the industrial complex was the first in Paris to use reinforced concrete. For the best view of the startling lime-green 'wave' that now dances across its vast, water-facing glass facade, cross the Seine over Pont Charles de Gaulle or hop aboard a Voguéo river metro.

MANUFACTURE DES GOBELINS
Map p164

☎ 01 44 08 52 00; 42 av des Gobelins, 13e; adult/7-25yr €8/6; ⓨ tours 1pm, 1.15pm, 2.45pm & 3pm Tue-Thu; Ⓜ Les Gobelins

The Gobelins Factory has been weaving *haute lisse* (high relief) tapestries on specialised looms since the 18th century along with Beauvais-style *basse lisse* (low relief) ones and Savonnerie rugs. Visits (1½ hours), by guided tour, takes you through the *ateliers* (workshops) and exhibits of the thousands carpets and tapestries woven here. Buy tickets in advance at Fnac (p294) or turn up well before 1pm for same-day tickets.

MONTPARNASSE & 15E

Drinking p291; Eating p270; Shopping p212; Sleeping p349

Less flamboyant than the Latin Quarter, less hip than Bastille and less audacious than Bercy, the unpretentious 14e arrondissement aka Montparnasse strikes a better balance than some, perhaps: buzzing cafés, brasseries where Picasso and his mates put 1930s Paris to rights, a cemetery with plenty of personality, and urban grit in the shape of a mainline train station and ugly tower with panoramic views to challenge Mme Eiffel.

Peer long and hard (and long and hard again) at the touristy restaurants and cafés around the unfortunate 1960s Gare Montparnasse complex and glimmers of the area's bohemian past occasionally emerge: after WWI writers, poets and artists of the avant-garde abandoned Montmartre on the Right Bank and crossed the Seine, shifting the centre of Paris' artistic ferment to the area around blvd du Montparnasse. Chagall, Modigliani, Léger, Soutine, Miró, Kandinsky, Stravinsky, Hemingway, Ezra Pound and Cocteau, as well as such political exiles as Lenin and Trotsky, all hung out here, talking endlessly in the cafés and restaurants for which the quarter became famous. It remained a creative hub until the mid-1930s.

Drift west, away from the energising hubbub of the train station area and its neon-lit nightlife, into the 15e arrondissement and suddenly things become more gentrified and

top picks

MONTPARNASSE & 15E

- Catacombes (p167) Go gruesome in Paris' most macabre sight – home to more skulls than you're ever likely to see again.
- Tour Montparnasse (p171) Ignore its outer appearance: the view from the top is a stunner.
- Cimetière de Montparnasse (p170) Pay your respects to crooner Serge Gainsbourg (bring a metro ticket), philosopher Sartre and others in this enormous cemetery.
- Fondation Cartier pour l'Art Contemporain (p171) Be thrilled by some striking contemporary art in this gem of a designer building.
- Musée Bourdelle (p171) No museum and garden is lovelier than this artistic ensemble for savouring the flavour of belle époque Paris.

residential. After the war, battalions of steelworkers clocked in every morning at the Citroën factory or one of the neighbourhood's numerous aeronautical companies. Av de la Motte-Picquet, blvd Pasteur and av Félix Faure are peaceful places – too peaceful for some tastes. For Unesco, the area seemed just right, and not far away the republic's future officers converge on the majestic École Militaire (p117).

But the 15e offers much more than bourgeois homes and institutions. Parisians flock to the shops and restaurants that line rue de la Convention, rue de Vaugirard (the longest street in Paris), rue St-Charles and rue du Commerce. On the quays, the towers of the Centre Beaugrenelle have long since abandoned their monopoly on futurism to the stylish, functional buildings occupied by TV stations Canal+ and France Télévision, and Parisians with their heart in the country can enjoy the Parc André-Citroën, one of the capital's most beautiful open spaces.

Mainline train station Gare Montparnasse, with its own metro station, is the natural transport hub. From here bus 91 goes to Gare d'Austerlitz, Gare de Lyon and Bastille; bus 92 to Charles de Gaulle–Étoile; and bus 94 to Sèvres Babylone (Le Bon Marché). Pick up bus 82 on blvd du Montparnasse for Invalides and the Eiffel Tower; and the 95 on rue de Rennes for St-Germain des Prés, Quai Voltaire, the Louvre, Palais Royal, Opéra and Lamarck–Caulaincourt (Montmartre).

LES CATACOMBES Map p168

☎ 01 43 22 47 63; www.catacombes.paris.fr, in French; 1 av Colonel Henri Roi-Tanguy, 14e; adult/14-26yr €8/4; ⏰ 10am-5pm Tue-Sun; Ⓜ Denfert–Rochereau

Paris' most gruesome and macabre sight: in 1785 it was decided to solve the hygiene and aesthetic problems posed by Paris' overflowing cemeteries by exhuming the bones and storing them in the tunnels of three disused quarries. The Catacombes is one such ossuary, created in 1810. After descending 20m (130 steps) from street level, visitors follow 1.7km of underground corridors in which a mind-boggling amount of bones and skulls of millions of Parisians

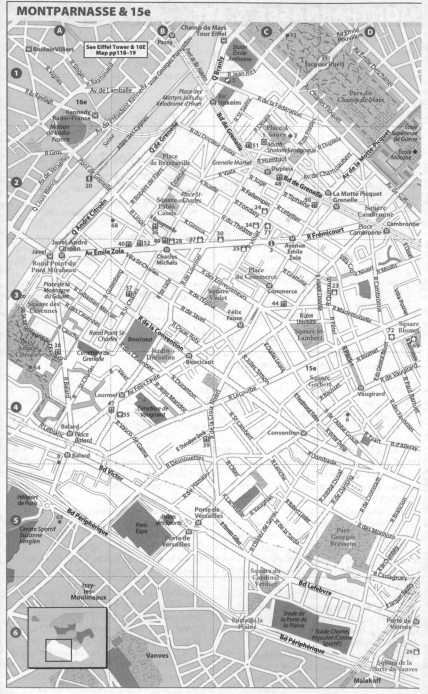

See Eiffel Tower & 16E
Map pp118–19

BoulainVilliers

Champ de Mars
Tour Eiffel

Passy

Stade
Émile
Anthoine

Av Émile
Pouvillon

Av Émile-Deschanel

R Vignes
R Singer
R Ravignan
R du Ranelagh

R de Lamballe

R Jean Rey

Pl
Jacques Ruell

Parc du
Champ de Mars

16e

Kennedy
Radio–France

Av du Président Kennedy   Voie Georges Pompidou

Place des
Martyrs Juifs du
Vélodrome d'Hiver

Bir
Hakeim

R de la Fédération

Av Charles Floquet

École
supérieure
de Guerre

Maison
de Radio
France

R Gros

Av de Versailles

Seine

Allée des Cygnes

Q de Grenelle

R du Docteur Finlay

Place A
Sauvy

Adath
Shalom Synagogue

École
Militaire

Av de la Motte-Picquet

Q de Versailles

Pont de Grenelle

Place
de Brazzaville

Grenelle Market

R Humblot

R de Suffren

R Louis Bleriot

Bd de Grenelle

Q Louis Blériot

Q André Citroën

R Robert de Flers

R Emerau

Square
Pablo Casals

Place St-
Charles

R Viala

R Juge

Bd de Grenelle

Av de Champaubert

La Motte Picquet
Grenelle

Square
Cambronne

R Linois

R Ginoux

R Fallempin

R Tiphaine

R Letellier

Place
Cambronne

Cambronne

Javel–André
Citroën

Av Émile Zola

R Beaugrenelle

R du Théâtre

R Violet

R Frémcourt

Javel

Rond Point du
Pont Mirabeau

Charles
Michels

Avenue
Émile
Zola

Place de la
Montagne
du Goulet

R Sébastien Mercier

R St-Charles

Gutenberg

Vasco de Gama

Square des
Cévennes

R des Cévennes

R de Javel

R de l'Église

Place
du Commerce

R de l'Entrepreneurs

Square
Violet

Félix
Faure

R Glinière

Commerce

R Léon
Thermitte

R Joseph Liouville

R Mademoiselle

R Péclet

Villa Croix Nivert

R Miollis

R Cambronne

Villa Poirier

Square
Blomet

Parc
André
Citroën

R Cauchy

R de la Montblanche

R de la Convention

R Oscar Roty

R des Cévennes

Rond Point St-
Charles

Boucicaut

Jardin
Duranton

Boucicaut

R Jules Simon

R Chalres Lecoq

R Blomet

15e

R de Vaugirard

Square
Gerbert

R Bausset

Vaugirard

R Paul Barruel

R des Favorites

R Balard

R Sébastien

Lourmel

Av Félix Faure

R Duranton

R Lecourbe

Ferdinand Faure

R de l'Abbé Groult

R Fizeau

R d'Alleray

R Leblanc

R Lacordaire

Cimetière de
Vaugirard

R Théodore Deck

R de la Croix Nivert

R St-Lambert

Convention

R Dombasle

Balard

Place
Balard

R Vasco de Gama

R Desnouettes

R Olier

R Lecuche

Heliport
de Paris

Bd Victor

R du Hameau

R Vaugelas

R Robert Linder

R de Dantzig

R Castagnary

R Brancion

Centre Sportif
Suzanne
Lenglen

Bd Périphérique

Paris
Expo

Palais
des Sports

Porte de
Versailles

Porte de
Versailles

Av Ernest Renan

R Olivier de Serres

R de la Saïda

Parc
Georges
Brassens

R de Chambéry

Issy-
les-
Moulineaux

Square du
Cardinal
Verdier

Bd Lefebvre

Vanves

Porte de la
Plaine

Porte de la
Plaine

Stade
de la Porte de
la Plaine

Stade Charles
Rigoulot (Centre
Sportif)

Porte de
Vanves

Bd Périphérique

Square de la
Porte de Vanves

Malakoff

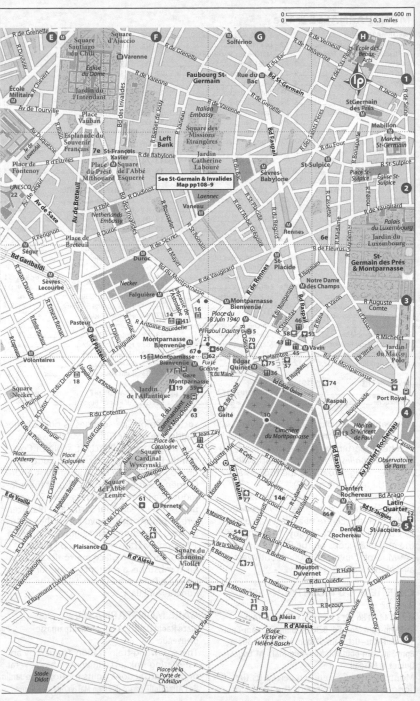

MONTPARNASSE & 15e

INFORMATION
Adath Shalom Synagogue 1 C2
Australian Embassy & Trade
  Commission 2 C1
Coin-Cuisine 3 C3
Copy-Top 4 F3
Cyber Cube 5 G3
École Le Cordon Bleu 6 D4
Fat Tire Bike Tours Office 7 C2
iXAir 8 A4

SIGHTS   pp167–72
Catacombes 9 H5
Centre d'Animation Garef
  Océanographique .... (see 17)
Cimetière du Montparnasse 10 G4
Fat Tire Bike Tours Departure
  Point 11 C1
First Church of Christ Scientist 12 H5
Fondation Cartier pour l'Art
  Contemporain 13 H4
Memorial du Marechal Leclerc
  de Hauteclocque et de la
  Liberation de Paris .... (see 17)
Musée Bourdelle 14 F3
Musée de la Poste 15 F3
Musée du Montparnasse 16 F3
Musée Jean Moulin 17 F4
Musée Pasteur 18 E4
Observatoire Météorologique
  Sculpture 19 F4
Pari Roller Ramble .... (see 67)
Statue of Liberty Replica 20 A2
Tour Montparnasse 21 F3
Unesco Building 22 E2

SHOPPING   pp191–212
Cacherel .... (see 32)
Canicrèche 23 D3

L'Arbre à Beurre 24 C2
Le Petit Bazar 25 C3
Marché aux Puces de la Porte
  de Vanves 26 D6
Mini Paris 27 B3
Mistigriff 28 B3
Naf Naf Stock 29 F6
Puzzle Michèle Wilson 30 C3
Dorotennis Stock 31 G6
SR Store 32 G6
SR Store 33 G6
Vitra 34 C2

EATING   pp213–74
Au Goût du Jour 35 B2
Boulevard Edgar Quinet Food
  Market 36 G4
Chez Nous, Chez Vous 37 B3
Fiori 38 A4
Jadis 39 B4
Kim Anh 40 B3
La Cabane à Huîtres 41 F3
La Cagouille 42 F4
La Closerie des Lilas .... (see 56)
La Coupole 43 G3
Le Cristal de Sel 44 C3
Le Dôme 45 G3
Le Parc au Cerfs 46 G3
L'Entrepôt .... (see 61)
L'Os à Moëlle 47 B4
Marché Biologique Brancusi .... (see 43)
Marché Grenelle 48 C2
Marché St-Charles 49 B3
Monoprix 50 C2
Poîlane 51 C2
Sawadee 52 B3

DRINKING   pp275–92
Cubana Café 53 G3

Félicie 54 G5
La Cave de l'Os Moëlle 55 B4
La Closerie des Lilas 56 H4
Le Rosebud 57 G4
Le Select 58 G3

NIGHTLIFE   pp293–308
Dancing de la Coupole .... (see 43)
Le Petit Journal 59 F4
Le Redlight 60 G3
L'Entrepôt 61 F5

THE ARTS   pp293–308
Kiosque Théâtre
  Montparnasse 62 F3

SPORTS & ACTIVITIES   pp309–16
Le Bowling 63 F4
Ballon Air de Paris 64 A4
Forest Hill Aquaboulevard 65 A5
Maison Roue Libre 66 H5
Patinoire de
  Montparnasse 67 F3
Piscine Keller 68 B2

SLEEPING   pp323–51
Aloha Hostel 69 D3
Celtic Hôtel 70 G3
Hôtel Amiral Fondary 71 C2
Hôtel Carladez
  Cambronne 72 D3
Hôtel de Blois 73 G5
Hôtel de la Paix 74 H4
Hôtel Delambre 75 G4
La Maison 76 F5
Petit Palace Hôtel 77 G5

TRANSPORT   pp383–90
Air France Buses 78 F4

are neatly packed along each and every wall. During WWII these tunnels were used as a headquarters by the Resistance; so-called *cataphiles* looking for cheap thrills are often caught roaming the tunnels at night (there's a fine of €60).

The route through the Catacombes begins at a small, dark-green *belle époque* building in the centre of a grassy area of av Colonel Henri Roi-Tanguy. The exit is at the end of 83 steps on rue Remy Dumoncel (M Mouton-Duvernet), 700m southwest of av Colonel Henri Roi-Tanguy.

CIMETIÈRE DU MONTPARNASSE
Map p168

☎ 01 44 10 86 50; 3 blvd Edgar Quinet, 14e; ⊙ 8am-6pm Mon-Fri, 8.30am-6pm Sat, 9am-6pm Sun mid-Mar–Oct, 8am-5.30pm Mon-Fri, 8.30am-6pm Sat, 9am-6pm Sun Nov–mid-Mar; M Edgar Quinet or Raspail

Montparnasse Cemetery received its first 'lodger' in 1824. It contains the tombs of

such illustrious personages as poet Charles Baudelaire, writer Guy de Maupassant, playwright Samuel Beckett, sculptor Constantin Brancusi, painter Chaim Soutine, photographer Man Ray, industrialist André Citroën, Captain Alfred Dreyfus of the infamous affair (see p31), actress Jean Seberg, philosopher Jean-Paul Sartre and his lover, writer Simone de Beauvoir, and the crooner Serge Gainsbourg, whose grave in division 1 just off av Transversale is a pilgrimage site for fans, who place metro tickets atop his tombstone, a reference to his famous song 'Le Poinçonneur des Lilas' (The Ticket Puncher of Lilas).

GARE MONTPARNASSE Map p168
place Raoul Dautry, 14e; M Montparnasse–Bienvenüe

This sprawling train station, fronted by an ice-skating rink (p313) in winter, has several unusual attractions on its rooftop. The Jardin de l'Atlantique (place des Cinq Martyr du Lycée Buffon,

14e), whose 3.5 hectares of green park terraces carpet the roof of the station, offers a bit of greenery and tranquillity in the heart of a very busy district. In the middle of the garden the futuristic **Observatoire Météorologique** 'sculpture' measures precipitation, temperature and wind speed.

Next to the garden the small **Musée Jean Moulin** (☎ 01 40 64 39 44; www.ml-leclerc-moulin.paris. fr, in French; 23 allée de la 2e DB, 14e; temporary exhibitions adult/14-25yr/under 14yr €4/3/2, permanent collections free; ✆ 10am-6pm Tue-Sun) is devoted to the WWII German occupation of Paris, with its focus on the Resistance and its leader, Jean Moulin (1899–1943). The attached **Mémorial du Maréchal Leclerc de Hauteclocque et de la Libération de Paris** shows a panoramic film on the eponymous general (1902–47), who led the Free French units during the war and helped to liberate the city in 1944.

Kids explore the marine world at the **Centre d'Animation Garef Océanographique** (☎ 01 40 64 11 99; www.garef.fr/oceano, in French; 26 allée du Chef de Escradon de Guillebon, 14e; ✆ 9am-12.30pm & 1.30-6pm Mon & Fri, to 7.30pm Tue & Thu, to 8pm Wed, 1.30-6pm Sat), a dynamic oceanographic centre with permanent and temporary exhibitions on the seafaring environment, and a shoal of workshops (from age six years) on underwater photography, diving, archaeology, seafood cuisine, marine flora and fauna, and so on.

To reach all these attractions, walk up the metal staircase next to platform 1 inside the station.

TOUR MONTPARNASSE Map p168
☎ 01 45 38 52 56; www.tourmontparnasse56.com; rue de l'Arrivée, 15e; adult/student & 16-20yr/7-15yr €11/8/4.70; ✆ 9.30am-11.30pm daily

Apr-Sep, to 10.30pm Sun-Thu, to 11pm Fri & Sat Oct-Mar; Ⓜ Montparnasse–Bienvenüe
The 210m-high Montparnasse Tower, a startlingly ugly, oversized lipstick tube built in 1973 with steel and smoked glass and housing offices for 5000 workers, affords spectacular views over the city. A lift whisks visitors up in 38 seconds to the indoor observatory on the 56th floor, with exhibition centre, video clips, multimedia terminals and Paris' highest café. Finish with a hike up the stairs to the open-air terrace on the 59th floor. To know what you're looking at, buy the multilingual *Paris vu d'en haut* guide (€3) from the ticket office before hiking up.

FONDATION CARTIER POUR L'ART CONTEMPORAIN Map p168
☎ 01 42 18 56 50; www.fondation.cartier.fr; 261 blvd Raspail, 14e; adult/11-26yr €7.50/5; ✆ 11am-10pm Tue, to 8pm Mon & Wed-Sun; Ⓜ Raspail
This stunning contemporary building, designed by Jean Nouvel, is a work of art. It hosts temporary exhibits on contemporary art (from the 1980s to today) in a wide variety of media – from painting and photography to video and fashion.

MUSÉE BOURDELLE Map p168
☎ 01 49 54 73 73; www.bourdelle.paris.fr, in French; 18 rue Antoine Bourdelle, 15e; adult/14-26yr €7/3.50; ✆ 10am-6pm Tue-Sun; Ⓜ Falguière
The Bourdelle Museum contains monumental bronzes in the house and workshop where sculptor Antoine Bourdelle (1861–1929), a pupil of Rodin, lived and worked. The three sculpture gardens are particularly lovely and impart a flavour of *belle époque* and post-WWI Montparnasse. The museum

LA POLLUTION CANINE: WATCH YOUR STEP

Every sixth person in France owns a dog, and Parisians are no exception. Problem is, that's a lot of dog dirt – an estimated 150,000 pooches here produce some 16 tonnes of the stuff every day, a lot of which ends up on the streets. The Paris municipality has made some valiant attempts in the past, most notably with the introduction of the *moto-crottes* (motorised pooper-scooters) by then mayor Jacques Chirac in the 1980s. At one stage, the city was spending up to €11 million each year to keep the city's pavements free of *la pollution canine*, but the machines were eventually abandoned as expensive and ineffective. Plastic-bag dispensers with the words '*J'aime mon chien, je ramasse*' (I love my dog, I pick up) have been placed strategically throughout the city, but the campaign has had less-than-howling success: only 60% of dog owners admit to doing their own scooping. Evidence to this effect takes the form of 'souvenirs' left by recently walked poodles and other breeds, often found smeared along the pavement (www.filthyfrance.com) by daydreaming strollers, one assumes – or guidebook writers absorbed in jotting down something important. And it gets more serious than that: more than 600 people are admitted to hospital each year after slipping on a *crotte*. Until Parisians – and their beloved canines – change their dirty ways, the word on the street remains the same: watch your step.

NICOLA'S TOP PARIS DAY

When Matthias sought to convince me too many years ago now that France was the country we should plump for, he sensibly whisked me to Paris, where we spent a whirlwind week of perfect days…zigzagging around Daniel Buren's zebra columns at the Palais Royal (p78), visiting Musée Picasso (p146) and Musée Rodin (p111), marvelling at that incredible blue at Ste-Chapelle (p97), ogling at the view of La Grande Arche (p176) slotted like a toy brick inside the Arc de Triomphe (p124) from place de la Concorde and the Champs-Élysées, eating ice cream on Île St-Louis (p227) and lounging *forever* in the Jardin du Luxembourg (p106) on those mythical sage-green chairs we then yearned to buy for years (Fermob, p212, was finally allowed to reproduce the 1923 original – mine's fuschia pink, his, boy-blue). These still are my perfect Parisian days, pebble-dashed with fave-of-the-moment food and drink addresses: L'Entrepôt (p272), Au Sauvignon (p283), Le Verre à Pied (p280), Curio Parlor Cocktail Club (p279) and KGB (p232).

usually has a temporary exhibition going on alongside its permanent collection (free on the rare occasion there's no exhibition).

MUSÉE DE LA POSTE Map p168

☎ 01 42 79 24 24; www.ladressemuseedelaposte. fr; 34 blvd de Vaugirard, 15e; adult/13-18yr 13yr €6.50/5; ⌚ 10am-6pm Mon-Sat; Ⓜ Montparnasse–Bienvenüe or Pasteur

Marketed as L'Adresse (the Address), Montparnasse's surprisingly contemporary Postal Museum delves into travel and exploration with its bevy of inspired temporary exhibitions. The main collection – the history of the French postal service – is spread across several rooms on several floors and is equally impressive. Upon departure, don't miss the shop selling every imaginable French stamp, from Harry Potter designs to romantic red heart-shaped stamps.

MUSÉE DU MONTPARNASSE Map p168

☎ 01 42 22 91 96; www.museedumontparnasse. net, in French; 21 av du Maine, 15e; adult/12-18yr €5/4; ⌚ 12.30-7pm Tue-Sun; Ⓜ Montparnasse– Bienvenüe

Housed in the studio of Russian cubist artist Marie Vassilieff (1884–1957) down a

surprisingly leafy alleyway off av du Maine, Montparnasse Museum doesn't have a permanent collection; rather it recalls the great role Montparnasse played during various artistic periods of the 20th century, offered through temporary exhibitions.

MUSÉE PASTEUR Map p168

☎ 01 45 68 82 83; www.pasteur.fr, in French; Institut Pasteur, 25 rue du Docteur Roux, 15e; adult/student €7/3; ⌚ 2-5.30pm Mon-Fri Sep-Jul; Ⓜ Pasteur

Housed in the apartment where the famous chemist and bacteriologist spent the last seven years of his life (1888–95), a tour of this museum takes you through Pasteur's private rooms, a hall with such odds and ends as gifts presented to him by heads of state and drawings he did as a young man. After Pasteur's death, the French government wanted to entomb his remains in the Panthéon, but his family, acting in accordance with his wishes, obtained permission to have him buried at his institute. The great savant lies in the basement crypt. Note that you will need to show a passport or ID card to gain entrance.

BEYOND CENTRAL PARIS

Eating p272; Shopping p212

Central Paris is enclosed by *le périphérique*, a ring road built on the site of the 19th-century city walls in the 1970s. The city proper is therefore sometimes referred to as *intra-muros* (inside the walls); and indeed the busy '*périph*' – eight lanes wide in most places – is still something of a physical and socioeconomic barrier that has kept the city from merging fluidly into the surrounding suburbs.

To the southeast and the southwest are the 'lungs' of Paris, the Bois de Vincennes (p122)and the Bois de Boulogne (p122), the municipality's largest green spaces and important recreational areas. To the north is St-Denis, France's royal resting place and the site of an impressive medieval basilica. The modern business district, La Défense, lies to the northwest and is so different from the rest of centuries-old Paris that it's worth a visit to put it all in perspective.

top picks

BEYOND CENTRAL PARIS

- **Basilique de St-Denis** (p173) Commune with the spirits of kings and queens in France's royal crypt.
- **Grande Arche de la Défense** (p176) The Arc de Triomphe goes modern.
- **Château de Vincennes** (p161) Erstwhile 'hunting lodge' turned royal château, with a picture-perfect keep.
- **Jardin d'Acclimatation** (p122) & **Parc Floral** (p161) Set the kids free in the playgrounds.
- **Stade de France** (p174) Catch Les Bleus for a home game.

ST-DENIS

Today no more than a poor suburb to the north of Paris, St-Denis was for some 1200 years the burial place of the kings of France. The ornate royal tombs, adorned with some truly remarkable statuary, and the Basilique de St-Denis (the world's first major Gothic structure) containing them are worth a visit and the town is easily accessible by metro (line 13 – be sure to take the St-Dénis Université branch) in just 20 minutes or so. St-Denis also boasts the Stade de France, the futuristic stadium just south of the Canal de St-Denis where France beat Brazil to win the World Cup at home in 1998.

BASILIQUE DE ST-DENIS Map p174

☎ 01 48 09 83 54; www.monuments-nationaux.fr; 1 rue de la Légion d'Honneur; tombs adult/senior, student & 18-25yr €7/4.50, EU resident under 26yr & everyone under 18yr free, 1st Sun of month Nov-Mar free, basilica admission free; 🕑 10am-6.15pm Mon-Sat, noon-6.15pm Sun Apr-Sep, 10am-5.15pm Mon-Sat, noon-5.15pm Sun Oct-Mar; Ⓜ Basilique de St-Denis (Line 13)

St-Denis Basilica was the burial place for all but a handful of France's kings and queens from Dagobert I (r 629–39) to Louis XVIII (r 1814–24), constituting one of Europe's most important collections of funerary sculpture; today the remains of 43 kings and 32 queens repose here. The single-towered basilica, begun around 1136, was the first major structure to be built in the Gothic style, serving as a model for other 12th-century French cathedrals, including the one at Chartres (p370). Features illustrating the transition from Romanesque to Gothic can be seen in the **choir** and **double ambulatory**, which are adorned with a number of 12th-century **stained-glass windows**. The **narthex** (the portico running along the western end of the basilica) also dates from this period. The **nave** and **transept** were built in the 13th century.

During the Revolution and the Reign of Terror, the basilica was devastated; remains from the royal tombs were dumped into two big pits outside the church. The mausoleums were put into storage in Paris, however, and survived. They were brought back in 1816, and the royal bones were reburied in the crypt a year later. Restoration of the structure was begun under Napoleon, but most of the work was carried out by the Gothic Revivalist architect Eugène Viollet-le-Duc from 1858 until his death in 1879. The **tombs** in the crypt are decorated with life-sized figures of the deceased. Those built before the Renaissance are adorned with *gisants* (recumbent figures). Those made after 1285 were carved from death masks and are thus fairly, well, lifelike; the 14 figures commissioned under Louis IX (St Louis; r 1214–70) are depictions of how earlier rulers *might* have looked. The oldest tombs (from around 1230) are those of Clovis I (d 511) and his son Childebert I (d 558). On no account should you miss the white marble catafalque tomb of Louis XII and Anne of Bretagne that dates from 1597. If you look carefully you'll see graffiti etched on the arms of the seated figures dating from the early 17th century. The Bourbon sepulchral vault contains the remains of Louis XVI and Marie-Antoinette but not of the king's younger brother Charles X; there's a tomb, but his bones lie in a church in Nova Gorica in Slovenia.

Self-paced 1¼-hour audioguide tours of the basilica and tombs cost €4 (€6.50 for two people sharing), available at the crypt ticket kiosk.

MUSÉE D'ART ET D'HISTOIRE
Map p174

☎ 01 42 43 05 10; www.musee-saint-denis.fr, in French; 22bis rue Gabriel Péri; adult/student, senior & everyone on Sun €5/3, 1st Sun of month free; ⏰ 10am-5.30pm Mon, Wed & Fri, to 8pm Thu, 2-6.30pm Sat & Sun; Ⓜ St-Denis-Porte de Paris (Line 13)

To the southwest of the basilica is the Museum of Art & History, housed in a restored Carmelite convent founded in 1625 and later presided over by Louise de France, the youngest daughter of Louis XV. Displays include reconstructions of the Carmelites' cells, an 18th-century apothecary section and, in the archaeology section, items found during excavations around the St-Denis Basilica. There's a section on modern art, with a collection of work by

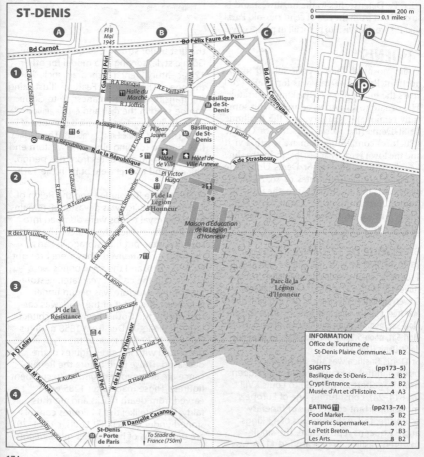

ST-DENIS

INFORMATION	
Office de Tourisme de St-Denis Plaine Commune....1	B2

SIGHTS	(pp173–5)
Basilique de St-Denis................2	B2
Crypt Entrance.............................3	B2
Musée d'Art et d'Histoire.........4	A3

EATING 🍴	(pp213–74)
Food Market...............................5	B2
Franprix Supermarket...............6	A2
Le Petit Breton.............................7	B3
Les Arts..8	B2

a local son, the surrealist artist Paul Éluard (1895–1952), as well as an important collection of politically charged posters, cartoons, lithographs and paintings from the 1871 Paris Commune.

STADE DE FRANCE
Map p174

☎ 08 92 70 09 00; www.stadefrance.com; rue Francis de Pressensé, ZAC du Cornillon Nord, 93216 St-Denis la Plaine; adult/student & 6-11yr €12/8, family pass €32; ⊙ tours on the hr in French 10am-5pm daily Apr-Aug, 4 to 5 tours per day Sep-Mar Tue-Sun, in English 10.30am & 2.30pm Apr-Aug; Ⓜ St-Denis-Porte de Paris (Line 13) or La Plaine Stade de France (RER B)

The 80,000-seat Stadium of France, just south of central St-Denis and in full view from rue Gabriel Péri, was built for the 1998 football World Cup, which France won by miraculously defeating Brazil 3-0. The futuristic and quite beautiful structure, with a roof the size of place de la Concorde, is used for football and rugby matches, major gymnastic events and big-ticket music concerts. It can be visited on guided tours only.

LA DÉFENSE
It was one of the world's most ambitious civil-engineering projects when development of Paris' skyscraper business district, west of the 17e arrondissement, began in the 1950s. Today La Défense counts more than 100 buildings, including headquarters of three-quarters of France's largest 20 corporations, and showcases extraordinary monumental art (see p176). By day more than 150,000 city-dwellers – mainly suits and execs – transform the oversized, nocturnal ghost town into a hive of high-flying urban activity; 20,000 people live here.

Architecture buffs will have a field day. First-generation buildings like the Centre des Nouvelles Industries et Technologies (Centre for New Industries & Technologies) – a giant 'pregnant oyster' inaugurated in 1958, extensively rebuilt 30 years later and revamped in 2008 as a shopping centre – feel tired. But later generations still excite: the 187m-high Total Coupole (1985) shimmers metallic blue and silver as its rises 48 floors up to the sky. The twin towers of the 161m-tall Cœur Défense (Défense Heart) stand over a light-filled atrium bigger than Notre Dame's nave. Diagonally

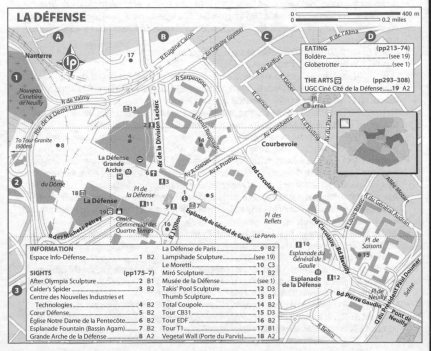

LA DÉFENSE

INFORMATION		La Défense de Paris.....................9 B2
Espace Info-Défense.........................1 B2		Lampshade Sculpture................(see 19)
		Le Moretti.............................10 C3
SIGHTS	(pp175-7)	Miró Sculpture..........................11 B2
After Olympia Sculpture.................2 B1		Musée de la Défense..................(see 1)
Calder's Spider...............................3 B2		Takis' Pool Sculpture...................12 D3
Centre des Nouvelles Industries et		Thumb Sculpture.......................13 B1
Technologies...............................4 B2		Total Coupole...........................14 B2
Cœur Défense...............................5 B2		Tour CB31...............................15 D3
Église Notre Dame de la Pentecôte...6 B2		Tour EDF................................16 B2
Esplanade Fountain (Bassin Agam)...7 B2		Tour T1.................................17 B1
Grande Arche de la Défense...........8 A2		Vegetal Wall (Porte du Parvis).....18 A2

EATING   (pp213-74)
Boldère...........................(see 19)
Globetrotter.......................(see 1)

THE ARTS 🎭   (pp293-308)
UGC Ciné Cité de la Défense......19 A2

opposite, the elongated, oval-shaped Tour EDF (2001) – a triumphal solution to a relatively small space and as attractive a steel-and-glass skyscraper as you'll find – almost undulates in the breeze that forever whips across place de la Défense. Recent additions include Tour T1, a 185m-high sail in glass; Société General's Tour Granite, which post-September 11 was scaled down from 230m to 183m; and Tour CB31, a renovation of the drab 1970s Tour Axa that now reaches a height of 220m.

Sky-high future creations throw caution to the wind: the Tour Air 2 (2012), a demolition-reconstruction job of the stubbier 1970s American architect Thom Mayne's Tour Phare (2013) will resemble a coiled sheet of woven metal and stand a record-breaking 300m tall, as will the Tour Generali (2013), which should practically tickle the clouds with its cluster of spiky spires.

Reach La Défense by taking metro line 1 to the terminus (La Défense Grande Arche).

RER Line A also serves the same station; but remember that La Défense is in zone 3 and therefore will cost extra.

GARDENS & MONUMENTS Map p175

Le Parvis, place de la Défense & Esplanade du Général de Gaulle; Ⓜ **La Défense–Grande Arche or Esplanade de la Défense**

The Parvis, place de la Défense and Esplanade du Général de Gaulle – a pleasant 1km walkway – is an open-air contemporary art gallery. Calder, Miró, Agam, César and Torricini are among the international artists behind the colourful and often surprising sculptures and murals on Voie des Sculptures (Sculptures Way), the Quartier du Parc (Park District) west of the Grande Arche and Jardins de l'Arche, a 2km-long extension of the Axe Historique. Meandering around this skyscraper district in search of these works of art is fun.

A WORK OF ART

La Défense is not only about architecture. A 12m-high thumb, an antique giant, a chunk of the Berlin Wall and a serpent that snakes underground with kids inside are among the many larger-than-life artworks that loiter between skyscrapers. Grab a copy of the illustrated *Guide to Works of Art* (€2) from La Défense's information office (p406) and hunt for art. Or stroll 'blind' and see what new treasures you find; a few more appear each year.

- *The Esplanade Fountain* (1975). Also called Bassin Agam or Fontaine Agam after its Palestinian kinetic-art creator, Yaacov Agam, this is actually a colourful, 86m-long pool tiled with Venetian mosaics and pierced by 66 fountains that dance to music at certain times of day (5pm to 7pm Sunday to Friday, to 8.30pm Friday and Saturday). Find it behind the tourist office.
- *Calder's Spider* (1974). It looks like a spider no one in their right mind would want to meet. Giant-sized and ferocious red, it struts its leggy stuff on place de la Défense.
- *Vegetal Wall* (2006). A mini version of the vertical garden that blooms on the Musée du Quai Branly (p116), this living wall of green shares the same creator, budding Parisian botanical artist Patrick Blanc. Find it next to the Porte du Parvis entrance of the Centre Commercial des Quatre Temps.
- *The Lampshade* (2006). Step inside the shopping centre through Porte du Parvis to see this fabulous light sculpture hanging from the ceiling. Kiko Lopez crafted it from thousands of Swarovski crystals.
- *The Thumb* (1994). The 12m-tall bronze thumb that gives the thumbs-up on place Carpeaux is not any old thumb. Its maker, Marseille-born César, made it from a cast of his own. Left or right?
- *Le Moretti* (1990). Candy-striped with myriad reds, blues, yellows (19 colours in total), this industrial, 32m-tall ventilation shaft on place de l'Iris is one of several shafts in La Défense to be transformed as art. Nice-born Taymond Moretti (1931–2005) did it using 672 fibreglass tubes. Lit at night, it's inspirational.
- *Takis' Pool* (1987). Plump on that historic axis is this large pool of water studded with 49 multicoloured lights strung atop spiral metal poles of varying heights. The crystal-clear reflection of the surrounding buildings in the water is a quintessential photo-op.
- *The Four Heads* (2002). London artist Emily Young, one of several artists whose works mingle with skyscrapers in the Triangle de l'Arche district of La Défense, ranks among Britain's top female sculptors. Masculine stone heads are what you're looking for.
- *After Olympia* (1986–87) Olympia's Greek temple's ornamental facade is the inspiration behind the 23m-long heap of rusted painted steel on av de la Division Leclerc. The work of English sculptor Anthony Caro, its reflections in the glassy buildings around it are as much a work of art as the work itself.
- Miró figures (1976). Ridiculing the strict symmetry of the surrounding blocks is this comic pair of bright blue, yellow and red figures in front of the Centre Commerical des Quatre Temps. In keeping with the oversized scale of things in La Défense, the Catalan surrealist's figures stand 11m and 12m tall.

GRANDE ARCHE DE LA DÉFENSE
Map p175

☎ 01 49 07 27 27; www.grandearche.com; 1 Parvis de la Défense; adult/6-17yr €10/8.50, family pass €25, ⊙ 10am-8pm Apr-Aug, to 7pm Sep-Mar; Ⓜ La Défense–Grande Arche

La Défense's draw card is the Grande Arche (Great Arch) – a remarkable, cube-like structure, 110m square, of white Carrara marble, grey granite and glass. It's constructed out of 3600 prefabricated cases, each 2.8m square and 800g in weight, and the entire construction rests on a dozen 30m-tall underground pillars. Scale the cigarette-butt-littered steps to the foot of this incredible arch free of charge and ponder its meaning as 'a window to the world, a symbol of hope for the future; that all men can meet freely'. Or pay to travel 1.6m per second to the 'roof' on the 35th floor, where temporary art exhibitions hang out alongside scaled models of the arch, a video showing its construction, a museum that presents the history of computing (Musée de l'Informatique), a ticky-tacky souvenir shop and a soulless restaurant that, incredibly, boasts no view (avoid).

Most interesting is the outlook from the roof terrace over the 8km-long Axe Historique (Historic Axis), begun in 1640 by André Le Nôtre of Versailles fame and stretching from the Louvre's glass pyramid, along av des Champs-Élysées to the Arc de Triomphe, Porte Maillot and finally the Esplanade du Général de Gaulle. The Grande Arche, home to government and business offices, marks the western end of this axis, although its maker, Danish architect Johan-Otto von Sprekelsen, deliberately placed the arch fractionally out of alignment with the Axe Historique (who wants perfection?!). Be aware that access to the roof was suspended indefinitely for security reasons in 2010; it may reopen by the time this book is in print, but check first.

WHAT'S IN A NAME?

Skyscraper-camouflaged military installations, subterranean bunkers and a different James Bond gadget embedded in every mirrored window...forget it. There's nothing militaristic about La Défense except its name, derived from a simple sculpture: La Défense de Paris was erected on place de la Défense in 1883 to commemorate the defence of Paris during the Franco-Prussian War of 1870–71.

MUSÉE DE LA DÉFENSE Map p175

☎ 01 47 74 84 24; www.ladefense.fr; 15 place de la Défense; admission free; ⊙ 10am-6pm Sun-Fri, 10am-7pm Sat; Ⓜ La Défense–Grande Arche

A trip to this space located just below the Espace-Info information centre is a real highlight. Drawings, architectural plans and scale models trace the development of the district from the 17th century to the present day. Especially fascinating are the projects that were never built: the 750m-tall Tour Tourisme TV (1961) by the Polak brothers; Hungarian-born artist Nicholas Schöffer's unspeakable Tour Lumière Cybernetique (1965), a 'Cybernetic Light Tower' that, at 324m, would stand at the same height as the Eiffel Tower; and the Tour sans Fin, a 'Never-Ending Tower' that would be 425m high, but just 39m in diameter. Ouch.

ÉGLISE NOTRE DAME DE LA PENTECÔTE Map p175

☎ 01 47 75 83 25; http://catholiques.aladefense. cef.fr, in French; 1 place de la Défense; ⊙ 8am-6.30pm Mon-Fri; Ⓜ La Défense–Grande Arche

When the crowds of suits gets you down, head for the futuristic Our Lady of the Pentecost Catholic Church and its sublime interior. Check out the flame-shaped pulpit, the image of the Virgin Mary that looks uncannily like the Buddha, and the individual chairs that unfold to create benches.

MONTMARTRE ART ATTACK

For centuries Montmartre was a simple country village filled with the *moulins* (mills) that supplied Paris with its flour. But when it was incorporated into the capital in 1860, its picturesque charm and low rents attracted painters and writers – especially after the Communard uprising of 1871 (see p31), which began here. The late 19th and early 20th centuries were Montmartre's heyday, when Toulouse-Lautrec drew his favourite cancan dancers and Picasso and Braque introduced the world to Cubism.

1 Moulin Rouge

Begin the walk at Place Blanche, whose name ('White Square') derives from the plaster (made from the locally mined gypsum) that was carted through the area. To the northwest of the square is the legendary Moulin Rouge (p295) beneath its trademark red windmill – it first opened as a dance hall in 1889.

2 Musée de l'Érotisme

Appropriately located to the right is the Musée de l'Érotisme (p135), an institution that portrays itself as educational rather than titillating. Yeah, right.

3 Café des Deux Moulins

Walk up rue Lepic, which is lined with food shops, and halfway up on the left is the Café des Deux Moulins (☎ 01 42 54 90 50; 15 rue Lepic, 18e; ☽ 7am-2am), where Amélie worked in the eponymous film.

4 Van Gogh's house

Follow the curve to the west; Théo Van Gogh owned the house at No 54; his brother, the artist Vincent, stayed with him on the 3rd floor for two years from 1886.

5 Passage de la Sorcière

After rue Lepic curves back east you'll see a steep private stairway, nicknamed the 'Passage de la Sorcière' (the Witch's Alleyway). At one time, an old lady, who local children believed to be a witch, lived in one of the houses at the top. Unfortunately for the woman, the name stuck. Today, the plush Hôtel Particulier Montmartre (p340) is located here, across from the 'Witch's Rock'.

6 Moulin Blute-Fin

In the 17th and 18th centuries, Montmartre was dotted with windmills, used to grind wheat into flour. Today only two remain, the Moulin Blute-Fin and the Moulin Radet. The Debray family, who owned both, turned them into a popular open-air dance hall (called Le Moulin de la Galette) in the 19th century, which was immortalised by Renoir in his 1876 tableau *Le Bal du Moulin de la Galette*.

7 Moulin Radet

About 100m to the east is the second windmill, the Moulin Radet, which is now a restaurant (also called le Moulin de la Galette). *Galette* was the name of the rye bread that the Drebays sold to Parisians, accompanied with a glass of milk.

8 Passe-Muraille statue

Crossing through place Marcel Aymé, you'll see a curious statue of a man emerging from a stone wall. It portrays Dutilleul, the hero of Marcel Aymé's short story *Le Passe-Muraille* (The Walker through Walls), who finally became trapped halfway inside a wall. Aymé lived in the adjacent apartment building from 1902 to 1967.

9 Statue of St-Denis

Cross the street to sq Suzanne Buisson, where you'll find a statue of St-Denis, the 3rd-century bishop of Paris who was beheaded by the Romans. According to legend, after his execution he washed his head in the fountain here before continuing north (still preaching), eventually stopping at the site where the Basilique de St-Denis (p173) was later built.

10 Cimetière St-Vincent

Exit the park and turn left (north) into rue Girardon, and pass the Allée des Brouillards ('Fog Alley'), named after the adjacent 'Fog Castle', where several artists squatted in the late 19th century; Renoir lived at No 8 from 1890 to 1897. Descend the stairs from place Dalida into rue St-Vincent; on the other side of the wall is Cimetière St-Vincent, final resting place of Maurice Utrillo (1883–1955), the 'painter of Montmartre'.

11 Au Lapin Agile

Just over rue des Saules is the celebrated cabaret Au Lapin Agile (p304), whose name seems to suggest a nimble rabbit but actually comes from *Le Lapin à Gill*, a mural of a rabbit jumping out of a cooking pot by caricaturist André Gill, which can still be seen on the western exterior wall. Among the cabaret's regulars was the poet Guillaume Apollinaire, the great proponent of cubism and futurism, who was killed in combat in 1918.

12 Clos Montmartre Take a right (south) into rue des Saules. Just opposite is the Clos Montmartre, a small vineyard dating from 1933 (originally planted to thwart real-estate development), whose 2000 vines produce an average of 800 bottles each October (p20). They're auctioned off for charity in the 18e. Just opposite is the Maison Rose, the famous subject of an Utrillo painting; it now houses a restaurant.

13 Musée de Montmartre The Musée de Montmartre (p132) is on rue Cortot at No 12–14, the first street on the left after the vineyard. The museum is housed in Montmartre's oldest building, a manor house built in the 17th century, and was the one-time home to painters Renoir, Utrillo and Raoul Dufy.

14 Eric Satie's house The celebrated composer lived from 1890 to 1898 in the house at 6 rue Cortot.

15 Water tower At the end of rue Cortot turn right (south) onto rue du Mont Cenis

(the attractive water tower just opposite dates from the early 20th century), left onto (tiny) rue de Chevalier de la Barre and then right onto rue du Cardinal Guibert.

16 Basilique du Sacré Cœur The entrance to the Basilique du Sacré Cœur (p132) and the stunning vista over Paris from the steps are just to the south.

17 Église St-Pierre de Montmartre From the basilica follow rue Azaïs west, then turn north to the Église St-Pierre de Montmartre. It was built on the site of a Roman temple to Mars (or Mercury) – some say that the name Montmartre is derived from 'Mons Martis' (Latin for Mount of Mars); others prefer the Christian 'Mont Martyr' (Mount of the Martyr).

lonelyplanet.com

WALK FACTS

Start Metro Blanche
End Metro Abbesses
Distance 2.5km
Time Two hours
Fuel stops Le Coquelicot (p248), Le Sancerre (p284)

NEIGHBOURHOODS   WALKING TOURS

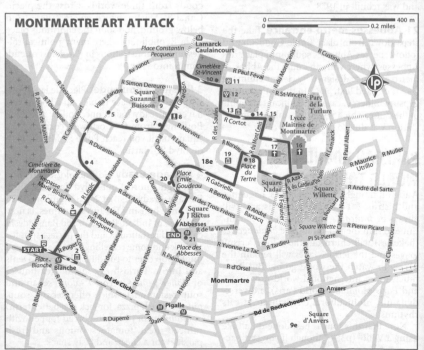

MONTMARTRE ART ATTACK

18 Place du Tertre Across from the church is the place du Tertre (p133) – arguably the most touristy place in all of Paris but still fun. Cossack soldiers allegedly first introduced the term *bistro* (Russian for 'quickly') into French at No 6 (La Mère Catherine) in 1814. On Christmas Eve, 1898, Louis Renault's first car was driven up the Butte to Place du Tertre, marking the start of the French auto industry.

19 Dalí Espace Montmartre Just off the southwestern side of the square is rue Poulbot, leading to the Dalí Espace Montmartre (p135) – surprisingly, the only art museum on the Butte.

20 Bateau Lavoir From place du Calvaire take the steps into rue Gabrielle, turning right (west) to reach place Émile Goudeau. At No 11bis is the site of the Bateau Lavoir, where Kees Van Dongen, Max Jacob, Amedeo Modigliani and Pablo Picasso, who painted his seminal *Les Demoiselles d'Avignon* (1907) here, once lived in great poverty. An old piano factory later used as a laundry, Jacob dubbed it the 'Laundry Boat' because of the way it swayed in a strong breeze. Originally at No 13, the Bateau Lavoir burned down in 1970 and was rebuilt in 1978.

21 Abbesses metro entrance Take the steps down from place Émile Goudeau and follow rue des Abbesses south into place des Abbesses, where you can't miss the Abbesses metro entrance designed by Hector Guimard (see the boxed text, p103). In the 18th century gypsum miners excavated significant amounts of the Butte, which is why the Abbesses metro station was dug so deeply.

PARISIAN ROUND-THE-WORLD TOUR

And you thought it was all berets, baguettes and bistros... To be sure, Paris is and will always be *français* – the couturiers will continue to spin their glad rags, the *boulangeries* (bakeries) will churn out those long, crispy loaves and the terrace cafés will remain the places to watch the world go by. But it's a much more international world nowadays, and *Paris Mondial* (World Paris), a diverse, dynamic, multicultural city, vibrates to its rhythms.

Note that this tour is best done on a bike using a Vélib' (p384), though if you can't access the bike-share system, you can still do it as a walk. In any case, the stations around Belleville are generally short of bikes (most get taken on the morning commute), so it's best to count on walking until you reach République.

1 Boulevard de Belleville Start the walk on blvd de Belleville. This street is a microcosm of *Paris Mondial* and on market mornings (see p222), you might think you've been transported to the Mediterranean, Africa or even Asia. Along the southwestern side of the street you'll find lots of North African bakeries selling delicious sweet pastries. At No 39 is the Mosquée Abou Bakr as Saddiq, just a few doors down from the modern Église Notre Dame Réconciliatrice, a Sri Lankan Christian church at No 57. About 100m up on the right-hand – or Tunisian – side of the street is the Synagogue Michkenot Yaachov at No 118, in dire need of renovation.

2 Rue du Faubourg du Temple Turn left (west) onto the vibrant rue du Faubourg du Temple. La Java (p303) at No 105, where Edith Piaf once warbled, now stands across from the Épicerie Asie, Antiles, Afrique, which sells goods from three worlds. Cross the placid Canal St-Martin, which emerges here from below ground, and soon the enormous place de la République, where many political rallies and demonstrations in Paris start or end, comes into view.

3 Rue René Boulanger Place de la République is a good place to pick up a bike if you haven't already found one. Follow rue René Boulanger from the northwest corner of the square until you reach Porte St-Martin (p144) on blvd St-Martin.

4 Passage Brady Go one block and then turn right (north) onto blvd de Strasbourg. Passage Brady (p251) at No 33, built in 1828 and once housing 100 tiny boutiques, is now a warren of Indian, Pakistani and Bangladeshi cafés and restaurants and the perfect spot for a break and some refuelling. Alternatively you might pop over to rue du Faubourg St-Denis and into a Turkish *çay salonu* (tea house) or *döner yemek ve çorba salon* (kebab and soup restaurant), which offer kebabs, soup, *pide* (Turkish pizza, for lack of a better term) and *lahmacun* (thin pitta bread topped with minced meat, tomatoes, onions and fresh parsley) for a cheap and tasty snack.

5 Marché Couvert St-Quentin Continue up blvd de Strasbourg (or rue du Faubourg St-Denis if on foot) and turn left onto blvd de Magenta at the lovely Gothic Église St-Laurent (15th century). Carry on north past the 19th-century Marché St-Quentin (p222), the Gare du Nord and the elevated metro line 2. The blvd de Magenta is a long stretch and best done on a bike.

6 La Goutte d'Or The big pink sign announcing the Tati department store (p204) marks the start of La Goutte d'Or, the neighbourhood called the 'Drop of Gold' after a white wine that was produced here in the 19th century. Today it's home to a diverse community of North African and West and Central African immigrants. Turn east into rue de la Goutte d'Or and park your Vélib' bike here if you have one.

7 Rue des Gardes Walk down rue de la Goutte d'Or and turn left onto rue des Gardes. Almost every address on this street belongs to an up-and-coming fashion designer – at last count there were eight studio-boutiques – and it's a good place to browse for original clothing, jewellery, bags and home design. Many of the labels are international in outlook, with designers looking to Iran, Brazil, Comoros and even the melting pot of la Goutte d'Or for inspiration.

8 Rue des Poissonniers
Take a left into rue Polonceau, lined with African and North African textile shops, and then turn right onto rue des Poissonniers (the 'Street of Fishmongers') where you'll find halal butchers offering special deals on sheep heads and 5kg packets of chicken but no fish. Rue Myrha on your right is the frontier between Central and West Africa and the Maghreb; *rai* music gives way to Cameroonian *bikutsi* (a fusion of ancestral rhythms and fast electric guitars) and Senegalese *mbalax* (drum music).

WALK FACTS

Start Metro Couronnes
End Metro Château Rouge
Distance 7km
Time 1½ to 2½ hours
Fuel stop Istanbul (p251), Passage Brady (p251), Olympic Café (p284)

PARISIAN ROUND-THE-WORLD TOUR

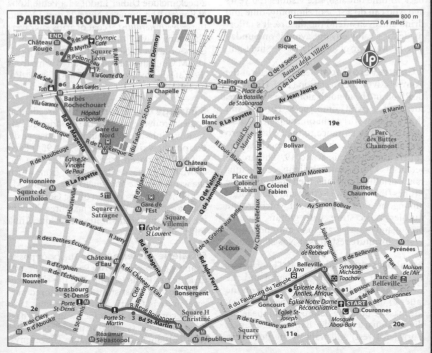

9 Rue Dejean After crossing over rue Myrha, turn left (west) into rue Dejean, where an open-air market is held from 8am to 1pm on Sundays and 3.30pm to 7.30pm Tuesdays to Saturdays. Here you *will* find fish and lots of it, especially fresh *capitaine* (Nile perch) and *thiof* from Senegal, alongside stalls selling fiery Caribbean Scotch Bonnet chillies, plantains and the ever-popular *dasheen* (taro). If you want to linger, the neighbourhood Olympic Café (p284) is back east down rue de Suez; otherwise, the Château Rouge metro station is a few steps to the southwest.

RIGHT BANK TIME PASSAGES

Stepping into the *passages couverts* (covered shopping arcades) of the Right Bank is the most simple way to get a feel for what life was like in early 19th-century Paris. These arcades emerged during a period of relative peace and prosperity under the restored House of Bourbon after Napoleon's fall and the rapid growth of the new industrial classes; by the mid-19th century Paris counted around 150 of these sumptuously decorated temples to Mammon.

On this walking tour, not only will you step back in time but also, like visitors 150 years ago, you can do a spot of shopping, dine and drink and even attend the theatre. It's tailor-made for a rainy day but avoid it on Sunday when at least two of the galleries are shut tight.

1 Galerie Véro Dodat Begin the walk at the Louvre–Rivoli metro station (1er). Cross rue de Rivoli and head north along rue du Louvre, turning left (west) onto rue St-Honoré and then right (north) again on rue Jean-Jacques Rousseau. The entrance to the Galerie Véro Dodat, built in 1823 by two well-heeled *charcutiers* (butchers), is at No 19. The arcade retains its 19th-century skylights, ceiling murals, Corinthian columns, tiled floor, gas globe fittings (though now electric) and shop fronts, among the most interesting of which are the Luthier music store, with guitars, violins, banjos and ukuleles, at No 17 and the Marini France furniture restorers at Nos 28 to 30.

2 Galeries du Palais Royal The gallery's western exit leads to rue du Bouloi and rue Croix des Petits Champs. Head north on the latter to the corner of rue du Colonel Drian; the massive building before you on the left is the headquarters of the Banque de France. Turn left (west) and walk to rue de Valois.

Ahead of you at No 5 is one of the entrances to the Galeries du Palais Royal. Strictly speaking, these galleries are not *passages* as they are arcaded rather than covered, but since they date from 1786 they are considered to be the prototypes of what was to come.

3 Galerie de Montpensier The Café de Foy, from where the Revolution broke out on a warm mid-July day just three years after the galleries opened, once stood on the western side of the Galeries du Palais Royal, at what is today's Galerie de Montpensier. Galerie de Montpensier has several traditional shops, including A Bacqueville at Nos 6 to 8, with Légion d'Honneur–style medals and ribbons; Didier Ludot (p211) at both Nos 19 and 20 and 23 and 24, with exquisite antique clothes; and in between Dugrenot with curios and antiques at Nos 21 and 22.

4 Galerie de Valois This *passage* on the eastern side, where Charlotte Corday, Jean-Paul Marat's assassin, once worked in a shop, is more upmarket, with posh galleries and designer shops such as Stella McCartney at Nos 114 to 121 and Pierre Hardy with bags and shoes at Nos 155 to 161. Other shops worth a peek include Didier Ludot's La Petite Robe Noire (p211) boutique at Nos 125 and 126 and the *graveur héraldiste* (coat of arms engraver) Guillaumot, which has been printing family coats-of-arms at Nos 151 to 154 since 1785. Did M Guillaumot heed the call to arms from the Café de Foy a mere four years after setting up shop?

5 Passage du Perron The tiny arcade that doglegs from the north of the Galeries du Palais Royal into rue de Beaujolais is passage du Perron; the writer Colette (1873–1954) lived out the last dozen years of her life in a flat above here (9 rue de Beaujolais), from which she wrote *Paris de Ma Fenêtre* (Paris from My Window), her description of the German occupation of Paris. There are just three shops in the arcade, including Boîtes à Musique Anna Joliet (p195).

6 Galerie Vivienne Diagonally opposite from where you exit from Passage du Perron at 4 rue des Petits Champs are the entrances to two of the most stunningly restored *passages* in Paris. Galerie Vivienne, built in 1826 and decorated on the upper walls with bas-reliefs of snakes (signifying prudence), scales (justice), anchors (hope), lute (harmony), cockerel (vigilance) and beehives (industry), as well as floor mosaics, was (and still is) one of the poshest of the *passages*. As you enter, look to the stairwell to the left at No 13 for its false marble walls; François Eugène Vidocq (1775–1857), master burglar *and* later the chief of detectives in Paris in the early 19th century, lived upstairs. Some shops to check out are Legrand Filles et Fils (p195), which sells wine and wine-related paraphernalia, at Nos 5 to 11 and opposite at No 14; Wolff et Descourtis and its silk scarves at No 18; L'Atelier Emilio Robbo, one of the most beautiful flower shops in Paris, at Nos 29 to 33; and the Librairie Ancienne & Moderne at No 45 and 46, which Colette frequented.

7 Galerie Colbert The major draw of the Galerie Colbert, which runs parallel to Galerie Vivienne, is its glass dome and rotunda. Built in 1826 and now part of the University of Paris system, the *passage* served as a car workshop and garage as recently as the early 1980s. Check out the bizarre fresco above the exit to the rue des Petits Champs; it's completely disproportionate. Enter and exit from rue des Petits Champs.

8 Passage Choiseul West of the Galerie Colbert at 40 rue des Petits Champs is the entrance to passage Choiseul. Passage Choiseul (1824), some 45m long and containing scores of shops, is more ordinary than many of the other *passages* on this tour but is refreshing for that. There are discount and vintage clothing shops (Nos 7 to 9, 28, 42 and 51 to 53), Asian fast-food outlets (eg Nos 19, 32 and 48) and secondhand bookshops (Nos 74 to 76). The *passage* has a long literary pedigree: Paul Verlaine (1844–96) drank absinthe here and Céline (1894–1961) grew up in his mother's lace shop at No 62, which now sells beads and costume jewellery. Check out the Théâtre des Bouffes Parisiens, where comedies are performed, at No 61 (the main theatre is around the corner at 4 rue Monsigny, 2e).

9 Bourse de Commerce Leave passage Choiseul at 23 rue St-Augustin and walk eastwards to where the street meets rue du Quatre Septembre. The building across the square is the Bourse de Commerce (p80), built in 1826. Turn left and head north up rue Vivienne, and then east (right) along rue St-Marc.

10 Passage des Panoramas The entrance to the mazelike passage des Panoramas is at 10

WALK FACTS

Start Metro Louvre-Rivoli
End Metro Le Peletier
Distance 3km
Time Two hours
Fuel stops Le Véro Dodat (p225), À Priori Thé (p279), L'Arbre à Cannelle p225)

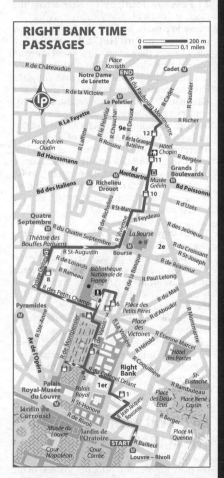

RIGHT BANK TIME PASSAGES

rue St-Marc. Built in 1800, passage des Panoramas is the oldest covered arcade in Paris and the first to be lit by gas (1817). It was expanded in 1834 with the addition of four other interconnecting *passages*: Feydeau, Montmartre, St-Marc and Variétés. It's a bit faded around the edges now, but is full of popular eateries including L'Arbre à Cannelle (p225). Keep an

183

eye open for Jean-Paul Belmondo's Théâtre des Variétés at No 17, the erstwhile vaudeville Théâtre d'Offenbach, from where spectators would come out to shop during the interval, the old engraver Stern (now a publisher called Maury) at No 47 and the autograph dealer Arnaud Magistry at No 60. Exit at 11 blvd Montmartre.

11 Passage Jouffroy Directly across the road, at 10–12 blvd Montmartre, is the entrance to passage Jouffroy, the last major *passage* to open in Paris (1847); the opening five years later of the capital's first *grand magasin* (department store), Le Bon Marché, would sound the death knell for *passages couverts*. Passage Jouffroy, the first to use metal and glass in its skylights and to have central heating, remains a personal favourite. There are two hotels here, including the Hôtel Chopin (p340), as well as the Musée Grévin (p131) of wax figures. There are also wonderful boutiques including M&G Segas (No 34), where Toulouse-Lautrec bought his walking sticks; Brésilophile (No 40) filled with colourful rocks and minerals; the old bookshop Paul Vulin (Nos 46 to 50); and the silversmith Olivier at No 63.

12 Passage Verdeau Leave passage Jouffroy at 9 rue de la Grange Batelière, cross the road to No 6, and enter passage Verdeau, the last and most modest of this stretch of covered arcades. Verdeau wasn't particularly successful because of its 'end-of-the-line' location. Still, there's lots to explore here: vintage Tintin and comic books at Librairie Roland Buret (No 6); needlepoint at Le Bonheur des Dames (No 8); Le Cabinet des Curieux (No 12) with weird and wonderful objects; and daguerreotypes at Photo Verdeau (No 14). The northern exit from passage Verdeau is at 31bis rue du Faubourg Montmartre.

MEDIEVAL MEANDERINGS IN THE MARAIS

Not long after Henri IV began construction of the place Royale (now place des Vosges) in the early 17th century, aristocrats began building the *hôtels particuliers* (private mansions) so characteristic of the Marais district. These gold- and cream-coloured brick buildings are among the most beautiful Renaissance structures in the city and, because so many were built at more or less the same time, the Marais enjoys an architectural harmony unknown elsewhere in Paris. Many of the *hôtels particuliers* house government offices, libraries and – importantly – museums. While doing this walk, you can also tick off such must-sees as the Musée Picasso and the Musée Carnavalet, which deals with the history of Paris.

1 Hôtel d'Aumont Begin the tour at St-Paul metro station on rue François Miron, 4e, facing rue de Rivoli. Walk south on narrow rue du Prévôt to rue Charlemagne, once called rue des Prestres (Street of the Priests). To the right (west) on the corner of rue des Nonnains d'Hyères at 7 rue de Jouy stands the majestic Hôtel d'Aumont, built around 1650 for a financier and one of the most beautiful *hôtels particuliers* in the Marais. It now contains offices of the Tribunal Administratif, the body that deals with – *sacré bleu!* – internal disputes in the bloated and litigious French civil service. Opposite Hôtel d'Aumont, on the corner of rue de Jouy and rue de Fourcy, is a wonderful 17th-century relief of a winemaker.

2 Hôtel de Sens Continue further south along rue des Nonnains d'Hyères, past the Hôtel d'Aumont's geometrical gardens on the right and turn left (east) onto rue de l'Hôtel de Ville. On the left at 1 rue du Figuier is Hôtel de Sens, the oldest private mansion in the Marais, with another geometric garden and a neo-Gothic turret. Begun around 1475, it was built as the Paris digs for the powerful archbishops of Sens, under whose authority Paris fell at the time. When Paris was made an archbishopric, the Hôtel de Sens was rented out to coach drivers, fruit sellers, a hatter, a glassblower and even a jam-maker. It was heavily restored in mock Gothic style in 1911; today it houses the Bibliothèque Forney (Forney Library; ☎ 01 42 78 14 60; admission free; ⊙ 1-7.30pm Tue, Fri & Sat, 10am-7.30pm Wed & Thu). Temporary exhibitions here will allow you to explore at least part of the building.

3 Philippe-Auguste's enceinte Continue southeast along rue de l'Ave Maria and then go northeast along rue des Jardins de St-Paul. The two truncated and crumbling towers across the sports fields on the left are all that remain of Philippe-Auguste's *enceinte*, a fortified medieval wall built around 1190 and once guarded by 39 towers. They are now part of the prestigious Lycée Charlemagne. On the opposite side of rue des Jardins de St-Paul are the entrances to Village St-Paul, a courtyard of antique shops and designer boutiques that has somehow never really taken off.

4 Église St-Paul St-Louis Cross over rue Charlemagne and duck into narrow rue Eginhard, a street with a tiny courtyard and a grated well built during the reign of Louis XIII. The street doglegs into rue St-Paul; on the corner above 23 rue Neuve St-Pierre, housing a bedlinen shop, are the remains of the medieval Église St-Paul. A bit further north, tiny passage St-Paul leads to the side entrance of the Église St-Paul St-Louis (☎ 01 42 72 30 32; ☉ 8am-8pm Mon-Fri, 8am-7.30pm Sat, 9am-8pm Sun) at No 7, a Jesuit church completed in 1641 during the Counter-Reformation.

5 Former boulangerie-pâtisserie Rue St-Paul debouches into rue St-Antoine. Turn left, passing the front entrance of Église St-Paul St-Louis at No 99, cross over rue de Rivoli and head north up rue Malher. A former

boulangerie–pâtisserie, or bakery–cake shop, at No 13 (now a clothes store) has fine old shop signs advertising *pains de seigle et gruau* (rye and wheaten breads), *gateaux secs* (biscuits) and *chaussons de pommes* (apple turnovers).

6 Hôtel Lamoignon Continue north on rue Pavée (Paved Street), the first cobbled road in Paris. At No 24 stands Hôtel Lamoignon,

WALK FACTS

Start Metro St-Paul
End Hôtel de Sully (Metro St-Paul)
Distance 2km
Time 1½ hours
Fuel stops Café Suédois (p287), Café Hugo (p258)

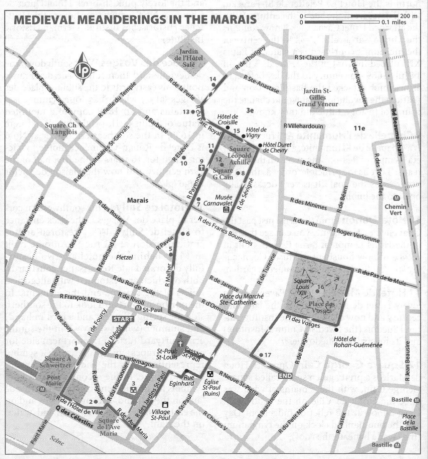

MEDIEVAL MEANDERINGS IN THE MARAIS

built between 1585 and 1612 for Diane de France (1538–1619), duchess of Angoulême and legitimised daughter of Henri II. It is a fine example of late Renaissance architecture; note the Corinthian capitals and stained glass in the courtyard and, above the main gate, the cherubs holding a mirror (symbolising truth) and a snake (for prudence). It now houses the Bibliothèque Historique de la Ville de Paris (☎ 01 44 59 29 40; ⏱ 10am-6pm Mon-Sat).

7 Hôtel Carnavalet

Walk north along rue Payenne. The building immediately on the right at No 2 is the back of the mid-16th century, Renaissance-style Hôtel Carnavalet, built between 1548 and 1654 and home to the letter-writer Madame de Sévigné (1626–96).

8 Hôtel Le Peletier de St-Fargeau

Further north is the Hôtel Le Peletier de St-Fargeau, which dates from the late 17th century. With the attached Hôtel Carnavalet, it now contains the Musée Carnavalet (p146). In the centre of the museum's courtyard is a statue of Louis XIII placed in front of the Hôtel de Ville on 14 July 1689 – a century to the day before an armed mob attacked the Bastille prison and sparked the revolution that would change the course of history. Little did they know...

9 Chapelle de l'Humanité

At 5 rue Payenne is a Chapelle de l'Humanité, a Revolutionary-era 'Temple of Reason'; the quote on the façade reads: 'Love as the principle, order as the base, progress as the goal'. It is very occasionally open to the public.

10 Hôtel Donon

From the grille just past the Chapelle de l'Humanité, you can see the rear of the Hôtel Donon at 8 rue Elzévir, built in 1598 and now housing the Musée Cognacq-Jay (p147). It too has a lovely geometric garden.

11 Hôtel de Marle

At 11 rue Payenne is the lovely Hôtel de Marle, built in the late 16th century and now containing the Institut Culturel Suédois (the Swedish Cultural Institute) and its lovely Café Suédois (p287).

12 Square George Cain

Opposite Hôtel de Marle is a pretty green space called square George Cain, with the remains of what was once the Hôtel de Ville on the south wall. Have a look at the relief of Judgement Day and the one-handed clock on the tympanum (the façade beneath the roof).

13 Hôtel de Libéral Bruant

From the square walk a short distance northwest to more spectacular 17th-century *hôtels particuliers*: Hôtel de Libéral Bruant at 1 rue de la Perle. It has been a museum and a gallery over the years but is now in private hands.

14 Hôtel Salé

Northeast of Hôtel de Libéral Bruant is another prize example of a 17th-century *hôtel particulier*: Hôtel Salé at 5 rue de Thorigny, whose three floors and vaulted cellars house the Musée Picasso (p146).

15 Rue du Parc Royal

Retrace your steps to rue du Parc Royal. Heading east you'll pass three buildings all of which date from about 1620 and do civic duty as archives and historical libraries: the unimpressive Hôtel de Croisille at No 12, Hôtel de Vigny at No 10 and the lovely pinkish-brick Hôtel Duret de Chevry at No 8, which now houses the Deutsches Historisches Institut (German Historic Institute).

16 Place des Vosges

Walk south down rue de Sévigné and then follow rue des Francs Bourgeois eastwards to the sublime place des Vosges (p146), which has four symmetrical fountains and an 1829 copy of a mounted statue of Louis XIII, originally placed here in 1639. In the southeastern corner at No 6 is Hôtel de Rohan-Guéménée, home to Victor Hugo for 16 years in the first half of the 19th century and now the Maison de Victor Hugo (p146).

17 Hôtel de Sully

In the southwestern corner of place des Vosges is the back entrance to Hôtel de Sully (p146), a restored aristocratic mansion at 62 rue St-Antoine built in 1625. Behind the hôtel are two beautifully decorated late Renaissance courtyards, both of which are festooned with allegorical reliefs of the seasons and the elements. In the northern courtyard look to the southern side for spring (flowers and a bird in hand) and summer (wheat sheaves); in the southern courtyard turn to the northern side for autumn (grapes) and winter, with a symbol representing both the end of the year and the end of life. In the second courtyard are symbols for the elements: on the western side 'air' on the left and 'fire' on the right and on the eastern side 'earth' on the left and 'water' on the right.

LATIN QUARTER LITERARY LOOP

It wasn't just Paris' reputation for liberal thought and relaxed morals that lured writers and artists in the 1920s. Left Bank Paris was cheap and in France, unlike in Prohibition-era America, you could drink alcohol to your heart's content.

1 James Joyce's flat Start at the Cardinal Lemoine metro station, 5e. Walk southwest along rue du Cardinal Lemoine, peering down the passageway at No 71. Irish writer James Joyce (1882–1941) lived in the courtyard flat at the back marked 'E' when he arrived in Paris in 1921; he finished editing *Ulysses* here.

2 Ernest Hemingway's apartment Further south at 74 rue du Cardinal Lemoine is the apartment where Ernest Hemingway (1899–1961) lived with his first wife Hadley from January 1922 until August 1923. Just below was Bal au Printemps, a popular *bal musette* (dancing club) that served as the model for the one where Jake Barnes meets Brett Ashley in Hemingway's *The Sun Also Rises*.

3 Paul Verlaine's garret Hemingway lived on rue du Cardinal Lemoine but wrote in a top-floor garret of a hotel round the corner at 39 rue Descartes, the very hotel where the poet Paul Verlaine (1844–96) died. Ignore the incorrect plaque.

4 Place de la Contrescarpe Rue Descartes runs south into place de la Contrescarpe, now a well-scrubbed square with four Judas trees and a fountain, but once a 'cesspool' (said Hemingway), especially Café des Amateurs at No 2–4, now Café Delmas (p280).

5 George Orwell's boarding house Rue Mouffetard (from *mofette,* meaning 'skunk') runs south of place de la Contrescarpe. Turn right onto rue du Pot de Fer where in 1928 George Orwell (1903–50) stayed in a cheap boarding house above No 6 while working as a dishwasher. Read about it and the street, which he called 'rue du Coq d'Or' (Street of the Golden Rooster), in *Down and Out in Paris and London* (1933).

6 Place du Panthéon Turn north onto rue Tournefort (the street where much of Balzac's novel *Père Goriot* takes place) and go left into

rue de l'Estrapade. From here follow Hemingway's own directions provided in *A Moveable Feast* as he made his way to a favourite café on place St-Michel. Turn north onto rue Clotilde and walk along the eastern side of vast place du Panthéon to the corner of rue Clovis. Just around the corner on rue Clovis is Église St-Étienne du Mont (p104).

7 Boulevard St-Michel Continue around the northern edge of place du Panthéon and walk west along rue Soufflot. Turn right onto blvd St-Michel, past the Musée National du Moyen Age (p104). The cafés on place St-Michel were taken over by tourists decades ago, and Shakespeare & Company (p197) around the corner has nothing to do with the bookshop frequented by Hemingway & co.

8 Jack Kerouac's hotel Follow the Seine west along quai des Grands Augustins, past the *bouquinistes* (secondhand booksellers) that Hemingway so loved. South at 9 rue Gît le Cœur is the Relais Hôtel du Vieux Paris, a favourite of poet Allen Ginsberg (1926–97) and Beat writer Jack Kerouac (1922–69) in the 1950s. Ginsberg and Kerouac drank down the road in bar Le Gentilhomme at 28 rue St-André des Arts (now an Irish pub).

9 Picasso's studio Pablo Picasso (1881–1973) lived in his studio at 7 rue des Grands Augustins from 1936 to 1955 and completed his masterpiece *Guernica* here in 1937 – a century after Balzac's *Le Chef d'Œuvre Inconnu* (The Unknown Masterpiece), set in this *hôtel particulier,* was published.

10 Shakespeare & Company – The Original Walk south to rue St-André des Arts, follow it west and turn south through Cour du Commerce Saint André, a covered passage that empties into blvd St-Germain. At 12 rue de l'Odéon stood the original Shakespeare & Company bookshop where founder–owner Sylvia Beach (1887–1962) lent books to Hemingway, and edited, retyped and published *Ulysses* for Joyce in 1922. The bookshop was closed during the occupation when Beach refused to sell her last copy of Joyce's *Finnegan's Wake* to a Nazi officer.

11 Sartre & de Beauvoir's hang-outs Return to blvd St-Germain and walk west to Les Deux Magots (p282) and Café de Flore (p281), favourite cafés of post-war Left Bank intellectuals Jean-Paul Sartre and Simone de Beauvoir.

12 Henry Miller's room From place St-Germain des Prés walk north along rue Bonaparte to No 36 where Henry Miller (1891–1980) stayed in a 5th-floor mansard room in 1930. He later wrote about the experience in *Letters to Emil* (1989).

WALK FACTS

Start **Metro Cardinal Lemoine**
End **Le Dôme or Select (Metro Vavin)**
Distance **7km**
Time **Three hours**
Fuel stops **Les Deux Magots** (p282) **or Café de Flore** (p281)

13 Oscar Wilde's hotel Continue north on rue Bonaparte and turn east onto rue des Beaux-Arts to No 13 (L'Hôtel, p334), the former Hôtel d'Alsace where Oscar Wilde died of meningitis in 1900. Argentine writer Jorge Luis Borges (1899–1986) stayed in the same hotel in the 1970s and '80s.

14 Rue Jacob This street has literary associations from the sublime to the ridiculous. At No 44, Hôtel d'Angleterre (p334) is where Hemingway spent his first night in Paris; and No 56 is where David Hartley, George III's representative, met with Benjamin Franklin, John Adams and John Hay on 3 September 1783 to sign the treaty recognising American independence.

No 52 rue Jacob was the fashionable restaurant Michaud's where Hemingway stood

LATIN QUARTER LITERARY LOOP

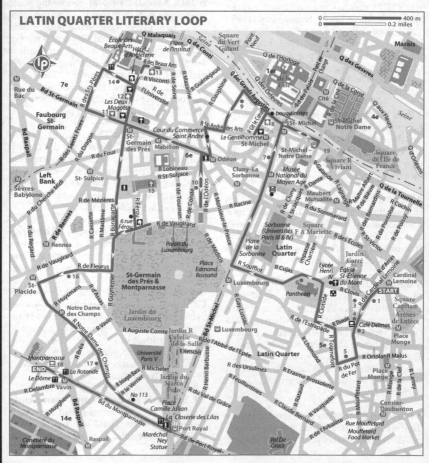

outside watching Joyce and his family dine and where a memorable event may have taken place. According to Hemingway in *A Moveable Feast*, writer F Scott Fitzgerald (1896–1940), concerned about not being able to sexually satisfy his wife Zelda, asked Hemingway to inspect him in the café's toilet. 'It is not basically a question of the size in repose…' Hemingway advised him.

15 Église St-Sulpice Go south on rue des Saints Pères, then east on blvd St-Germain and south on rue Bonaparte. Follow it past Église St-Sulpice (p106), where a pivotal clue is left and a murder takes place in Dan Brown's *The Da Vinci Code*.

16 Gertrude Stein's home After slumming it for a few years in the Latin Quarter, Hemingway and others of the so-called Lost Generation moved to this area. In 1925 William Faulkner (1897–1962) spent a few months at 42 rue de Vaugirard. Hemingway spent his last years in Paris in a rather grand flat at 6 rue Férou, within easy striking distance of 27 rue de Fleurus where American novelist Gertrude Stein (1874–1946) lived and entertained such luminaries as Matisse, Picasso, Braque, Gauguin and Pound.

17 Rue Notre Dame des Champs Nearby, in a flat filled with Japanese paintings and packing crates posing as furniture, lived Ezra Pound (1885–1972) at 70bis rue Notre Dame des Champs. Hemingway's first apartment in this area was above a sawmill at 113 rue Notre Dames des Champs. Further east is La Closerie des Lilas (p270) where Hemingway drank.

18 Literary Cafés Port Royal metro station is just opposite. West of here are two café–restaurants that have hosted more literary luminaries than any others in the world: Le Dôme (p270) and Select' (p291).

top picks

- E Dehillerin (p196)
- L'Écritoire (p196)
- Fromagerie Alléosse (p202)
- I Love My Blender (p205)
- Clair de Rêve (p196)
- Merci (p206)
- Puzzle Michèle Wilson (p209)
- Ivoire (p198)
- Lin et Cie (p199)
- Le Bon Marché (p199)

SHOPPING

When it comes to shopping, Paris naturally has it all: large boulevards lined with international chains, luxury avenues with designer fashion, famous *grands magasins* (department stores) and fabulous flea markets (see p212). But the real charm of Parisian shopping resides in a peripatetic stroll through the side streets, where tiny speciality shops and quirky boutiques selling everything from strawberry-scented Wellington boots to candles scented like heaven alternate with cafés, galleries and churches. These original addresses are what we focus on in this chapter.

As in many capital cities, shops are spread out across different neighbourhoods, inspiring very different styles of shopping. If what the French do best – fashion (see p41) – is what you're after, tread the *haute couture* (high fashion), luxury jewellery and designer perfume boardwalks in the Étoile and Champs-Élysées. For original fashion, both street and vintage, the addictive maze of boutique shopping in the Marais and St-Germain will keep you on your toes. For the full lowdown on shopping areas in Paris see p193.

Fashion is but one wallet temptation. Parisian shopping is an exquisite Pandora's Box of fine food, wine and tea, books, beautiful stationery, fine art, antiques and original collectables. Be it a music box to enchant, a hammock to string between trees or a truffle to shave on pasta, you won't be stuck for gifts and souvenirs to take home. For our favourite gift ideas under €25 see p195.

Should you not look like a millionaire, trying to raise a smile out of frosty, poker-faced staff in certain designer boutiques (or indeed attracting their attention to let you in; most require you to buzz) can be disheartening. To navigate what can be an intimidating scene, gen up on our shopping tips on p194.

Costs

With its catwalk fashion and boutique fare, Parisian shopping is not really for the dedicated bargain hunter. But there are bargains to be had – at the city's clutch of flea markets and twice a year during the annual *soldes* (sales) which see prices slashed by as much as 50%: sales usually last a month, starting in mid-January and again in mid-June.

CONSUMER TAXES & BARGAINING

Non-EU residents can get a TVA (VAT; sales tax) refund of up to 19.6% on spends of more than €175 in any one store on one day; see p404.

Some larger department stores and duty-free shops might give discounts of 10% to foreign passport holders if asked; otherwise bargaining is reserved for flea markets.

Opening Hours

Opening hours are generally between 10am and 7pm Monday to Saturday. Smaller shops often shut all day on Monday; on other days, their proprietors may close from noon to around 2pm for a long and lazy lunch. Many larger stores hold *nocturnes* (late-night shopping) on Thursday, remaining open until around 10pm. For Sunday shopping, the Champs-Élysées (p201), Montmartre (p203), Marais (p205) and Bastille (p210) areas are the liveliest.

LOUVRE & LES HALLES

Though you'll find any number of specialist boutiques selling everything from music boxes to kitchenware here, the 1e and 2e arrondissements are mostly about fashion. Indeed, the Sentier garment district has become a centre for fashion, while rue Étienne Marcel, place des Victoires and rue du Jour beside the Église St-Eustache (Map p76) offer prominent labels and shoe shops. Nearby rue Montmartre and rue Tiquetonne are known for their streetwear and avant-garde designs. Les Halles itself, once the city's food market, is now a vast underground shopping complex. It's flanked to the east by the sleaze and sports stores of rue St-Denis, and to the south by the chain stores of rue de Rivoli. The easternmost part of the 1e around Palais Royal is far more conservative, with fancy period and label fashion.

Most of the many museums in this neighbourhood have excellent in-house shops. For a preview of what to expect, check out the Les Boutiques de Musées (www.boutiquesdemusees.fr/en) website.

CARROUSEL DU LOUVRE

Map p76   Shopping Mall

☎ 01 43 16 47 10; www.carrouseldulouvre.com, in French; 99 rue de Rivoli, 1er; ⏱ 8am-11pm; Ⓜ Palais Royal–Musée du Louvre

Built around IM Pei's inverted glass pyramid beneath the place du Carrousel, this shopping centre contains more than 30 upmarket shops (⏱ 10am-8pm daily), more than a dozen restaurants and even the Comédie Française Studio Théâtre (p307).

BRENTANO'S Map p72   Books & Comics

☎ 01 42 61 52 50; www.brentanos.fr, in French; 37 av de l'Opéra, 2e; ⏱ 10am-7.30pm Mon-Sat, 1-7pm Sun; Ⓜ Opéra

Situated midway between the Louvre and Palais Garnier, this totally renovated bookshop is the last survivor of the once ubiquitous US chain. It's a good shop for tracking down American books, including fiction, business and children's titles, as well as magazines.

LIBRAIRIE GOURMANDE

Map p72   Books & Comics

☎ 01 43 54 37 27; www.librairie-gourmande.fr, in French; 92 rue Montmartre, 2e; ⏱ 11am-7pm Mon-Sat; Ⓜ Sentier

The city's leading bookshop dedicated to things culinary and gourmet is conveniently just up the road from kitchenware shops A Simon and E Dehillerin. All the classic texts are here, along with new recipe collections.

WH SMITH Map p72   Books & Comics

☎ 01 44 77 88 99; www.whsmith.fr; 248 rue de Rivoli, 1er; ⏱ 9am-7pm Mon-Sat, 12.30-7.30pm Sun; Ⓜ Concorde

This branch of the British-owned chain, supposedly the largest English-language bookshop in Paris, counts some 70,000 titles in stock, as well as a good selection of international magazines, DVDs and greetings cards.

AGNÈS B FEMME

Map p76   Fashion & Accessories

☎ 01 45 08 56 56; www.agnesb.com; 6 rue du Jour, 1er; ⏱ 10 or 10.30am-7 or 7.30pm Mon-Sat; Ⓜ Les Halles

Style stalwart agnès b excels in extremely durable, comfortable and sometimes quirky clothes. The foundations are excellent; the rest has somewhat lost its cachet of late. On the same street you'll find agnès b homme (Map p76; ☎ 01 42 33 04 13; 3 rue du Jour, 1er) for

men and agnès b enfant (Map p76; ☎ 01 40 39 96 88; 2 rue du Jour, 1er) for children.

ANDRÉ Map p76   Fashion & Accessories

☎ 01 53 40 96 84; www.andre.fr, in French; 106 rue de Rivoli, 1er; ⏱ 9am-8pm Mon-Sat; Ⓜ Châtelet

This branch of a footwear chain is where ordinary (and still very stylish) Parisian women buy their shoes and boots. At the same time each year André invites hot new designers to create new lines of shoes and handbags at affordable prices.

ANTOINE Map p72   Fashion & Accessories

☎ 01 42 96 01 80; 10 av de l'Opéra, 2e; ⏱ 10.30am-3pm & 4-6.30pm Mon-Sat; Ⓜ Pyramides or Palais Royal–Musée du Louvre

Founded in 1745, Antoine is the place to come if you're in the market for a bespoke

top picks

SHOPPING AREAS

Key areas to mooch with no particular purchase in mind are the Marais in the 3e and 4e, around St-Germain des Prés in the 6e, and parts of Montmartre and Pigalle in the 9e and 18e. Or perhaps you have something specific to buy?

- **Designer Haute Couture** The world's most famous designers stylishly jostle for window space on av Montaigne, av George V and rue du Faubourg St-Honoré, 8e (p203).
- **Chain-Store Fashion** Find Gap, H&M, Zara and other major, supersized chain stores on rue de Rivoli in the 1er, Les Halles in the 2e, and av des Champs-Élysées, 8e (p192).
- **Department Stores** On and around bd Haussmann, 9e (p201).
- **Factory Outlets** Price-cut fashion for men, women and kids the length of rue d'Alésia, 14e (p211).
- **Hip Fashion & Art** Young designers crowd rue Charlot in the 3e, and beyond in the northern Marais (p205 and p210).
- **Stuff for Kids** Fashion and toys, including Petit Bateau, Jacardi and Du Pareil au Même, around rue Vavin, 6e (p198).
- **Fine Art & Antiques** Right-bank place des Vosges, 4e (p205) and left-bank Carré Rive Gauche, 6e (p198).
- **Design** Eames, eat your heart out! Boutique galleries specialising in modern furniture, art and design (1950s to present) stud rue Mazarine and rue de Seine, 6e (p199).

cane, umbrella, fan or pair of gloves. It sells both new and vintage items.

BARBARA BUI

Map p76   Fashion & Accessories

☎ 01 40 26 43 65; www.barbarabui.com; 23 rue Étienne Marcel, 2e; ⏰ 11am-7.30pm Mon-Sat; Ⓜ Étienne Marcel

Franco-Vietnamese Barbara Bui's nearby Kabuki Femme (p194) was an instant success here in Paris and she went on to open her own shops, known for their elegant modernism and beautifully cut trousers. There's also a Marais branch (Map p152; ☎ 01 53 01 88 05; 43 rue des Francs Bourgeois, 4e; ⏰ 12.30-7pm Mon, 10.30am-7pm Tue-Sat, 1-7pm Sun; Ⓜ St-Paul).

BONPOINT

Map p72   Fashion & Accessories

☎ 01 40 26 20 90; www.bonpoint.com; 50 rue Étienne Marcel; ⏰ 10am-7pm Mon-Sat; Ⓜ Étienne Marcel

This is an immaculate collection of classic children's clothes (newborn to 14 years). It's a longstanding tradition for the chic *bébés* of Paris to be besuited by their grannies in Bonpoint, but if you're looking to buy into it, expect to pay €90 for a pair of perfectly crafted first-time booties.

COLETTE

Map p72   Fashion & Accessories

☎ 01 55 35 33 90; www.colette.fr; 213 rue St-Honoré, 1er; ⏰ 11am-7pm Mon-Sat; Ⓜ Tuileries

This Japanese-inspired concept store has clothes and accessories as well as books, art, music and beauty products. Limited-edition sneakers, candles that smell like sex (so say staff, anyway), cutting-edge clocks – it's worth a look even if you're not buying. Colette's famous sales see huge reductions on the designer stock, including Comme des Garçons, Marc Jacobs and far more. The Water Bar café-restaurant in the basement features still and sparkling water from around the world.

EKIVOK Map p76   Fashion & Accessories

☎ 01 42 21 98 71; www.ekivok.com, in French; 39 bd de Sébastopol, 1er; ⏰ 11am-7.30pm Mon-Sat; Ⓜ Les Halles

You'll find hoodies, sweats and jeans at this graffiti-covered outlet, including labels of the moment such as Carhartt, Bullrot, Skunk Funk and Hardcore Session. Good music too.

KABUKI FEMME

Map p76   Fashion & Accessories

☎ 01 42 33 55 65; www.barbarabui.com; 25 rue Étienne Marcel, 2e; ⏰ 11am-7.30pm Mon-Sat; Ⓜ Étienne Marcel

Opened some 20 years ago, this is the shop that brought Barbara Bui to world attention. Her own eponymous store is next door (p194) and you'll find Kabuki Homme (Map p76; ☎ 01 42 33 13 44; 21 rue Étienne Marcel, 2e), for men, two doors down. In addition to Bui's own designs there's a judicious selection from other brands, including Prada, Balenciaga, Stella McCartney, Yves Saint Laurent and Dior.

KENZO Map p76   Fashion & Accessories

☎ 01 40 28 11 80; www.kenzo.com; 1 rue du Pont Neuf, 1er; ⏰ noon-7.30pm Mon, 11am-7.30pm Tue-Sat; Ⓜ Pont Neuf

While Kenzo himself may have retired from designing some time ago, his successor Antonio Marras has brought a new *joie de vivre* to the label. The Pont Neuf flagship store is spread over five floors and is a tantalising temple to fashion and beauty for both men and women.

top picks

TOP TIPS

- Start with an overview of Paris fashion at department stores like Le Bon Marché (p199), Galeries Lafayette (p202) and Le Printemps (p202).
- The most exclusive designer boutiques require customers to buzz to get in – don't be shy about ringing the bell.
- Clothes shopping in France is 'look but don't touch' style, meaning no disturbing perfectly folded piles of T-shirts or trying on shades without asking.
- Returning or exchanging a purchase without the *ticket de caisse* (receipt) is impossible. Keep the receipt safe and know you have one month to change the item.
- Buying a present for someone or simply fancy your purchase exquisitely gift-wrapped? Ask for *un paquet cadeau* (gift-wrapping). It costs nothing and is something practically every shop does – and very beautifully too.
- Don't want to DIY? Invest in a personalised shopping tour by foot or chauffeur: www.secretsofparis.com and www.chicshoppingparis.com are two of many.

top picks

GIFTS UNDER €25

- Guerlain (p202), L'Artisan Parfumeur (p205) & Fragonard (p205) Perfume and scented candles.
- La Tour d'Argent (p227) An edible, oenological or silver souvenir that says 'quack' from the upmarket boutique of Paris' famous duck restaurant.
- Mélodies Graphiques (p209), L'Agenda Moderne (p209) & L'Écritoire (p196) Beautiful stationery.
- Atelier d'Autrefois (p208) & Clair de Rêve (p196) A music box.
- E Dehillerin (p196) Oyster mitts to save yours when cracking a dozen open from the king of kitchen shops.
- La Boutique des Inventions (p209) The next best thing by a French inventor.
- Boutique Obut (p208) A three-ball *pétanque* (French boules) set.

KILIWATCH
Map p72   Fashion & Accessories

☎ 01 42 21 17 37; www.kiliwatch.fr, in French; 64 rue Tiquetonne, 2e; ◷ 2-7pm Mon, 11am-7.30pm Tue-Sat; Ⓜ Étienne Marcel

A Parisian institution, Kiliwatch is always packed with hip guys and gals rummaging through rack after rack of new and used streetwear and designs. There's a startling vintage range including hats and boots, plus art/photography books, eyewear and the latest sneakers.

MARIA LUISA FEMME
Map p72   Fashion & Accessories

☎ 01 47 03 96 15; www.marialuisaparis.com; 7 rue Rouget de l'Isle, 1er; ◷ 10.30am-7pm Mon-Sat; Ⓜ Concorde

Every fashionista knows the eminent selection of classic and avant-garde designers at this shop, which also carries a range of swimwear. Around the corner you'll find an accessories branch (Map p72; ☎ 01 42 60 99 83; 38 rue du Mont Thabor, 1er; Ⓜ Concorde).

MARITHÉ & FRANÇOIS GIRBAUD
Map p72   Fashion & Accessories

☎ 01 53 40 74 20; www.girbaud.com; 38 rue Étienne Marcel, 2e; ◷ 11.30am-7.30pm Mon, 10.30am-7.30pm Tue-Sat; Ⓜ Étienne Marcel

This globetrotting designer couple call themselves 'jeanologists', having devoted themselves to more than 30 years of denim. They have four other boutiques in Paris, including a Marais branch (Map p152; ☎ 01 44 54 99 01; 20 rue Malher, 4e; ◷ 11am-7pm Mon-Sat, 2-7pm Sun; Ⓜ St-Paul) and a St-Germain branch (Map p112; ☎ 01 53 63 53 63; 7 rue du Cherche Midi, 6e; ◷ 11.30am-7.30pm Mon, 10.30am-7.30pm Tue-Sat; Ⓜ St-Sulpice) with its own 'vegetation wall' inside (p57).

LAVINIA
Map p72   Food & Drink

☎ 01 42 97 54 50; www.lavinia.com, in French; 3 bd de la Madeleine, 1er; ◷ 10am-8pm Mon-Sat; Ⓜ Madeleine

Among the largest (and certainly most exclusive) drinks shops is this bastion of booze near Madeleine. To be sure, come here for the fruit of the vine but we usually visit to top our collection of exclusive *eaux-de vie* (fruit brandies).

LEGRAND FILLES & FILS
Map p72   Food & Drink

☎ 01 42 60 07 12; www.caves-legrand.com, in French; 1 rue de la Banque, 2e; ◷ 11am-7pm Mon, 10am-7.30pm Tue-Fri, 10am-7pm Sat; Ⓜ Pyramides

This shop in the covered arcade (5-11 Galerie Vivienne) sells not just fine wines but also all the accoutrements: corkscrews, tasting glasses, decanters etc. It also has a fancy wine bar and espace dégustation (tasting room; 14 Galerie Vivienne; ◷ noon-7pm Mon-Sat).

BOÎTES À MUSIQUE ANNA JOLIET
Map p72   Gifts & Souvenirs

☎ 01 42 96 55 13; www.boitesamusique-paris.com, in French; passage du Perron, 9 rue de Beaujolais, 1er; ◷ 10am-7pm Mon-Sat; Ⓜ Pyramides

This wonderful (and tiny) shop at the northern end of the Jardin du Palais Royal specialises in music boxes, both new and old, from Switzerland. Just open the door and see if you aren't tempted in (and/or can recognise the tune).

CANICRÈCHE
Map p72   Gifts & Souvenirs

☎ 01 42 71 59 09; www.canicreche.fr, in French; 32 rue de Turbigo, 3e; ◷ 8am-8pm Mon-Fri, 10am-8pm Sat; Ⓜ Arts et Métiers

And where do the chic *chiens* (dogs) of Paris go? They head for this friendly boutique, which moonlights as a canine hotel, for their collars, toys, bedding and stunning little outfits. There's a branch in the 15e (Map p168; ☎ 01 43 06 64 34; 9 rue Quinault, 15e; ◷ 8am-8pm Mon-Fri, 8am-7pm Sat; Ⓜ Commerce).

L'ÉCRITOIRE Map p76   Gifts & Souvenirs
☎ 01 42 78 01 18; www.ecritoire.fr; 61 rue St-Martin, 4e; ⏱ 11am-7pm Mon-Sat; Ⓜ Châtelet or Hôtel de Ville
This bijou of a shop so beloved by young Japanese tourists sells anything and everything to do with writing – from pens and ink in a rainbow of colours to seals, sealing wax and origami-like handmade envelopes. It's been here since 1975.

A SIMON Map p72   Home & Garden
☎ 01 42 33 71 65; www.simon-a.com; 48 & 52 rue Montmartre, 2e; ⏱ 1.30-6.30pm Mon, 9am-6.30pm Tue-Fri, 10am-6.30pm Sat; Ⓜ Étienne Marcel
A more modern kitchenware shop than nearby E Dehillerin (p196), A Simon has more pots, pans, mixing bowls and utensils (as well as crockery and cutlery) than you thought existed, in two separate shops.

ASTIER DE VILLATTE
Map p76   Home & Garden
☎ 01 42 60 74 13; www.astierdevillatte.com; 173 rue St-Honoré, 1er; ⏱ 11am-7.30pm Mon-Sat; Ⓜ Palais Royal–Musée du Louvre
The only Parisian outlet of the exclusive manufacturer of ceramic tableware displays its settings (and candles and beauty products) in a wonderfully old-fashioned shop just west of the Palais Royal.

E DEHILLERIN Map p76   Home & Garden
☎ 01 42 36 53 13; www.dehillerin.com; 18-20 rue Coquillière, 1er; ⏱ 9am-12.30pm & 2-6pm Mon, 9am-6pm Tue-Sat; Ⓜ Les Halles
Founded in 1820, this two-level shop carries an incredible selection of professional-quality *matériel de cuisine* (kitchenware). You're sure to find something you desperately need, such as a *coupe volaille* (poultry scissors) or even a *turbotiére* (turbot poacher).

THE ISLANDS

Despite their small size, the islands (particularly the Île de St-Louis) are a shopper's delight. The Île de la Cité is best for souvenirs and other tourist kitsch.

LIBRAIRIE ULYSSE Map p82   Books & Comics
☎ 01 43 25 17 35; www.ulysse.fr, in French; 26 rue St-Louis en l'Île, 4e; ⏱ 2-8pm Tue-Fri; Ⓜ Pont Marie

A delightful shop on historic Île de St-Louis stocking some 20,000 travel guides, magazines and maps. Count on sage advice from well-travelled staff. They'll open Saturday morning if you phone in advance.

SOBRAL Map p82   Fashion & Accessories
☎ 01 43 25 80 10; www.sobraldesign.com; 79 rue St-Louis en l'Île, 4e; ⏱ 11am-7.30pm Mon-Sat, to 7pm Sun; Ⓜ Pont Marie
Brighten up your life with a bangle, pendant, pair of earrings or other costume jewellery pieces made from recycled resin by Brazilian jeweller Carlos Sobral. Yes, he makes toilet seats and Eiffel Towers, too.

LA PETITE SCIERIE Map p82   Food & Drink
☎ 01 55 42 14 88; www.lapetitescierie.fr; 60 rue St-Louis en l'Île, 4e; ⏱ 11am-7pm Thu-Mon; Ⓜ Pont Marie
This hole-in-the-wall shop called the 'Little Sawmill' sells every permutation of duck edibles with the emphasis – *naturellement* – on foie gras. The products come direct from the shop's own farm with no intermediary involved, so you can be assured of the highest quality.

CLAIR DE RÊVE Map p82   Kids
☎ 01 43 29 81 06; www.clairdereve.com, in French; 35 rue St-Louis en l'Île, 4e; ⏱ 11am-1pm & 2.45-7.45pm Mon-Sat; Ⓜ Pont Marie
This shop is all about puppets – mostly marionettes, which sway and bob suspended from the ceiling. Wooden ones start at around €50, papier-mâché and leather ones are twice that and ceramic

top picks

BOOKSHOPS

- Librairie Gourmande (p193) Gourmet and culinary.
- Les Mots à la Bouche (p318) Gay and lesbian.
- Red Wheelbarrow Bookstore (p205) Literature and 'serious reading' in English.
- Shakespeare & Company (p197) Paris' legendary English-language bookshop.
- Tea & Tattered Pages (p198) Secondhand books in English.
- Village Voice (p198) Superb English-language bookshop loaded with North American fiction and European literature.

more expensive still. It also sells wind-up toys and music boxes (from €8).

THE LATIN QUARTER

Bookworms in particular will love this part of the Left Bank, not particularly known for its shopping but home to some fine bookshops nonetheless, Paris' most famous English-language bookshop included.

ABBEY BOOKSHOP Map p100 Books & Comics
☎ 01 46 33 16 24; 29 rue de la Parcheminerie, 5e; ⏱ 10am-7pm Mon-Sat; Ⓜ Cluny–La Sorbonne
This mellow, Canadian-owned bookshop is known for its free tea and coffee (sweetened with maple syrup) sipped over new and secondhand books, fiction and non-fiction.

ALBUM Map p100 Books & Comics
☎ 01 53 10 00 60; 67 bd St-Germain, 5e; ⏱ 10am-8pm Mon-Sat, noon-7pm Sun; Ⓜ Maubert–Mutualité
The ultimate in adult fantasy: *bandes dessinées* (comic books) – *huge* in France – is the speciality here. Browse for hours in its twinset of shops on bd St-Germain.

LIBRAIRIE EYROLLES
Map p100 Books & Comics
☎ 01 44 41 11 72; www.eyrolles.com, in French; 61 bd St-Germain, 5e; ⏱ 9.30am-7.30pm Mon-Sat; Ⓜ Maubert–Mutualité
Art, design, architecture, dictionaries and kids' books are the mainstay of this large bookshop with titles in English and bags of browsing space. For maps, guides and travel lit hop two doors over to its Librairie de Voyage (Map p100; ☎ 01 46 34 82 75; 63 bd St-Germain, 5e; ⏱ 10.30am-7.30pm Mon, 9.30am-7.30pm Tue-Fri, 9.30am-8pm Sat; Ⓜ Maubert Mutualité).

SHAKESPEARE & COMPANY
Map p100 Books & Comics
☎ 01 43 26 96 50; 37 rue de la Bûcherie, 5e; ⏱ 10am-11pm Mon-Fri, 11am-11pm Sat & Sun; Ⓜ St-Michel Notre Dame
Paris' most famous English-language bookshop sells new and used books and is a charm to browse (grab a read and sink into one of the two cinema chairs near the stairs out back); the staff's picks are worth noting and there's a dusty old library on the 1st floor. This isn't the original Shakespeare & Company owned by Sylvia Beach, who

published James Joyce's *Ulysses;* that one was closed down by the Nazis.

AU VIEUX CAMPEUR
Map p100 Games & Hobbies
☎ 01 53 10 48 48; www.auvieuxcampeur.fr, in French; 48 rue des Écoles, 5e; ⏱ 11am-8pm Mon-Wed & Fri, to 9pm Thu, 10am-8pm Sat; Ⓜ Maubert–Mutualité or Cluny La Sorbonne
This sporting-gear chain runs 26 shops in the Latin Quarter, each selling equipment for a specific outdoor activity. Find walking gear at 2-4 rue Thénard; camping gear and a fabulous range of accessories (torches, knives, flasks, folding buckets, pack showers…) at 6 rue Thénard; clothing for *le froid urbain* (city cold) at 50 rue des Écoles and 3 rue de Latran; and Paris' most complete range of maps and guides at 2 rue de Latran (Map p100).

LA BOUTIQUE DU CRÉATEUR DE JEUX Map p100 Games & Hobbies
☎ 0 875 976 963; www.laboutiqueducreateurdejeux.com, in French; 40 rue St-Jacques, 5e; ⏱ 11.30am-7pm Tue-Sat; Ⓜ Cluny–La Sorbonne
A real gem, this shop sells brand-new board and card games created in the last couple of years in France; several are bilingual (French and English). Its *jeux de mesure* are made-to-measure, limited editions often focusing on a social issue such as alcohol abuse, immigrant equality etc.

MAGIE Map p100 Games & Hobbies
☎ 01 43 54 13 63; www.mayette.com, in French; 8 rue des Carmes, 5e; ⏱ 1-8pm Mon-Sat; Ⓜ Maubert–Mutualité
One of a kind, this 19th-century (1808) magic shop is said to be the world's oldest, and since 1991 in the hands of world-famous magic pro Dominique Duvivier. Professional and hobbyist magicians flock here to discuss king sandwiches, reverse assemblies, false cuts and other card tricks with him and his daughter, Alexandra. Should you want to learn the tricks of the trade, Duvivier has magic courses up his sleeve.

PLAY FACTORY Map p100 Games & Hobbies
☎ 01 53 10 00 35; www.playfactory.fr, in French; 85 bd St-Michel, 5e; ⏱ 10.30am-10pm Tue, to 11pm Wed-Fri, to 7pm Sat; Ⓜ Luxembourg
The clientele is predominantly male and teen at this toy shop, not quite like any other. Pokemon, Dungeons & Dragons

and other 'collectable' card games – for adults as much as kids – is its speciality and anyone can come here to play as well as buy. Wednesday evening is role games, Thursday figurine painting and Friday Pokemon et al. Dozens more game tables fill the basement.

ST-GERMAIN & INVALIDES

The northern wedge of the 6e between Église St-Germain des Prés and the Seine is a dream to mooch with its bijou art galleries, antique shops, stylish vintage clothes (p211) and mid-range fashion boutiques (Ventilo, Cacherel, Penny Black, Vanessa Bruno, Joseph etc). Don't miss Cour du Commerce St-André (Map p112), an enchanting glass-covered passageway built in 1735 to link a pair of Jeu de Paume (old-style tennis) courts. By the water, square on quai Voltaire and a trio of parallel streets south, 120 art and antiques galleries gather under the exclusive Carré Rive Gauche (www.carrerivegauche. com; Ⓜ Rue du Bac or Solférino) umbrella.

In the more austere 7e, St-Germain des Prés' natural style continues along the western half of bd St-Germain and rue du Bac – two streets with a striking collection of contemporary furniture, kitchen and design shops, including Kartell (Map p112), Conran Shop and Paris' biggest shop window in the shape of Knoll (Map p108).

No boutique is sweeter in this chic part of town – think the most extraordinary gateaux showcased gallery-style – than Philippe Conticini's La Pâtisserie des Rêves (p235).

HAPART Map p112 — Art & Antiques
☎ 01 56 24 94 34; 72 rue Mazarine, 6e; ☽ 2-7pm Tue-Sun; Ⓜ Odéon
A lovely one to idle in, this collector's delight the size of a pocket handkerchief recalls lost childhood with its romantic selection of old and antique toys.

IVOIRE Map p112 — Art & Antiques
☎ 01 43 54 71 09; 57 rue Bonaparte, 6e; ☽ 9am-noon & 2-6pm Tue-Fri; Ⓜ St-Germain des Prés
This family-run business dating from 1913 is a two-man team comprising father Pierre Heckmann (in his mid-eighties) and son Jean-Pierre (apprenticed at age 14 and not far from retirement himself). Sculpting and restoring ivory, bone and nacre is their trade,

and their art is extraordinary. The workshop interior, last refitted in 1937, is original.

LIBRAIRIE LE MONITEUR
Map p112 — Books & Comics
☎ 01 44 41 15 75; www.librairiedumoniteur.com, in French; 7 place de l'Odéon, 6e; ☽ 10am-7pm Mon-Sat; Ⓜ Odéon
This specialist bookshop sports books relating to design, architecture and urbanism, including the annual French–English *Paris Design Guide* published by bilingual design mag *Intramuros*.

TASCHEN Map p112 — Books & Comics
☎ 01 40 52 79 22; 2 rue du Buci, 6e; ☽ 11am-8pm Sun-Wed, to midnight Thu & Fri; Ⓜ Odéon
Illustrated books on art, design, architecture, fashion and urban culture is what this innovative book publisher is about. Equally striking is its shop design by Philippe Starck. Bargain buys begging to be browsed fill stands on the pavement outside.

TEA & TATTERED PAGES
Map p108 — Books & Comics
☎ 01 40 65 94 35; 24 rue Mayet, 6e; ☽ 11am-7pm Mon-Sat, noon-6pm Sun; Ⓜ Duroc
More than 15,000 volumes are squeezed onto two floors at this secondhand English-language bookshop with tearoom.

VILLAGE VOICE
Map p112 — Books & Comics
☎ 01 46 33 36 47; www.villagevoicebookshop. com; 6 rue Princesse, 6e; ☽ 2-7.30pm Mon, 10am-7.30pm Tue-Sat, noon-6pm Sun; Ⓜ Mabillon
With an excellent selection of contemporary North American fiction and European literature, lots of readings and helpful staff, the Village Voice is a favourite.

SHU UEMURA Map p112 — Cosmetics
☎ 01 45 48 02 55; 176 bd St-Germain, 6e; ☽ 11am-8pm Sun-Wed, to midnight Thu & Fri; Ⓜ St-Germain des Prés
Curly fake eyelashes, lime-marmalade lip gloss (yep, it's green), 71 shades of lipstick and badger-hair make-up brushes: this Japanese cosmetics boutique founded by the Hollywood make-up guru who painted Shirley MacLaine's face in the film *My Geisha* (1962) is extraordinary. Treat yourself to a 1½-hour lesson (€150) at its make-up school.

LE BON MARCHÉ Map p108   Department Store
☎ 01 44 39 80 00; www.bonmarche.fr, in French;
24 rue de Sèvres, 7e; ⏱ 10am-8pm Mon-Wed & Fri,
10am-9pm Thu & Sat; Ⓜ Sèvres-Babylone
Built by Gustave Eiffel as Paris' first department store in 1852, Le Bon Marché
(which translates as 'good market' but also
means 'bargain') is less frenetic than its
rivals across the river, and no less chic. It
has excellent men's and women's fashion
collections, and a designer *'snack chic'* café
on the 1st floor. But the icing on the cake
is its glorious food hall, La Grande Épicerie
de Paris (Map p108; 26 rue de Sèvres; ⏱ 8.30am-
9pm Mon-Sat, Ⓜ Sèvres-Babylone), which sells,

top picks

TAKE-HOME ART

Meandering the galleries on rue Mazarine, rue Jacques
Callot, rue des Beaux Arts and rue de Seine is a real feast
for the designer soul.

- Downtown (Map p112; ☎ 01 46 33 82 41; www.
  galeriedowntown.com; 33 rue de Seine, 6e; Ⓜ St-
  Germain des Prés) Designer furniture has been this
  gallery's exclusive forte for 25 years.
- Galerie Loft (Map p112; ☎ 01 46 33 18 96;
  www.galerieloft.com; 3bis rue des Beaux Arts, 6e;
  Ⓜ St-Germain des Prés) All forms of art (digital
  video and performance photography included) by
  contemporary Chinese artists is the striking focus
  of this courtyard gallery.
- Galerie Loevenbruck (Map p112; ☎ 01 53 10 85
  68; www.loevenbruck.com; 40 rue de Seine, 6e;
  Ⓜ St-Germain des Prés) Larger-than-life pop art.
- Galerie Onega (Map p112; ☎ 01 40 46 81
  25; www.galerie-onega.com, in French; 60 rue
  Mazarine, 6e; Ⓜ St-Germain des Prés) Street art
  and graffiti – a bold statement indeed.
- La Galerie Moderne (Map p112; ☎ 01 46 33 13
  59; www.lagaleriemoderne.com; 52 rue Mazarine,
  6e; Ⓜ St-Germain des Prés) Original designer
  furniture and lights from the 1950s, '60s and '70s.
- Pièce Unique Variations (Map p112; ☎ 01 43
  26 85 93; www.galeriepieceunique.com; 26-28 rue
  Mazarine, 6e; Ⓜ St-Germain des Prés) Permanent
  collection of works and installations by contemporary artists; its single-room gallery (4 rue Jacques
  Callot, 6e) showcases one (usually very large) piece
  especially created for this *pièce unique* (unique
  room), illuminated until 2am.

among other edibles, vodka-flavoured
lollipops with detoxified ants inside and
fist-sized Himalayan salt crystals to grate
over food.

ALEXANDRA SOJFER
Map p112   Fashion & Accessories
☎ 01 42 22 17 02; www.alexandrasojfer.fr, in
French; 218 bd St-Germain, 7e; ⏱ 9.30am-7pm;
Ⓜ Rue du Bac
Become Parisian chic with a frivolous, frilly,
fantastical or frightfully fashionable *parapluie* (umbrella), parasol or walking cane,
handcrafted by Alexandra Sojfer at this
parapluie-packed St-Germain boutique, in
the trade since 1834.

GALERIE FRANÇOIS RÉNIER
Map p112   Fashion & Accessories
☎ 01 45 49 26 88; www.unjourunsac.com;
27 bd Raspail, 7e; ⏱ 10am-7pm Tue-Sat;
Ⓜ Sèvres-Babylone
Un jour un sac (a bag a day) is the philosophy of handbag designer François Rénier,
who creates bags from paper, fabric or
leather and leaves his customer to pick
which handles to attach. Buy a couple to
mix 'n' match at home.

LIN ET CIE
Map p108   Fashion & Accessories
☎ 01 43 54 43 32; www.linetcie.com, in French; 16
rue Bréa, 6e; ⏱ 1-6pm Mon, 11am-7pm Tue-Sat;
Ⓜ Notre Dame des Champs
Simplicity is the charm of the organic jewellery created for mother and baby at this
unusual boutique. The nail-sized silver, pre-
cious stone or porcelain motifs delicately
strung on nylon and tied with knots can
also be ordered online.

CACAO ET CHOCOLAT
Map p112   Food & Drink
☎ 01 46 33 77 63; www.cacaoetchocolat.com; 29
rue du Buci, 6e; ⏱ 10.30am-7.30pm; Ⓜ Mabillon
You haven't tasted chocolate till you've
had a hot chocolate (€3.50) spiced with
cinnamon, ginger or cayenne pepper at
this exotic shop showcasing cocoa beans
in every guise. Citrus, spice and chilli are
among the flavoured bars to buy here or
at its outlets in the Marais (Map p152; ☎ 01 42
71 50 06; 36 rue Vieille du Temple, 4e; ⏱ 11am-7.30pm;
Ⓜ St-Paul) and on Île St-Louis (Map p82; ☎ 01
46 33 33 33; 63 rue St-Louis en l'Île, 4e; ⏱ 10.30am-
7.30pm; Ⓜ Pont Marie).

CAVE ST-SULPICE Map p112   Food & Drink

☎ 01 53 10 01 00; www.cavesaintsulpice.com, in French; 3 rue St-Sulpice, 6e; ⏰ 11am-8.15pm Mon-Fri, 10am-1pm Sat; Ⓜ Odéon

Take one look at the shop front of this lovely little boutique and there's no guessing what single product it sells – Champagne. Spend as little or as much as you fancy; on a half bottle, bottle or magnum; pink, white or designer.

HUILERIE J LEBLANC ET FILS

Map p112   Food & Drink

☎ 01 46 34 61 55; www.huile-leblanc.com; 6 rue Jacob, 6e; ⏰ 11am-7pm Tue-Sat; Ⓜ St-Germain des Prés

The Leblanc family has made the smoothest of culinary oils (almonds, pistachios, sesame seeds, pine kernels, peanuts etc) at its stone mill in Burgundy since 1878. Taste and buy.

LA DERNIÈRE GOUTTE

Map p112   Food & Drink

☎ 01 43 29 11 62; www.laderniauregoutte.net; 6 rue du Bourbon le Château, 6e; ⏰ 10.30am-1.30pm & 3-8.30pm Mon-Fri, 10am-8.30pm Sat, 11am-7pm Sun; Ⓜ Mabillon

'The Last Drop' is the lovechild of sommelier Juan Sánchez, the Cuban-American behind the extraordinary wine list to grace Fish La Boissonerie (p236). His tiny wine shop is packed with exciting French *vins de propriétaires* (estate-bottled wines) made by small independent producers. Saturday evening ushers in a talk and tasting.

PÂTISSERIE SADAHARU AOKI

Map p108   Food & Drink

☎ 01 45 44 48 90; www.sadaharuaoki.com; 35 rue de Vaugirard, 6e; ⏰ 11am-7pm Tue-Sat, 10am-6pm Sun; Ⓜ Rennes or St-Sulpice

'Exquisite' fails to describe the creations of one of Paris' top pastry chefs, Tokyo-born Sadaharu Aoki. Almost too beautiful to eat, his gourmet works include boxes of 72 different flavoured macaroons and green-tea chocolate. He also has a boutique in the Latin Quarter (Map p100; ☎ 01 45 35 36 80; 56 bd de Port Royal, 5e; ⏰ 10am-7pm Tue-Sat, to 6pm Sun; Ⓜ Port Royal) and inside Galeries Lafayette (p202).

PIERRE HERMÉ Map p112   Food & Drink

☎ 01 43 54 47 77; www.pierreherme.com; 72 rue Bonaparte, 6e; ⏰ 10am-7pm Sun-Fri, to 7.30pm Sat; Ⓜ Odéon or Luxembourg

It's the size of a chocolate box but once in, your tastebuds will go wild. Pierre Hermé is one of Paris' top chocolatiers and his two boutiques are a veritable feast of perfectly presented petits fours, cakes, chocolate, nougats, macaroons and jam. His second branch (☎ 01 47 83 89 96; 185 rue Vaugirard, 15e; ⏰ 10am-7pm Mon-Wed, to 7.30pm Thu-Sat, to 6pm Sun; Ⓜ Pasteur) is in the 15e arrondissement.

AU PLAT D'ÉTAIN

Map p112   Games & Hobbies

☎ 01 43 54 32 06; http://auplatdetain.com, in French; 16 rue Guisarde, 6e; ⏰ 11am-12.30pm & 2-7pm Tue-Sat; Ⓜ Odéon

People do collect tin (*étain*) and lead soldiers, as this fascinating boutique crammed with nail-sized, hand-painted soldiers, snipers, cavaliers, military drummers and musicians attests. In business since 1775, the shop itself is practically a collectable.

LA MAISON DE POUPÉE

Map p112   Games & Hobbies

☎ 01 46 33 74 05, 06 09 65 58 68; 40 rue de Vaugirard, 6e; ⏰ 10am-7pm Mon-Sat; Ⓜ Odéon or Luxembourg

Poupées anciennes (antique dolls) is what this enchanting boutique opposite the residence of the French Senate's president sells.

ROUGE ET NOIR Map p108   Games & Hobbies

☎ 01 43 26 05 77; www.rouge-et-noir.fr, in French; 26 rue Vavin, 6e; ⏰ 11am-7pm Tue-Sat; Ⓜ Vavin

Trivial Pursuit Paris, Rubik's cubes, juggling balls, backgammon, chess, tarot and playing cards… This small family-run boutique specialising in traditional and not-so-traditional games promises bags of fun.

DEYROLLE Map p108   Home & Garden

☎ 01 42 22 30 07; 46 rue du Bac, 7e; ⏰ 10am-1pm & 2-7pm Mon, 10am-7pm Tue-Sat; Ⓜ Rue du Bac

This shop, born in 1831, has to be seen to be believed. Be it a stuffed white stork, baby chick, butterfly or tiger you want to hang in your home, you can buy one here. A quick chat with a member of staff confirmed that Deyrolle stocks every animal species legally allowed. Buy rare and unusual seeds (including many old types of tomato), gardening tools and accessories on the ground floor.

FLAMANT HOME INTERIORS

Map p112   Home & Garden

☎ 01 56 81 12 40; www.flamant.com; 8 place de Furstenberg & 8 rue de l'Abbaye, 6e; ⏲ noon-7pm Mon, 10.30am-7pm Tue-Sat; Ⓜ Mabillon

Silverware, curtains, cutlery, tableware, linen and other quality home furnishings: this maze of a concept store with two entrances is the place where moneyed Parisians shop for the household.

LES BEAUX DRAPS DE JEANINE CROS

Map p112   Home & Garden

☎ 01 45 48 00 67; 11 rue d'Assas, 6e; ⏲ 10am-7pm Mon-Sat; Ⓜ Rennes

Restoring old fabrics is the highly specialist trade of passionate seamstress Jeanine Cros, and this old-style boudoir – a Pandora's box of fabric – is draped with layer after layer of exquisite old linen, materials tinted with natural pigments etc.

BONTON BAZAR Map p108   Kids

☎ 01 42 22 77 69; www.bonton.fr; 122 rue du Bac, 7e; ⏲ 10am-7pm Mon-Sat; Ⓜ Sèvres-Babylone

This ode to childhood is an old-fashioned delight. It sells a mix of toys, kids' chopsticks (handy for families dining out a lot in Paris), kitchen and bathroom wares (polka-dotted cutlery, black rubber ducks with fishing rods), bedroom decorations, pedal-powered metal cars and so on. Quaint, retro fashion of the same timeless ilk for babies (from 12 months on) and kids respectively is the focus of nearby Bébé Bonton (Map p108; ☎ 01 44 39 12 01; 82 rue de Grenelle, 7e; Ⓜ Rue du Bac) and Grenelle Bonton (Map p108; ☎ 01 44 39 20 01; 82 rue de Grenelle, 7e; Ⓜ Rue du Bac). In 2010 the St-Germain reference jumped the river to open Grand Bonton (☎ 01 42 72 34 69; www.bonton.fr; 5 bd des Filles-du-Calvaire, 3e; ⏲ 10am-7pm Mon-Sat), its 800-sq-m concept store on the Right Bank.

CHAMPS-ÉLYSÉES & GRANDS BOULEVARDS

Global chains line the Champs-Élysées, but it's the luxury fashion houses in the Triangle d'Or that make the area famous. For more on the wonderful window-shopping here, see the boxed text, p203.

If the big fashion houses reign mainly on the other side of the Champs-Élysées, the class and couture continues along rue du Faubourg

St-Honoré and its eastern extension, rue St-Honoré in the 1e, where designer shops – and designer shoppers – abound. This area is also home to the grand gourmet food stores of place de la Madeleine and the luxury jewellery of place Vendôme.

The area around Opéra and the Grands Boulevards is where you'll find Paris' most popular *grands magasins*. North toward Pigalle, there's a handful of interesting boutiques opened by young designers along rue Clauzel and rue Henry Monnier.

HÔTEL DROUOT

Map p126   Art & Antiques

☎ 01 48 00 20 20; www.drouot.com; 7-9 rue Drouot, 9e; ⏲ sales 2-6pm; Ⓜ Richelieu Drouot

Paris' most established auction house has been selling fine lots for more than a century. The bidding is in rapid-fire French (now also available on the website) and a 10% to 15% commission is charged on top of the purchase price. Viewings (always a vicarious pleasure) are usually from 11am to 6pm the day before and from 10.30am to 11.30am the morning of the auction. Further details can be found in the weekly *Gazette de l'Hôtel Drouot* (www.gazette-drouot.com; €3.40), available at the auction house and selected newsstands on Friday, as well as on the main Hôtel Drouot website.

GUERLAIN Map p126   Cosmetics

☎ 01 45 62 52 57; www.guerlain.com; 68 av des Champs-Élysées, 8e; ⏰ 10.30am-8pm Mon-Sat, noon-7pm Sun; Ⓜ Franklin D Roosevelt

Guerlain is Paris' most famous parfumerie, and its shop (dating from 1912) is one of the most beautiful in the city. With its shimmering mirror and marble art-deco interior, it's a reminder of the former glory of the Champs-Élysées. For total indulgence, make an appointment at their decadent spa (☎ 01 45 62 11 21).

SÉPHORA Map p126   Cosmetics

☎ 01 53 93 22 50; www.sephora.com; 70-72 av des Champs-Élysées, 8e; ⏰ 10am-midnight; Ⓜ Franklin D Roosevelt

Séphora's flagship store features more than 12,000 fragrances and cosmetics for your sampling pleasure. You can spend hours in here and will invariably come out with bags of stuff (and maybe a headache from all the scent in the air).

GALERIES LAFAYETTE

Map p126   Department Store

☎ 01 42 82 36 40; www.galerieslafayette.com, in French; 40 bd Haussmann, 9e; ⏰ 9.30am-8pm Mon-Wed, Fri & Sat, to 9pm Thu; Ⓜ Auber or Chaussée d'Antin

Probably the best known of the big Parisian department stores, Galeries Lafayette is spread across three buildings: the main store, the men's store (and Lafayette Gourmet, p202) and the home-design store. Not counting the hours of shopping, there's quite a bit to do in the main store. You can check out modern art in the new gallery (1st fl; ⏰ 11am-7pm Mon-Sat), take in a fashion show (☎ bookings 01 42 82 30 25; ⏰ Mar-Jul & Sep-Dec) at 3pm on Fridays, or ascend to the rooftop for a windswept Parisian panorama (free). When your legs need a break, head up to Lafayette Café on the 6th floor, the rooftop restaurant (⏰ May-Oct) or the champagne bar on the 1st floor.

LE PRINTEMPS Map p126   Department Store

☎ 01 42 82 57 87; www.printemps.com; 64 bd Haussmann, 9e; ⏰ 9.35am-8pm Mon-Wed, Fri & Sat, to 10pm Thu; Ⓜ Havre Caumartin

This is actually three separate stores – Le Printemps de la Mode (women's fashion), Le Printemps de l'Homme (for men) and Le Printemps de la Beauté et Maison (for beauty and household goods) – offering a staggering display

of perfume, cosmetics and accessories, as well as established and up-and-coming designer wear.

ERES Map p126   Fashion & Accessories

☎ 01 47 42 28 82; www.eres.fr; 2 rue Tronchet, 8e; ⏰ 10am-7pm Mon-Sat; Ⓜ Madeleine

You will pay an arm and a leg for a swimsuit here, but anyone who has despaired at buying one in the past will understand why these have become a must-have item for those in the know. The stunning swimsuits are cut to suit all shapes and sizes, with bikini tops and bottoms sold separately. It also stocks magnificent lingerie.

FROMAGERIE ALLÉOSSE

Map p136   Food & Drink

☎ 01 46 22 50 45; www.alleosse.com; 13 rue Poncelet, 17e; ⏰ 9.30am-1pm & 4-7pm Tue-Thu, 9am-1pm & 3.30-7pm Fri & Sat, 9am-1pm Sun; Ⓜ Ternes

In our opinion, this is the best cheese shop in Paris and worth a trip across town. Cheeses are sold as they should be – grouped into five main categories: *fromage de chèvre* (goat's milk cheese), *fromage à pâte persillée* (veined or blue cheese), *fromage à pâte molle* (soft cheese), *fromage à pâte demi-dure* (semihard cheese) and *fromage à pâte dure* (hard cheese). Ask for advice.

HÉDIARD Map p126   Food & Drink

☎ 01 43 12 88 88; www.hediard.fr; 21 place de la Madeleine, 8e; ⏰ 9am-9pm Mon-Sat; Ⓜ Madeleine

This famous luxury food shop established in 1854 consists of two adjacent sections selling prepared dishes, teas, coffees, jams, wines, pastries, fruits, vegetables and so on, as well as a popular restaurant (☎ 01 43 12 88 99; ⏰ 8.30am-9pm Mon-Fri, to 10pm Sat), where tea is served from 3pm to 6pm. There's also a George V branch (Map p126; ☎ 01 47 20 44 44; 31 av George V, 8e; ⏰ Sun; Ⓜ George V).

LAFAYETTE GOURMET

Map p126   Food & Drink

☎ 01 42 82 36 40; www.galerieslafayette.com, in French; 40 bd Haussmann, 9e; ⏰ 8.30am-9.30pm Mon-Sat; Ⓜ Auber or Chaussée d'Antin

On the 1st floor of the Galeries Lafayette men's store is Lafayette Gourmet, an entire floor dedicated to the art of pleasing the palate. You'll find perfect pastries, chocolates, fondants, cheeses, pâté, organic muffins, you name it. There's also an excellent wine shop that has a surprisingly affordable selection.

LA MAISON DU MIEL Map p126 Food & Drink
☎ 01 47 42 26 70; www.maisondumiel.com, in French; 24 rue Vignon, 9e; ⏰ 9.30am-7pm Mon-Sat; Ⓜ Madeleine

In this sticky, very sweet business since 1898, 'the Honey House' stocks more than 50 kinds of honey, with such flavours as Corsican chestnut flower, Turkish pine and Tasmanian leatherwood.

LES CAVES AUGÉ Map p126 Food & Drink
☎ 01 45 22 16 97; www.cavesauge.com, in French; 116 bd Haussmann, 8e; ⏰ 9am-7.30pm Mon-Sat; Ⓜ St-Augustin

Founded in 1850, this fantastic wine shop with bottles stacked in every conceivable nook and cranny should be your first choice if you trust the taste of Marcel Proust, who was a regular customer. The shop organises tastings every other Saturday (see website), where you can meet local winemakers from different regions.

PLACE DE LA MADELEINE
Map p126 Food & Drink

place de la Madeleine, 8e; Ⓜ Madeleine

Ultragourmet food shops are the treat here; if you feel your knees start to go all wobbly in front of a display window, you know you're in the right place. The most notable

names include truffle dealers La Maison de la Truffe (☎ 01 42 65 53 22; www.maison-de-la-truffe.com, in French; 19 place de la Madeleine; ⏰ 10am-10pm Mon-Sat); luxury food shop Hédiard (p202); mustard specialist Boutique Maille (☎ 01 40 15 06 00; www.maille.com; 6 place de la Madeleine; ⏰ 10am-7pm Mon-Sat); and Paris' most famous caterer, Fauchon (☎ 01 70 39 38 00; www.fauchon.fr; 26 & 30 place de la Madeleine; ⏰ 8.30am-7pm Mon-Sat), selling incredibly mouth-watering delicacies, from foie gras to jams, chocolates and pastries.

VIRGIN MEGASTORE
Map p126 Books & Comics, Music

☎ 01 49 53 50 00; 52-60 av des Champs-Élysées, 8e; ⏰ 10am-midnight Mon-Sat, noon-midnight Sun; Ⓜ Franklin D Roosevelt

This French-owned version of the huge British music and bookshop chain has the largest music collection in Paris, as well as English-language books.

MONTMARTRE, PIGALLE & 17E

Montmartre is swimming in souvenirs, and yet there is much more here to discover. The area around rues des Martyrs, Yvonne le Tac, Vieuville and Houdon constitutes a good stroll for the patient shopper. You'll find little designer-clothing shops (for women and children), a few larger Parisian labels – Antoine

HISTORIC HAUTE COUTURE

A stroll around the legendary Triangle d'Or (av Montaigne and av George V) and along rue du Faubourg St-Honoré, all in the 8e (Map p126; Ⓜ George V), constitutes the walk of fame of top French fashion. Rubbing shoulders with the world's top international designers are Paris' most influential French fashion houses:

- **Chanel** (Map p126; ☎ 01 47 23 74 12; www.chanel.com; 42 av Montaigne, 8e) Box jackets and little black dresses, chic ever since their first appearance in the 1920s.
- **Christian Dior** (Map p126; ☎ 01 40 73 73 73; www.dior.com; 30 av Montaigne, 8e) Post-WWII, Dior's creations dictated style, re-establishing Paris as the world fashion capital.
- **Christian Lacroix** (Map p126; ☎ 01 42 68 79 04; www.christianlacroix.com; 73 rue du Faubourg St-Honoré, 8e) Taffeta and lace flirt with denim and knits in this designer's theatrical combinations.
- **Givenchy** (Map p126; ☎ 01 44 31 51 25; www.givenchy.com; 3 av George V, 8e) The first to present a luxurious collection of women's prêt-à-porter.
- **Hermès** (Map p126; ☎ 01 40 17 47 17; www.hermes.com; 24 rue du Faubourg St-Honoré, 8e) Founded in 1837 by a saddle-maker, Hermès' famous scarves are *the* fashion accessory.
- **Jean-Paul Gaultier** (Map p126; ☎ 01 44 43 00 44; www.jeanpaulgaultier.com; 44 av George V, 8e) A shy kid from the Paris suburbs, JPG morphed into the *enfant terrible* of the fashion world with his granny's corsets, men dressed in skirts and Madonna's conical bra.
- **Louis Vuitton** (Map p126; ☎ 01 53 57 52 00; www.vuitton.com; 101 av des Champs-Élysées, 8e) Take home a Real McCoy canvas bag with the 'LV' monogram.

et Lili (p204) for one – not to mention some excellent, typically French food stores. Also worth checking out are the fashion designers on rue des Gardes (p181) in the Goutte d'Or neighbourhood.

TATI
Map p134   Department Store

☎ 01 55 29 52 20; www.tati.fr, in French; 4 bd de Rochechouart, 18e; ⏰ 10am-7pm Mon-Fri, 9.30-7pm Sat; Ⓜ Barbès Rochechouart

With its war cry of *les plus bas prix* (the lowest prices) – and quality to match, some would say – Tati has been Paris' great working-class department store for more than half a century. Don't be surprised to see trendy Parisians fighting for bargains hidden in the crammed bins and piled onto tables. There's a smaller 3e branch (Map p148; ☎ 01 48 87 72 81; 172-174 rue du Temple, 3e; ⏰ 9.30am-7.30pm Mon-Fri, 10am-7pm Sat; Ⓜ Temple or République) as well.

LA CITADELLE
Map p134   Fashion & Accessories

☎ 01 42 52 21 56; 1 rue des Trois Frères, 18e; ⏰ 11am-8pm Mon-Sat, to 7pm Sun; Ⓜ Abbesses

This designer discount shop hidden away in Montmartre has some real finds from new French, Italian and Japanese designers. Look out for such labels as Les Chemins Blancs and Yoshi Kondo.

ETS LION
Map p134   Food & Drink

☎ 01 46 06 64 71; www.epicerie-lion.fr, in French; 7 rue des Abbesses, 18e; ⏰ 10.30am-8pm Tue-Sat, 11am-7pm Sun; Ⓜ Abbesses

Another stop on the foodie trail is this gourmet and gardening shop, selling homemade jams, packaged *riz au lait* (rice pudding), multicoloured Eiffel Tower pasta and olive oils. They carry a good selection of organic products.

KINDAL
Map p136   Home & Garden

☎ 01 42 61 70 78; www.kindal.net, in French; 23bis rue de Constantinople, 8e; ⏰ 11am-6pm Tue-Sat; Ⓜ Europe or Rome

In the market for something sharp? This *coutellerie* (cutlery shop) sells everything that slices and dices – from table and pocket knives to razors and Japanese swords. We even saw some stunning nail clippers on sale here.

GARE DU NORD & CANAL ST-MARTIN

This area has recently emerged as a trendy shopping district. Lots of little boutiques have sprung up in the past few years and it's an enjoyable place to window-shop. The main strip is rue Beaurepaire, which has lots of little-known fashion designers, while rue de Marseille has larger Parisian brands like APC (p206) at No 5.

ANTOINE ET LILI
Map p140   Fashion & Accessories, Home & Garden

☎ 01 40 37 41 55; www.antoineetlili.com; 95 quai de Valmy, 10e; ⏰ 11am-2.30pm Mon, to 8pm Tue-Sat, children's store also 11am-7pm Sun; Ⓜ République or Gare de l'Est

All the colours of the rainbow and all the patterns in the world congregate in this wonderful Parisian institution with designer clothing for women (pink store) and children (green store), and hip home decorations (yellow store). There are five other locations in Paris, including a Marais store (Map p152; ☎ 01 42 72 26 60; 51 rue des Francs Bourgeois, 3e; Ⓜ St-Paul), which keeps the same hours.

BAZAR ÉTHIC
Map p140   Fashion & Accessories, Home & Garden

☎ 01 42 00 15 73; www.bazarethic.com; 25 rue Beaurepaire, 10e; ⏰ 11am-7pm Mon-Sat, 2-7pm Sun; Ⓜ République or Jacques Bonsergent

An excellent shop for a browse, Bazar Éthic specialises in chic fair-trade and ecofriendly

top picks

SPECIALITY STREETS

- Rue de Paradis, 10e (Map p140; Ⓜ Château d'Eau) Crystal, glass and tableware.
- Rue Drouot, 9e (Map p126; Ⓜ Richelieu Drouot) Collectable postage stamps.
- Rue du Pont Louis-Philippe, 4e (Map p152; Ⓜ Pont Marie) Stationery and fine paper.
- Rue Keller, 11e (Map p158; Ⓜ Ledru Rollin) Comic books, mangas, DVDs.
- Rue Martel, 10e (Map p140; Ⓜ Château d'Eau) Sewing machines.
- Rue Victor Massé, 9e (Map p126; Ⓜ Pigalle) Musical instruments.

products. It carries a range of clothing (organic cotton jeans, children's wear) and home-design handicrafts, such as lacquered bamboo bowls.

LIZA KORN
Map p140

☎ 01 42 01 36 02; 19 rue Beaurepaire, 10e; www.liza-korn.com; ⏰ 11.30-7.30 Mon-Sat; Ⓜ Jacques Bonsergent

From rock 'n' roll fashion to a new children's line, this designer's tiny boutique is a portal into a rich and playful imagination.

MAJE
Map p140   Fashion & Accessories

☎ 01 42 38 96 67; www.maje-paris.fr; 6 rue de Marseille, 10e; ⏰ 11am-8pm Tue-Sat, 1.30-7pm Sun & Mon; Ⓜ Jacques Bonsergent

A Parisian prêt-à-porter brand featured regularly on the pages of *Elle, Glamour* and *Marie Claire*, Maje doesn't come cheaply – that is, unless you know about this outlet store, which sells most items at a 30% discount.

MARAIS & MÉNILMONTANT

The Marais can boast some excellent speciality stores and an ever-expanding fashion presence. Note that the hip young designers are colonising the upper reaches of the 3e towards rue Charlot (Map p148) as well as rue de Turenne (Map p152). Meanwhile, rue des Francs Bourgeois and, towards the other side of rue de Rivoli, rue François Mirron in the 4e have well-established boutique shopping for clothing, hats, home furnishings and stationery. Place des Vosges is lined with very high-end art and antique galleries with some amazing sculpture for sale.

I LOVE MY BLENDER
Map p152   Books & Comics

☎ 01 42 77 50 32; www.ilovemyblender.fr; 36 rue du Temple, 4e; ⏰ 10am-7.30pm Tue-Sun; Ⓜ Rambuteau

As far removed from kitchenware as you can imagine, this bookshop run by a former advertising executive is stocked almost exclusively with books written in English, whatever the provenance. They're available here in their original editions and in French translation.

LIBRAIRIE DE L'HÔTEL DE SULLY
Map p152   Books & Comics

☎ 01 44 61 21 75; www.editions.monuments-nationaux.fr; 62 rue St-Antoine, 4e; ⏰ 10am-7pm; Ⓜ St-Paul

This early 17th-century aristocratic mansion housing the Centre des Monuments Nationaux (Monum), the body responsible for many of France's historical monuments, has one of the best bookshops in town for titles related to Paris. From historical texts and biographies to picture books and atlases, it's all here.

RED WHEELBARROW BOOKSTORE
Map p148   Books & Comics

☎ 01 48 04 75 08; www.theredwheelbarrow.com; 22 rue St-Paul, 4e; ⏰ 10am-6pm Mon, to 7pm Tue-Sat, 2-6pm Sun; Ⓜ St-Paul

This impeccably run English-language bookshop of the old school has arguably the best selection of literature and 'serious reading' in Paris, and helpful, well-read staff. It's always a pleasure to visit.

FRAGONARD
Map p152   Cosmetics

☎ 01 44 78 01 32; www.fragonard.com; 51 rue des Francs Bourgeois, 4e; ⏰ 10.30am-7.30pm Mon-Sat, noon-7pm Sun; Ⓜ St-Paul

This Parisian perfume maker has alluring natural scents in elegant bottles as well as candles, essential oils and soaps. In addition to the splendid smells, there's a small, expensive and very tasteful selection of clothing, hand-stitched linen tablecloths and napkins, as well as jewellery. There's also a St-Germain branch (Map p112; ☎ 01 42 84 12 12; 196 bd St-Germain, 6e; Ⓜ St-Germain des Prés), and Fragonard runs the Musée du Parfum (p130), which has its own shop.

L'ARTISAN PARFUMEUR
Map p152   Cosmetics

☎ 01 48 04 55 66; www.artisanparfumeur.com; 32 rue du Bourg Tibourg, 4e; ⏰ 10.30am-7.30pm Mon-Sat; Ⓜ St-Paul

This artisan has been making exquisite original scents and candles for decades. The products are expensive but of very high quality and attractively packaged. There are more than half a dozen other outlets across town, as well as stands at the Galeries Lafayette and Le Printemps department stores.

BAZAR DE L'HÔTEL DE VILLE

Map p152   Department Store

☎ 01 42 74 90 00; www.bhv.fr, in French; 14 rue du Temple, 4e; ⏰ 9.30am-7.30pm Mon, Tue, Thu & Fri, to 9pm Wed, to 8pm Sat; Ⓜ Hôtel de Ville
Though renovated and expanded in recent years, BHV ('bay-ash-vay') is still pretty much a straightforward (though now flashier) department store – apart from its huge hardware/DIY department in the basement, with every possible type of hammer, power tool, nail, plug or hinge you could ask for. The eating options on the 5th floor, notably Ma Cantine (p261), are worth considering.

MERCI Map p148   Department Store

☎ 01 42 77 00 33; www.merci-merci.com, in French; 111 bd Beaumarchais, 3e; ⏰ 10am-7pm Mon-Sat; Ⓜ St-Sébastien Froissart
The landmark pink Fiat Cinquecento in the courtyard marks the entrance to this unique multistorey concept store whose rallying cry is one-stop shopping. Clothing, household goods, gifts, books – it has the lot, as well as the wonderful Cantine Merci in the basement to drop in before and while you shop. Merci is the brainchild of the people behind the exclusive children's outfitters Bonpoint (p194), and all the proceeds go to a children's charity in Madagascar.

ABOU D'ABI BAZAR

Map p152   Fashion & Accessories

☎ 01 42 71 13 26; www.aboudabibazar.com; 125 rue Vieille du Temple, 3e; ⏰ 2-7.15pm Mon, 10.30am-7.15pm Tue-Sat; Ⓜ Chemin Vert
This fashionable boutique is a treasure trove of smart and affordable ready-to-wear pieces from such young designers as Paul & Joe and Isabel Marant. There's also a Latin Quarter branch (Map p152; ☎ 01 42 77 96 98; 15 rue Soufflot, 5e; ⏰ 10.30am-7.15pm Tue-Sat, 2-7pm Sun & Mon; Ⓜ Luxembourg).

ALTERNATIVES Map p152   Fashion & Accessories

☎ 01 42 78 31 50; 18 rue du Roi de Sicile, 4e; ⏰ 1-7pm Tue-Fri, by appointment Sat; Ⓜ St-Paul
This resale shop stocking mostly men's high-end fashion has great bargains in superb condition. This is an excellent place to pick up Japanese designer wear at a third of the original price. You can also come across Miu Miu, Prada, Martin Margiela, Comme des Garçons and Rick Owens here on a good day.

APC

Map p152   Fashion & Accessories

☎ 01 42 78 18 02; www.apc.fr; 112 rue Vieille du Temple, 3e; ⏰ 11.30am-8pm; Ⓜ Chemin Vert
The hip streetwear of the renovated and expanded Atelier de Production et Création (Production and Creation Workshop) is very popular with those young Parisian guys with pop-rock haircuts, white sneakers and jeans. The focus is on simple lines and straight cuts, though some pieces are more adventurous. It also has women's clothes. There's also a branch on rue de Marsaille (Map p140; ☎ 01 42 39 84 46; 5 rue de Marseille, 10e; ⏰ 11.30am-8pm; Ⓜ Jacques Bonsergent).

EROTOKRITOS

Map p152   Fashion & Accessories

☎ 01 42 78 14 04; www.erotokritos.com; 99 rue Vieille du Temple; ⏰ 1-7.30pm Mon, 11am-7.30pm Tue-Sat, 12.30-6.30pm Sun; Ⓜ Filles du Calvaire
Greek-Cypriot Erotokritos' clothes are chic and colourful, combining and contrasting fabrics with amazing prints. They're also quite affordable, considering the designer's reputation. There's also a Les Halles branch (Map p72; ☎ 01 42 21 44 60; 58 rue d'Argout, 2e; ⏰ 1-7.30pm Mon, 11am-7.30pm Tue-Sat; Ⓜ Sentier).

L'ÉCLAIREUR

Map p152   Fashion & Accessories

☎ 01 48 87 10 22; www.leclaireur.com; 40 rue de Sévigné, 4e; ⏰ 11am-7pm Mon-Sat; Ⓜ St-Paul
Part art space, part lounge and part deconstructionist fashion statement, this new shop for women is known for having the next big thing first. You'll find Dries Van Noten rubbing shoulders with objects by Piet Hein Eek and Piero Fornasetti. Just down the road is another stunning Marais branch (Map p152; ☎ 01 44 54 22 11; 12 rue Malher, 4e; Ⓜ St-Paul), for men and converted from an old warehouse.

L'HABILLEUR

Map p152   Fashion & Accessories

☎ 01 48 87 77 12; 44 rue de Poitou, 3e; ⏰ noon-7.30pm Mon-Sat; Ⓜ St-Sébastien Froissart
For 15 years this shop has been known for its discount designer wear – offering 50% to 70% off original prices. It generally stocks last season's collections including such lines as Paul & Joe, Giorgio Brato and Belle Rose. The selection of men's clothes is quite extensive.

SHINE Map p152 Fashion & Accessories

☎ 01 48 05 80 10; 15 rue de Poitou, 3e; ⏰ 11am-7.30pm Tue-Sat; Ⓜ Filles du Calvaire

Another limited but discerning collection of designer stuff in the trendsetting 3e. Young women's clothing and some excellent shoes and handbags have been astutely selected, with plenty of Marc Jacobs, See by Chloé and K by Karl Lagerfeld, as well as jewellery by Bijoux de Sophie.

SIC AMOR Map p152 Fashion & Accessories

☎ 01 42 76 02 37; www.french-jewellery.fr; 20 rue du Pont Louis-Philippe, 4e; ⏰ 11am-7.30pm Mon-Sat, noon-7pm Sun; Ⓜ Pont Marie

This shop sells contemporary jewellery by local designers from a shop located opposite the headquarters of the all-but-moribund Partie Communiste Française. For hats and scarves head south along the same street to Mi Amor (Map p152; ☎ 01 42 71 79 29; 10 rue du Pont Louis-Philippe, 4e; Ⓜ Pont Marie).

SURFACE TO AIR
Map p152 Fashion & Accessories

☎ 01 44 61 76 27; www.surfacetoair.com; 108 rue Vieille du Temple, 3e; ⏰ 11.30am-7.30pm Mon-Sat, noon-6pm Sun; Ⓜ St-Sébastien Froissart

This shop has very edgy clothing as well as arty books and accessories. With an exceedingly up-to-date collection of daring local and international designs, the space also welcomes regular installations and collaborative events with artists. Its other Marais branch (Map p148; ☎ 01 44 61 76 27; 68 rue Charlot, 3e; ⏰ by appointment; Ⓜ Filles du Calvaire) is smaller and more exclusive.

À L'OLIVIER Map p152 Food & Drink

☎ 01 48 04 86 59; www.alolivier.com; 23 rue de Rivoli, 4e; ⏰ 2-7pm Mon, 9.30am-7pm Tue-Sat; Ⓜ St-Paul

'At the Olive Tree' has been the place for oil, from olive and walnut to soy and sesame, since 1822; buy it from one of the stainless vats on display in this Marais shop. It also offers olive-oil tastings and olive-oil beauty products, as well as good vinegars, jams and honeys.

JULIEN CAVISTE Map p148 Food & Drink

☎ 01 42 72 00 94; 50 rue Charlot, 3e; ⏰ 10am-1.30pm & 3.30-8pm Tue-Sat, 10am-1.30pm Sun; Ⓜ Filles du Calvaire

This independent wine shop at the southern end of hip rue Charlot focuses on small, independent producers and organic wines. There's a unique selection of Rhône, Languedoc and Loire vintages and exceptional sparkling wines. The enthusiastic merchant Julien will locate and explain (and wax lyrical about) the wine for you, whatever your budget.

LE PALAIS DES THÉS
Map p152 Food & Drink

☎ 01 48 87 80 60; www.palaisdesthes.com; 64 rue Vieille du Temple, 3e; ⏰ 10am-8pm Mon-Sat; Ⓜ Hôtel de Ville or St-Paul

The 'Palace of Teas' is not as well established as Mariage Frères (p207), but the selection is as large and the surroundings much more 21st century. There are four other outlets in Paris, including a 6e branch (Map p168; ☎ 01 42 22 03 98; 61 rue du Cherche Midi, 6e; ⏰ 10.30am-7pm Mon, 10am-7pm Tue-Sat; Ⓜ Rennes).

LE REPAIRE DE BACCHUS
Map p148 Food & Drink

☎ 01 48 87 73 68; 40 rue de Bretagne, 3e; ⏰ 5-8.30pm Mon, 10am-8.30pm Tue-Sat, 10am-1.30pm Sun; Ⓜ Arts et Métiers

'The Den of Bacchus' stocks a good selection of New World wines along with an excellent supply of French vintages, as well as Cognac, Armagnac and whiskies.

MARIAGE FRÈRES Map p152 Food & Drink

☎ 01 42 72 28 11; www.mariagefreres.com; 30, 32 & 35 rue du Bourg Tibourg, 4e; ⏰ shop 10.30am-7.30pm, tearooms noon-7pm; Ⓜ Hôtel de Ville

Founded in 1854, this is Paris' first and arguably finest teashop. Choose from more than 500 varieties of tea sourced from some 35 countries. Mariage Frères has four other outlets, including the 6e branch (Map p112; ☎ 01 40 51 82 50; 13 rue des Grands Augustins; Ⓜ Odéon) and the 8e branch (Map p126; ☎ 01 46 22 18 54; 260 rue du Faubourg St-Honoré, 8e; Ⓜ Ternes).

PRODUITS DES MONASTÈRES
Map p152 Food & Drink

☎ 01 48 04 98 98; 10 rue des Barres, 4e; ⏰ 9.30am-noon & 2-7pm Tue-Fri, 10am-noon & 2-6.20pm Sat, 12.20-1pm Sun; Ⓜ Hôtel de Ville or Pont Marie

This shop on an ancient cobbled street just down from Église St-Gervais-St-Protais sells jams, biscuits, cakes, muesli, honey, herbal teas and other comestibles made at Benedictine and Trappist monasteries in Jerusalem. For linens, candles, sandals and

LOCAL KNOWLEDGE: PATRICIA WELLS

The only American considered to have truly captured the soul of French cuisine, writer, cookery teacher and author of *The Food Lover's Guide to Paris*, Patricia Wells (www.patriciawells.com) has lived, cooked and shopped in Paris since 1980. 'Only the best' is the label on the fresh fish, meat, cheese, breads and other market produce that guests at her St-Germain des Prés cooking studio use in class. So just where does she shop? Nicola Williams finds out.

What is it that makes Paris so wonderful for culinary shopping? The tradition, the quality, the quantity, the atmosphere and physical beauty!

Where do you buy your weekly groceries? All over: the Sunday organic market (Map p112; bd Raspail, 7e; Ⓜ Rennes) at Rennes; Poilâne (p215) for bread; Quatrehommes (p238) for cheese; Poissonnerie du Bac (Map p108; 69 rue du Bac, 7e; Ⓜ Rue du Bac) for fish; also the Marché Président Wilson (p222).

And for that extraspecial gourmet meal? I shop regularly at Le Bon Marché's La Grande Épicerie de Paris (p199) because it is right down the street from me. But for special meals I always order things in advance and go from shop to shop. That is the fun of Paris and of France.

Favourite markets & and top tips? I love the dried fruits and nuts at the Sunday Rennes market, *all* the fish stands at the President Wilson market, the Planet Fruits and Daguerre Marée stands at the Rue Poncelet market (rue Poncelet, 17e; Ⓜ Ternes). If you live in Paris, become a *client fidèle* so they reach in the back and give you the best stuff. If you only go once in a while, just smile and be friendly.

Your top specialist addresses? Poilâne (bread; p215); Maison du Chocolat (Map p112; 19 rue de Sèvres, 6e) and Pierre Hermé (chocolate and cakes; p200); La Dernière Goutte (wine; p200).

A creative idea for a culinary souvenir from Paris? Fragonard (p205), the perfume maker, has a great shop on bd St-Germain. They have a changing litany of *great* things for the home, such as fabulous vases with an Eiffel Tower theme, lovely embroidered napkins with a fish or vegetable theme, great little spoons with a cake or pastry theme. Nothing is very expensive and the offerings change every few months, so you have to pounce when you find something you love. The gift wrapping in gorgeous Fragonard bags is worth it alone!

Interviewed by Nicola Williams

---

ceramics sourced from the same places, go around the corner to Monastica (Map p152; ☎ 01 48 87 85 13; 11 rue du Pont Louis-Philippe, 4e; ◷ 10am-6pm Tue-Fri, 10am-noon & 1.15-6.30pm Sat; Ⓜ Pont Marie).

VERT D'ABSINTHE
Map p152   Food & Drink
☎ 01 42 71 69 73; www.vertdabsinthe.com; 11 rue d'Ormesson, 4e; ◷ noon-7pm Tue-Sat; Ⓜ St-Paul
Fans of the *fée verte* (green fairy), as absinthe was known during the belle époque, will think they've died and gone to heaven here. You can buy not only bottles of the best-quality hooch here but all the paraphernalia as well: glasses, water jugs and tiny slotted spoons for the all-important sugar cube.

BOUTIQUE OBUT
Map p148   Games & Hobbies
☎ 01 47 00 91 38; www.labouleobut.com; 60 av de la République, 11e; ◷ 10am-noon & 12.30-6.30pm Tue-Sat; Ⓜ Parmentier
This is the Parisian mecca for fans of *pétanque* or the similar (though more formal) game of boules, a form of bowls played with heavy steel balls wherever a

bit of flat and shady ground can be found. It will kit you out with all the equipment necessary to get a game going and even has team uniforms. Three-ball sets start at €24.

LA MAISON DE L'ASTRONOMIE
Map p148   Games & Hobbies
☎ 01 42 77 99 55; www.maison-astronomie.com, in French; 33-35 rue de Rivoli, 4e; ◷ 10.30am-6.40pm Tue-Sat; Ⓜ Hôtel de Ville
If you've ever had the inclination to gaze at the stars, visit this large shop just west of the Hôtel de Ville. The 1st floor is positively crammed with telescopes, some of which can run into tens of thousands of euros. It also stocks astronomical books, periodicals, sky maps, binoculars and globes.

ATELIER D'AUTREFOIS
Map p148   Gifts & Souvenirs
☎ 01 42 77 35 56; 61 bd Beaumarchais, 3e; ◷ 10am-6pm; Ⓜ Chemin Vert
This treasure chest of a shop stocks exquisite music boxes – both new and antique – and will repair any that are ailing. It's a shop that will attract both collectors and souvenir-hunters.

CSAO BOUTIQUE & GALLERY

Map p152   Gifts & Souvenirs

☎ 01 42 71 33 17; www.csao.fr, in French; 9 & 9bis rue Elzévir, 3e; ☼ 11am-7pm Tue-Fri, 11am-7.30pm Sat, noon-7pm Sun; Ⓜ St-Paul or Chemin Vert

This wonderful shop and gallery, owned and operated by the charitable Compagnie du Sénégal et de l'Afrique de l'Ouest (CSAO; Senegal and West Africa Company), distributes the work of African craftspeople and artists. Many of the colourful fabrics and weavings are exquisite. Included are items handmade from recycled handbags, aluminium cans and tomato-paste tins.

LA BOUTIQUE DES INVENTIONS

Map p148   Gifts & Souvenirs

☎ 01 42 71 44 19; www.la-boutique-des -inventions.com; 13 rue St-Paul, 4e; ☼ 11am-7pm Wed-Sun; Ⓜ St-Paul

This unique shop in the heart of Village St-Paul, a delightful little shopping square with boutiques and galleries, is a forum for inventors and their inventions. Be the first on the block to own a shaker that sprinkles its own salt, a pepper grinder that twists itself or a miraculous filter that turns water into wine. Lots of wacky designs, too.

LA CHARRUE ET LES ÉTOILES

Map p152   Gifts & Souvenirs

☎ 01 48 87 39 07; 19 rue des Francs Bourgeois, 4e; ☼ 11am-7pm; Ⓜ St-Paul or Chemin Vert

Presumably named after Sean O'Casey's 1926 play (though the Irish connection is lost on us), 'the Plough and Stars' may look like just another gift shop but stocks an unusual collection of figurines modelled after celebrated works of art (eg *Vertumnus* and *The Librarian* by Arcimboldo) and miniature soldiers.

L'AGENDA MODERNE

Map p152   Gifts & Souvenirs

☎ 01 44 54 59 20; www.agenda-moderne.com; 42 rue de Sévigné, 3e; ☼ 10am-4.30pm Mon-Fri; Ⓜ St-Paul

Subtitled 'the Shop of Days', this boutique sells handmade diaries beautifully bound in natural or dyed alligator or calves' leather. And, fear not, they're bilingual, so the Monday morning blues will not become *les blues de lundi matin*.

MÉLODIES GRAPHIQUES

Map p152   Gifts & Souvenirs

☎ 01 42 74 57 68; 10 rue du Pont Louis-Philippe, 4e; ☼ 2-7pm Mon, 11am-7pm Tue-Sat; Ⓜ Pont Marie

Here you'll find all sorts of items made from exquisite Florentine *papier à cuve* (paper hand-decorated with marbled designs). There are several other fine stationery shops along the same street.

BAINS PLUS Map p152   Home & Garden

☎ 01 48 87 83 07; www.parismarais.com/shopping -guide/bains-plus-spa; 51 rue des Francs Bourgeois, 3e; ☼ 11am-7.30pm Tue-Sat, 2-7pm Sun & Mon; Ⓜ Hôtel de Ville

A bathroom supplier for the 21st century and true to its name, 'Baths Plus' stocks luxurious robes and gowns, soaps, salts and oils, shaving brushes and mirrors.

LA MAISON DU HAMAC

Map p148   Home & Garden

☎ 01 47 00 66 00; www.lamaisonduhamac.com, in French; 57 rue de Malte, 11e; ☼ 10.45am-7pm Tue-Sat; Ⓜ République

'The House of the Hammock' specialises in just that – a movable bed you string between two trees and rock till you (don't) drop. Choose anything from a brightly coloured net specimen from Brazil, Colombia or Nicaragua, or one shrouded in mosquito netting for napping by the water.

L'OURS DU MARAIS Map p152   Kids

☎ 01 42 77 60 43; www.oursdumarais.com, in French; 18 rue Pavée, 4e; ☼ 11.30am-7.30pm Tue-Sat, 2-7.30pm Sun; Ⓜ St-Paul

'The Marais Bear' doesn't focus on Smoky or Yogi but on Teddy – there are more versions of the popular cuddly toy in this crowded little boutique than you could fill a bear's den with.

PUZZLE MICHÈLE WILSON

Map p148   Games & Hobbies

☎ 01 47 00 12 57; www.puzzles-et-jeux.com; 39 rue de la Folie Méricourt, 11e; ☼ 10am-6pm Tue-Fri, 2-7pm Sat; Ⓜ St-Ambroise

Puzzleurs and *puzzleuses* will love the selection of hand-cut wooden jigsaw puzzles available in this shop. Ranging in size (and degree of difficulty) from 80 to – wait for it – 5000 pieces, the puzzles depict for the most part major works of art; everyone from Millet and Bosch to the impressionists is represented. The ones of medieval stained glass and 18th-century fans are particularly fine. There are two other outlets, including a 15e branch (Map p168; ☎ 01 45 75 35 28; 97 av Émile Zola, 15e; ◷ 9am-7pm Mon-Fri, 10am-7pm Sat; Ⓜ Charles Michels).

TUMBLEWEED Map p152   Kids, Games & Hobbies
☎ 01 42 78 06 10; www.tumbleweedparis.com; 19 rue de Turenne, 4e; ◷ 11am-7pm Mon-Sat, 2-7pm Sun; Ⓜ St-Paul or Chemin Vert
This gorgeous little shop, which specialises in *l'artisanat d'art ludique* (crafts of the playing art), stocks wonderful handmade wooden toys, some of which look too nice to play with. The brain-teasers and puzzles for adults are exquisitely made; we especially love the Japanese 'spin' and 'secret' boxes that defy entry.

BASTILLE & GARE DE LYON

The neighbourhoods around Bastille in the 11e have some interesting shops, including rue Keller (Map p158), where you'll find young designers, records and manga/comics shops; and rue de Charonne, known for its cut-rate clothes shops. The upmarket boutiques of Bercy have transformed the 12e and are always packed with shoppers. Elsewhere in the 12e, the area near the Viaduc des Arts has discerning furniture, antiques and art. The flea market at place d'Aligre is a must.

ALBUM
Map p158   Books & Comics, Games & Hobbies
☎ 01 53 33 87 88; www.album.fr, in French; 46 cour St-Émilion, 12e; ◷ 11am-9pm; Ⓜ Cour St-Émilion
Album specialises in *bandes dessinées* (comics), which have an enormous following in France, with everything from Tintin and Babar to erotic comics and the latest Japanese manga. There are four more outlets in Paris, including a Latin Quarter branch (Map p100; ☎ 01 53 10 00 60; 67 bd St-Germain, 5e; ◷ 10am-8pm Mon-Sat, noon-7pm Sun).

ISABEL MARANT
Map p158   Fashion & Accessories
☎ 01 43 26 04 12; www.isabelmarant.tm.fr; 16 rue de Charonne, 11e; ◷ 10.30am-7.30pm Mon-Sat; Ⓜ Bastille
Great cardigans and trousers, interesting accessories, ethnic influences and beautiful fabrics: just a few reasons why Isabel Marant has become the *chouchou* (darling) of Paris fashion. Bohemian and stylish, these are clothes that people actually look good in.

MARCHÉ AUX PUCES D'ALIGRE
Map p158   Flea Market
place d'Aligre, 12e; ◷ 8am-1pm Tue-Sun; Ⓜ Ledru Rollin
Smaller but more central (and, punters say, more trustworthy) than Paris' other flea markets (p212), this is one of the best places to rummage through boxes of clothes and accessories worn decades ago by those fashionable (and not-so-fashionable) Parisians, as well as their bric-a-brac.

CHEMINS DE BRETAGNE
Map p158   Food & Drink
☎ 01 43 07 61 32; www.chemins-de-bretagne. com, in French; 15 rue de Prague, 12e; ◷ 10.30am-2pm & 3.30-7pm Tue-Sat; Ⓜ Ledru Rollin
Can't live without buttery *kouign amann* (a kind of Breton cake)? Sights set on *cidre* (cider)? This is the place to go for all things Breton – from fish and shellfish products and cakes to organic herbal teas and sea salts.

PREMIÈRE PRESSION PROVENCE
Map p158   Food & Drink
☎ 01 53 33 03 59; www.ppprovence.com; 3 rue Antoine Vollon, 12e; ◷ 11am-2.30pm & 3.30-7pm Tue-Fri, 11am-7pm Sat, 11am-2pm Sun & Mon; Ⓜ Ledru Rollin
By and large France does not make a lot of olive oil – a mere 0.02% of world production, in fact – but what it does press is lighter, more fruity and easier to digest than the olive oils of Spain, Italy or Greece. 'First Provence Pressing' is where to buy the finest AOC-rated cold-pressed *huile d'olive* (olive oil) from Provence.

LA MAISON DU CERF-VOLANT
Map p158   Gifts & Souvenirs, Games & Hobbies
☎ 01 44 68 00 75; www.lamaisonducerfvolant. com, in French; 7 rue de Prague, 12e; ◷ 11am-7pm Tue-Sat; Ⓜ Ledru Rollin
'The Kite House' has just that – kites in every conceivable size, shape, colour and design, as well as kits with which to make them. You'll also find quite a nice collection of boomerangs and Frisbees, including ones that light up in the dark.

DRESS FOR LESS

When I shop secondhand in Paris I don't want to rummage through sloppy piles of someone else's has-beens. That's fine in my own village hall, but not in Paris.

First stop on my carefully researched list of designer outlets specialising in *grandes marques* (big names) was **Mistigriff** (Map p168; ☎ 01 53 95 32 40; www.mistigriff.fr, in French; 83-85 rue St-Charles, 15e; **M** Charles Michels), a shop that got rave reports online. But in the flesh its neon-lit facade screamed 'tack', the security guard was snarling and the heaps of strings spilling onto the floor just didn't ooze the elegance I'd set my heart on.

One peg up but still cut from the same soulless cloth was **Mouton à Cinq Pattes** (Map p108; ☎ 01 45 48 86 26; 8 & 18 rue St-Placide, 6e; **M** Sèvres-Babylone), two shops with €1 bargain trough and scruffy notice on the door requesting *sacs de courses* (shopping bags) to be left *à la caisse* (at the checkout). But its tightly packed rows of clothes oozed choice and at €119 the Jean-Paul Gaultier bustiers (sorry, no conical cups) were a snip of the **Triangle d'Or** (p203) price tag.

A pleasant surprise was **La Clef des Marques** (Map p108; ☎ 01 45 49 31 00; www.laclefdesmarques.com, in French; 122-126 bd Raspail, 6e; **M** Vavin), despite its hackles-raising door policy: surrender your handbag in exchange for a ticket or keep it and be searched later. I swallowed my pride and left an hour later with a last-season Emilio Pucci ski top (€50), classic Ralph Lauren jumper (€80) and a note in my diary to bring my husband here for business suits next time. Its extensive designer lingerie (loads of Calvin Klein), children's fashion (Le Petit Bateau, Diesel, Ralph Lauren) and sportswear sections were equally impressive.

I could have spent all day browsing *les bonnes affaires* – a mix of last-season leftovers at half the price and the current season's collection costing 10% to 15% less – on **Rue d'Alésia**, 14e (Map p168; **M** Alésia). Fascinating was the rail of prototypes of this summer's frocks in **Cacharel** at No 114. There was only one of each design and each a *taille unique* (one size), but at €90 what a find. Exiting the metro station, walk west along rue d'Alésia to uncover its line-up of outlets, including Sonia Rykiel in the SR Store at Nos 64 and 112, Dorotennis at No 74, and Naf Naf Stock at No 143.

My foray into current designer secondhand was short and sweet: Parisian pioneer of *dépôt-vente* (secondhand) in 1970, **Chercheminippes** (Map p108; www.chercheminippes.com, in French; 102, 109-111 & 124 rue du Cherche Midi, 6e; **M** Vaneau) in St-Germain des Prés was everything I could dream of in the shape of five beautifully presented boutiques on one street, each specialising in a different genre (*haute couture*, kids, menswear etc) and perfectly ordered by size and designer. There were even changing rooms.

The single biggest draw of shopping for **vintage** in Paris is not the promise of Parisian chic but price. Secondhand *haute couture* from previous decades costs 20% to 30% less in Paris than in London, says Lawrence Carlier at **Le Dépôt-Vente de Buci** (Map p112; ☎ 01 46 34 28 28; 4 rue Bourbon le Château, 6e; **M** Mabillon). She stocks hand-me-downs brought in from well-off ladies in the 6e arrondissement, returning anything that hasn't sold after three months. 'My vintage is mainly from the 1960s, very à la mode again', she adds, as I mentally calculate if my bank account can handle pea-green cowboy boots, a Chanel jacket *and* an A-line skirt smothered in sequins. This stylish 'boutique of curiosities' with black wooden facade and a hip wine shop as neighbour is right up my alley – as is Madame Auguet's **Ragtime** (Map p112; ☎ 01 56 24 00 36; 23 rue de l'Échaude, 6e; **M** Mabillon) selling *vêtements anciens* (vintage clothes) from 1870 to 1970, and elegant **L'Embellie** (Map p112; ☎ 01 45 48 29 82; 2 rue du Regard, 6e; **M** Sèvres-Babylone). Count anything upwards of €100 for a designer dress at all three. For old-fashioned accessories like gentlemen's pocket watches, ladies' hats and walking canes, browse **Aspasie & Mathieu** (Map p100; 10 rue des Carmes, 5e; **M** Maubert–Mutualité) in the Latin Quarter.

Paris being Paris, there's secondhand…and secondhand: in the rag trade since 1975, collector Didier Ludot not only sells the city's finest couture creations of yesteryear in his exclusive twinset of boutiques **Didier Ludot** (Map p72; ☎ 01 42 96 06 56; www.didierludot.com; 20 & 24 Galerie de Montpensier, 1er; **M** Palais Royal–Musée du Louvre), he also hosts fashion exhibitions in the neighbouring galleries of the Palais Royal, and has published a book portraying the evolution of the little black dress, brilliantly brought to life in his boutique that sells just that, **La Petite Robe Noire** (Map p72; ☎ 01 40 15 01 04; 125 Galerie de Valois, 1er; **M** Palais Royal–Musée du Louvre). Shop mannequins modelled a 1960s Chanel and 2006 Lanvin the day we were there.

Prize for innovation goes to **Andrea Crews** (Map p134; ☎ 01 45 26 36 68; www.andreacrews.com; 10 rue Frochot, 9e; **M** Pigalle), a creative collective that added a whole new dimension to my quest to dress for less. Using everything from discarded clothing to electrical fittings and household bric-a-brac, the team chops, sews, recycles and reinvents to create the most extraordinary new fashion not everyone (few?) would wear. 'Sustainable secondhand' is its motto.

Nicola Williams

FERMOB Map p158 Home & Garden

☎ 01 43 07 17 15; www.fermob.com; 81-83 av Ledru-Rollin, 12e; 🕑 10am-7pm Mon-Sat; Ⓜ Ledru Rollin

If you want to create the 'Jardin du Luxembourg look' in your own backyard or garden, head for Fermob. It makes French park-style benches and folding chairs in a range of yummy colours – from carrot and lemon to fuchsia and aubergine.

MONTPARNASSE & 15E

There might be just one *raison d'être* to shop in the 14e arrondissement, but it's alfresco and bargain-packed. The neighbouring 15e is hardly a frantic shopping district, but it is privy to a clutch of specialist addresses.

MARCHÉ AUX PUCES DE LA PORTE DE VANVES Map p168 Flea Market

av Georges Lafenestre & av Marc Sangnier, 14e; 🕑 7am-6pm or later Sat & Sun; Ⓜ Porte de Vanves

The Porte de Vanves flea market is the smallest and, some say, friendliest of the lot. Av Georges Lafenestre has lots of 'curios' that don't quite qualify as antiques. Av Marc Sangnier is lined with stalls of new clothes, shoes, handbags and household items for sale.

L'ARBRE À BEURRE
Map p168 Food & Drink, Cosmetics

☎ 01 78 09 56 30; www.codina.net, in French; 24 rue Violet, 15e; 🕑 11am-7pm Tue-Sat; Ⓜ Av Émile Zola

Organic oils (pumpkin-seed oil, avocado oil, daisy oil, carrot, cashew and cherry) are made by at this sky-blue Codina atelier. Be it your hair or health you need to boost, Codina has something to suit.

MINI PARIS Map p168 Games & Hobbies

☎ 01 56 77 00 00; www.miniparis.fr, in French; 91-93 av Émile Zola, 15e; 🕑 8.30am-7pm Mon-Fri; Ⓜ Charles Michels or Avenue Émile Zola

Tricky to take a Mini Cooper home, yes, but this showroom is a must – not only for the gorgeous, top-of-the-range convertibles it showcases but also for its interior design. Buy a pedal-powered version of the peppy little cult car for your kid or simply enjoy the glam experience it promises.

VITRA Map p168 Home & Garden

☎ 01 56 77 07 77; www.vitra.com; 40 rue Violet, 15e; 🕑 9am-6pm Mon-Thu, to 5pm Fri; Ⓜ Charles Michels or Avenue Émile Zola

The classics from the history of furniture design can be ogled in this crisp, white space in life-size or miniature form. Go to the back of this inspiring showroom to fully appreciate its own industrial, glass-roofed design.

LE PETIT BAZAR Map p168 Kids

☎ 01 76 90 73 17; www.lepetitbazar.com, in French; 128 av Émile Zola, 15e; 🕑 1.15-6.15pm Mon, 10am-6.30pm Tue-Sat; Ⓜ Avenue Émile Zola

A real *quartier* (neighbourhood) boutique with a distinctly 'green' philosophy, this emporium for tots has it all: imaginative games and toys, clothes, bedroom furnishings and accessories, stuff for school and babycare products – all organic, recycled or made by local artisans. Top it off with a coffee corner to help yourself to a herbal tea or juice and slice of homemade cake (fill in your own bill and pay at the counter), not to mention a clutch of music workshops for toddlers (aged one to five).

BEYOND CENTRAL PARIS

MARCHÉ AUX PUCES DE ST-OUEN
Off Map p134 Flea Market

www.parispuces.com; 140 rue des Rosiers, St Ouen; 🕑 9am-6pm Sat, 10am-6pm Sun, 11am-5pm Mon; Ⓜ Porte de Clignancourt

This vast flea market, founded in the late 19th century and said to be Europe's largest, has more than 2500 stalls grouped into a dozen *marchés* (market areas), each with its own speciality (eg Paul Bert for 17th-century furniture, Malik for clothing, Biron for Asian art). There are miles upon miles of 'freelance' stalls; come prepared to spend some time.

top picks

- Jadis (p270)
- Chez Janou (p252)
- Le Hangar (p252)
- La Gazetta (p261)
- Derrière (p252)
- Bistrot du Sommelier (p240)
- Chez Michel (p248)
- L'Astrance (p238)
- L'Agrume (p227)
- La Cabane à Huîtres (p270)

French cuisine is the West's most important and influential style of cooking. With the arguable exception of the Chinese, no other cuisine can compare to French for freshness of ingredients and reliance on natural flavours – that's not a trend for things 'green' or 'organic' but a predilection that dates back centuries. Add to that the use of refined, often very complex cooking methods and the typical Parisian's passion (some would say obsession) for anything connected with the table and you will soon realise what everyone else here already knows: you are in a gourmet's paradise.

Do not think for a moment, though, that this passion for things culinary means that eating out or dining in a private home here has to be a ceremonious or even formal occasion, one full of pitfalls for the uninitiated. Indeed, approach food and wine with half the enthusiasm that the Parisians themselves do, and you will be warmly received, tutored, encouraged and, of course, well fed.

Indeed, the latest buzzword in Paris is the *néo-bistro* (new bistro). Usually a small, relatively informal venue serving outstanding cuisine under the tutelage of a talented (and often 'name') chef, the *néo-bistro* is the biggest growth industry in Paris. It's not a return to basics; it's the way things have always been – with a new twist. As they say in French: *plus ça change, plus c'est la même chose* (the more things change, the more they stay the same).

ETIQUETTE

It is not easy to cause offence at a French table, and manners here have more to do with common sense than learned behaviour. Still, there are subtle differences in the way French people handle themselves while eating that are worth pointing out.

A French table will be set for all courses at restaurants (not always at home), with two forks, two knives and a large spoon for soup or dessert. When diners finish each course, they cross their knife and fork (not lay them side by side) face down on the plate to be cleared away. If there's only one knife and fork at your setting, you should place the cutlery back on the table after each course.

At a dinner party courses may not be served in the order to which you are accustomed; salad may follow the main course, for example, and cheese *always* precedes dessert (p214). A separate plate for bread may or may not be provided. If it is missing, rest the slice on the edge of the main plate or on the tablecloth itself. It is quite acceptable – in fact, encouraged – to sop up sauces and juices with slices of bread.

You will not be expected to know the intricacies of how to cut different types of cheese but at least try to remember the basic rules (see p215). If there are wine glasses of varying sizes at each place setting, the larger one (or ones) will be for red wine (and water), the smaller one for white wine. In general it's better to wait for the host to pour the wine rather than helping yourself, but this depends on your relationship and the tone of the evening. Tasting the wine in restaurants and pouring it at home have traditionally been male tasks, but these days many women will happily serve and more enlightened *sommeliers* (wine waiters) will ask which one of a mixed couple would like to try the wine.

STAPLES & SPECIALITIES

Every nation or culture has its own staples dictated by climate, geography and tradition.

ORDERLY EATING

At a blow-out traditional French meal – be it lunch starting at around 1pm or dinner at about 8.30pm – courses are served as follows:

- **Apéritif** – a preprandial drink
- **Hors d'œuvre** – appetisers; cold and/or warm snacks served before the start of the meal
- **Entrée** – first course or starter
- **Plat principal** – main course
- **Salade** – salad, usually a relatively simple green one with vinaigrette dressing
- **Fromage** – cheese
- **Dessert** – anything from homemade tarte Tatin to something from the local pâtisserie
- **Fruit** – sometimes served in place of dessert
- **Café** – coffee, almost always drunk black
- **Digestif** – digestive; an after-dinner drink

French cuisine has long stood apart for its great use of a variety of fresh and seasonal foods – beef, lamb, pork, poultry, fish and shellfish, cereals, vegetables and legumes – but its three most important staples are the 'holy trinity' of the French kitchen: bread, cheese and *charcuterie* (cured, smoked or processed meat products). And as for regional specialities, well, *tout est possible* (the sky's the limit).

Staples
BREAD

Nothing is more French than *pain* (bread). More than three-quarters of all French people eat it at every meal, and it comes in an infinite variety.

All bakeries have *baguettes* (and the somewhat similar *flûtes*), which are long, thin and crusty loaves weighing 250g. What is simply called a *pain* (400g) is wider, softer on the inside and has a less crispy crust. Both types are at their best if eaten within four hours of baking; if you're not very hungry, ask for a *demi baguette* or a *demi pain*, which is half a loaf. A *ficelle* is a thinner, crustier 200g version of a baguette – not unlike a very thick breadstick.

Bread has experienced a renaissance here in recent years, and most bakeries also carry heavier, more expensive breads made with all sorts of grains and cereals; you will also find loaves studded with nuts, raisins or herbs. These heavier breads keep much longer than baguettes and standard white-flour breads.

Bread is baked at various times during the day, so it's available fresh as early as 6am and also in the afternoon. Most bakeries close for one day a week but you'll always find one open in the neighbourhood – even on Sunday morning

CHEESE

France counts upwards of 500 varieties of *fromage* (cheese) made of cow's, goat's or ewe's milk. Bear in mind, though, that there are just five basic types (see the boxed text, p216), which can be raw, pasteurised or *petit-lait* ('little milk'; the whey left over after the milk fats and solids have been curdled with rennet, an enzyme derived from the stomach of a calf or young goat).

When cutting cheese at the table, remember that a small circular cheese such as a Camembert is cut in wedges like a pie. If a larger cheese (eg a Brie) has been bought already sliced into a wedge shape, cut from the tip to the rind; cutting off the top is just not on.

top picks

BAKERIES

- **Boulangerie Bazin** (Map p158; ☎ 01 43 07 75 21; 85bis rue de Charenton, 12e; ⏰ 7.30am-8pm Fri-Tue; Ⓜ Bastille) Belle époque bakery dating from 1906 churns out award-winning baked goods.
- **Boulangerie Eric Kayser** (Map p100; ☎ 01 44 07 01 42; www.maison-kayser.com, in French; 8 rue Monge, 5e; ⏰ 6.45am-8.30pm Wed-Mon; Ⓜ Maubert–Mutualité) One of 15 branches in Paris, this artisan bakery has become a household name in Paris.
- **Du Pain et des Idées** (Map p140; ☎ 01 42 40 44 52; www.dupainetdesidees.com; 34 rue Yves Toudic, 10e; ⏰ 6.45am-8pm Mon-Fri; Ⓜ Jacques Bonsergent) Award-winning baker churns out fruit and herbal breads and brioches from this museum-quality shop.
- **L'Autre Boulange** (Map p158; ☎ 01 43 72 86 04; www.lautreboulange.com; 43 rue de Montreuil, 11e; ⏰ 7.30am-1.30pm & 4-7.30pm Mon-Fri, 7.30am-1.30pm Sat; Ⓜ Faidherbe Chaligny) Fans of organic wholemeal, rye and sourdough breads can choose from among two dozen varieties.
- **Moisan** (Map p158; ☎ 01 43 45 46 60; www.painmoisan.fr, in French; 5 place d'Aligre, 12e; ⏰ 7am-8pm Tue-Sat, 7am-2pm Sun; Ⓜ Ledru-Rollin) Organic breads and *viennoiseries* (baked goods) keep punters at the nearby market happy and full.
- **Poilâne** (Map p112; ☎ 01 45 48 42 59; www.poilane.fr; 8 rue du Cherche Midi, 6e; ⏰ 7.15am-8.15pm Mon-Sat; Ⓜ Sèvres–Babylone) A legend in its own lifetime, the famous sourdough loaf is France's most famous bread. There's a 15e branch (Map p168; ☎ 01 45 79 11 49; 49 blvd de Grenelle, 15e; ⏰ 7.15am-8.15pm Tue-Sun; Ⓜ Dupleix).

Slice cheeses whose middle is the best part (eg blue or veined cheeses) in such a way as to take your fair share of the rind. A flat piece of semi-hard cheese like Emmental is usually just cut horizontally in hunks.

Wine and cheese is often a match made in heaven. It's a matter of taste, but in general, strong, pungent cheeses require a young, full-bodied red or a sweet wine, while soft cheeses with a refined flavour call for more quality and age in the wine. Some classic pairings include:

THE FIVE BASIC CHEESE TYPES

The choice on offer at a *fromagerie* (cheese shop) can be overwhelming, but *fromagers* (cheese merchants) always allow you to sample what's on offer before you buy, and they are usually very generous with their guidance and pairing advice. The following list divides French cheeses into five main groups – as they are usually divided in a shop – and recommends several types in each family to try.

Fromage à pâte demi-dure 'Semi-hard cheese' means uncooked, pressed cheese. Among the finest are Tomme de Savoie, made from either raw or pasteurised cow's milk; Cantal, a cow's milk cheese from Auvergne that tastes something like Cheddar; Saint Nectaire, a strong-smelling pressed cheese that has a strong, complex taste; and Ossau-Iraty, a ewe's milk cheese made in the Basque Country.

Fromage à pâte dure 'Hard cheese' is always cooked and then pressed. Among the most popular are: Beaufort, a grainy cow's milk cheese with a slightly fruity taste from Rhône-Alpes; Comté, a cheese made with raw cow's milk in Franche-Comté; Emmental, a cow's milk cheese made all over France; and Mimolette, an Edam-like dark-orange cheese from Lille that can be aged for up to 36 months.

Fromage à pâte molle 'Soft cheese' is moulded or rind-washed. Camembert, a classic moulded cheese from Normandy that for many is synonymous with 'French cheese', and the refined Brie de Meaux are both made from raw cow's milk; Munster from Alsace, mild Chaource and strong-smelling Langres from Champagne, and the odorous Époisses de Bourgogne are rind-washed, fine-textured cheeses.

Fromage à pâte persillée 'Marbled' or 'blue cheese' is so called because the veins often resemble *persille* (parsley). Roquefort is a ewe's milk veined cheese that is to many the king of French cheeses. Fourme d'Ambert is a mild cow's milk cheese from Rhône-Alpes. Bleu du Haut Jura (also called Bleu de Gex) is a mild, blue-veined mountain cheese.

Fromage de chèvre 'Goat's milk cheese' is usually creamy and both sweet and slightly salty when fresh, but hardens and gets much saltier as it matures. Among the best varieties are: Sainte Maure de Touraine, a creamy, mild cheese from the Loire region; Crottin de Chavignol, a classic though saltier variety from Burgundy; Cabécou de Rocamadour from Midi-Pyrenées, often served warm with salad or marinated in oil and rosemary; and Saint Marcellin, a soft white cheese from Lyon.

Alsatian Gewürztraminer and Munster; Côtes du Rhone red with Roquefort; Côte d'Or (Burgundy) red and Brie or Camembert; and mature Bordeaux with Emmental or Cantal. Even Champagne can get into the act; drink it with Chaource, a mild cheese that smells of mushrooms.

CHARCUTERIE

Traditionally *charcuterie* is made only from pork, though a number of other meats – from beef and veal to chicken and goose – are now used in making sausages, blood puddings, hams, and other cured and salted meat products. Pâtés, terrines and *rillettes* – potted meat or even fish that is shredded, seasoned, mixed with fat and spread cold, like pâté, over bread or toast – are essentially *charcuterie* and are prepared in many different ways.

While every region in France produces standard *charcuterie* favourites as well as its own specialities, Alsace, Lyon and the Auvergne produce the best sausages, and Périgord and the north of France, some of the most popular pâtés. Some very popular types of *charcuterie* include *andouillette* (soft raw sausage made from the pig's small intes-

tines that is grilled and eaten with onions and potatoes); *boudin noir* (blood sausage or pudding made with pig's blood, onions and spices, and usually eaten hot with stewed apples and potatoes); *jambon* (ham, either smoked or salt-cured); *saucisse* (usually a small fresh sausage that is boiled or grilled before eating); *saucisson* (usually a large salami eaten cold); and *saucisson sec* (air-dried salami).

Specialities

La cuisine parisienne (Parisian cuisine) and that of the Île de France surrounding the capital are basically indistinguishable from the cooking of France in general. Dishes associated with these places are few – *vol-au-vent*, a light pastry shell filled with chicken or fish in a creamy sauce; *potage Saint-Germain*, a thick green pea soup; *gâteau Paris-Brest*, a ring-shaped cake filled with *praline* (butter cream) and topped with flaked almonds and icing sugar; and the humble onion soup and pig's trotters described so intimately in Ernest Hemingway's *The Sun Also Rises*. Deep-fried potatoes (*frites*) and other dishes such as *steak-frites* have always been a Parisian speciality. Today very few dishes are associated with the capital as such, though certain side dishes bear the names of some of its suburbs (p217).

The surfeit of other cuisines available in Paris – from Lyonnais and Corsican to Vietnamese and Moroccan – is another story, and will have you spoilt for choice and begging for more.

Snacks & Street Food

Though Parisians may snack or eat between meals, they do not seem to go in for street food in a big way; hot-dog stands and noodle carts are nowhere to be seen and eating in public is considered somewhat *anglo-saxon* (English or American) and hence rude! You may encounter a crêpe-maker on a busy street corner in the Marais or Latin Quarter, or someone selling roasted *châtaignes* (chestnuts) in autumn and winter, but generally people duck into a café for *un truc à grignoter* (something to nibble on) or a patisserie for a slice of something sweet to be eaten at the desk.

WHERE TO EAT

An English menu posted outside an eatery is not necessarily an indication that the establishment attracts only tourists and serves inferior quality food; it's a global world, after all. But a menu in several languages with those little flag insets is a definite no-no-no. Be on the lookout for handwritten menus, preferably in pen on paper or chalk on blackboard rather than with done a felt-tip or that white stuff on mirror or glass. This is a sign that your chef reinvents the menu daily, according to seasonal and market offerings.

There are a vast number of eateries in Paris where you can get breakfast or brunch, a full lunch or dinner, and a snack between meals.

Most have defined roles, though some definitions are less strict nowadays and some have even become blurred.

Bistro

Sometimes written *bistrot*, this can be a fully fledged restaurant or something akin to a bar serving snacks and light meals. The *néo-bistro* is a new term for an establishment that combines the conviviality and relaxation of a bistro with the cuisine of a *grand restaurant*.

Brasserie

Unlike the vast majority of restaurants in Paris, brasseries – which can look very much like cafés – serve full meals from morning till 11pm or even later. The featured dishes almost always include *choucroute* (sauerkraut with assorted meats) and sausages because the brasserie, which means 'brewery' in French, originated in Alsace.

Café

Cafés are an important focal point for social life in Paris, and sitting in a café to read, write, talk with friends or just daydream is an integral part of many people's daily life here.

The main focus here, of course, is coffee, and only basic food is available at most cafés. Common options include a baguette filled with Camembert or pâté with *cornichons* (gherkins), a *croque-monsieur* (grilled ham and cheese sandwich) or a *croque-madame* (a croque-monsieur topped with a fried egg).

Three factors determine how much you'll pay in a café: where the café is located, where you are sitting within the café, and what time of day it is. Progressively more expensive tariffs apply at the *comptoir* or *zinc* (counter or bar), in the *salle* (inside seating area) and on the *terrasse* (pavement terrace), the best

---

SAVOURING THE SUBURBS

The *maraîchers* (market gardeners) of the Île de France encircling Paris traditionally supplied the capital with fresh produce. Today, while the Île de France is less important agriculturally and encompasses the eight *départements* that make up the urbanised Région Parisienne (Parisian Region), the green and gentle 'Island of France' has clung to many of the products it knows best.

A list of fruits and vegetables from the region reads like an RER map: *asperges d'Argenteuil* (Argenteuil asparagus), *carottes de Crécy* (Crécy carrots), *cerises de Montmorency* (Montmorency cherries), *fraises de Palaiseau* (Palaiseau strawberries), *pétales de roses de Provins* (Provins rose petals, used to make jam), *tomates de Montlhéry* (Montlhéry tomatoes), *champignons de Paris* (Paris mushrooms, grown *for* – not *in* – the capital) and so on. A dish served *à la parisienne* (in the Parisian style) is a combination of vegetables along with potato balls that have been sautéed in butter, glazed in meat drippings and sprinkled with parsley.

vantage point from which to see and be seen. A café on a major boulevard, such as blvd du Montparnasse or the av des Champs-Élysées, will charge considerably more than a place that fronts a quiet side street in the 3e. The price of drinks usually goes up after 8pm.

Ordering a cup of coffee (or anything else, for that matter) earns you the right to occupy the seat for as long as you like. You will never feel pressured to order something else.

Cafétéria

Paris has several chains of *cafétérias* (cafeteria restaurants), including Flunch, that offer a decent and cheap (menus from €7.50) selection of dishes that you can see before ordering, a factor that can make life easier if you're travelling with kids.

Crêperie

Crêperies specialise in ultra-thin pancakes cooked on a flat surface and then folded or rolled over a filling. Sometimes the word 'crêpe' is used to refer only to sweet crêpes made with *farine de froment* (wheat flour), whereas a savoury crêpe, more accurately a *galette*, is made with *farine de sarrasin* (buckwheat flour), and filled with cheese, mushrooms, eggs and the like.

Restaurant

Unlike a brasserie, a restaurant is usually open only for lunch and dinner. Almost all restaurants close for at least one and a half days (ie a full day and either one lunch or dinner period) each week, and this schedule is usually posted on the front door. Chain restaurants are usually open throughout the day, seven days a week.

Restaurants generally also post a *carte* (menu) outside, so you can decide before going in whether the selection and prices are to your liking and/or budget. Most offer at least one fixed-price, multicourse meal known in French as a *menu, menu à prix fixe* or *menu du jour* (daily menu). This almost always costs much less than ordering à la carte.

When you order a three-course *menu*, you usually get to choose an entrée, a main course (one of several meat, poultry or fish dishes, including the *plat du jour,* or the 'daily special'); and either cheese or dessert. Some places offer a *formule,* which allows you to pick two of three courses – an entrée and a main course, say, or a main course and a dessert.

Boissons (drinks), including wine, cost extra unless the menu says *boisson comprise* (drink included), in which case you may get a beer or a glass of mineral water. If the *menu* says *vin compris* (wine included), you'll probably be served a 25cL *pichet* (jug) of house red or white. The waiter will always ask if you would like coffee to end the meal, but this will almost always cost extra.

Restaurant meals in Paris are almost always served with bread, which is never accompanied by butter.

Restaurant Libre-Service

A *restaurant libre-service* is a self-service restaurant not unlike a *cafétéria.*

Restaurant Rapide

A *restaurant rapide* is a fast-food place, be it imported (eg McDonald's) or home-grown, such as Quick.

Restaurant Universitaire

The University of Paris system has some 14 subsidised *restaurants universitaires* (canteens or refectories) and 23 *cafétérias* (p219) serving very cheap meals.

Salon de Thé

A *salon de thé* (tearoom) is a trendy, somewhat expensive establishment that offers a variety of quiches, salads, cakes, tarts, pies and pastries, in addition, of course, to various types of tea.

VEGETARIANS & VEGANS

Vegetarians and vegans make up a small minority in a country where *viande* (meat) once also meant 'food', and they are not particularly well catered for; specialist vegetarian restaurants are few and far between in Paris. In fact, the vegetarian establishments that do exist in France often look more like laid-back, 'alternative lifestyle' cafés than restaurants. On the bright side, more and more restaurants are offering vegetarian choices on their set *menus.*

Strict vegetarians and vegans should note that most French cheeses are made with rennet, an enzyme derived from the stomach of a calf or young goat, and that some red wines (especially Bordeaux) are often clarified with the albumin of egg whites.

PRACTICALITIES
Opening Hours

Restaurants generally open from noon to 2.30pm or 3pm for lunch and from 7pm or 7.30pm to between 10pm and midnight for dinner. Only brasseries serve full meals continuously throughout the day (usually from 11am or noon to as late as 1am). National and local laws require that restaurants close for one and a half days a week; that means most eateries will be shut for a full day and (usually) an afternoon. Be advised that the vast majority of restaurants in Paris close on Sunday (and there's a distressing tendency for many to shut down for the entire weekend). Due to

---

CHEAP EATS

Along with the less-expensive places listed at the end of each neighbourhood in this chapter, French chain and university restaurants offer excellent value for those counting their euros.

Chain Restaurants

A number of local chain restaurants have outlets around Paris with good-value fixed price menus. They are definitely a cut above fast-food outlets and can be a boon in areas like the av des Champs-Élysées, where restaurants tend to be overpriced.

Bistro Romain (www.bistroromain.fr, in French; starters €4.30-17.50, pasta €11-14.90, mains €12.70-19.50, menu €9.90-26.90; 🕑 11am-midnight Sun-Thu, to 1am Fri & Sat) This ever-popular Italian-ish bistro–restaurant chain, which has a dozen branches in Paris proper and seven in the *banlieues* (suburbs), is a surprisingly upmarket place for its price category, and service is always pleasant and efficient. The Champs-Élysées branch (Map p126; ☎ 01 43 59 93 31; 122 av des Champs-Élysées, 8e; Ⓜ George V) is a stone's throw from place Charles de Gaulle and the Arc de Triomphe.

Buffalo Grill (www.buffalo-grill.fr, in French; starters €5.20-8.50, mains €9.50-18.30, menu €7.90-14.90; 🕑 11am-11pm Sun-Thu, to midnight Fri & Sat) This successful chain has seven branches in central Paris, including the Gare du Nord branch (Map p140; ☎ 01 40 16 47 81; 9 blvd de Denain, 10e; Ⓜ Gare du Nord), where – not surprisingly – the emphasis is on grills and steak.

Hippopotamus (www.hippopotamus.fr, in French; starters €4.30-9.90, mains €11.90-29.90, menu €14.90-29.90; 🕑 11.45am-midnight Sun-Thu, to 12.30 or 1am Fri & Sat) This spreading chain, which has 22 branches in Paris proper, specialises in solid, steak-based meals and is always fun. Five of the outlets here stay open to 3am Sunday to Thursday and to 5am at the weekend, including the Opéra branch (Map p72; ☎ 01 47 42 75 70; 1 blvd des Capucines, 2e; Ⓜ Opéra).

Léon de Bruxelles (www.leon-de-bruxelles.com, in French; starters €5.70-9.90, mains €13.90-17.70, menu €11.70-17.90; 🕑 11.45am-11pm) At Léon the focus is on one thing and one thing only: *moules* (mussels). Meal-size bowls of the meaty bivalves, served with chips and bread, start at about €10.50 and are exceptionally good value, especially at lunch. On Sundays eat as much as you like for €15.90. There are nine Léons in central Paris, including the Les Halles branch (Map p76; ☎ 01 42 36 18 50; 120 rue Rambuteau, 1er; Ⓜ Les Halles).

University Canteens

Stodgy but filling *cafétéria* food is available in copious quantities at Paris' 14 *restaurants universitaires* (student restaurants). Another 23 cafeterias (sometimes in the same building) serve drinks, snacks and lighter meals from 8am to between 3pm and 6pm on weekdays. Tickets for three-course meals at Paris' university restaurants are €2.90/4.90 for local students with a French university or college ID card/visiting students with an ISIC or youth card. Guests accompanied by a CROUS cardholder pay €6.80.

Centre Régional des Œuvres Universitaires et Scolaires (CROUS; ☎ 01 40 51 36 00; www.crous-paris.fr, in French) restaurants (usually called *restos U*) have variable hours that change according to university holiday schedules and weekend rotational agreements; check the schedule posted outside any of the following or the CROUS website for current times. The only one open all year and on Sunday (for brunch) is Bullier.

Branches include Bullier (Map p100; 39 av Georges Bernanos, 5e; 🕑 11.30am-2pm daily, 6.15-8pm Mon-Sat; Ⓜ Port Royal); Censier (Map p100; 31 rue Geoffroy St-Hilaire, 5e; 🕑 11am-2.30pm Mon-Fri; Ⓜ Censier–Daubenton or Jussieu); Châtelet (Map p100; 10 rue Jean Calvin, 5e; 🕑 11.30am-2pm Mon-Fri; Ⓜ Censier–Daubenton); Mabillon (Map p112; 3 rue Mabillon, 6e; 🕑 11.30am-2.30pm & 6-8pm Mon-Sat; Ⓜ Mabillon); and Mazet (Map p112; 5-5bis rue André Mazet, 6e; 🕑 11.30am-2pm Mon-Fri; Ⓜ Odéon).

the quirkiness of restaurant opening hours, we have listed them all under each review.

How Much?

When it comes to eating out in Paris, the question 'How much?' is like asking 'How long is a piece of string?' It all depends... A three-course dinner *menu* (fixed-price meal with two or three courses) can be had for as little as €12 at budget places, and one-plate *plats du jour* (daily specials) at lunch are sometimes available for under €10. On the other hand, three courses for lunch at Le Grand Véfour (p221) overlooking the Jardin du Palais Royal will set you back €88, and dinner is three times that amount.

In general, however, you should be able to enjoy a substantial sit-down lunch for under around €15 and an excellent three-course dinner for around €35.

Lower-priced good-value *menus* that are available at lunch only (and usually just on weekdays) are noted as such throughout the chapter. Generally, higher-priced *menus* are available at dinner.

Booking Tables

It is always advisable to book in advance at midrange restaurants and absolutely mandatory at top-end ones. If you do arrive at a restaurant without a reservation, you will be treated more seriously if you state the number of *couverts* (covers) required upon entry. If you're just a party of two, ask *Avez-vous deux couverts?*

Tipping

French law requires that restaurant and café bills include the service charge, which is usually between 12% and 15%. But a word of warning is in order. *Service compris* (service included, sometimes abbreviated as 'sc' at the bottom of the bill) means that the service charge is built into the price of each dish; *service non-compris* (service not included) or *service en sus* (service in addition) means that the service charge is calculated after the food and/or drink you've consumed has been added up. In either case you pay only the total of the bill so a *pourboire* (tip) on top of that is neither necessary nor expected in most cases. However, many Parisians will leave a few coins on the table in a restaurant, unless the service was particularly bad. They almost never tip in cafés and bars when they've just had a coffee or a drink, however.

Self-Catering

Many people in Paris buy at least some of their food from a series of small neighbourhood shops, each with its own speciality, though, as everywhere, more and more people are relying on supermarkets these days. Having to go to a series of shops and stand in several queues to fill the fridge (or assemble a picnic) may seem rather a waste of time, but the whole ritual is an important part of the way many Parisians live their daily lives. And as each *commerçant* (shopkeeper) specialises in purveying only one type of food, he or she can almost always provide a variety of useful tips: which round of Camembert is ripe, which wine will complement a particular food, which type of pot to cook rabbit in and so on.

As these shops are geared to people buying small quantities of fresh food each day, it's perfectly acceptable to purchase only meal-size amounts: a few *tranches* (slices) of meat to make a sandwich, say, or a *petit bout* (small hunk) of sausage. You can also request just enough for *une/deux personne(s)* (one/two persons). If you want a bit more, ask for *encore un petit peu*, and if you are being given too much, say *'C'est trop'*.

Fresh bread is baked and sold at *boulangeries;* mouth-watering pastries are available at *pâtisseries*. A *fromagerie* can supply you with cheese that is *fait* (ripe) to the exact degree that you request. A *charcuterie* offers sliced meat, pâtés and so on. Fresh fruit and vegetables are sold at *épiceries* (greengrocers) and open-air markets. A *traiteur* (caterer or delicatessen) sells prepared dishes that are often ready to eat.

A *boucherie* is a general butcher, but for specialised poultry you have to go to a *marchand de volaille*. A *boucherie chevaline*, easily identifiable by the gilded horse's head above the entrance but scarce as hens' teeth these days, sells horse meat, which some people prefer to beef or mutton. Fresh fish and seafood are available from a *poissonnerie*.

Neighbourhood *marchés alimentaires* (food markets) are equally a part of life here. The city's *marchés découverts* (open-air markets) – some 70 of which pop up in public squares around the city two or three times a week – are usually open from about 7am or 8am to 2pm or 3pm, depending on the time of year. The dozen marchés couverts (covered markets) keep more regular hours: 8am or 9am to 1pm and 3.30pm or 4pm to 7pm or 7.30pm from Tuesday to Saturday and till lunch time on Sunday. Completing the picture are numerous independent rues commerçantes, pedestrian streets where the shops set up outdoor stalls. To find out when there's a market near you, check out the list on p222, enquire at your hotel or hostel or ask anyone who lives in the neighbourhood. Self-catering details are included at the end of each of the neighbourhood sections in this chapter.

The trade of produits sans chimiques (products without additives) or produits biologiques is carefully government-regulated and very much on the increase in France. Look for the Label Agriculture Biologique (white letters 'AB' against a green background), which guarantees that the product is 95% organic.

LOUVRE & LES HALLES

The area between Forum des Halles (1er) and the Centre Pompidou (4e) is filled with a number of trendy restaurants, but most of them cater to tourists and few of them are especially good. Streets lined with places to eat include rue des Lombards, the narrow streets to the north and east of Forum des Halles and pedestrian-only rue Montorgueil, a market street that's probably your best bet for something quick. In addition, there are several worthwhile places in the passages couverts (covered shopping arcades; p182).

Those in search of Asian food should head for rue Ste-Anne and other streets of Paris' so-called Japantown, which is just west of the Jardin du Palais Royal. There are also some good-value restaurants serving other Asian cuisines in the area.

LE GRAND VÉFOUR Map p72   French €€€
☎ 01 42 96 56 27; www.grand-vefour.com, in French; 17 rue de Beaujolais, 1er; starters €79-92, mains €75-108, menus €88 (lunch only) & €268; ☽ lunch Mon-Fri, dinner to 9.30pm Mon-Thu; Ⓜ Pyramides
This 18th-century jewel on the northern edge of the Jardin du Palais Royal has been a dining favourite of the Parisian elite since 1784; just look at who gets their names ascribed to each table – from Napoleon to Victor Hugo and Colette (who lived next door). The food is tiptop; expect a voyage of discovery in one of the most beautiful restaurants in the world.

PRICE GUIDE

The symbols below indicate the cost for a two-course meal at the restaurant in question.

€	under €20
€€	€20-40
€€€	more than €40

DROUANT Map p72   French €€€
☎ 01 42 65 15 16; www.drouant.com; 16-18 place Gaillon, 2e; starters €20, mains €30, menus €43 (lunch only), €42 & €54; ☽ lunch & dinner to midnight; Ⓜ Quatre Septembre
If you're something of a literary groupie, you've just got to make your way to the restaurant where they award the Prix Goncourt, France's equivalent of the Booker or Pulitzer. Of course you might also come for the superb food, prepared by Alsatian chef Antoine Westerman, who cut his teeth at the Mon Vieil Ami (p226). Food comes bite-sized and in lots of four; think tapas and get ready to share. It fronts a lovely square unfortunately full of parked cars. The plat du jour is a snip at €17.50.

KAÏ Map p76   Japanese €€€
☎ 01 40 15 10 99; 18 rue du Louvre, 1er; starters €16-24, mains €28-32, menus €28-42 (lunch only) & €69; ☽ lunch Tue-Sat, dinner to 10.30pm Tue-Sun; Ⓜ Louvre–Rivoli
This exquisite (if pricey) Japanese restaurant is where we want to go when we die (and have been deemed worthy of paradise). The décor – bamboo ceiling, blond-wood flooring – is an exercise in restraint. The food is out of this world with its own style of making sushi and excellent grilled dishes (try the aubergine with miso).

RESTAURANT DU PALAIS ROYAL
Map p72   International €€€
☎ 01 40 20 00 27; www.restaurantdupalaisroyal .com, in French; 110 galerie de Valois, 1e; starters €12-23, mains €26-40; ☽ lunch & dinner to 10pm Mon-Sat; Ⓜ Palais Royal–Musée du Louvre
The terrace of this stunner overlooking the Palais Royal has become one of the most coveted covers in fine weather in recent years. In colder months the redder-than-red dining room is both cosy and stylish and chef Bruno Hees turns out some award-wishing international dishes with an Italian spin, especially pasta and risotto (€18 to €30) ones and osso buco à la Milanese (€24).

IN THE MARKET

The following is a list of Paris markets selected according to the variety of their produce, their ethnicity and the neighbourhood. They are *la crème de la crème* of what's on offer in Paris. They are ordered here by arrondissement.

Rue Montorgueil (Map p72; rue Montorgueil btwn rue de Turbigo & rue Réaumur, 2e; 8am-7.30pm Tue-Sat, to noon Sun; Les Halles or Sentier) One of our favourite streets to shop for food in Paris, this *rue commerçante* is the closest market to Paris' 700-year-old wholesale market, Les Halles, which was moved from this area to Rungis in 1969.

Marché Couvert des Enfants Rouges (Map p148; 39 rue de Bretagne, 3e; 9am-2pm & 4-8pm Tue-Thu, 9am-8pm Fri & Sat, 9am-2pm Sun; Filles du Calvaire) This covered market south of place de la République has ethnic (Italian, Moroccan, Japanese etc) stalls as well as French ones.

Marché Maubert (Map p100; place Maubert, 5e; 7am-2.30pm Tue, Thu & Sat; Maubert–Mutualité) This market, spread over a small triangle of intersecting streets, reigns over St-Germain des Prés, the poshest part of the bohemian 5e.

Marché Monge (Map p100; place Monge, 5e; 7am-2pm Wed, Fri & Sun; Place Monge) This is one of the better open-air neighbourhood markets on the Left Bank.

Rue Mouffetard (Map p100; rue Mouffetard around rue de l'Arbalète, 5e; 8am-7.30pm Tue-Sat, 8am-noon Sun; Censier–Daubenton) Rue Mouffetard is the city's most photogenic commercial market street and it's the place where Parisians send tourists (travellers go to Marché Bastille or Rue Montorgueil).

Marché Raspail (Map p112; blvd Raspail btwn rue de Rennes & rue du Cherche Midi, 6e; 7am-2.30pm Tue & Sun; Rennes) This traditional open-air market north of Rennes metro station turns into an organic market on Sunday from 9am to 3pm.

Rue Cler (Map p108; rue Cler, 7e; 7am or 8am-7pm or 7.30pm Tue-Sat, 8am-noon Sun; École Militaire) This commercial street in the 7e is a breath of fresh air in a sometimes stuffy *quartier* and can almost feel like a party at the weekend when the whole neighbourhood turns out en masse.

Marché Biologique Batignolles (Map p136; blvd des Batignolles btwn rue des Batignolles & rue Puteaux, 8e & 17e; 9am-2pm Sat; Place de Clichy or Rome) The first of Paris' *marchés biologiques* (organic markets).

Marché Couvert St-Quentin (Map p140; 85bis blvd de Magenta, 10e; 8am-1pm & 3.30-7.30pm Tue-Sat, 8am-1pm Sun; Gare de l'Est) This iron-and-glass covered market, built in 1866, is a maze of corridors lined mostly with gourmet and upmarket food stalls.

Marché Bastille (Map p158; blvd Richard Lenoir, 11e; 7am-2.30pm Thu & Sun; Bastille or Richard Lenoir) Stretching as far north as the Richard Lenoir metro station, this is arguably the best open-air market in Paris, with a fair number of ethnic food stalls now in attendance.

Marché Belleville (Map p148; blvd de Belleville btwn rue Jean-Pierre Timbaud & rue du Faubourg du Temple, 11e & 20e; 7am-2.30pm Tue & Fri; Belleville or Couronne) This market offers a fascinating entry into the large, vibrant ethnic communities of the *quartiers de l'est* (eastern neighbourhoods), home to African, Middle Eastern and Asian immigrants as well as artists and students.

Marché Couvert Beauvau (Map p158; place d'Aligre, 12e; 8am-1pm & 4-7.30pm Tue-Sat, 8am-1pm Sun; Ledru Rollin) This covered market remains a colourful Arab and North African enclave not far from Bastille.

Marché Biologique Brancusi (Map p168; place Constantin Brancusi, 14e; 9am-2pm Sat; Vavin) This weekly open-air market specialises in organic produce.

Marché Grenelle (Map p168; blvd de Grenelle btwn rue de Lourmel & rue du Commerce, 15e; 7am-2.30pm Wed & Sun; La Motte-Picquet–Grenelle) Arranged below an elevated railway and surrounded by stately Haussmann boulevards and art nouveau apartment blocks, the Grenelle market attracts a well-heeled clientele.

Marché St-Charles (Map p168; rue St-Charles btwn rue de Javel & rond-point St-Charles, 15e; 7am-2.30pm Tue & Fri; Charles Michels or Javel–André Citroën) This market may appear somewhat far-flung off in the western 15e, but shoppers will go any distance for its quality produce, including organic goods.

Marché Président Wilson (Map p118; av du Président Wilson btwn rue Debrousse & place d'Iéna, 16e; 7am-2.30pm Wed & Sat; Iéna or Alma–Marceau) This upscale market attracts a *bobo* crowd from the 16e.

CHEZ LA VIEILLE Map p76 French €€€

☎ 01 42 60 15 78; 1 rue Bailleul & 37 rue de l'Arbre Sec, 1er; starters €15-23, mains €24-30, menu €26 (lunch only); ⊗ lunch Mon-Fri, dinner to 9.45pm Mon, Tue, Thu & Fri; Ⓜ Louvre–Rivoli

'At the Old Lady's', a favourite little restaurant south of Bourse, is on two floors, but don't expect a slot on the more rustic ground floor; that's reserved for regulars. The small menu reflects the size of the place but is universally sublime. Try the excellent mushroom raviolis (€15) or the beef Stroganoff (€26) .

LE GRAND COLBERT Map p72 French €€€

☎ 01 42 86 87 88; www.legrandcolbert.fr; 2 rue Vivienne, 2e; starters €9.20-23.50, mains €21.50-35, 2-/3-course menus €22.50 & €29.50 (lunch only); ⊗ noon-1am; Ⓜ Pyramides

This former workers' *cafétéria* transformed into a *fin de siècle* showcase is more relaxed than many similarly restored restaurants and a convenient spot for lunch if visiting Galerie Vivienne and Galerie Colbert or cruising the streets at night (last orders: midnight). Don't expect gastronomic miracles, but portions are big and service is friendly.

CAFÉ MARLY Map p76 French, Café €€€

☎ 01 46 26 06 60; cour Napoléon du Louvre, 93 rue de Rivoli, 1er; starters €10-26, mains €20-30; ⊗ 8am-2am; Ⓜ Palais Royal–Musée du Louvre

This classic venue facing the Louvre's inner courtyard serves contemporary French fare throughout the day under the palace colonnades. The views of the glass pyramid are priceless – if you don't know you're in Paris now, you never will – and depending on how *au courant* (familiar) you are with French starlets and people who appear in *Match,* you should get an eyeful. Decent pastas are €18 to €24 while sandwiches and snacks are from €12 to €18.

AUX LYONNAIS Map p72 French, Lyonnais €€

☎ 01 42 96 65 04; www.auxlyonnais.com; 32 rue St-Marc, 2e; starters €10.50-14, mains €19-25, 2-/3-course menus €26/34; ⊗ lunch Tue-Fri, dinner to 11pm Tue-Sat; Ⓜ Richelieu–Drouot

This is where Alain Ducasse (who's got three Michelin stars at his restaurant over at the Plaza Athénée) and his followers 'slum' it. The venue is an art nouveau masterpiece that feels more real than movie set and the food is restructured Lyonnais classics on the short, seasonal menu; any item based

on *cochon* (pig) comes with an ironclad guarantee to satisfy; and everything goes well with Beaujolais. Two complaints: there are too many covers in the small space and service is rushed and impersonal.

L'ARDOISE Map p72 French, Bistro €€

☎ 01 42 96 28 18; www.lardoise-paris.com; 28 rue du Mont Thabor, 1er; menu €34; ⊗ lunch Tue-Sat, dinner to 11pm Tue-Sun; Ⓜ Concorde or Tuileries

This is a lovely little bistro with no menu as such (*ardoise* means 'blackboard', which is all there is), but who cares? The food – fricassee of corn-fed chicken with morels, pork cheeks in ginger, hare in black pepper, prepared dextrously by chef Pierre Jay (ex–Tour d'Argent) – is superb, the menu changes every three weeks and the three-course *prix fixe* (set menu) offers good value. L'Ardoise is bound to attract a fair number of tourists due to its location, but generally they too are on a culinary quest.

WILLI'S WINE BAR Map p72 French, Bistro €€

☎ 01 42 61 05 09; www.williswinebar.com; 13 rue des Petits Champs, 1er; starters €10, mains €18.50, menus €20 & €26 (lunch only), €32 & €35; ⊗ lunch & dinner to 11pm Mon-Sat; Ⓜ Bourse

This civilised and very convivial wine bar-cum-bistro was opened in 1980 by British expats who introduced the wine-bar concept to Paris. The food by chef François Yon is still excellent, the wines (especially Côtes du Rhône) well chosen and Willi's legendary status lives on.

LE PETIT MÂCHON
Map p76 French, Lyonnais €€

☎ 01 42 60 08 06; 158 rue St-Honoré, 1er; starters €7.50-13.50, mains €17-25.50, menu €16.50 (lunch only); ⊗ lunch & dinner to 11pm Tue-Sun; Ⓜ Palais Royal–Musée du Louvre

Close to the Louvre, this upbeat bistro serves some of the best Lyons-inspired specialities in town and the welcome is always warm. It takes its name from a Burgundian variety of *galette des rois* (kings' cake), a puff pastry filled with frangipane cream that is eaten at Epiphany (Twelfth Night) or 6 January. The *plat du jour* is €18.50.

AU PIED DE COCHON
Map p76 French, Brasserie €€

☎ 01 40 13 77 00; www.pieddecochon.com; 6 rue Coquillère, 1er; starters €6.90-18.50, mains €17.20-35.90, menus €16.30 (lunch only) & €21.90; ⊗ 24hr; Ⓜ Les Halles

This venerable establishment, which once satisfied the appetites of both market porters and theatre-goers with its onion soup and *pieds de cochon* (pig's feet or trotters), has become more uniformly upmarket and touristy since Les Halles was moved to the suburbs, but it still opens round the clock seven days a week as it has since the end of WWII.

LE VAUDEVILLE Map p72 French, Brasserie €€

☎ 01 40 20 04 62; www.vaudevilleparis.com; 29 rue Vivienne, 2e; starters €6.50-18.50, mains €17.50-32, menus €24 & €30; ⏲ lunch & dinner to 1am; Ⓜ Bourse

This stunning brasserie opposite the stock exchange is to art deco what the Left Bank's *Bouillon Racine* (p234) is to art nouveau. OK, the food – steaks, fish, oysters – might be something of an afterthought at this branch of the Flo chain, but at least you can be guaranteed a certain standard. Come for the fabulous décor – engraved glass, extravagant lighting, domed ceiling and intricate ironwork – designed in the 1920s by the Solvet brothers, who also did *La Coupole* (p270).

L'ÉPI D'OR Map p76 French, Bistro €€

☎ 01 42 36 38 12; 25 rue Jean-Jacques Rousseau, 1er; starters €6-16, mains €17-24, 2-/3-course menus €17/23; ⏲ lunch Mon-Fri, dinner to 11.30pm Mon-Sat; Ⓜ Louvre–Rivoli

The 'Golden Sword' has been an institution since the *belle époque,* when it would open at 10pm to serve the *'forts des halles'*, the brutes who stacked the *'devils'*, huge bags of potatoes and cabbage, all night at the old Marché des Halles. Today it's an oh-so-Parisian bistro with 1940s décor and well-prepared, classic dishes – *gigot d'agneau* (leg of lamb; €18) cooked for seven hours, *magret de canard* (sliced duck breast; €22) – to a surprisingly well-heeled crowd. The *menus* are available at lunch and till 9pm only.

COMPTOIR DE LA GASTRONOMIE

Map p72 French €€

☎ 01 42 33 31 32; www.comptoir-gastronomie. com, in French; 34 rue Montmartre, 1er; starters €6-16, mains €16-25; ⏲ noon-11pm Mon-Thu, to midnight Fri & Sat; Ⓜ Les Halles

This striking art nouveau establishment, here since 1894, has an elegant dining room where dishes are constructed around such delicacies as foie gras, truffles and caviar. The adjoining épicerie fine (specialist grocer; ⏲ 6am-8pm Mon, 9am-8pm Tue-Sat) stocks a scrumptious array of gourmet goods to take away.

CAFÉ BEAUBOURG

Map p76 French, International €€

☎ 01 48 87 63 96; 100 rue St-Martin, 4e; starters €9-14, mains €15-21; ⏲ 8am-1am Sun-Wed, to 2am Thu-Sat; Ⓜ Châtelet–Les Halles

This upbeat minimalist café across from the Centre Pompidou has been drawing a well-heeled crowd for breakfast and brunch (from €13 to €24) on its terrace for two dozen years now. The leather chairs and books on shelves give the main room a clubby feel, the *plats du jours* are €15 to €19 and there's always free entertainment on the *parvis* (large square) just opposite.

JOE ALLEN Map p76 American €€

☎ 01 42 36 70 13; www.joeallenrestaurant.com; 30 rue Pierre Lescot, 1er; starters €7.90-11.10, mains €14-26.50, menus €14 (lunch only), €18.10 & €22.50; ⏲ noon-2am; Ⓜ Étienne Marcel

An institution in Paris since 1972, Joe Allen is a little bit of New York in Paris, with a great atmosphere and a good selection of Californian wines. There's an excellent brunch (€19.50 to €23.50) from noon to 4pm at the weekend, where many can be seen slumped over a Bloody Mary and trying to make sense of the night – or was that the morning? – before. The food is simple but finely prepared; the ribs (€18.50) are particularly recommended and some people think Joe Allen serves the best hamburgers in town.

DJAKARTA BALI Map p76 Indonesian €

☎ 01 45 08 83 11; www.djakarta-bali.com; 9 rue Vauvilliers, 1er; starters €10.50-14.50, mains €11-22; ⏲ dinner to 11pm Tue-Sun; Ⓜ Louvre–Rivoli

OK, it might look like Hollywood's idea of an Indonesian restaurant with all those Balinese handicrafts adorning the walls, but this is the real thing, run by the progeny of an Indonesian diplomat exiled when President Sukarno was overthrown in 1967. If you think you can handle it, order one of four *rijstafels* (Dutch for 'rice table'), priced from €20 to €45: they are feasts of between seven and 10 courses that just won't stop coming. Those with nut allergies beware: peanuts seem to appear in one form or another in most dishes.

BAAN BORAN
Map p72   Thai €

☎ 01 40 15 90 45; www.baan-boran.com, in French; 43 rue de Montpensier, 1er; starters €8-20, mains €11.40-21; ⏱ lunch Mon-Fri, dinner to 11pm Mon-Sat; Ⓜ Palais Royal–Musée du Louvre or Pyramides

The fare at this eatery behind the Palais Royal is provincial Thai and about as authentic as you'll find in this part of Paris. It makes a convenient stop before or after touring the Louvre. There are several vegetarian dishes, priced between €8 and €12.30. If you just want something quick and on the trot, visit Baan Boran à Emporter (Map p76; ☎ 01 40 13 96 70; 103 rue St-Honoré, 1er; dishes €6-7.50, menu €8.90 & €9.50; ⏱ 11am-8pm Mon-Sat; Ⓜ Châtelet or Pont Neuf), which has takeaway service and counter seating.

L'ARBRE À CANNELLE
Map p72   French, Bistro €

☎ 01 45 08 55 87; www.arbre-a-cannelle.fr; 57 passage des Panoramas, 2e; starters €6.90-12.80, mains €12.90-15.90; ⏱ lunch Mon-Sat, dinner till 11pm Wed-Sat; Ⓜ Grands Boulevards

The 'Cinnamon Tree', until recently a simple tearoom with tartes salées (savoury pies) and salads has developed into a full-fledged bistro with large assiettes (platters) that are meals in themselves. The original 19th-century décor is worth a visit in itself; seating is on the ground and 1st floors and gets packed at lunch-time.

PORTA DA SELVA
Map p72   Brazilian €

☎ 06 66 66 93 85; 152 rue St-Denis, 2e; starters €6-10, mains €11-15, menu €12 (lunch only); ⏱ lunch Sun-Fri, dinner to 11pm daily; Ⓜ Étienne Marcel

Step into this sunny space and the warm yellows and greens of the Brazilian flag give the game away. For Brazilian and Portuguese specialities like feijoada (a rich meat and bean stew; €14) and various bacalhau (dried cod) dishes we know of no better place than the 'Jungle Door' (which may be referring to the Amazon or the immediate district of whorehouses and sex shops). Plats du jours are €11 and there's brunch (€12) on Sunday.

LES TROUBADOURS
Map p72   French, Bistro €

☎ 01 40 26 67 10; 10 passage des Panoramas, 2e; 2-/3-course menus €16/19.50; ⏱ lunch daily, dinner to 11pm Mon-Sat; Ⓜ Grands Boulevards

Should you be touring or shopping in the Passage des Panoramas (p182) and feel peckish, you could do no better than stop for lunch at this very intime old-style bistro serving the most traditional of French dishes. Service is uniformly friendly and helpful, the plat du jour €13 and the chocolate cake not to be missed.

SAVEURS VÉGÉT'HALLES
Map p76   Vegetarian €

☎ 01 40 41 93 95; www.saveursvegethalles.fr; 41 rue des Bourdonnais, 1er; starters & salads €4.90-11.90, mains €12.90-17.90, menus €9.90-15.90 (lunch only), €15.90 & €18.90; ⏱ lunch & dinner to 10.30pm Mon-Sat; Ⓜ Châtelet

Due south of the Forum des Halles, this vegan eatery is egg-free and offers quite a few mock-meat dishes, such as poulet végétal aux champignons ('chicken' with mushrooms) and escalope de seitan (wheat gluten 'escalope'; both €12.90). No alcohol is served here.

LE VÉRO DODAT
Map p76   French €

☎ 01 45 08 92 06; 1st fl, 19 Galerie Véro Dodat, 2 rue du Bouloi, 1er; mains €13.50, menu €16.50; ⏱ lunch & dinner to 10.30 Mon-Sat; Ⓜ Louvre–Rivoli

This friendly little place in the heart of the Véro Dodat passage couvert (p182) has seating both downstairs and upstairs. At lunchtime it's popular with workers from the nearby Bourse de la Commerce, who come for the reasonably priced plats du jour.

SCOOP
Map p76   International €

☎ 01 42 60 31 84; www.scoopcafe.com, in French; 154 rue St-Honoré, 1er; dishes €9.90-15.50; ⏱ 11am-4pm Tue, 11am-4pm & 7-10pm Wed-Sat, 11am-5pm Sun; Ⓜ Louvre–Rivoli

This American-style ice-cream parlour has also been making quite a splash with its excellent wraps, burgers, tarts and soups and central, very fashionable location. The upstairs lounge is made for a tête-à-tête, and Sunday brunch (€18 to €25) includes pancakes with maple syrup.

KUNITORAYA
Map p72   Japanese €

☎ 01 47 03 33 65; www.kunitoraya.com, in French; 39 rue Ste-Anne, 1er; dishes €9-18, menu €12.50 (lunch only); ⏱ 11.30am-10pm; Ⓜ Pyramides

With seating across two floors, this simple and intimate restaurant offers a wide and excellent range of Japanese shop-made noodle dishes and set lunches and dinners. If headed here, aim to arrive before 1pm for lunch or before 8pm for dinner to beat the crowds.

ALSO RECOMMENDED

Higuma (Map p76; ☎ 01 58 62 49 22; 163 rue St-Honoré, 1er; mains €6.50-15, menus €10-18; ☺ lunch & dinner to 10.30pm; Ⓜ Palais Royal–Musée du Louvre) Authentic, no-nonsense Japanese noodle shop offers great value, particularly for its location opposite the Comédie Française.

Khatag (Map p76; ☎ 01 48 87 51 25; 68 rue Quincampoix & 66 rue Rambuteau, 3e; starters €4.50-5.50, mains €9.50-10.50, menus €13-22; ☺ lunch & dinner to 11pm Tue–Sun; Ⓜ Rambuteau) This oasis of calm in frenetic Les Halles decorated with wall hangings and *khatag* (offering scarves) is thought to have some of the best Tibetan food in Paris.

Ta Sushi (Map p76; ☎ 01 42 33 52 02; 4 rue Étienne Marcel, 2e; sushi & rolls €3.80-5.80; ☺ lunch & dinner to 11pm; Ⓜ Étienne Marcel) Arguably the pick of the crop of affordable sushi bars that have sprouted up in Paris in recent years.

La Table des Gourmets (Map p76; ☎ 01 40 27 00 87; 14 rue des Lombards, 4e; 2-/3-course menu €15/18; lunch & dinner to 11pm Mon-Sat; Ⓜ Hôtel de Ville) Come here for the venue – a 12th-century chapel with vaulted ceilings – not the standard French dishes at this Chinese-owned establishment.

Thai Classic (Map p76; ☎ 01 48 87 22 04; www.thaiclassic.fr; 26 rue des Lombards, 1er; starters €6.50-12.50, mains €11.10-15.20, menus €15-25; ☺ lunch & dinner till 11.30pm; Ⓜ Châtelet) Long-awaited avatar of our favourite Thai place in Belleville has all the old favourites, including soups, and 10 vegetarian mains.

SELF-CATERING

Rue Montorgueil (Map p72), one of the busiest and best-stocked *rues commerçantes* (commercial streets, not unlike open-air markets) in Paris, is north of Les Halles.

There are several supermarkets around Forum des Halles, including Franprix Les Halles branch (Map p76; 35 rue Berger, 1er; ☺ 8.30am-9pm Mon-Sat, 9am-1.30pm Sun; Ⓜ Châtelet). On the south side of rue de Rivoli you'll find the Franprix Châtelet branch (Map p76; 16 rue Bertin Poirée, 1er; ☺ 8.30am-9pm Mon-Sat, 9am-1pm Sun; Ⓜ Châtelet).

THE ISLANDS

Famed more for its ice cream than dining options, Île St-Louis is a pricey place to eat, although there are a couple of fine places worth a brunch or lunchtime munch with, depending on which you choose and where you sit, some great street entertainment (p295) thrown in for free. As for Île de la Cité, forget it – recommended eating spots are almost nonexistent.

LE TASTEVIN
Map p82   French €€€

☎ 01 43 54 17 31; www.letastevin-paris.com; 46 rue St-Louis en l'Île, 4e; starters €16-24.50, mains € 23-31, menus €28-67; ☺ lunch Wed-Sun, dinner to 11pm Tue-Sun; Ⓜ Pont Marie

This restaurant in a building dating back to the 17th century is an excellent choice if you are looking for very traditional French dishes like escargots, salad of foie gras and green beans, *sole meunière* and profiteroles. One group of readers enjoyed the place so much they ate almost every meal here during their visit.

MON VIEIL AMI
Map p82   French, Alsatian €€€

☎ 01 40 46 01 35; www.mon-vieil-ami.com; 69 rue St-Louis en l'Île, 4e; starters/mains/dessert €11/22/8, menu €41; ☺ lunch & dinner to 10.15pm Wed-Sun; Ⓜ Pont Marie

You're treated like an old friend – hence the name – from the minute you enter this sleek black bistro in one of Paris' most sought-after neighbourhoods. The pâté in pastry crust is a fabulous starter and any of the Alsatian *plats du jours* (€13) is worth exploring. The chocolate tart is the pick of the desserts.

LES FOUS DE L'ÎLE
Map p82   French, Brasserie €€

☎ 01 43 25 76 67; www.lesfousdelile.com; 33 rue des Deux Ponts, 4e; 2-/3-course menus from €23/26; ☺ 10am-2am; Ⓜ Pont Marie

No longer the arty café-cum-*salon de thé* that served somewhat uneven dishes and hung artwork of varying degrees of ability, this place has reinvented itself as a somewhat genteel brasserie, retaining the open kitchen and adding a cockerel theme (we don't know either) throughout. Try any of their Spanish-inspired tapas or the 'real' (their claim, not ours) *cassoulet* (hearty casserole or stew with beans and meat).

LE FLORE EN L'ÎLE Map p82   French, Café €

☎ 01 43 29 88 27; www.lefloreenlile.com; 42 quai d'Orléans, 4e; snacks €8, lunch €16; ☺ 8am-1am; Ⓜ Pont Marie

A tourist crowd piles into this excellent people-watching spot for several very good reasons – its simple coffee 'n' croissant breakfast and Full Monty bacon 'n' egg brunch (€22); its club sandwich–style lunches (€14); its afternoon crêpes (€8); its Berthillon ice-cream shakes and sundaes (from €9 to €11.80); and its prime views of the buskers on Pont St-Louis.

BERTHILLON Map p82   Ice Cream €

☎ 01 43 54 31 61; 31 rue St-Louis en l'Île, 4e; ice creams €2.10-5.40; ☺ 10am-8pm Wed-Sun; Ⓜ Pont Marie

Berthillon is to ice cream what Château Lafite Rothschild is to wine and Valhrona is to chocolate. And with nigh on to 70 flavours to choose from, you'll be spoiled for choice. While the fruit-flavoured sorbets (eg cassis, blackberry etc) produced by this celebrated *glacier* (ice-cream maker) are renowned, the chocolate, coffee, *marrons glacés* (candied chestnuts), Agenaise (Armagnac and prunes), *noisette* (hazelnut) and *nougat au miel* (honey nougat) are richer. The takeaway counter of this café has one/two/three/four small scoops for €2.10/3.20/4.30/5.40.

SELF-CATERING

There are a couple of *fromageries* on rue St-Louis en l'Île, 4e, as well as a small supermarket called Le Prestige d'Alimentation (Map p82; 67 rue St-Louis en l'Île, 4e; ☺ 8am-10pm Wed-Mon). The Boulangerie St-Louis (Map p82; 80 rue St-Louis en l'Île, 4e; ☺ 7am-8pm Wed-Mon) sells filled sandwiches, quiche slices and cheese-topped hot dogs in baguettes to take away.

THE LATIN QUARTER

From chandelier-lit palaces loaded with history to cheap-eat student haunts, the 5e arrondissement has something to suit every budget and culinary taste. Rue Mouffetard is famed for its food market and food shops, while its side streets, especially pedestrian rue du Pot au Fer, cook up some fine budget dining.

A tourist-busy concentration of ethnic restaurants is squeezed into the maze of narrow streets, a duck and a dive from Notre Dame across the Seine, between rue St-Jacques, blvd St-Germain and blvd St-Michel: rue Boutebrie alone cooks up Georgian, Tunisian, Japanese and South American; rue Xavier Privas, rue St-Steven and rue de la Huchette heave with budget restaurants flaunting €15 *menus*.

LA TOUR D'ARGENT

Map p100   French, Classical €€€

☎ 01 43 54 23 31; www.latourdargent.com; 15 quai de la Tournelle, 5e; menu lunch €75, dinner €160; ☺ lunch Wed-Sun, dinner to 9pm Tue-Sun; Ⓜ Cardinal Lemoine or Pont Marie

A much-vaunted riverside address, the 'Silver Tower' is famous – for its *caneton* (duckling), Michelin stars that come and go, rooftop garden with Notre Dame view and fabulous history harking back to 1582. Its wine cellar is one of Paris' best; dining is dressy and exceedingly fine. Reserve eight to 10 days ahead for lunch, three weeks ahead for dinner. Buy fine food and accessories in its boutique opposite.

BISTROT LES PAPILLES

Map p100   French, Bistro €€

☎ 01 43 25 20 79; www.lespapillesparis.com, in French; 30 rue Gay Lussac, 5e; 2-course menu Tue-Fri €22 & €24.50, 4-course menu €31; ☺ lunch & dinner Tue-Sat; Ⓜ Luxembourg

This hybrid bistro, wine cellar and *épicerie* with sunflower-yellow façade is one of those fabulous dining experiences that packs out the place (reserve a few days in advance to guarantee a table). Dining is at simply dressed tables wedged beneath bottle-lined walls, and fare is market-driven: each weekday cooks up a different *marmite du marché* (€16). But what really sets it apart is its exceptional wine list. Taste over lunch then stock your own *cave* (wine cellar) at Les Papilles' *cave à vin*.

L'AGRUME Map p100   French, Bistro €€

☎ 01 43 31 86 48; 15 rue des Fossés St-Marcel, 5e; starters/mains €14/30, menu lunch €14 & €16, dinner €35; ☺ lunch & dinner Tue-Sat; Ⓜ Censier–Daubenton

Lunching at this much-vaunted, pocket-sized contemporary bistro on a little-known street on the Latin Quarter's southern fringe is magnificent value and a real gourmet experience. Watch chefs work with seasonal products in the open kitchen while you dine – at table, bar-stool seating or *comptoir* (counter). Evening dining is an exquisite, no-choice *dégustation* (tasting) melody of five courses, different every day. Snagging a table at L'Agrume – meaning 'Citrus Fruit' – is tough; reserve several days ahead.

L'AOC Map p100 French, Classical €€

☎ 01 43 54 22 52; www.restoaoc.com; 14 rue des Fossés St-Bernard, 5e; 2-/3-course lunch €21/29; ☺ lunch & dinner to 11.30pm Tue-Sat; Ⓜ Cardinal Lemoine

'Bistrot carnivore' is the strapline of this tasty little number concocted around France's most respected culinary products. The concept here is AOC (*appellation d'origine contrôlée*), meaning everything has been reared or made according to strict guidelines designed to protect a product unique to a particular village, town or area. The result? Only the best! Rare is the chance to taste *porc noir de Bigorre,* a type of black piggie bred in the Pyrénées.

LE COUPE-CHOU

Map p100 French, Romantic €€

☎ 01 46 33 68 69; www.lecoupechou.com, in French; 9 & 11 rue de Lanneau, 5e; starters €9.50-20.90, mains €17.60-34, menu lunch €18, dinner €28.50; ☺ lunch & dinner to 11.30pm Mon-Sat; Ⓜ Maubert–Mutualité

Well hidden but well known among Paris expats, this maze of candle-lit rooms snaking through a vine-clad 17th-century townhouse is overwhelmingly romantic. Ceilings are beamed, furnishings are antique, and background classical music mingles with the intimate chatter of diners. Le Coupe-Chou, incidentally, has nothing to do with cabbage *(chou)*; rather it's named after the barber's razor once wielded with a deft hand in one of its seven rooms. As in the days when Marlene Dietrich et al dined here, advance reservations are all essential.

LE PETIT PONTOISE

Map p100 French, Bistro €€

☎ 01 43 29 25 20; 9 rue de Pontoise, 5e; starters €8-13.50, starters €10-15, mains €17.50-25; ☺ lunch & dinner to 10.30pm daily; Ⓜ Maubert– Mutualité

Plop yourself down at a wooden table, note the lace curtains hiding you from the world, and pig out on fantastic old-fashioned classics like *rognons de veau à l'ancienne* (calf kidneys), *boudin campagnard* (black pudding) and sweet apple purée or roast quail with dates at this great bistro. Dishes might seem simple, but you'll leave pledging to return.

CHEZ RENÉ Map p100 French, Bistro €€

☎ 01 43 54 30 23; 14 blvd St-Germain, 5e; starters €6-10, mains €15-29; ☺ lunch & dinner to 11pm Tue-Sat; Ⓜ Cardinal Lemoine or Maubert–Mutualité

Proud owner of one of blvd St-Germain's busiest pavement terraces, Chez René has been an institution since the 1950s. Perfect for punters seeking no surprises, cuisine is quintessentially bistro: think *pot au feu* (beef stew), *coq au vin* (chicken cooked in wine), *rognons de veau* (calf kidneys) etc accompanied by your pick of *garnitures* (fries, boiled potatoes, fresh spinach or other veg of the season etc) and sauces.

LA MOSQUÉE DE PARIS

Map p100 North African €€

☎ 01 43 31 38 20; www.la-mosquee.com; 39 rue Geoffroy St-Hilaire, 5e; starters €5.50-7, mains €15-20; ☺ lunch & dinner to 10.30pm daily; Ⓜ Censier–Daubenton or Place Monge

Dig into one of 11 types of couscous (from €12 to €21), two hands' worth of *tajines* (from €13.50 to €17) or a meaty grill (€14.50) at this authentic restaurant tucked within the walls of the city's central mosque (p99). Feeling decadent? Plump for a peppermint tea and calorie-loaded *pâtisserie orientale* between trees and chirping birds in the North African–style tearoom (☺ 9am-11.30pm) or, better still, a *formule orientale* (€58), which includes a body scrub, 10-minute massage and lounge in the *hammam* (Turkish bath) as well as lunch, mint tea and sweet pastry.

CHEZ LÉNA ET MIMILLE

Map p100 French €€

☎ 01 47 07 72 47; www.chezlenaetmimille.fr; 32 rue Tournefort, 5e; plat du jour €9.50, mains €15-26; ☺ lunch Tue-Fri, dinner to 11pm Tue-Sat; Ⓜ Censier–Daubenton

One of Paris' *bonnes tables* with a fabulous terrace, this intimate restaurant peeps down on a tiny park with fountain and comical equestrian statue. Its notably varied and choice-loaded menu, moreover, allows diners to decide just how fine or otherwise the experience will be. Fancy a simple plate of finely sliced Iberian salami over a lazy glass of wine? Or you want the whole multiple-course hog? Then the *Menu*

Note à Note (€55), finely tuned to the culinary principles of molecular gastronomy, is an exquisite choice.

MOISSONIER Map p100 French, Lyonnais €€

☎ 01 43 29 87 65; 28 rue des Fossés St-Bernard, 5e; starters/mains €10/20; ☻ lunch & dinner to 9.30pm Tue-Sat; Ⓜ Cardinal Lemoine

It's Lyon, not Paris, that French gourmets venerate as the French food capital (they have a point). Indeed, take one bite of a big fat *andouillette* (pig-intestine sausage), *tablier de sapeur* (breaded, fried stomach), traditional *quenelles* (fish-flavoured dumplings) or *boudin noir aux pommes* (black pudding with apples) and you'll realise why. A perfect reflection of one of France's most unforgettable regional cuisines, Moissonier is worth the wait. Look for the elegant oyster-grey façade opposite the university.

LE BABA BOURGEOIS

Map p100 French €€

☎ 01 44 07 46 75; http://lebababourgeois.com, in French; 5 quai de la Tournelle, 5e; menus lunch €16.90 & €19.90, dinner €25.90 & €29.90; ☻ lunch & dinner to 10.30pm Tue-Sat, brunch Sun; Ⓜ Cardinal Lemoine or Pont Marie

It's all very trendy, le BB. Bang-slap on the Seine with a pavement terrace facing Notre Dame, this contemporary eating and drinking space is a former architect's studio. Its interior screams 1970s Italian design and the menu – *tartes salées* (savoury tarts) and salads – makes for a simple stylish bite any time. Sunday ushers in a splendid all-day buffet brunch, *à volonté* (all you can eat for €27).

LE PRÉ VERRE Map p100 French, Bistro €€

☎ 01 43 54 59 47; 25 rue Thénard, 5e; starters €5-10, mains €15, 2-/3-course menu €13.50/28; ☻ lunch & dinner Tue-Sat; Ⓜ Maubert–Mutualité

Noisy, busy and buzzing, this jovial bistro run by the Delacourcelle brothers plunges diners into the heart of a Parisian's Paris. At lunchtime join the flock and go for the fabulous-value *formule dejeuner* (€13) – the day we were there it had curried chickpea soup, guinea-fowl thigh spiced with ginger on a bed of red and green cabbage, a glass of wine and loads of ultra-crusty, ultra-chewy baguette (the best). Desserts mix Asian spices with traditional French equally well. Philippe cooks but is constantly in and out of the kitchen, throwing around

top picks

FOOD STREETS

- **Av de Choisy, av d'Ivry and rue Baudricourt** (Map p164) All three have a plethora of good and quite cheap Chinese and Southeast Asian (especially Vietnamese) eateries.
- **Blvd de Belleville** (Map p148) This is the place for North African (Algerian, Tunisian) food, especially couscous.
- **Passage Brady** (Map p140) This covered arcade is your magnet for Indian, Pakistani and Bangladeshi dishes.
- **Rue Cadet, rue Richer and rue Geoffroy Marie** (Map p126) This triangle of streets has restaurants serving Jewish (mostly Sephardic) and kosher food.
- **Rue Montorgueil** (Map p72) This pedestrians-only market street is one of the best places around for something quick to eat. Tiptop quality.
- **Rue Mouffetard** (Map p100) 'La Mouffe' is not just a food market but also an excellent street to find ethnic and French restaurants in the budget category.
- **Rue Rosiers** (Map p152) In the heart of the Pletzl, this is the best hunting grounds for Ashkenazic Jewish kosher food, especially felafel.

his charm, while Marc is the man behind the interesting wine list, which features France's small independent *vignerons* (wine producers).

LES PIPOS

Map p100 French, Wine Bar €€

☎ 01 43 54 11 40; www.les-pipos.com, in French; 2 rue de l'École Polytechnique, 5e; plats du jour €15.90-28.50; ☻ 8am-2am Mon-Sat; Ⓜ Maubert–Mutualité

A feast for the eyes and the senses, this *bar à vins* is constantly propped up by a couple of regulars over 60. Bistro tables wear red and white, and are so close you risk disturbing the entire house should you need the loo midway through your meal. Its *charcuteries de terroir* (regional cold meats and sausages) is mouth-watering, as is its cheese board, which includes all the gourmet names (bleu d'Auvergne, St-Félicien, St-Marcellin etc). Indeed, take one glance at the titles on the bookshelf (feel free to browse) and you'll realise Les Pipos' overtly casual, laidback scene is a guise for feasting on the finer things in a French foodie's life. No credit cards.

THE TEA CADDY

Map p100   Tearoom €€

☎ 01 43 54 15 56; www.the-tea-caddy.com; 14 rue St-Julien le Pauvre, 5e; mains €8.40-12.80, menu brunch/lunch €28/30; ⏰ 11am-6pm Wed-Mon; Ⓜ St-Michel–Notre Dame

Arguably the most English of the 'English' tearooms in Paris, this institution, founded in 1928, is a fine place to break for lunch or a nice cuppa tea with a Devon scone, double cream and jam after a tour of nearby Notre Dame, Ste-Chapelle or the Conciergerie.

LE COMPTOIR DU PANTHÉON

Map p100   Café, Bar, Brasserie €

☎ 01 43 54 75 56; 5 rue Soufflot, 5e; salads €10-15; bar ⏰ 7am-2am Mon-Sat, to 11pm Sun; brasserie ⏰ 11am-11pm Mon-Sat, to 7pm Sun; Ⓜ Luxembourg or Cardinal Lemoine

Salads…enormous salads, creative salads, fabulous meal-sized salads are the reason to pick this busy café as dining spot. Magnificently placed across from the domed Panthéon on the shady side of the street, its pavement terrace is big, busy and oh so Parisian in feel – turn your head away from Voltaire's burial place and Mademoiselle Eiffel pops into view. Service is super speedy to boot and food is handily served all day.

MACHU PICCHU Map p100   South American €

☎ 01 43 26 13 13; 9 rue Royer-Collard, 5e; starters €6.50-8.20, mains €8.50-14.90, menu lunch €10.50; ⏰ lunch & dinner to 10.30pm Mon-Fri; Ⓜ Luxembourg

Students adore this place, named after the lost city of the Incas in Peru. But doesn't Peruvian food mean guinea-pig fricassee? No. This hidey-hole, going strong since the 1980s, serves excellent meat and seafood dishes as well as a bargain-basement lunch *menu* and *plats du jour* (€6). No credit cards.

LE JARDIN DES PÂTES

Map p100   Organic, Pasta €

☎ 01 43 31 50 71; 4 rue Lacépède, 5e; pasta €9-14; ⏰ lunch & dinner to 11pm daily; Ⓜ Place Monge

A crisp white-and-green façade handily placed next to a Vélib' station flags the Pasta Garden, a simple, smart 100% *bio* (organic) place where pasta comes in every guise imaginable – barley, buckwheat, rye, wheat, rice, chestnut and so on. Our favourite: *pâtes de chataignes* (chestnut pasta) with duck breast, nutmeg, crème fraîche and mushrooms.

LE PUITS DE LÉGUMES

Map p100   Vegetarian €

☎ 01 43 25 50 95; lapuitdelegumes@hotmail.fr; 18 rue du Cardinal Lemoine, 5e; plat du jour €13; ⏰ lunch & dinner to 10pm Mon-Sat; Ⓜ Cardinal Lemoine

Homemade tarts, quiches and rice dishes smacking of fresh seasonal vegetables are the draw of the 'Vegetable Well', a sweet vegetarian address much loved by students in the Latin Quarter. From the tiny kitchen out back a comforting waft of homemade cooking pervades the simple dining room, filled with a handful of condiment-clad tables. Specials are chalked on the board outside. Before leaving, dedicated vegetarians can buy a copy of *Organic & Vegetarian Paris* (www.vegeparis.com), an English-language guide listing other veggie restaurants, juice bars, organic food shops and so on in the city.

KOOTCHI

Map p100   Afghan €

☎ 01 44 07 20 56; 40 rue du Cardinal Lemoine, 5e; mains €12, menus €9.20-15.50; ⏰ lunch & dinner to 10.30pm Mon-Sat; Ⓜ Cardinal Lemoine

A menagerie of carpets, traditional instruments and other jumble lend this Afghan restaurant a definite Central–Asian caravanserai air. The welcome is warm and the food is warming. Specialities include *qhaboli palawo* (veal stew with nuts and spices); *dogh,* a drink not unlike salted Indian lassi; and traditional *halwa* (a type of sweet cake) perfumed with rose and cardamom. Vegetarians keen to spice up their culinary life should plump for *borani palawo* (spicy vegetable stew) as their main course.

LA SALLE À MANGER

Map p100   French €

☎ 01 55 43 91 99; 138 rue Mouffetard, 5e; lunch €10-15; ⏰ 8.30am-6.30pm Mon-Fri, to 7pm Sat & Sun; Ⓜ Censier–Daubenton

With a sunny pavement terrace beneath trees enviably placed at the foot of foodie street rue Mouffetard, the 'Dining Room' is prime real estate. Its 360-degree outlook – market stalls, fountain, church and garden with playground for tots – could not be prettier and its salads, *tartines* (open toasted sandwiches), tarts and pastries ensure packed tables at breakfast, lunch and weekend brunch.

AUX CÉRISES DE LUTÈCE

Map p100   Tearoom €

☎ 01 43 31 67 51; 86 rue Monge, 5e; mains €10;
🕑 11am-6.30pm Tue-Sat; Ⓜ Place Monge
A feast for the eyes and tastebuds, this cosy
eating space, heaped with colourful tea
pots, jugs and jumble, is the type of place
that would wear flowery wellies. As much
café and tearoom as lunchtime restaurant,
it serves breakfast all day (from €8 to €14)
alongside salads, quiches and *tartines*. Market mornings see punters clawing for the
trio of tables on the pavement out front.

TASHI DELEK Map p100   Tibetan €

☎ 01 43 26 55 55; 4 rue des Fossés St-Jacques, 5e;
soups & bowls €4-7, mains €7.50-14; 🕑 lunch &
dinner to 11pm Mon-Sat; Ⓜ Luxembourg
Gourmet it might not be; cheap, tasty and
inexpensive, it is. Tickle the tastebuds with
a *tsampa* (vegetable and barley soup),
followed by delicious *daril seu* (meatballs
with garlic, ginger and rice) or *tselmok*
(cheese and vegetable ravioli). Then wash
the whole lot down with traditional or
salted-butter tea. Don't forget to say 'tashi
delek' upon entering – it means 'bonjour'
in Tibetan.

LE FOYER DU VIETNAM

Map p100   Vietnamese €

☎ 01 45 35 32 54; 80 rue Monge, 5e; starters €3-6,
mains €6-10; 🕑 lunch & dinner to 10pm Mon-Sat;
Ⓜ Place Monge
The 'Vietnam Club', with its self-proclaimed
ambiance familiale (family atmosphere),
might be nothing more than a long room
with peeling walls and tables covered in
oilcloths and plastic flowers, but everyone
flocks here to feast on its hearty house specialities, 'Saigon' or 'Hanoi' soup (noodles,
soya beans and pork flavoured with lemon
grass, coriander and chives) included.
Dishes come in medium or large portions
and the price:quality ratio is astonishing.
Students can fill up for €7.

SELF-CATERING

Shop with Parisians at a trio of lively outdoor
food markets, framed (as with every market),
by some lovely food shops: Marché Maubert, rue
Mouffetard and Marché Monge (p222).

There are also good supermarket options,
including Carrefour Market (Map p100; 34 rue Monge, 5e;
Ⓜ Cardinal Lemoine), Marché Franprix (Map p100; 82 rue

Mouffetard, 5e; Ⓜ Place Monge) and Monoprix (Map p100;
24 blvd St-Michel, 5e; 🕑 9am-midnight Mon-Sat).

ST-GERMAIN & INVALIDES

There's far more to this fabled pocket of
Paris – effectively the 6e arrondissement and
eastern half of the neighbouring 7e – than
the literary cafés (see p281) of Sartre or the
picnicking turf of the Jardin de Luxembourg.
Rue St-André des Arts and its continuation,
rue du Buci, are lined with places to dine as
lightly or lavishly as your heart desires, as
is the stretch between Église St-Sulpice and
Église St-Germain des Prés (especially rue des
Canettes, rue Princesse and rue Guisarde).

Quintessential Parisian bistros abound here
but if contemporary design à la Terence Conran is more your style, restaurant Alcazar (p282)
is the choice spot to see and be seen. Build
the king of picnics at the Harrods food hall of
Paris, Le Bon Marché (p199), or the food shops
on pedestrian rue Cler. For afternoon tea,
weekend brunch (€35) or a light lunch with
the girls, no address is sweeter than legendary
Ladurée (p235). Les Pâtes Vivantes (p240) is an excellent address for dining with kids.

LE SALON D'HÉLÈNE

Map p112   French, Contemporary €€€

☎ 01 42 22 00 11; www.helenedarroze.com; 4
rue d'Assas, 6e; menu lunch €28 or €35 incl wine,
dinner €85 or €105 incl wine; 🕑 lunch & dinner to
10.15pm Tue-Sat; Ⓜ Sèvres Babylone
While culinary star and media darling
Hélène Darroze has a fine-dining Michelin-
starred restaurant (called La Salle à Manger) upstairs, this more casual 'salon' is
far more fun. The best way to experience
her wonderful creations come dusk is to
persuade your table to each order the
tapas-sized tasting menu with or without
wine. Five courses come in matched pairs,
each dish with descriptions longer than
this review.

L'ATELIER DE JOËL ROBUCHON

Map p112   International €€€

☎ 01 42 22 56 52; www.restaurants-joel-robuchon
.com; 5 rue de Montalembert, 7e; starters/mains
€30/40, menu €150; 🕑 lunch & dinner to midnight
daily; Ⓜ Rue du Bac
It's a mean feat to snag a seat at this
celebrity-chef address, which accepts

reservations from 11am to 12.30pm the day you want to dine out at precisely 6.30pm for dinner. Once in, you'll realise what all the fuss is about. Diners are taken on a mind-blowing culinary tour of the finer things in French gastronomy, lobster, sardines, foie gras and milk-fed lamb included. And with accolades like 'chef of the century' and 'world's best restaurant' under Joël Robuchon's belt, you know it'll be good. Dining is stool-style around a U-shaped black lacquer bar and the décor (bamboo in glass vases and the like) throws in a touch of Japan.

TOYO Map p108   Franco-Japanese, Contemporary €€€

☎ 01 43 54 28 03; 4 rue Jules Chaplain, 6e; menu lunch €35 & €45, dinner €55 & €75; ☯ lunch & dinner to 10pm Tue-Sat; Ⓜ Vavin

Toyo … Toyomitsu Nakayama is the name that's been on many a Parisian's lips since this up-to-the-minute dining address opened. The culinary flair behind the place is the former private chef of fashion designer Kenzo and the concept is a fabulous fusion of French and Japanese cuisine that seats diners side by side at a stylish wooden bar – prime real estate for watching Toyo chop.

SENSING Map p108   French, Contemporary €€€

☎ 01 43 27 08 80; www.restaurantsensing.com; 19 rue Bréa, 6e; starters €21-24, mains €32-37, menu 2-/3-course lunch €25/35 & €55, dinner €75 & €95; ☯ dinner to 10.30pm Mon, lunch & dinner to 10.30pm Tue-Sat; Ⓜ Vavin

Don't worry about arriving at this elegant address with a hair out of place or smudged lipstick – a quick preen in the mirrored door upon entering will sort it out. The swanky 'affordable-bistro' creation of Michelin-starred celebrity chef Guy Martin, Sensing is one of those try-hard New York–type places with an interior design so cutting edge it seriously distracts from the food. 'Snacking' is the trendy name for pre-dinner nibbles.

CAFÉ DE L'ESPLANADE

Map p108   Fusion €€€

☎ 01 47 05 38 80; 52 rue Fabert, 7e; starters €15-20, mains €25-45; ☯ lunch & dinner to 12.30am daily; Ⓜ La Tour Maubourg

An address to impress (so dress to impress), Café de l'Esplanade might well be one of those chic, hobnobbing society places to be seen in between business deals – it *is*

of the same Costes brothers ilk as Café Marly (p223) et al, much loved by politicians and journalists. But take one look at the astonishing view and you'll understand why. This is, after all, the only café–restaurant on the magnificent Esplanade des Invalides. No menus – just *à la carte* until half-past midnight.

CASA BINI Map p112   Italian €€

☎ 01 46 34 05 60; www.casabini.fr, in French; 36 rue Gregoire de Tours, 6e; starters €10-15, pasta €15-22, mains €25-40, 2-/3-course lunch menu €23/27; ☯ lunch & dinner until 11.30pm daily; Ⓜ Odéon

With classical façade and sober interior, the décor clearly plays second fiddle to cuisine at this highly recommended Italian restaurant where homemade pasta is cooked to al dente perfection and children are treated like gods. Be it squid and creamed courgette soup, *tagliolini* studded with white summer truffles or a classic veal *saltimbocca* (veal escalope flavoured with ham, thyme and sage), tastebuds won't be disappointed. Lunch, which has a different menu from that after dusk (including a tasty €16 *carpaccio de jour),* is a more affordable affair.

KGB Map p112   Fusion €€

☎ 01 46 33 00 85; http://zekitchen-galerie.fr, in French; 25 rue des Grands Augustins, 6e; menu lunch €27 & €34, pasta/mains €21/28; ☯ lunch & dinner to 11pm Tue-Sat; Ⓜ St-Michel

KGB (as in 'Kitchen Galerie Bis') is the latest creation of William Ledeuil of Ze Kitchen Galerie fame. Overtly art gallery in feel, this small dining space plays to a hip crowd with its casual platters of Asian-influenced *hors d'œvres* (€16/19/22 for 4/5/6), creative pastas (*orecchiette* studded with octopus, squid and crab the day we were here) and marmite-cooked meats. Roast pigeon with ginger and cranberry condiment anyone?

ZE KITCHEN GALERIE Map p112   Fusion €€€

☎ 01 44 32 00 32; http://zekitchen-galerie.fr, in French; 4 rue des Grands Augustins, 6e; starters/mains €15/25, menu lunch/dinner €26.50/65; ☯ lunch & dinner to 11pm Mon-Fri, dinner to 11.30pm Sat; Ⓜ St-Michel

William Ledeuil's passion for Southeast Asian travel oozes out of the feisty dishes he creates in his Michelin single-starred glass-box kitchen, which hosts three to five different art exhibitions a year. The menu is a vibrant feast of broths loaded with Thai herbs and coconut milk, meat and fish cooked *à la plancha* and inventive desserts like sweet chestnut-and-vanilla soup. Service is speedy and lunch *menus* include a glass of wine and coffee.

BRASSERIE THOUMIEUX
Map p108   French, Brasserie €€

☎ 01 47 05 49 75; www.thoumieux.com, in French; 79 rue St-Dominique, 7e; starters/mains €10/25, menus €15 (lunch only) & €35; ⏱ lunch & dinner to 11.30pm daily; Ⓜ La Tour Maubourg

Chef Christian Beguet has been here since 1979 – and that's just the tip of the iceberg. Founded in 1923, Thoumieux is an old-school institution just south of the Seine, loved by politicians and tourists alike. Duck thighs, veal, snails…the menu is typical brasserie and the service silky smooth. It has 10 rooms up top should you need to crash.

LE PETIT ZINC Map p112   French, Brasserie €€

☎ 01 42 86 61 00; www.petit-zinc.com, in French; 11 rue St-Benoît, 6e; starters/mains €15/30, 2-course lunch €20.30; ⏱ noon-2am daily; Ⓜ St-Germain des Prés

Not a 'little bar' as its name would suggest, but a wonderful, large brasserie serving mountains of fresh seafood, traditional French cuisine and regional specialities from the southwest in true art nouveau splendour. The term 'brasserie' is used loosely here; you'll feel more like you're in a starred restaurant, so book ahead and dress accordingly.

CHEZ ALLARD Map p112   French, Bistro €€

☎ 01 43 26 48 23; 41 rue St-André des Arts, 6e; starters €8-20, mains €25, menu €34; ⏱ lunch & dinner to 11.30pm Mon-Sat; Ⓜ St-Michel

A definite Left Bank favourite is this charming bistro where the staff couldn't be kinder or more professional – even during its enormously busy lunchtime. And the food is superb. Try a dozen snails, some *cuisses de grenouilles* (frogs' legs) or *un poulet de Bresse* (France's most legendary chicken, from Burgundy) for two. Enter from 1 rue de l'Éperon.

MATTEO ET PAOLA Map p112   Tearoom €

☎ 01 45 49 33 64; 20 rue du Cherche Midi, 6e; starters €15 mains €22; ⏱ 9am-9pm Mon-Sat, 10.30am-9pm Sun; Ⓜ Sèvres–Babylone

A youthful mix of tearoom-cum-trendy-café-bar, this popular weekend spot on a quiet shopping street near Le Bon Marché (p199) is perfect for a lazy breakfast over newspapers, brunch or indeed a light savoury-tart lunch. Most food has gone by 7pm when regulars stream in for an aperitif on the small pavement terrace.

LE COMPTOIR DU RELAIS
Map p112   French, Bistro €€€

☎ 01 44 27 07 97; 9 Carrefour de l'Odéon, 6e; starters/mains €15/20, menu €50; ⏱ lunch & dinner to 12.30am daily; Ⓜ Odéon

Simply known as Le Comptoir (the Counter) among the in crowd, this gourmet bistro has provoked a real stir ever since it opened. The culinary handiwork of top chef Yves Camdeborde, it cooks up seasonal bistro dishes with a seriously creative and gourmet twist – fancy asparagus and foie gras salad? Bagging a table at lunchtime is just about doable providing you're here at 12.30pm sharp, but forget evening dining – more gastronomic than at *midi* – unless you have a table reservation (weeks in advance for weekends).

BELLOTA BELLOTA
Map p108   Spanish, Tapas €€

☎ 01 53 59 96 96; www.bellota-bellota.com; 18 rue Jean Nicot, 7e; mains €19, 2-/3-course menu €24/29; ⏱ lunch & dinner to 11pm Tue-Sat; Ⓜ La Tour Maubourg

This Spanish-style tapas bar with a clutch of great big Iberian hams strung in the window is a perfect spot for lunch before or after the Musée d'Orsay (p107), or, for that matter, an aperitif at the end of the day. As much drinking as dining venue, this atmospheric little place lures punters in with a fabulous tiled floor, grey painted chairs and more black-footed piggy legs than you'll ever be able to eat dangling from the ceiling.

LES ÉDITEURS Map p112   French, Café €€

☎ 01 43 26 67 76; 4 Carrefour de l'Odéon, 6e; starters €10-18, mains €18-25; ⏱ 8am-2am daily; Ⓜ Odéon

This place goes to great lengths to describe itself as café, restaurant, library, bar and *salon de thé,* but for us it's a place to eat and/or people-watch. It is intended for writers – there are more than 5000 books on hand and it's done up to feel like a slightly faded and dingy library – but it has floor-to-ceiling windows through which you can watch the Germanopratin (yes, there is an adjective for St-Germain des Prés) goings-on. Breakfasts and Sunday brunch are big here.

LES COCOTTES

Map p108   French, Contemporary €€

www.leviolondingres.com; 135 rue Ste-Dominique, 7e; cocottesstarters/mains/desserts €11/16/7; ⏲ lunch & dinner to 10.30pm Mon-Sat; Ⓜ École Militaire or Port de l'Alma

Cocottes are casseroles and that is precisely what Christian Constant's chic concept space is about. Day in day out, its contemporary interior is jam-packed with a buoyant crowd feasting on inventive seasonal creations cooked to perfection in little black enamel, oven-to-table *cocottes* (casserole dishes). Seating is on bar stools around high tables and the place doesn't take reservations. Get here at noon sharp or 7.15pm (or before) to get a table. If the queue's out the door, nip a couple of doors down for a drink at Café Constant (p234).

CAFÉ CONSTANT

Map p108   French, Contemporary €€

☎ 01 47 53 73 34; www.cafeconstant.com, in French; 139 rue Ste-Dominique, 7e; starters/mains/ desserts €11/16/7; ⏲ lunch & dinner to 10.30pm Tue-Sun; Ⓜ École Militaire or Port de l'Alma

Take a former Michelin-starred, dead-simple corner café and what do you get? This jam-packed address with original mosaic floor, simple wooden tables and a huge queue out the door every meal time. The pride and joy of Christian and Catherine Constant, the café doesn't take reservations but you can enjoy a drink at the bar (or on the pavement outside) while you wait. Cuisine is creative bistro, mixing old-fashioned grandma staples like *purée de mon enfance* (mashed potato from my childhood) with Sunday treats like foie-gras-stuffed quail and herb-roasted chicken. Les Cocottes (p234), a couple of doors down on the same street, is another Constant hit.

BOUILLON RACINE

Map p112   French, Classical €€

☎ 01 44 32 15 60; 3 rue Racine, 6e; starters €6.50-14.50, mains €15.50-28, menus €14.90 (lunch) & €29.50; ⏲ lunch & dinner to 11pm daily; Ⓜ Cluny–La Sorbonne

We've never seen anything quite like this 'soup kitchen', built in 1906 to feed market workers. A gorgeous art nouveau palace with mirrored walls, floral motifs and ceramic tiling, the interior is a positive delight. Oh, and the food? Wholly classic inspired by age-old recipes such as roast snails, *caille confite* (preserved quail) and lamb shank with liquorice. Finish off your foray in gastronomic history with an old-fashioned sherbet.

CHEZ HANAFOUSA

Map p112   Japanese €€

☎ 01 43 26 50 29; 4 passage de la Petite Bouche-rie, 6e; menus €13.50 (lunch) & €29-72; ⏲ lunch & dinner to 11.30pm daily; Ⓜ St-Germain des Prés

Dining at this understated Japanese restaurant is a spectacular choice guaranteed to impress. Sit around a steely-topped U-shaped 'hot table' and watch fish, meat, spices, vegetables and herbs chopped, sliced, ground and flamed before your very eyes – all the set menus (bar the quick, good-value miso-and-sushi lunchtime choice) feature *teppanjaki* (hot plate cooking). End the show with a flaming vanilla ice-cream fritter or less flamboyant green-eat cheesecake with wasabi ice-cream.

L'ARBUCI

Map p112   French, Brasserie €€

☎ 01 44 32 16 00; 25 rue du Buci, 6e; starters €8-20, mains €15-25; ⏲ noon-midnight daily; Ⓜ Mabillon

A popular choice for breakfast or brunch, this airy lounge bar with big, street-facing windows buzzes. Its décor is a contemporary take on traditional brasserie-style and the easygoing menu caters to all tastes, including those whose buds go wild over bottomless plates of oysters. Prime real estate, the packed tables on the pavement terrace in front see you vying for foot space with passing pedestrians. Live jazz in the basement on Fridays and Saturdays.

BRASSERIE LIPP

Map p112   French, Brasserie €€

☎ 01 45 48 53 91; www.brasserie-lipp.fr; 151 blvd St-Germain, 6e; starters €10-15, mains €15-25; ⏲ 9-1am daily; Ⓜ St- Germain des Prés

Politicians rub shoulders with intellectuals, while waiters in black waistcoats, bow ties and long white aprons serve brasserie favourites like *choucroute garnie* and *jarret de porc aux lentilles* (pork knuckle with lentils) at this celebrated wood-panelled café, opened by Léonard Lipp in 1880.

CRÈMERIE RESTAURANT POLIDOR
Map p112   French €€

☎ 01 43 26 95 34; http://restaurantpolidor.info, in French; 41 rue Monsieur le Prince, 6e; starters €4.50-17, mains €11-22, menus €22 & €32;

🕙 lunch & dinner to 12.30am Mon-Sat, to 11pm Sun; M Odéon

A meal at this quintessentially Parisian *crèmerie-restaurant* is like a trip to Victor Hugo's Paris: the restaurant and its décor

SWEET MEMORIES

Like all French people, Parisians love *sucreries* (sweet things) and fruit and, judging from the eye-catching and saliva-inducing window displays at pastry shops throughout the city, they can't get enough of either in combination. The following are some of our favourite *pâtisseries* in Paris, but be aware that the list is *not* comprehensive; there are plenty more out there just waiting to be discovered.

Boulangerie-Pâtisserie Stéphane Secco (Map p108; ☎ 01 43 17 35 20; 20 rue Jean Nicot, 7e; 🕙 8am-8.30pm Tue-Sat; M La Tour-Maubourg) Try M Secco's flagship *Paris-Brest* (choux pastry with butter cream and almonds), *madeleines* (lemon-flavoured shell-shaped cake) and 0% fat cheesecake (we don't know either).

Boulangerie Bruno Solques (Map p100; ☎ 01 43 54 62 33; 143 rue St-Jacques, 5e; 🕙 6.30am-8pm Mon-Fri; M Luxembourg) Arguably the most inventive pâtissier in Paris, Bruno Solques excels at oddly shaped flat tarts with mashed fruit and fruit-filled brioches. Kids from the school across the way can't get enough.

Dalloyau (Map p148; ☎ 01 48 87 89 88; www.dalloyau.fr; 5 blvd Beaumarchais, 4e; 🕙 9am-9pm; M Bastille) Specialities include *pain aux raisins* (raisin bread), *millefeuille* (pastry layered with cream), *tarte au citron* (lemon tart) and famously its *opéra*, with coffee-flavoured almond cake and chocolate. There's also a 8e branch (Map p126; ☎ 01 42 99 90 00; 101 rue du Faubourg St-Honoré, 8e; 🕙 8.30am-9pm; M St-Philippe du Roule), which has an adjoining tearoom.

Gérard Mulot (Map p108; ☎ 01 43 26 85 77; www.gerard-mulot.com, in French; 76 rue de Seine, 6e; 🕙 6.45am-8pm; M Odéon or Mabillon) Specialities include various fruit tarts (peach, lemon, apple), *tarte normande* (apple cake) and *clafoutis* (upside-down custard and cherry tart). There a new **Marais branch** (Map p148; ☎ 01 42 78 52 17; 6 rue du Pas de la Mule, 3e; 🕙 8am-8pm Tue-Sun; M Chemin Vert) north of place des Vosges.

La Fougasse (Map p148; ☎ 01 42 72 36 80; 25 rue de Bretagne, 3e; 🕙 7am-8pm Tue-Sat, 7am-2pm Sun; M Filles du Calvaire) Come here for the scrumptious *marrons glacés* (candied chestnuts), *sablés* (rich shortbread biscuit) and *tarte aux abricots* (apricot tart).

Ladurée (Map p126; ☎ 01 40 75 08 75; www.laduree.fr; 75 av des Champs-Élysées, 8e; 🕙 7.30am-11.30pm Sun-Thu, 7.30-12.30am Fri, 8.30am-12.30am Sat; M George V) Specialities at this most famous and decadent of Parisian pâtisseries include its own invention, *macarons* (especially the chocolate and pistachio variety) and *le baiser Ladurée* (layered almond cake with strawberries and cream). There's also a **St-Germain branch** (Map p112; ☎ 01 40 44 07 64 87; 21 rue Bonaparte, 7e; 🕙 8.30am-7.30pm Mon-Fri, 8.30am-8.30pm Sat, 10am-7.30pm Sun; M St-Germain des Prés)

Le Nôtre (Map p148; ☎ 01 53 01 91 91; www.lenotre.fr, in French; 10 rue St-Antoine, 4e; 🕙 9am-9.30pm; M Bastille) This branch of the famous *traiteur* chain at the corner of rue des Tournelles has some of the most delectable pastries and chocolate in Paris. There are 10 more outlets sprinkled across the capital.

La Pâtisserie des Rêves (Map p108; ☎ 01 42 84 00 82; www.lapatisseriedesreves.com; 93 rue du Bac, 7e; 🕙 10am-8.30pm Tue-Sat, 8.30am-2pm Sun; M Rue du Bac) The most extraordinary cakes, far too beautiful to eat, are showcased beneath glass domes at the oh-so-chic 'art' gallery of big-name pâtissier Philippe Conticini. Each month cooks up a different fruit tart – banana in January, almond in March, purple figs and quince in November and so on.

Sacha Finkelsztajn (Map p152; ☎ 01 42 72 78 91; www.laboutiquejaune.com, in French; 27 rue des Rosiers, 4e; 🕙 11am-7pm Wed-Mon; M St-Paul) Known in some circles as 'La Boutique Jaune', this very 'yellow shop' has scrumptious Jewish and Central European breads and pastries, including apple strudel, poppy-seed cakes and sernik (Jewish cheese cake).

Stohrer (Map p72; ☎ 01 42 33 38 20; www.stohrer.fr, in French; 51 rue Montorgueil, 2e; 🕙 7.30am-8.30pm; M Les Halles or Sentier) Specialities include its very own *baba au rhum* (sponge cake soaked in rum-flavoured syrup) and *puits d'amour* (puff pasty with vanilla cream and caramel).

date from 1845 and everyone knows about it (read: touristy). Still, *menus* of tasty, family-style French cuisine ensure a never-ending stream of punters eager to sample *bœuf bourguignon*, *blanquette de veau à l'ancienne* (veal in white sauce) and the most famous *tarte Tatin* in Paris! Expect to wait. No credit cards.

ROGER LA GRENOUILLE

Map p112   French €€

☎ 01 56 24 24 34; 26-28 rue des Grands Augustins, 6e; frogs' legs starter/main €24/31, menus €19 (lunch) & €24; ⏰ dinner to 11pm Mon, lunch & dinner to 11pm Tue-Sat; Ⓜ St-Michel

Roger the Frog is an appealing chap, known very much for one thing – frogs' legs, simmered and stewed in a variety of guises. À la Provençale is with tomato, Orientale sees the pin-sized legs spiced with pine kernels and fresh mint, while Indienne has a splash of curry thrown in. B&W pictures of 1920s Paris bedeck the white-washed walls and an array of old lamps light up the low nicotine-coloured ceiling. Reserve in advance to ensure a table.

HUÎTERIE REGIS Map p112   Oyster Bar €€

☎ 01 44 41 10 07; 3 rue de Montfaucon, 6e; dozen oysters & glass wine €23.50; ⏰ 11am-midnight Tue-Sun mid-Sep–mid-Jul; Ⓜ Mabillon

Hip, trendy, tiny and white, this is *the* spot for revelling in oysters on crisp winter days. They come only by the dozen, along with fresh bread and butter, but wash them down with a glass of chilled Muscadet and *voilà*, one perfect lunch. Add coffee and a glass of Sancerre (€26) or be a devil and have some king prawns too (€27.50). A twinset of tables loiter on the pavement outside; otherwise it's all inside.

FISH LA BOISSONNERIE

Map p112   Seafood €€

☎ 01 43 54 34 69; 69 rue de Seine, 6e; starters/mains €8/15; ⏰ lunch & dinner to 10.45pm Tue-Sun; Ⓜ Mabillon

A hybrid of a Mediterranean place run by a New Zealander (of Cosi fame; p237) and an American, with its rustic communal seating and bonhomie, Fish has surely taken its cue from London, where such places have been a mainstay for several years. The wine selection is excellent – it's almost as much a wine bar as a restaurant – and the wonderful old mosaic on the front façade is a delight.

LE MÂCHON D'HENRI Map p112   French €€

☎ 01 43 29 08 70; 8 rue Guisarde, 6e; starters €7-10, mains €15; ⏰ lunch & dinner until 11.30pm daily; Ⓜ St-Sulpice or Mabillon

What with the gaggle of hungry customers constantly waiting for a seat and the extraordinary proximity of the 10 marble-topped tables, this is one busy, tiny bistro. But the staff, seemingly exclusively male and over a certain age, are smile and charm personified. And the menu, crammed with feisty French staples like *boudin noir aux pommes* (black pudding with apples) from Lyon, *saucisse de Morteau* (a type of sausage) and lentils from the Jura or tripe cooked Caen-style, guarantees you'll leave absolutely stuffed.

LE CHERCHE MIDI Map p112   Italian €€

☎ 01 45 48 27 44; www.lecherchemidi.fr; 22 rue du Cherche Midi, 6e; starters/mains €12/15; ⏰ lunch & dinner to 11.45pm daily; Ⓜ Sèvres– Babylone

This popular restaurant with red awning and classic interior buzzes all the more at weekends when shoppers (Saturday) and those out for a stroll (Sunday) make a beeline for Le Cherche Midi's small sunlit pavement terrace. Cuisine is Italian, classic and elegant. Get here by 12.30pm and 8pm respectively to be sure of getting a table.

DA ROSA Map p112   Mediterranean, Delicatessen €

☎ 01 45 21 41 30; www.restaurant-da-rosa.com; 62 rue de Seine, 6e; cheese, meat & fish platters €10-30; ⏰ 10&m-11pm daily; Ⓜ Mabillon

Gourmets can spend a little or a lot at this modern *épicerie* (delicatessen) and *cantine* (hip, casual eating place), a real foodie address with its vast array of savoury hams, salamis, pâtés, caviars, cheeses and other unique savoury products from France; Spain, Portugal and Italy. Be it foie gras, smoked salmon, Iberian ham or marble-cooled *lardo di colonnata* from Carrara, 'only the best' is very much the philosophy at Da Rosa. Everything on the menu can be bought to take home.

LA GRANDE ÉPICERIE

Map p108   Wok & Sandwich Bar €

☎ 01 46 39 81 00; www.lagrandeepicerie.fr; 26 rue de Sèvres, 7e; lunch €10-15; ⏰ 8.30am-9pm Mon-Sat; Ⓜ Sèvres–Babylone

Join the hordes of workers from the offices in this area for a quick tasty lunch at the

Espace Pic Nic, in the ground-floor food hall of stylish Le Bon Marché department store (p199). Hover around the bar over a wok-cooked hot dish, a design-your-own sandwich (pick the bread type and fillings yourself; a self-designed salad or an 11-piece sushi plate. Pay marginally less to take the same away, or build your own gourmet picnic from the food hall.

AU PIED DE FOUET Map p112 French €
☎ 01 43 54 87 83; 50 rue St-Benoît, 6e; starters €3-5, mains €10; ⏱ lunch & dinner Mon-Sat; Ⓜ St-Germain des Prés
If it's an authentic bistro experience you are after, this busy address with traditional Bordeaux façade, tightly packed tables and devout crowd of regulars is a perfect choice. Its wholly classic bistro dishes such as *entrecôte* (steak), *confit de canard* (duck cooked very slowly its own fat) and *foie de volailles sauté* (pan-fried chicken livers) moreover are astonishingly good value. Round off your meal with a quintessential *tarte Tatin* (upside-down apple pie), wine-soaked prunes or a simple bowl of *fromage blanc* (a cross between yoghurt, sour cream and cream cheese).

MAMIE GÂTEAUX Map p108 Tearoom €
☎ 01 42 22 32 15; www.mamie-gateaux.com, in French; 66-70 rue du Cherche Midi, 6e; lunch €10-15; ⏱ 11.30am-6pm Tue-Sat; Ⓜ St-Placide or Sèvres–Babylone
A perfect light-lunch spot after a taxing morning savouring the stylish boutiques around nearby Le Bon Marché (p199), this retro tearoom with lace curtains and a *brocante* (secondhand) décor positively heaves at lunchtime. Funnily enough for this hot shopping area, the clientele is predominantly female and chatty, as the electrifying buzz of happy shoppers chomping into homemade quiches, savoury cakes, tarts and salads testifies. For us, the ratatouille-and-mozzarella tart is the icing on the cake.

CHEZ LES FILLES Map p108 Tearoom €
☎ 01 45 48 61 54; 64 rue du Cherche Midi, 6e; lunch €10-15; ⏱ 11.30am-4.30pm Mon-Fri, 11.30am-6pm Sat; Ⓜ St-Placide or Sèvres–Babylone
If Mamie Gâteaux is full, try this other female-filled hot spot, which – unlike its grandmotherly neighbour – transports an eager lunch crowd into the land of the Orient. Salads, *tajines*, savoury tarts and a

fantastic value *plat du jour* (€13) make for a colourful lunch. Mid-afternoon, refresh parched souls with a *pâtisserie orientale* and cup of sweet mint tea.

CUISINE DE BAR Map p112 Sandwich €
☎ 01 45 48 45 69; 8 rue du Cherche Midi, 6e; breakfast €7.60-12, lunch €12; ⏱ 8.30am-7pm Tue-Sat; Ⓜ Sèvres–Babylone; 🛜
As next-door neighbour to one of Paris' most famous bakers (p215), this is not any old sandwich bar. Rather, it is a chic spot to lunch between designer boutiques on open sandwiches cut from that celebrated Poilâne bread and fabulously filled with gourmet goodies such as foie gras, smoked duck, gooey St-Marcellin cheese and Bayonne ham. Its breakfasts and afternoon teas are equally lush.

LA JACOBINE Map p112 Tearoom €
☎ 01 46 34 15 95; 59-61 rue St-André des Arts, 6e; lunch €10-15; ⏱ 11.30am-11.30pm daily; Ⓜ Odéon
What a sweet find! An olde-worlde hybrid tearoom and busy lunch spot, La Jacobine is packed to the rafters by noon with punters keen to fill up on homemade tarts, giant-sized salads and crêpes. Its lovely location inside Cour du Commerce St-André, a glass-covered passageway built in 1735 to link two Jeu de Paume (old-style tennis) courts, makes it all the more romantic.

COSI Map p112 Sandwich Bar €
☎ 01 46 33 35 36; 54 rue de Seine, 6e; sandwich menus €10-15; ⏱ noon-11pm daily; Ⓜ Odéon
An institution in the 6th for a quick cheap eat in or out, Cosi could easily run for Paris' most imaginative sandwich maker: with sandwich names like Stonker, Tom Dooley and Naked Willi, how could you expect otherwise? Classical music playing in the background and homemade Italian bread, still warm from the oven, only adds to Cosi's natural sex appeal, which, incidentally, is of New Zealand origin.

AMORINO
Map p112 Ice Cream €
☎ 01 43 26 57 46; 4 rue de Buci, 6e; ⏱ noon-midnight daily; Ⓜ St-Germain des Prés
Though not such dedicated *lécheurs* (lickers) as some, we're told that Berthillon (p227) has serious competition and Amorino's homemade ice cream (yogurt, caramel, kiwi, strawberry etc) is, in fact, better. It

has no less than 10 other branches in Paris, including **Amorino Luxembourg** (Map p108; ☎ 01 42 22 66 86; 4 rue Vavin, 6e; Ⓜ Vavin); **Amorino Île St-Louis** (Map p82; ☎ 01 44 07 48 08; 47 rue St-Louis en l'Île, 4e; Ⓜ Pont Marie); and **Amorino Cler** (Map p108; 42 rue Cler, 6e; Ⓜ École Militaire).

SELF-CATERING

Food shops cluster along rue de Seine and rue de Buci. The covered **Marché St-Germain** (Map p112; 4-8 rue Lobineau, 6e; ⏰ 8.30am-1pm & 4-7.30pm Tue-Sat, 8.30am-1pm Sun; Ⓜ Mabillon) and open-air food markets **Rue Cler** (Map p108; p222) and organic **Marché Raspail** (Map p112; p222) have huge arrays of fine fresh produce.

Baguettes might be a common-as-muck staple but watching them being made is a rare treat that can be enjoyed at *boulangerie* Besnier (☎ 01 45 51 24 29; 40 rue de Bourgogne, 7e; ⏰ 7am-8pm Mon-Fri Sep-Jul).

Buy the best of every French cheese you can find, many with an original take (eg Epoisses boxed in chestnut leaves, Mont d'Or flavoured with black truffles, spiced honey and Roquefort bread etc), at king of *fromageries* Quatre-hommes (Map p108; ☎ 01 47 34 33 45; 62 rue de Sèvres, 6e; ⏰ 8.45am-1pm & 4-7.45pm Tue-Thu, 8.45am-7.45pm Fri & Sat; Ⓜ Vanneau). The smell alone as you enter is heavenly.

Decent supermarkets options in the area include **Carrefour Market** (Map p112; 79 rue de Seine, 6e; ⏰ 1-9pm Mon, 8.40am-9pm Tue-Sat, 9am-1pm Sun; Ⓜ Mabillon) and **Monoprix** (Map p112; 24 blvd St-Michel, 6e; ⏰ 8.30am-11.50pm Mon-Sat; Ⓜ Cluny–La Sorbonne).

EIFFEL TOWER & 16E

The 16e arrondissement is best known for its monuments and museums and, conveniently, there are a number of good restaurants located in the sights themselves. Around the Eiffel Tower you can grab picnic supplies at rue Cler (p222) or choose from the restaurants on rue de Montessuy. And, for a truly memorable experience, you can even dine in the icon itself (p239).

L'ASTRANCE Map p118 French €€€
☎ 01 40 50 84 40; 4 rue Beethoven, 16e; lunch menus €70/120, dinner menu €190; ⏰ Tue-Fri; Ⓜ Passy
It's been over a decade now since Pascal Barbot's dazzling cuisine at the three-star

L'Astrance made its debut, but it has shown no signs of losing its cutting edge. Look beyond the complicated descriptions on the menu – what you should expect are teasers of taste that you never even knew existed, and a presentation that is an art unto itself. A culinary experience unique to Paris, you'll need to reserve two months in advance (one month for lunch).

LE CRISTAL ROOM Map p118 French €€€
☎ 01 40 22 11 10; www.baccarat.com; 11 place des États-Unis, 16e; mains €37-40, menus €29/36/55 (lunch only) & €150; ⏰ lunch & dinner to 10pm Mon-Sat; Ⓜ Iéna
Located on the first floor of the Galerie-Musée Baccarat (p121), this stunner of a venue features interiors conceived by the over-employed Philippe Starck: mirrors, crystal and even a black chandelier. The menu by Thierry Burlot is excellent but expensive. Note that you will need to book well in advance.

LES OMBRES Map p118 French €€€
☎ 01 47 53 68 00; www.lesombres-restaurant.com; 27 quai Branly, 7e; starters €21-34, mains €28-45; menus €26/38 (lunch only) & €95; ⏰ lunch & dinner to 10.30pm Sun-Thu, to 11pm Fri & Sat; Ⓜ Pont de l'Alma or Alma-Marceau
Paris gained not only a museum in the Musée du Quai Branly (p117) but also this glass-enclosed rooftop restaurant on the 5th floor. Named the 'Shadows' for the patterns cast by the Eiffel Tower's webbed ironwork, the dramatic views are complemented by Sébastien Tasset's elegant creations, such as roasted turbot and cantal cheese with a buckwheat crêpe, or chicken stuffed with lemon confit.

CAFÉ DE L'HOMME
Map p118 International €€€
☎ 01 44 05 30 15; www.restaurant-cafedelhomme. com; 17 place du Trocadéro, 16e; starters €15-24, mains €22-35; ⏰ lunch & dinner to 11.30pm daily; Ⓜ George V
You probably wouldn't cross town for the food at the Café de L'Homme, the plush restaurant sharing the same wing of the Palais de Chaillot as the Musée de l'Homme and the Musée de la Marine (p117); it's overpriced and designed for the beautiful people who are flocking here at the moment. But you would travel for the view; virtually any spot at any table is a front-row seat before the Eiffel Tower. This is why you came to Paris.

58 TOUR EIFFEL Map p118 French €€

☎ 01 45 55 20 04; www.restaurants-toureiffel.
com; 1st level, Champ de Mars, 7e; mains €14-16,
menus €17.50/22.50 (lunch), mains €20-33, menu
€65 (dinner); ☷ 11.30am-5.30pm & 6.30-11pm;
Ⓜ Champ de Mars–Tour Eiffel or Bir Hakeim
If you're intrigued by the idea of a meal
in the Tower, the 58 Tour Eiffel is a pretty
good choice. It may not be the caviar and
black truffles of Jules Verne (on the 2nd
level), but Alain Ducasse did sign off on the
menu, ensuring that this is much more than
just another tourist cafeteria. That said,
it's really the views from the 1st-floor bay
windows that make it something special.
For lunch, go first to the restaurant's outside kiosk (near the north pillar); for dinner,
reserve online or by telephone.

FIRMIN LE BARBIER
Map p118 French €€

☎ 01 45 51 21 55; www.firminlebarbier.fr; 20 rue
de Monttessuy, 7e; starters €9, mains €22, plat
du jour €14 (lunch only); ☷ lunch Wed-Fri & Sun,
dinner Tue-Sun; Ⓜ Pont de l'Alma
This discreet brick-walled bistro was opened
by a retired surgeon turned gourmet, and
his passion for a good meal is apparent in
everything from the personable service to

top picks

BUDGET FRENCH

- Les Troubadours (p225) Time-warp bistro serves
  old-style food in the 19th-century Passage des
  Panorama.
- Breizh Café (p259) Affordable Breton fare: crêpes,
  galettes and maybe even a couple of oysters.
- L'Encrier (p266) Everyone's favourite cheapie
  Frenchie in the Bastille area, with menus from €12.
- Au Trou Normand (p258) The 'Norman Hole'
  serves affordable dishes and not all are from
  Normandy.
- Chartier (p243) You can't beat the belle époque
  atmosphere in the turn-of-the-century soup
  kitchen off the Grands Boulevards.
- Le Bastringue (p251) Minor foodie destination
  with a clever café menu and relaxed canal-side
  location.
- Le Pré Verre (p229) Recommended Latin Quarter
  lunch date with local Parisians.
- Chez Gladines (p269) Cheap Basque eats bistro-
  style in the irresistible Buttes aux Cailles district.

the wine list. The menu is traditional French
(faux filet with polenta, decadent boeuf
bourguignon), while the modern interior
is bright and cheery and even benefits
from an open kitchen – a rarity in smaller
Parisian restaurants. The good news: it's a
five-minute walk from the Eiffel Tower. The
bad: it doesn't seat much more than 20
people – be sure to reserve.

LE PETIT RÉTRO
Map p118 French €€

☎ 01 44 05 06 05; www.petitretro.fr, in French;
5 rue Mesnil, 16e; starters €6-14, mains €15-29,
menus €25 (lunch only), €30 & €35; ☷ lunch &
dinner to 10.30pm Mon-Fri; Ⓜ Victor Hugo
From the gorgeous 'Petit Rétro' embla-
zoned on the zinc bar to the art nouveau
folk tiles, this is a handsome space and
one that serves up hearty dishes year-
round. With dishes such as rognons de
veau poêles (potted veal kidneys) and
choucroute maison as house specials, it's
hearty, heart-warming stuff. They've expanded in recent years, making the seating less cramped.

LA CANTINE RUSSE
Map p118 Russian €€

☎ 01 47 20 56 12; www.lacantinerusse.com; 26
av de New York, 16e; starters €9-22, mains €15-24,
menus €17 (lunch only) & €32; ☷ lunch & dinner to
midnight Mon-Sat; Ⓜ Alma–Marceau
Established for the overwhelmingly Russian
students at the prestigious Conservatoire
Rachmaninov in 1923, this 'canteen' is still
going strong more than eight decades
later. At communal tables you can savour
herrings served with blinis, aubergine
'caviar', chicken Kiev, beef Stroganov,
chachliks (marinated lamb kebabs) and, to
complete the tableau, vatrouchka (cream
cheese cake).

BERT'S
Map p118 Café €

☎ 01 47 23 43 37; www.berts.com; 4 av du
Président Wilson, 8e; sandwiches €5.80-6.90, salads
€5.90-8.40; ☷ 8am-8pm Mon-Fri, 10.30am-8pm
Sat, 11am-8pm Sun; Ⓜ Alma–Marceau
Elsewhere this modern café chain with worn
leather couches and comfy armchairs might
not stand out, but in this part of town it's
a good address to have on hand – not
least because it's open daily. Sandwiches
are served on organic bread and there are
plenty of veggie options available.

SELF-CATERING

If you're planning on a picnic near the Eiffel Tower, you can stock up on supplies at rue Cler (p222). Across the river, the open-air Marché Prèsident Wilson (p222) is convenient to the neighbourhood.

CHAMPS-ÉLYSÉES & GRANDS BOULEVARDS

The 8e arrondissement around the Champs-Élysées is known for its big-name chefs (Alain Ducasse, Pierre Gagnaire, Guy Savoy) and culinary icons (Taillevent), but there are all sorts of under-the-radar restaurants scattered in the back streets, where the Parisians who live and work in the area actually dine. If you're just looking for a simple breakfast or lunch, head to rue de Ponthieu, which runs parallel to the Champs (to the north), where you'll find several bakeries, cafés and pasta bars catering to the office workers in the area. Note most will be closed in the evenings and on weekends.

Further east are the landmark Opéra and place de la Madeleine, the latter encircled by gourmet food shops. In between the two is rue Godot de Mauroy, a good spot for lunch with Italian, Greek and crêpe restaurants as well as soup and wine bars.

L'Opéra marks the start of the Grands Boulevards and the 9e arrondissement, where shoppers can break from an afternoon in the department stores for a coffee or meal in Galeries Lafayette (p202). Just north of here the area becomes more residential, and the diversity increases accordingly: kosher delis, handmade Chinese noodles, organic cafés and Michelin-starred chefs are just some of the many culinary riches awaiting.

JEAN Map p126   French €€€

☎ 01 48 78 62 73; www.restaurantjean.fr; 8 rue St-Lazare, 9e; starters €15-24, mains €33-41, menus €46/75/95; ✆ lunch & dinner Mon-Fri; Ⓜ Notre Dame de Lorette

This stylish gourmet restaurant manages to balance just the right amounts of sophistication and genuine warmth. Dark-red banquette seats liven up the large, quiet dining room. A sample meal might include *fricassée de langoustines* (scampi) served with a julienne of vegetables, *magret de canard rôti au miel et ses navets et échalotes confites* (honey-roasted fillet of duck breast served with preserved turnips and shallots)

and a modern version of profiteroles – a scoop of vanilla ice cream between two crunchy, chocolate-coated meringues.

BISTROT DU SOMMELIER
Map p126   French €€€

☎ 01 42 65 24 85; www.bistrotdusommelier.com; 97 blvd Haussmann, 8e; starters €13.50-22, mains €24-30, lunch menu €33, with wine €43, dinner menus €65/80/110; ✆ lunch & dinner to 10.30pm Mon-Fri; Ⓜ St-Augustin

This is the place to choose if you are as serious about wine as you are about food. The whole point of this attractive eatery is to match wine with food, and owner Philippe Faure-Brac, one of the world's foremost sommeliers (see p241), is at hand to help. The best way to sample his wine-food pairings is on Friday, when a three-course tasting lunch with wine is €50 and a five-course dinner with wine is €75. The food, prepared by chef Jean-André Lallican, is hearty bistro fare and, surprisingly, not all the wines are French.

SPOON Map p126   Fusion €€€

☎ 01 40 76 34 44; www.spoon-restaurants.com; 14 rue de Marignan, 8e; starters €10-19, mains €19-36, menu €33 (lunch only) & €75; ✆ lunch & dinner to 11pm Mon-Fri; Ⓜ Franklin D Roosevelt

Diners at this Ducasse/Starck-inspired venue are invited to mix and match their own main courses and sauces – pan-seared red mullet, say, with a choice of barbecue, lemon or sesame sauces or duckling with peppers, lemon-parsley butter or crushed olives. There are a few vegetarian options on the menu, which has kept its popular with the stay-slim fashion crowd. It has an excellent selection of New World and non-French European wines.

MARKET Map p126   Fusion €€€

☎ 01 56 43 40 90; www.jean-georges.com; 15 av Matignon, 8e; starters €10-27, mains €18-39, two-dish tasting menu €34 (lunch and early dinner till 8.30pm); ✆ lunch Mon-Fri, brunch noon-4.30pm Sat & Sun, dinner to 11.30 daily; Ⓜ Franklin D Roosevelt

Alsatian chef Jean-Georges Vongerichten's swish fusion restaurant focuses on fresh market produce delivered with his signature eclectic combinations and Asian leanings. For flavours that are going somewhere unexpected, sample sea bream in a sweet-and-sour broth, duck filet with cocoa beans and fig chutney, or black truffle and fontina cheese pizza. Like his restaurants in Manhattan and Shanghai (among others), Market stands out in the crowd, though it's rare JG is actually in the kitchen. Lunch attracts a predominantly business crowd; dinner is a much sexier proposition.

CASA OLYMPE Map p126   French €€€
☎ 01 42 85 26 01; www.casaolympe.com; 48 rue St-Georges, 9e; menus €34 (lunch only) & €43; ☽ lunch & dinner to 11pm Mon-Fri; Ⓜ St-Georges
This very smart (if somewhat sombre) restaurant run by Dominique Versini, the first female chef in France to be awarded a Michelin star, serves excellent and rather inventive dishes in surprisingly ample sizes. We loved our pot of warming winter vegetables with bacon followed by a veal chop cooked with bay leaf and *pleurotte* mushrooms. The artwork on the walls was done by the chef-owner's mother.

LE BOUDOIR Map p126   French €€€
☎ 01 43 59 25 29; www.brasserieleboudoir.com; 25 rue du Colisée, 8e; starters €14-18, mains €17-40, menus €19 (lunch) & €50; ☽ lunch Mon-Fri, dinner

Tues-Sat; Ⓜ St-Philippe du Roule or Franklin D Roosevelt
Spread across two floors, the quirky salons here – Marie Antoinette, Palme d'Or and the Red Room – are individual works of art with a style that befits the name. The menu runs from upscale bistro fare (duck fricassée with cherries and baked butternut squash) to more adventurous creations, such as grilled tandoori scallops and saffron rice with mango. In a move towards yesteryear decadence, there's even a private smoking room hidden on the premises. The *prix fixe* lunch is an excellent deal.

MAKOTO AOKI
Map p126   French €€€
☎ 01 43 59 29 24; 19 rue Jean Mermoz, 8e; lunch/dinner menus €21/40; ☽ lunch Mon-Fri, dinner to 11pm Mon-Sat; Ⓜ Franklin D Roosevelt
In an arrondissement known for superstar chefs who are often elsewhere, grandiose dining rooms and €5 coffees, this intimate neighbourhood favourite off the Champs Élysées is a real find. The Japanese chef is a haute-cuisine perfectionist – lunch might include

---

LOCAL KNOWLEDGE: PHILIPPE FAURE-BRAC

The much-decorated Philippe Faure-Brac – he was named Best Sommelier in France in 1988 and Best Sommelier in the World four years later – owns and operates the highly successful Bistrot du Sommelier (p240), produces his own label (a Côtes du Rhône Villages called Domaine Duseigneur) and has written half a dozen books on the subject of wine, wine tasting (*Comment Goûter un Vin*, 2007) and wine and food pairing (*Exquisite Matches*, 2005).

Bring me a bottle of... Red from the Rhône Valley – a Châteauneuf-du-Pape, maybe – or a good-quality Riesling from Alsace.

Let's cut to the chase. Is there life beyond French wines? Yes, of course, but understand that my references are French. Parisians are very keen on so-called New World wines and we list bottles from three dozen different countries on our card. The best Sauvignon outside France is made in New Zealand, Shiraz from Australia is especially good and the best Malbec is from Argentina.

I'm going to have a glass of red wine with the chicken and my friend wants white with the lamb. OK with you? The *code de couleur* does not have to be rigid. What you drink is really a matter of taste; at the end of the day a good wine is a good wine. The question you have to ask yourself is: 'What is the dominant characteristic of the food?' Cream sauces can go well with red wine, for example, shellfish with Champagne and certain cheeses (Chaource, Comté) with Rosé.

Then what should I have with my Mexican chilli and my (even spicier) Thai tom yum gung? These two cuisines are especially difficult to pair with wines. Try a white or, even better, a rosé. Avoid reds, especially complex ones.

About wine whiners... What do you do when someone claims a wine is corked and you know it isn't? We always smell it first, which tells us whether the wine is off. But one can make mistakes, and the customer is always right. Of course we will change it even if we don't believe it is corked.

It's a kind of snobbery, isn't it? It's not easy to stay a wine snob for long. A blind taste test is a great equaliser. Wine snobs don't tend to come here. Instead we get guests who are particularly knowledgeable about wine. If they're not French, they're often Belgian or English.

Interviewed by Steve Fallon

an extravagant bacon–morel brioche; dinner a heavenly risotto with John Dory or truffles.

LE PERSIL FLEUR
Map p126   French €€

☎ 01 42 65 40 19; www.persilfleur.com; 8 rue Boudreau, 9e; starters €8-17, mains €17-26, menus €34/39 (dinner only); ☽ lunch & dinner Mon-Fri; Ⓜ Auber or Havre–Caumartin

Le Persil Fleur is the type of old-fashioned French restaurant where the patron welcomes customers, chats extensively with the regulars and personally checks on each table as meals progress. Don't be put off by the somewhat faded décor – if this place remains popular, it's because the food is consistently good. Expect French standards that offer a departure from the usual sauces – lamb with cumin and mint, beef filet with cocoa or duck with caramelised onions.

LE J'GO
Map p126   Southwest French €€

☎ 01 40 22 09 09; www.lejgo.com; 4 rue Drouot, 9e; starters €9-12, mains €18-25, lunch menus €15/20; ☽ lunch Mon-Fri, dinner Mon-Sat; Ⓜ Richelieu–Druot

This contemporary Toulouse-style bistro is meant to magic you away to southwestern France for a spell (perfect on a grey Parisian day), its bright yellow walls decorated with bull-fighting posters and flavourful regional cooking based around the rotisserie – not to mention other Gascogne standards like cassoulet and foie gras. For the full experience, it's best to go in a small group with time to spare: the roasting takes a minimum 20 minutes, which gives you the opportunity to sample their choice selection of sunny southern wines.

LA BOULE ROUGE
Map p126   Jewish, Kosher €€

☎ 01 47 70 43 90; 1 rue de la Boule Rouge, 9e; starters €5-8, mains €15-28; menus €20 (lunch only) & €26/33; ☽ lunch & dinner to midnight Mon-Sat; Ⓜ Cadet or Grands Boulevards

Though this Tunisian stalwart has been *in situ* for three decades, the 'Red Ball' has been getting a lot of press – good, bad or otherwise – only since Monsieur Sarkozy was spotted dining here. It's a lovely space, with a wonderful caravan mural on the ceiling and photos of politicians and celebs on the walls. Some of the couscous dishes served here – mince with okra, spinach, spicy chicken with corn – are unusual and the three-course *menu* includes an excel-

lent array of *kemia* (vegetarian meze) plus a drink.

LE HIDE
Map p126   French €€

☎ 01 45 74 15 81; www.lehide.fr; 10 Rue du Général Lanrezac, 17e; starters €8.50, mains €16, menus €22/29; ☽ lunch Mon-Fri, dinner to 11pm Mon-Sat; Ⓜ Charles de Gaulle–Étoile

A reader favourite, Le Hide is another tiny neighbourhood bistro (seating 33 people) serving scrumptious traditional French fare: snails, baked shoulder of lamb, monkfish in lemon butter. As at Aoki, the chef is Japanese, which in Paris is an indication of top quality – this place fills up faster than you can scurry down the steps at the nearby Arc de Triomphe. Reserve well in advance.

LE ROI DU POT AU FEU
Map p126   French €€

☎ 01 47 42 37 10; 34 rue Vignon, 9e; starters €4-7, pot-au-feu €17, menus €21/28; ☽ noon-10.30pm Mon-Sat; Ⓜ Havre–Caumartin

A typical Parisian bistro atmosphere, '30s décor and checked tablecloths all add to the charm of the 'King of Hotpots'. What you really want to come here for is a genuine pot-au-feu, a stockpot of beef, aromatic root vegetables and herbs stewed together, with the stock served as an entree and the meat and vegetables as the main course. You drink from an open bottle of wine and pay for what you've consumed. No reservations accepted.

LES AILES
Map p126   Jewish, Kosher €€

☎ 01 47 70 62 53; www.lesailes.fr; in French; 34 rue Richer, 9e; mains €16-29; ☽ lunch & dinner to 11.30pm daily; Ⓜ Cadet

With an adjoining bakery and delicatessen, 'Wings' is a kosher North African (Sephardic) restaurant that has superb couscous with meat or fish (€18 to €24) and grills as well as light meals of salad and pasta (€11 to €19.50). Don't even consider a starter; you'll be inundated with little plates of salad, olives etc before you can say *shalom*. Sabbath meals (pre-ordered and prepaid) are also available.

NOUVEAU PARIS-DAKAR
Map p126   African, Senegalese €€

☎ 01 42 46 12 30; www.lenouveauparisdakar.com, in French; 11 rue de Montyon, 9e; starters €7-8, mains €14-22, menus €10.90 (lunch only) & €26/36/40; ☽ lunch Mon-Thu, Sat & Sun, dinner to 1am daily; Ⓜ Grands Boulevards

This is a little bit of Senegal in Paris, with Mamadou still reigning as the 'King of Dakar'. Specialities here include *yassa* (chicken or fish marinated in lime juice and onion sauce; €14) and *maffé Cap Vert* (lamb in peanut sauce; €14). There's live African music most nights.

HÔTEL AMOUR

Map p126   Bistro €

☎ 01 48 78 31 80; www.hotelamourparis.fr; 8 rue Navarin, 9e; mains €13-17; ⏰ 8am-midnight;
Ⓜ St-Georges or Pigalle; ⏴
Attached to the arty hotel of the same name (p339), this buzzing hotspot is a cross between an American diner and a hip French bistro. The food is definitely not gourmet (croque monsieur, bacon cheeseburger), but it is served nonstop until midnight, making this a great after-hours stop. There is also fantastic garden seating – if you can get it.

BUGSY'S

Map p126   American €

☎ 01 42 68 18 44; 15 rue Montlivet, 8e; salads €12-13, mains €11.50-19; ⏰ lunch & dinner to 11pm daily; Ⓜ Madeleine
This immensely popular place – it's heaving at lunchtime, especially with expats – is done up to resemble a Prohibition-era Chicago speakeasy from the 1920s. Food is the please-everyone easy option: Tex-Mex, salads, ploughman's lunches, burgers (€12.50 to €14.50) and the intriguing *entrecôte irlandaise* (Irish rib steak). The huge bar keeps going till 1am daily.

CHARTIER

Map p126   French, Bistro €

☎ 01 47 70 86 29; www.restaurant-chartier.com; 7 rue du Faubourg Montmartre, 9e; starters €2.20-6.80, mains €8.50-13.50, menu with wine €19.40; ⏰ lunch & dinner to 10pm daily; Ⓜ Grands Boulevards
Chartier, which started life as a *bouillon*, or soup kitchen, in 1896, is a real gem that is justifiably famous for its 330-seat belle époque dining room. It's no longer as good a deal as it once was, but for a taste of old-fashioned Paris, the atmosphere is definitely unbeatable. Note that reservations are not accepted and some readers have been turned away at the last minute on busy nights – if there's a long queue, head elsewhere.

SUPERNATURE

Map p126   Organic, Vegetarian €

☎ 01 47 70 21 03; www.super-nature.fr; 8 & 12 rue de Trévise, 9e; mains €11, menu €13.60;
⏰ lunch Mon-Fri, brunch Sun;
Ⓜ Cadet or Grands Boulevards
A funky organic café, Supernature has some clever creations on the menu, like curried split-pea soup and a cantaloupe, pumpkin seed and feta salad. Though there are plenty of veggie options available, it's not all légumes – this is France after all – and you can still order a healthy cheeseburger with sprouts if so inclined. Everything is made fresh daily, and there's even a takeaway branch two doors down (at no 8) that serves sandwiches (€4.20), salads (from €4.80) and thick slices of sweet potato and gorgonzola quiche.

LES PÂTES VIVANTES

Map p126   Chinese €

☎ 01 45 23 10 21; 46 du Faubourg Montmartre, 9e; noodles €9.50-12; ⏰ lunch & dinner Mon-Sat;
Ⓜ Le Peletier
This is one of the few spots in Paris for hand-pulled noodles (*là miàn*) made to order in the age-old northern Chinese tradition. It packs in a crowd, so arrive early to stake out a table on the ground floor and watch as the nimble noodle maker works his magic. There's also a St-Germain branch (☎ 01 40 46 84 33; 22 blvd St-Germain, 5e;
Ⓜ St-Germain des Prés) .

COJEAN Map p126   Sandwich Bar €

☎ 01 45 61 07 33; www.cojean.fr, in French; 25 rue Washington, 8e; salads €3.90-6.10, sandwiches €4.80-5.90; ⏰ Mon-Fri 10am-4pm;
Ⓜ George V; ⏴
Cojean is one of the places that redefined the Parisian idea of a quick lunch. Where are those buttered baguettes with processed ham, hi-cal saucisson and chicken slathered in mayonnaise? Gone, gone and gone. Instead you get a Champs-Élysées chic interior and health-conscious fare that probably would have met with bewildered looks a mere decade ago. Go for the delicious – albeit small – salads (kasha and tuna, the B12), quiches, sandwiches, fresh juice and even vegetarian lasagne and risotto (€8.90). Handy branches include Grands Boulevards (17 bd Haussmann, 9e; ⏰ 8.30am-7pm Mon-Fri, 10am-7pm Sat; Ⓜ Chaussée d'Antin).

SELF-CATERING

In the Champs Élysées area, Rue Poncelet and rue Bayen have some excellent food shops, including the incomparable Fromagerie Alléosse (p202). The sprawling Monoprix (Map p126; 62 av des Champs-Élysées, 8e; 9am-midnight Mon-Sat; Franklin D Roosevelt) at the corner of rue la Boétie has a big supermarket section in the basement, and there's a Franprix (Map p126; 12 rue de Surène, 8e; 8.30am-8pm Mon-Sat; Madeleine) near place de la Madeleine.

Farther east on av de l'Opéra and rue de Richelieu are several supermarkets, including a large Monoprix (Map p72; 21 av de l'Opéra, 2e; 9am-10pm Mon-Fri, to 9pm Sat; Pyramides). To the north is a convenient Franprix Rodier (Map p126; 52 rue Rodier, 9e; 9am-9pm Mon-Sat; St-Georges or Cadet), south of square d'Anvers.

MONTMARTRE, PIGALLE & 17E

The 18e arrondissement, where you'll find Montmartre and the northern boundary of Pigalle, thrives on crowds and little else. When you've got Sacré Coeur, place du Tertre and Paris literally at your feet, who needs decent restaurants? But that's not to say that everything is a write-off in this well-trodden tourist area. You just have to pick and choose a bit more carefully than elsewhere in Paris. As a general rule, the lower down the hill you go, the better the options. Note that in Montmartre many restaurants are open for dinner only.

Further west is the 17e, a residential neighbourhood that is not of enormous interest when it comes to eating out. There are a few choices around place de Clichy, which isn't too far from Montmartre and is less touristy.

CHARLOT, ROI DES COQUILLAGES

Map p136   French, Seafood €€€
☎ 01 53 20 48 00; www.charlot-paris.com, in French; 12 place de Clichy, 9e; starters €9.30-18.50, mains €15.50-35.90, menus €22.10 & €29.50 (lunch only); lunch & dinner to midnight Sun-Wed, to 1am Thu-Sat; Place de Clichy
'Charlot, the King of Shellfish' is an art deco palace that some Parisians think is the best place in town for no-nonsense seafood. The seafood platters and oysters are why everyone is here, but don't ignore the wonderful fish soup and mains, such as grilled sardines, sole meunière and bouillabaisse (€36).

LA MASCOTTE
Map p134   French, Seafood €€
☎ 01 46 06 28 15; www.la-mascotte-montmartre.com; 52 rue des Abbesses, 18e; starters €9-12, mains €20-30, menu €20 (lunch only) & €38; lunch & dinner to midnight daily; Abbesses
La Mascotte is a small, unassuming spot much frequented by regulars who can't get enough of its seafood and regional cuisine. In winter, don't hesitate to sample the wide variety of seafood, especially the shellfish. In summer sit on the terrace and savour the delicious fricassée de pétoncles (fricassee of queen scallops). Meat lovers won't be disappointed with various regional delicacies, including Auvergne sausage and Troyes andouillette (veal tripe sausage).

À LA CLOCHE D'OR
Map p134   French €€
☎ 01 48 74 48 88; www.alaclochedor.com, in French; 3 rue Mansart, 9e; starters €7-14, mains €18-30; menus €18.50 (lunch only), €29.50 & €32; lunch Mon-Fri, dinner to 5am Mon-Sat; Blanche or Pigalle
This place, at the foot of the Butte Montmartre since 1928 and once the property of actress Jeanne Moreau's parents, is the antithesis of trendy. Decorated in 'old bistro' style with photos of stars of stage (mostly) and screen (some) plastering the walls, the 'Gold Bell' serves up favourites like steak tartare (its signature dish), massive steaks and fish of the day. Order the baked Camembert and, in winter, sit by the fire.

CHEZ TOINETTE
Map p134   French €€
☎ 01 42 54 44 36; 20 rue Germain Pilon, 18e; starters €7-13, mains €17-22; dinner to 11.15pm Mon-Sat; Abbesses
The atmosphere of this convivial restaurant is rivalled only by its fine cuisine. In the heart of one of the capital's most touristy neighbourhoods, Chez Toinette has kept alive the tradition of old Montmartre with its simplicity and culinary expertise. Game lovers won't be disappointed; perdreau (partridge), biche (doe), chevreuil (roebuck) and the famous filet de canard à la sauge et au miel (fillet of duck with sage and honey) are the house specialities and go well with a glass of Bordeaux.

LE MIROIR
Map p134   French €€
☎ 01 46 06 50 73; 94 rue des Martyrs, 18e; starters €9, mains €17, menus €18 (lunch only) & €25 & €32; lunch Tue-Sun, dinner Tue-Sat; Abbesses

This unassuming modern bistro is smack in the middle of the Montmartre tourist trail, yet it remains a local favourite. There are lots of delightful pâtés and rillettes to start off with – guinea hen with dates, duck with mushrooms, haddock and lemon – followed by well-prepared standards like stuffed veal shoulder. The €18 lunch special includes a glass of wine (FYI, they've conveniently opened a new wine shop right across the street), coffee and dessert; the Sunday brunch (€26) also gets the thumbs up.

CAFÉ BURQ Map p135 French €€
☎ 01 42 52 81 27; 6 rue Burq, 18e; menus €26 & €30; 7pm-2am Tue-Sat; Ⓜ Abbesses
This convivial, retro bistro in the heart of Montmartre is always buzzing; make sure you book ahead – especially at the weekend. Don't come for the décor or the space, though; both are nonexistent. Instead visit for the unfussy but well-prepared dishes like baked Camembert and lamb shoulder.

MICHELANGELO
Map p134 Italian €€
☎ 01 42 23 10 77; 3 rue André-Barsacq, 18e; menu around €25; dinner Tue-Sat; Ⓜ Anvers or Abbesses
A one-man show, chef Michelangelo does it all – the shopping, the chopping, the table-waiting, the cooking, the sitting down with guests for a glass of wine while the pasta is boiling…it is, in fact, the equivalent of being invited over to a Sicilian chef's house for dinner. There are things to know, of course: 1) there are only 14 chairs (everyone eats at a long table in front of the open kitchen) so reservations are mandatory; 2) Michelangelo chooses the menu (three courses, about €25, cash only), so you have to be somewhat adventurous; and 3) all the products – the olive oil, the wine (from €28 per bottle), the cheese – come from Sicily, so if there's no more oregano the restaurant may suddenly close for a week while he goes to stock up.

CHEZ PLUMEAU Map p134 French €€
☎ 01 46 06 26 29; 4 place du Calvaire, 18e; starters €8.50-9.50, mains €15.50-21.50; lunch & dinner to 11.30pm Thu-Tue Apr-Sep, lunch & dinner to 11.30pm Thu-Mon Oct-Mar; Ⓜ Abbesses
Once the popular Auberge du Coucou restaurant and cabaret, today's 'Feather Duster' caters mainly to tourists fresh from having their portraits done on place du Ter-

tre. But for a tourist haunt it's not too bad and the back terrace is great on a warm spring or summer afternoon. Plats du jour are a snip at €17.

LE MAQUIS
Map p134 French €€
☎ 01 42 59 76 07; 69 rue Caulaincourt, 18e; starters €10, mains €17, menus €14 (lunch only), €21 & €32; lunch & dinner to 10pm Tue-Sat; Ⓜ Lamarck–Caulaincourt
If you're in Montmartre and despairing over the choice of eateries (overpriced with poor service), give the Butte the boot and head the short distance north to rue Caulaincourt and this typical bistro with *cuisine traditionelle* (traditional cooking). The name refers to the neighbourhood and not the French Resistance or the herbal underbrush of Corsica. The set lunch includes a 25cL *pichet* of wine.

LE CHÉRI-BIBI
Map p134 French €€
☎ 01 42 54 88 96; 15 rue André del Sarte, 18e; menus €21 & €25; dinner to 11.30pm Tue-Sat; Ⓜ Barbès–Rochechouart
Taking its name from the series of detective novels by Gaston Leroux (1868–1927), this odd little place can be found (with some difficulty, it must be said) on a grotty street on the 'other' (read: wrong) side of the Butte de Montmartre and when you arrive you won't even know it as there is no sign outside. Just look for the thick black drapes in the shopfront window and enter what feels like the 1950s, with its postwar décor and excellent 'family' cooking (try the *boeuf bourguignon*).

LE CAFÉ QUI PARLE
Map p134 French €€
☎ 01 46 06 06 88; www.lecafequiparle.com; 24 rue Caulaincourt, 18e; starters €8-14, mains €15-26; menus €12.50 & €17; closed Sun dinner; Ⓜ Lamarck–Caulaincourt or Blanche;
The 'Talking Café' is a fine example of where modern-day eateries are headed in Paris. It offers inventive, reasonably priced dishes prepared by owner-chef Damian Moeuf and cuisine amid comfortable surroundings. We love the art on the walls and the ancient safes down below (the building was once a bank), but not as much as we do their brunch (€17), served from 10am on Saturdays and Sundays.

AU PETIT BUDAPEST

Map p134   Hungarian €€

☎ 01 46 06 10 34; 96 rue des Martyrs, 18e; starters €7.50-17.50, mains €14.50-22, menu €19.50; 🕑 dinner Tue-Sun, lunch Sat & Sun; Ⓜ Abbesses
With its old etchings and some requisite Gypsy music, this little eatery does a reasonable job of recreating the atmosphere of a late 19th-century Hungarian *csárda* (traditional inn). From the chicken paprika to the *crêpe à la Hortobagy* (crêpe with meat and crème fraîche; €10.50), these are refined versions of popular Hungarian dishes. For dessert try the ever-rich *Gundel palacsinta* (flambéed pancake with chocolate and nuts).

LA GAIETÉ COSAQUE

Map p136   Russian €€

☎ 01 44 70 06 07; 6 rue Truffaut, 17e; starters €2.50-10.50, mains €17.50-21.50, menus €10.50 & €12.50 (lunch only), €25 & €29; 🕑 lunch & dinner to 11.45pm Mon-Sat; Ⓜ Place de Clichy or Rome

top picks

DINING WITH A VIEW

- **Café Beaubourg** (p224) The terrace at this café offers front-row seats to the Centre Pompidou and the entertainers performing in front of it.
- **Café Marly** (p223) Priceless views of the Louvre, its glass pyramids and the Tuileries.
- **Ma Cantine** (p261) A bird's-eye view of the Marais from the BHV department store's top-floor restaurant.
- **Café Hugo** (p258) Its terrace under the arcades of the place des Vosges looks onto what is arguably the most beautiful square in Paris.
- **Le Flore en l'Île** (p227) This excellent venue offers prime views of Notre Dame Cathedral and the buskers on Pont St-Louis.
- **Les Ombres** (p238) A rooftop restaurant that takes its name from the patterns cast by the Eiffel Tower's webbed ironwork.
- **Lafayette Café** (p202) Once you've finished shopping, head up to the top floor of the Galeries Lafayette for a well-deserved break.
- **58 Tour Eiffel** (p239) The new Eiffel Tower restaurant that serves lunch, dinner and classic Parisian panoramas.
- **Le Comptoir du Panthéon** (p230) It's busy, it's budget and it's smack bang opposite the neoclassical domes of the Latin Quarter's Panthéon.

This bistro-like restaurant with the oxymoronic name (Cossack Cheerfulness indeed!) is the place for *zakouski* (Russian hors d'oeuvres), typically drunk with ice-cold vodka. Among the stand-outs are *salades de choux blancs aux baies roses* (a coleslaw-like salad with bay leaves), the various herring dishes and aubergine 'caviar'. Hearty mains include *chachlyik* (lamb kebab; €19) and *koulbiaka* (pie filled with fish, rice, veg and boiled eggs; €20.50).

BISTRO DES DAMES

Map p136   French €€

☎ 01 45 22 13 42; 18 rue des Dames, 17e; starters €7-15, mains €14-20; 🕑 lunch & dinner to 11.30pm; Ⓜ Place de Clichy
This charming little bistro will appeal to lovers of simple, authentic cuisine, such as hearty salads, tortillas and glorious *charcuterie* platters of *pâté de campagne* and paper-thin Serrano ham. The dining room, which looks out onto the street, is lovely, but during those humid Parisian summers it's the cool and tranquillity of the small back garden that pulls in the punters.

IL DUCA

Map p134   Italian €€

☎ 01 46 06 71 98; 26 rue Yvonne le Tac, 18e; starters €8-13.50, mains €11-18, menu €14 (lunch only); 🕑 lunch & dinner to 11.30pm daily; Ⓜ Abbesses
This intimate little Italian restaurant has good, straightforward food, including homemade pastas (€11 to €15). The selection of Italian wine and cheese is phenomenal; themed weeks, with various regions and types of produce, are scheduled throughout the year.

CUL DE POULE

Map p126   French €€

☎ 01 53 16 13 07; 53 rue des Martyrs, 9e; 2/3-course menus €14/17 (lunch), €22/26 (dinner); 🕑 closed Sun; Ⓜ Pigalle; 🛜
With plastic orange cafeteria seats outside, you probably wouldn't wander into the Cul de Poule by accident – in fact, if you're like most people, you'll probably be tempted to head straight next door to L'Épicerie (p247). But the light-hearted spirit (yes, there is a mounted chicken's derrière on the wall) is deceiving; this is one of the best and most affordable kitchens in the Pigalle neighbourhood, with excellent *néo-bistro* fare that emphasises quality ingredients from the French countryside.

LA TÊTE DE GOINFRE
Map p136   French, Café €€

☎ 01 42 29 89 80; 16 rue Jacquemont, 18e; starters €6-7.50, mains €12-18; ☷ lunch & dinner to 10.30pm Mon-Sat; Ⓜ La Fourche

This funny place, whose name translates as 'Glutton Head', has a piggy theme, and cute little figurines pepper the joint. As for the joints and other comestibles on the plate, it's (mostly) pork – from the *charcuterie* to munch on while you wait for a table to the *l'os à moëlle* (marrow bone) and *confit de porc* (pork confit). It's a lively place, always packed and an evening to experience. Just go with a carnivore.

À LA GRANDE BLEUE
Map p136   North African, Berber €

☎ 01 42 28 04 26; 4 rue Lantiez, 17e; starters €4.50-7.50, mains €10-18.50, menu €10.90 (lunch only); ☷ lunch Mon-Sat, dinner to 10.30pm Mon-Sat, closed Aug; Ⓜ Brochant or Guy Moquet

You'll find unusual barley couscous (€11.80 to €18.50) prepared in the style of the Berbers (Kabyles) of eastern Algeria, as well as the usual semolina variety (€10 to €17.50), *tajines* (€13 to €23) and savoury-sweet *pastilla au poulet* (chicken pastilla; €18.50). The rare *crêpes berbères* (Berber crêpes, €8.50 to €11.50) require a minimum of four people. We love the blue and yellow décor, the art on the walls and the warm welcome.

AUX NÉGOCIANTS
Map p134   French €

☎ 01 46 06 15 11; 27 rue Lambert, 18e; starters €5.30-6.80, mains €12-14.50; ☷ lunch & dinner to 10.30pm Mon-Fri; Ⓜ Château Rouge

This old-style wine bar and bistro is far enough from the madding crowds of Montmartre to attract a faithful local clientele. Pâtés, terrines, traditional mains like *bœuf bourguignon,* and wine paid for according to consumption – it all feels like the Paris of the 1950s (or even earlier).

LE MONO
Map p134   African, Togolese €

☎ 01 46 06 99 20; 40 rue Véron, 18e; starters €4-6.50, mains €11-14.50; ☷ dinner to 1am Thu-Tue; Ⓜ Abbesses or Blanche

Le Mono, run by a cheery Togolese family, offers West African specialities, including *lélé* (flat, steamed cakes of white beans and shrimp; €6.50), *azidessi* (beef or chicken with peanut sauce; €12), *gbekui* (goulash with spinach, onions, beef, fish and shrimp; €13) and *djenkoumé* (grilled chicken with

semolina noodles; €12). The rum-based punches are an excellent prelude.

LE REFUGE DES FONDUS
Map p134   French, Savoie €

☎ 01 42 55 22 65; www.lerefugedesfondus.com, in French; 17 rue des Trois Frères, 18e; menu €17; ☷ dinner to 2am daily; Ⓜ Abbesses or Anvers

This odd place has been a Montmartre favourite for nigh on four decades. The single *menu* provides an aperitif, hors d'oeuvre, red wine (or beer or soft drink) in a *biberon* (baby bottle) and a good quantity of either *fondue savoyarde* (melted cheese) or *fondue bourguignonne* (meat fondue). The last sitting is at midnight.

LE RELAIS GASCON
Map p134   French, Southwest €

☎ 01 42 58 58 22; www.lerelaisgascon.fr, in French; 6 rue des Abbesses, 18e; starters €6.50-11, mains €10.50-16, menus €9 (lunch only), €15.50 & €25.50; ☷ 10am-2pm daily; Ⓜ Abbesses

Situated just a short stroll from the place des Abbesses, the Relais Gascon has a relaxed atmosphere and authentic regional cuisine at very reasonable prices. The *salades géantes* (giant salads, a house speciality) and the *confit de canard* will satisfy big eaters, while the traditional *cassoulet* and *tartiflette* are equally tasty and filling. Another branch (☎ 01 42 52 11 11; 13 rue Joseph de Maistre) is just down the street. No credit cards at the main restaurant.

L'ÉPICERIE
Map p126   Italian €

☎ 01 48 78 07 50; www.fuxia.fr, in French; 51 rue des Martyrs, 9e; starters €3-7, dishes €10-18; ☷ 10am-10pm daily; Ⓜ Pigalle

A buzzy Italian caterer, L'Épicerie serves all sorts of delicacies from the Boot, including succulent risottos (artichokes, peppers and olives), plates of pasta, and stuffed veggies and cannelloni. Meal times are less formal here than elsewhere, and you can even order out for an improv picnic.

AU BON COIN
Map p136   French, Café €

☎ 01 58 60 28 72; 52 rue Lemercier, 17e; starters €3.50-5.50, mains €9.50-12; ☷ lunch Mon-Fri, dinner to midnight Tue-Fri; Ⓜ La Fourche

There's nothing particularly spectacular about this café up from place de Clichy that moonlights as a restaurant four nights a week. In fact, it's crowded and rather noisy. But if you are looking for solid café food and a quintessential Parisian eating experience, look no further than 'At the Right Corner'.

JOY IN FOOD Map p136 Vegetarian €

☎ 01 43 87 96 79; 2 rue Truffaut, 17e; starters €5, mains €10, menus €13 & €17; Ⓧ lunch Mon-Fri; Ⓜ Place de Clichy

This cosy little place just northwest of the place de Clichy serves homemade vegetarian dishes including omelettes and savoury tarte. The plat du jour might be couscous or vegetarian gratin and the huge desserts (apple crumble, chocolate cake) are legendary.

AU GRAIN DE FOLIE

Map p134 Vegetarian €

☎ 01 42 58 15 57; 24 rue de la Vieuville, 18e; salads €11, menus €12 & €16; Ⓧ lunch 1pm-2.30pm Tue-Sun, dinner to 10.30pm Tue-Sat; Ⓜ Abbesses

This hole-in-the-wall macrobiotic and organic eatery run by a woman from Cambridge and in business for over 25 years has excellent vegetarian pâté and vegan quiche. There are also lots of good dippy things like hummus and guacamole.

ISAAN Map p134 Thai €

☎ 01 42 80 09 72; 1 rue de Calais, 9e; starters €4.50-8, mains €7-10.50, menus €10 (lunch only) & €13.90; Ⓧ lunch Mon-Fri, dinner to 11pm daily; Ⓜ Blanche

The name of this friendly little eatery just south of Montmartre refers to Thailand's northeast, which produces the spiciest dishes in the realm. While we can't say the dishes blew our tops off, they were certainly authentic. Go for the basics: chicken green curry and pad tai noodles.

LA MAFFIOSA DI TERMOLI

Map p136 Italian, Pizzeria €

☎ 01 55 30 01 83; 19 rue des Dames, 17e; pizzas & pasta €8.10-10.40; Ⓧ lunch Mon-Sat, dinner to 11pm daily; Ⓜ Place de Clichy

This place has more than 40 pizzas that are too good to ignore, as well as decent garlic bread with or without Parma ham. It does a thriving takeaway business, too.

CRÊPERIE PEN-TY Map p134 Crêpes €

☎ 01 48 74 18 49; 65 rue de Douai, 9e; galettes €3-8.80, crêpes €3.50-6.80; Ⓧ lunch & dinner to 11pm Mon-Sat; Ⓜ Place de Clichy

Hailed as the best crêperie in northern Paris, Pen-Ty is worth the detour. Alas, the place

is tiny, so be sure to book ahead. Need to brush up on Breton Cuisine 101? A galette is a savoury crêpe made from buckwheat; a regular crêpe is sweet and made from white flour.

LE COQUELICOT Map p134 Café €

☎ 01 46 06 18 77; www.coquelicot-montmartre. com; 24 rue des Abbesses, 9e; omelettes €6.50, quiche with salad €4.20; Ⓧ 8.30am-5pm; Ⓜ Abbesses

Although nothing to excitedly blog about, the Coquelicot bakery is nonetheless a good spot for an easy meal, offering omelettes, quiches, sandwiches and yummy pastries. The outdoor tables occupy a prime location alongside rue des Abbesses.

SELF-CATERING

Towards place Pigalle there are lots of groceries, many of them open until late at night; try the side streets leading off blvd de Clichy (eg rue Lepic). Heading south from blvd de Clichy, rue des Martyrs, 9e, is lined with food shops almost all the way to the Notre Dame de Lorette metro station. For picnic supplies you can also head to the Marché des Gastronomes (Map p134; 9 place Pigalle; Ⓧ 10am-9pm Tue-Sat, 10am-7pm Sun, 5pm-9pm Mon; Ⓜ Pigalle), a supermarket with all sorts of French specialties. Another supermarket in the area is 8 à Huit (Map p134; 24 rue Lepic, 18e; Ⓧ 8.30am-10.30pm Mon-Sat; Ⓜ Abbesses). The bakery Le Grenier à Pain (Map p134; 38 rue des Abbesses, 18e; Ⓧ 7.30am-8pm Thu-Mon; Ⓜ Abbesses) is not one to miss, with delicious fougasses and a baguette à la tradition that won the best baguette in Paris award in 2010.

Near place de Clichy, the Marché Batignolles-Clichy (p222) is excellent for produits biologiques (organic food products).

GARE DU NORD & CANAL ST-MARTIN

Great things await along the cobbled banks of the Canal St-Martin. Eating out here is often a fun, laid-back experience, and kitchens aren't afraid to add a dash of creativity to spice up French standards. Also of note are the ethnic eats in the neighbourhoods around rue du Faubourg St-Denis and northeast of the Gare du Nord.

CHEZ MICHEL Map p140 French €€

☎ 01 44 53 06 20; 10 rue de Belzunce, 10e; menu €32; ⏰ Tue-Fri lunch, Mon-Fri dinner; Ⓜ Gare du Nord

If all you know about Breton cuisine is crêpes and cider, a visit to Chez Michel is in order. The formula here is simple – you order the three-course menu, and then if you want to add a twist, you replace an item with one of the 25 specialities chalked up on the blackboard (supplement €5 to €30). But even the 'regular' menu is outstanding (particularly the thick, creamy fish soup served in a large pitcher). If you can't book a table, don't despair – they also prepare four-course-with-wine picnic baskets (€43 for two people) if you order ahead. Two doors down is little brother Chez Casimir (6 rue de Belzunce; menus €22/29; ⏰ lunch & dinner Mon-Fri, 10am-7pm Sat & Sun), a café-bar-restaurant.

AUX DEUX CANARDS

Map p140 French €€

☎ 01 47 70 03 23; www.lesdeuxcanards.com; 8 rue du Faubourg Poissonnière, 10e; starters €4-7.50, mains €12.50-28, menus €32/39/52; ⏰ lunch Tue-Fri, dinner to 10.15pm Mon-Sat; Ⓜ Bonne Nouvelle

The tradition at this long-established inn-like place is that you ring first (is this a speakeasy or what?) before you are allowed entry. The name of the restaurant – 'At the Two Ducks' – reflects much of the menu (there's everything from foie gras to à l'orange), but you'll find starters as diverse as mussels with leek and a salad of Jerusalem artichoke and sheep's cheese. The host is a true, err, ham and performs to an appreciative, mostly English-speaking audience.

TERMINUS NORD

Map p140 French, Brasserie €€

☎ 01 42 85 05 15; www.terminusnord.com; 23 rue de Dunkerque, 10e; starters €7.80-19, mains €16.30-33.50, menus €23.50 & €31.50; ⏰ 8am-1am daily; Ⓜ Gare du Nord

The 'North Terminus' is a brasserie with a copper bar, waiters in white uniforms, brass fixtures and mirrored walls that look as they did when it opened in 1925. Breakfast (€7.90) is available from 8am to 11am, and full meals are served continuously from 11am to 1am. It's a museum-quality time piece and an excellent place for a final meal before returning home.

LA PAELLA Map p140 Spanish €€

☎ 01 46 07 28 89; www.restaurantlapaella.com, in French; 50 rue des Vinaigriers, 11e; starters €6.50-14.50, mains €16-30.50, menu €29; ⏰ lunch & dinner to 11pm Tue-Sun; Ⓜ Jacques Bonsergent

This homely place, which almost feels like a buzzy café (especially on weekend nights), specialises in Spain's most famous culinary export – though it does a mean *zarzuela de pescado* (Spanish 'bouillabaisse'; €27) as well. The paella is cooked to order so count on at least a 30-minute wait and don't overdo the tapas.

L'OFFICE Map p140 French €€

☎ 01 47 70 67 31; 3 rue Richer, 9e; lunch menus €17/21, dinner around €30-35; ⏰ lunch Thu & Fri, dinner Tue-Sat; Ⓜ Poissonnière or Bonne Nouvelle

Straddling the east-west Paris divide, L'Office is off the beaten track but unusual enough to merit a detour for those serious about their food. You might be misled by the name, but that's part of its underground charm – this is more of a place for creative types than white-collar workers. The market-inspired menu is short – as in there are only two choices for lunch – but often outstanding (seafood ragout with red rice and blood oranges, gnocchi with braised lamb and smoked ricotta) and there are excellent wines on offer.

HÔTEL DU NORD Map p140 French €€

☎ 01 40 40 78 78; www.hoteldunord.org; 102 quai de Jemmapes, 10e; starters €8-15.50, mains €15-23, menu €13.50 (lunch only); ⏰ 9am-2.30am; Ⓜ Jacques Bonsergent; 📶

The setting for the eponymous 1938 film starring Louis Jouvet and Arletty (p143), the interior of this vintage café feels as if it was stuck in a time warp with its zinc counter, red velvet curtains and old piano. The food is definitely modernist, though – grilled scallops in orange butter with quinoa, ricotta raviolis in a sweet-and-sour sauce, and pumpkin soup with chestnuts are just some of the palate pleasers on offer.

LA MARINE Map p140 French €€

☎ 01 42 39 69 81; 55bis quai de Valmy, 10e; starters €7-13, mains €14.50-21, menu weekday/weekend lunch €14/16; ⏰ 8am-midnight Mon-Fri, 9am-midnight Sat & Sun; Ⓜ République; 📶

This large, airy bistro overlooking Canal St-Martin is a favourite, especially in the warmer months, among *les branchés du quartier* (neighbourhood trendies), who nibble on dishes like *millefeuille de rouget à la vinaigrette* (mullet in layered pastry with vinaigrette) and *brick de poisson à la crème océane* (fish fritter with seafood sauce).

JAMBO Map p140 — African €€

☎ 01 42 45 46 55; 23 rue Ste-Marthe, 10e; menus €13 (lunch) & €25 (dinner); ⓨ lunch & dinner Tues-Sat; Ⓜ Belleville

This charming restaurant, decorated with shields and masks from different parts of Africa, was opened by a former aid worker and his Rwandan wife. The cuisine draws on dishes from Central Africa, and many of the ingredients have been imported directly from Kigali, the Rwandan capital.

LE CHANSONNIER Map p140 — French €€

☎ 01 42 09 40 58; www.lechansonnier.com, in French; 14 rue Eugène Varlin, 10e; starters €8.20, mains €17, menus €11.60 (lunch only) & €24; ⓨ lunch & dinner Mon-Fri, dinner only Sat-Sun; Ⓜ Château Landon or Louis Blanc

The 'Singer' (named after the 19th-century Lyonnais socialist singer–songwriter Pierre Dupont) could be a film set, with its curved zinc bar and Art Nouveau mouldings. The food is very substantial; try the *noix St-Jacques provençal* (scallops in herbed tomato sauce), bouillabaisse or *daube de sanglier* (boar stew) as a main course.

LA CANTINE DE QUENTIN

Map p140 — French €€

☎ 01 42 02 40 32; 52 Rue Bichat, 10e; starters €7-12, mains €13-18, lunch menu €16; ⓨ lunch noon-3.30pm Tue-Sun, shop 10am-7.30pm; Ⓜ Jacques Bonsergent or Gare de l'Est

A bewitching combination of gourmet food shop and lunchtime bistro, La Cantine de Quentin stocks quality products from the countryside (cassoulet, *charcuterie*, wine, tapenade, vinegar, mushrooms), many of which find their way into the back-room kitchen. You won't leave empty handed.

CHEZ PAPA Map p140 — French, Southwest €€

☎ 01 42 09 53 87; www.chezpapa.fr, in French; 206 rue La Fayette, 10e; starters & salads €7.65-11.45, mains €10.65-19.80; ⓨ noon-midnight daily; Ⓜ Louis Blanc

Chez Papa serves all sorts of specialities of the southwest, including cassoulet (€17.95), *pipérade* (€15.40) and *garbure* (€18.05), but most diners are here for the famous *salade Boyarde*, an enormous bowl filled

with lettuce, tomato, sautéed potatoes, two types of cheese and ham – all for the princely sum of €8.90 (or €9.75 if you want two fried eggs thrown in). There's a Grands Boulevards branch (Map p72; ☎ 01 40 13 07 31; 153 rue Montmartre, 2e; Ⓜ Grands Boulevards) and a 8e branch (Map p126; ☎ 01 42 65 43 68; 29 rue de l'Arcade, 8e; Ⓜ St-Augustin), which open noon to midnight Sunday to Thursday and till 1am at the weekend.

MADAME SHAWN Map p140 — Thai €€

☎ 01 42 38 07 37; www.mmeshawn.com; 56 rue de Lancry, 10e; starters €7, mains €11.50-17.50 (add €1 to prices for dinner); ⓨ lunch & dinner; Ⓜ Jacques Bonsergent

The Mme started out in a humble French café that was deftly transformed into a sophisticated Thai restaurant. The heat may be turned down a few degrees, but you can still taste the flavours of Chiang Mai in the *tôm yam* soup, invigorating green curries and…chocolate *nem* for dessert? There are now a handful of locations, including the casual canal-side café Ari (☎ 01 46 07 02 00; 3 rue des Récollets, 10e; ⓨ 9am-2am; Ⓜ Jacques Bonsergent or Gare de l'Est; 🛜).

LE RÉVEIL DU XE

Map p140 — French, Wine €

☎ 01 42 41 77 59; 35 rue du Château d'Eau, 10e; starters €5-10, mains €12.50-15; ⓨ lunch Mon-Sat, dinner to 11pm Mon-Fri; Ⓜ Chateau d'Eau

This corner wine bar is slightly out of the way, but if you're in search of a locals' place you won't regret the trip. Plates of *charcuterie* (saucisson, rillettes, pâté) and Auvergne cheeses (cantal, st-nectaire, bleu) supplement French bistro standards (*confit de canard* and garlic-fried potatoes), and there are even mixed salads (€ 10.50) for those hoping for a glimpse of the colour green.

LE VERRE VOLÉ Map p140 — French, Wine €

☎ 01 48 03 17 34; 67 rue de Lancry, 10e; starters €6.50-8.50, mains €12; ⓨ lunch & dinner to 11pm; Ⓜ Jacques Bonsergent

The tiny 'Stolen Glass' – a wine shop with a few tables – is just about the most perfect wine-bar-cum-restaurant in Paris, with excellent wines (€5 to €60 a bottle, €4.50 per glass) and expert advice. Unpretentious and hearty *plats du jour* are excellent. Reserve well in advance for meals, or just stop by for a tasting.

LE BASTRINGUE Map p140 French, Café €

☎ 01 42 09 89 27; 67 quai de la Seine, 19e; lunch menu €10.80, dinner mains €10-17; ☾ Mon-Fri 9am-2am, Sat 5pm-2am; Ⓜ Riquet

One of the better dining options in the 19e, the quay-side Bastringue rose from humble origins (café by day, bar by night) to become a minor foodie destination in its own right. The drinks are still available late into the night (along with games like Boggle), but it's the generous portions of hefty quiches (salmon and spinach), clever salads (tagliatelle with pesto, cantal cheese and walnuts) and other tantalising creations (grilled turkey and prunes) that have won it a following.

PASSAGE BRADY

Map p140 Indian, Pakistani €

46 rue du Faubourg St-Denis & 33 blvd de Strasbourg, 10e; veggies €6.50-10, mains €12-14.50; ☾ lunch & dinner to 11pm; Ⓜ Château d'Eau

This old-style covered arcade has long been the place to go to for inexpensive Indian meals. While the Gare du Nord has since become a better destination for curry fiends, Passage Brady is a reliable standby that's closer to central Paris. Among the many choices, the pick of the crop are Palais des Rajpout (☎ 01 42 46 23 75; 64-66 passage Brady), Passage de Pondicherry (☎ 01 53 34 63 10; 84 passage Brady) and Pooja (☎ 01 48 24 00 83; 91 passage Brady). Prix-fixe lunches are usually around €7 to €8.

PINK FLAMINGO Map p140 Pizza €

☎ 01 42 02 31 70; www.pinkflamingopizza.com; 67 rue Bichat, 10e; pizzas €10.50-16; ☾ lunch & dinner Tue-Sat, 1pm-11pm Sun; Ⓜ Jacques Bonsergent

Not another pizza place? Mais non, chérie! Once the weather warms up, the Flamingo unveils its secret weapon – pink helium balloons that the delivery guy uses to locate you and your perfect canal-side picnic spot (GPS not needed). Order a Poulidor (duck, apple and chèvre) or a Basquiat (gorgonzola, figs and cured ham), pop into Le Verre Volé (p250) across the canal for the perfect bottle of vino and you're set.

LE CAMBODGE

Map p140 Cambodian €

☎ 01 44 84 37 70; www.lecambodge.fr, in French; 10 av Richerand, 10e; dishes €8.50-13; ☾ lunch & dinner to 11.30pm Mon-Sat; Ⓜ Goncourt

Hidden in a quiet street between the gargantuan Hôpital St-Louis and Canal St-Martin, this favourite spot among students serves enormous rouleaux de printemps (spring rolls; €6.50) and the ever-popular pique-nique Angkorien ('Angkor picnic' of rice vermicelli and sautéed beef, which you wrap up in lettuce leaves; €11.50). The food tastes homemade (if not especially authentic) and the vegetarian options (€8.50 to €11.50) are especially good.

ISTANBUL Map p140 Turkish €

☎ 01 48 00 98 10; 66 rue du Faubourg St-Denis, 10e; starters €5.60-9, mains €8.50-10.80; ☾ lunch & dinner to 11pm Sun-Thu, to 11.30 Fri & Sat; Ⓜ Château d'Eau

Our favourite Turkish restaurant in the heart of Turkey Town serves all our favourites – Iskender kebab (lamb slices served with pide bread and yogurt), imam bayildi ('the imam fainted'; an eggplant dish) – and the combination meze platter (€9) is a meal in itself. What friendly and generous staff: the baklava, fruit slices and mint tea kept coming after we had settled the bill!

JARDIN DES VOLUPTÉS

Map p140 Organic €

☎ 01 48 24 38 68; 10 rue de l'Échiquier, 10e; mains €11.90, 2/3-course menus €13.90/20; ☾ 11am-4pm Mon-Sat, 10am-3pm Sun; Ⓜ Strasbourg–St-Denis

A cosy teahouse attached to a bona fide qigong (ch'i kung) centre, this health-oriented place would have no trouble fitting in in California. What's surprising is how popular it is with Cartesian-esque Parisians (particularly local families), attracted by both the quality of the organic ingredients and the original cooking. Kids might shy away from the quinoa vegetable stir-fry, but other dishes (meatless chilli, salmon-and-leek gratin, dairy-free lemon meringue pie) can do no wrong. Sunday brunch is by reservation only.

DISHNY Map p140 Indian €

☎ 01 40 05 18 36; 212 rue du Faubourg St-Denis, 10e; mains €6-13, menus €7 (lunch only), €9 & €16; ☾ lunch & dinner to midnight; Ⓜ La Chapelle or Gare du Nord

Probably the most famous Indian restaurant situated along rue Cail – Paris' new Little India – the Dishny offers an array of inexpensive choices, many from the south. It's not far from the Gare du Nord for those in need of a curry fix.

KRISHNA BHAVAN

Map p140   Indian, Vegetarian €

☎ 01 42 05 78 43; 24 rue Cail, 10e; dishes
€1.50-7, menu €13; ⏲ lunch & dinner to 11pm;
Ⓜ La Chapelle

This is about as authentic an Indian vegetarian canteen as you'll find in Paris. If in
doubt as to what to order, ask for a *thaali*
(€8), a circular steel tray with samosas,
dosas and other wrapped goodies. Wash it
all down with a yoghurt-based lassi, which
comes in five flavours, including mango
and rose.

BOB'S JUICE BAR

Map p140   Vegetarian €

☎ 09 50 06 36 18; www.bobsjuicebar.com; 15 rue
Lucien Sampaix, 10e; juice €4-6.50, breakfast from
€3.75, sandwiches €6, menu €6.50-11; ⏲ 7.30am-
3pm Mon-Fri; Ⓜ République; 🛜

In need of some vitamin C? Sweet potato
soup? This tiny outpost (and do note that it
is tiny) with bags of rice flour and flax seed
lining the walls serves delicious smoothies, freshly squeezed organic juices, vegan
breakfasts, hummus sandwiches…in short,
all those things you might have trouble
finding elsewhere in Paris. There's another
branch (Map p145; ☎ 09 52 55 11 66; 74 rue des Gravilliers, 3e; ⏲ 8am-3pm Mon-Fri, 10am-4pm Sat & Sun;
Ⓜ Arts et Metiers) that also serves up a popular brunch at weekends.

SELF-CATERING

Two covered markets in this area are the
Marché aux Enfants Rouges and the Marché
St-Quentin. For details, see p222. For a gourmet picnic, stock up specialties at La Cantine
de Quentin (p250).

Rue du Faubourg St-Denis, 10e, which links
blvd St-Denis and blvd de Magenta, is one of
the cheapest places to buy food, especially fruit
and vegetables; the shops at Nos 23, 27–29 and
41–43 are laden with produce. The street has
a distinctively Middle Eastern air, and quite
a few of the groceries offer Turkish, North
African and subcontinental specialities. Many
of the food shops, including the *fromagerie* at
No 54, are open Tuesday to Saturday and until
noon on Sunday.

Supermarkets convenient to this area include Franprix St-Denis branch (Map p174; 7-9 rue des
Petites Écuries,10e; ⏲ 9am-8.20pm Mon-Sat; Ⓜ Château
d'Eau) and Franprix Magenta branch (Map p140; 57 blvd
de Magenta, 10e; ⏲ 9am-8pm Mon-Sat; Ⓜ Gare de l'Est).

MARAIS & MÉNILMONTANT

The Marais, filled with small restaurants of
every imaginable type, is one of Paris' premier
neighbourhoods for eating out. Make sure to
book ahead at the weekend.

Towards République there's a decent selection of ethnic places. If you're after authentic
Chinese food but can't be bothered going to
the larger Chinatown in the 13e (see p268),
check out the small noodle shops and restaurants along rue Au Maire, 3e (Map p148). The
Jewish restaurants (some Ashkenazic, some
Sephardic, not all kosher) along rue des Rosiers (Map p152), the so-called Pletzl area, serve
specialities from Central Europe, North Africa
and Israel. Be aware: many are closed on Friday evenings, Saturdays and Jewish holidays.
Takeaway falafel and *shwarma* (kebabs) are
available at several places along the street.

In the northern part of the 11e and into the
19e and 20e arrondissements, rue Oberkampf
and its extension, rue de Ménilmontant, are
popular with diners and denizens of the night,
though rue Jean-Pierre Timbaud, running
parallel to the north, has been giving them a
bit of competition. Rue de Belleville and the
streets running off it are dotted with Chinese, Southeast Asian and Middle Eastern
places; blvd de Belleville has some couscous
restaurants.

LE CHATEAUBRIAND

Map p148   French, Bistro €€€

☎ 01 43 57 45 95; 129 av Parmentier, 11e;
2-/3-course menu €16/22 (lunch only) & €45;
⏲ lunch Tue-Fri, dinner to 10pm Tue-Sat;
Ⓜ Goncourt

The quintessential *néo-bistro* (p217) Le
Chateaubriand is a simple but elegantly
tiled art deco dining room with some of
the most imaginative cuisine in town. Chef
Iñaki Aizpitarte – a name that could only
be Basque – is well travelled and his dishes
show that global exposure again and again
in its odd combinations (watermelon and
mackerel, milk-fed veal with langoustines
and truffles). Dinner is a five-course tasting
menu with no choices. Trust us, you'll love
them all.

BISTROT DE L'OULETTE

Map p148   French, Southwest €€€

☎ 01 42 71 43 33; www.l-oulette.com; 38 rue
des Tournelles, 4e; starters €11-18, mains €19-23,

2-/3-course menus €13/18 (lunch only), €26/33;
🕑 lunch Mon-Fri, dinner to 11pm Mon-Thu, to
midnight Fri & Sat; Ⓜ Bastille or Chemin Vert
A younger cousin of the chic L'Oulette (p261)
in Bercy, this bistro bustles by day and
night with a mix of locals and tourists who
are here for the capable southwestern provincial cooking. Duck features heavily – try
the *foie gras de canard* (€18) or the *magret
de canard* (fillet of duck breast; €19). Wines
include almost a dozen from the southwest.

LE VILLARET Map p148 French €€€
☎ 01 43 57 89 76; 13 rue Ternaux, 11e; starters
€9-22, mains €19-38, menu €20 & €25 (lunch only);
🕑 lunch Mon-Fri, dinner to 11.30pm Mon-Sat;
Ⓜ Parmentier
An excellent neighbourhood bistro serving very rich food, Le Villaret has diners
coming from across Paris to sample the
house specialities. The *velouté de cèpes* (cep
mushroom soup) and the *jarret de veau à
la poudre foie gras* (veal shank sprinkled
with foie gras) are recommended, but only
the chef knows what will be available as
he changes the menu daily. Tasting menus
start at €52.

LE DÔME BASTILLE
Map p148 French, Seafood €€€
☎ 01 48 04 88 44; 2 rue de la Bastille, 4e; starters
€8.50-16.50, mains €20-31; 🕑 lunch & dinner to
11pm; Ⓜ Bastille
This lovely restaurant, little sister to the
more established (and touristy) Dôme (p270)
in Montparnasse and awash in pale yellows, specialises in superbly prepared fish
and seafood dishes. The blackboard menu
changes daily. Wines are a uniform €23.90
per bottle.

LE REPAIRE DE CARTOUCHE
Map p148 French €€€
☎ 01 47 00 25 86; 8 blvd des Filles du Calvaire &
99 rue Amelot, 11e; starters €9-18, mains €20-28,
menu €25 (lunch only); 🕑 lunch & dinner to 11pm
Tue-Sat; Ⓜ St-Sébastien–Froissart
With entrances at both front and back,
'Cartouche's Den' – a reference to the
18th-century Parisian 'Robin Hood' Louis-
Dominique Cartouche – looks to the past
and the future. It's an old-fashioned place
that takes a very modern, innovative
approach to French food under the direction of Norman chef Rodolphe Paquin. As
its name implies and the rifle on the wall
underscores, it focuses on meat and game,

though there are some excellent fish and
shellfish dishes on the menu.

DERRIÈRE Map p148 French €€€
☎ 01 44 61 91 95; 69 rue des Gravilliers, 3e; starters €12-15, mains €18-26; 🕑 lunch Tue-Fri, dinner
to 11pm daily; Ⓜ Arts et Métiers
So secretive it's almost a speakeasy, 'Behind' is just that – set in a lovely courtyard
between (and behind) the 404 (p256) restaurant and the Andy Walhoo (p288) bar and club.
Chilled in a 'shoes-off' kind of way with
distressed armchairs and newspapers on
the coffee tables, this place is a lot more
serious behind the scenes, serving up
both classic French bistro dishes and more
inventive ones (eg suckling pig braised
in ginger and lime with lentils, macaroni
gratin with taramasalata). Vegetarians:
more than half the starters are meatless.
Smokers: there's a *fumoir* behind the closet
door upstairs.

BOFINGER Map p148 French, Brasserie €€€
☎ 01 42 72 87 82; www.bofingerparis.com; 5-7 rue
de la Bastille, 4e; starters €9-18.50, mains €16.90-
35, 2-/3-course menus €25/30; 🕑 lunch & dinner to
midnight or 12.30am; Ⓜ Bastille
Founded in 1864, Bofinger is reputedly the
oldest brasserie in Paris, though its polished art nouveau brass, glass and mirrors
throughout flags a redecoration a few decades later. As at most Parisian brasseries,
specialities include Alsatian-inspired dishes
such as *choucroute* (sauerkraut with assorted meats; €19.80 to €21), and seafood
dishes. Ask for a seat downstairs and under
the *coupole* (stained-glass dome); it's the
prettiest part of the restaurant. Just opposite Le Petit Bofinger (☎ 01 42 72 05 23; 6 rue de
la Bastille, 4e; starters €6.20-19.30, mains €14.90-25.80,
menus with wine €18 & €25.50; 🕑 lunch & dinner to
midnight daily; Ⓜ Bastille) is the brasserie's less
brash (and cheaper) little sister.

LE BARATIN Map p148 French, Bistro €€€
☎ 01 43 49 39 70; 3 rue Jouye-Rouve, 20e; starters
€8-10, mains €18-24, menu €16 (lunch only);
🕑 lunch Tue-Fri, dinner to midnight Tue-Sat;
Ⓜ Pyrénées or Belleville
Baratin (chatter) rhymes with *bar à vin*
(wine bar) in French and this animated
place just a step away from the lively Belleville quarter does both awfully well. In
addition it offers some of the best (and very
affordable) French food in the 20e on its

ever-changing blackboard. The selection of wine (some of it organic) by the glass or carafe is excellent; most are between €24 and €36 a bottle.

AUBERGE NICOLAS FLAMEL

Map p148   French €€€

☎ 01 42 71 77 78; www.auberge-nicolas-flamel. fr, in French; 51 rue de Montmorency, 3e; starters €10, mains €17; 2-/3-course menu €18.50/25 (lunch only), €31 & €46 ☯ lunch & dinner to 11pm Mon-Sat; Ⓜ Rambuteau or Arts et Métiers

A visit to this charming restaurant, with its higgledy-piggledy rooms on two floors, is not so much about the food as the location: this was once the residence of celebrated alchemist and writer Flamel (1330–1417) and is the oldest building still standing in Paris. Expect dishes that are correct but not earth-moving – duck foie gras, lamb cooked in a *tajine* and so on. Ask about wine tastings in the atmospheric (read: spooky) cellar.

AU BASCOU

Map p148   French, Basque €€€

☎ 01 42 72 69 25; 38 rue Réaumur, 3e; starters €10, mains €17, menu €19 (lunch only); ☯ lunch & dinner to 10.30pm Mon-Fri; Ⓜ Arts et Métiers

This is a popular eatery serving such classic Basque dishes as *pipérade* (peppers, onions, tomatoes and ham cooked with scrambled eggs), *axoa* (ragout of ground veal with a sauce of pimento and peppers) and Bayonne ham in all its guises. Round off the meal with a piece of Ardi Gasna *brebis* (a Basque ewe's milk cheese) or a slice of *gâteau basque*, a layer cake filled with cream and cherry jam.

LE TEMPLE

Map p148   French, Corsican €€

☎ 01 42 72 30 76; www.la-grande-assiette-corse. com; 87 rue de Turbigo, 3e; starters €10.90-20.50, mains €17.50-20.50, menu €11.50 (lunch only); ☯ 11.30am-10pm daily; Ⓜ Temple

Here be witches, we were told, and it does feel like a fortune-teller's parlour, this place, with its masks and heads and faux leopard skin throughout. A very friendly eatery specialising in traditional Corsican *mets* (victuals, for lack of a better term), the *tripes de sanglier à la corse* (Corsica-style boar tripe) may not tickle your fancy but the cannelloni stuffed with fresh *brocciu* cheese, the grilled *figatelli* ham and the chestnut cake surely will. We shall return – for sure.

L'ENOTECA

Map p148   Italian €€€

☎ 01 42 78 91 44; www.enoteca.fr, in French; 25 rue Charles V, 4e; starters €9-14, mains €17-19, menus €14 (lunch only), €28 & €43; ☯ lunch & dinner to 11.30pm; Ⓜ Sully–Morland or Pont Marie

The 'Vinotheque', a *trattoria* in the historic Village St-Paul quarter of the Marais, serves *haute cuisine à l'italienne,* and there's an excellent list of Italian wines by the glass (€3.50 to €9). It's no secret that this is one of the few Italian wine bars in Paris to take its *vino* seriously (there are 400 labels in the cellar), so book ahead. Pasta dishes (€13 to €18) are good, as is the generous *tavola antipasti* (antipasto buffet table) at lunch.

L'ALIVI

Map p152   French, Corsican €€€

☎ 01 48 87 90 20; www.restaurant-alivi.com, in French; 27 rue du Roi de Sicile, 4e; starters €9-16, mains €16-23, menus €27 & €31; ☯ lunch & dinner to 11.30pm; Ⓜ St-Paul

The ingredients at this fashionable Corsican restaurant in the heart of the Marais are always fresh and refined, with *brocciu* cheese (eg in cannelloni), charcuterie and basil featuring strongly on the menu. Try the chestnut and mushroom cream soup and the eggplant with brebis (ewe's-milk cheese) with a Leccia wine to fully experience the pleasures of what the French call *l'Île de Beauté* (the beautiful island).

LE PETIT MARCHÉ

Map p148   French, Bistro €€

☎ 01 42 72 06 67; 9 rue de Béarn, 3e; starters €9.50-15, mains €16-24, menu €12.50 (lunch only); ☯ lunch & dinner to midnight; Ⓜ Chemin Vert

This great little bistro just up from the place des Vosges fills up at lunch and then again in the evening with a mixed crowd who come to enjoy the hearty cooking and friendly service. The salad starters are popular, as are the *selle d'agneau au basilique* (saddle of lamb with basil). The open kitchen also offers a fair few vegetarian choices.

CHEZ NÉNESSE

Map p152   French, Bistro €€

☎ 01 42 78 46 49; 17 rue de Saintonge, 3e; starters €8-16, mains €17-18; ☯ lunch & dinner to 10.30pm Mon-Fri; Ⓜ Filles du Calvaire

The atmosphere at this bistro is very 'old Parisian café' and unpretentious. Fresh, high-quality ingredients are used to make the dishes, such as *salade de canard au*

top picks

LATE-NIGHT BITES

- **Marche ou Crêpe** (p260) Sweet or savoury, the pancakes are yours till at least midnight.
- **Joe Allen** (p224) Always eager to please, JA is the place for late-night ribs that will stick to your, well, ribs.
- **Le Grand Colbert** (p223) The portions are huge at this *fin-de-siècle* brasserie serving food late.
- **Chez Papa** (p250) It might not be *haute cuisine*, but this Gascogne eatery ensures you won't walk away hungry.
- **Hôtel Amour** (p243) Hip French-bistro-meets-American-diner in Pigalle.
- **Terminus Nord** (p249) Step into the Parisian past at this traditional brasserie across from the Gare du Nord.
- **Le Petit Zinc** (p233) Feast on seafood platters at this historic St-Germain brasserie with fabulous art nouveau interior.
- **Les Pipos** (p229) Meaty bistro dining around tightly packed tables dressed in red-and-white checks.
- **Brasserie Lipp** (p234) Parisians have been packing out this St-Germain brasserie since 1880.
- **La Coupole** (p270) Late-night dining like Sartre did in 1920s Paris.

vinaigre d'hydromel (duck salad with honey vinegar) and *fricassée de volaille aux morilles* (poultry fricassee with morel mushrooms). The lunchtime starters are €4 and *plats du jour* are €9.50 or €10.

LE DÔME DU MARAIS
Map p152   French €€
☎ 01 42 74 54 17; 53bis rue des Francs Bourgeois, 4e; starters €5-18, mains €18-28, 2-/3-course menus €19/25 (lunch only); ☽ lunch & dinner to 11pm Tue-Sat; Ⓜ Rambuteau
This place serves classic French dishes such as *joues de bœuf* (beef cheeks) as well as hare and lighter fare – often shellfish and fish. The location is sublime: a pre-Revolution building and former auction room with a glassed-in courtyard just down from the Archives Nationales. The octagonal-shaped dining room is a knock-out, as is the 'Humeur du Chef' (Chef's Mood) tasting menu at €52.

LE HANGAR Map p152   French, Bistro €€
☎ 01 42 74 55 44; 12 Impasse Berthaud, 3e; starters €9-10, mains €16-20; ☽ lunch & dinner to 11pm Tue-Sat; Ⓜ Les Halles
Unusual for big mouths like us, we almost balk at revealing details of this perfect little restaurant tucked away just south of the Musée de la Poupée (p150). It serves all the bistro favourites – rillettes, foie gras, steak tartare – in relaxing, very quiet surrounds. The terrace is a delight in fine weather and the service both professional and personal.

CHEZ JENNY Map p148   French, Alsatian €€
☎ 01 44 54 39 00; www.chezjenny.com; 39 blvd du Temple, 3e; starters €6.40-17.50, mains €17.50-27, 2-/3-course menus €17.50 & €27.50; ☽ noon-midnight Sun-Thu, to 1am Fri & Sat; Ⓜ République
This cavernous brasserie dating from 1932 serves a huge *choucroute garnie* and, at the weekend, excellent *baeckeoffe* (€23), an Alsatian stew made of meat and several types of vegetables, but we suspect that most people visit to admire the stunning marquetry of Alsatian scenes by Charles Spindler on the 1st floor. A quick and tasty lunch here is *flammekuche* (€10.50 to €15.50), an Alsatian-style tart made with cream, onion, bacon and cheese.

CHEZ JANOU
Map p148   French, Provencal Bistro €€
☎ 01 42 72 28 41; www.chezjanou.com; 2 rue Roger Verlomme, 3e; starters €9.50-11, mains €14.50-19, menu €12.50 (lunch only); ☽ lunch & dinner to midnight; Ⓜ Chemin Vert
Not exactly 'French bistro' as ordered by Central Casting but close to it, this lovely little spot just east of place des Vosges attracts celebs (last seen: John Malkovich) and hangers on with its inspired Provençal cooking, 80 different types of pastis and excellent service. Try the superb ratatouille with anchovy and black olive dips and the spelt risotto with scallops.

LE POTAGER DU MARAIS
Map p152   Vegetarian €€
☎ 01 42 74 24 66; 22 rue Rambuteau, 3e; starters €6.50-10, mains 15-17, 3-course menu €25; ☽ lunch & dinner to 10.30pm; Ⓜ Rambuteau
A very welcome addition to the Marais dining scene is this organic vegetarian restaurant within easy reach of the Centre Pompidou. The décor is rustic, with lots of lush plants inside, and there's a full page of

options for vegans. We especially enjoyed the onion soup. The 'Marais Vegetable Garden' is not cheap, but it makes for a refreshing change from the usual run-of-the-mill veggie eateries that feel more like canteens or at best cafeterias.

BISTRO FLORENTIN Map p148 Italian €€

☎ 01 43 55 57 00; 40 rue Jean-Pierre Timbaud, 11e; starters €8.50-17, mains €15-17, menu €12 (lunch only); ☾ lunch Mon-Fri, dinner to 11pm Mon-Sat; Ⓜ Parmentier

Expect excellent Italian fare amid cosy surrounds: grilled, finely seasoned aubergine for starters, tiramisu as light as a feather for dessert and, in between, a wide choice of mains and pastas (€12 to €17). The *penne à la crème d'artichauts* (penne with cream and artichokes; €15) is superb as is the *ravioli à la gorgonzola aux épinards* (spinach and cheese ravioli). Pizzas are €8 to €13.

404 Map p148 North African, Moroccan €€

☎ 01 42 74 57 81; 69 rue des Gravilliers, 3e; starters €7-9, couscous & tajines €15-24, menus €17 (lunch only); ☾ lunch Mon-Fri, dinner to midnight daily, brunch noon-4pm Sat & Sun; Ⓜ Arts et Métiers

As comfortable a Maghreb (North African) caravanserai as you'll find in Paris, the 404 has not only excellent couscous and *tajines* but also superb grills (€13 to €24) and fish *pastilla* (€18). The *brunch berbère* (Berber brunch; €21) is available at the weekend. You'll just love the One Thousand and One Nights décor with antiques and curios.

L'AMBASSADE D'AUVERGNE
Map p148 French, Auvergne €€

☎ 01 42 72 31 22; www.ambassade-auvergne.com; 22 rue du Grenier St-Lazare, 3e; starters €8-17, mains €14-23, menu €20 (lunch only) & €28; ☾ lunch & dinner to 10pm; Ⓜ Rambuteau

The 'Auvergne Embassy' is the place to head if you are a truly hungry carnivore. This century-old restaurant offers traditional dishes from the Auvergne such as *salade tiède de lentilles vertes du Puy* (warm salad of green Puy lentils; €9), a great lead-up to the house speciality: *saucisse de Parlan à l'aligot* (Auvergne-style pork sausage served with a potato and cheese purée; €14).

AUX VINS DES PYRÉNÉES
Map p148 French €€

☎ 01 42 72 64 94; 25 rue Beautreillis, 4e; starters €8.50-15, mains €14.50-19, menu €13.50 (lunch only); ☾ lunch Sun-Fri, dinner to 11.30pm; Ⓜ St-Paul or Bastille

Located in a former wine warehouse, this is a good place to enjoy a unpretentious French meal with a lot of wine. The place has been able to retain its old-world charm and it's not surprising that a crowd of *bobo* (bohemian bourgeois) locals, a few *showbiz parisien* types among them, have set up headquarters here. The fish, meat and game dishes are all equally good, but worth a special mention is the foie gras and the top-notch *pavé de rumsteak* (thick rump steak). The wine list offers a wide choice of celebrated and little-known estate wines.

MAI THAI Map p148 Thai €€

☎ 01 42 72 18 77; www.maithai.fr, in French; 24bis rue St-Gilles, 3e; starters €9-11, mains €13-20, menu €13.50 (lunch only); ☾ lunch & dinner to 11pm daily; Ⓜ Chemin Vert

This rather stylish place, done up in warm tones of orange, red and yellow with Buddha figures, the *sine qua non* of Thai restaurants, throughout, has a loyal clientele so you should book in advance for dinner. Among *les classiques de la cuisine du Siam* (classics of the cuisine of Siam) on offer is chicken cooked with sacred basil (€15) and the unusual spicy Thai sausages (€13).

LE CLOWN BAR Map p148 French, Bistro €€

☎ 01 43 55 87 35; 114 rue Amelot, 11e; starters €7.50-12, mains €15-19, menu €25; ☾ lunch Wed-Sat, dinner to 1am Mon-Sat; Ⓜ Filles du Calvaire

A wonderful wine-bar-cum-bistro next to the Cirque d'Hiver (Map p148) dating from 1852, the Clown Bar is like a museum with its painted ceilings, mosaics on the wall, lovely zinc bar and circus memorabilia that touches on one of our favourite themes of all time: the evil clown. The food is simple and unpretentious traditional French; the *charcuterie* platter is substantial and goes well with a half-bottle of Brouilly, while the *Parmentier de boudin à la normande* (black pudding Parmentier with apple) is one of the restaurant's most popular dishes.

MAISON MARAIS
Map p152 Korean €€

☎ 01 48 87 28 15; www.maisonmarais.com; 3 rue Ferdinand Duval, 4e; starters €10-18, mains €13-18, menu €9.50 (lunch only); ☾ lunch and dinner to 11pm Tue-Sun; Ⓜ St-Paul

Things Korean – especially films – seem to be taking the world by storm these days and Paris is no exception. This place in the heart of the Marais has excellent barbecues on offer, but we particularly like the *bibimbab* (from €12, rice served in a sizzling pot topped with thinly sliced beef (or other meat) and cooked with preserved vegetables, then bound by a raw egg and flavoured with chilli-laced soy paste. Staff are welcoming but language can be an issue.

LES CAVES ST-GILLES Map p148   Spanish €€

☎ 01 48 87 22 62; www.caves-saint-gilles.fr; 4 rue St-Gilles, 3e; tapas €5.50-26, mains €12-18; ☺ lunch & dinner to 11.30pm daily; Ⓜ Chemin Vert

This Spanish wine bar a short distance northeast of place des Vosges is the most authentic place on the Right Bank for tapas, paella (at the weekend only; €19) and sangria (€28 for 1.4cL). If you're unsure, just ask the Spanish expats who arrive here in droves.

LE TIRE BOUCHON

Map p148   French €€

☎ 01 47 00 43 50; 5 rue Guillaume Bertrand, 11e; starters €7.50-14, mains €15-18, menus €12 & €15 (lunch only), €26.50; ☺ lunch & dinner to 11pm Mon-Sat; Ⓜ St-Maur

This mock old-style bistro close to the flashy rue Oberkampf has a dozen tables with gingham tablecloths arranged around a polished wooden bar. Add a few old photographs of the *quartier,* a touch of greenery and some decent bottles of wine and *voilà*: the 'Corkscrew'. The *cassoulet* (casserole or stew with beans and meat) and the fillet of sea bream in a lobster sauce will tickle your taste buds. Expect friendly, attentive service but book in advance.

CAFFÉ BOBOLI

Map p152   Italian €€

☎ 01 42 77 89 27; www.caffeboboli.com; 13 rue du Roi de Sicile, 4e; starters €8.90-12.50, mains €13.60-17.80; ☺ lunch Tue-Sun, dinner to 11pm Mon-Sat; Ⓜ St-Paul

Affordable Italian fare in the heart of the Marais? Not as preposterous a notion as you might think with this small restaurant run by two young Florentines. The food is very wholesome and based on vegetables, cheese and *charcuterie* like Parma ham and beef carpaccio. On the walls are original paintings and photographs that are changed every few months.

LE PETIT DAKAR

Map p152   African, Senegalese €€

☎ 01 44 59 34 74; 6 rue Elzévir, 3e; starters €6-8, mains €14-16, menu €15 (lunch only); ☺ lunch Tue-Sat, dinner to 11pm Tue-Sun; Ⓜ St-Paul

Some people think this is the most authentic Senegalese restaurant in Paris; the *tiéboudienne* (rice, fish and vegetables) is particularly well received. And with the CSAO Boutique & Gallery (p209) just up the road, it does feel like a little bit of Africa has fallen onto a quiet Marais street.

EL PALADAR Map p148   Cuban €€

☎ 01 43 57 42 70; 26bis rue de la Fontaine au Roi, 11e; starters €5-7, mains €14-18, 2-/3-course menus €12/14 (lunch only); ☺ lunch & dinner to midnight mon-Sat; Ⓜ Goncourt

While the name of this place suggests the restaurants run from private homes in today's cash-strapped Havana (and the US greenback is on their calling card), the food and sheer exuberance recalls the Cuba of the 1950s, when everything was plentiful. It's a convivial, graffiti-covered place with super *caipirinhas* (€6) – cocktails made from a sugarcane-based alcohol, lime juice and sugarcane syrup – and such authentic dishes as *pescado guisado* (fried fish), *pollo piopio* (chicken cooked with citrus) and *yuca con mojo* (manioc with onions and garlic).

CURIEUX SPAGHETTI

Map p152   International €€

☎ 01 42 72 75 97; www.curieuxspag.com; 14 rue St-Mérri, 4e; starters €7-12, mains €12-18; ☺ noon-2am Sun-Wed, to 4am Thu-Sat; Ⓜ Rambuteau

This very upbeat restaurant-cum-bar hip hangout always attracts a young crowd with its mountain-sized portions of pasta, test-tube shots of unusually flavoured vodka (bubblegum, anyone?) and great canned music. The weekly calendar's red-letter event is the weekend buffet brunch (€256) from 11am or noon to 4pm.

LE TRUMILOU Map p152   French, Bistro €€

☎ 01 42 77 63 98; www.letrumilou.com; 84 quai de l'Hôtel de Ville, 4e; starters €4-14, mains €15-22, 2-/3-course menu €16.50/19.50; ☺ lunch & dinner to 11pm; Ⓜ Hôtel de Ville

This no-frills bistro just round the corner from the Hôtel de Ville and facing the posh Île de St-Louis square is a Parisian institution in situ for over a century. If you're looking for an authentic menu from the early 20th century and prices (well, almost) to match, you won't do better than this. Specialities of the house include *canard aux pruneaux* (duck with prunes; €17) and *ris de veau grand-mère* (veal sweetbreads in mushroom cream sauce; €22).

L'AVE MARIA Map p148 — Fusion €€
☎ 01 47 00 61 73; 1 rue Jacquard, 11e; dishes €15-17; ◷ dinner to midnight daily; Ⓜ Parmentier
This colourful canteen combines the flavours of the southern hemisphere and creates hearty, hybrid and harmonious dishes. You might be treated to West African *mafé de poulet fermier* (farm chicken simmered in peanut sauce), the Amazonian fish and chips, the 'Voyage to Madras' vegetarian curry or the Thai chicken satay. The music livens up towards midnight and goes on to 1 or 2am.

SOYA CANTINE BIO
Map p148 — Vegetarian €€
☎ 01 48 06 33 02; www.soya75.fr; 20 rue de la Pierre Levée, 11e; starters €5-8.50, mains €13.50-17, menu €15 (lunch only); ◷ lunch daily, dinner to 11pm Tue-Sat; Ⓜ Goncourt
Housed in a former *atelier* (workshop) in what was until recently a very working-class district, Soya is a full-on vegetarian eatery serving dishes (many based around tofu and its variations) that are 95% organic. The décor is a bit brutal with its bare cement and metal columns but we love the glass floor that floods the basement area with light. Brunch (€22.50) is available till 3.30pm at the weekend.

AU TROU NORMAND Map p148 — French €€
☎ 01 48 05 80 23; 9 rue Jean-Pierre Timbaud, 11e; starters €6.50-12.10, mains €12.50-18, 2-/3-course menus €13.50/15.50 (lunch only); ◷ lunch & dinner to 11.30pm Sun-Thu, to midnight Fri & Sat; Ⓜ Oberkampf
The 'Norman Hole' remains something of a budget *cafétéria* in the trendy 11e arrondissement. The dishes served are simple and portions fairly generous. There are dozens of starters to choose from; main courses include *confit de canard* (duck confit; €15.50), *brandade de morue* (cod puréed with potatoes; €14) and various cuts of beef (tournedos, steak tartare etc) served with chips made on the premises.

GEORGET (ROBERT ET LOUISE)
Map p152 — French €€
☎ 01 42 78 55 89; 64 rue Vieille du Temple, 3e; starters €5.20-15.80, mains €11.40-18, menu €12 (lunch only); ◷ lunch Wed-Sun, dinner to 11pm daily; Ⓜ St-Sébastien–Froissart
This 'country inn', complete with its red gingham curtains, offers delightful, simple and inexpensive French food, including *côte de bœuf* (side of beef; €40), which is cooked on an open fire and prepared by the original owners' daughter, Georget, and her husband. If you arrive early, choose to sit at the farmhouse table, right next to the fireplace. It's a jolly, truly Rabelaisian evening. The *plat du jour* is a snip at €12.

CAFÉ HUGO Map p148 — French, Café €€
☎ 01 42 72 64 04; 22 place des Vosges, 4e; starters €6.10-6.90, mains €10.70-13.30; ◷ 8am-2am; Ⓜ Chemin Vert
Named after the 19th-century novelist whose home (now a museum, p146) was a mere 200m south on place des Vosges is our favourite affordable eatery on Paris' most beautiful square. The *plat du jour* with a glass of wine is but €12.50 and brunch is €16.20. For this location those are bargain-basement prices. A bonus is the warm and friendly welcome.

KRUNG THEP
Map p148 — Thai €€
☎ 01 43 66 83 74; 93 rue Julien Lacroix, 20e; starters €7-10, mains €8-20; ◷ lunch Sat & Sun, dinner to 11pm; Ⓜ Pyrénées
Krung Thep, which means 'Bangkok' in Thai, is a small – some might say cramped – and kitsch place with all our favourite dishes (and then some – there are dozens and dozens of dishes on the menu): green curries, *tom kha goong* (spicy soup with prawns; €20), fish steamed in banana leaves and *som dom* (spicy shredded green papaya; €8). There is also a generous number of vegetarian dishes.

REUAN THAI Map p148 — Thai €€
☎ 01 43 55 15 82; 36 rue de l'Orillon, 11e; starters €6-16, mains €9-18; ◷ lunch & dinner to 10.30pm daily; Ⓜ Belleville
This fragrant place offers some of the most authentic Thai food in Paris and has all your favourite Thai dishes. About half a dozen of the choices are vegetarian. Décor is on the kitsch side, but we weren't here for the

figurines and the bolsters piled up almost to the ceiling. The lunch-time buffet (€9.50) is good value.

LA PERLA Map p152
Mexican €€

☎ 01 42 77 59 40; www.cafepacifico-laperla. com; 26 rue François Miron, 4e; starters €6.10-9.10, mains €8.50-10.70, menu €9.90 (lunch only); ⊗ lunch & dinner to midnight daily; Ⓜ St-Paul or Hôtel de Ville

A cousin of the long-established Cafe Pacifico in both London and Sydney, this Californian-style Mexican bar and restaurant has excellent guacamole (€7.20), nachos (from €6.30) and quesadillas (€6.30 to €7.80), the 'Pearl' is best known as the 'kingdom of tequila', with some 60 varieties on the shelf. Knock it back neat with salt and lemon or disguised in a margarita (€9.40 to €11). The bar is open from noon to 2am daily, with happy hour from 5pm to 8pm.

NEW NIOULLAVILLE
Map p148
Asian €€

☎ 01 40 21 96 18; www.nioullaville.com, in French; 32-34 rue de l'Orillon, 11e; starters €6-10.80, mains €7.50-16.50, menus €7-14; ⊗ lunch & dinner to 1am daily; Ⓜ Belleville or Goncourt

This cavernous, 400-seat place with 500 menu entries tries to please all of the people all of the time. As a result the food is a bit of a mishmash – dim sum sits next to beef satay, as do scallops with black bean alongside Singapore noodles, though whether they do so comfortably is another matter. Order carefully and you should get some authenticity. Rice and noodle dishes are between €6.50 and €9.

CHEZ MARIANNE
Map p152
Jewish €

☎ 01 42 72 18 86; 2 rue des Hospitalières St-Gervais, 4e; dishes €4.60-21; ⊗ noon-midnight; Ⓜ St-Paul

This is a Sephardic alternative to the Ashkenazi fare usually available at Pletzl eateries. Platters containing four to 10 different meze (such as falafel, hummus, purées of aubergine and chickpeas) cost from €12 to €26. The takeaway window sells falafel in pita for €5 and there's also a bakery attached. Chez Marianne's set menus include a number of vegetarian options but note that food served here is not Beth Din kosher.

BREIZH CAFÉ
Map p152
French, Breton €

☎ 01 42 72 13 77; www.breizhcafe.com; 109 rue Vieille du Temple, 4e; crêpes & galettes €3.80-10.50; ⊗ lunch & dinner to 11pm Wed-Sun; Ⓜ St-Sébastien Froissart

It may use a minority language in its name (breizh is 'Breton' in Breton), but we doubt you'll hear much of that Celtic tongue spoken here. Concentrate instead on the sound of Cancale oysters being sucked, crêpes of organic flour prepared on a grill autrement (in a different way) and any of the 20 types of cider on offer being uncorked. This is definitely a cut-above crêperie.

ASIANWOK Map p148
Asian €

☎ 01 43 57 63 24; 63 rue Oberkampf, 11e; starters €3.50-6.50, mains €7.50-11, 2-/3-course menus €13.90/15.90; ⊗ lunch & dinner to 10pm Mon-Sat; Ⓜ Parmentier

We can't get enough of the wonderful stir-fries, big salads and ample platters and soup bowls (€11) served at this pan-Asian eatery housed in a vintage bar-café along trendy rue Oberkampf. The welcome from the young Asian staff is always warm and the two-course formule (available any time) a snip at €13.90.

LE POROKHANE
Map p148
African, Senegalese €

☎ 01 40 21 86 74; www.leporokhane.com, in French; 3 rue Moret, 11e; 2-course menu €15; ⊗ dinner to 2am; Ⓜ Ménilmontant or Parmentier

A large dining room in hues of ochre and terracotta, this cheapie is a popular meeting place for Senegalese artists. The clientele has un peu tendance show-biz, we're told – and live kora (a traditional string instrument) music is not unusual at the weekend. Try the tiéboudienne, yassa or mafé.

TAEKO Map p148
Japanese €

☎ 01 48 04 34 59; 39 rue de Bretagne, 3e; menus €9.20-12.50; ⊗ 9am-6pm Tue-Sat, to 3pm Sun; Ⓜ Marais

Just about the last thing you would expect to find in the Marché des Enfants Rouges (p222), one of the oldest markets in Paris, is this homely Japanese eatery. There's sushi and sashimi and salmon tartar to start and delightful warm dishes like codfish balls and chicken cooked with soy sauce. Sit at the communal table near the entrance – if there's room! Otherwise buy a takeaway bento (lunchbox; €11.90)

TAI YIEN Map p148   Chinese €

☎ 01 42 41 44 16; 5 rue de Belleville, 19e; starters €3.80-6.90, mains €7.50-10.70; ☼ lunch & dinner to midnight; Ⓜ Belleville

This is usually where we head when we are looking for a fix of rice or noodles, especially late in the evening. It's a Hong Kong–style 'steam restaurant' and the real McCoy: it's hard to imagine better *char siu* (barbecued pork) outside Chinatown.

BREAKFAST IN AMERICA

Map p152   American, Deli €

☎ 01 42 72 40 21; www.breakfast-in-america.com; 4 rue Malher, 4e; meals €6.95-11.50; ☼ 8.30am-11.30pm daily; Ⓜ St-Paul

This American-style diner, complete with red banquettes and Formica surfaces, is as authentic as you'll find outside the US of A. Breakfast, served all day and with free coffee refills, starts at just under €7, and there are generous burgers, chicken wings and fish and chips (€8.50 to €11.50). There's also a Latin Quarter branch (Map p100; ☎ 01 43 54 50 28; 17 rue des Écoles, 5e; Ⓜ Cardinal Lemoine) that opens the same hours.

DONG HUONG Map p148   Vietnamese €

☎ 01 43 57 42 81; 14 rue Louis Bonnet; dishes €6.50-9.50; ☼ lunch & dinner to 10.30pm Wed-Mon; Ⓜ Belleville

Despite a name that sounds like a Spanish Lothario, this no-frills Vietnamese noodle-shop-cum-restaurant serves up great bowls of *pho* to rooms full of appreciative regulars. The fact that the regulars are all Asian (and mainly Vietnamese) and the food comes out so fast is a testament to its authenticity and freshness.

GRAND APPÉTIT Map p148   Vegetarian €

☎ 01 40 27 04 95; 9 rue de la Cerisaie, 4e; soups €3.40-4.40, dishes €5.40-12.30; ☼ lunch Mon-Fri, dinner to 9pm Mon-Thu; Ⓜ Bastille or Sully Morland

Set back from Bastille in a small, quiet street, this place offers light fare such as miso soup and cereals plus strength-building *bols garnis* (bowls of rice and mixed vegetables) and *assiettes* (platters) for those with a *grand appétit* (big appetite). The menu features delicious, filling dishes

served with 100% organic cereals, raw and cooked vegetables and seaweed. Next door there's an excellent organic and macrobiotic grocery store (☼ 9.30am-noon & 4-7pm Mon-Sat).

MARCHE OU CRÊPE

Map p148   French, Breton €

☎ 01 43 57 04 78; www.marcheoucrêpe.com; 88 rue Oberkampf, 11e; crêpes & galettes €2.20-7.80; ☼ 6pm-midnight Tue-Thu, 6pm-2am Fri & Sat, 5pm-midnight Sun; Ⓜ Parmentier

A favourite new place for both savoury galettes and sweet crêpes, this little outlet just south of the bars and clubs along rue Jean-Pierre Timbaud has the added advantage of staying open late, particularly at the weekend. They also have homemade soups and salads.

L'AS DE FELAFEL Map p152   Jewish, Kosher €

☎ 01 48 87 63 60; 34 rue des Rosiers, 4e; dishes €5-7; ☼ noon-midnight Sun-Thu, to 5pm Fri; Ⓜ St-Paul

This has always been our favourite place for those deep-fried balls of chickpeas and herbs (€5) and serves turkey and lamb shwarma sandwiches (€7) too. It's always packed, particularly at weekday lunch, so avoid that time if possible.

POZZETTO

Map p152   Ice Cream €

☎ 01 42 77 08 64; www.pozzetto.biz; 39 rue du Roi de Sicile, 4e; ice creams €3.50-8; ☼ 11.30-9pm Mon-Thu, to 11.30pm Fri-Sun; Ⓜ St-Paul

Urban myth tells us that this gelato maker opened up when a group of friends from northern Italy couldn't find their favourite ice cream here in Paris so they imported the ingredients to create it from scratch. Flavours – spatula'd, not scooped – include *gianduia torinese* (hazelnut chocolate from Turin) and *zabaione*, made from egg yolks, sugar and sweet Marsala wine, along with the more usual peach, pistachio and poire William.

ALSO RECOMMENDED

Happy Nouilles (Map p148; ☎ 01 44 59 31 22; 95 rue Beaubourg, 3e; dishes €5.50-10.50; ☼ lunch daily, dinner to 11.30pm Wed-Mon; Ⓜ Arts et Métiers) *Nouilles* means noodles and this is the place to taste the real Chinese McCoy hand-pulled for your pleasure in the window.

La Briciola (Map p148; ☎ 01 42 77 34 10; 64 rue Charlot, 3e; starters & salads €8-15, pizzas €9.50-19; ☼ lunch &

dinner to 11pm Mon-Sat; **M** Oberkampf) Excellent pizzas, salads and wine at this friendly hole-in-the-wall Italian eatery in the northern Marais.

Ma Cantine (Map p148; ☎ 01 42 74 90 00; 5th fl, BHV, 14 rue du Temple, 4e; menus €11-15.60; ⏱ 11.15am-6pm Mon, Tue, Thu-Sat, to 8.30pm Wed; **M** Hôtel de Ville) Should you get peckish while shopping at the BHV department store, this top-floor restaurants offers three good-value *menus* and views to die for.

Merguez Factory (Map p148; ☎ 01 48 06 37 34; 123 rue Oberkampf, 11e; dishes €5.50-6.50, menus €8-10; ⏱ lunch daily, dinner to midnight Mon-Thu, to 2am Fri & Sat; **M** Ménilmontant) If you're keen to try the spicy red North African sausage – with chips or in a sandwich – this is the place to head to.

SELF-CATERING

In the Marais, there are a number of food shops and Asian delicatessens on the odd-numbered side of *rue St-Antoine*, 4e (Map p152; **M** St-Paul), as well as several supermarkets, including **Monoprix** (Map p152; basement, 71 rue St-Antoine, 4e; ⏱ 9am-10pm daily; **M** St-Paul), **Franprix Marais** (Map p152; 135 rue St-Antoine, 4e; ⏱ 9am-10pm Mon-Sat; **M** St-Paul) and **Supermarché G20 Bastille** (Map p152; 115 rue St-Antoine, 4e; ⏱ 9am-8.30pm Mon-Sat; **M** St-Paul).

To the west you'll find **Ed l'Épicier** (Map p148; 80 rue de Rivoli, 4e; 9am-8pm Mon-Sat; **M** Hôtel de Ville) and, almost side by side, **Franprix** (Map p72; 87 rue de la Verrerie, 4e; ⏱ 9am-10pm daily; **M** Hôtel de Ville) and **Supermarché G20** (Map p76; 81-83 rue de la Verrerie, 4e; ⏱ 8.30am-9pm Mon-Sat; **M** Hôtel de Ville).

To the north and over in Ménilmontant, there's the **Franprix Bretagne branch** (Map p148; 49 rue de Bretagne, 3e; ⏱ 2-10pm Mon, 8.30am-10pm Tue-Sat, 9am-2.30pm Sun; **M** Arts et Métiers), **Franprix Jean-Pierre Timbaud branch** (Map p148; 23 rue Jean-Pierre Timbaud, 11e; ⏱ 8.30am-10pm Mon-Sat, 9am-6pm Sun; **M** Oberkampf) and **Franprix Jules Ferry branch** (Map p148; 28 blvd Jules Ferry, 11e; ⏱ 8.30am-9pm Tue-Sun; **M** République or Goncourt). **Marché Belleville** (p222) is one of the most exotic markets in Paris.

BASTILLE & GARE DE LYON

Bastille is another area chock-a-block with restaurants, some of which have added a star or two to their epaulettes in recent years. Narrow rue de Lappe and rue de la Roquette (11e), just east of place de la Bastille, may not be as hip as they were a dozen years ago, but they remain popular streets for nightlife and attract a young, alternative crowd.

The waterfront southwest of Gare de Lyon has got a new lease on life in recent years. The development of the old wine warehouses in Bercy Village (p156) attract winers and diners till the wee hours. There are loads of decent restaurants on the roads fanning out from huge place de la Nation.

L'OULETTE Map p158   French, Southwest €€€
☎ 01 40 02 02 12; www.l-oulette.com; 15 place Lachambeaudie, 12e; starters €16-32, mains €26-41, 2-/3-course menus €38/42, with wine €44/48; ⏱ lunch & dinner to 10.15pm Mon-Fri; **M** Cour St-Émilion
Big brother (or is that sister?) to the Bistrot de l'Oulette (p252) in the Marais, this is a lovely (and pricey) restaurant with a terrace overlooking a pretty church in a rather dreary neighbourhood. Owner-chef Marcel Baudis' *menu du saison* (seasonal menu; €38) might include *veloute de potimarron et moules* (cream of pumpkin soup with mussels) and *cuisses de canettes au genièvre* (duckling thighs with juniper).

LE TRAIN BLEU Map p158   French, Brasserie €€€
☎ 01 43 43 09 06; www.le-train-bleu.com; 1st fl, Gare de Lyon, 26 place Louis Armand, 12e; starters €18-28, mains €22-38, menus €52 (lunch only), €64 & €97; ⏱ 7.30am-11pm Mon-Sat, 9am-11pm Sun; **M** Gare de Lyon
We can state in all confidence that you've never – ever – seen a railway station restaurant as sumptuous as this heritage-listed belle époque showpiece that has been the backdrop of a fair few films in the past. This is the top-end spot to dine on such fare as foie gras with a confiture of red onions, grapes and hazelnuts, Charolles beef steak tartare and chips and the house-made *baba au rhum*. Sunday brunch is from 11.30am to 2.30pm, just enough time before boarding that train to the Côte d'Azur.

SARDEGNA A TAVOLA
Map p158   Italian, Sardinian €€€
☎ 01 44 75 03 28; 1 rue de Cotte, 12e; starters & pasta €10-26, mains €24-38; ⏱ lunch Tue-Sat, dinner to 11pm Mon-Sat; **M** Ledru–Rollin
'Sardinia at the Table' claims it will introduce you to '*les saveurs, les couleurs et les odeurs de la Méditerranée*' (the flavours, colours and fragrances of the Mediterranean) and you barely have to walk though the door for the last two. But stick around

GUESS WHO'S COMING TO DINNER?

Jim Haynes' (p273) may have been the first, but his is hardly the only supper club in Paris. As in so many other world-class cities – London and Hong Kong (where they're called speakeasies) spring to mind – they're popping up like toadstools after rain all over the French capital. But where *dîner chez Jim* is less about the food and more about socialising and perhaps even pulling, the newer clubs focus on multicourse gastronomic meals (eg Hidden Kitchen, see below) and visiting the 'in' *adresse* (restaurant) of the moment with a local foodie (eg Paris Supper Club). You'll get an excellent meal and they're still great places for meeting people. The following are the names and locations of some of the most popular ones. Expect to pay from €80 per person and be sure to book well in advance. If you don't get a spot bear in mind that many post on Twitter if they have a cancellation or last-minute place available.

Chez Nous, Chez Vous (Map p168; ☎ 01 45 30 58 92; www. cheznouschezvous.com; 116bis rue St-Charles, 15e; Ⓜ Charles Michels)

Hidden Kitchen (Map p72; www.hkmenus.com; 28 rue de Richelieu, 1er; Ⓜ Palais Royal–Musée du Louvre)

Paris Soirees (☎ 06 43 79 35 15; www.parissoirees.com) Twice-weekly Paris events hosted on the Île de la Cité by Patricia Laplante-Collins.

Paris Supper Club (www.thepar
iskitchen.com/paris-supper-club) Run by the excellent local dining blog the Paris Kitchen.

Talk Time (☎ 01 43 25 86 55, 06 20 87 76 69; www.meetup.com/TalkTime) Michael Muszlak's Saturday night food-and-bilingual-chat in the Latin Quarter, organised through the New York based group Meetup (www.meetup.com).

for the flavours and you won't be disappointed. Try the *poêlon* (pot) of mixed seafood cooked with parsley, tomatoes and garlic and the distinctly Sardinian spaghetti with *bottarga* (cured mullet roe) cooked with oil, garlic, parsley and red-pepper flakes.

LA GAZZETTA Map p158 French €€€
☎ 01 43 47 47 05; www.lagazzetta.fr; 29 rue de Cotte, 12e; menus €16 (lunch only), €38 & €50; Ⓨ lunch Tue-Sat, dinner to 11pm Mon-Sat; Ⓜ Ledru–Rollin
This *néo-brasserie* has gained a substantial (and international) following under the tutelage of Swedish chef Peter Nilsson who is as comfortable producing dishes like scallops with cress and milk-fed lamb confit and ice Bleu d'Auvergne cheese as he is mini anchovy pizzas. The lunchtime menu is excellent and the welcome especially warm. Go to dinner hungry; the fixed-price menus count five and seven courses.

L'ÉCAILLER DU BISTROT
Map p158 French, Seafood €€€
☎ 01 43 72 76 77; 22 rue Paul Bert, 11e; starters €10-25, mains €22-36; Ⓨ lunch & dinner to 11.30pm Tue-Sat; Ⓜ Faidherbe Chaligny
Oyster lovers should make a beeline for the 'Bistro Shucker', a neighbourhood resto owned by the daughter of a famous Breton oyster culturist, which serves up to a dozen

varieties of fresh bivalves, freshly shucked and accompanied by a little lemon juice. Other delights are platters of seafood, a half-dozen *oursins* (sea urchins), minute-cooked tuna steak with sesame oil and the extravagant lobster *menu* (€55).

UNICO Map p158 Argentian €€€
☎ 01 43 67 68 08; www.resto-unico.com, in French; 15 rue Paul Bert, 11e; starters €8-18, mains €23-35, menu €17 (lunch only); Ⓨ lunch & dinner to 11pm Mon-Sat; Ⓜ Faidherbe Chaligny
This very trendy, very orange Argentine *parillada* (steakhouse) has taken over an old butcher and put a modern (well, sort of 1970s, but it works) spin on it. Unico is all about meat – especially the barbecued *entrecôte* (rib steak) with chunky *frites* (chips); look at the 'map' of a steer provided and choose your 'territory'. Good wine selection.

LES AMIS DE MESSINA
Map p158 Italian, Sicilian €€€
☎ 01 43 67 96 01; www.lesamisdesmessina.com; 204 rue du Faubourg St-Antoine, 12e; starters €8.10-17, mains €19.20-25; Ⓨ lunch Mon-Fri, dinner to 11.30pm Mon-Sat; Ⓜ Faidherbe–Chaligny
The décor of this little neighbourhood trattoria is stylish, with clean lines, an open kitchen and the inevitable Italian football pennant. For starters, try the *tortino di melanzane* e zucchine (eggplant and courgette casserole) or share a mixed antipasto

(€19.80). For mains, the *escalope farcie aux oignons, jambon et fromage* (veal escalope stuffed with onions, ham and cheese; €19.80) is a huge hit, or go for any of the exquisite Sicilian pastas (€13.50 to €17).

AU VIEUX CHÊNE Map p158 French €€
☎ 01 43 71 67 69; 7 rue du Dahomey, 11e; starters €10-16, mains €21-24, menus €13 (lunch only), €28 & €33; ☾ lunch & dinner to 10.30pm Mon-Fri; Ⓜ Faidherbe–Chaligny

Along a quiet side street in a neighbourhood full of traditional woodworking studios, 'At the Old Oak' bistro offers an excellent seasonal menu and some well-chosen wines. The surrounds are fabulous and very retro. Three of the cast-iron columns holding the place up are registered monuments.

ATHANOR Map p158 Romanian €€
☎ 01 43 43 49 15; 4 rue Crozatier, 12e; starters €9-12, mains €19-25, menus €13 (lunch only) & €22; ☾ lunch & dinner to 11pm Tue-Sat; Ⓜ Reuilly– Diderot

It's not easy to get a fix of Romanian cuisine here, but Athanor can provide. The décor (puppets, red curtains, old carpets) is theatrical in the extreme; grab a vodka and tune in to the folk music playing. Try the blinis with *tarama* (fish-roe dip) and herrings in cream. Seasoned soup of freshwater river fish or potted pike perch are specialities, though you must not miss the *sarmale* (stuffed cabbage or grape leaves; €19), the national dish.

CHEZ RAMULAUD Map p158 French €€
☎ 01 43 72 23 29; 269 rue du Faubourg St-Antoine, 11e; starters €9, mains €19, menus €14-16 (lunch only) & €29; ☾ lunch Mon-Fri, dinner to 11pm Mon-Sat; Ⓜ Faidherbe–Chaligny

With its peaceful, retro atmosphere, this enormous establishment is reminiscent of an established provincial restaurant. The blackboard offerings are not overly adventurous but are comforting and substantial – daily soups, terrine, *œufs cocotte aux champignons de saison* (coddled eggs with seasonal mushrooms). For mains, the fish dishes are usually winners. The *plat du jour* is good value at €10.

L'ÉBAUCHOIR Map p158 French €€
☎ 01 43 42 49 31; 45 rue de Cîteaux, 12e; starters €8-14, mains €18-24, menus €12 & €13 (lunch only), €22.50 & €25; ☾ lunch Tue-Sat, dinner to 11pm Mon-Sat; Ⓜ Faidherbe–Chaligny

This convivial one-time workers' eatery attracts a loyal clientele who mix with an 'outside' crowd who have discovered it. The usual menu of bistro food is well prepared and such dishes as marinated herrings, *crème de lentilles au Beaufort* (creamed lentils with Beaufort cheese) and *foie de veau au miel* (veal liver with honey sauce) keep customers coming back.

LA MUSE VIN Map p158 French, Wine €€
☎ 01 40 09 93 05; 101 rue de Charonne; starters €8, mains €18, menus €9 & with wine €15.50 (lunch only), €25 & €30; ☾ lunch Mon-Fri, dinner to 11pm Mon-Sat; Ⓜ Charonne

Primarily a wine bar and bottle shop, the very pink (or is that Rosé?) 'Wine Muse' also does food both day (*plat du jour* €9) and night and its offerings go well beyond plates of cold meats and cheese. In fact, the evening menu changes every three weeks. It takes its 150 wines very seriously, though, so keep that foremost in your mind.

COMME COCHONS Map p158 French €€
☎ 01 43 42 43 36; 135 rue de Charenton, 12e; starters €8, mains €18, 2 /3-course menus €23/27; ☾ lunch & dinner to 11pm; Ⓜ Gare de Lyon

You may not be attracted by the name but the excellent *cuisine du terroir* (country cooking) and the sunny terrace at 'Like Pigs' will undoubtedly change your mind. This bistro is like a page out of the past – only the contemporary paintings on the wall by local artists will keep you in the present. Among the specialities are potted *pleurotte* mushrooms with foie gras and *potée limousine côte de cochon* (pork and vegetable 'stew' cooked in a clay pot). There's live jazz some nights.

KHUN AKORN Map p158 Thai €€
☎ 01 43 56 20 03; 8 av de Taillebourg, 11e; starters €10-14, mains €16; ☾ lunch & dinner to 11pm Tue-Sun; Ⓜ Nation

This long-established Thai eatery near place de la Nation is an oasis of sophisticated good taste – in every sense. Among the traditional dishes, the *tom yum,* and the beef and chicken satays with scrumptious peanut sauce are outstanding. More innovative offerings include *fruits de mer grillés sauce barbecue maison* (grilled seafood with barbecue sauce) and the *larmes du tigre* ('tears of the tiger'; grilled fillet of beef marinated in honey and herbs at €17). In fine weather, try the upstairs terrace.

LE SQUARE TROUSSEAU
Map p158   French €€

☎ 01 43 43 06 00; www.squaretrousseau.com; 1 rue Antoine Vollon, 12e; starters €8-14, mains €17-23; ☽ lunch & dinner to midnight; Ⓜ Ledru-Rollin
This vintage (c 1900) bistro with etched glass, zinc bar and polished wood panelling is comfortable rather than trendy and attracts a jolly, mixed clientele. Most people come to enjoy the lovely terrace overlooking a small park. The paper table covering and crayons lark has been done to death everywhere – but it's still fun.

MANSOURIA
Map p158   North African, Moroccan €€

☎ 01 43 71 00 16; www.fatemahalreceptions.com, in French; 11 rue Faidherbe, 11e; starters €8-17, mains €17-25, menus €28 & €36; ☽ lunch Wed-Sat, dinner to 11pm Mon-Sat; Ⓜ Faidherbe–Chaligny
This is an especially attractive Moroccan restaurant that serves excellent milk-fed steamed lamb, if not the best *kascsou* (couscous) and *touagin* (tajine) in town. Someone in your group should definitely order the *mourouzia* (€19), lamb simmered in a complex combination of some 27 spices and served with a sauce of honey, raisins and almonds.

LES GRANDES MARCHES
Map p158   French, Brasserie €€

☎ 01 43 43 90 32; 6 place de la Bastille, 12e; starters €8-17.50, mains €16-39, 3-course menu €20 (lunch only); ☽ noon-midnight daily; Ⓜ Bastille
This futuristic modern brasserie next to the 'Great Steps' of the Opéra Bastille was designed by Elisabeth and Christian Portzamparc for the Flo group. The result has been less than impressive both in décor and food served but it has a convenient (and much-coveted) location and good value at lunch when the *plat du jour* is €13.50. The bar stays open till 2am daily.

BISTROT PAUL BERT
Map p158   French, Bistro €€

☎ 01 43 72 24 01; 18 rue Paul Bert, 11e; menus €16.50 (lunch only) & €34; ☽ lunch & dinner to 11pm Tue-Sat; Ⓜ Faidherbe–Chaligny
This enormous traditional bistro on one of our favourite dining streets may look like it's been here since time immemorial but

top picks

VEGETARIAN RESTAURANTS

- Soya Cantine Bio (p258) Vegetarian food that's 95% organic served in a former workshop.
- Le Potager du Marais (p255) Arguably the finest (and cosiest) vegetarian restaurant in Paris.
- Saveurs Végét'halles (p225) Totally vegan and 'dry' restaurant in the heart of the Marais.
- Grand Apétit (p264) For those with a 'big appetite' this place serves generous platters and bowls of veggies.
- Au Grain de Folie (p248) Uninspired by the tourist fare in Montmartre? Try this tiny macrobiotic eatery.
- Super Nature (p264) OK, not everything is veggie in this funky organic café – but it sure is delicious.
- Krishna Bhavan (p252) Get your curry fix at this authentic Indian vegetarian canteen.
- Bob's Juice Bar (p252) From smoothies and hummus sandwiches to vegan muffins.
- Gentle Gourmet (p338) A vegan B&B that does dinner too.
- Le Puits de Légumes (p230) Dining here is like dining at home; wash it down with bio wine or freshly squeezed veggie juice.
- Bioart (p268) Organic is the green thrust of this contemporary Seine-side space near the National Library.

it opened only in 1997. Still, it's *steak-frites* and *Paris-Brest* (ring-shaped cake filled with butter cream and topped with flaked almonds) have punters coming back for more. Be sure to book.

LE MOUTON NOIR Map p158   French, Bistro €€
☎ 01 48 07 05 45; www.lemoutonnoir.fr; 65 rue de Charonne, 11e; starters/mains/desserts €8/16/8, 3-course menu €29; ☽ dinner to 10.30pm Tue-Sat, noon-3pm Sat & Sun; Ⓜ Charonne
This tiny place with a mere two-dozen covers west of Bastille is a neighbourhood secret, which we've now gone and blown. The idea here is to use unusual product in traditional French cooking – they call it 'cuisine hippy groove' for some inexplicable reason – in a warm and welcoming atmosphere and they've succeeded on both accounts; try the crab bisque with red curry and lentils and the sea bass with La Vache qui Rit cheese and eggplant with thyme. Brunch (€19) is a weekend tradition.

LES DOMAINES QUI MONTENT

Map p158   French, Wine €€

☎ 01 43 56 89 15; www.lesdomainesquimontent.
com, in French; 136 blvd Voltaire, 11e; menus
€14.50 & €24.50; ✇ lunch Mon-Sat daily;
Ⓜ Voltaire

What better way to enjoy wine with a meal
than at a wine merchant's establishment
amid shelves and cartons of bottles? The
optimistically named 'Estates on the Rise'
serves a *table d'hôtes* – a set meal with little
or no choice – at lunchtime of a cheese
and charcuterie or a *plat du jour* or a more
ambitious five-course *menu*. These can
be paired expertly with any of the wine
around you and expert advice is included
in the price!

LE SOUK Map p158   North African €€

☎ 01 49 29 05 08; www.lesoukfr.com, in French;
1 rue Keller, 11e; starters €7-15, mains €15-20,
menus €19.50 & €26.50; ✇ lunch & dinner to
11.30pm Tue-Sat; Ⓜ Ledru-Rollin

We like coming here almost as much for
the décor as the food – from the clay pots
overflowing with spices on the outside to
the exuberant (but never kitsch) Moroccan
interior. And the food? As authentic as the
decoration, notably the duck *tajine*, the
pigeon pastilla and vegetarian couscous. Be
warned: mains are enormous, so this might
have to be a one-dish meal.

CHEZ PAUL Map p158   French, Bistro €€

☎ 01 47 00 34 57; www.chezpaul.com, in French;
13 rue de Charonne, 11e; starters €5.60-17, mains
€15-23; ✇ lunch & dinner to 12.30am daily;
Ⓜ Ledru-Rollin

When they put up a 'French restaurant' film
set in Hollywood, this ever-expanding bistro is what it must look like. An extremely
popular bistro, it has traditional French
main courses handwritten on a yellowing
menu and brusque service – Paris in true
form! Stick with the simplest of dishes – the
steak or foie gras with lentils – and make
sure you've booked ahead.

À LA RENAISSANCE

Map p158   French, Café €€

☎ 01 43 79 83 09; 87 rue de la Roquette, 11e;
starters €8.50-14.50, mains €13-21, menus €22
(lunch only) & €30; ✇ lunch & dinner to 11.30pm
daily; Ⓜ Voltaire

This large, café-like *bistro de quartier* has a
huge bar (open 8am or 9am to 2am) with

large plate-glass windows and terrace
looking onto the street. Food is reliable if
unadventurous – herring fillets on a bed
of warm potatoes, mackerel *rillettes*, steak
tartare and that all-time favourite, *œufs à
la coq aux tartines* (soft-boiled eggs with
toast). Sunday brunch is €22.

LE VIADUC CAFÉ

Map p158   International, Café €€

☎ 01 44 74 70 70; 43 av Daumesnil, 12e; starters
€7.50-16, mains €14-20, menu €15.50 (lunch only)
& €25.50; ✇ 9am-2am; Ⓜ Gare de Lyon

This New York–style café-bar with a terrace in one of the glassed-in arches of the
Viaduc des Arts (p157) is an excellent spot to
while away the early hours (though food
is served noon to 11pm daily) and enjoy
brunch (€22) from noon to 4pm on Sundays. The terrace is a great spot for people
watching.

PARIS MAIN D'OR

Map p158   French, Corsican €€

☎ 01 44 68 04 68; 133 rue du Faubourg St-Antoine,
11e; starters €7.50-15, mains €14-20, menu €13;
✇ lunch & dinner to 11pm Mon-Sat;
Ⓜ Ledru-Rollin

The unprepossessing, cafélike 'Paris Golden
Hand' serves authentic Corsican dishes to
an appreciative audience, many of them
coppers (traditionally the preferred form
of employment among Corsicans in the
capital). *Sturza preti* (spinach and fine *brocciu* cheese; €9) and traditional omelette
with *brocciu* and *jambon sec* (dried ham,
matured for two years) are some of the appetisers on the menu. For mains, favourites
include the *tian d'agneau aux olives* (lamb
ragout with olives; €18) and the *caprettu
arrustini* (roast kid; €21). Pasta dishes come
in at about €11, the *plat du jour* is €9.50.

LES GALOPINS Map p158   French, Bistro €€

☎ 01 47 00 45 35; www.lesgalopins.fr; 24 rue
des Taillandiers, 11e; starters €6.50-10.50, mains
€14.50-20, menus €14.50 & €17.50 (lunch only);
✇ lunch Mon-Fri, dinner to 11pm Mon-Thu, to
11.30pm Fri & Sat; Ⓜ Bastille or Voltaire

The décor of this cute neighbourhood bistro is simple, the meals are straightforward
and in the best tradition of French cuisine,
with such offerings as *raviolis de pétoncles*
(queen scallops ravioli), *médaillons de lotte
au gingembre* (monkfish medallions with
ginger) and *côte de veau aux pleurotes* (veal
chop with mild white mushrooms). It's not

a secret find, so it can feel like a bit of a factory during lunch or on a weekend night.

SWANN ET VINCENT

Map p158   Italian €€

☎ 01 43 43 49 40; 7 rue St-Nicolas, 12e; starters €6-14, mains €13.50-18, menu €15.90 (lunch only); ☻ lunch & dinner to 11.45pm; Ⓜ Ledru-Rollin

Unpretentious French staff can help you select from the huge blackboard, where at least two of the starters, pastas and main dishes change every day. Go slow on the complimentary basket of olive-and-sweet-herb bread, though; you need to leave room for the tiramisu (€6.50). And, if you must know, Swann and Vincent, whose larger-than-life portraits as children face you through the front window opposite at No 14, are the sons of the owner.

BISTROT LES SANS CULOTTES

Map p158   French, Bistro €€

☎ 01 48 05 42 92; www.lessansculottesfr.com, in French; 27 rue de Lappe, 11e; starters €6-13, mains €13-18, menus €18 & €23; ☻ lunch & dinner to 11pm Tue-Sun; Ⓜ Bastille

You wouldn't cross Paris to eat at Sans Culottes – the place takes its name from the working-class 'men without breeches' who fought in the French Revolution – but in a neighbourhood that has become somewhat trendy it's a comforting reminder of the past. The interior, with frosted glass, huge zinc bar, ornate ceilings and wooden floors, positively glows in the evening. The range of food is uneven, though relatively low-priced; service is friendly and attentive.

WALY FAY

Map p158   African, Creole €€

☎ 01 40 24 17 79; 6 rue Godefroy Cavaignac, 11e; starters €6-8, mains €10-15, menu €25; ☻ dinner to 11.30pm daily; Ⓜ Charonne

This easygoing 'loungin' restaurant' attracts a rather hip crowd for the African food with a West Indian twist served to the sounds of soul and jazz. For starters, the *pepe* (fish soup) is deliciously smooth and highly spiced. For mains, the *tiéboudienne* (rice, fish and vegetables), Senegal's national dish, and beef *n'dole* with wild greens are recommended by the staff; you might also consider the copious *mafé* (beef simmered in peanut sauce) served with rice and *aloko* (fried plantain bananas). The distressed walls and low lighting add warmth to the surrounds. The ginger ice cream goes down a treat.

L'ENCRIER

Map p158   French, Bistro €

☎ 01 44 68 08 16; 55 rue Traversière, 12e; starters €5.50-11.50, mains €10-19, 2-/3-course menus €12/13.90 (lunch only) & €18.90-23.30; ☻ lunch Mon-Fri, dinner to 11pm Mon-Sat; Ⓜ Ledru-Rollin or Gare de Lyon

Always heaving but especially at lunch, the 'Inkwell' attracts punters with its classic salmon *assiette de foie gras* and less-common dishes like *cervelle des canuts* (a herbed cheese from Lyons). To follow, try the *bar entier grillé* (whole grilled bass) or delicate *joues de cochon aux épices* (pig's cheeks with spices). A variety of set *menus*, an open kitchen, exposed beams and a large picture window make this a winner.

AGUA LIMÓN

Map p158   Spanish €

☎ 01 43 44 92 24; www.restaurant-agualimon. com, in French; 12 rue Théophile Roussel, 12e; tapas €5-13.50; 2-/3-course menus €11.50/16 (lunch only); ☻ lunch & dinner Tue-Sat; Ⓜ Ledru Rollin

Considered by some to have the best tapas in Paris, 'Lemon Water' is an attractive bar-restaurant within easy walking distance of Bastille. Go for the *boquerones* (whitebait) in vinegar, the octopus Catalan-style and the excellent *patatas bravas*. There's a decent selection of Spanish wines, including Riojas, and a *plat du jour* at €9.50.

À LA BANANE IVOIRIENNE

Map p158   African, Côte d'Ivoire €

☎ 01 43 70 49 90; 10 rue de la Forge Royale, 11e; starters €5-7.50, mains €10-16.50, menu with wine €28; ☻ dinner to midnight Tue-Sat; Ⓜ Ledru-Rollin

West African specialities (including a generous vegetarian platter; €12) are served in a relaxed and friendly setting, with lots of West African gewgaws on display. It's been an African institution in Paris for over 20 years and is said to served the best Ivorian food in the capital. There's live African music in the cellar restaurant starting at 10pm on Fridays.

CAFÉ DE L'INDUSTRIE

Map p158   French, Café €

☎ 01 47 00 13 53; 16 & 17 rue St-Sabin, 11e; starters €4.40-8, mains €8-16, menu €10.50 (lunch only); ☻ 9am-2am daily; Ⓜ Bastille

This popular café-restaurant with neocolonial décor has two locations directly opposite one another. It's a pleasant space and the perfect spot to meet a friend instead of at one of the crowded cafés or bars in Bastille. Food is competitively priced but not always up to scratch; to avoid disappointment stick with the simple entrées or just graze off the fabulous dessert table (€4 to €6). The *plats du jours* are between €9 and €11.50.

LA PARTIE DE CAMPAGNE

Map p158   French €

☎ 01 43 40 44 11; 36 cour St-Émilion, 12e; dishes €11-14.50; ⏱ 8am-2am daily; Ⓜ Cour St-Émilion
Located in one of the old *chais* (wine warehouses) of Bercy, the 'Country Outing' serves some of the best food in the area. Business people and strollers from the Jardin de Bercy sit cheek by jowl at a large communal table set up at the back of the room, and order from a menu that includes soups, *tartines*, pies and crêpes (€4.20 to €5.50). It's also a great place for breakfast, and the inviting terrace is open in the warmer months.

CHEZ HEANG Map p158   Korean €

☎ 01 48 07 80 98; 5 rue de la Roquette, 11e; barbecue €8.50-17.50, menus €8.80 (lunch only) & €12-23.80; ⏱ lunch & dinner to midnight; Ⓜ Bastille
Also known as 'Barbecue de Seoul', this tiny place is where you cook your food on a grill in the middle of your table and eat little side dishes known as *banchan* that include the Korean staple *kimchi* (spicy-hot pickled cabbage). The *fondue maison*, a kind of spicy hotpot in which you dip and cook your food, costs €28 per person (minimum two).

PATATI PATATA Map p158   International, Café €

☎ 01 48 05 94 90; 51 rue de Lappe, 11e; dishes €5.50-6.50, menus €7.80-8.50; ⏱ lunch & dinner to midnight Mon-Sat; Ⓜ Bastille or Ledru-Rollin
If you're looking for something cheap and filling at almost any time of the day, visit this simple little caff with Formica tables that dispenses *pommes de terre au four* (baked or jacket potatoes) with toppings to the appreciative masses of Bastille.

LINA'S Map p158   Sandwich Bar €

☎ 01 43 40 42 42; www.linasparis.com, in French; 102 rue de Bercy, 12e; soups & salads €5.90-8.10, sandwiches €3.20-7.10, menus €10-12.40 ⏱ 8.30am-4.30pm Mon-Sat; Ⓜ Bercy)
This branch of a popular chain of lunch spots (some 14 outlets in central Paris) has upmarket sandwiches, salads and soups.

Another convenient outlet is the Victoires branch (Map p72; ☎ 01 42 21 16 14; 50, rue Étienne Marcel, 2e; Ⓜ Étienne Marcel).

CRÊPERIE BRETONNE FLEURIE DE L'ÉPOUSE DU MARIN

Map p158   French, Breton €

☎ 01 43 55 62 29; 67 rue de Charonne, 12e; starters €4-8.50, crêpes & galettes €2.40-8.50; ⏱ lunch Mon-Fri, dinner to 11.30pm Mon-Sat; Ⓜ Charonne
Head to the 'Sailor's Wife' if you fancy savoury buckwheat *galettes* – try the ham, cheese and egg *complète* – or a sweet crêpe and wash it down with dry *cidre de Rance* (Rance cider; €6.50 for 50cL) served in a teacup (as is traditional). The Breton paraphernalia and B&W photos will keep you occupied if there's a lull in the chatter.

ALSO RECOMMENDED

La Plancha (Map p158; ☎ 01 48 05 20 30; 34 rue Keller, 11e; tapas €9, mains €9-16; ⏱ dinner to 1.30am Tue-Sat; Ⓜ Bastille) This tiny Spanish-Basque *bodega* (note the *pelota* baskets and bullfighting photos) serves up the best tapas in the neighbourhood till the wee hours.

Nicolas (Map p158; ☎ 01 44 74 62 65; www.nicolas. com; 36 cour St-Émilion, 12e; dishes €7-12.90, menu with wine €15.80; ⏱ noon-11pm daily; Ⓜ Cour St-Émilion) Not just France's largest chain of wine shops, Nicolas also serves food – salads, quiches and more hearty *assiettes* (platters) – at its Bercy Village outlet throughout the day.

Paris Hanoi (Map p158; ☎ 01 47 00 47 59; 74 rue de Charonne, 11e; starters €3.50-11, mains €9.50-11; ⏱ lunch & dinner to 10.30pm daily; Ⓜ Charonne) This upbeat, very yellow restaurant is an excellent place to come for *pho* (soup noodles, usually with beef) and shrimp noodles.

SELF-CATERING

The incomparable (and open-air) **Marché Bastille** (p222) is our favourite market in Paris. Also in the Bastille area there are lots of food shops along **rue de la Roquette** (Map p158; Ⓜ Voltaire or Bastille) towards place Léon Blum.

Monoprix Bastille branch (Map p158; 97 rue du Faubourg St-Antoine, 11e; ⏱ 9am-9.45pm Mon-Sat; Ⓜ Ledru-Rollin) and the late-opening **Monop'** (Map p158; 62-64 rue de la Roquette, 11e; ⏱ 8.30am-midnight Mon-Sat, 10am-10pm Sun; Ⓜ Voltaire) are convenient supermarkets.

West of the Parc de Bercy there's a **Franprix** (Map p158; 3 rue Baron le Roy, 12e; ⏱ noon-9pm Mon, 8.30am-9pm Tue-Sun; Ⓜ Cour St-Émilion) that's open every day.

PLACE D'ITALIE & CHINATOWN

With the Simone de Beauvoir footbridge (p163) making Bercy (p156) mere footsteps away from the 13e, foodies are hot-footing it to Paris' Chinatown in search of Asian food: Av de Choisy, av d'Ivry and rue Baudricourt are streets to try.

North around the Bibliothèque Nationale de France and MK2 entertainment complex (p305), stretching north along av Pierre Mendès to Gare d'Austerlitz, is the land of opportunity where a new cutting-edge dining or drinking venue appears to crop up every day. To wine and dine afloat (starters/mains €10/18, menu lunch/dinner €19/25) board Le Batofar (p297).

Westwards is the gritty, real-life 'village' of Butte aux Cailles, chock-a-block with interesting addresses. Or book a table at L'Agrume (p227), one of the city's most raved about contemporary bistros – it's just across the arrondissement border on the 13e's northern fringe.

CHEZ JACKY Map p164 French €€

☎ 01 45 83 71 55; www.chezjacky.fr, in French; 109 rue du Dessous des Berges, 13e; starters/mains €20/30, menu €23, with wine €44; ⏱ lunch & dinner to 10.30pm Mon-Fri; Ⓜ Bibliothèque

In the shadow of the national library, Chez Jacky is a serious, traditional restaurant with thoughtful service and a nice, old-fashioned provincial atmosphere. The brothers in charge know how to find good regional produce and present it with great panache, even if originality isn't their cardinal virtue.

CHEZ NATHALIE

Map p164 French, Contemporary €€

☎ 01 45 80 20 42; 41 rue Vandrezanne, 13e; starters €10-15, mains €20-25; ⏱ lunch & dinner to 11pm daily; Ⓜ Corvisart or Place d'Italie

Refreshingly different with summertime tables on car-quiet rue Vandrezanne, this pocket-sized dining spot is a lovely spot to dine tête à tête. Transparent Kartell chairs and deep purple table tops ooze modernity, as does the menu, which fuses traditional French with world food in the guise of a pressed artichoke heart with foie gras, wild boar with celery puree, squid pan-fried with chilli and so on.

LES CAILLOUX

Map p164 Italian, Contemporary €€

☎ 01 45 80 15 08; www.lescailloux.fr; 58 rue des Cinq Diamants, 13e; pasta/mains €15/20; ⏱ lunch & dinner to 11pm daily; Ⓜ Corvisart or Place d'Italie

It is pricey and chic and its pavement terrace smart in the heart of Butte aux Cailles is without question the spot to sit and be seen. In keeping with the cool crowd that gathers here, décor is minimalist: think understated chocolate façade, shabby-chic wooden floor and simple tables lit by low-hanging lamps. Almost secondary to this hip-hangout scene is the food – Italian and delicious.

CHEZ PAUL Map p164 French €€

☎ 01 45 89 22 11; 22 rue de la Butte aux Cailles, 13e; starters €10-15, mains €18-21; ⏱ lunch & dinner to midnight daily; Ⓜ Corvisart or Place d'Italie

Paul's pad is a classic in Butte aux Cailles. Soak up the relaxed, chatty feel and indulge in Frencher-than-French dishes cooked to perfection. Despite its name gras double (double fat) is not fatty; rather, it's belly pan-fried with garlic and parsley, as the friendly note on the menu thoughtfully explains.

BIOART Map p164 Organic €€

☎ 01 45 85 66 88; www.restaurantbioart.fr; 1 quai François Mauriac, 13e; starters/mains €12/25, 2-/3-course menu €28/36; ⏱ lunch & dinner to 11.30pm Mon-Fri; Ⓜ Bibliothèque

Split across two floors, this Seine-side eating space with neon lighting and glass windows is 100% bio. Snacks, salads and bowls of pasta 'n' risotto make up the ground-floor Green Café menu, while the risotto au cognac à la crème is typical of the more formal fare served upstairs. Savouring 'un plaisir naturel' (a natural pleasure) is the hip but laidback mood here.

L'AVANT GOÛT Map p164 French, Bistro €€

☎ 01 53 80 24 00; www.lavantgout.com, in French; 26 rue Bobillot, 13e; starters/mains €10/16.50, menu lunch/dinner €14/31; ⏱ lunch & dinner to 10.45pm Tue-Sat; Ⓜ Place d'Italie

A prototype of the Parisian néo-bistro, the 'Foretaste' has chef Christophe Beaufront serving some of the most inventive modern cuisine around. The place gets noisy, tables count little more than a dozen, and service is stern. But the food is different and divine.

Advance reservations are vital but, should you not get in, grab a takeaway from its wine shop (p270).

LA FLEUVE DE CHINE Map p164 — Chinese €€
☎ 01 45 82 06 88; 15 av de Choisy, 13e; starters €5-10, mains €7-15; ⏱ lunch & dinner to 11pm Fri-Wed; Ⓜ Porte de Choisy

Here you'll find the most authentic Cantonese and Hakka food in Paris and, as is typical, both the surroundings and the service are forgettable. Go for the superb dishes cooked in clay pots. La Fleuve de Chine can also be reached through the Tour Bergame housing estate at 130 blvd Masséna.

LA CHINE MASSÉNA Map p164 — Chinese €€
☎ 01 45 83 98 88; 18 av de Choisy, 13e; soups & starters €5-12, mains €6.50-15; ⏱ lunch & dinner to 11pm daily; Ⓜ Porte de Choisy

This enormous restaurant specialising in Cantonese and Chiu Chow cuisine is a real favourite in Chinatown; to ensure it would have good joss for the coming year we fed the dragon lettuce at the last Lunar New Year celebrations. The dim sum here is especially good and women still go around the dining area with trolleys calling out their wares.

LE TEMPS DES CÉRISES Map p164 — French €
☎ 01 45 89 69 48; 18-20 rue de la Butte aux Cailles, 13e; starters/mains €7/13; ⏱ lunch Mon-Fri, dinner to 11.30pm Mon-Fri, to midnight Sat; Ⓜ Corvisart or Place d'Italie

There's no beating about the bush at the 'Time of Cherries' (ie 'days of wine and roses' to English speakers), an easygoing restaurant run by a workers' cooperative for three decades. Switch off your mobile (lest there be hell to pay) before entering, plonk yourself down at a table and while away several hours munching on faithfully solid fare in a quintessentially Parisian atmosphere. Buy their coton-bio T-shirt upon departure.

CHEZ GLADINES Map p164 — French, Basque €
☎ 01 45 80 70 10; 30 rue des Cinq Diamants, 13e; starters €5-10, mains €6-10; ⏱ lunch & dinner to midnight Sun-Tue, to 1am Wed-Sat; Ⓜ Corvisart

Enormous 'meal-in-a-metal-bowl' salads and potato platters guaranteed to reap change from a €10 note is the prime draw of this down-to-earth Basque bistro in Buttes aux Cailles. It buzzes with students and spendthrift diners under 30, and is always a hoot. Traditional Basque specialities to munch on atop red-and-checked cloth tables include pipérade and poulet basque (chicken cooked with tomatoes, onions, peppers and white wine). Arrive early to grab a pew.

FIL 'O' FROMAGE Map p164 — French, Cheese €
☎ 01 53 79 13 35; www.filofromage.com; 12 rue de Tolbiac, 13e; sandwiches €6, mains €15, lunch menu €10; ⏱ 10am-7.30pm Mon-Wed, to 10.30pm Thu-Sat; Ⓜ Bibliothèque

This fromagerie offering lunches and light meals throughout the day six days a week is godsend in an area that is not overly endowed with places to eat, especially budget ones. Everything here involves cheese, including the assiette froide (cold plate) of three cheese, three cold meats and salad and the poêlons (pots) of warm cheese.

LA MAISON DES FRIGOS
Map p164 — Japanese, Art Gallery €
☎ 01 44 23 76 20; 19 rue des Frigos, 13e; 2-course lunch €14; ⏱ lunch to 3.30pm Mon-Sat; Ⓜ Bibliothèque

The location of this tiny hybrid gallery–lunch spot – on the ground floor of the graffiti-decorated art squat Les Frigos (p166) – could not be more apt. Grab a table

top picks

ASIAN RICE & NOODLES

- **Happy Nouilles (p260)** The noodle shop of choice among Asian students on the Right Bank.
- **Asianwok (p259)** Upbeat and chilled; come here for wontons after a heavy night out.
- **Thai Classic (p226)** A favourite pit stop, especially for pad thai (Thai fried rice).
- **Paris Hanoi (p267)** Nothing faux about the pho (Vietnamese vermicelli and beef soup) here – it's the real McCoy.
- **Ta Sushi (p226)** We give thanks to one of the best affordable sushi bars in Paris.
- **Les Pâtes Vivantes (p243)** Northern-style Chinese noodles pulled into shape before your eyes.
- **Le Foyer du Vietnam (p231)** Cheap 'n' cheerful footsteps from place Monge in the Latin Quarter.
- **Chez Hanafousa (p234)** Dining at this Japanese gem tucked down an alley off blvd St-Germain is spectacular – quite literally.

between flower pots outside or between art and industrial piping inside, and tuck into the '100% *maison*' cuisine of Japanese cook Mairko. Very much a one-man show, her *okonomiyaki* (Japanese crêpes) are simple, wholesome and delicious. No credit cards.

SELF-CATERING

Wines selected by and dishes created by top Parisian chef Christophe Beaufront are sold to take home at L'Avant-Goût Coté Cellier (Map p164; ☎ 01 53 81 14 06; www.lavantgout.com, in French; 37 rue Bobillot, 13e; ❤ noon-8pm Tue-Fri, 10.30am-1.30pm & 3.30-8.30pm Sat; Ⓜ Place d'Italie). Don't miss his signature dish, *pot au feu au cochon aux épices* (spicy pork stew).

MONTPARNASSE & 15E

Since the 1920s, the area around blvd du Montparnasse has been one of the city's premier avenues for enjoying Parisian café life, though younger Parisians deem the place somewhat *démodé* and touristy these days. Glam it's not. But it does boast a handful of legendary brasseries and cafés which warrant a culinary visit. Made famous by writers (see p187) and artists like Picasso, Dalí and Cocteau between the wars, these same cafés attracted exiles such as Lenin and Trotsky before the Russian Revolution.

With its dearth of food shops and twin-set of quintessential café-cum-bars on seemingly every pair of street corners, the neighbouring 15e arrondissement is one area where you know real Parisians really live. Solidly down to earth and stoically free of trendy concept dining, this quarter cooks up some fabulous bistro fare – well worth the trip. Rue de la Convention, rue de Vaugirard, rue St-Charles, rue du Commerce and those south of blvd de Grenelle are key streets.

LE DÔME Map p168 French, Seafood €€€
☎ 01 43 35 25 81; 108 blvd du Montparnasse, 14e; starters/mains €20/40; ❤ lunch & dinner to 11.30pm daily; Ⓜ Vavin
A 1930s art deco extravaganza, Le Dôme is a monumental place for a meal service of the formal white-tablecloth and bow-tied waiter variety. Stick with the basics at this historical venue, opting perhaps for an impressive shellfish platter piled high with fresh oysters, king prawns, crab claws and so on, followed by creamy homemade *millefeuille*. Wheeled in on a trolley and cut

in front of you, the traditional French dessert is a deliciously decadent extravaganza not to be missed.

LA CLOSERIE DES LILAS
Map p168   French, Brasserie €€€
☎ 01 40 51 34 50; www.closeriedeslilas.fr; 171 blvd du Montparnasse, 6e; restaurant/brasserie starters €23-46/11-21, mains €22-42/23-27, menu lunch €45; ❤ restaurant lunch & dinner to 11.30pm, brasserie noon-1am, piano bar 11am-1am; Ⓜ Port Royal
As anyone who has read Hemingway will know, what is now the American Bar at the 'Lilac Enclosure' is where Papa did a lot of writing, drinking and oyster slurping; brass plaques tell you exactly where he and other luminaries such as Picasso, Apollinaire, Man Ray, Jean-Paul Sartre and Samuel Beckett stood or sat (or fell) and whiled away the hours. The place is split into piano bar, chic restaurant and more lovable (and cheaper) brasserie with hedged-in pavement terrace.

LA COUPOLE Map p168   French, Brasserie €€€
☎ 01 43 20 14 20; www.lacoupoleparis.com, in French; 102 blvd du Montparnasse, 14e; starters €6.50-20, mains €12.50-35; ❤ 8.30am-1am Sun-Thu, to 1.30am Fri & Sat; Ⓜ Vavin
The famous mural-covered columns (painted by such artists as Brancusi and Chagall), dark wood panelling and soft lighting have hardly changed an iota since the days of Sartre, Soutine, Man Ray, the dancer Josephine Baker and other regulars. The reason for visiting this enormous, 450-seat brasserie, designed by the Solvet brothers and opened in 1927, is more history than gastronomy. You can book for lunch, but you'll have to queue for dinner; though there's always breakfast. The more expensive *menus* are available until 6pm and after 10.30pm.

JADIS Map p168   French, Bistro €€€
☎ 01 45 57 73 20; www.bistrot-jadis.com, in French; 202 rue de la Croix Nivert, 15e; starter/main €9/19, menu (lunch) €25 & €32, dinner €45 & €65; ❤ lunch & dinner to 11pm Mon-Fri; Ⓜ Boucicaut
This upmarket *néo-bistro* with sober Bordeaux façade and white lace curtains on the corner of a very unassuming street in the 15e is one of Paris' most raved about (read: reserve in advance to avoid disappointment). Traditional French dishes pack a modern punch thanks to rising-star chef

top picks

PLACES FOR BRUNCH

- **Curieux Spaghetti** (p257) There's got to be a morning after…and this is the place for it in the heart of the Marais.
- **Le Train Bleu** (p261) This opulent eatery in the Gare de Lyon offers a very special Chattanooga Choo Choo moment even for those staying put.
- **Le Viaduc Café** (p265) Breakfast 'under the arches' takes on a new meaning south of Bastille.
- **Le Mouton Noir** (p264) Tiny but almost perfect, the 'Black Sheep' lives up to its uniqueness.
- **Le Café qui Parle** (p245) Quality brunches in the café that doesn't break the bank.
- **Bob's Juice Bar** (p252) Get your health-conscious wake-up call here.
- **Le Miroir** (p244) Reflections of Sunday morning decadence in a local Montmartre favourite.
- **L'Entrepôt** (p272) There are few leafier, prettier gardens to tuck into Sunday brunch than this.
- **Les Éditeurs** (p233) The buzz never dies at this busy café, an institution for ions in chic St-Germain.
- **Matteo et Paola** (p233) Laze away the weekend with regulars at this youthful tearoom-cum-café bar between designer boutiques.

Guillaume Delage who dares to do things like braise pork cheeks in beer and use black rice instead of white. The lunch *menu* is extraordinarily good value and the chocolate soufflé – order it at the start of your meal – is nothing other than to-die-for heavenly.

LA CAGOUILLE Map p168   French, Seafood €€

☎ 01 43 22 09 01; www.la-cagouille.fr; 10 place Constantin Brancusi, 14e; starters €10-15, mains €16-45, 2-/3-course menu €23/38; ⏰ lunch & dinner to 10.30pm daily; Ⓜ Gaîté
Chef Gérard Allemandou, one of the best seafood cooks (and cookery book writers) in Paris, gets rave reviews for his fish and shellfish dishes at this café–restaurant opposite 23 rue de l'Ouest. The *menus* here are exceptionally good value.

LE PARC AUX CERFS Map p108   French €€

☎ 01 43 54 87 83; 50 rue Vavin, 6e; starters €10.50, mains €19, 2-/3-course menu €29.50/36; ⏰ lunch & dinner daily Sep-Jul; Ⓜ Notre Dame de Champs
Evening reservations are essential at this small, stylish restaurant known for its crea-

tive dishes: two-cabbage salad, *tartare de saumon* (raw chopped salmon) with pink peppercorns and grapefruit, goat's cheese 'n' almonds and so on. Elegant air and friendly service aside, the icing on the cake has to be its delightful patio garden out back.

L'OS À MOËLLE Map p168   French, Bistro €€

☎ 01 45 57 27 27; 3 rue Vasco de Gama, 15e; menus lunch €17 (vegetarian), €21 & €28, dinner €35; ⏰ lunch & dinner to 11.30pm Tue-Fri, dinner to midnight Sat; Ⓜ Lourmel
Marrowbone chef Thierry Faucher (ex-Hotel Crillon) makes no bones about his outstanding cuisine wholly inspired by 'the market, the season and the humour of the moment'. His six-course sampling menus are among the most affordable in town, embracing delicacies like scallops with coriander, sea bass in cumin butter or half a quail with endives and chestnuts, while his chocolate *quenelle* (dumpling) with saffron cream is award-winning. Should you fail to snag a table, try his wine bar (p292) opposite.

SAWADEE Map p168   Thai €€

☎ 01 45 77 68 90; 53 av Émile Zola, 15e; menus €15 (lunch) & €21-33; ⏰ lunch & dinner to 10.30pm Mon-Sat; Ⓜ Charles Michels
For 20 years this well-known restaurant has been bidding *sawadee* (welcome) to Thai-food lovers – and is in most guidebooks to prove it. The décor is rather impersonal, but the sophisticated cuisine more than makes up for it. Twist your tongue around prawn or chicken soup flavoured with lemon grass, spicy beef salad (a real treat), satay sticks (chicken, beef, lamb and pork) with peanut sauce and other classic dishes of Siam.

LE CRISTAL DE SEL p168   French €€

☎ 01 42 50 35 29; www.lecristaldesel.fr, in French; 13 rue Mademoiselle, 15e; starters €10-15, mains €20-28, 2-/3-course lunch menu €15/18; ⏰ lunch & dinner to 10pm Tue-Sat; Ⓜ Commerce
The raved-about stage of young rising chef Karl Lopez, this modern bistro has a distinct kitchen feel with its small brightly lit white walls, white-painted beams and gaggle of busy chefs behind the bar. The only decorative feature is a candle-lit crystal of rose-tinted salt on each table – a sure sign that food is what the 'Salt Crystal' is all about. Lopez's *tarte à la bergamote fraîche*

meringuée (lemon meringue pie) – divine – has to be the zestiest in Paris. Reservations essential.

KIM ANH Map p168 Vietnamese €€

☎ 01 45 79 40 96; 49 av Émile Zola, 15e; starters €13-15, mains €20, menu €34; ⊙ dinner to 10.30pm Tue-Sun; Ⓜ Charles Michels
A travel guide hotspot situated across the road from Sawadee, this place is the antithesis of the typically Parisian canteen-style Vietnamese restaurant. Kim Anh greets its customers with tapestries, white tablecloths, fresh flowers and extraordinarily fresh and flavoursome food, all elaborately presented. The *émincé de bœuf à la citronnelle* (beef with lemon grass) is a skilful combination of flavours, but the true sensation is the caramelised langoustine.

L'ENTREPÔT Map p168 French €€

☎ 01 45 40 07 50; 7-9 rue Francis de Préssensé, 14e; starters/mains €6/15; ⊙ lunch & dinner daily; Ⓜ Pernety or Plaisance
Industrial in mood and open-minded in spirit (all ages come here), this dynamic cultural centre (p303) happens to be a fantastic place to eat too. Service is fast, friendly and French – start with goat's cheese marinated in nut oil or half a dozen snails followed by ravioli in chestnut cream or chicken and chunky hand-cut fries. But the real show stealer, live bands line-up aside, is its leafy back garden with dozens of tables beneath trees. Reserve tables al fresco in advance, especially for Sunday brunch.

AU GOÛT DUJOUR Map p168 French, Bistro €

☎ 01 45 71 68 36; www.au-gout-dujour.com, in French; 12 rue Beaugrenelle, 15e; 2-/3-course menu €18/25; ⊙ lunch & dinner Mon-Fri, dinner Sat; Ⓜ Charles Michel
Denis Dujour is the chef behind this overtly 'local *quartier*' bistro with jolly burgundy-red canopy and market-driven dishes chalked on several blackboards. Be it roast cod with polenta and white asparagus in May or chestnuts in autumn, cuisine here is strictly seasonal – and some of the best value in town.

FIORI Map p168 Italian, Pizza €

☎ 01 45 54 90 90; 52-56 rue Balard, 15e; pizza €9-12, pasta €10-16; ⊙ lunch & dinner daily; Ⓜ Balard

Breadsticks, spiced olive oil…you'll find all the trademarks of a good Italian at this down-to-earth address, smart on the edge of Parc André-Citroën. Come lunchtime it gets packed with hungry suits from nearby offices and families out for a romp in the park. Grab a seat on its sunny pavement terrace and dig into a Real McCoy pizza.

LA CABANE À HUÎTRES

Map p168 French, Oysters €

☎ 01 45 49 47 27; 4 rue Antoine Bourdelle, 14e; starters €10-17, dozen oysters €13-17, menu €18; ⊙ lunch & dinner Wed-Sat; Ⓜ Montparnasse-Bienvenüe
One of Paris' best oyster addresses; this earthy wooden-styled *cabane* (cabin) with just nine sought-after tables is the pride and joy of fifth-generation oyster farmer Françis Dubourg, who splits his week between the capital and his oyster farm in Arcachon on the Atlantic Coast. Geared totally towards dedicated gourmets, the fixed menu features a dozen oysters, foie gras de Landes (from Gascony in southwest France) or *magret de canard fumé* (smoked duck breast) followed by Pyreneen *brebis* cheese or sweet *canelé* (a rum, vanilla and cinnamon-spiced cake).

SELF-CATERING

Opposite Tour Montparnasse is the open-air Blvd Edgar Quinet food market (Map p168; blvd Edgar Quinet, 14e; ⊙ 7am-2pm Wed & Sat; Ⓜ Edgar Quinet or Montparnasse Bienvenüe). Find supermarkets on rue du Commandant René Mouchotte, 14e.

The 15e has two markets, Marché Grenelle and Marché St-Charles (p222); ample supermarkets including Monoprix (Map p168; 2 rue du Commerce, 15e; ⊙ 9am-10pm Mon-Sat; Ⓜ La Motte Picquet-Grenelle); and a branch of Poilâne (Map p168; p215), one of Paris' most famous bakeries.

BEYOND CENTRAL PARIS
LA DÉFENSE

Quick eats form the backbone of La Défense's dining scene. The 3rd floor of the Centre Commercial des Quatre Temps (☎ 01 47 73 54 44; www.les4temps. com, in French; 15 Parvis de la Défense; ⊙ 9am-10pm Mon-Fri, 8.30am-10pm Sat) alone is loaded with lunch

LOCAL KNOWLEDGE: JIM HAYNES

A Louisianan raised in Venezuela, who did his US military service in Edinburgh, started a theatre in London's Covent Garden and spent 30 years teaching sexual politics (in English) at university in Paris, where he hung out with the likes of Allen Ginsburg, William Burroughs and James Baldwin, Jim Haynes has a CV that just won't quit. But he's best known for the Sunday night dinners chez Jim (☎ 01 43 27 17 67; www.jim-haynes.com; Atelier A2, 83 rue de la Tombe Issoire, 14e; Ⓜ Alésia) in a *belle époque* atelier in the 14e. It's the original Paris supper club (p262), where people meet, greet, eat, drink and, well, do whatever people then do together – all for a suggested donation of €25.

Same old song: how long has this been going on? It all started in 1978. I've always had house guests – it's hard not to in places like Edinburgh, London and Paris – and I once put up a ballet dancer who liked to cook. She made dinner for me and my friends once or twice a week, which turned into a regular Sunday night event for everybody. And when Cathy couldn't cook we began to have guest chefs.

So still crazy after all these years about entertaining? People ask me all the time why I continue. I don't know. Inertia? I just think, well, it's Sunday. It's time to do dinner.

Overnight sensation or slow boil? The event grew organically from the beginning but right now we're full every week. I did an interview with NPR (National Public Radio) in the USA early in 2009 and then the mint-makers After Eight shot a TV advert here. That pushed the numbers way up. In good weather the crowd spills into garden and can go as high as 130 but I prefer between 60 to 70 people.

It was standing-room-only crowd last night, a veritable club frotti/frotta (roughly 'rub club') About 130,000 people have passed through the front door and many romances leading to relationships, marriages and babies have started in this room. I watched a shy French gal and a timid German guy who could barely communicate sit on that sofa one Sunday night. They've now been married for 18 years and have three kids. And they speak three languages fluently!

Has travel – have travellers – changed since you fed your first? People haven't changed. I think there will always be two basic ways to travel: to go around the world and see things as a tourist or to participate in local life as a traveller. Why do people like one city and dislike another? They got involved with locals in some way in the first and not the second. All the people who come to my dinners are travellers as they are getting involved – even if they don't always know it.

What keeps you glued to the spot? I love all big cities but particularly Paris because it's a small big city. Each arrondissement is like a little town; I rarely leave mine as I've got everything I need here. And I'm a real local now; everyone calls me Mr Jim. It's endearing.

Words of wisdom for the Paris virgins out there? Talk to people – even it just involves a 'Pass the salt, please' directed at the next table. A lot of friendships have started that way. But bear in mind one rule among the Parisians: never, ever, start a conversation without saying 'Bonjour' first. Ignore that and you'll be dismissed as impolite. In fact, you're a rude bastard.

Thank you.

Interviewed by Steve Fallon

spots, be it pizza or pancakes, Häagen-Dazs ice cream, Starbucks coffee, soup 'n' juice or Japanese.

GLOBETROTTER Map p175   Island Cuisine €€
☎ 01 55 91 96 96; www.globetrottercafe.com; 16 place de la Défense; starters €9.50-18, mains €15-33; Ⓨ restaurant noon-2.30pm, café 7.30am-9.30pm Mon-Fri; Ⓜ La Défense Grande Arche
La Défense's *gens d'affaires* (businesspeople) come to this tropical restaurant to embark on a culinary tour of the world through various islands. Think swordfish carpaccio with Caribbean pineapple or duck breast with dried fruit. Tables on the wooden-deck terrace face La Grande Arche

and those inside woo diners with first-row seats at the Bassin Agam (p176). Shoeboxshaped, this must be the stubbiest building in La Défense!

BOLDÈRE Map p175   Salad Bar €
☎ 01 47 73 54 44; 15 Parvis de la Défense; salad with 3 toppings €6.80; Ⓨ noon-3pm Mon-Fri; Ⓜ La Défense Grande Arche
On the 3rd floor of Les Quatre Temps, health-conscious punters build their salad from a hundred and one different ingredients or plump for one of four different homemade soups. It's a decent alternative to the fast food that pervades the rest of the mall.

ST-DENIS

There's little reason to linger in St-Denis; the cafés outside the Basilique are the best bet for a coffee, mint tea or a meal.

LES ARTS Map p174   North African, French €€
☎ 01 42 43 22 40; 6 rue de la Boulangerie; starters €6-7, mains €8.50-17, menu €21.90; ⏱ lunch & dinner to 10.30pm; Ⓜ Basilique de St-Denis
This welcoming restaurant has mostly Maghreb cuisine (couscous, *tajines*, etc), with a few traditional French dishes as well, and comes recommended by locals.

They also serve some refreshing mint tea, preceded by a rinsing of the hands with fragrant orange blossom water. It's just opposite the basilica.

LE PETIT BRETON Map p174   French, Breton €
☎ 01 48 20 11 58; 18 rue de la Légion d'Honneur; menus €12 & €15; ⏱ 11.30am-2.30pm Mon-Sat; Ⓜ St-Denis Porte de Paris
The 'Little Breton' is a decent spot for a lunch of traditional French café fare (escalope Normande, steaks). The *plat du jour* is a bargain-basement €8.

DRINKING

top picks

- **Le Fumoir** (p278)
- **Le Pure Café** (p289)
- **Le Bistrot du Peintre** (p290)
- **L'Apparemment Café** (p288)
- **Le Cochon à l'Oreille** (p277)
- **Delaville Café** (p285)
- **Café Chéri(e)** (p285)
- **Prescription Cocktail Club** (p281)
- **Au Sauvignon** (p283)
- **Le 10** (p282)

What's your recommendation? www.lonelyplanet.com/paris

DRINKING

Yearning for a chilled venue where you don't need a gold-plated credit card or membership of the local anarchists' association to feel at ease? Don't despair: there's far more to the Parisian drinking scene than chic, design-driven lounge bars brimming with beautiful people or tatty, dime-a-dozen *tabacs* (bar-tobacconists) with thin-haired regulars propping up the bar.

Drinking in Paris as salt-of-the-earth Parisians do means: savouring wafer-thin slices of *saucisson* (sausage) over a glass of sauvignon on a pavement terrace at sundown; meeting after work for *une verre* (a glass) and *tartines* (open sandwiches) cut from Poilâne bread; quaffing an early-evening apéritif in the same literary café as Sartre and Simone did; dancing on tables to bossa nova beats; hovering at a zinc counter with locals; indulging in a spot of *dégustation* (tasting; see the boxed text, p278); sipping martinis on a dark leather couch while listening to live jazz; sipping *gyokuro* in a trendy Japanese *salon de thé* (tearoom).

In a country where eating and drinking are as inseparable as cheese and wine, it's inevitable that the line between bars, cafés and bistros is blurred at best (no, you haven't drunk too much – indeed the French rarely go drunk-wild and really rather frown upon it). Practically every place serves food of some description, but those featured in this chapter are favoured, first and foremost, as happening places to drink – be it alcohol, coffee or tea.

The distinct lack of any hardcore clubbing circuit in the French capital, moreover, only serves to spice up Paris' drinking scene still further; what might appear as a simple café at 5pm can morph quite comfortably to DJ bar and pounding dance floor as the night rolls on.

PRACTICALITIES

Drinking in Paris essentially means paying the rent for the space you take up. So it costs more sitting at tables than standing at the counter, more on a fancy square than a backstreet, more in the 8e than in the 18e. Come 10pm many cafés apply a pricier *tarif de nuit* (night rate).

A glass of wine starts from €3 or €4, a cocktail costs €10 to €15 and a *demi* (half-pint) of beer is between €3 and €5. In clubs and chic bars, prices can be easily double this. To hunt down the place with the cheapest drinks, just follow the trail of students. Most mainstream bars and international-styled pubs have a 'happy hour' – called just that (no French translation) – which ushers in reduced-price drinks for a good two or three hours no less, usually from around 5pm to 9pm. A service charge between 12% and 15% is included as part of the advertised café and restaurant prices, meaning there is no expectation or obligation – including in bars – to add a tip.

Closing time tends to be 2am, though some bars have licences until dawn. See p296 for clubbing spots and p299 for live music venues – great places to drink, too.

The Parisian drinking scene is smoke-free, kind of. Following the blanket smoking-in-public-places ban imposed in 2008, smokers have simply moved from inside to out, socialising on the street in front of bars instead or lighting up on tightly packed pavement terraces which, heated and plastic-covered during the colder months, are now smokier than ever!

LOUVRE & LES HALLES

Some great bars skirt the no-man's-land of Les Halles, but avoid crossing the garden above the Forum des Halles at night. Rue des Lombards is celebrated for its jazz venues (p301), while sophisticated bars are grouped towards the Louvre and Palais Royal. Rue Tiquetonne and rue Montorgueil in the Étienne Marcel area have a fine selection of hip cafés. This area is right next to the happening bars of rue Montmartre.

LE CAFÉ NOIR Map p72   Bar
☎ 01 40 39 07 36; 65 rue Montmartre, 2e;
🕑 8am-2am Mon-Fri, 4pm-2am Sat; Ⓜ Sentier
An excellent, dependable bar on the edge of the Sentier garment district, the 'Black Café' is, in fact, predominantly red, and one of those bars you decide to turn into a regular haunt. It's always packed, with a mix of French and Anglophone imbibers attracted by the friendly and very hip ambience.

LE CŒUR FOU Map p72   Bar
☎ 01 42 33 91 33; 55 rue Montmartre, 2e;
🕑 5pm-2am; Ⓜ Étienne Marcel

The 'Crazy Heart' is hip without attaining that too-cool-by-half pretentiousness that reigns in the Étienne Marcel environs. It's a tiny, gallery-like bar with little candles nestled in whitewashed walls, a dapper late-20s crowd that doesn't keep to itself, and rotating art exhibitions.

L'IMPRÉVU Map p76   Bar
☎ 01 42 78 23 50; 9 rue Quincampoix, 4e;
⊗ 3pm-2am; Ⓜ Rambuteau

The 'Unexpected' is just that – something of an oasis in the busy Les Halles area. It's a relatively inexpensive and gay-friendly bar, with mismatched furniture and a relaxed, distressed charm. The bar is quite large but the different rooms and corners mean you'll soon find your niche.

CAFÉ LA FUSÉE
Map p76   Bar, Café
☎ 01 42 76 93 99; 168 rue St-Martin, 3e;
⊗ 10am-2am; Ⓜ Rambuteau or Étienne Marcel

Close to the Pompidou Centre but away from the crowds, this hip café, strung with coloured lights, is a lively and laid-back local hangout. The wine selection is particularly good and the music excellent.

LE COCHON À L'OREILLE
Map p72   Bar, Café
☎ 01 42 36 07 56; 15 rue Montmartre, 1er;
⊗ 10am-11pm Tue-Sat; Ⓜ Les Halles or Étienne Marcel

A Parisian *bijou* (jewel), this heritage-listed hole-in-the-wall retains its belle époque tiles with market scenes of Les Halles and just eight tiny tables. There's a small but excellent menu (mains €12.50 to €16, lunch menu €10.50) of traditional bistro fare.

LE TAMBOUR Map p72   Bar, Café
☎ 01 42 33 06 90; 41 rue Montmartre, 2e;
⊗ 8am-6am; Ⓜ Étienne Marcel or Sentier

Some people will say that the 'Drummer', a Paris mecca for night owls, with generously long hours and friendly service, is a restaurant. And they do serve straightforward dishes till as late as 3.30am or 4am. But we enjoy it as a late-night drinking venue and its mixed, somewhat boisterous crowd. You'll enjoy the recycled street furniture, the transport bits 'n' bobs and the cocky staff.

LE CAFÉ DES INITIÉS
Map p76   Café
☎ 01 42 33 78 29; 3 place des Deux-Écus, 1er;
⊗ 7.30am-2am Mon-Fri, 9am-2am Sat & Sun;
Ⓜ Louvre–Rivoli

This modern-design café almost on rue du Louvre is popular with journalists and communications types. While not a late-night venue, it has a pleasant terrace and is great for evening drinks, coffees and even meals (a two-course menu is just €14.50). Slick service, nondeafening music and good food attract a trendy 30-something mix.

HARRY'S NEW YORK BAR
Map p72   Cocktail Bar
☎ 01 42 61 71 14; 5 rue Daunou, 2e; ⊗ 10.30am-4am; Ⓜ Opéra

One of the most popular American-style bars in the prewar years (when there were

HOW TO DRINK LIKE A PARISIAN

Kick off the day with *un café* (a short sharp shot of espresso) standing up at the bar or *comptoir* (counter). If milky coffee's more your thing, this is your chance to enjoy *un café au lait* or cappuccino – both are perfectly acceptable at breakfast but a real no go as a drink to round off any other meal.

Noon beckons with an aperitif on a sunny café terrace (p286) – try a kir (white wine with a dash of blackcurrant syrup) – followed by wine (exclusively French in the main) with lunch. Most restaurants serve two or three different wines by the glass in addition to a good-value, perfectly drinkable house white and red. Other staples are *une carafe d'eau* (free jug of tap water) and *un café* with the bill.

Few Parisians take tea in the afternoon. Rather, it's *un café au lait*, cappuccino or a long cold drink such as *un citron pressé* (fresh lemon juice mixed to taste with water and sugar). Then, of course, there are those wacky one-off events like Sunday-afternoon pyjama cocktail parties (silk please) at the Prescription Cocktail Club (p281).

Come 6pm: Oh my! *Apéro* (aperitif) time again, be it *une pression* (33cl glass of draught beer), aniseed-flavoured pastis, glass of chilled rosé, *une coupe de Champagne* (a glass of Champagne) or ice- and mint-packed mojito. Don't be shy in asking the waiter or barman if he has any nuts or olives, or play chic and head to one of the city's impossibly trendy cocktail bars (p282) where complimentary nibbles are a given on a cocktail list starring new house creations alongside fabulous old-fashioned favourites.

several dozen in Paris), Harry's once welcomed such habitués as literature writers F Scott Fitzgerald and Ernest Hemingway, who no doubt sampled the bar's unique cocktail and creation: the Bloody Mary (€12.50). The Cuban mahogany interior dates from the mid-19th century and was brought over from a Manhattan bar in 1911. There's a basement piano bar called Ivories where Gershwin supposedly composed *An American in Paris* and, for the peckish, old-school hot dogs (€6) and generous club sandwiches to snack on. The advertisement for Harry's that occasionally appears in the papers still reads 'Tell the Taxi Driver Sank Roo Doe Noo' and is copyrighted.

LE FUMOIR Map p76 — Cocktail Bar
☎ 01 42 92 00 24; 6 rue de l'Amiral de Coligny, 1er; ⏲ 11am-2am; Ⓜ Louvre–Rivoli
This colonial-style bar-restaurant opposite the eastern flank of the Louvre is a fine place to sip top-notch gin from quality glassware while nibbling on olives from the vintage mahogany bar; during happy hour (6pm to 8pm) the cocktails, usually €8.50 to €11, drop to €7. There's a buoyant, corporate crowd on weekday evenings. The restaurant is popular for late breakfast during the week and brunch on Sundays; try to get a seat in the 'library'.

CAFÉ OZ Map p76 — Pub
☎ 01 40 39 00 18; 18 rue St-Denis, 1er; ⏲ 5pm-3am Sun-Thu, 5pm-5am Fri, 1pm-5am Sat; Ⓜ Châtelet
A militantly Aussie pub at the bottom of sleazy rue St-Denis, Oz tries to be authentic – from its green-and-ochre décor to its strong commitment to maximising your drink intake of Aussie and Kiwi beers. Convivial bordering on raucous, it's popular with Anglos but the French love it too. The place is packed on Friday and Saturday nights, when it heats up with DJs and dancing. Happy hour is 5pm to 8pm. There are a couple more branches, including Pigalle's Café Oz Blanche (☎ 01 40 16 11 16; 1 rue de Bruxelles, 9e; ⏲ 5pm-2am Mon-Wed, 5pm-4am Thurs, 5pm-10am Fri, 2pm-10am Sat, 2pm-2am Sun; Ⓜ Blanche).

WHERE TO TASTE WINE IN PARIS

Sorting the good wines from the inferior ones when it comes to serious wine-tasting in Paris is no mean feat. Dozens of courses exist, but few come recommended.

One man in the capital who really knows his stuff is sommelier Juan Sánchez, who holds talks and *dégustations* (tastings) most Saturday evenings with independent French wine growers he buys from at his wine shop La Dernière Goutte (p200) in St-Germain des Prés. Legrand Filles & Fils (p195) is another well-informed wine shop with tasting room and all the accoutrements a wine lover could want. Le Pré Verre (p229), Tandem (p291) and Au Sauvignon (p283), a classic wine bar around since 1954, are informal, atmospheric places on the Left Bank to taste interesting wines by small producers over a meal or *casse-croûte* (quick light snack).

Oenophiles aspiring to headier heights should aim for one of the Saturday tastings with French winemakers held in Paris' oldest wine shop, Les Caves Augé (p203; ☎ 01 45 22 16 97; 116 blvd Haussmann, 8e; Ⓜ St-Augustin), in business since 1850. On the same street, one of the world's foremost sommeliers, Philippe Faure-Brac, pairs food and wine to perfection for a price at Bistrot du Sommelier (p241). Cellar tastings with wine growers pre-empt Friday's brilliantly matched three-/five-course lunch/dinner (€50/75).

To learn how to sort the wheat from the chaff, embark on a wine-tasting course at the highly esteemed Centre de Dégustation Jacques Vivet (Map p112; ☎ 01 43 25 96 30, 06 07 28 61 85; www.ecoledegustation.fr, in French; 48 rue de Vaugirard, 6e; Ⓜ Luxembourg), opposite Jardin de Luxembourg. As well as one-day tasting courses and introductory wine courses (in English and French), it runs advanced *cours d'oenologie* (in French only) focusing on several wines from one appellation or grape variety.

Then there's Ô Château (Map p76; ☎ 01 44 73 97 80; www.o-chateau.com; 52 rue de l'Arbre Sec, 1er; Ⓜ Louvre–Rivoli), a young fun-charged company run by bilingual sommelier Olivier Magny that offers the full range of tastings and experiences in a 17th-century vaulted stone cellar near the Louvre: wine-tasting over dinner (€130) or a cheese lunch (€75), with chocolate (€65), *grands crus* master classes (€95) and so on. It also organises day trips to Champagne to taste you know what (€150), Champagne river cruises (€45) and, by night, Champagne bus parties (€60) with music that include, hmm, learning how to open a bottle of champers with a sword in front of the Eiffel Tower.

For an updated and comprehensive monthly calendar of wine tastings in the city there is no better source than Paris by Mouth (www.parisbymouth.com).

À PRIORI THÉ Map p72   Tea Room

☎ 01 42 97 48 75; 35-37 Galerie Vivienne, 2e;
🕙 9am-6pm Mon-Fri, 9am-6.30pm Sat, 12.30-
6.30pm Sun; Ⓜ Pyramides
This cute little tearoom set up by two
Americans (the bad pun gives the game
away) 20 years ago is just the ticket if
you're shopping in the covered shopping
arcades and want to stop – now! Good
lunches but even better cakes (€3.50 to €7).

ANGÉLINA Map p72   Tea Room

☎ 01 42 60 82 00; 226 rue de Rivoli, 1er; 🕙 8am-
7pm Mon-Fri, 9am-7pm Sat & Sun; Ⓜ Tuileries
Take a break from the long trek along the
Tuileries gardens and line up for a table at
Angélina, along with lunching ladies, their
posturing poodles and half the students
from Tokyo University. This beautiful, high-
ceilinged tearoom has exquisite furnishings, mirrored walls and fabulous fluffy
cakes. More importantly, it serves the best
and most wonderfully sickening 'African'
hot chocolate in the history of time (€6.90),
served with a pot of whipped cream. It's a
positive meal replacement (though breakfast is €16.50 to €27.50).

THE ISLANDS

Drinking venues on the islands are as scarce
as hens' teeth. They do exist but use them as
a starting point as very few places stay open
after the bewitching hour of midnight.

TAVERNE HENRI IV Map p82   Bar

☎ 01 43 54 27 90; 13 place du Pont Neuf, Île de la
Cité, 1er; 🕙 11.30am-10pm Mon-Fri, noon-6pm
Sat; Ⓜ Pont Neuf
One of the very few places to drink on the
Île de la Cité, this is a serious wine bar dating back to 1885 and a decent place for a
nibble, with a choice of inexpensive *tartines*
(€4.40 to €8.80), *charcuterie* (cold cooked
meats; €9 to €13), cheese and quiche. This
place attracts lots of legal types from the
nearby Palais de Justice and has become
something of an institution.

LA CHARLOTTE EN ÎLE
Map p82   Tea Room

☎ 01 43 54 25 83; 24 rue St-Louis en l'Île, Île de
St-Louis, 4e; 🕙 2-8pm Thu-Sun; Ⓜ Pont Marie
This tiny place is one of the loveliest *salons
de thé* (tearooms) in all of Paris and definitely worth crossing the bridge for. The

top picks

BAR-HOPPING STREETS

Prime drinking spots in Paris, perfect for evening meandering to soak up the scene.
- **Rue Vieille du Temple & surrounding streets, 4e**
  (p286) Marais cocktail of gay bars and chic cafés.
- **Rue Oberkampf & rue Jean-Pierre Timbaud,**
  11e (p286) Hip bars, bohemian hang-outs and
  atmospheric cafés.
- **Rue de la Roquette, rue Keller & rue de Lappe,**
  11e (p289) Whatever you fancy; Bastille has the
  lot.
- **Rue Montmartre, 2e** (p276) Modern, slick bars
  and pubs.
- **Canal St-Martin, 10e** (p285) Heady summer
  nights in casual canal-side cafés.
- **Rue Princesse & rue des Canettes, 6e** (p281) On
  the other side of the Seine, hit this pedestrian duo
  for student, sports 'n' tapas bars and pubs.

fairy-tale theme adds flavour (as if any was
needed) to the chocolate and pastries, and
the dozens of teas on offer are superbly
chosen. Marionette shows usually take
place on Wednesday. Pass by to get the
latest flyer.

THE LATIN QUARTER

Rive Gauche romantics, well-heeled café society types and students by the gallon drink
in the 5e arrondissement, where old-but-good
recipes, nostalgic formulas and a flurry of
early-evening happy hours ensure a quintessential Parisian soirée. It's all good fun here,
though nothing ground-breaking.

CURIO PARLOR COCKTAIL CLUB
Map p100   Bar, Club

☎ 01 44 07 12 47; 16 rue des Bernardins, 5e;
🕙 7pm-2am Tue-Thu, 7pm-4am Fri & Sat;
Ⓜ Maubert–Mutualité
Run by the same switched-on, chilled-out
team as the Experimental (p307) and Prescription Cocktail Clubs (p281), this hybrid
bar-club looks to the inter-war *années folles*
(crazy years) of 1920s Paris, London and
New York for inspiration. Its racing-green
façade with simple brass plaque on the
door is the height of discretion: go to its
Facebook page to find out which party is
happening when.

LE CROCODILE Map p100 Bar

☎ 01 43 54 32 37; 6 rue Royer Collard, 5e;
🕑 10pm-6am Mon-Sat; Ⓜ Luxembourg

This bar with racing-green wooden shutters has been dispensing cocktails (more than 200 on the list) since 1966. Apparently the '70s were 'epic' in this bar, and the dream kicks on well into the wee hours of the new century. Arrive late for a truly eclectic crowd, including lots of students, and an atmosphere that can go from quiet tippling to raucous revelry.

LE PIANO VACHE Map p100 Bar

☎ 01 46 33 75 03; 8 rue Laplace, 5e; 🕑 noon-2am Mon-Fri, 9pm-2am Sat & Sun; Ⓜ Maubert–Mutualité

Down the hill from the Panthéon, this bar is covered in old posters above old couches and is drenched in 1970s and '80s rock ambience. Effortlessly underground and a real student fave, bands and DJs play mainly rock, plus some goth, reggae and pop.

LE VIEUX CHÊNE Map p100 Bar

☎ 01 43 37 71 51; 69 rue Mouffetard, 5e; 🕑 4pm-2am Sun-Thu, to 5am Fri & Sat; Ⓜ Place Monge

This rue Mouffetard institution is reckoned to be Paris' oldest bar. Indeed, a revolutionary circle met here in 1848 and it was a popular *bal musette* (dancing club) in the late 19th and early 20th centuries. Today it's popular with students, and hosts jazz at weekends.

CAFÉ DELMAS Map p100 Café

☎ 01 43 26 51 26; 2 place de la Contrescarpe, 5e; 🕑 8am-2am Sun-Thu, to 4am Fri & Sat; Ⓜ Cardinal Lemoine

Enviably situated on tree-studded place de la Contrescarpe, the Delmas is a hot spot for chilling over *un café*/cappuccino or all-day breakfast (€12). Sit comfortably beneath overhead heaters outside to soak up the street atmosphere or snuggle up between books in the library-style interior – awash with students from the nearby universities. Should you need the loo, Jacqueline is for women, Jacques for men.

LE VERRE À PIED Map p100 Café

☎ 01 43 31 15 72; 118bis rue Mouffetard, 5e; 🕑 8am-9pm Tue-Sat, to 4pm Sun; Ⓜ Censier–Daubenton

This *café-tabac* is a pearl of a place where little has changed since 1870. Its nicotine-hued mirrored wall, moulded cornices and original bar make it part of a dying breed, but the place oozes the charm, glamour and romance of an old Paris everyone loves. Stall holders from the rue Mouffetard market yo-yo in and out, contemporary photography and art adorns one wall. Lunch is a busy, lively affair, and live music quickens the pulse a couple of evenings a week.

CAVE LA BOURGOGNE

Map p100 Café, Wine Bar

☎ 01 47 07 82 80; 144 rue Mouffetard, 5e;
🕑 9am-10.30pm; Ⓜ Censier–Daubenton

A prime spot for lapping up rue Mouffetard's contagious 'saunter-all-day' spirit, this neighbourhood hang-out sits on square St-Médard, one of the Latin Quarter's loveliest squares: think flower-bedecked fountain, centuries-old church and tastebud-titillating market stalls spilling across one side. Inside, old ladies and their pet dogs meet for coffee around dark wood tables alongside a local wine-sipping set. In summer everything spills outside.

LE PUB ST-HILAIRE Map p100 Pub

2 rue Valette, 5e; 🕑 11am-2am Mon-Thu, to 4am Fri, 4pm-4am Sat, 3pm-midnight Sun; Ⓜ Maubert–Mutualité

'Buzzing' fails to do justice to the pulsating vibe inside this student-loved pub. Generous happy hours last several hours and a trio of pool tables, board games, music on two floors and various gimmicks to rev up the party crowd (a metre of cocktails, 'be your own barman' etc) keep the place packed. Pay €3.50/5.50/10 for a *demi/pinte/litre* of *bière pression* (draught beer).

LE VIOLON DINGUE Map p100 Pub

☎ 01 43 25 79 93; 46 rue de la Montagne Ste-Geneviève, 5e; 🕑 8pm-5am Tue-Sat; Ⓜ Maubert–Mutualité

A loud, lively bar adopted by revolving generations of students, the 'Crazy Violin' attracts lots of young English-speakers with big-screen sports shown upstairs and the flirty 'Dingue Lounge' downstairs. The name 'Crazy Violin' is a pun on the expression *le violon d'Ingres*, meaning 'hobby' in French, because the celebrated painter Jean-Auguste-Dominique Ingres used to play fiddle in his spare time.

ST-GERMAIN & INVALIDES

While much of the 6e is sleepy and snobby, Carrefour de l'Odéon has a cluster of lively bars and cafés. Rue de Buci, rue St-André des Arts and rue de l'Odéon enjoy a fair slice of night action with their arty cafés and busy pubs, while place St-Germain des Prés buzzes with the pavement terraces of St-Germain's beloved literary cafés. The local and international student hordes pile into the bars and pubs on atmospheric '*rue de la soif*' (street of thirst), aka rue Princesse and rue des Canettes.

An undisputable day rather than night venue, with government ministries and embassies outweighing drinking venues hands-down, the neighbouring 7e arrondissement does have a redeeming feature for socialites, in the shape of three very lovely cafés.

LE ZÉRO DE CONDUITE Map p112   Bar
☎ 01 46 34 26 35; www.zerodeconduite.fr, in French; 14 rue Jacob, 6e; 🕑 8.30pm-1.30am Mon-Thu, 6pm-2am Fri & Sat, 9pm-1am Sun; Ⓜ Odéon
Originality, if nothing else, ensures that this *bijou* drinking hole, in the house where Richard Wagner lived briefly in the 1840s, gets a mention. Serving cocktails in *biberons* (baby bottles) and throwing *concours de grimaces* (face-pulling competitions), it goes all out to rekindle your infancy. Bizarre, yes, but obviously some enjoy sucking vodka and banana liqueur shaken with grenadine and orange juice through a teat. Board games, dice, cards and Trivial Pursuit complete the playful scene. Advance table reservations are strongly recommended.

LES ETAGES ST-GERMAIN Map p112   Bar
☎ 01 46 34 26 26; 5 rue de Buci, 6e; 🕑 11am-2am daily; Ⓜ Odéon
Busy and bustling on shop-lined rue de Buci, this terrace bar with shabby-chic army-green façade and retro stooling makes a great people-watching pit stop between boutiques. Grab a coffee or summertime strawberry mojito (€7.50) in the sun, or plump for happy hour when cocktails plummet to €5.50 a shot.

L'URGENCE BAR Map p112   Bar
☎ 01 43 26 45 69; www.urgencebar.com, in French; 45 rue Monsieur-le-Prince, 6e; 🕑 9pm-4am Tue-Sat; Ⓜ Luxembourg

Just south of the École de Médecine is located this medical-themed 'emergency room'. Here are the future doctors of France, busy imbibing luridly coloured liquor from babies' bottles and test tubes, loosening their stethoscopes and pointing to the 'X-ray art' – making comments like '*Mais non! Clarisse, that's so not the tibia!*' Even if you don't understand French, its website gives a good sense of the vibe here.

PRESCRIPTION COCKTAIL CLUB
Map p112   Bar, Club
☎ 01 46 34 67 73; 23 rue Mazarine, 6e; 🕑 7pm-2am Mon-Thu, 7pm-4am Fri & Sat; Ⓜ Odéon
With bowler and flat-top hats as lampshades and a 1930s speakeasy New York air to the place, this cocktail club – one in a trio run by the same massively successful team as Curio Parlor (p279) and Experimental (p307) – really is an address to safeguard in your little black book. It's all very Parisian-cool and getting past the doorman can be tough, but once in it's friendliness and old-fashioned cocktails all round. Watch its Facebook page for events (our favourite to date: its Sunday afternoon Mad Hatters pyjama parties).

CAFÉ DE FLORE Map p112   Café
☎ 01 45 48 55 26; 172 blvd St-Germain, 6e; 🕑 7.30am-1.30am; Ⓜ St-Germain des Prés
The red upholstered benches, mirrors and marble walls at this art deco landmark haven't changed much since the days when Jean-Paul Sartre, Simone de Beauvoir, Albert Camus and Pablo Picasso wagged their chins here. Its busy terrace draws in lunching ladies, posh business-folk and foreigners in search of the past.

CAFÉ DU MUSÉE RODIN Map p108   Café
☎ 01 44 18 61 10; 77 rue de Varenne, 7e; 🕑 9.30am-6.45pm Tue-Sun Apr-Sep, to 5pm Tue-Sun Oct-Mar; Ⓜ Varenne
A serene beauty pervades the garden of the Musée Rodin (p111), with the great master's sculptures popping up among the roses and lime trees that line the pathways. If the weather is fine you can have a drink and a snack at one of the tables hidden behind the trees (garden admission €1).

CAFÉ LE BASILE Map p112   Café
☎ 01 42 22 59 46; 34 rue de Grenelle, 7e; 🕑 7am-9pm Mon-Sat; Ⓜ Rue du Bac
Don't bother looking for a name above this hip student café, framed by expensive

designer fashion shops – there isn't one. Well-worn Formica tables, petrol-blue banquettes and a fine collection of 1950s lights and lampshades keep the sleek crowd out, the retro crowd in. A fabulous find for a hot chocolate or beer, light lunch or flop between lectures.

CAFÉ THOUMIEUX Map p108   Café
☎ 01 45 51 50 40; 4 rue de la Comète, 7e; ☺ noon-2am Mon-Fri, 5pm-2am Sat; Ⓜ La Tour-Maubourg
The trendy tapas annexe of Brasserie Thoumieux (p233) is always full of well-heeled young people who seem to enjoy the Iberian ambience. Tapas and San Miguel beer set the scene, but perfumed vodka is the house speciality, with no fewer than 40 different types (including chocolate, fig, watermelon and mint tea) to pick from.

LES DEUX MAGOTS Map p112   Café
☎ 01 45 48 55 25; 170 blvd St-Germain, 6e; ☺ 7am-1am; Ⓜ St-Germain des Prés
This erstwhile literary haunt dates from 1914 and is known as the favoured hangout of Sartre, Hemingway and André Breton. Its name refers to the two *magots* (grotesque figurines) of Chinese dignitaries at the entrance. It's touristy, but just once you should give in to nostalgia and sit on this inimitable terrace where passing celebrities, retiring philosophers and remnants of noblesse sip its famous shop-made hot chocolate, served in porcelain jugs.

CAFÉ LA PALETTE Map p112   Café, Bar
☎ 01 43 26 68 15; 43 rue de Seine, 6e; ☺ 8am-2am Mon-Sat; Ⓜ Mabillon
In the heart of gallery land, this *fin-de-siècle* café and erstwhile stomping ground of Paul Cézanne and Georges Braque attracts a grown-up set of fashion people and local art dealers. Its summer terrace is beautiful.

ALCAZAR Map p112   Cocktail Bar
☎ 01 53 10 19 99; www.alcazar.fr; 62 rue Mazarine, 6e; ☺ noon-3pm & 7pm-2am; Ⓜ Odéon
Also known as 'La Mezzanine', this hip bar inside Alcazar has got Conran's name all over it. Narcissistic but alluring, it's a modern white-and-glass mezzanine overlooking the restaurant (brunch €34, lunch/dinner menu €20 to €34/40) with fancy cocktails, *nouvelle cuisine* dinners and a fashionable supper-club clientele. Wednesday to Saturday, DJs 'pass records' in the corner – this place is

top picks

FOR COCKTAILS

Feeling fancy? Flit into urban high life for a taste of Paris at its most chic:

- **Buddha Bar** (p283) Chill-out soundtrack and Buddha-ful décor.
- **Ice Kube** (p285) Vodkatinis at five below.
- **Andy Walhoo** (p288) Bar 'with nothing' has everything and everybody knows it.
- **Le China** (p290) The name may have changed (slightly) but the Asian clubby verve, jazz and dim sum remain.
- **Alcazar** (p282) Cocktails on the Left Bank à la Monsieur Terence Conran – inevitably hip.
- **Le Fumoir** (p278) Promise of a smoke in a stylish boozer around from the Louvre.
- **Experimental** (p307), **Curio Parlor** (p279) & **Prescription Cocktail Club** (p281) This glam trio of cocktail-bar siblings has reinvented the bar scene, New Yorker–style.
- **Lizard Lounge** (p288) Ultra-chilled Marais landmark does cocktails and more.

famous for its excellent trip-hop/house/lounge music compilations. Next door is Conran's club Le Wagg (p298). Flyers for all three are posted at www.blogalcazar.fr.

LE 10 Map p112   Pub
☎ 01 43 26 66 83; 10 rue de l'Odéon, 6e; ☺ 5.30pm-2am; Ⓜ Odéon
A local institution, this cellar pub groans with students, smoky ambience and cheap sangria. Posters adorn the walls and an eclectic selection emerges from the jukebox – everything from jazz and the Doors to *chanson française* ('French song'; traditional musical genre in which lyrics are paramount). It's the ideal spot for plotting the next revolution or conquering a lonely heart.

KILÀLI Map p112   Tearoom
☎ 01 43 25 65 64; 3-5 rue des Quatre Vents, 6e; ☺ noon-10pm Tue-Sat, 1-9pm Sun; Ⓜ Odéon
Style personified, this Japanese tearoom-cum-art gallery is a peaceful oasis amid the bustling shops. Finesse, nobility and other elevated adjectives describe the different varieties of green teas served in pottery teapots with matching *yunomi* (goblets). Request a refill of water after you've drained the pot.

COMPTOIR DES CANNETTES

Map p112   Wine Bar

☎ 01 43 26 79 15; 11 rue des Canettes, 6e;
🕙 noon-2am Tue-Sat, closed Aug; Ⓜ Mabillon
In the biz since 1952, a faithful local following pours into this cellar, a stuffy, atmospheric tribute to downtrodden romanticism complete with red tablecloths, melting candles and nostalgic photos of musicians. The wine is cheap, the regulars incorrigible and on a good night the whole thing spills up the stairs and onto the street.

AU SAUVIGNON

Map p108   Wine Bar, Café

☎ 01 45 48 49 02; 80 rue des Sts-Pères, 7e;
🕙 8am-midnight daily; Ⓜ Sèvres–Babylone
There is no more authentic *bar à vin* than this, footsteps from Le Bon Marché in the shop-chic 7e. Grab a table in the evening sun or opt for the quintessential bistro interior, a vibrant affair with original zinc bar, tightly packed tables and hand-painted ceiling celebrating French viticultural tradition. To savour this wine bar at its best, choose from 11 reds, six whites and two rosés served by the glass (€4.70 to €6.20) and order a plate of *casse-croûtes au pain Poilâne* – ham, pâté, terrine, smoked salmon, foie gras and so on sandwiches with the city's most famous bread.

CHAMPS-ÉLYSÉES & GRANDS BOULEVARDS

The Champs-Élysées is still a popular place for drinking but the vast majority of venues are terribly expensive and tend to be either tacky tourist traps or exceedingly pretentious lounges. As far as nightlife is concerned, this is a better area to come to for clubbing (p296).

Haussmann's windswept boulevards have plenty of brasseries that are good for a coffee break or post-shopping drink, but for the most part, Paris' more atmospheric bars and cafés tend to be elsewhere.

AU GÉNÉRAL LA FAYETTE

Map p126   Café

☎ 01 47 70 59 08; 52 rue La Fayette, 9e; 🕙 10am-4am daily; Ⓜ Le Peletier
With its all-day menu, archetypal belle époque décor and special beers on offer, this old-style brasserie is an excellent stop for an afternoon coffee, evening drink or

typical French meal outside normal restaurant hours.

BUDDHA BAR Map p126   Cocktail Bar

☎ 01 53 05 90 00; 8-12 rue Boissy d'Anglas, 8e; 🕙 noon-2am Sun-Thu, 4pm-3am Fri & Sat; Ⓜ Concorde
Although moving in and out of A-list status as the fickle übercrowd comes and goes, Buddha Bar has made a name for itself with its Zen lounge music CDs and remains a hit – especially with tourists. The décor is simply spectacular, with a two-storey golden Buddha, millions of candles, intimate corners and supremely attitudinous staff. Go for the cocktails (from €16) and Asian-inspired bar snacks.

CRICKETER Map p126   Pub

☎ 01 40 07 01 45; 41 rue des Mathurins, 8e; 🕙 noon-2am; Ⓜ Madeleine or Havre–Caumartin; 🛜
This self-proclaimed 'English sports pub' can stake a claim to authenticity – it was transported lock, stock and barrel from Ipswich. It's not a happening venue at night, but with Newcastle Brown on tap, salt 'n' vinegar chips, Brit tabloids and quiz night every Tuesday it is as close to Old Blighty as you'll find on this side of the Channel.

O'SULLIVAN'S Map p126   Pub

☎ 01 40 26 73 41; www.osullivans-pubs.com; 1 blvd Montmartre, 2e; 🕙 noon-5am Sun-Thu, to 7am Fri & Sat; Ⓜ Grands Boulevards; 🛜
From the outside this looks like just another supermarket-chain Irish pub, but O'Sullivan's is so much more. It's hugely popular thanks to its prominent location and friendly vibe. The spacious surrounds are always packed for big sporting events, plus concerts (jazz, rock, pop, Irish music) on Thursdays and DJs at the weekend. Different available areas such as the 1st floor and the outdoor terrace mean you can (almost) always find a tranquil place to chat.

AU LIMONAIRE Map p126   Wine Bar

☎ 01 45 23 33 33; http://limonaire.free.fr; 18 cité Bergère, 9e; 🕙 7pm-midnight Mon, 6pm-midnight Tue-Sun; Ⓜ Grands Boulevards
This little wine bar is one of the best places to listen to traditional French *chansons* and local singer-songwriters. Performances begin at 7pm on Sunday and at 10pm Tuesday to Saturday. It's free entry, and simple meals are served for between €8.50 and €11. Reservations are recommended.

MONTMARTRE, PIGALLE & 17E

Crowded around the hill side of Montmartre you'll find an eclectic selection of places to drink. This area offers an unusual medley of tourist-trap *chanson* bars at Sacré Cœur, picturesque Parisian spots around Abbesses, anything-goes venues (from hostess bars to Irish pubs) at Pigalle and cool African outposts at Château Rouge.

Rue des Dames in the 17e arrondissement is a particularly rewarding street when in search of a libation or a laugh – there are a handful of good wine bars here.

LA FOURMI Map p134   Bar
☎ 01 42 64 70 35; 74 rue des Martyrs, 18e; ☺ 8am-2am Mon-Thu, to 4am Fri & Sat, 10am-2am Sun; Ⓜ Pigalle

A Pigalle stayer, the 'Ant' hits the mark with its lively yet unpretentious atmosphere. The décor is hip but not overwhelming, the zinc bar is long and inviting and the people are laid-back. The music is mostly rock – quality, well-known tunes that get you going while leaving space in the airways for the rise and fall of unbridled conversation. If you're hungry, its *plat du jour* costs €9.

LE SANCERRE Map p134   Bar
☎ 01 42 58 08 20; 35 rue des Abbesses, 18e; ☺ 7am-2am; Ⓜ Abbesses; 🛜

Le Sancerre is a popular, rather brash bistro-cum-bar that's often crowded to capacity in the evening, especially on Saturdays. Scruffy yet attractive with its classic bistro décor and hip local mood, it has a prized terrace that gets the late morning sun. It serves bistro food and breakfasts from 11.30am to 11.30pm. Happy hour is 5.30pm to 8pm.

LUSH BAR Map p136   Bar
☎ 01 43 87 49 46; 16 rue des Dames, 17e; ☺ 5pm-2am; Ⓜ Place de Clichy

This Clichy post has made a name for itself with a relaxed-but-hip local following and Anglo expats. It has excellent cocktails including killer white Russians, as well as wines and, in true English (or Irish – there are photos of the Emerald Isle on the walls) style, affordable beers. DJs often play at weekends.

OLYMPIC CAFÉ Map p134   Bar
☎ 01 42 52 29 93; www.rueleon.net; 20 rue Léon, 18e; ☺ 11am-2am Tue-Sat; Ⓜ Château Rouge

This community bar in the Goutte d'Or neighbourhood is full of surprises. From plays and film screenings to concerts of Guinean *griot*, Balkan folk, Cameroon hip-hop and so on in the basement (tickets €1 to €5), this is a breeding ground for creative young people bursting with original ideas. The monthly program available at the bar also includes events (tickets adult/concession €15/10) at the Lavoir Moderne Parisien (Map p134; ☎ 01 42 52 09 14; 35 rue Léon, 18e), another springboard for young talent down the road.

AU RENDEZ-VOUS DES AMIS
Map p134   Bar, Café
☎ 01 46 06 01 60; 23 rue Gabrielle, 18e; ☺ 8am-2am; Ⓜ Abbesses

If you need to ease your way up or down the steps of Montmartre, look no further than this kick-back café-bar, which serves €1 espresso and €10 pitchers of beer. Sandwiches and snacks are prepared in Hell's Kitchen.

CHÀO BÀ CAFÉ Map p134   Café
☎ 01 46 06 72 90; 22 blvd de Clichy, 18e; ☺ 8.30am-2am Sun-Wed, to 4am Thu, to 5am Fri & Sat; Ⓜ Pigalle; 🛜

This comfortable café-restaurant on two levels is decorated in colonial Oriental style with huge plants, ceiling fans and bamboo chairs. It serves great cocktails (from €9.50) in goldfish-bowl-sized glasses, and somewhat bland Franco-Vietnamese fusion food. And by the way: *chào bà* means *bonjour madame* in Vietnamese.

LE PROGRÈS Map p134   Café
☎ 01 42 64 07 37; 7 rue des Trois Frères, 18e; ☺ 9am-2am; Ⓜ Abbesses

A real live *café du quartier* perched in the heart of Abbesses, the 'Progress' occupies a corner site with huge windows and simple seating and attracts a relaxed mix of local artists, shop staff, writers and hangers-on. It's great for convivial evenings, with DJs and bands some nights, but it's also a good place to come for inexpensive meals and daytime coffees.

O P'TIT DOUAI Map p134   Café
☎ 01 53 21 91 35; 92 rue Blanche, 9e; ☺ 8am-2am; Ⓜ Blanche

This colourful neighbourhood café is just down the street from the Moulin Rouge, but it might as well be light years away. Trade in the mayhem for some tranquillity over coffee, wines by the glass (from €2.50) or some traditional Parisian fare at mealtimes.

LE WEPLER Map p136 — Café
☎ 01 45 22 53 24; 14 Place de Clichy, 18e; ☽ 8am-1am; Ⓜ Place de Clichy

Though this large café-brasserie founded in 1892 is celebrated for its oysters, we go across the road to Charlot, Roi des Coquillages (p244) for our bivalves and to the Wepler to sit in the large covered terrace and enjoy the hubbub and scenery of Place de Clichy. Great people-watching; friendly service.

ICE KUBE Map p134 — Cocktail Bar
☎ 01 42 05 20 00; 1-5 passage Ruelle, 18e; ☽ 7pm-1.30am Wed-Sat, 2-11pm Sun; Ⓜ La Chapelle

Every city worth its, err, salt, has got to have an ice bar nowadays, and this *temple de glace* (ice temple) on the 1st floor of the *très boutique* Kube Hôtel (p340) is the French capital's first. The temperature is set at -5°C, there are down jackets on loan and the bar is a shimmering block of carved ice. For €38 you get four vodka cocktails and 30 minutes of chill time.

BAR À VINS DU CINÉMA DES CINÉASTES Map p136 — Wine Bar
☎ 01 53 42 40 34; 7 av de Clichy, 17e; ☽ 6pm-midnight; Ⓜ Place de Clichy

This excellent wine bar is seldom filled to capacity, presumably because most people are downstairs, watching a film at the Cinéma des Cinéastes (p305). The selection of wines by the glass, *pichet* (50cL) or bottle is excellent, there is a brief but well-considered menu and the first Sunday of each month hosts a music night starting at 6pm.

GARE DU NORD & CANAL ST-MARTIN

Canal St-Martin offers a trendy bohemian atmosphere and wonderful summer nights (and days) in casual canal-side cafés. The proliferation of bars and cafés in the 10e is gradually joining this area up with Belleville and Ménilmontant (see p286).

LE JEMMAPES Map p140 — Bar
☎ 01 40 40 02 35; 82 quai de Jemmapes, 10e; ☽ 11am-2am daily; Ⓜ Jacques Bonsergent or Goncourt

This canal-side bar has several Belgian beers on tap as well as no-frills plastic cups for when the party spills outside in nicer weather.

CAFÉ CHÉRI(E) Map p140 — Bar, Café
☎ 01 42 02 02 05; 44 blvd de la Villette, 19e; ☽ noon-1am; Ⓜ Belleville; ☎

Very reminiscent of Belleville before all the changes, this successful bar-café has a lively, gritty, art-chic crowd and electro DJs Thursday to Saturday. An imaginative, colourful bar with its signature red lighting, infamous *mojitos* and *caiparinhas* and commitment to quallty tunes, it's become everyone's *chéri(e)* (darling) and the first port of call on a night out in this part of town.

CHEZ PRUNE Map p140 — Bar, Café
☎ 01 42 41 30 47; 71 quai de Valmy, 10e; ☽ 8am-2am Mon-Sat, 10am-2am Sun; Ⓜ République

This Soho-*boho* café put Canal St-Martin on the map. It's a classic Parisian bar-café, nicely rough around the edges, with good vibes – a terrace opposite the Canal St-Martin open in summer and a cosy atmosphere in winter. Brunch on Sundays (noon to 4pm) is popular.

DELAVILLE CAFÉ Map p140 — Bar, Café
☎ 01 48 24 48 09; 34 blvd de Bonne Nouvelle, 10e; ☽ 11am-2.30am; Ⓜ Bonne Nouvelle; ☎

This grand erstwhile brothel has an alluring mix of restored history (original mosaic tiles, distressed walls) and industrial chic. Between the high-ceilinged restaurant (mains €14 to €19), the extensive terrace (one of the best along the *grands boulevards*) and the bar–lounge areas, you're sure to find your niche somewhere. DJs play Thursday to Saturday, making it a quality 'before' venue for the nearby Rex Club (p297).

LA SARDINE Map p140 — Bar, Café
☎ 01 42 49 19 46; www.barlasardine.com; 32 place Ste-Marthe, 10e; ☽ 9am-2am daily Apr-Sep, 9am-2am Tue-Sun Oct-Mar; Ⓜ Belleville; ☎

Out in the western flanks of Belleville, it's easy to miss the rue Ste-Marthe, filled with colourful restaurants and bars exerting a dilapidated, funky charm. At the top, literally and figuratively, is this splendid and convivial café-wine-bar, a bit of Marseille in Paris, with an enormous terrace on sheltered place Ste-Marthe. It's brilliant for warm afternoons, casual meals (tapas €3 to €6, lunch menu €11) and to sample a few organic wines.

L'ATMOSPHÈRE Map p140   Bar, Café
☎ 01 40 38 09 21; 49 rue Lucien Sampaix, 10e; ⊙ 9.30am-1.45am Mon-Sat, till midnight Sun; Ⓜ Jacques Bonsergent or Gare de l'Est
Another nod to the 1938 flick *Hôtel du Nord* (see p143), this timber-and-tile café along the canal has an arty, spirited ambience, well-priced drinks and decent food.

MARAIS & MÉNILMONTANT

The Marais is an excellent spot for a night out. It's a lively mix of gay-friendly (and gay-only) café society and bourgeois arty spots, with an interesting sprinkling of eclectic bars and relatively raucous pubs.

Rue Oberkampf is the essential hub of the Ménilmontant bar crawl, springing from a few cafés to being the epicentre of a vibrant, rapidly expanding bar scene. But as Oberkampf commercialises, the arty/edgy crowd has been moving steadily outwards, through cosmopolitan Belleville and towards La Villette (see p139).

AU PETIT FER À CHEVAL Map p152   Bar
☎ 01 42 72 07 27; 30 rue Vieille du Temple, 4e; ⊙ 8am-2am; Ⓜ Hôtel de Ville or St-Paul; 🛜
The original (1903) horseshoe-shaped zinc bar leaves little room for much else, but nobody seems to mind at this genial place. It overflows with friendly regulars enjoying a drink or a sandwich (simple meals are served from noon to 1.15am). The stainless-steel toilets are straight out of a Flash Gordon film even after all this time.

AU P'TIT GARAGE Map p148   Bar
☎ 01 48 07 08 12; 63 rue Jean-Pierre Timbaud, 11e; ⊙ 6pm-2am; Ⓜ Parmentier
Just about the last 'neighbourhood' bar in the *quartier*, the 'Little Garage' attracts local custom (think grease monkeys and others with cleaner hands) with its rock 'n' roll, laid-back staff and rough-and-ready décor. It's still our favourite venue on rue JPT.

top picks

CAFÉ TERRACES

Languish on a café terrace and watch the capital enjoy life over that all-essential, early-evening *apéro* (aperitif).

- Delaville Café, 10e (p285) Erstwhile brothel offers the best terrace on the *grands boulevards*.
- Pause Café, 11e (p290) All-weather terrace provides the quintessential meeting place for *riverains* (local residents)
- Le Café des Initiés, 1er (p277) Hobnob with local scribes at this venue near the Louvre.
- Les Funambules, 11e (p289) Delightful place – inside or out – to while away a summer's evening.
- Chai 33, 12e (p290) Not one but two terraces at this converted wine warehouse in Bercy.
- Chez Prune, 10e (p285) Canal-side trendsetters.
- La Sardine, 10e (p285) A gem of local's wine bar on a hidden square.
- Le Sancerre, 18e (p284) On the sunny side of the rue in Montmartre.
- Café La Palette, 6e (p282) Parisians have hung out at this Left Bank address framed by art galleries since the 1930s.
- Café Delmas, 5e (p280) Drink al fresco on one of the Latin Quarter's leafiest squares.

LA CARAVANE
Map p148   Bar
☎ 01 49 23 01 86; 35 rue de la Fontaine au Roi, 11e; ⊙ 11am-2am; Ⓜ Goncourt; 🛜
This funky, animated bar is a little jewel tucked away between République and Oberkampf; look for the tiny campervan above the pavement. The bar is surrounded by colourful kitsch furnishings, and the people around it and behind it are amiable and relaxed. The kitchen was into a rather odd hybrid cuisine – Thai noodles, Indian korma, Provençal dishes – the last time we looked.

LA CHAISE AU PLAFOND Map p152   Bar
☎ 01 42 76 03 22; 10 Rue du Trésor, 4e; ⊙ 10am-2am; Ⓜ Hôtel de Ville or St-Paul
The 'Chair on the Ceiling' is a peaceful, warm place, with wooden tables outside on a terrace giving onto tranquil passage du Trésor. It's a real oasis from the frenzy of the Marais and worth knowing about in summer.

LA PERLE Map p152 Bar

☎ 01 42 72 69 93; 78 rue Vieille du Temple, 3e; ⏲ 6am-2am Mon-Fri, 8am-2am Sat & Sun; Ⓜ St-Paul or Chemin Vert

This is where *bobos* (bohemian bourgeois) come to slum it over *un rouge* (glass of red wine) until the DJ arrives and things liven up. We like the (for real) distressed look of the place and the model locomotive over the bar.

L'ALIMENTATION GÉNÉRALE

Map p148 Bar

☎ 01 43 55 42 50; 64 rue Jean-Pierre Timbaud, 11e; ⏲ 5pm-2am Wed, Thu & Sun, 5pm-4am Fri & Sat; Ⓜ Parmentier

Another rue JPT stalwart, the 'Grocery Store' is a massive space, with crazy retro décor and some outrageous toilets. Music is a very big deal here. DJs rock the joint at weekends; expect to pay €10 with a drink for big names.

LES ÉTAGES Map p152 Bar

☎ 01 42 78 72 00; 35 rue Vieille du Temple, 4e; ⏲ 5pm-2am; Ⓜ Hôtel de Ville or St-Paul; 🛜

Students and expats find the 'Storeys' (all three floors) a viable alternative to the standard Marais fare, and happily appropriate the upgraded lounge rooms upstairs. Before 9pm certain cocktails are €5 instead of the usual €8. Happy hour is 5pm to 9pm.

POP IN Map p148 Bar

☎ 01 48 05 56 11; 105 rue Amelot, 11e; ⏲ 6.30pm-1.30am; Ⓜ St-Sébastien–Froissart

All skinny jeans and cultivated pop-rock nonchalance, the Pop In somehow got itself on the in-crowd map but maintains a relaxed regulars' vibe. It's popular with expats and Parisian students starting out the evening, and the drinks are reasonably priced. Whisper sweet nothings as you leave; they've had a lot of problems with noise-sensitive neighbours.

CAFÉ BAROC Map p152 Bar, café

☎ 01 48 87 61 30; 37 rue du Roi de Sicile, 4e; ⏲ 5pm-2am Tue-Sat, 3pm-2am Sun; Ⓜ St-Paul

The old cinema seats here are ideal for sipping flavoured beer (a big deal here). Normally a chilled, almost classy little place, things get hyper when bar staff play fabulously camp 1980s tunes. Open mic from 4pm till closing on Sunday lets you try at being just as good (or bad).

CAFÉ CHARBON Map p148 Bar, Café

☎ 01 43 57 55 13; 109 rue Oberkampf, 11e; ⏲ 9am-2am Sun-Wed, to 4am Thu-Sat; Ⓜ Parmentier; 🛜

With its post-industrial belle époque ambience, the Charbon was the first of the hip cafés and bars to catch on in Ménilmontant. It's always crowded and worth heading to for the distressed décor with high ceilings, chandeliers and perched DJ booth. The food (mains €14 to €18) is good; it's a popular spot for brunch (€15) between noon and 4pm on Sundays.

LE PICK-CLOPS Map p152 Bar, Café

☎ 01 40 29 00 87; 16 rue Vieille du Temple, 4e; ⏲ 7am-2am Mon-Sat, 8am-2am Sun; Ⓜ Hôtel de Ville or St-Paul; 🛜

This buzzy bar-café – all shades of yellow and lit by neon – has Formica tables, ancient bar stools and plenty of mirrors. Attracting a friendly flow of locals and passers-by, it's a great place for morning or afternoon coffee, or that last drink alone or with friends. Great rum punch (from €6.60) served with copious amounts of peanuts.

AU CHAT NOIR Map p148 Café

☎ 01 48 06 98 22; 76 rue Jean-Pierre Timbaud, 10e; ⏲ 9am-2am Mon-Sat, 11am-2am Fri & Sat, noon-2am Sun; Ⓜ Parmentier or Couronnes; 🛜

Slightly removed from the overexcitement of Oberkampf and with a slightly older crowd, this attractive corner café with high ceilings and a long, wooden bar is a happening but relaxed drinking space at night. It's also a great café in which to hang out or read emails during the day. Downstairs is more animated, with occasional live concerts.

CAFÉ DES PHARES Map p148 Café

☎ 01 42 72 04 70; 7 place de la Bastille, 4e; ⏲ 7.30am-3am Sun-Thu, to 4am Fri & Sat; Ⓜ Bastille

The 'Beacons Café' is best known as the city's original *philocafé* (philosophers' café). If you feel like debating such topics as 'What is a fact?' and 'Can people communicate?', head for this place at 11am on Sunday; the debate lasts for two hours. It may sound posy but this is Paris.

CAFÉ SUÉDOIS Map p152 Café

☎ 01 44 78 80 20; 11 rue Payenne, 3e; ⏲ noon-6pm Tue-Sun; Ⓜ Chemin Vert; 🛜

Housed in the beautiful 16th-century Hôtel de Marle, this gorgeous café in the Swedish Cultural Institute hosts a variety of exhibitions, concerts and debates, with rich resources on Swedish history and culture. But what we're interested in here are the delicious soups, sandwiches and cakes (€4 to €6) and the tables outside in the tranquil paved courtyard.

L'APPAREMMENT CAFÉ Map p152   Café
☎ 01 48 87 12 22; 18 rue des Coutures St-Gervais, 3e; ☼ noon-2am Mon-Sat, to midnight Sun; Ⓜ St-Sébastien–Froissart
This place is a tasteful haven tucked behind the Musée Picasso and at a merciful distance from the madding crowds of the Marais. It's a bit like a private living room, with wood panelling, leather sofas, scattered parlour games, dog-eared books – and Parisians languidly studying their 'lounch' (their word, not ours) and (on Sunday till 6pm) their brunch – or is that 'brounch'? – menus.

L'AUTRE CAFÉ Map p148   Café
☎ 01 40 21 03 07; 62 rue Jean-Pierre Timbaud, 11e; ☼ 8am-2am; Ⓜ Parmentier; 🛜
A young mixed crowd of locals, artists and party-goers remains faithful to this quality café with its long bar, spacious seating areas, relaxed environment, reasonable prices and exhibition openings. It's a great place to do a little work, and there is a small lounge upstairs. Sunday brunch (€18) is from noon to 5pm.

ANDY WALHOO Map p148   Cocktail Bar
☎ 01 42 71 20 38; 69 rue des Gravilliers, 3e; ☼ 5.30pm-2am Tue-Sat; Ⓜ Arts et Métiers
Casablanca meets pop-artist Andy Warhol in this cool, multicoloured cocktail lounge hidden away just north of the Centre Georges Pompidou. Its clever name means 'I have nothing' in Arabic and is a major misnomer: the acid colours, sweet cocktails, pushy staff and loud house music may be a bit too much for some palates. Happy hour is 5pm to 8pm. The courtyard behind is paradise for smokers and pullers.

LIZARD LOUNGE Map p152   Pub
☎ 01 42 72 81 34; 18 rue du Bourg Tibourg, 4e; ☼ noon-2pm; Ⓜ Hôtel de Ville or St-Paul
A quality outpost of Anglo-Saxon attitude in the heart of the Marais, this relaxed pub has beer on tap, cocktails and food

(think club sandwiches and burgers), with a popular brunch (€12 to €18) on Sunday. Young expats with clutch purses file straight downstairs to the cellar, complete with stone walls, a DJ at the weekend, and magnanimous little corners in which to schmooze. Happy hour is 8pm to 10pm.

PURE MALT Map p152   Pub
☎ 01 42 76 03 77; 4 rue Caron, 4e; ☼ 5pm-2am; Ⓜ St-Paul
A little Scottish pub-bar just south of the lovely place du Marché Ste-Catherine, the Pure Malt is for the whisky connoisseur. More than 150 types of whisky are on hand to try at from €9 a glass. It concentrates mainly on single malts, though there's beer available for €6 or €7 a pint (cheaper at happy hour: 5pm to 7pm). It's a great place for watching sport.

QUIET MAN Map p152   Pub
☎ 01 48 04 02 77; 5 rue des Haudriettes, 3e; ☼ 5pm-2am; Ⓜ Rambuteau
This is about the most authentic Irish pub Paris has to offer, with a real live Irish musicians playing real live Irish music. The only fake about it is its name, which comes from John Ford's 1932 film starring John 'Call Me Paddy' Wayne. There are frequent trad sets in the basement and darts tournaments every two weeks. Happy hour is from 5pm to 8pm daily.

STOLLY'S STONE BAR Map p152   Pub
☎ 01 42 76 06 76; 16 rue de la Cloche Percée, 4e; ☼ 4.30pm-2am; Ⓜ Hôtel de Ville or St-Paul
This itty-bitty Anglophone pub on a tiny street just above rue de Rivoli is always crowded, particularly during the 5pm to 8pm happy hour, when a pint/pitcher of cheap *blonde* (that's the house lager – not the Monroe double propping up the bar) costs €5/12. When big football matches are on and you're looking forward to a quiet drink, go elsewhere.

LE LOIR DANS LA THÉIÈRE
Map p152   Tea Room
☎ 01 42 72 90 61; 3 rue des Rosiers, 4e; ☼ 9.30am-7pm; Ⓜ St-Paul
Its cutesy name ('Dormouse in the Teapot') notwithstanding, this is a wonderful old space filled with retro toys, comfy couches and scenes of *Through the Looking Glass* on the walls. It serves up to a dozen different types of tea, excellent savoury tarts and

sandwiches (€8.50 to €12), desserts like apple crumble (€6.50), and brunch (€19.50) at the weekend.

LA TARTINE Map p152 — Wine Bar
☎ 01 42 72 76 85; 24 rue de Rivoli & 17 rue du Roi de Sicile, 4e; ☻ 8am-2am; Ⓜ St-Paul

A wine bar where little has changed since the days of gas lighting (some of the fixtures are still in place), this place offers 15 selected reds, whites and rosés by the *pot* (46cL). There's not much to eat except lots of *tartines* (open-faced sandwiches).

BASTILLE & GARE DE LYON

Bastille has become increasingly *démodé* (unfashionable) and even crass over the years, but it invariably draws a crowd, particularly to heaving rue de Lappe. Things get progressively quieter – and better – as you go further up rue de la Roquette and rue de Charonne. Rue Keller has some good cafés and a decent gay bar (see p320).

Once a desert when it came to drinking and carousing, Bercy is an increasingly happening place that draws in crowds for its cinemas and wine bars, though it's a somewhat artificially created scene. Gare de Lyon and Nation are close to drinking spots in Bastille, and to the eastern side of the 11e.

IGUANA CAFÉ Map p158 — Bar
☎ 01 40 21 39 99; 15 rue de la Roquette, 11e; ☻ 3pm-5am; Ⓜ Bastille

A contemporary, two-level, backlit café-pub whose clientele is slipping progressively from 30-somethings to early-20s punters. It's the best of a mediocre bunch and we love the red, black and silver décor on two levels. It has the advantage of closing late – or would that be early? – every night, and there's a DJ on the weekend, with themed nights. Happy hour is 6pm to 9pm.

LA LIBERTÉ Map p158 — Bar
☎ 0143 72 11 18; 196 rue de Faubourg St-Antoine, 12e; ☻ 10am-2am Mon-Sat, 11am-2am Sun; Ⓜ Faidherbe–Chaligny; 🛜

A delightfully messy local institution infused with the spirit of the '68 revolution, the 'Liberty' does simple meals and wine by day, and is a heaving mix of regulars and drop-ins, raspy-voiced arguments and

glasses going clink by night. It's the kind of place where *bobos*, artists and old rockers find their common point: a passionate love of drink and talk. Great music.

LES FUNAMBULES Map p158 — Bar
☎ 01 43 70 83 70; 12 rue Faidherbe, 11e; ☻ 7.30am-2am Mon-Sat, noon-midnight Sun; Ⓜ Faidherbe–Chaligny; 🛜

Like so many small cafés in east Paris, the 'Tightrope Walkers' has been transformed into a fashionable bar. While the original architecture provides character (check out the frescoes), nowadays the terrace is crammed with beautiful people on warm summer evenings. The rest of the year customers take shelter inside under the stunning coffered ceiling with chandelier and bird cages and enjoy a cocktail at the bar or a snack of tapas (€4.20 to €5.30) in the back room.

SANZ SANS Map p158 — Bar
☎ 01 44 75 78 78; 49 rue du Faubourg St-Antoine, 11e; ☻ 9am-2am Mon, 9am-5am Tue-Sat, 6pm-5am Sun; Ⓜ Bastille

A little cheesy, a little sleazy, this lively bar clad in red velvet and zebra stripes continues to hold out as a busy drinking venue on the Bastille beat. DJs play a very mixed bag of music, mostly electronic or funk and soul, and the crowd is similarly unpredictable. It's always good fun. There's a €5 cover charge at the weekend. Happy hour is from 5pm to 8pm.

TROLL CAFÉ Map p158 — Bar, Café
☎ 01 43 42 10 75; 27 rue de Cotte, 12e; ☻ 5pm-2am; Ⓜ Ledru-Rollin

This music and beer bar just up from the Marché Couvert Beauvau (p222) takes Brittany as its theme (at least the eponymous Troll, 90 years old if a day, is supposedly from there) but mixes in something of a northern France thing by selling Ch'ti beer. It's a young place, somewhat silly but fun for that.

LE PURE CAFÉ Map p158 — Café
☎ 01 43 71 47 22; 14 rue Jean Macé, 11e; ☻ 7am-2am; Ⓜ Charonne

This old café, which should be declared a national monument (if it already hasn't been), moonlights as a restaurant with a modern kitchen and some dishes that veer toward 'world' food (mains €17.50 to €21). But we like it as it was intended to be, especially over a *grand crème* (large white coffee) and the papers on Sunday morning. It has appeared as Central Casting's 'typical French café' in a number of films, including the 2004 British film *Before Sunset*.

PAUSE CAFÉ Map p158
Café

☎ 01 48 06 80 33; 41 rue de Charonne, 11e; ⊙ 8am-2am Mon-Sat, 9am-8pm Sun; Ⓜ Ledru-Rollin
Principally a restaurant with *plats du jour* for €11 to €14, this attractive café with lots of windows remains a popular destination for drinks, meals, coffee or brunch. Well situated a little away from the fray of Bastille, its generous terrace (covered and heated in winter) fills up with fashionable locals and the almost famous.

LE CHINA Map p158
Cocktail Bar

☎ 01 43 46 08 09; 50 rue de Charenton, 12e; ⊙ 7pm-2am; Ⓜ Ledru-Rollin or Bastille
The much-loved (and missed) China Club, with its Oriental gentlemen's club feel, huge bar and high ceilings, has metamorphosed into the 'China' and who can tell the difference? There's still jazz in the basement that harkens back to the Shanghai of the 1930s and a well-reputed menu with dim sum between €8 and €12.

CHAI 33 Map p158
Wine Bar

☎ 01 53 44 01 01; 33 cour St-Émilion, 12e; ⊙ noon-11pm Sun & Mon, to midnight Tue, to 12.30am Wed & Thu, to 1.30am Fri & Sat; Ⓜ Cour St-Émilion
The converted wine warehouses (*chais* in French) in Bercy Village house a variety of restaurants and bars, including this enormous wine-oriented concept space with a restaurant, lounge, tasting room and shop. Wine, both French and foreign, is divided into six colour-coded categories: purple is 'fruity and intense', green is 'light and spirited', yellow is 'dry and soft' etc. There's decent food (*menus* €16 to €29) here, too, as well as two terraces.

LE BARON ROUGE Map p158
Wine Bar

☎ 01 43 43 14 32; 1 rue Théophile Roussel, 12e; ⊙ 10am-2pm & 5-10pm Mon-Thu, 10am-10pm Fri & Sat, 10am-3pm Sun; Ⓜ Ledru-Rollin
To our mind just about the ultimate Parisian wine bar experience, this place has a dozen barrels of the stuff stacked up against the bottle-lined walls and sells wine by the glass. As unpretentious as you'll find, it's a local meeting place where everyone is welcome and is especially busy on Sundays

after the flea market at the Marché Couvert Beauvau (p222) wraps up.

LE BISTROT DU PEINTRE
Map p158
Wine Bar

☎ 01 47 00 34 39; 116 av Ledru-Rollin, 11e; ⊙ 7am-2am Mon-Sat, 8am-2am Sun; Ⓜ Bastille; ⊙
This lovely belle époque bistro and wine bar should really count more as a restaurant than a drinking place; after all, the food is great. But the 1902 art nouveau bar, elegant terrace and spot-on service put this place on our apéritif A-list – and that of local artists, *bobos* and local celebs.

LE CAFÉ DU PASSAGE Map p158
Wine Bar

☎ 01 49 29 97 64; 12 rue de Charonne, 11e; ⊙ 6pm-2am; Ⓜ Ledru-Rollin
This is the destination of choice for wine buffs, who relax in armchairs while sampling vintages from the excellent range on offer. The 'Arcade Café' has hundreds of wines available, including many by the glass (from €4.80). Whisky aficionados are also catered for and won't be disappointed by the selection of single malts. It's a warm, cosy place, and gourmet snacks and light meals (€7.50 to €18) are available.

PLACE D'ITALIE & CHINATOWN

While Chinatown isn't a hopping spot for bars, the area around the Butte aux Cailles, a kind of molehill southwest of Place d'Italie, has some good options. It is a pretty area that is popular with students and local residents: places in this area tend to have die-hard regulars.

SPUTNIK Map p164
Bar

☎ 01 45 65 19 82; 14 rue de la Butte aux Cailles, 13e; ⊙ 2pm-2am Mon-Sat, 4pm-midnight Sun; Ⓜ Corvisart or Place d'Italie; ⊙
This large bar with wi-fi zone and a dozen machines to surf is far more than an internet café. With its buzzing pavement terrace on one of Paris' hippest streets, Sputnik is a place to be seen. Students love it, particularly between 6pm and 8pm during happy hour.

THE FROG & BRITISH LIBRARY
Map p164
Pub

☎ 01 45 84 34 26; 114 av de France, 13e; ⊙ 7.30am-2am Mon-Fri, noon-2am Sat & Sun; Ⓜ Bibliothèque; ⊙

A hybrid English pub–French brasserie, this spacious drinking venue around the corner from the Bibliothèque Nationale is propped up by French students who flock here between library visits for food (mains €13.50, lunch menus €15) such as apple pie and custard, weekend brunches, potato wedges and cheese nachos washed down with a pint. The pick of the drinks list is the six beers brewed on the premises. The enormous Frog at Bercy Village (Map p158; ☎ 01 43 40 70 71; 25 cour St-Émilion, 12e; ☼ noon-2am; M Cour St-Émilion) is just across the river.

TANDEM Map p164
Wine Bar

☎ 01 45 80 38 39; 10 rue de la Butte aux Cailles, 13e; ☼ noon-2.30pm & 7.30-11pm Tue-Sat; M Corvisart or Place d'Italie

If wine's your love, make a beeline for this overwhelmingly old-fashioned *bar à vins* crammed with regulars. The lovechild of two brothers with a fierce oenological passion, Tandem homes in on 'boutique' *(vins de propriétés)* and organic wines as well as those produced by new *vignerons* (winemakers). A traditional bistro menu complements the wine list.

ALSO RECOMMENDED

Friendly and convivial, Le Merle Moqueur (Map p164; 11 rue de la Butte aux Cailles, 13e; ☼ 5pm-2am; M Corvisart) stocks the largest selection of rum punches we've seen. Two doors down at La Taverne de la Butte (Map p164; 13 rue de la Butte aux Cailles, 13e; ☼ 5pm-2am; M Corvisart) a pint of Guinness is the choice drink.

MONTPARNASSE & 15E

The scene here is far from rocking, but the pace is not slow thanks to the comings and goings of the train station, a dynamic cultural centre called L'Entrepôt (p272) and a trio of legendary café-bars.

LE SELECT Map p168
Café

☎ 01 42 22 65 27; 99 blvd du Montparnasse, 6e; ☼ 7.30am-2.30am; M Vavin

Along with La Coupole (p270) and Le Dôme (p270), this café is a Montparnasse institution that has changed little since 1923. Students congregate in the early evening; regulars take over as the night wears on. *Tartines* made with Poilâne bread (see p215) are a speciality.

FÉLICIE Map p168
Café, Bar

☎ 01 45 41 05 75; www.felicie.info; 174 ave du Maine, 14e; ☼ 7am-2am; M Lourmel

Be it breakfast, lunch, pre- or post-dinner drinks, this unpretentious neighbourhood brasserie-cum-bar with big heated pavement terrace is a quintessentially Parisian spot to Zen any time of day. Chuck in Sunday brunch, 'express' lunch deals (€12.50 and €18) built around bistro classics like steak tartare and a laid-back late-night vibe, and there's no saying you won't be back time and time again.

CUBANA CAFÉ Map p168
Cocktail Bar

☎ 01 40 46 80 81; 47 rue Vavin, 6e; ☼ 11am-3am Sun-Wed, to 5am Thu-Sat; M Vavin

This is the perfect place for cocktails and tapas shared among friends. A post-work crowd sinks into the comfy leather armchairs and flops beneath oil paintings of daily life in Cuba.

LE ROSEBUD Map p168
Cocktail Bar

☎ 01 43 35 38 54; 11bis rue Delambre, 14e; ☼ 7pm-2am; M Edgar Quinet or Vavin

Like the sleigh of that name in *Citizen Kane*, Rosebud harkens to the past. In this case it's

top picks

FOR TEA

Salons de thé – English, Japanese or North African – are chic in Paris.

- À Priori Thé, 1er (p279) Punny little place in the heart of Paris' most exclusive shopping arcade.
- Le Loir dans la Théière, 4e (p288) Probably the best tearoom in Paris (and we're not the only ones who think that).
- La Mosquée de Paris, 5e (p228) Peppermint tea and syrupy pastries between trees at the city's central mosque, across from the Jardin des Plantes.
- Kilàli, 6e (p281) A heady oasis of Japanese Zen on the left bank, perfectly placed between designer boutiques.
- Mariage Frères, 6e (p207) With tearooms in the Marais, St-Germain de Prés and on rue Faubourg St Honoré, there's no excuse to miss this 1854 institution.
- Tea Caddy, 5e (p230) Afternoon tea the English way, traditional Devon scones with lashings of cream included.

to the time of the Montparnos (painters and writers who frequented Montparnasse during the early 20th century). Enjoy a Champagne cocktail amid the quiet elegance of polished wood and aged leather.

LA CAVE DE L'OS À MOËLLE

Map p168   Wine Bar

☎ 01 45 57 28 28; rue Vasco de Gama, 15e; ⏰ noon-3pm & 7.30-10.30pm Tue-Sat, noon-4pm & 7.30-10.30pm Sun; Ⓜ Lourmel

Warming the cockles with a *vin chaud* (mulled wine) and *pain d'épice* (honey spiced bread) around a wine-barrel-turned-table on the pavement outside this cosy wine bar is a real winter delight. The lunchtime *formule à buffet* (€22.50) is excellent value.

BEYOND CENTRAL PARIS

CHEZ LOUISETTE Off Map p134

☎ 01 40 12 10 14; Marché aux Puces de St-Ouen; ⏰ noon-5pm Sat-Mon; Ⓜ Porte de Clignancourt

Here since 1967, this little bistro is a highlight of any visit to Paris' largest flea market, Marché aux Puces de St-Ouen (p212). Market-goers crowd around little tables to eat lunch (mains €15 to €20) and hear old-time *chanteuses* and *chanteurs* (they change regularly) belt out numbers by Piaf and other classic French singers, accompanied by accordion music; you might even get to see an inspired diner jump up to dance *la guingette* (the jig) in the aisles.

NIGHTLIFE & THE ARTS

top picks

- Comédie Française (p307)
- Cinémathèque Française (p305)
- L'Attirail (p303)
- Salle Pleyel (p301)
- Cabaret Sauvage (p302)
- Point Éphemère (p300)
- Palais Garnier (p306)
- Le Batofar (p297)
- L'Entrepôt (p303)
- La Pagode (p305)

A night out in Paris can mean anything from swilling Champagne on the Champs-Elysées to opening unmarked doorways in search of a new club in the *banlieues* (suburbs) or dancing on tables till dawn in a mad-loud DJ bar (see p276). From jazz cellar to comic theatre, garage beat to go-go dancer, world-class art gallery to avant-garde artist squat, this is *the* capital of *savoir-vivre*, with spectacular entertainment to suit every budget and every taste.

The French capital holds a firm place on the touring circuit of the world's finest artists and boasts dozens of historic and/or legendary concert venues: seeing a performance here is a treat. French and international opera, ballet and theatre companies (not to mention cabaret's incorrigible cancan dancers) take to the stage in a clutch of venues of mythical proportion – the Palais Garnier, Comédie Française and the Moulin Rouge included. Away from the bright lights and media glare, a flurry of young, passionate, highly creative musicians, theatre aficionados and artists make the city's fascinating fringe art scene what it is.

The film-lover's ultimate city, Paris provides the best seat in the house to catch new flicks, avant-garde cinema and priceless classics. Its inhabitants are film fetishists *par excellence*, with wonderful movie theatres – 1930s Chinese pagoda to Seine-side cutting-edge shoebox – to prove it.

So go out. Delve into the Parisian night.

Information & Listings

'Theatre', 'Kids', 'Outings & Leisure', 'Cinema', 'Restaurants', 'Festivals', 'Music', 'The Arts' and 'Paris by Nights' are the key headings in the index of *Pariscope* (€0.40), the capital's primary weekly listings guide published every Wednesday. Its 230-odd pages – B&W with the odd splash of colour – are almost too packed with information, but everything you need to know about what's on and happening is there. Many find Paris' other weekly listings bible, *L'Officiel des Spectacles* (€0.35; www.offi.fr, in French), also out on Wednesday, easier to handle. Buy both (in French only) at any newsstand.

Rock, jazz, world and *chanson* (song) are among the many genres covered by *Les Inrockuptibles* (www.lesinrocks.com, in French; €3.30), a national weekly music mag published every Wednesday with a strong Paris focus and great soiree and concert listings.

Of the surfeit of various French-language freebies, easy to pick up on the street and great for a gander between metro stops, *A Nous Paris* (www.anous.fr/paris, in French) is among the most informed and posts its entire magazine online. Pocket-sized booklet *LYLO* (short for *Les Yeux, Les Oreilles*, meaning 'eyes and ears'), freely available at bars and cafés, is a fortnightly lowdown on the live music, concert and clubbing scene and runs an information line (☎ 0 892 68 59 56; www.lylo.fr, in French). Flyers, schedules and programmes for cultural events float around the ticket office areas in Fnac (p294).

Digital links finely tuned to the music, clubbing, theatre scene etc right now are listed in the respective sections of this chapter.

Tickets & Reservations

Purchase tickets for concerts, theatre performances and other cultural events at the *billeteries* (ticket offices) in Fnac (rhymes with 'snack') and Virgin Megastore. Both offices take reservations by phone and the internet, and accept most credit cards. Tickets can't usually be returned or exchanged unless a performance is cancelled.

Some Fnac (☎ 0 892 68 36 22; www.fnacspectacles. com, in French) outlets:

Champs-Élysées (Map p126; 74 av des Champs-Élysées, 8e; ☉ 10am-midnight Mon-Sat, noon-midnight Sun; M Franklin D Roosevelt)

Étoile (Map p136; 26-30 av des Ternes, 17e; ☉ 10am-7.30pm Mon-Sat; M Ternes)

Forum des Halles (Map p76; Forum des Halles shopping centre, level 3, 1-7 rue Pierre Lescot, 1er; ☉ 10am-8pm Mon-Sat; M Châtelet–Les Halles)

Montparnasse (Map p108; ☎ 01 49 54 30 00; 136 rue de Rennes, 6e; ☉ 10am-7pm Mon-Sat; M St-Placide)

St-Lazare (Map p136; 109 rue St-Lazare, 9e; ☉ 10am-7.30pm Mon-Wed & Sat, to 8.30pm Thu & Fri; M St-Lazare).

Branches of Virgin Megastore (☎ 08 25 12 91 39; www.virginmega.fr, in French):

Barbès (Map p134; ☎ 01 56 55 53 70; 15 blvd Barbès, 18e; ⏰ 10am-9pm Mon-Sat; Ⓜ Barbès–Rochechouart)

Champs-Élysées (Map p126; ☎ 01 49 53 50 00; 52-60 av des Champs-Élysées, 8e; ⏰ 10am-midnight Mon-Sat, noon-midnight Sun; Ⓜ Franklin D Roosevelt)

Galerie du Carrousel du Louvre (Map p76; ☎ 01 44 50 03 10; 99 rue de Rivoli, 1er; ⏰ 10am-8pm Mon & Tue, to 9pm Wed-Sun; Ⓜ Palais Royal–Musée du Louvre)

Gare Montparnasse (Map p168; place Raoul Dautry, 14e; ⏰ 7am-8.30pm Mon-Thu, to 9pm Fri, 8am-8pm Sat; Ⓜ Montparnasse–Bienvenüe)

Other ticketing box offices:

Agence Marivaux (Map p72; ☎ 01 42 97 46 70; 7 rue de Marivaux, 2e; ⏰ 11am-7.30pm Mon-Fri, noon-4pm Sat; Ⓜ Richelieu–Drouot) Paris' oldest ticket agency, just opposite the Opéra Comique.

Agence Perrossier & SOS Théâtres (Map p126; ☎ 01 42 60 26 87, 01 42 60 58 31; www.agencedetheatresdeparis.fr; 6 place de la Madeleine, 8e; ⏰ 10am-7pm Mon-Sat; Ⓜ Madeleine)

Discount Tickets

Come the day of a performance, pick up a half-price ticket for ballet, theatre, opera etc at discount-ticket outlets Kiosque Théâtre Madeleine (Map p126; www.kiosquetheatre.com; opp 15 place de la Madeleine, 8e; ⏰ 12.30-8pm Tue-Sat, to 4pm Sun; Ⓜ Madeleine), Kiosque Théâtre Ternes (Map p126; place des Ternes, 8e; ⏰ 12.30-8pm Tue-Sat, to 4pm Sun; Ⓜ Ternes) and Kiosque Théâtre Montparnasse (Map p168; Parvis Montparnasse, 15e; ⏰ 12.30-8pm Tue-Sat, to 4pm Sun; Ⓜ Montparnasse Bienvenüe). They all charge €3 commission.

CABARET

Parisians don't tend to watch the city's risqué cabaret revues – tourists do. Times and prices for the dazzling, pseudo-bohemian productions starring women in two beads and a feather (or was that two feathers and a bead?) vary: first shows often begin between 8.15pm and 9.30pm, second shows between 10.45pm

DIGITAL DISCOUNT TICKETING

- www.billetreduc.com
- www.ticketac.com
- www.webguichet.com

top picks

FREE SHOWS

Paris' eclectic gaggle of clowns, mime artists, living statues, acrobats, roller-bladers, buskers and other street entertainers can be bags of fun and costs substantially less than a theatre ticket (a few coins in the hat is a sweet gesture). Some excellent musicians perform in the long echo-filled corridors of the metro, a highly prized privilege that artists do audition for. Outside, you can be sure of a good show at:

- **Place Georges Pompidou, 4e** (Map p76) The huge square in front of the Centre Pompidou.
- **Pont St-Louis, 4e** (Map p82) The bridge linking Paris' two islands (best enjoyed with Berthillon ice cream in hand; p227).
- **Pont au Double, 4e** (Map p82) The pedestrian bridge linking Notre Dame with the Left Bank (grab a Berthillon ice cream to enjoy here, too; p227).
- **Place Jean du Bellay, 1er** (Map p76) Musicians and fire-eaters near the Fontaine des Innocents.
- **Parc de la Villette, 19e** (p140) African drummers at the weekend.
- **Place du Tertre, Montmartre, 18e** (Map p134) Montmartre's original main square wins hands down as Paris' busiest busker stage.

and 11.30pm. They all have lunch specials and additional evening shows at the weekend. Tickets cost anything from €55 to €100 per person (€140 to €280 with swish dinner and Champagne). All venues sell tickets online.

CRAZY HORSE Map p126

☎ 01 47 23 32 32; www.lecrazyhorseparis.com; 12 av George V, 8e; Ⓜ Alma Marceau

This popular cabaret, whose dressing (or, rather, undressing) rooms were featured in Woody Allen's film *What's New Pussycat?* (1965), now promotes fine art – abstract 1960s patterns as they appear superimposed on the female nude form.

MOULIN ROUGE Map p134

☎ 01 53 09 82 82; www.moulinrouge.fr; 82 blvd de Clichy, 18e; Ⓜ Blanche

Ooh la la… What is probably Paris' most celebrated cabaret was founded in 1889 and its dancers appeared in the celebrated posters by Toulouse-Lautrec. It sits under its trademark red windmill (actually a 1925 replica of the 19th-century original) and attracts viewers and voyeurs by the busload.

LE LIDO DE PARIS Map p126
☎ 01 40 76 56 10; www.lido.fr; 116bis av des Champs-Élysées, 8e; Ⓜ George V
Founded at the close of WWII, this gets top marks for its sets and the lavish costumes of its 70 artistes, including the famed Bluebell Girls and now the Lido Boy Dancers.

CLUBBING

Paris is *not* London, Berlin or New York when it comes to clubbing, and hardcore clubbers from other European capitals might be surprised by the pick of Paris clubs. Lacking a mainstream scene, clubbing here tends to be underground and extremely mobile, making blogs, forums and websites the savviest means of keeping apace with what's happening (loads of clubs/events are on MySpace). The best DJs and their followings have short stints in a certain venue before moving on, and the scene's hippest *soirées clubbing* (clubbing events) float between a clutch of venues – including the city's many dance-driven bars (see p276).

But the beat is strong. Electronic music is of particularly high quality in Paris' clubs, with some excellent local house and techno. Funk and groove have given the whimsical predominance of dark minimal sounds a good pounding, and the Latin scene is huge; salsa dancing and Latino music nights pack out plenty of clubs. R 'n' B and hip-hop pickings are decent, if less represented than in, say, London.

Club admission costs anything from nothing to €20; admission is usually cheaper before 1am and men can't always get in unaccompanied by a woman. Drink prices start at around €6 for a beer and €8 for a mixed drink or cocktail, but are often more.

FOLIE'S PIGALLE Map p134
☎ 01 48 78 55 25; www.lefoliespigalle.com; 11 place Pigalle, 9e; admission €20; ⏰ 10pm-dawn Mon-Thu, to noon Fri & Sat, 6pm-dawn Sun; Ⓜ Pigalle
Folie's Pigalle is a heaving place with a mixed gay and straight crowd that is great for cruising from the balcony above the dancefloor. There are theme nights and concerts (usually at 2am) throughout the week. Sunday evening is the 'Original Gay Tea Party', followed by 'Las Bibas', Paris' only transsexual theme night, with R 'n' B, dance, techno and house.

LA DAME DE CANTON Map p164
☎ 01 53 61 08 49; www.damedecanton.com, in French; opp 11 quai François Mauriac, 13e; admission €6-10; ⏰ 7pm-2am Tue-Thu, to dawn Fri & Sat; Ⓜ Quai de la Gare or Bibliothèque
This floating *boîte* (club) aboard a three-masted Chinese junk with a couple of world voyages under its belt is moored opposite the Bibliothèque Nationale de France. Called *Cabaret Pirate* and *Guinguette Pirate* in previous lives, it re-adopted its maiden name – the 'Lady from Canton' – in 2008 to mark its 30th birthday. Concerts (8.30pm) range from pop and indie to electro, hip hop, reggae and rock; afterwards, DJs keep the young crowd moving.

LA SCÈNE BASTILLE Map p158
☎ 01 48 06 50 70; www.scenebastille.com; admission €12-15; 2bis rue des Taillandiers, 11e; concerts from 7.30pm, club nights midnight-6am Mon-Sat; Ⓜ Bastille or Ledru-Rollin)
The 'Bastille Scene' puts on a mixed bag of concerts but focuses on electro, funk and hip hop Thursday to Saturday. Unpretentious venue – the kind of place where local DJs go to relax and listen to music.

LE BALAJO Map p158
☎ 01 47 00 07 87; www.balajo.fr; 9 rue de Lappe, 11e; admission from €12; ⏰ 10pm-2am Tue & Thu, 11pm-5am Fri & Sat, 3-7.30pm Sun; Ⓜ Bastille
A mainstay of Parisian nightlife since 1936, this ancient ballroom is devoted to salsa classes and Latino music during the week. Weekends see DJs spinning a very mixed bag of rock, disco, funk, R 'n' B and house. While a bit lower-shelf these days, it scores a mention for its historical value and its old-fashioned *musette* (accordion music) gigs on Sundays: waltz, tango and cha-cha for aficionados of retro tea-dancing.

DIGITAL CLUBBING

Track tomorrow's hot 'n' happening *soirée* with these finger-on-the-pulse Parisian nightlife links (in French).

- www.gogoparis.com (in English)
- www.lemonsound.com
- www.novaplanet.com
- www.parisbouge.com
- www.parissi.com
- www.tribudenuit.com

LE BATOFAR Map p164

☎ 01 53 16 70 30; www.batofar.org, in French; opp 11 quai François Mauriac, 13e; admission free-€15; ☽ 9pm-midnight Mon & Tue, to 4am or later Wed-Sun; Ⓜ Quai de la Gare or Bibliothèque

This incongruous, much-loved, red-metal tugboat has a rooftop bar that's terrific in summer, while the club underneath provides memorable underwater acoustics between its metal walls and portholes. Le Batofar is known for its edgy, experimental music policy and live performances, mostly electro-oriented but also incorporating hip hop, new wave, rock, punk or jazz. Sometimes it doesn't open until 10pm.

LE DIVAN DU MONDE Map p134

☎ 01 40 05 06 99; www.divandumonde.com; 75 rue des Martyrs, 18e; admission €10-15; ☽ 11pm-5am Fri & Sat; Ⓜ Pigalle

Take some cinematographic events, Gypsy gatherings, *nouvelles chansons françaises* (new French songs). Add in soul/funk fiestas, air-guitar face-offs and rock parties of the Arctic Monkeys/Killers/Libertines persuasion and stir with an Amy Winehouse swizzle stick. You may now be getting some idea of the inventive, open-minded approach at this excellent cross-cultural venue in Pigalle. It sometimes open for events Monday to Friday.

LE DJOON Map p164

☎ 01 45 70 83 49; www.djoon.fr, in French; 22-24 blvd Vincent Auriol, 13e; admission €10-12; ☽ 7pm-midnight Thu, 11.30pm-5am or 6am Fri & Sat, 6pm-midnight Sun; Ⓜ Quai de la Gare

In an area increasingly known for its cutting-edge venues, this urbanite, New York–inspired loft club and restaurant has carved out a name for itself as a super-stylish weekend venue for soul, funk, deep house, garage and disco, courtesy of different visiting DJs. Thursday and Sunday evenings are tamer but still 100% DJ-fed dance. Look for the striking glass-and-steel façade.

LE NOUVEAU CASINO Map p148

☎ 01 43 57 57 40; www.nouveaucasino.net, in French; 109 rue Oberkampf, 11e; club admission €5-10, concerts €8-22; ☽ 7.30pm or midnight to 2am or 5am Tue-Sun; Ⓜ Parmentier

This club–concert annexe of the Café Charbon (p287) has made a name for itself amid the

top picks

CLUBS

- **La Scène Bastille** The name says it all – get the latest on what's really happening on the Paris clubbing scene.
- **Le Nouveau Casino** Everyone ends up at the flagship club of Ménilmontant.
- **Le Divan du Monde** Cultural cocktails unique to Paris at this Montmartre venue.
- **Le Batofar** Float on the Seine aboard this old tugboat, around for aeons and one of the city's edgiest venues.
- **Le Balajo** Still crazy (and just as much fun) after all these years.

bars of Oberkampf with its live music concerts (usually Tuesday, Thursday and Friday) and lively club nights at the weekend. Electro, pop, deep house, rock – the program is eclectic, underground and always up to the minute. Check the website for up-to-date listings.

LE REDLIGHT Map p168

☎ 01 42 79 94 53; www.leredlight.com, in French; 34 rue du Départ, 14e; admission €15-20; ☽ 11pm or midnight to 5am or 6am Sat & Sun; Ⓜ Montparnasse–Bienvenüe

It seems that this underground (literally) venue beneath Tour Montparnasse, fittingly called *l'enfer* (hell) in a previous life, will never perish. Up there among Paris' busiest house, techno and electro clubs, its podiums get packed out with a young, dance-mad crowd well past dawn. French Kiss 'after' parties often kick off at 6am. Huge and laser-lit, its hours vary depending on the *soirée* – see its website for flyers – and admission is often half-price before 1am.

LE REX CLUB Map p72

☎ 01 42 36 10 96; www.rexclub.com; 5 blvd Poissonnière, 2e; admission free-€12; ☽ 11.30pm-6am Wed-Sat; Ⓜ Bonne Nouvelle

The Rex reigns majestic in the house and techno scene, always has and probably always will. The sound system is impeccable but getting in is more a question of lining up than looking right. Friday nights are a techno institution in Paris.

LE WAGG Map p112

☎ 01 55 42 22 00; www.wagg.fr, in French; 62 rue Mazarine, 6e; admission incl 1 drink Fri & Sat €12, Sun €12, before/after midnight Thu free/€10; ⊙ 11pm-6am Thu-Sat, 3pm-midnight Sun; Ⓜ Odéon

The Wagg is a UK-style Conran club (associated with the popular Fabric in London), beautifully dressed in slick fixtures and contemporary design, but with a somewhat stifled vibe. Last time we looked it had been taken over by the salsa craze – indeed, it opens early on Sunday to host a two-hour salsa class followed by *une soirée 100% cubaine*. Find event flyers posted on the blog (www.blogalcazar.fr) of the neighbouring Conran restaurant.

LES BAINS DOUCHES Map p76

☎ 01 48 87 01 80; www.lesbainsdouchesparis.com, in French; 7 rue du Bourg l'Abbé, 3e; admission €10-20; ⊙ 11.30pm-5am Wed-Sun; Ⓜ Étienne Marcel

Housed in a refitted old Turkish *hammam*, this darling of the 1990s, famous for its glamorous clientele and impassable door complete with blocking limo, has sought to shake off its inaccessible image with a new mix of theme nights, Sunday morning 'afters' and gay soirées. It's working, but only just, and memories do linger: Friday is still 'Famous Club' night.

PENICHE EL ALAMEIN Map p164

☎ 01 45 86 41 60, 06 88 99 20 58; http://elalamein.free.fr, in French; opp 11 quai François Mauriac, 13e; admission €8; ⊙ 8.30pm-2am Sep-Jun; Ⓜ Quai de la Gare or Bibliothèque

The third in the trendy trio afloat opposite the library, this deep-purple boat is strung with terracotta pots of flowers from head to toe, making it a lovely spot on the Seine to sip away summer evenings – the deck is open from 4.30pm when the sun shines. Sit amid flowering tulips and enjoy live bands playing from 9pm; flyers are stuck on the lamppost in front. Its sound – less hectic than its next-door neighbours, hence the older crowd – embraces jazz, world and Piaf-style *chansons françaises* (French songs) of 1930s Paris.

QUEEN Map p126

☎ 01 53 89 08 90; www.queen.fr; 102 av des Champs-Élysées, 8e; admission €20; ⊙ 11.30pm-10am; Ⓜ George V

Once the king (as it were) of gay discos in Paris, Le Queen now reigns supreme

---

CLUBBING IN PARIS: BEFORE, AFTER & D'AFTER

Seasoned Parisian clubbers, who tend to have a finely tuned sense of the absurd, split their night into three parts. First, *la before* – drinks in a bar that has a DJ playing (loads listed in the Drinking chapter, p276). Second, they head to a club for *la soirée*, which rarely kicks off before 1am or 2am. When the party continues (or begins) at around 5am and goes until midday, it's the third in the trio – *l'after*. Invariably, though, given the lack of any clear-cut distinction between Parisian bars and clubs, the before and after can easily blend into one without any real 'during'. *'After d'afters'*, meanwhile, kicks off in bars and clubs on Sunday afternoons and evenings, with a mix of strung-out hardcore clubbers pressing on amid less-mad socialites out for a party that doesn't take place in the middle of the night.

with a very mixed crowd, though it still has a mostly gay Disco Queen on Monday. While right on the Champs-Élysées, it's not as difficult to get into as it used to be – and not nearly as inaccessible as most of the nearby clubs. There's a festive atmosphere and mix of music with lots of house and electro.

REGINE'S Map p126

☎ 01 43 59 21 13; www.leregines.com; 49-51 rue de Ponthieu, 8e; admission €10; ⊙ midnight-dawn Fri & Sat; Ⓜ Franklin D Roosevelt

Done up in red seats, funky prints and mirrors, Regine's attracts top electro and techno DJs (Jeff Mills, Miss Kittin, Marco Resmann) to this revamped space off the Champs Élysées.

SHOWCASE Map p126

☎ 01 45 61 25 43; www.showcase.fr; Port des Champs Élysées, under Pont Alexandre III, 8e; admission €15; ⊙ 11.30pm-dawn Fri & Sat; Ⓜ Invalides or Champs Élysées–Clemenceau

This gigantic electro club has solved the neighbour-versus-noise problem that haunts so many other Parisian nightlife spots: it's secreted away beneath a bridge alongside the Seine. Unlike many of the other exclusive backstreet clubs along the Champs, the Showcase can pack 'em in (up to 1500 clubbers) and is less stringent about its door policy, though you'll still want to look like a star.

SOCIAL CLUB Map p72

☎ 01 40 28 05 55; www.parissocialclub.com;
142 rue Montmartre, 2e; admission free-€15;
⊗ 11pm-3am Wed & Sun, to 6am Thu-Sat;
Ⓜ Grands Boulevards

This vast and very popular club is set up in three stonewalled underground rooms and fills somewhat of a gap in inner-city clubbing. Musically it's on to it, with a serious sound system offering electro, hip hop and funk, as well as live acts.

COMEDY

Surprising to some perhaps, Parisians do like to laugh, and the capital is not short of comedy clubs, where such comedians as Bourvil, Fernandel, Bernard Blier, Louis de Funès, Francis Blanche, Jean Poiret, Michel Serrault, Smaïn and the duo Elie Kakou and Guy Bedos have enjoyed enormous popularity over the years. The 'one-man show' (say it with a French accent) is increasingly popular, while English-language comedy is a growing scene.

An outfit called **Laughing & Music Matters** (☎ 01 53 19 98 88; www.anythingmatters.com), with no fixed address, presents some of the best English-language laugh-fests in town, with both local and imported talent (last seen: Jools Holland from the UK). It usually puts on shows at La Java (p303). See the website for details.

POINT VIRGULE Map p152

☎ 01 42 78 67 03; www.lepointvirgule.com, in French; 7 rue Ste-Croix de la Bretonnerie, 4e; 1/2/3 shows adult €17/29/36, per show student except Sat €13; Ⓜ Hôtel de Ville

This tiny and convivial comedy spot in the Marais has been going strong for well over five decades. It offers café-theatre at its best – stand-up comics, performance artists, musical acts. The quality is variable, but it's great fun and the place has a reputation for discovering new talent. There are at least three shows daily, usually at 7pm, 8pm and 9.15pm, with additional ones at 2.30pm, 4pm and 5.30pm on Saturday and Sunday.

MUSIC

Music thrives in cosmopolitan Paris, a first-class stage for classical music and big-name rock, pop and independent acts, not to mention world-renowned jazz. A musical culture deeply influenced by rich immigration, vibrant subcultures and an open-minded public make it a fervent breeding ground for experimental music: Paris-bred world music, especially from Africa and South America, is renowned. As with the hybrid drinking–clubbing scene, bars (p276) are as much a space to revel in these sounds as specific music venues.

Festivals for just about every music genre going ensure that everyone gets to listen in; to check what's on, see p294. Street music is a constant in this busker-merry city (p295), summer adding a soul-stirring string of open-air concerts along the Seine and in city parks to the year-round hum of accordion players on the metro and amateur opera singers around the Centre Pompidou.

And should classical music be your love, don't forget Paris' beautiful churches – wonderful places to listen to organ music – in addition to the theatres and concert halls listed in this chapter: the magnificent Sunday-afternoon concerts in the Église St-Sulpice (p106) are nothing short of earth-shattering.

ROCK, POP & INDIE

With several venues in and around the city regularly hosting international performers, it can be easier to see big-name Anglophone acts in Paris than in their home countries. **Palais Omnisports de Paris-Bercy** (Map p158; ☎ 08 92 39 01 00; www.bercy.fr, in French; 8 blvd de Bercy, 12e; Ⓜ Bercy); **Stade de France** (off Map p174; ☎ 08 92 39 01 00; www.stadefrance.com; rue Francis de Pressensé, ZAC du Cornillon Nord, St-Denis La Plaine; Ⓜ St-Denis-Porte de Paris); and **Le Zénith** (Map p140; ☎ 08 90 71 02 07, 01 55 80 09 38; www.le-zenith.com, in French; 211 av Jean Jaurès, 19e; Ⓜ Porte de Pantin) in Parc de la Villette are the largest (and most impersonal) venues. But it's is the smaller concert halls with real history and charm that most fans favour.

ALHAMBRA Map p140

☎ 01 40 20 40 25; www.alhambra-paris.com;
21 rue Yves Toudic, 10e; admission €24-41;
Ⓜ République or Jacques Bonsergent

M Ward and Natalie Merchant are among the artists who have recently played at this 1930s cinema-theatre, which now serves as a music hall for pop, rock and soul concerts.

LA CIGALE Map p134

☎ 01 49 25 81 75; www.lacigale.fr; 120 blvd de Rochechouart, 18e; admission €25-60;
Ⓜ Anvers or Pigalle

Now classed as a historical monument, this music hall dates from 1887 but was redecorated 100 years later by Philippe Starck. Having welcomed artists from Jean Cocteau to Sheryl Crow, today it prides itself on its avant-garde program, with rock and jazz concerts by French and international acts.

LA FLÈCHE D'OR Map p158

☎ 01 44 64 01 02; www.flechedor.fr; 102bis rue de Bagnolet, 20e; admission free-€8; ✆ 8pm-2am Mon-Thu, to 6am Fri & Sat, noon-2am Sun; Ⓜ Alexandre Dumas or Gambetta

Just over 1km northeast of place de la Nation and housed in a former railway station on the outer edge of central Paris, this music bar has reinvented itself attracting a young and alternative crowd with not just its indie rock concerts but also its house/electro DJ nights. The 'Golden Arrow' – that was the train to Calais in the 1930s – has a solid reputation for promoting young talent.

LE BATACLAN Map p148

☎ 01 43 14 00 30; www.myspace.com/bataclan paris; 50 blvd Voltaire, 11e; admission €25-65; ✆ varies; Ⓜ Oberkampf or St-Ambroise

Built in 1864 and Maurice Chevalier's debut venue in 1910, this excellent little concert hall draws big-ticket French (eg Pony Pony Run Run) and some international rock and pop legends. Now a symphony of lively red, yellow and green hues, the Bataclan also masquerades as a theatre and dance hall.

LE MOTEL Map p158

☎ 01 58 30 88 52; www.myspace.com/lemotel; 8 passage Josset, 11e, admission free; ✆ 6pm-1.45am Tue-Sun; Ⓜ Ledru-Rollin

This hole-in-the wall venue in the hot-to-the-boiling-point 11e can feel more Camden (Tribute to the Cure, Jesus and Mary Chain) than Bastille some nights but its tiny stage manages to attract some of the best new local around. Please leave quietly or there may not be a Motel to come back to.

LES DISQUAIRES Map p158

☎ 06 61 16 19 84; www.lesdisquaires.com, in French; 6 rue des Taillandiers, 11e; admission free-€10; ✆ 6pm-2am; Ⓜ Ledru-Rollin or Bastille

There's something for everybody at this new oh-so-Bastille club and music venue with nightly concerts (rock, folk, pop, jazz) from 8pm. After about 10.30pm from Wednesday to Saturday the party continues with DJs like Goldrush taking to the decks.

DIGITAL MUSIC

Tune into the latest sounds and the concerts they spawn with these useful sites (in French). Most listed on p296 also cover the music scene.

- www.figaroscope.fr (great search tool for concerts by arrondissement – click on the map)
- www.france-techno.fr
- www.paris.fr (click 'Paris Actu' then 'Culture')

L'ÉLYSÉE-MONTMARTRE Map p134

☎ 01 44 92 45 47; www.elyseemontmartre.com; 72 blvd de Rochechouart, 18e; admission €17-45; Ⓜ Anvers

A huge old music hall with a great sound system, L'Élysée-Montmartre is one of the better venues in Paris for one-off hip-hop and indie concerts (ex-Wu Tang Clan, Hush Puppies, Morgan Heritage, Sabotage). It opens for concerts at 6.30pm and hosts club events and big-name DJs at 11.30pm on Fridays and Saturdays.

L'OLYMPIA Map p126

☎ 08 92 68 33 68; www.olympiahall.com; 28 blvd des Capucines, 9e; admission €35-110; Ⓜ Opéra

The Olympia was opened by the founder of the Moulin Rouge in 1888 and is said to be the oldest concert hall in Paris. It's an atmospheric venue of manageable size, with a sloping floor. It has hosted all the big names over the years, from Johnny Halliday to Jimi Hendrix. This is the hallowed venue of one of Édith Piaf's last performances, and what Jeff Buckley considered his best ever concert, the seminal *Live at l'Olympia* in 1995.

POINT ÉPHEMÈRE Map p140

☎ 01 40 34 02 48; www.pointephemere.org; 200 quai de Valmy, 10e; admission free-€21; ✆ bar noon-2am Mon-Sat, 1pm-9pm Sun; Ⓜ Louis Blanc

This self-proclaimed 'centre for dynamic artists' has a great location by the Canal St-Martin, with indie concerts and the odd electro dance night. There's also a bar, restaurant and exhibit area on the scene.

CLASSICAL

The city hosts dozens of orchestral, organ and chamber-music concerts each week. In addition to the theatres and concert halls listed here, Paris' beautiful churches have much-celebrated organs and can be wonderful places to hear music. Many concerts don't keep to any fixed schedule, but are simply advertised on posters around town. Admission fees vary, but usually cost from €20 for adults and half that for students.

CONSERVATOIRE NATIONAL SUPÉRIEUR DE MUSIQUE ET DE DANSE Map p140

☎ 01 40 40 45 45; www.cnsmdp.fr; 209 av Jean Jaurès, 19e; ⏰ box office noon-6pm Tue-Sat, 10am-6pm Sun, to 8pm on day of performance; Ⓜ Porte de Pantin

Students at France's National Higher Conservatory of Music and Dance put on free orchestra concerts and recitals several times a week, in the afternoon or evening; check its website for the monthly schedule (currently accessible only through the French-language portal).

LUCINAIRE Map p108

☎ 01 42 22 26 50, reservations ☎ 01 45 44 57 34; www.lucinaire.fr, in French; 53 rue Notre Dame des Champs, 6e; admission Sun-Thu €12, Fri & Sat €14, under 25yr €10; box office ⏰ 11.30am-12.30pm & 1.30pm-10.30pm, restaurant & bar ⏰ 10am-11pm; Ⓜ Notre Dame des Champs

Sunday-evening concerts are a permanent fixture on the impressive repertoire of this dynamic Centre National d'Art et d'Essai (National Arts Centre) sandwiched between the Jardin du Luxembourg and Montparnasse. Be it classical guitar, baroque, French *chansons* or oriental music, these weekly concerts starting at 6.30pm are a real treat. Art and photography exhibitions, cinema, theatre, lectures, debates and guided walks round off the packed cultural agenda.

SALLE PLEYEL Map p126

☎ 01 42 56 13 13; www.sallepleyel.fr; 252 rue du Faubourg St-Honoré, 8e; tickets €30-85; ⏰ box office noon-7pm Mon-Sat, to 8pm on day of performance, by telephone 11am-7pm daily; Ⓜ Ternes

This highly regarded hall dating from the 1920s hosts many of Paris' finest classical music recitals and concerts, including those by the celebrated Orchestre de Paris (www.orches tredeparis.com). It has recently emerged from a protracted renovation and now looks (and sounds) even more *magnifique*.

THÉÂTRE DU CHÂTELET Map p76

☎ 01 40 28 28 40; www.chatelet-theatre.com, in French; 1 place du Châtelet, 1er; concert tickets €10-85, opera & musicals €10-125; ⏰ box office 11am-7pm Mon-Sat, 1hr before performance Sun, closed Jul & Aug; Ⓜ Châtelet

This central venue hosts concerts as well as operas, musical performances, theatre and ballet. Subject to availability, anyone under 26 or over 65 can get reduced-price tickets from 15 minutes before curtain time. The Sunday concerts (☎ 01 42 56 90 10; adult/under 26yr €23/12) at 11am are a popular fixture.

JAZZ & BLUES

Paris became Europe's most important jazz centre after WWII and, niche as the style has since become, the city's best clubs and cellars still lure international stars – as does the wonderful Paris Jazz Festival (www.parcfloraldeparis.com or www.paris.fr) that sets the Parc Floral buzzing each year in June and July. Big-name talent is likewise on the billing at Banlieues Bleues (Suburban Blues; www.banlieuesbleues.org), a jazz festival held mid-March to mid-April in St-Denis and other Parisian suburbs.

Download podcasts, tunes, concert information and all that jazz to listen to on your iPod from Paris' soothing jazz radio station, TFS (89.9 MHz FM; www.tsfjazz.com).

CAFÉ UNIVERSEL Map p100

☎ 01 43 25 74 20; www.myspace.com/cafe universel; 267 rue St-Jacques, 5e; admission free; ⏰ 7.30pm-2am Tue-Sat; Ⓜ Port Royal

Café Universel hosts a brilliant array of live concerts with everything from bebop and Latin sounds to vocal jazz sessions. Plenty of freedom is given to young producers and artists, and its convivial relaxed atmosphere attracts a relaxed mix of students and jazz lovers. Particularly lively are its vocal jam sessions, every Tuesday from 9pm until just after midnight. Its complete monthly agenda is posted online.

CAVEAU DE LA HUCHETTE Map p100

☎ 01 43 26 65 05; www.caveaudelahuchette.fr; 5 rue de la Huchette, 5e; admission Sun-Thu €12, Fri & Sat €14, under 25yr €10; ⏰ 9.30pm-2.30am Sun-Wed, to 4am Thu-Sat; Ⓜ St-Michel

Housed in a medieval *caveau* (cellar) used as a courtroom and torture chamber during the Revolution, this club is where virtually all the jazz greats have played since the end of WWII. It's touristy, but the atmosphere can be more electric than at the more serious jazz clubs. Sessions start at 10pm.

LE BAISER SALÉ Map p76

☎ 01 42 33 37 71; www.lebaisersale.com, in French; 58 rue des Lombards, 1er; admission free-€20; ☽ 5pm-6am; Ⓜ Châtelet

One of several jazz clubs located on this street, the *salle de jazz* (jazz room) on its 1st floor has concerts of jazz, Afro and Latin jazz and jazz fusion. Combining big names and unknown artists, it is known for its relaxed vibe and has a gift for discovering new talents. Sets start at 7.30pm and 10pm. The Monday night *soirée bœuf* (jam session) is free.

LE PETIT JOURNAL ST-MICHEL
Map p100

☎ 01 43 26 28 59; www.petitjournalsaintmichel. com, in French; 71 blvd St-Michel, 5e; admission incl 1 drink adult €17-20, student €11-15; ☽ 6pm-2am Mon-Sat; Ⓜ Luxembourg

Classic jazz concerts kick off at 9.15pm in the atmospheric downstairs cellar – think St-Germain des Prés during the 1950s – of this sophisticated jazz venue across from the Jardin du Luxembourg. Everything ranging from Dixieland and vocals to big band and swing sets punters' toes tapping, and Monday-night jam sessions are free entry. Dinner (*menus* €44 and €47) is served at 8pm, should you wish to make a meal of it.

Concerts at St-Michel's sister club near Gare de Montparnasse, Le Petit Journal Montparnasse (Map p168; ☎ 01 43 21 56 70; www. petitjournal-montparnasse.com; 13 rue du Commandant René Mouchotte, 14e; admission incl 1 drink adult/student & under 25yr €25/15, with dinner €55; ☽ 8pm-2am Mon-Sat), start at 10pm and meals are likewise served.

NEW MORNING Map p140

☎ 01 45 23 51 41; www.newmorning.com, in French; 7-9 rue des Petites Écuries, 10e; admission €15-21; ☽ 8pm-2am; Ⓜ Château d'Eau

New Morning is a highly regarded auditorium with excellent acoustics that hosts big-name jazz concerts as well as a variety of blues, rock, funk, salsa, Afro-Cuban and Brazilian music. Concerts take place three to seven nights per week at 9pm, with the second set ending at around the 1am mark. Tickets can usually be purchased at the door.

SUNSET/SUNSIDE Map p76

☎ 01 40 26 46 60; www.sunset-sunside.com; 60 rue des Lombards, 1er; admission free-€25; ☽ 8pm-4am; Ⓜ Châtelet

Two venues in one at this trendy, well-respected club. The Sunset downstairs has electric jazz and fusion concerts beginning at 9.30pm or 10pm. It leans towards world music and sometimes runs salsa sessions during the week. The Sunside picks things up upstairs with jazz acoustics and concerts starting at 8pm or 9pm.

WORLD & LATINO

Sono mondiale (world music) is a big deal in Paris, where everything – from Algerian *raï* and other North African music to Senegalese *mbalax* and West Indian *zouk* – goes at clubs. Latino music, especially Cuban salsa, has been overwhelmingly popular over the past decade or so. Many of the concert and clubbing venues listed have salsa classes; look for summertime dancing on the banks of the Seine.

BARRIO LATINO Map p158

☎ 01 55 78 84 75; www.buddhabar.com; 46-48 rue du Faubourg St-Antoine, 11e; admission free-€8; ☽ noon-2am Sun-Thu, to 3pm Fri & Sat; Ⓜ Bastille

Still squeezing the salsa theme for all that it's worth, this enormous over-the-top bar-restaurant with serious dancing – distantly related to Buddha Bar (p283) – is spread over three highly impressive floors. It attracts Latinos, Latino wannabes and Latino wannahaves and a gay crowd. The delicious *mojitos* go down a treat.

CABARET SAUVAGE Map p140

☎ 01 42 09 03 09; www.cabaretsauvage.com; Parc de la Villette, 221 av Jean Jaurès, 19e; tickets €8-34; ☽ 7pm-2am Tue-Sun; Ⓜ Porte de la Villette

This very cool space in the Parc de la Villette (it looks like a gigantic yurt) is host to African, reggae and raï concerts as well as DJ nights that last till dawn. There are also occasional hip-hop and indie acts that pass through.

CITÉ DE LA MUSIQUE Map p140

☎ 01 44 84 44 84; www.citedelamusique.fr; 221 av Jean Jaurès, 19e; tickets €8-38; ☽ box office noon-6pm Tue-Sat, 10am-6pm Sun, to 8pm on day of performance, by telephone 11am-7pm daily; Ⓜ Porte de Pantin

At the Parc de la Villette, every imaginable type of music and dance, from Western classical to North African and Japanese, is hosted at this venue's oval-shaped, 1200-seat main auditorium. Smaller concerts are in the little Amphithéâtre du Musée de la Musique.

DANCING LA COUPOLE Map p168

☎ 01 43 27 56 00; 102 blvd du Montparnasse, 14e; admission €10-12; ◷ 7pm-3am Tue & Fri, 8pm-3am & Sat; Ⓜ Vavin

Above the restaurant of the same name, this established club is famed for its salsa nights, which were credited with single-handedly passing Latin fever to most of Paris. Salsa and Latino nights still take place, but the venue also hosts other kinds of music like *zouk,* reggae, funk and garage.

LA CHAPELLE DES LOMBARDS
Map p158

☎ 01 43 57 24 24; www.la-chapelle-des-lombards. com; 19 rue de Lappe, 11e; admission free-€20; ◷ 11.30pm-6am Tue-Thu & Sun, 8.30pm-6am Fri & Sat; Ⓜ Bastille

This perennially popular Bastille dance club has happening Latino DJs and reggae, funk and Afro jazz concerts – in a word, a bit of everything. Concerts usually take place at 8.30pm on Friday and Saturday.

LA FAVELA CHIC Map p148

☎ 01 40 21 38 14; www.favelachic.com; 18 rue du Faubourg du Temple, 10e; admission free-€10; ◷ 8pm-2am Tue-Thu, to 4am Fri & Sat; Ⓜ République

It starts as a chic, convivial restaurant (open for lunch and dinner to 11pm) and gives way to *caipirinha-* and *mojito*-fuelled bumping, grinding, flirting and dancing (mostly on the long tables). The music is traditionally bossa nova, samba, *baile* (dance) funk and Brazilian pop, and it can get very crowded and hot. They've become so popular they've opened a branch in London's Hoxton.

LA JAVA Map p148

☎ 01 42 02 20 52; www.la-java.fr, in French; 105 rue du Faubourg du Temple, 10e; admission €5-24; ◷ 8pm-3am Mon-Thu, 9pm-6am Fri, midnight-6am Sat, 2pm-2am Sun; Ⓜ Goncourt

Built in 1922, this is the dance hall where Édith Piaf got her first break, and it now reverberates to the sound of live salsa, rock and world music. Live concerts usually take place during the week at 8pm

top picks

LIVE MUSIC BARS

- Au Limonaire (p283) Intimate wine bar with French *chansons.*
- Olympic Café (p284) One of the few smaller places to catch world music, with an accent on l'Afrique.
- Quiet Man (p288) Irish pub offering real-live Irish music sessions.
- Le Vieux Chêne (p280) Weekend jazz at Paris' oldest bar slash 19th-century *bal musette* (dancing club).
- Curio Parlor Cocktail Club (p279) Catch live music Fridays from 9pm at this happening Left Bank cocktail bar.

or 9pm. Afterwards a festive crowd gets dancing to electro, house, disco and Latino DJs.

L'ATTIRAIL Map p148

☎ 01 42 72 44 42; www.lattirail.com; 9 rue au Maire, 3e; admission free; ◷ 10.30am-1.30am Mon-Sat, 3pm-1.30am Sun; Ⓜ Arts et Métiers

There are free concerts of *chansons françaises* and world music (incorporating Hungarian and Balkan Gypsy music, Irish folk, *klezmer* and southern Italian folk) almost daily at 9.30pm at this cosmopolitan enclave next door to the popular club Le Tango (p320). Manic but friendly customers crowd into the Formica bar, with its cheap *pots* (460mL bottle) of wine and friendly staff.

L'ENTREPÔT Map p168

☎ 01 45 40 07 50; www.lentrepot.fr, in French; 7-9 rue Francis de Préssensé, 14e; Ⓜ Pernety or Plaisance

Loud orange flags mark the industrial-styled entrance of this dynamic cultural space, a real mixed-bag venue near Gare Montparnase.

SATELLIT CAFÉ Map p148

☎ 01 47 00 48 87; www.satellit-cafe.com; 44 rue de la Folie Méricourt, 11e; admission free-€12; ◷ 8pm-1am Tue & Wed, 8pm-dawn Thu, 10pm-dawn Fri & Sat; Ⓜ Oberkampf or St-Ambroise

A great venue for world music, and not as painfully trendy as some others in Paris. Come here to hear everything from blues and flamenco to African and Bollywood.

Concerts usually take place at 9pm Tuesday to Thursday, with dancing starting at 11pm.

FRENCH CHANSONS

Think of French music and accordions or *chansonniers* (cabaret singers) like Édith Piaf, Jacques Brel, Georges Brassens and Léo Ferré float through the air. But though you may stumble upon buskers performing *chansons françaises* or playing *musette* (accordion music) in the markets, it is harder than you'd imagine to catch traditional French music in a more formal setting. Try the venues listed here to hear it in both traditional and modern forms.

AU LAPIN AGILE Map p134

☎ 01 46 06 85 87; www.au-lapin-agile.com; 22 rue des Saules, 18e; adult €24, student except Sat €17; ⊙ 9pm-2am Tue-Sun; Ⓜ Lamarck–Caulaincourt
This rustic cabaret venue was favoured by artists and intellectuals in the early 20th century and *chansons* are still per-

formed here. The four-hour show starts at 9.30pm and includes singing and poetry. Some love it, others feel it's a bit of a trap. Admission includes one drink (€6 or €7 subsequently). It's named after *Le Lapin à Gill*, a mural of a rabbit jumping out of a cooking pot by caricaturist André Gill, which can still be seen on the western exterior wall.

LE VIEUX BELLEVILLE

Map p148

☎ 01 44 62 92 66; www.le-vieux-belleville.com; 12 rue des Envierges, 20e; admission free; ⊙ performances at 8pm Thu-Sat; Ⓜ Pyrénées
This old-fashioned bistro at the top of Parc de Belleville is an atmospheric venue for performances of *chansons* featuring accordions and an organ grinder three times a week. It's a lively favourite with locals, though, so booking ahead is advised. The 'Old Belleville' serves classic bistro food (open for lunch Monday to Friday and dinner Tuesday to Saturday).

ÉDITH PIAF: URCHIN SPARROW

Like her American contemporary Judy Garland, Édith Piaf was not just a singer but also a tragic and stoic figure whom the nation took to its heart yet never let go.

She was born Édith Giovanna Gassion to a street acrobat and a singer in the working-class district of Belleville in 1915. Spending her childhood with an alcoholic grandmother who neglected her, and a stint with her father's family, who ran a local brothel in Normandy, Piaf's beginnings were far from fortunate. On tour with her father at the age of nine, by 15 she had left home to sing alone in the streets of Paris. It was her first employer, Louis Leplée, who dubbed her *la môme piaf* (urchin sparrow) and introduced her to the cabarets of the capital.

When Leplée was murdered in 1935 Piaf faced the streets again, but along came Raymond Asso, an ex-French Legionnaire who became her Pygmalion. He forced her to break with her pimp and hustler friends, put her in her signature black dress and was the inspiration for her first big hit, *'Mon Légionnaire'* ('My Legionnaire') in 1937. When she signed a contract with what is now La Java (p303), one of the most famous Parisian music halls of the time, her career skyrocketed.

This frail woman, who sang about street life, drugs, unrequited love, violence, death and whores, seemed to embody all the miseries of the world, yet sang in a husky, powerful voice with no self-pity. Her tumultuous love life earned her the reputation as *une dévoreuse d'hommes* (a man-eater); in fact she launched the careers of several of her lovers, including Yves Montand and Charles Aznavour. When one of her lovers, world middleweight boxing champion Marcel Cerdan, died suddenly in a plane crash, Piaf insisted that the show go on – and fainted on stage in the middle of *'L'Hymne à l'Amour'* ('Hymn to Love'), a song inspired by her late lover.

After suffering serious injuries in a car accident in 1951, Piaf began drinking heavily and became addicted to morphine. Despite her rapidly declining health she continued to take the world stage, including New York's Carnegie Hall in 1956, and recorded some of her biggest hits such as *'Je ne Regrette Rien'* ('I regret nothing') and *'Milord'* ('My Lord'). In 1962, frail and once again penniless, Piaf married a 20-year-old hairdresser called Théophanis Lamboukas (aka Théo Sarapo), recorded the duet *'À Quoi ça sert l'Amour?'* ('What Use is Love?') with him and left Paris for the south of France, where she died the following year. Some two million people attended her funeral in Paris, and the grave of the beloved and much-missed Urchin Sparrow at Père Lachaise Cemetery is still visited and decorated by thousands of loyal fans each year. Public interest in her life and work lives on: the biopic film *La Môme* (p54) was an international success and won several major awards, including an Academy Award for Marion Cotillard, who played Piaf.

LES TROIS BAUDETS Map p134

☎ 01 42 62 33 33; www.lestroisbaudets.com, in French; 64 blvd de Clichy, 18e; ⊙ 6.30pm-1.30am Tue-Sat; Ⓜ Blanche

Diverse French performers take to the stage at this legendary music hall.

DANCE

The Ballet de l'Opéra National de Paris (www.opera-de-paris.fr) performs at both Palais Garnier (p306) and the Opéra de Paris Bastille (p306). Other important venues for both classical and modern dance are the Théâtre du Châtelet and those listed here.

THÉÂTRE DE LA VILLE Map p76

☎ 01 42 74 22 77; www.theatredelaville-paris.com, in French; 2 place du Châtelet, 4e; adult €13-26, student & under 30yr €10-23; ⊙ box office 11am-7pm Mon, to 8pm Tue-Sat; Ⓜ Châtelet

While the Théâtre de la Ville also hosts theatre and music, it's most celebrated for its contemporary dance productions by such noted choreographers as Merce Cunningham, Angelin Preljocaj and Maguy Marin. Depending on availability, students and those under 30 can buy up to two tickets from €10 on the day of the performance. There are no performances in July and August. Its sister venue, the Théâtre de la Ville-Salle Abbesses (Map p134; ☎ 01 42 74 22 77; 31 rue des Abbesses, 18e; ⊙ box office 5-8pm Tue-Sat; Ⓜ Abbesses), stages more avant-garde productions.

LE REGARD DU CYGNE Map p140

☎ 01 43 58 55 93; www.leregarducygne.com, in French; 210 rue de Belleville, 20e; admission €5-13; Ⓜ Place des Fêtes

Le Regard du Cygne prides itself on being an independent, alternative performance space. Situated in the creative 20e, this is where many of Paris' young and daring talents in movement, music and theatre congregate to perform. If you're in the mood for some innovative and experimental modern dance, performance or participation, this is the place to come. The box office is open one hour before performances.

FILM

Both *Pariscope* and *L'Officiel des Spectacles* (p294) list the full crop of Paris' cinematic pickings and screening times; online check out http://cinema.leparisien.fr. Going to the cinema in Paris is not cheap: expect to pay around €10 for a first-run film. Students, under 18s and over 60s get discounted tickets (usually just under €7) every night except Friday, and all day Saturday and on Sunday matinées. Wednesday yields discounts for everyone. English-language films with French subtitles are labelled 'VO' (*version originale*).

There are a few noteworthy movie theatres over and above mainstream cinemas showing Hollywood blockbusters:

CINÉMA DES CINÉASTES Map p136

☎ 08 92 68 97 17; www.cinema-des-cineastes.fr, in French; 7 av de Clichy, 17e; adult €8.90, student & child €6.90, morning screenings €6; Ⓜ Place de Clichy

Founded by the three Claudes (Miller, Berri and Lelouch) and *Betty Blue* director Jean-Jacques Beneix, this is a three-screen theatre dedicated to quality cinema, be it French or foreign, but always avant-garde. Thematic showings, documentaries and meet-the-director sessions round out the repertoire. Don't miss the excellent Bar à Vins du Cinéma des Cinéastes (p285) on the 1st floor.

CINÉMATHÈQUE FRANÇAISE
Map p158

☎ 01 71 19 33 33; www.cinemathequefrancaise.com; 51 rue Bercy, 12e; adult/student/child under 12yr €6.50/5/3.50; ⊙ box office noon-7pm Mon, Wed, Fri & Sat, to 10pm Thu, 10am-8pm Sun; Ⓜ Bercy

This national institution is a temple to the 'seventh art' and always leaves its foreign offerings – often rarely screened classics – in their original versions. The association is a nonprofit collective and also holds debates, cultural events, workshops and exhibitions. For information on its exhibitions see p161.

LA PAGODE Map p108

☎ 01 45 55 48 48; 57bis rue de Babylone, 7e; adult/student €7/5; Ⓜ Vaneau

A classified historical monument, this Chinese-style pagoda was shipped to France, piece by piece, in 1895 by Monsieur Morin (the then proprietor of Le Bon Marché), who had it rebuilt in his garden on rue de Babylone as a love present for his wife. The wife clearly wasn't too impressed – she left him a year later. But Parisian *cinéphiles* who flock here to revel in its eclectic programme are. La Pagode has been a fantastic, atmospheric cinema since 1931 – don't miss a moment or two in its bamboo-enshrined garden.

LE CHAMPO Map p100

☎ 01 43 54 51 60; www.lechampo.com, in French; 51 rue des Écoles, 5e; adult/student & under 20yr €7.50/6, 2pm matinée €5;
Ⓜ St-Michel or Cluny–La Sorbonne

This is one of the most popular of the many Latin Quarter cinemas, featuring classics and retrospectives looking at the films of such actors and directors as Alfred Hitchcock, Jacques Tati, Alain Resnais, Frank Capra and Woody Allen. One of the two *salles* (cinemas) has wheelchair access. A couple of times a month Le Champo screens films all night for night owls kicking off at midnight (three films plus breakfast €15).

MK2 BIBLIOTHÈQUE Map p164

☎ 08 92 69 84 84; www.mk2.com; 128-162 av de France, 13e; adult/student/under 18yr €10.50/7/5.90, everyone before noon €6;
Ⓜ Bibliothèque

This branch of the ever-growing chain (nine outlets at the most recent count) next to the Bibliothèque Nationale is the most ambitious yet, with 14 screens, a trendy café, brasserie, restaurant, late-night bar and a trio of shops specialising in DVDs, books and comics and graphic novels respectively. MK2 Bibliothèque cinemas show a variety of blockbusters and studio films, so there's always something for everyone. Don't miss MK2 Quai de Seine (Map p140; ☎ 08 92 69 84 84; 14 quai de Seine, 19e; Ⓜ Jaurès or Stalingrad) and MK2 Quai de Loire (Map p140; ☎ 08 92 69 84 84; 7 quai de Loire, 19e; Ⓜ Jaurès or Stalingrad), which face one another across from the canal and are linked by ferry boat.

UGC CINÉ CITÉ LA DÉFENSE Map p175

☎ 08 92 70 00 00; www.ugc.fr; 15 Parvis de la Défense; adult/student/under 18yr €10.40/6.90/5.90, everyone before noon €5.90;
Ⓜ La Défense Grande Arche

One of a dozen-odd UGC cinemas in Paris, this modern 16-screen venue inside the Centre Commercial des Quatre Temps shows all the latest box-office hits, many in VO (undubbed).

OPERA

The Opéra National de Paris (ONP) divides its performance schedule between the Palais Garnier, its original home (completed in 1875), and the modern Opéra de Paris Bastille, which opened its doors in 1989. Both opera houses also stage ballets and classical-music concerts performed by the ONP's affiliated orchestra and ballet companies. The opera season runs between September and July.

OPÉRA DE PARIS BASTILLE Map p158

☎ 0 892 899 090, 01 72 29 35 35; www.opera-de-paris.fr, in French; 2-6 place de la Bastille, 12e; opera €5-172, ballet €5-87, concerts €5-49;
Ⓜ Bastille

Despite some initial resistance to this 3400-seat venue, the main opera house in the capital, it's now performing superbly. While less alluring than the Palais Garnier (p306), at least all seats in the main hall have an unrestricted view of the stage. Ticket sales begin at a precise date prior to each performance, with different opening dates for bookings by telephone, online or from the box office (Map p158; 130 rue de Lyon, 11e; ☎ 10.30am-6.30pm Mon-Sat). The cheapest opera seats are €7 and are sold only from the box office. Note: on the first day they are released, box office tickets can be bought only from the opera house at which the performance is to be held. At Bastille, standing-only tickets for €5 are available 1½ hours before performances begin. Just 15 minutes before the curtain goes up, last-minute seats at reduced rates (usually €20 for opera and ballet performances) are released to people aged under 28 or over 60 but this is a very rare occurrence indeed.

PALAIS GARNIER Map p126

☎ 08 92 89 90 90; www.opera-de-paris.fr; place de l'Opéra, 9e; Ⓜ Opéra

The city's original opera house is smaller and more glamorous than its Bastille counterpart, and boasts perfect acoustics. Due to its odd shape, however, some seats have limited or no visibility. Ticket prices and conditions (including last-minute discounts) at the box office (☼ 11am-6.30pm Mon-Sat, at the corner of rues Scribe and Auber) are identical to those at the Opéra de Paris Bastille (p306).

OPÉRA COMIQUE Map p72

☎ 0 825 010 123; www.opera-comique.com;
1 place Boïeldieu, 2e; tickets €6-108;
Ⓜ Richelieu–Drouot

This century-old hall has premiered many
important French operas and continues
to host classic and less-known works. Buy
tickets online or from the box office (⊙ 11am-
7pm Mon-Sat, to 5pm Sun) on the other side of
the square from the theatre. Subject to
availability, students and those under 28
can buy tickets from €15 (but often not for
weekend performances).

THEATRE

The majority of theatre productions in Paris,
including those originally written in other languages, are – naturally enough – performed
in French. Only very occasionally does the
odd itinerant English-speaking troupe play at
smaller venues in and around town. Consult
Pariscope or *L'Officiel des Spectacles* (p294) for
details.

COMÉDIE FRANÇAISE Map p76

☎ 0 825 101 680; www.comedie-francaise.fr; place
Colette, 1er; tickets €5-37; ⊙ box office 11am-
6pm; Ⓜ Palais Royal–Musée du Louvre

Founded in 1680 under Louis XIV, the
'French Comedy' theatre bases its repertoire around the works of classic French
playwrights such as Molière, Racine, Corneille, Beaumarchais, Marivaux and Musset,
although in recent years contemporary
and even – shock, horror! – non-French

LOCAL KNOWLEDGE: PARIS VIBES

Tariq Krim, charismatic founder of Netvibes.com and Jolicloud.com, is among a clutch of young innovators credited with
making the internet what it is. Be it tracking the future in digital space or the next best bar in his city, he is a Parisian
in tune with the vibe. He has clubbed with Paris' finest first-generation electronic-music DJs, his music taste is eclectic
and as work increasingly takes him around the world, he is enjoying a new weekend affair with his city. So where does
he go on Saturday night? He opened his address book to Nicola Williams.

You go out a lot, right? I'm not very often here any more (always travelling with Jolicloud), and when I am
it's for fun; it's interesting because now I'm experiencing Paris at the weekend. I'm very loyal to lots of places. I grew
up in the Marais and spent almost all my life there and the Bastille. The 11e is my all-time favourite neighbourhood:
I'm very much this side of the Seine, but you know the story... If I have to go to St-Germain I don't know where to go.

Your ideal night out? Two kinds: when you have no voice because you have to yell over the music and places
where you can actually talk.

Perfect lose-your-voice places? Chez Janou (p255), one of my favourite restaurants in France, period. It's
been there for 10 years and is an institution, the canteen of people like John Malkovich. I call it Little New York now
because so many people speak English there these days. Or Café de l'Industrie (p266); that's a loud place. Then drinks at
L'Aréa (☎ 01 42 72 96 50; www.lareaforever.com, in French; 10 rue Tournelles, 4e; Ⓜ Bastille), a Lebanese-Brazilian
restaurant with lots of music. The owner, Édouard, is an amazing guy, super-nice, and knows where to send you next,
which clubs... I used to go to the Rex (p297). Now there's the Social Club (p299).

For something quieter? An Italian restaurant I love, it could be the perfect date restaurant: Swann et Vincent
(p266). Then I go for a cocktail. Le Fumoir (p278) has the best collection of vodka martinis and is very quiet, especially
the last room at the back. I love the idea of a vintage club with armchairs, a library full of books and international magazines, and people drinking very nice cocktails. The décor is also amazing: art deco – lost in New York after Prohibition.

The other place I go is the Experimental Cocktail Club (☎ 01 45 08 88 09; www.myspace.com/experimental-
cocktailclub; 37 rue St-Saveur, 2e; ⊙ 6pm-2am Sun-Thu, to even later Fri & Sat; Ⓜ Réaumur–Sébastopol), a similar
concept to Milk & Honey – amazing cocktails, people super-nice and it's small.

Another, already known by a bunch of people, but one I love is the literary café with bar L'Étoile Manquante (☎ 01
42 72 48 34; www.cafeine.com; 34 rue du Vieille du Temple, 4e; Ⓜ Hôtel de Ville or St-Paul Café).

Best neighbourhood bar? Le Fée Verte (☎ 01 43 72 31 24; 108 rue de la Roquette, 11e; Ⓜ Voltaire): I
started Netvibes here three years ago – imagine the perfect dream bar with wi-fi; it was one of the first. I love the idea
of being in contact with the world and saying 'Can I have another cappuccino, please?'!

Nightlife philosophy? You can be in the best place by yourself or the worst place with your friends; I would
always go for the second.

Interviewed by Nicola Williams

works (in translation, of course) have been staged.

There are three venues: the main Salle Richelieu on place Colette just west of the Palais Royal; the Studio Théâtre (Map p76; ☎ 01 44 58 98 58; Galerie du Carrousel du Louvre, 99 rue de Rivoli, 1er; ☺ box office 2-5pm Wed-Sun; Ⓜ Palais Royal–Musée du Louvre) and the Théâtre du Vieux Colombier (Map p112; ☎ 01 44 39 87 00; 21 rue du Vieux Colombier, 6e; ☺ box office 11am-6pm; Ⓜ St-Sulpice).

Tickets for regular seats at the Salle Richelieu cost €11 to €37; tickets for the 65 places near the ceiling (€5) go on sale one hour before curtain time (usually 8.30pm) at the discount ticket window (Map p76) around the corner from the main entrance and facing place André Malraux. Those aged under 28 can purchase any of the better seats remaining one hour before curtain time for between €5.50 and €14 at the main box office.

top picks

- Bike tours (p400)
- Espace St-Louis (p311)
- Hammam de la Mosquée de Paris (p310)
- Ice skating at the Hôtel de Ville (p313)
- Piscine de la Butte aux Cailles (p314)
- Piscine Joséphine Baker (p314)
- Stade de France (p315)

SPORTS & ACTIVITIES

Hot, sticky sports and ice-cool Parisians seemingly don't go together. *Au contraire:* not only are Parisians mad about watching sport, they play it too. The only trifling difference between us and them is that they wouldn't be seen dead walking down the street in their tracksuit (or working out in their lunch hour).

As the French capital, Paris is privy to big games in world-class stadiums, and there are bags of opportunities to see great sporting moments unfold before your very eyes. Out of the arena, it's dead easy for all those closet *sportifs* (sportspeople) to stay fit (and sickeningly slim). Be it cycling, swimming, lounging on the beach, street blading with the masses or practising the silent art of t'ai chi in the Jardin du Luxembourg, this urban landscape is action-packed.

The best single source of information on sports – spectator and participatory – is the free, 500-page *Parisports: Le Guide du Sport à Paris* (www.paris.fr, 'Sport' menu, in French), published online and on paper by the **Mairie de Paris** (Paris Town Hall; Map p152; ☎ 39 75; www.paris.fr; Hôtel de Ville, 29 rue de Rivoli, 4e; Ⓜ Hôtel de Ville); *mairies* (town halls) in every arrondissement have information on sports in their own patch. For an abbreviated version in English, click on the 'Well Being' menu at www.parisinfo.com.

HEALTH & FITNESS

Whether you want to hobnob with the stars at a *spa de luxe* or get a *savon noir* (black soap) exfoliation at the neighbourhood hammam, Paris has spaces to suit every whim. Spoil yourself.

HAMMAMS & SPAS

Nothing beats a lavender-and-ginger massage, perfumed foot soak or flop in a traditional Turkish bath (hammam) between sips of *thé à la menthe* (mint tea) after a hard day slogging the city sights.

ESPACE JOÏYA Map p126

☎ 01 40 70 16 49; www.joiya.fr; 6 rue de la Renaissance, 8e; per 30/60/90min €50/95/130; ⏱ 11am-7.30pm Mon-Wed & Sat, 11am-9pm Thu & Fri; Ⓜ Alma–Marceau

The creation of former Russian model Julia Lemigova (she looks like Julia Roberts), who is mad about Asia, this exclusive spa unwinds wound-up city slickers with detox and de-stress massages using natural and essential oils.

HAMMAM DE LA MOSQUÉE DE PARIS
Map p100

☎ 01 43 31 38 20; www.la-mosquee.com; 39 rue Geoffroy St-Hilaire, 5e; admission €15; ⏱ men 2-9pm Tue, 10am-9pm Sun, women 10am-9pm Mon, Wed, Thu & Sat, 2-9pm Fri; Ⓜ Censier Daubenton or Place Monge

Massages at this atmospheric hammam cost €1 a minute and come in 10-, 20- or 30-minute packages. Should you fancy an exfoliating body scrub and mint tea, get the 10-/30-minute massage *formule* (€38/58). There are lunch deals for rumbling tummies. Bring a swimsuit but hire a towel/dressing gown (€4/5). No kids under 12.

HARNN & THANN Map p72

☎ 01 40 15 02 20; www.harnn-spa.fr; 11 rue Molière, 1e; 1hr massage from €75; ⏱ 11am-8pm Mon-Wed, Fri & Sat, 11am-10pm Thu; Ⓜ Pyramides

This relaxing 'natural home spa' in a secret courtyard is another heady one for the senses. Masseuses soothe muscles with traditional Thai massage techniques and an aromatic mix of herbs and essential oils. Particularly inventive are its Wednesday Les Petit Duos (€50) – a 30-minute massage for one worn-out mum or dad plus kid (aged six to 12 years) – and its after-work *bien-être* (well-being; €250) deal for couples, which includes a foot bath, massage *en duo* and dinner at a neighbouring Thai restaurant. A 20-minute lounge in the peacock-blue hammam costs €20.

LES BAINS DU MARAIS Map p152

☎ 01 44 61 02 02; www.lesbainsdumarais.com, in French; 31-33 rue des Blancs Manteaux, 4e; massage from €70; ⏱ 10am-8pm Mon, Fri & Sat, 10am-11pm Sun, Tue-Thu; Ⓜ Rambuteau or Hôtel de Ville

Luxury personified, this hammam (€35) combines the classical with modern – mint tea and Levantine decor with as many pampering treatments as you'd care to name. The hammam is reserved for men and for women on certain days; 'mixed days', when bathing suits are obligatory, are Wednesday evening and all day Saturday and Sunday.

SPA NUXE Map p76

☎ 01 55 80 71 40; www.nuxe.com; 32 rue Montorgueil, 1e; massage from €80; ⏰ 9.30am-9pm Mon-Fri, 9.30am-7.30pm Sat; Ⓜ Les Halles
A regular in *Elle* and other French glossies, this recently overhauled spa lounging in a medieval wine cellar with old stone walls and wood-beamed ceilings is where stars and supermodels find peace. Spa Nuxe offers an orgy of 45-minute massages (Thai, ayurvedic, Californian, shiatsu), including rhythmic ones to music; skin treatments; French pedicures and manicures; and so on.

HAMMAM MEDINA Map p140

☎ 01 42 02 31 05; www.hammam-medina.com, in French; 43-45 rue Petit, 19e; €39-150; ⏰ 11am-10pm Mon-Fri, 10am-9pm Sat, 9am-7pm Sun; Ⓜ Laumière
It might not be close to the centre of Paris, but this is nevertheless a notable hammam: it is one of the city's largest, it has an attached North African tearoom and restaurant, and it is one of the few to accept men as well as women (Saturdays only; swimwear required). Basic admission includes the sauna, spa and exfoliation rubdown.

GYMS

Many Paris gyms and fitness clubs allow one-off or short-term memberships.

CLUB MED GYM

☎ 0 820 202 020; www.clubmedgym.com
In addition to 17 gyms (one day pass €26) in greater Paris, Club Med runs Club Med Waou (basically, 'Club Med Wow'; €35) centres offering luxurious settings and spa facilities; check the website for the five locations. Club Med Gym branches include Palais Royal (Map p76; ☎ 01 40 20 03 03; 147bis rue St-Honoré, 1er; ⏰ 7.30am-10pm Mon, Thu & Fri, 7.30am-11pm Tue & Wed, 9am-7pm Sat & 5pm Sun; Ⓜ Palais Royal-Musée du Louvre); République (Map p148; ☎ 01

47 00 69 98; 10 place de la République, 11e; ⏰ 7.30am-10pm Mon-Fri, 8am-7pm Sat, 9am-7pm Sun; Ⓜ République), which is entered via rue du Faubourg du Temple; and the 20e (Map p158; ☎ 01 43 70 07 07; 63-65 rue de Bagnolet, 20e; ⏰ 7.30am-10pm Mon-Fri, 8.30am-6pm Sat; Ⓜ Alexandre Dumas).

ESPACE ST-LOUIS Map p82

☎ 09 50 52 67 43; www.espace-saint-louis.com, in French; 51-53 rue St-Louis en l'Île, 2e; 1/10/20 sessions €18/150/280; Ⓜ Pont Marie
Take your pick of keep-fit courses at this fun fitness place: pilates, hatha or ashtanga yoga, qigong, salsa, samba, flamenco, modern jazz. Pay €10 to try a one-hour *cour* or buy a carnet. Recommended are the classes aboard a *péniche* (barge) on the Seine near Notre Dame or the Louvre. Details are online.

VIT'HALLES BEAUBOURG Map p152

☎ 01 42 77 21 71; www.vithalles.com, in French; 48 rue de Rambuteau, 3e; day pass €25, 10-entry carnet €199; ⏰ 8am-10.30pm Mon-Fri, 9am-7pm Sat, 10am-7pm Sun; Ⓜ Rambuteau
This squeaky-clean health club gets fabulous reviews from local residents and blow-ins; it follows the Les Mills fitness program. There are nine other branches in greater Paris, including Vit'halles Nation (Map p158; ☎ 01 43 43 57 57; 164 blvd Diderot, 12e; Ⓜ Nation), which keeps the same hours.

ACTIVITIES

Entertainment weeklies *Pariscope* and *L'Officiel des Spectacles* (p294) list what's on.

CYCLING

Plenty more Parisians are pedal-powered thanks to Vélib' (see p384 for details); for all things Velib' related, check out the blog (http://blog.velib.paris.fr/blog, in French).

Paris is aiming for some 600km of *pistes cyclables* (cycling lanes) running throughout the city by 2013, if you count the Bois de Boulogne (16e) and Bois de Vincennes (12e). On Sunday and holidays, large sections of road are reserved for pedestrians, cyclists and skaters under the scheme *Paris Respire* (p312).

The Mairie de Paris (Map p152; ☎ 39 75; www.paris. fr; Hôtel de Ville, 29 rue de Rivoli, 4e; Ⓜ Hôtel de Ville) is an invaluable source of information for cyclists. It allows free downloads online at www.velo. paris.fr (in French) of its *carte des itineraries* cyclables (map of cycling itineraries) mapping every Parisian cycling lane; pick up a paper version at local *mairies*. This is also the place to source itineraries, rules and regulations detailed in its free booklet *Paris à Vélo* (Paris by Bicycle). Even more detailed are maps and guides such as *Paris Vélo! Pocket Plan* (€2.95) or *Paris Vélo Pratique* (*Paris by Bike*; €6.95), sold in bookshops and some newspaper stands.

For information on guided bicycle tours, see p400.

Bicycle Hire

FAT TIRE BIKE TOURS Map p168

☎ 01 56 58 10 54; www.fattirebiketoursparis.com; 24 rue Edgar Faure, 15e; 1hr/day/week €4/25/100; ⏱ 9am-7pm, after 11.30am only May-Aug; Ⓜ La Motte-Picquet–Grenelle

Fat Tire is a friendly Anglophone outfit that rents three-speed cruisers, kids' bikes, trailers, tandems and so on. Show a driver's licence or passport and leave €250 deposit on your credit card. It organises fantastic bike tours too; see p400.

GEPETTO & VÉLOS Map p100

☎ 01 43 54 19 95; www.gepetto-et-velos.com, in French; 59 rue du Cardinal Lemoine, 5e; half-/full day/weekend/week €9/15/25/60; ⏱ 9am-1pm & 2-7.30pm Tue-Sat; Ⓜ Cardinal Lemoine

New and secondhand bicycles, plus repairs. To rent, show your passport and leave a €325 deposit.

PARIS À VÉLO, C'EST SYMPA! Map p148

☎ 01 48 87 60 01; www.parisvelosympa.com; 22 rue Alphonse Baudin, 11e; half-/full day/weekend /week €12/15/25/60; ⏱ 9.30am-1pm & 2-6pm Mon-Fri, 9am-1pm & 2-7pm Sat & Sun; Ⓜ St-Sébastien–Froissart

Cringeworthy name ('Paris by Bike, it's Nice!'), yes, but this super-friendly outfit rents tandems for the price of two bikes and organises great thematic bike tours around Paris (p401). Deposit €250 (€900 for a tandem) with a credit card or your passport.

VÉLO CITO Map p148

☎ 01 43 38 47 19; www.velocito.fr, in French; 7 rue St-Ambroise, 11e; day €25; ⏱ 10am-7pm Mon-Sat; Ⓜ St-Ambroise

The pedal-weary can opt for extra power with a smart electric bicycle to cruise around the city from this outlet located between Bastille and République; rental is by the day only and you need to leave your passport as a deposit. It distributes an excellent free map (1:53:000) detailing some lovely *pistes cyclables* starting at RER stations around Paris.

FREESCOOT Map p100

☎ 01 44 07 06 72; www.scooter-rental-paris.com; 63 quai de la Tournelle, 5e; bike/tandem half-day €10/22, day €15/32; ⏱ 9am-1pm & 2-7pm Mon-Sat year-round plus Sun mid-Apr–mid-Sep; Ⓜ Maubert–Mutualité

This scooter and bike-rental shop is the outfit to come to if you fancy pedalling Paris on the back of a tandem. Well-equipped bikes come with helmet, lock, basket and windbreaker, and require a passport or ID card and €300 as deposit. Its Voltaire branch (☎ 01 44 93 04 03; 144 blvd Voltaire, 11e; ⏱ 9am-1pm & 2-7pm Mon-Fri) opens Monday

PARIS BREATHES

Now a well-established operation, Paris Respire ('Paris Breathes') kicks motorised traffic off certain streets at certain times to let pedestrians, cyclists, in-line skaters and other nonmotorised cruisers breathe. While it drives its usual traffic jams and pollution to other spots in the city instead, it makes Sundays very pedal-pleasurable.

The tracks listed here are off-limits to cars on Sunday and public holidays. Due to the number of areas now included, not everything has been listed here. For updates on exact routes and detailed maps see www.velo.paris.fr.

- By the Seine: central areas along both banks (from 9am to 5pm).
- Marais: almost all of the central Marais (from 10am to 7.30pm summer, 10am to 6pm winter).
- Latin Quarter, 5e: along rue Mouffetard extending north along rue Descartes (from 10am to 6pm).
- Bastille, 11e: Rue de la Roquette and surrounding streets (from 10am to 6pm).
- Montmartre, 18e: all the streets in Montmartre (from 11am to 6pm).
- Canal St-Martin, 10e: quai de Valmy and quai de Jemmapes (from 10am to 6pm winter, 10am to 8pm summer); expanded in July and August.
- Bois de Boulogne: (from 9am to 6pm Saturday and Sunday) and Bois de Vincennes (from 9am to 6pm Sunday).
- Jardin du Luxembourg, 6e: immediate surrounding streets (from 10am to 6pm March to November).

to Friday only. It also rents snazzy motor scooters; see p387 for details.

AU POINT VÉLO HOLLANDAIS
Map p100

☎ 01 43 45 85 36; www.pointvelo.com; 83 blvd St-Michel, 5e; ⏰ 10am-7.30pm Mon-Sat; Ⓜ Luxembourg Cruise Paris on a trusted Dutch Gazelle, silky-smooth ride guaranteed. The shop, next to Jardin du Luxembourg, repairs bikes too and leaves a pump outside for passing cyclists with flats.

JOGGING

Jogging through Paris is a real temptation, but you have to pick the time and place carefully. It's definitely an early morning activity; the narrow streets quickly become crowded as the day's commute begins. The 42km Paris Marathon (www.parismarathon.com) takes place every April and is quite popular with French and international runners. Registration begins in mid-September and costs from €58 to €90.

Also look out for the Paris Running Tour (www.parisrunningtour.com), a new tour group that specialises in cross-town jogs. Oh, and watch out for the dog poop.

SKATING

Be it across tarmac or ice, skating is big – see p295 for street spots to catch entertaining free demos. See p312 for details of traffic-free streets to cruise down on Sundays.

In-line Skating

Serious bladers use the bus lanes; others scoot along pavements and cycling lanes. Up to 15,000 take part in the weekly *randonnées en roller* (skating rambles).

The 30km Pari Roller Ramble (aka Friday Night Fever, www.pari-roller.com) kicks off on place Raoul Dautry, 14e (Map p168; Ⓜ Montparnasse–Bienvenüe) at 10pm Friday (arrive at 9.30pm), returning at 1am.

The Rollers & Coquillages Ramble (☎ 01 44 54 07 44; www.rollers-coquillages.org, in French) afternoon skate departs from behind the Nomades bike shop (p313) on Sunday at 2.30pm, returning around 5.30pm. It is better suited for novices than the evening skate.

NOMADES Map p148

☎ 01 44 54 07 44; www.nomadeshop.com, in French; 37 blvd Bourdon, 4e; half-/full day Mon-Fri €5/8, Sat & Sun €6/9, full week €30; ⏰ 11.30am-7.30pm Tue-Fri, 10am-7pm Sat, noon-6pm Sun; Ⓜ Bastille

Paris' 'Harrods for roller-heads' rents and sells equipment and accessories, and gives courses costing from €12 to €40 per person per hour depending on the number of participants. Renting elbow and knee guards/helmets costs €1/2 and you'll need a deposit of €150 or an identity card or passport.

Ice Skating

From December to early March, the city maintains several pretty-as-a-picture outdoor *patinoires de Noël* (Christmas ice-skating rinks; www.paris.fr, in French). Access is free but *patins/casques* (skates/safety helmets) cost €5/3 to rent. Rinks include Patinoire de l'Hôtel de Ville (Map p152; ☎ 39 75; place de l'Hôtel de Ville, 4e; ⏰ noon-10pm Mon-Fri, 9am-10pm Sat & Sun; Ⓜ Hôtel de Ville) and the Patinoire de Montparnasse (Map p168; ☎ 39 75; place Raoul Dautry, 14e; ⏰ noon-8pm Mon-Fri, 9am-8pm Sat & Sun; Ⓜ Montparnasse–Bienvenüe). The national library rink, Patinoire de la Bibliothèque François Mitterand (cnr rue des Moulins & av de France; ⏰ 9am-8pm late Dec–early Jan; Ⓜ Bibliothèque), opens late December to late January.

DJs turn Friday and Saturday evenings into something of an ice disco at the Patinoire Sonja Henie (Map p158; ☎ 01 40 02 60 60; www.bercy.fr, in French; 8 blvd de Bercy, 12e; adult/under 26yr €4/3, Fri & Sat €6/4, skate hire €3, helmet €1; ⏰ 3-6pm Wed, 9.30pm-12.30am Fri, 3-6pm & 9.30pm-12.30am Sat, 10am-noon & 3-6pm Sun Sep-May; Ⓜ Bercy), an indoor ice-skating rink in the Palais Omnisports de Paris-Bercy.

Art Deco in style, 800 sq metres in size and worth the trip is Patinoire Pailleron (Map p140; ☎ 01 40 40 27 70; 32 blvd Édouard Pailleron, 19e; adult before/after 8pm €4/6, carnet of 10 tickets before/after 8pm €34/26, skate hire €3; ⏰ noon-1.30pm & 4-10pm Mon, Tue & Thu, noon-10pm Wed, noon-1.30pm & 4pm-midnight Fri, noon-midnight Sat, 10am-6pm Sun during school term; noon-10pm Mon, Tue & Thu, 9am-10pm Wed, noon-midnight Fri, 9am-midnight Sat, 10am-6pm Sun during school holidays), open year-round except July and August.

BOULES & BOWLING

Don't be surprised to see groups of earnest Parisians (usually men) playing *boules* (known as *pétanque* in southern France) – France's most popular traditional game, similar to lawn bowls – in the Jardin du Luxembourg and other parks and squares with suitably flat, shady patches of gravel. The Arènes de

Lutèce *boulodrome* (www.arenesdelutece.com, in French) in a 2nd-century Roman amphitheatre in the Latin Quarter is a fabulous spot to absorb the scene. The player who tosses his *boules* (biased metal balls) nearest the small wooden *cochonnet* (jack) wins. Sports shops and supermarkets sell cheap sets of *boules*, should you have the urge to have a spin at it. There are usually places to play at Paris Plages (p19).

Come evening, tenpin bowling takes over. Prices for games depend on the time and day of the week. Among the best and/or most central alleys:

LE BOWLING Map p168

☎ 01 43 21 61 32; 25 rue du Commandant René Mouchotte, 14e; games €5-7.50 inc shoes; ❀ noon-2am Mon-Thu, noon-4am Fri, 10am-5am Sat, 10am-midnight Sun; Ⓜ Montparnasse–Bienvenüe
This centre, just opposite Gare Montparnasse, has 16 lanes.

BOWLING MOUFFETARD Map p100

☎ 01 43 31 09 35; www.bowling-mouffetard.abcsalles.com, in French; 13 rue Gracieuse & 73 rue Mouffetard, 5e; games €3.50-7, shoes €2; ❀ 3pm-2am Mon-Fri, 10am-2am Sat & Sun; Ⓜ Place Monge
Intimate, friendly place with eight lanes and two entrances.

SWIMMING

Paris has almost 40 public swimming pools. Most are short-length pools and finding a free lane to swim laps can be tricky. Opening times vary widely; Wednesdays (kids are off school) and weekends are the busiest. Unless noted otherwise, admission costs €3/24 for a single ticket/carnet of 10 and €1.70 a dip for Paris residents under 26 years.

Boys, no hiding what you don't have: Bermuda and boxer shorts are a no-go in public pools. With the exception of nudist Roger Le Gall, men and boys must don a pair of skintight trunks *(slips de bain)*. Most places also demand that everyone wears a *bonnet* (swimming hat), sold at most pools for a few euros.

FOREST HILL AQUABOULEVARD
Map p168

☎ 01 40 60 10 00; www.aquaboulevard.com, in French; 4-6 rue Louis Armand, 15e; adult/child 3-11yr €20/10, high season €25/10; ❀ 9am-11pm Mon-Thu, 9am-midnight Fri, 8am-midnight Sat, 8am-11pm Sun; Ⓜ Balard

This tropical 'beach' and aquatic park delights with water slides, waterfalls and wave pools. The less frivolous can keep fit with tennis, squash, golf, gym and dance classes. No children under three; last admission is 9pm.

PISCINE DE LA BUTTE AUX CAILLES
Map p164

☎ 01 45 89 60 05; 5 place Paul Verlaine, 13e; adult/child €3/1.70; ❀ 7am-8.30am, 11.30am-1.30pm & 4.30-9pm Tue, 7am-7pm Wed, 7am-8.30am & 11.30am-6.30pm Thu & Fri, 7am-8.30am & 10am-6.30pm Sat, 8am-6pm Sun; Ⓜ Place d'Italie

This stunning pool, built in 1924, takes advantage of the lovely warm water issuing from a nearby artesian well. Come summer, its two outdoor pools buzz with swimmers frolicking in the sun. Open extended hours during school holidays.

PISCINE JOSÉPHINE BAKER
Map p164

☎ 01 56 61 96 50; quai François Mauriac, 13e; adult 1/10 entries €3/24; ❀ 1-9pm Mon, Wed & Fri, 1-11pm Tue & Thu, noon-8pm Sat, 10am-8pm Sun; Ⓜ Bibliothèque or Quai de la Gare

This striking *piscine* afloat the Seine is style indeed (named after the sensual 1920s Afro-American singer, what else could it be?). More of a spot to be seen than thrash laps, the two 25m-by-10m pools lure Parisians like bees to a honey pot in summer when the roof slides back.

PISCINE KELLER Map p168

☎ 01 45 71 81 00; 14 rue de l'Ingénieur Keller, 15e; adult/child €3/1.70; ❀ noon-10pm Mon & Fri, 7-8.30am & noon-10pm Tue & Thu, 7am-8pm Wed, 9am-9pm Sat, 9am-7pm Sun; Ⓜ Charles Michels

This revamped 1960s indoor pool with state-of-the-art glass roof that slides back on warm days is a splash with Parisians keen to swim beneath the stars. It has slightly different hours during school holidays.

PISCINE PONTOISE Map p100

☎ 01 55 42 77 88; 19 rue de Pontoise, 5e; adult/concession €4.20/2.40, 10-entry carnet €33.20/21.20; ❀ during school holidays 7-8.30am & 11am-11.45pm Mon, 7am-7.30pm & 8.15-11.45pm Tue & Thu, 7-8.30am, 11.30am-7.30pm & 8.15-11.45pm Wed, 7-8.30am, 11am-8pm & 9-11.45pm Fri, 10am-7pm Sat, 8am-7pm Sun; Ⓜ Maubert–Mutualité

A beautiful Art Deco-style indoor pool in the heart of the Latin Quarter; a €9 evening ticket covers entry to pool, gym and sauna. It has shorter hours during term time.

PISCINE ROGER LE GALL Map p158

☎ 01 44 73 81 12; 34 blvd Carnot, 12e; ⏱ noon-2pm & 5-8pm Mon, Tue & Thu, 8am-9pm Wed, noon-2pm & 5-9pm Fri, noon-7pm Sat, 8am-7pm Sun; Ⓜ Porte de Vincennes

With its grassy lawns to lounge about on and twin-set of pools, indoor and out, many readers reckon this is Paris' best (blvd Périphérique is a tad close for our comfort). It is notably the only public *naturiste* pool in Paris where you can swim nude at selected times on certain days. In July and August admission costs more; open extended hours during school holidays.

TENNIS

Again, the Mairie de Paris (Map p152; ☎ 39 75, reservations 01 71 71 70 70; www.tennis.paris.fr; open court per hr adult/under 26yr €7.50/4.50, covered court €14/8) is the contact. The city runs approximately 170 covered and open tennis courts in dozens of locations (hours vary considerably); reserve by telephone or online. Courts include Candie (Map p158; ☎ 01 43 55 84 95; rue de Candie, 11e; Ⓜ Ledru Rollin) and Neuve St-Pierre (Map p148; ☎ 01 42 78 21 04; 5 rue Neuve St Pierre, 4e; Ⓜ St-Paul).

YOGA

Yoga is quite popular among Parisians; if you're in Paris for an extended stay you should be able to locate neighbourhood classes fairly easily (check with the local *mairie*). The Centre Sivananda (☎ 01 40 26 77 49; www.sivananda.org/paris; 140 rue du Faubourg St-Martin, 10e; 1/10 courses €15/115, plus €20 registration fee; Ⓜ Gare de l'Est) offers excellent classes, sometimes in English.

SPECTATOR SPORT

Depending on what time of year you're here, this is the city to see all types of matches and events. Follow the 'what's on' link at http://en.parisinfo.com or visit box offices – which sell tickets for most sports events – situated inside branches of Fnac and Virgin Megastore (p203) for info in English. If you can read French, sports daily *L'Équipe* (www.lequipe.fr) and entertainment and activities supplement *Figaroscope* (www.figaroscope.fr; published every Wednesday in *Le Figaro*), will provide more depth.

FOOTBALL

Paris' magnificent Stade de France (p175; tickets €20 to €100), north of the centre in St-Denis, is where France's home matches kick off.

The city's only top-division football team, Paris-St-Germain (www.psg.fr), wears red and blue

PARKOUR & FREERUNNING

Should you be stopped dead in your tracks on the streets of Paris by a feline figure scaling two buildings with a death-defying leap, vaulting a statue or springing off a lamppost, no sweat: that's Parkour. Throw in a 360° backflip and triple somersault and you have its more flamboyant acrobatic brother, Freerunning.

Born in the Parisian suburbs, the craze of getting from A to B without letting *anything* get in your way has since gained a cult following in cities worldwide. And anything really means *anything*, be it a stairwell, metro station entrance, Vélib' bike stand or 25m gap between rooftops. One YouTube video tags it as 'dudes fiddling around with buildings' (a fair enough assumption), but this is a discipline fusing sport, art and philosophy with serious backbone. Plain dangerous, in fact, whether you do or don't know what you're doing.

Two godlike men with a cinematic screen presence and muscles to die for are behind the French-bred discipline, which some say was the natural progression of New York's 1970s breakdance: David Belle (b 1973; http://kyzr.free.fr/davidbelle) and Sébastien Foucan (b 1974; www.foucan.com). The two played together as kids growing up in the Parisian suburb of Lisses, 40km south of the centre, and in 1989 as fearless adolescents they put a name to their increasingly dare-devil street antics – Parkour, from the French military's *parcours du combattant* (obstacle courses).

But in the 1990s, then a fireman, Foucan found his outlook shifting subtly away from Belle's as the philosophical lure of martial arts and yearning for greater freedom of expression kicked in. Thus, in 2001, he came up with his own, more expressive brand of Parkour called Freerunning. While Belle and his followers (known as *les traceurs*) ruthlessly track the shortest, most efficient route from A to B, Foucan's team focuses on aesthetics and creativity of movement – hence the gravity-defying stunts and acrobatics choreographed in most Freerunning movements. As much a mental as a physical challenge (indeed, 'obstacles' are not always what they seem), both brands advocate the extreme sport as a way of life in which inner balance plays as crucial a role as physical prowess.

and plays its home games at the 48,500-seat Parc des Princes (Map p118; ☎ 32 75; www.leparcdesprinces. fr; 24 rue du Commandant Guilbaud, 16e; tickets €20-150; ☺ box office 9am-7pm Mon-Fri & 3hr before match; Ⓜ Porte de St-Cloud), built in 1970.

RUGBY

When at home Paris-based team Stade Français CASG (☎ 01 40 71 71 00; www.stade.fr) plays north at the small Stade Jean Bouin (Map p118; ☎ 01 46 51 00 75; 26 av du Général Sarrail, 16e; tickets €5-35; box office ☺ 11am-2pm & 3-7pm Tue-Fri, 2-7pm Mon & Sat; Ⓜ Exelmans) and occasionally at the Stade de France (p175). There is talk of the team moving to a new stadium, though, at the time of research, nothing had been decided. The finals of the Championnat de France de Rugby take place in late May and early June.

TENNIS

By far the glitziest annual sporting event in Paris is the French Open, the second of four Grand Slam tennis tournaments, held on clay at the 16,500-seat Stade Roland Garros (off Map p118; www.billetterie.fft.fr; 2 av Gordon Bennett, 16e; Ⓜ Porte d'Auteuil) in the Bois de Boulogne from late May to mid-June. Tickets are expensive and like gold dust; they go on sale mid-December and bookings must be made by March. They are only available online or via mail. One week prior to the competition (on the first day of the qualifiers), remaining tickets are sold from the box office (☺ 9.30am-5.30pm Mon-Fri) at the entrance to the stadium.

The top indoor tournament is the Paris Tennis Open, usually held in late October or early November at the Palais Omnisports de Paris-Bercy (Map p158; ☎ 01 40 02 60 60, box office 08 92 39 01 00; www.bercy.fr, in French; 8 blvd de Bercy, 12e; Ⓜ Bercy).

CYCLING

Joining the tens of thousands of spectators along the av des Champs-Élysées to watch the final leg of the world's most prestigious cycling race, the three-week Tour de France (www. letour.fr), is a must for those in Paris towards the end of July.

The final day varies from year to year but is usually the 3rd or 4th Sunday in July, with the race finishing some time in the afternoon. If you want to see this exciting event, find a spot at the barricades before noon.

Track cycling, a sport at which France excels, is sometimes held in the velodrome of the Palais Omnisports de Paris-Bercy (Map p158; ☎ 01 40 02 60 60; www.bercy.fr, in French; 8 blvd de Bercy, 12e; Ⓜ Bercy).

HORSE RACING

Spend a cheap afternoon relaxing at the races with Parisians of all ages, backgrounds and walks of life. The easiest racecourse to get to is Hippodrome d'Auteuil (Map p118; ☎ 01 40 71 47 47; www.france-galop.com; Champ de Courses d'Auteuil, Bois de Boulogne, 16e; Ⓜ Porte d'Auteuil), host to steeplechases six times a month from February to late June or early July, and early September to early December. Admission is €3 to €4 (under 18s free).

GAY & LESBIAN PARIS

top picks

- Centre Gai et Lesbien de Paris Île de France (p321)
- Le Gai Moulin (p318)
- Le Tango (p320)
- Les Marronniers (p320)
- 3W Kafé (p319)

What's your recommendation? www.lonelyplanet.com/paris

GAY & LESBIAN PARIS

France is one of Europe's most liberal countries when it comes to homosexuality – in part because of the long French tradition of public tolerance towards groups of people who choose not to live by conventional social codes – and Paris is the epicentre.

While certainly not London, New York or even Berlin, the French capital is home to thriving gay and lesbian communities, and same-sex couples are a common sight on its streets, especially in the Marais district of the 4e. In 1999 the government enacted PACS (Pacte Civile de Solidarité) legislation, designed to give homosexual couples some of the legal protection (eg inheritance rights) it extends to married heterosexuals (though it falls well short of the laws since codified in Spain and the UK). In May 2001 Paris elected Bertrand Delanoë, the first openly gay mayor of a European capital. He was returned to office for a second six-year term in March 2008.

SHOPPING

LES MOTS À LA BOUCHE

Map p152   Books & Comics

☎ 01 42 78 88 30; www.motsbouche.com, in French; 6 rue Ste-Croix de la Bretonnerie, 4e; ⊗ 11am-11pm Mon-Sat, 1-9pm Sun; Ⓜ Hôtel de Ville

'On the Tip of the Tongue' is Paris' premier gay and lesbian bookshop. Most of the left-hand side of the shop on the ground floor is devoted to English-language books, including some guides and novels. If you're feeling naughty, go downstairs.

EATING

LE GAI MOULIN Map p152   French €€

☎ 01 48 87 06 00; www.le-gai-moulin.com, in French; 10 rue St-Merri, 4e; menus lunch €11.50 & €15.50, dinner €20.90; ⊗ lunch & dinner to midnight; Ⓜ Rambuteau

The friendly 'Gay Mill' (we don't get it either – unless they mean 'rumours') serves 'classic but honest' French cuisine, including decently priced set menus, to a mainly (but not exclusively) gay clientele. With the tables this close, there's no chance of not making a friend or two between (or even during) courses. We love the piano bar downstairs on Tuesday evenings.

VILLA PAPILLON Map p72   Thai €€

☎ 01 42 21 44 83; www.villa-papillon.com; 15 rue Tiquetonne, 2e; starters €8-11, mains €13-20, lunch menus €16 & €19; ⊗ lunch Mon-Sat, dinner to 11.30pm daily; Ⓜ Étienne Marcel

Charming, very welcoming Thai restaurant on a street where each restaurant is more original than the next, the 'Butterfly Villa'

offers authentic dishes at relatively affordable prices. Try assorted Thai 'tapas' for two (€17) and the *homok pla* (cod with coconut steamed in a banana leaf; €15). Lovely staff.

PAIN, VIN, FROMAGE Map p152   French €

☎ 01 42 74 07 52; www.painvinfromage.com; 3 rue Geoffroy l'Angevin, 4e; starters €4-10, mains €14.50-19; ⊗ dinner to 11.30pm; Ⓜ Rambuteau

This little place with wonderful farmhouse decor and a delightful vaulted cellar specialises in fondue (€14.50 to €16) and *raclette* (€15.50 to €19), though it also does a mean *tartiflette* (potatoes, cheese and bacon baked in a casserole; €13).

DRINKING & NIGHTLIFE

The Marais (4e), especially the areas around the intersection of rue Ste-Croix de la Bretonnerie and rue des Archives, and eastwards to rue Vieille du Temple, has been Paris' main centre of gay nightlife for more than two decades. There are also a few bars and clubs within walking distance of bd de Sébastopol. Other venues are scattered throughout the city.

The lesbian scene here is much less public than its gay counterpart, and centres around a few cafés and bars in the Marais, especially along rue des Écouffes.

In Paris, the need for exclusiveness appears to be relaxing, as is the general public's mentality towards homosexuality. Clubs are generally all gay-friendly, while specifically gay venues are increasingly mixing things up, becoming some of the coolest spots in Paris. The bars and clubs listed here are almost exclusively gay or lesbian. For mixed clubs or ones with gay and/or lesbian soirées (eg Les

Bains Douches), see the Nightlife & the Arts chapter (p293).

LOUVRE & LES HALLES

LA CHAMPMESLÉ Map p72   Bar

☎ 01 42 96 85 20; www.lachampmesle.com, in French; 4 rue Chabanais, 2e; ⌚ 4pm-dawn; M Pyramides

The *grande dame* of Parisian dyke bars, in situ since 1979, this is a cosy and very relaxed spot that tends to attract an older crowd – about 75% of whom are lesbians (the rest are mostly gay men). It's an active place, with a cabaret (often of *chansons françaises*) starting at 10pm on Thursday and Saturday, tarot-card reading and fortune-telling on Tuesday and exhibitions of works by female artists each month.

LE TROISIÈME LIEU Map p76   Bar

☎ 01 48 04 85 64; www.facebook.com/letroisieme lieuparis; 62 rue Quincampoix, 4e; ⌚ 6pm-2am Tue-Sun; M Rambuteau

Billing itself as *la cantine des ginettes armées* (canteen of armed gals), this kooky place for chic young lesbians – and, at times, for everyone else – is part bar, part club, part restaurant. There's a large, colourful bar and big wooden tables at street level, with good-value meals available. The vaulted cellar below leaves space for dancing to DJs (house, electro) and rock/alternative music concerts. On the last Saturday of the month it opens at 2pm. Happy hour is from 6pm to 8pm.

EAGLE PARIS Map p76   Bar

☎ 01 42 33 41 45; www.eagleparis.com; 33bis rue des Lombards, 1er; ⌚ 6pm-4am Sun-Thu, 6pm-6am Fri, 5pm-6am Sat; M Châtelet

The Eagle (from London) has landed (in Paris). And it's brought something for everyone: covered terrace, a couple of bars on two levels, a decent-sized dance floor (techno and house), a chill-out zone, a *fumoir* (smoking room) and, natch, a back room. Various themed nights are scheduled, including a 'tea dance' of the London-based Long Yang Club for Asians and 'rice queens' from 8.30pm Tuesday. Generous happy hour on beer till 11pm. Wear something leather.

WOLF BAR Map p76   Bar

☎ 01 40 28 02 52; www.wolfparis.com; 37 rue des Lombards, 1er; ⌚ 5pm-2am; M Châtelet

Bear bar a short distance from Forum des Halles attracts a *clientèle poilue* (hairy crowd) who are very seriously OFB (out for business). Happy hour is every day from opening to 9pm.

MARAIS & MÉNILMONTANT

3W KAFÉ Map p152   Bar

☎ 01 48 87 39 26; 8 rue des Écouffes, 4e; ⌚ 5.30pm-2am; M St-Paul

The name of this flagship cocktail bar/pub on a street with several dyke bars means 'Women with Women' so it can't be any clearer. It's relaxed and there's no ban on men (though they must be accompanied by a girl). On weekends there's dancing downstairs with a DJ and themed evenings take place regularly.

LE COX Map p152   Bar

☎ 01 42 72 08 00; www.coxbar.fr, in French; 15 rue des Archives, 4e; ⌚ 1pm-2am; M Hôtel de Ville

This small gay bar has become *the* meeting place for an interesting (and maybe interested) and cruisy crowd throughout the evening from 6 or 7pm. OK, we don't like the in-your-face name either, but what's a boy to do? Happy hour on beer is from 6pm to 9pm daily and the decor – be it a farm, be it a casino, be it a rodeo – changes every quarter.

LE QUETZAL Map p152   Bar

☎ 01 48 87 99 07; 10 rue de la Verrerie, 4e; ⌚ 5pm-2am; M Hôtel de Ville

This perennial favourite gay bar – one of the first in the Marais – is opposite rue des Mauvais Garçons (Bad Boys' Street), a road named after the brigands who congregated here in 1540. It's always busy, with house and dance music playing at night, and cruisy at all hours; plate-glass windows allow you to check out the talent before it arrives. During happy hour (5pm to 11pm) a pint costs just under €4.

LES JACASSES Map p152   Bar

☎ 01 42 71 15 51; 5 rue des Écouffes, 4e; ⌚ 5pm-2am Tue-Sun; M St-Paul

Girls looking for something a bit more authentic in the Marais should cross over rue des Écouffes to the 3W's (p319) sister-bar, which looks like it's been transplanted from Normandy. Softer music, more hard-core evenings.

LES MARRONNIERS Map p152   Bar, Café

☎ 01 40 27 87 72; 18 rue des Archives, 4e;
⏰ 9am-2am; Ⓜ Hôtel de Ville
Strictly speaking it's not gay, but in this part of town how do you tell? What this place has got is location cubed, and its enormous pavement terrace is the place in the Marais for both hunters and the hunted. Lots of decent munchies too.

LITTLE CAFÉ Map p152   Bar, Café

☎ 01 48 87 43 36; 62 rue du Roi de Sicile, 4e;
⏰ 9am-2am; Ⓜ St-Paul
This lesbian-owned bar-café is a local favourite, with great coffee and meals and a warm welcome for one and all. The clientele is relaxed, mixed and street-smart, with a penchant for electronic music and good wine.

OPEN CAFÉ Map p152   Bar, Café

☎ 01 42 72 26 18; www.opencafe.fr, in French; 17 rue des Archives, 4e; ⏰ 11am-2am Sun-Thu, 11am-4am Fri & Sat; Ⓜ Hôtel de Ville
A gay venue for all types at all hours, this bar-café seems to empty as Le Cox (p319) hots up a few doors southwards. Still, the large terrace and daytime schedule are draw cards, as is the four-hour happy hour starting at 6pm daily.

LE DUPLEX Map p148   Club

☎ 01 42 72 80 86; 25 rue Michel le Comte, 3e;
⏰ 8pm-2am; Ⓜ Rambuteau
Attracting a crowd that is *ni fashion ni folle* (neither into fashion nor queeny), the (very) long-established Duplex is comatose during the week but fills up at the weekend with 'boys next door' from out of town. Looking for a glitz-less shag? Come here.

LE TANGO Map p148   Club

☎ 01 42 72 17 78; www.boite-a-frissons.fr; 13 rue au Maire, 3e; admission €8; ⏰ 10.30pm-6am Fri & Sat, 5-11pm Sun; Ⓜ Arts et Métiers
Billing itself as a *boîte à frissons* (club of thrills), Le Tango brings in a mixed and cosmopolitan gay and lesbian crowd. Housed in a historic 1930s dancehall, its atmosphere and style is retro and festive. Dancing gets going when it opens, with waltzing, salsa and tango. From about 12.30am onwards DJs play. Sunday's gay tea dance is legendary.

RAIDD BAR Map p152   Club

☎ 01 42 77 05 13; www.raiddbar.com; 23 rue du Temple, 4e; ⏰ 5pm-4am; Ⓜ Hôtel de Ville
This is a club-bar that takes its cue from Splash in New York, with showering go-go boys behind glass (three times nightly from 11pm) and a terrace on which to cool off. The staff are pretty attitude-y and the drinks aren't cheap, but that's New York for you. Happy hour is 5pm to 9pm daily (till 11pm for beer).

BASTILLE & GARE DE LYON

L'INTERFACE Map p158   Bar

☎ 01 47 00 67 15; 34 rue Keller, 11e;
⏰ 3pm-2am; Ⓜ Ledru Rollin
No, not 'In yer face'… This is a laid-back gay bar that attracts locals and habitués of the nearby sex club Le Keller (☎ 01 47 00 05 39; 14 rue Keller, 11e). Unusual for a gay bar in Paris, it attracts customers in the afternoon and early evening, especially during happy hour (6pm to 9pm).

SLEEPING

HÔTEL CENTRAL MARAIS

Map p152   Hotel €€

☎ 01 48 87 56 08; www.hotelcentralmarais.com; 2 rue Ste-Croix de la Bretonnerie, 4e; s & d €89, tr €109; Ⓜ Hôtel de Ville; ▯
Still the only gay game in town, this small hotel in the centre of gay Paris caters essentially for men, though lesbians are also welcome. It's in a lovely 17th-century building and its seven rooms are spread over several floors; there is no lift. Also, there is only one bathroom for every two rooms, though the room on the 5th floor has an en suite bathroom and toilet. Reception, which is on the 1st floor, is open from 8am to 5pm; after that check in around the corner at Le Central Bar (Map p152; ☎ 01 48 87 99 33; 33 rue Vieille du Temple, 4e; ⏰ 4pm-2am Mon-Fri, 2pm-2am Sat & Sun; Ⓜ Hôtel de Ville), which is the oldest and most welcoming gay bar in Paris.

FURTHER RESOURCES

Most of France's major gay organisations are based in Paris. If you require a more complete list than we are able to provide here, pick up a copy of *Genres*, a listing of gay, lesbian, bisexual and transsexual organisations, at the Centre Gai et Lesbien de Paris Île de France or download it from its website, or consult the thorough *Le Petit Futé Paris Gay et Lesbien* guide.

Act Up Paris (☎ 01 48 06 13 89; www.actupparis.org, in French) Meetings of this association (known for its 'outings' of the not-always rich and famous and other extreme actions) are open to the public and are held every Thursday at 7pm at the École des Beaux-Arts (Map p108; Amphithéâtre des Loges, 14 rue Bonaparte, 6e; Ⓜ St-Germain des Prés).

Association des Médecins Gais (AMG; ☎ 01 48 05 81 71; www.medecins-gays.org, in French) The Association of Gay Doctors deals with gay-related health issues. Telephone advice on physical-health issues is available from 6pm to 8pm on Wednesday and 2pm to 4pm on Saturday. For counselling, call between 8.30pm and 10.30pm on Thursday.

Centre Gai et Lesbien de Paris Île de France (CGL; Map p148; ☎ 01 43 57 21 47; http://cglparis.org, in French; Ⓒ 6-8pm Mon, 3-8pm Tue & Thu, 2-8pm Wed, 12.30-8pm Fri & Sat, 4-7pm Sun; Ⓜ Rambuteau or Arts et Métiers) The Lesbian, Gay, Bisexual and Transsexual Centre, just north of the Centre Pompidou, is your single best source of information in Paris. The large library of gay books and periodicals is open from 6.30pm to 8pm on Monday, 6pm to 8pm Tuesday and Wednesday, 4pm to 6pm Friday and 5pm to 7pm Saturday.

Écoute Gaie (☎ 0 811 810 057; http://ecoute-gaie. france.qrd.org, in French; Ⓒ 6-10pm Mon-Fri) Established in 1982, this is the oldest hotline for gays and lesbians in Paris.

SOS Homophobie (☎ 0 810 108 135, 01 48 06 42 41; www.sos-homophobie.org; Ⓒ 6-10pm Mon & Fri, 8-10pm Tue-Thu, 2-4pm Sat, 6-8pm Sun) This hotline takes anonymous calls concerning discriminatory acts against gays and lesbians.

Of the gay and lesbian publications, *Têtu* (www.tetu.com, in French; €5) is a popular and widely circulated glossy monthly available at newsstands everywhere. Be on the lookout for bimonthly freebies such as *2X* (www.2xparis.

fr, in French), *Mâles-a-Bars* (www.males-a-bars.com, in French) and *Agenda Q* (www. agendaq.fr, in French), which have interviews, articles and listings of gay clubs, bars, associations and personal classifieds. You'll find them stacked up at most gay venues. The monthly magazine *Lesbia* (€4), established in 1983, looks at lesbian women's issues and gives a rundown of what's happening around the country. Also for women, *La Dixième Muse* (www.ladixiememuse.com, in French; €4.50) is more culturally oriented.

The following guidebooks list pubs, restaurants, clubs, beaches, saunas, sex shops and cruising areas; they are available from Les Mots à la Bouche bookshop (p318).

Le Petit Futé Paris Gay et Lesbien (www.petitfute.com, in French; €13.95) A French-language guide that goes well beyond hedonistic pursuits, with political, cultural, religious and health listings, along with bars and restaurants. Highly recommended.

Spartacus International Gay Guide (www.spartacus-world.com; €28.95) A male-only guide to just about every country in the world, with more than 70 pages devoted to France, almost half of which cover Paris.

Among some of the better gay and lesbian websites are the following:

CitéGay (www.citegay.com, in French) One of the best all-inclusive gay sites with a heavily political agenda.

Dyke Planet (www.dykeplanet.com, in French) French-language website for gay women.

La France Gaie & Lesbienne (www.france.qrd.org, in French) 'Queer resources directory' for gays and lesbians.

Le Gay Paris (www.legayparis.fr) Not unlike Paris Gay (see following) but not as up to date.

Paris Gay (www.paris-gay.com) Decent overview of what's up and what's on in the French capital.

Ze Girlz (www.zegirlz.com, in French) Something-for-everyone girls' site with podcasts, Q&As, forums etc.

lonely planet Hotels & Hostels

Want more sleeping recommendations than we could ever pack into this little ol' book? Craving more detail — including extended reviews and photographs? Want to read reviews by other travellers and be able to post your own? Just make your way over to **lonelyplanet.com/hotels** and check out our thorough list of independent reviews, then reserve your room simply and securely.

SLEEPING

top picks

- **Hidden Hotel** (p339)
- **Hôtel Amour** (p339)
- **Hôtel du Petit Moulin** (p343)
- **Hôtel Eldorado** (p341)
- **Hôtel La Demeure** (p349)
- **Hôtel Les Jardins du Marais** (p343)
- **Hôtel Particulier Montmartre** (p340)
- **Hôtel Relais St-Germain** (p333)
- **Le Relais du Louvre** (p329)
- **Oops** (p349)

Paris has a very wide choice of accommodation options, counting nearly 75,000 beds in some 2000 establishments that cater for all budgets throughout much of the city. There are four basic types: deluxe and top-end hotels, some of which count among the finest in the world; midrange hotels, many of which have personalities all of their own, and by and large offer very good value when compared with similarly priced places to stay in other European capitals; adequate but generally uninspiring budget hotels; and hostels, which run the gamut from cramped, airless cupboards to party places with bars worth a visit in their own right. In this chapter, accommodation options are listed according to the sections of the city as outlined in the Neighbourhoods chapter and appear in budget order, with the most expensive first. Prices are given for rooms with bathrooms unless otherwise noted.

The city of Paris levies a *taxe de séjour* (tourist tax) of between €0.20 (camp sites, 'NN' or unclassified hotels) and €1.50 (four-star hotels) per person per night on all forms of accommodation.

A note on the icons used in this chapter: most hotels and hostels in Paris have some form of internet access available nowadays. The wi-fi icon (📶 ; pronounced wee-fee in French) indicates wireless availability, generally free of charge. If there are fees we mention this. A computer icon (💻) indicates that the hotel allows guests to use a terminal in the lobby or reception area. Some establishments (usually hostels) charge their guests an access fee for this service, which we have usually noted in the review text.

Smoking is now officially banned in all Paris hotels, though not all managers are aware of this law. Don't be afraid to complain if you get a smoky room.

Most hotels with two or more stars in Paris are equipped with a lift but not much more for those in wheelchairs. In this chapter most of the hotels marked with a wheelchair icon (♿) have one or two guestrooms fully equipped for disabled guests (bathrooms big enough for a wheelchair user to turn around in, access door on bath tubs, grip bars alongside toilets etc), though we've included a few with guestrooms on the *rez-de-chaussée* (ground floor) that can be accessed by anyone in a wheelchair and may serve at a pinch.

ACCOMMODATION STYLES
Apartments & Flats

If you are interested in renting a furnished flat for anything from one night to one month, consult one of the many agencies listed under the heading 'Furnished Rentals' in the 'Hotels & Accommodation' section of the Paris Convention & Visitors Bureau (www.parisinfo.com) website. Accommodation for students and organisations that arrange it are listed under the heading 'Young Paris'.

Websites of commercial agencies that let studios and apartments to visitors, and have been recommended by both readers and Lonely Planet staff members, include the following:

A La Carte Paris Apartments (www.alacarte-paris-apartments.com) Mostly one- and two-bedroom flats, with studios starting at €700 per week.

Apartment in Paris (www.an-apartment-in-paris.com) A Marais studio for €460 per week.

Haven in Paris (http://haveninparis.com) Luxury apartments, with studios starting at €575 per week.

Lodgis (www.lodgis.com) Over 1600 available properties, with studios starting at €1000 per month. No weekly rentals.

Paris Accommodation Service (www.paris-accommodation-service.com) Over 500 available properties, with studios starting at €520 per week. Daily rentals possible.

Paris Apartments Services (www.paris-apts.com) Mostly studios and one-bedroom flats, with daily rates starting at €100.

Paris Attitude (www.parisattitude.com) Nearly 3000 available properties, with studios starting at €325.

Paris Stay (www.paristay.com) Over 200 vacation flats (ie convenient location), with studios starting at €300.

For information about longer-term apartment and flat rentals in Paris, see p326.

SERVICED APARTMENTS

Serviced apartments – like staying in a hotel without a lot of the extras – are an excellent option for those staying longer than a week, particularly if you're part of a small group, and don't feel like emptying the garbage yourself. There are quite a few of them around Paris, as listed in the 'Apartments At Your Serice' boxed text.

Hotels

Hotels in Paris are inspected by authorities at *département* (administrative division of France) level and classified into six categories – from no star to four-star 'L' (for *luxe*), the French equivalent of five stars. All hotels must display their rates, including TVA (VAT; valued-added tax) both outside the hotel and in guests' rooms.

Paris may not be able to boast the number of budget hotels it had a decade or so ago, but the choice is still more than ample, especially in the Marais, around the Bastille, and near the major train stations. Places with one star and those with the designations 'HT' (Hôtel de Tourisme) or 'NN' (Nouvelle Norme), which signifies that a hotel is awaiting its rating but remains of a certain standard of comfort, are much of a muchness. Remember: the overall consideration at these places is cost, never quality. Be advised that some budget hotels in Paris do not accept credit cards.

Breakfast – usually a simple continental affair of bread, croissants, butter, jam and coffee or tea, though American-style breakfast buffets are becoming more popular – is served at most hotels with two or more stars and usually costs around €8.

Some hotels in Paris have different rates according to the season and are noted as such throughout the chapter. The high season is (roughly) from April to September while the low season is from October to March. There are usually bargains to be had during the late autumn (say, November) and winter months (January and February).

Hostels

Paris is awash with hostels, but such budget accommodation isn't as cheap as it used to be. Expect a bed to cost between €20 to €30 – and up to €40 during summer holidays. Two people who don't mind sleeping in the same bed may find basic rooms in budget hotels a less-expensive proposition. Groups of three or four will save even more if they share two or three beds in a budget hotel.

Showers are always free at hostels in Paris, and rates often include a simple breakfast. Internet access (from about €1 for 15 minutes) is available at almost all the hostels listed here. If you don't have your own sheet bag, sheets can be rented at most hostels for a one-off charge of around €3 (plus deposit).

Some of the more institutional hostels allow guests to stay only a maximum of three nights, particularly in summer. Places that have upper age limits (for example, 30 years old) tend not to enforce them except at the busiest of times. Only the official *auberges de jeunesse* (youth hostels), of which there are just two in Paris, require guests to present Hostelling International (HI) cards or their equivalent. Curfew – if enforced – is generally at 1am or 2am.

Homestays & B&Bs

Under an arrangement known as *hôtes payants* (literally 'paying guests') or *hébergement*

APARTMENTS AT YOUR SERVICE

The following are among the three most popular chains of serviced apartments in Paris. Various discounts are usually offered depending upon your length of stay.

Apart'hotels Citadines (☎ 0 825 333 332, from abroad +33 1 41 05 79 05; www.citadines.com; ✉ 🖥 📶 ♿) This fabulously successful international chain has 17 properties in Paris. Prices vary depending on the season and the location but, in general, a small studio for two with fully equipped kitchen for just under a week costs from €118 to €289 per night and a one-bedroom flat sleeping four costs €173 to €462.

Adagio City Aparthotel (☎ 01 55 26 32 00; www.adagio-city.com; ✉ 🖥 📶) Adagio counts some 10 properties in greater Paris, including the **Adagio Montmartre City Aparthotel** (Map p134; ☎ 01 42 57 14 55; 10 place Charles Dullin, 18e; 2/3/4 person studios per night €160/176/207, 1/2 bed apt €255/319; Ⓜ Abbesses), an attractive *résidence* at the end of a leafy street in the heart of Montmartre with 76 studios and apartments for between two and six people.

Résidence Le St-Germain (Map p100; ☎ 01 46 34 22 33; www.franceloc.fr; 16 rue Boutebrie, 5e; 2-person studio €93-119, 4-person apt €143-158; Ⓜ St-Michel; 🖥) has 11 fully equipped studios and apartments measuring from 17 to 55 sq metres for between two and six people.

chez l'habitant (lodging with the occupants of private homes), students, young people and tourists can stay with French families. In general you rent a room and, for an additional fee, have access to the family's kitchen in the evening. Half and full board is also usually available. For a list of homestay venues see p327. Some private language schools (p393) can arrange homestays for their students.

Bed-and-breakfast (B&B) accommodation, known as *chambres d'hôte* in French, has never been anywhere near as popular in Paris as it has been in, say, London but that is changing. The city of Paris has inaugurated a scheme called Paris Quality Hosts (www.hqp.fr) to encourage Parisians to rent out their spare rooms. The idea is not just to offer visitors an alternative choice of accommodation but also to ease the isolation of some Parisians, half of whom apparently live alone. Expect to pay anything from €50 for a double. Most hosts will expect you to stay a minimum of three or four nights.

The following B&Bs are all members of the Paris Quality Hosts initiative. At least two have been recommended by readers.

Alcôve & Agapes (Alcoves & Feasts; ☎ 01 44 85 06 05; www.bed-and-breakfast-in-paris.com)

B&B Paris (☎ 01 82 88 01 45; www.2binparis.com)

Fleurs de Soleil (Sunflower; ☎ 08 26 62 03 22; www.fleursdesoleil.fr)

Good Morning Paris (☎ 01 47 07 28 29; www.goodmorningparis.fr)

Longer-term Rentals

Small (15 to 30 sq metres) studios with attached toilet in Paris average out around €30 per sq metre per month; you can find deals from about €800 for a one-bedroom flat and €600 for a studio, but they aren't easy to come by. The per-metre cost theoretically decreases the larger the place, the further away it is from the city centre and if it is a walk-up (ie does not have access to a lift).

BOOK ACCOMMODATION ONLINE

For more accommodation reviews and recommendations by Lonely Planet authors, check out the online booking service at www.lonelyplanet.com. You'll find the true, insider lowdown on the best places to stay. Reviews are thorough and independent. Best of all, you can book online.

TRAVELLING WITH CHILDREN

As far as accommodation goes, families should definitely consider renting an apartment (p325), which is particularly convenient if you have young children and is generally less expensive than staying in a hotel. If you prefer to stay in a hotel, or if you're only in Paris for the weekend, be aware that the majority of rooms are small and, for example, if you are a family of four, you will probably need to get two connecting rooms. If your children are too young to stay in their own room, it is possible to make do with triples, quads or suites in some places. Chain hotels, though they may be short on charm, are often very good candidates in these situations. Some to consider include Ibis (www.ibishotel.com), Mercure (www.mercure.com), Accor (www.accorhotels.com) and Novotel (www.novotel.com).

Under €500 a month will get you a tiny garret room with a washbasin but no landline telephone, proper cooking facilities or private toilet. There may not even be a communal shower. These rooms, often occupied by students, are usually converted *chambres de bonne* (maid's quarters) on the 6th or 7th floors of old apartment buildings without lifts, but in decent neighbourhoods.

The hardest time to find an apartment – especially a cheap one – in Paris is in September and October, when everyone is back from their summer holidays and students are searching for digs for the academic year. Moderately priced places are easiest to find towards the end of university semesters – ie between Christmas and early February and July to September.

If you've exhausted your word-of-mouth sources (expats, students, compatriots living temporarily in Paris), it's a good idea to check out the bulletin boards at the American Church (p402). People who advertise there are more likely to rent to foreigners, will usually speak at least some English and might be willing to offer a relatively short-term contract. *Fusac* (www.fusac.fr), a free periodical issued every two weeks, is another good English-language source.

If you know some French (or someone who does), you'll have access to a wider range of options, via several agencies online: *De Particulier à Particulier* (www.pap.fr; €2.95), which also has a print publication that comes out on Thursday (available at newsstands); *À Vendre, à Louer* (www.avendrealouer.fr);

and *Se Loger* (www.seloger.com). You'll have to do your calling in French, though. If you have access to a phone, you could place a want ad in *De Particulier à Particulier* and have people call you.

Allô Logement Temporaire (Map p152; ☎ 01 42 72 00 06; www.allo-logement-temporaire.asso.fr; 1st fl, 64 rue du Temple, 3e; ✆ noon-8pm Mon-Fri; Ⓜ Rambuteau) is a nonprofit organisation that links property-owners and foreigners looking for furnished apartments for periods of one week to one year. Small furnished studios of 15 to 18 sq metres cost around €800 per month while double that size starts from €950, depending on the location. October, when university classes resume, is the hardest month to find a place, but over summer and into September it's usually possible to rent something within a matter of days. Before any deals are signed, the company will arrange for you to talk to the owner by phone, assisted by an interpreter if necessary. There is a €55 annual membership fee and, in addition to the rent and one month's deposit (paid directly to the owner), you'll pay a charge of €35 for each month you rent.

RESERVATIONS

During periods of heavy domestic or foreign tourism – Christmas and New Year, the winter school holidays (February to March), Easter, July and August – a hotel reservation can mean the difference between a bed in a room and a bench in the park. For really popular places – think location and/or price – book several months ahead.

Many hotels, especially budget ones, accept reservations only if they are accompanied by *des arrhes* (a deposit). Some places, especially those with two or more stars, don't ask for a deposit if you give them your credit card number or if you send them confirmation of your plans by letter, fax or email in French or clear, simple English.

Most independent hotels will hold a room only until a set hour, rarely later than 6pm or 7pm without prior arrangement. If you're arriving later than expected and you haven't prepaid or given the hotel your credit-card details, let the staff know or they might rent your room to someone else.

The **Paris Convention & Visitors Bureau** (Office de Tourisme et de Congrès de Paris), particularly the Gare du Nord branch (p406), can find you a place to accomodate you for the night of the day you stop by and will make the booking for free. The only catch is that you have to use a credit card to reserve a room. Be warned: the queues can be very long in the high season.

ROOM RATES

When calculating accommodation costs, assume you'll spend a minimum €70 for a double room with shower. It's possible, but less common, to find old-style rooms with washbasin only, which can go for as cheaply as €45. Bear in mind that you may be charged extra (up to €3) to use communal showers in budget hotels. If you can't go without your daily ablutions, it can be a false economy staying at such places.

Midrange hotels in Paris offer some of the best value for money of any European capital city, outside Berlin and Madrid. Hotels at this level always have bathroom facilities (showers

---

PRICE GUIDE

The symbols below indicate the cost per night of a standard double room in high season.

€	under €80
€€	€81-180
€€€	over €180

or baths) unless noted otherwise. These hotels charge between €80 and €180 for a double and generally offer excellent value, especially at the higher end.

Top-end places run the gamut from tasteful and discreet boutique hotels to palaces with more than 100 rooms and will cost two people €180 or more a night. And brace yourself for the prices in this category; according to a report published by the tourist office, luxury hotels are more expensive in Paris than any other city in the world (with an average room costing €379 a night) – except Geneva.

LOUVRE & LES HALLES

The area encompassing the Musée du Louvre and the Forum des Halles, effectively the 1er and a small slice of the 2e, is very central but don't expect to find tranquillity or many bargains here. While it is more disposed to welcoming top-end travellers, there are some decent midrange places to choose from and the main branch of a popular hostel can also be found here.

HÔTEL RITZ PARIS Map p72   Hotel €€€
☎ 01 43 16 30 30; www.ritzparis.com; 15 place Vendôme, 1er; s & d €770-870; ste from €1020; Ⓜ Opéra; 🅇 🛜 🚇
So famous it's lent its name to the English lexicon, the incomparable, the unmistakable Ritz has 161 sparkling rooms and suites. Its L'Espadon restaurant has two Michelin stars and the Hemingway Bar (☎ 01 43 16 30 50; ⏰ 6.30pm-2am Tue-Sat) is where the American author imbibed once he'd made a name for himself and took charge of the place during the liberation of Paris. The Ritz is celebrated for its cooking school (p393). Wi-fi costs €25 extra.

HÔTEL MEURICE Map p72   Hotel €€€
☎ 01 44 58 10 10; www.meuricehotel.com; 228 rue de Rivoli, 1er; s & d €665-1030; ste from €1150; Ⓜ Tuileries; 🅇 🛜 ♿
With 160 rooms, many of them facing the Jardin des Tuileries, the Meurice's gold leaf

and art nouveau glass positively glisten, and its ground-floor restaurant, Le Meurice, is a mainstay of good taste (in more ways than one). The domed Le Dali restaurant with its astonishing canvas painted by Ara Starck, daughter of designer Philippe, and its whimsical furnishings, is a light-hearted addition to this otherwise bastion of tasteful reserve. Wi-fi costs €20.

HÔTEL BRITANNIQUE
Map p76   Hotel €€€
☎ 01 42 33 74 59; www.hotel-britannique.fr; 20 av Victoria, 1er; s €160, d & tw €190-221, tr €251, ste €279-325; Ⓜ Châtelet; 🅇 🛜
With all the plaid, the throw pillows with crosses of St George and the panelled, library-like lounge, you'd be excused for thinking you'd hopped over what the French called La Manche ('Sleeve', or English Channel). Still, the 40-room 'Britannic' remains a Gallic oasis above the brouhaha of Châtelet, and the rooms on the upper floors, some of which have balconies, look straight down to a row of plane trees. It's an excellent choice if you want to be near everything.

GRAND HÔTEL DE CHAMPAIGNE
Map p76   Hotel €€€
☎ 01 42 36 60 00; www.hotelchampaigneparis. com; 17 rue Jean Lantier & 12 rue des Orfèvres, 1er; s €155-189, d & tw €189-236, tr €210-257; Ⓜ Châtelet; 🛜
This very comfortable, three-star hotel is housed in the former Hôtel des Tailleurs, a stonecutters' mansion built in 1562 on a quiet street between rue Rivoli and the Seine. Some of the 44 guestrooms (eg the Louis XIII–style room) are almost over the top but, well, this is Paris. Some rooms have balconies.

HÔTEL THÉRÈSE Map p72   Hotel €€€
☎ 01 42 96 10 01; www.hoteltherese.com; 5-7 rue Thérèse, 1er; s €155-170, d & tw €185-280, ste from €300; Ⓜ Pyramides; 🅇 🛜
From the same people who brought you the Left Bank's Hotel Verneuil (p333), the Thérèse also has chic individually decorated rooms and suites – in this case 43 of them in eight basic colours. The décor is classic yet eclectic; larger rooms have tubs while smaller ones (and they are small) have showers. We love the linen panels on the windows that diffuse the light so nicely and the clubby library lounge.

LE RELAIS DU LOUVRE Map p76   Hotel €€
☎ 01 40 41 96 42; www.relaisdulouvre.com; 19 rue des Prêtres St-Germain l'Auxerrois, 1er; s €125, d & tw €170-215, tr €215, ste €244-435; Ⓜ Pont Neuf; ❌ 🛜

If you are someone who likes style but in a traditional sense, choose this lovely 21-room hotel just west of the Louvre and south of the Église St-Germain l'Auxerrois. The nine rooms facing the street and the church are on the petite side; if you are looking for something more spacious, ask for one of the five rooms ending in a '2' (eg 52). Room 2 itself has access to the garden. The apartment on the top floor sleeps five, boasts a fully equipped kitchen and has memorable views over the rooftops.

HÔTEL ST-MERRY Map p76   Hotel €€
☎ 01 42 78 14 15; www.hotelmarais.com; 78 rue de la Verrerie, 4e; s & d €135-230, tr €205-275, ste €250-407; Ⓜ Châtelet; ❌ 🛜

The interior of this 12-room hostelry, with beamed ceilings, church pews and wrought-iron candelabra, is a neo-Goth's wet dream; you have to see the architectural elements of room 9 (flying buttress over the bed) and the furnishings of 12 (choir-stall bed board) to believe them. On the downside there is no lift connecting the postage-stamp lobby with the four upper floors, and only some of the rooms have air-conditioning.

HÔTEL FAVART Map p72   Hotel €€
☎ 01 42 97 59 83; www.hotel-favart.com; 5 rue Marivaux, 2e; s €105-130, d €135-160, tr €145-180, q €155-200; Ⓜ Richelieu–Drouot; ❌ 🛜 ♿

This stylish art nouveau hotel with 37 rooms facing the Opéra Comique feels like it never let go of the belle époque. It's an excellent choice if you're interested in shopping, being within easy walking distance of the *grands magasins* on blvd Haussmann. We like the prints of Parisian scenes on the walls in the lobby and the dramatic wrought-iron staircase leading up to the 1st floor, but not those fake books. Goya slept here in 1824.

HÔTEL VIVIENNE Map p72   Hotel €
☎ 01 42 33 13 26; www.hotel-vivienne.com; 40 rue Vivienne, 2e; s €64-118, d & tw €79-118; Ⓜ Grands Boulevards; 🖥 🛜

This stylish two-star hotel is amazingly good value for Paris. While the 45 rooms are not huge, they have all the mod cons (some even boast little balconies), and the public areas are bright and cheery. Wi-fi is free in reception and there's a computer there too.

HÔTEL TIQUETONNE Map p72   Hotel €
☎ 01 42 36 94 58; fax 01 42 36 02 94; 6 rue Tiquetonne, 2e; s/d from €35/55; Ⓜ Étienne Marcel

If you're looking for excellent-value digs smack in the middle of party town, this vintage 47-room cheapie on a cobbled pedestrian street may not be inspirational but it's clean and comfortable. Some of the rooms are quite large. Forum des Halles is a short distance to the south.

HÔTEL DE LILLE Map p76   Hotel €
☎ & fax 01 42 33 33 42; 8 rue de Pélican, 1er; s €39-43, d €50-55, tr €85; Ⓜ Palais Royal–Musée du Louvre

This old-fashioned but spotlessly clean 13 room hotel is down a quiet side street from the Louvre in a 17th-century building. A third of the rooms have just a wash-basin and bidet (communal showers cost €3), while the rest have en suite showers. Some of the rooms, like No 1 with its Moroccan theme, have been refitted. The friendly and helpful manager speaks good English.

BVJ PARIS-LOUVRE Map p76   Hostel €
☎ 01 53 00 90 90; www.bvjhotel.com; 20 rue Jean-Jacques Rousseau, 1er; per person dm €29, d €35; Ⓜ Louvre–Rivoli; 🖥 🛜

This modern, 200-bed hostel run by the Bureau des Voyages de la Jeunesse (BVJ; Youth Travel Bureau) has doubles and bunks in a single-sex room for four to 10 people with showers down the corridor. Guests should be aged 18 to 35. Rooms are accessible from 2.30pm on the day you arrive and all day after that. There are no kitchen facilities. There is usually space in the morning, even in summer, so stop by as early as you can. Wi-fi internet access is available for €3 for two hours. The BVJ Paris-Quartier Latin (Map p100; ☎ 01 43 29 34 80; 44 rue des Bernardins, 5e; per person dm €29, s/d €45/35; Ⓜ Maubert Mutualité), its sister-hostel on the Left Bank, has 140 beds in singles, doubles and single-sex dorm rooms for four to 10 people. All rooms have showers and rates include breakfast.

THE ISLANDS

The smaller of the two islands in the middle of the Seine, the Île St-Louis, is by far the more romantic and has a string of excellent top-end hotels. It's an easy walk from central Paris. Oddly enough, the only hotel of any sort on the Île de la Cité is a budget one – at least for now.

HÔTEL DE LUTÈCE Map p82   Hotel €€€
☎ 01 43 26 23 52; www.paris-hotel-lutece.com; 65 rue St-Louis en l'Île, 4e; s/d/tr €155/195/230; Ⓜ Pont Marie; ✄ 🤶
An exquisite 23-room hotel, the Lutèce has an enviable spot on delightful Île St-Louis. The lobby–salon, with its ancient fireplace, wood panelling, antique furnishings and terracotta tiles, sets the inviting tone of the whole place; the comfortable rooms are tastefully decorated and the location is one of the most desirable in the city.

HÔTEL ST-LOUIS Map p82   Hotel €€
☎ 01 46 34 04 80; www.hotel-saint-louis.com; 75 rue St-Louis en l'Île, 4e; s & d €140-220, tr €270; Ⓜ Pont Marie; ✄ 🤶 ♿
One of several hotels lining posh rue St-Louis en l'Île, this 19-room hotel is getting a facelift that will have reached the nether regions by the time you arrive; check out room 52 at the top with its beams and balcony. The public areas, including the basement breakfast room dating from the early 17th century, have always been lovely and the welcome nothing short of passionate.

HÔTEL HENRI IV Map p82   Hotel €
☎ 01 43 54 44 53; www.henri4hotel.fr; 25 place Dauphine, 1er; s €42-69, d €52-76, tr €79-81; Ⓜ Pont Neuf or Cité; ♿
This place, known for its 15 worn and very cheap rooms, has always been a popular choice for its location, location and – above all else – location on the tip of the Île de la Cité. It would be impossible to find a hotel more romantically located at such a price in all of Paris – much less the Île de la Cité. What we long expected has happened. Under new management the hotel is cleaning up its act (it now has a website), refitting its room (check out room 4 with its ancient stone wall and wooden floor), and all but one room now has a shower. The views over the square are wonderful. Book well in advance.

THE LATIN QUARTER

There are dozens of attractive two- and three-star hotels in the Seine-side Latin Quarter (5e arrondissement), particularly popular with students since the Middle Ages and with visiting academics. This makes rooms hardest to find during conferences and seminars from March to June and in October.

The area generally offers better value than the well-heeled neighbouring 6e and has a handy airport link (p384) by RER and Orlyval to its Luxembourg and Port Royal RER stations.

HÔTEL RÉSIDENCE HENRI IV
Map p100   Hotel €€€
☎ 01 44 41 31 81; www.residencehenri4.com; 50 rue des Bernardins, 5e; d €230-340; Ⓜ Maubert–Mutualité; ✄ 🖥 ♿
This exquisite late 19th-century hotel at the end of a quiet cul-de-sac near the Sorbonne has eight rooms and five two-room apartments – all with kitchenette (microwave, fridge, stove, crockery and cutlery). They are of a generous size – a minimum 17 sq metres for the rooms and 25 sq metres for the apartments – and all look out onto the street and leafy square, while the bathrooms all face a courtyard. Room 1 on the ground floor is wheelchair accessible. Rates vary widely; check the internet.

HÔTEL HENRI IV RIVE GAUCHE
Map p100   Hotel €€
☎ 01 46 33 20 20; www.henri-paris-hotel.com; 9-11 rue St-Jacques, 5e; s/d/tr €159/185/210; Ⓜ St-Michel Notre Dame or Cluny–La Sorbonne; ✄ 🖥 🤶 ♿
This three-star hotel with 23 rooms awash with antiques, old prints and fresh flowers is an oasis in the Latin Quarter just steps from Notre Dame and the Seine. Exuding a real air of 'country chic', the lobby with its 18th-century fireplace, terracotta tiles and portraits could almost be in a manor house in Normandy. Front rooms have stunning views of the Église St-Séverin and its buttresses. Rates are cheapest online.

HÔTEL DE NOTRE DAME MAÎTRE ALBERT Map p100   Hotel €€€
☎ 01 43 26 79 00; www.hotel-paris-notredame. com; 19 rue Maître Albert, 5e; d €170-280; Ⓜ Maubert–Mutualité; ✄ 🖥 🤶
A lovely little number hidden down a quiet street paces from the Seine, this quaint hotel is something of a labyrinth

LOCAL KNOWLEDGE: ERIC GAUCHERON

The son of hoteliers, Eric Gaucheron owns and operates what many consider to be among the most welcoming and well-run hotels in Paris, the two-star Familia Hôtel and, just next door, the three-star Hôtel Minerve.

What's the worst thing about being a hotelier? Dealing with people's expectations. Guests sometimes expect things we just can't provide. In America, hotels have big guestrooms, for example; there's a lot of land there. Those who have travelled to Europe know that this is not the case here.

OK, and for the saints among the sinners out there, what's the best thing about your job? Learning from guests. Whether they're from Norway, New Zealand or China, my guests and I share ideas. Because I can't travel everywhere, I move with my guests.

Just how difficult can people be? People are a lot more demanding these days because life is so much faster. In fact, it's as fast as the internet. But in the end nothing is difficult, you just need to take your time. My ambition is to anticipate any problem a guest may have beforehand.

Any, err, particularly odd requests? Well, yes, the usual things. But there's always a way to refuse a request nicely. The key is discretion. A hotelier must above all be discreet. But it's become more and more difficult finding such people.

OK, the question we've all been wanting to ask: what's the shelf life for sheets and bedspreads? For sheets, 1½ to two years. For bedspreads, four to five years.

If there were no room at the inns Familia or Minerve, where would you stay? Probably the (four-star) Hôtel de l'Abbaye St-Germain (p333). I find some of the great five-star hotels overly serviced; they actually try to give too much. I prefer the feel of a local hotel.

On my perfect day, find me... Poking through old books and antiques at the Marché aux Puces d'Aligre (p210) or attending one of the auctions at the Hôtel Drouot (p201). I don't go just to collect things for the hotels but for my own pleasure as well.

Interviewed by Steve Fallon

with its long corridors bedecked in striking cobbled-stone patterned carpet and rooms with low-beamed ceilings, occasionally sloping. Bedrooms are brightly painted and modern, and marry perfectly with the soft muted colours of the beautiful tapestries covering the walls in reception.

SELECT HÔTEL Map p100 Boutique Hotel €€
☎ 01 46 34 14 80; www.selecthotel.fr; 1 place de la Sorbonne, 5e; d €164-205, tr €228-295; Ⓜ Cluny–La Sorbonne; ❄ ▯ ☎
Smack dab in the heart of the studenty Sorbonne area, the Select is a very Parisian art deco mini-palace, with an atrium and cactus-strewn winter garden, an 18th-century vaulted breakfast room and 67 stylish bedrooms. The rooms are not always as large as you'd hope for, but the design solutions are ingenious, making great use of a minimum of space. The 1920s-style cocktail bar with an attached 'library' just off the lobby is a delight.

HÔTEL ST-JACQUES Map p100 Hotel €€
☎ 01 44 07 45 45; www.hotel-saintjacques.com; 35 rue des Écoles, 5e; s €110, d €125-215, tr €200; Ⓜ Maubert–Mutualité; ❄ ▯ ☎ ♿
The very stylish 36-room Hôtel St-Jacques houses rooms with balconies overlooking

the Panthéon. Audrey Hepburn and Cary Grant, who filmed some scenes of *Charade* here in the 1960s, would surely commend the mod cons that complement the original 19th-century details (trompe l'oeil ceilings that look like cloud-filled skies, an iron staircase and so on). The cabaret-themed breakfast room and bowl of jelly beans in the lobby provide some welcome touches.

HÔTEL MINERVE
Map p100 Hotel €€
☎ 01 43 26 26 04; www.parishotelminerve.com; 13 rue des Écoles, 5e; s €96-126, d €126-142, tr €162; Ⓜ Cardinal Lemoine; ❄ ▯ ☎
Housed in two Haussman buildings and owned by the same family who run the Familia Hôtel (p332) next door, the Minerve has a reception area kitted out with Oriental carpets and antique books, which the affable owner–manager collects. Other pleasing touches include frescoes of French monuments and reproduction 18th-century wallpaper. Some 10 rooms have small balconies, eight with views of Notre Dame, and two have tiny courtyards that are swooningly romantic.

HÔTEL DES GRANDES ÉCOLES

Map p100   Hotel €€

☎ 01 43 26 79 23; www.hotel-grandes-ecoles.com; 75 rue du Cardinal Lemoine, 5e; d €115-140; Ⓜ Cardinal Lemoine or Place Monge; 🖥 🛜 ♿

This wonderful, very welcoming 51-room hotel just north of place de la Contrescarpe has one of the loveliest situations in the Latin Quarter, tucked away in a courtyard off a medieval street with its own private garden. Choose a room in one of three buildings but our favourites are those in the garden annexe, especially the five that are on the ground floor and have direct access to the garden (rooms 29 to 33).

HÔTEL ST-CHRISTOPHE Map p100 Hotel €€

☎ 01 43 31 81 54; www.charm-hotel-paris.com; 17 rue Lacépède, 5e; s/d €105/115; Ⓜ Place Monge; 🖥 ♿

This classy small hotel is located on a quiet street between rue Monge in the Latin Quarter and the Jardin des Plantes. The 32 rooms are hardly what you would call spectacular, but they are well equipped and there are five sizes and shapes to choose from. The welcome is always particularly warm at this Logis de France 'charm hotel'. Rates are cheapest online.

HÔTEL DU LEVANT Map p100   Hotel €€

☎ 01 46 34 11 00; www.hoteldulevant.com; 18 rue de la Harpe, 5e; s €76, d €103-170, tr €180-230, q €250-270; Ⓜ Cluny–La Sorbonne or St-Michel; ▨ 🖥 🛜

It's hard to imagine anything more central than this 47-room hotel in the heart of the Latin Quarter; you'll never lack for a kebab day or night. The lobby, done up in yellows and reds, is warm and welcoming; the breakfast room is nicely decorated with a large *faux naïf* mural and lots of 19th-century fashion engravings. Rooms are of a decent size, with furnishings two steps beyond pure functional, and feature modern bathrooms.

FAMILIA HÔTEL Map p100   Hotel €€

☎ 01 43 54 55 27; www.familiahotel.com; 11 rue des Écoles, 5e; s €86, d €97-127, tr/q €149/176; Ⓜ Cardinal Lemoine; ▨ 🖥 🛜

This very welcoming and well-situated family-run hotel has sepia murals of Parisian landmarks in most rooms and is one of the most attractive 'almost budget' options on this side of the Seine. Eight rooms have

little balconies, from which you can catch a glimpse of Notre Dame. We love the flower-bedecked window, the lovely parquet floors and the complimentary breakfast.

HÔTEL DU COLLÈGE DE FRANCE

Map p100   Hotel €€

☎ 01 43 26 78 36; www.hotel-collegedefrance.com; 7 rue Thénard, 5e; s €70-116, d €90-145; Ⓜ Maubert–Mutualité; 🖥

Close to its prestigious educational namesake, this hotel has 29 rooms that are basic and very similar; avoid the dark ones facing the courtyard and go for those overlooking the quiet street, especially the rooms with two windows. The lobby, with its fireplace, stained glass and statue of Joan of Arc (go figure – unless it's to remind visiting Brits of their dastardly deed), is welcoming.

HÔTEL ESMERALDA Map p100   Hotel €€

☎ 01 43 54 19 20; www.hotel-esmeralda.fr; 4 rue St-Julien le Pauvre, 5e; s €75, d €90-110, tr/q €130/150; Ⓜ St-Michel

Tucked away in a quiet street with million-dollar views of Notre Dame (choose room 12!), this no-frills place is about as central to the Latin Quarter as you're ever likely to get. Its charm is no secret though, so book at least two months in advance. At these prices and location, the 19 rooms – the three cheapest singles have washbasin only – are no great shakes, so expect little beyond the picture-postcard view through the window.

HÔTEL DE L'ESPÉRANCE Map p100 Hotel €

☎ 01 47 07 10 99; www.hoteldelesperance.fr; 15 rue Pascal, 5e; s/d €75/80; Ⓜ Censier–Daubenton; ▨ 🖥 🛜 ♿

An eclectic mix of B&W photos, paintings and a rather intrusive flat-screen TV strew the salon walls of this immaculately kept 38-room hotel, a couple of minutes' walk south of lively rue Mouffetard. Furnishings are *faux* antique: think floral canopy beds with drapes to match. The couple who run it are an absolute charm and very service oriented; grab ice for drinks in your room from the downstairs ice-machine.

PORT ROYAL HÔTEL Map p100   Hotel €

☎ 01 43 31 70 06; www.hotelportroyal.fr; 8 blvd de Port Royal, 5e; s €41-89, d €52.50-89; Ⓜ Les Gobelins; ♿

This 46-room hotel, owned and managed by the same family since 1931, is one of those refreshingly unassuming one-star hotels that really don't yearn for any more stars. Its six floors are served by a lift, but the cheapest (washbasin-clad) rooms share a toilet and shower (buy a token for €2.50 at reception). Rooms are spotless and very quiet, especially those that peep down on a small glassed-in courtyard. Predictably, this value-for-money place is no secret, so book ahead. No credit cards.

YOUNG & HAPPY HOSTEL

Map p100   Hostel €

☎ 01 47 07 47 07; www.youngandhappy.fr; 80 rue Mouffetard, 5e; dm €26-28, d per person €30; Ⓜ Place Monge; 🖳 🛜

Check in after 4pm, out before 11am at this friendly if frayed place in the heart of the Latin Quarter. Beds are in cramped rooms with washbasins, and accommodate three to 10 people – double rooms can be reserved in advance so get in quick! Rates include breakfast in the dark stone-vaulted cellar, sheets and towels (you need to leave a €5 and €1 respectively deposit for the latter two). Happy-go-lucky is the general mood of this busy hostel.

ST-GERMAIN & INVALIDES

Staying in the chic Left Bank neighbourhoods of St-Germain des Prés (6e) and the quieter 7e arrondissement next door is a delight, especially for those mad about boutique shopping. Excellent midrange hotels reign supreme: a particularly stylish crop of strikingly creative, designer boutique hotels is perfectly placed around the Vavin metro station between the Jardin du Luxembourg and Montparnasse. Predictably for such a well-heeled part of Paris, budget accommodation is seriously short-changed.

RELAIS CHRISTINE Map p112   Hotel €€€

☎ 01 40 51 60 80; www.relais-christine.com; 3 rue Christine, 6e; d/ste from €306.50/506.50; Ⓜ Odéon; ⚇ 🖳 🛜

Part of the Small Luxury Hotels (SLH) association, the Relais Christine is a beautiful property housed in what was once a Catholic college. Special features include an unforgettable courtyard entrance off a quiet street with a garden behind it, as well as a spa and fitness centre built in and

top picks

BOUTIQUE HOTELS

- **BLC Design Hotel (p347)** Like the inside of a milk bottle, this whiter-than-white hostelry is a Zen oasis east of Bastille.
- **Hidden Hotel (p339)** The environmental movement gets a Parisian-style makeover.
- **Hôtel du Petit Moulin (p343)** Chic boutique offering in the Marais from über-designer Christian Lacroix has 17 very different rooms.
- **Hôtel Le Placide (p335)** Elegance, style and discretion between fashion shops in the well-heeled 6e.
- **Kube Hôtel (p340)** In northern Paris, it's hip to be square.
- **Le Général Hôtel (p344)** Primary colours and gumdrops are memorable at this candy box of a hotel near République.
- **Le Six** One of those art addresses anyone into contemporary design will thoroughly enjoy – dig the four-star spa bar!

around an original 13th-century cellar. The 51 rooms are spacious and (unusual for a hotel of this category) the décor is more modern than classic.

LE SIX Map p108   Boutique Hotel €€€

☎ 01 42 22 00 75; www.hotel-le-six.com; 14 rue Stanislas, 6e; s & d €300-450, ste €600-700; Ⓜ Notre Dame des Champs; ⚇ 🖳 🛜

Push your way in using the black leather door handle and know you're entering the last word in contemporary design. From the funky red-leather reception bar to rotating art exhibitions, glass-topped courtyard salon and oh-so-cool spa bar, this four-star hotel will make art and design lovers swoon. For the ultimate luxury, check into the other-worldly penthouse suite (€1200).

HÔTEL RELAIS ST-GERMAIN

Map p112   Hotel €€€

☎ 01 43 29 12 05; www.hotel-paris-relais-saint -germain.com; 9 Carrefour de l'Odéon, 7e; s/d €220/285, ste €395; Ⓜ Odéon; ⚇ 🖳 🛜

What rave reports this elegant four-star hotel with flowerboxes and baby-pink awning gets, and for good reason. Ceilings are beamed, furniture is antique and fabrics are floral (and very fine indeed) inside this 17th-century townhouse. Mix this with a chic contemporary air, ample artwork to admire and one of Paris' most talked-about bistros Le Comptoir (p233) as next-door neighbour. Absolutely delicious, darling!

L'HÔTEL Map p112   Boutique Hotel €€€
☎ 01 44 41 99 00; www.l-hotel.com; 13 rue des Beaux Arts, 6e; d €280-740; ⓜ St-Germain des Prés;

With 20 rooms and a location tucked away in a quiet quayside street, this award-winning hostelry with the most minimal of names is the stuff of romance, Parisian myths and urban legends. Rock- and film-star patrons alike fight to sleep in room 16 where Oscar Wilde died in 1900 and now decorated with a peacock motif, or in the art deco room (No 36) of legendary dancer Mistinguett, with its huge mirrored bed. Rooms lead off a large circular atrium. Other features include a fantastic bar and restaurant under a glass canopy and, in the ancient cellar, a very modern swimming pool. Rates vary widely according to the seasons.

LA VILLA Map p112   Boutique Hotel €€€
☎ 01 43 26 60 00; www.villa-saintgermain.com; 29 rue Jacob, 6e; d €280-370, ste €470; ⓜ St-Germain des Prés;

This 31-room hotel helped set what has become almost a standard of the Parisian accommodation scene: small, minimalist, boutique. Fabrics, lighting and soft furnishings are all of the utmost quality and taste. Rooms are refreshingly modern (with a preference for chocolate browns, purples and burgundies) but subtly designed. Bathrooms are small but shimmering, and the lobby, with its popular bar, is large and bright.

HÔTEL DE L'ABBAYE SAINT GERMAIN Map p112   Hotel €€€
☎ 01 45 44 38 11; www.hotelabbayeparis.com; 10 rue Cassette, 6e; d €260-380, ste €477-538; ⓜ St-Sulpice;

It's the delightfully romantic outside areas that set this elegant abode apart from the four-star crowd. Swing through the wrought-iron gates and enjoy a moment in the lovely front courtyard, bedecked with bench to enjoy its potted plants and flowers. Next morning linger over breakfast served beneath ivy-clad walls on one of the city's prettiest patios.

HÔTEL LE CLOS MÉDICIS
Map p112   Hotel €€€
☎ 01 43 29 10 80; www.closmedicis.com; 56 rue Monsieur-le-Prince, 6e; s €175, d €215-270, tr €310, ste €495; ⓜ Luxembourg;

Someone has taken an 18th-century building and pushed it into the 21st century, with tasteful greys, blacks and burgundies in the 38 bedrooms. History stays for the most part in the lobby, with its antique furnishings, convivial bar and, in winter, open fireplace. The inner courtyard is a delight for drinks and/or breakfast in the warmer months.

HÔTEL D'ANGLETERRE Map p112   Hotel €€€
☎ 01 42 60 34 72; www.hotel-dangleterre.com; 44 rue Jacob, 6e; d €140, d €200-240, ste €320; ⓜ St-Germain des Prés;

The 'England Hotel' is a beautiful 27-room property in a quiet street close to busy blvd St-Germain and the Musée d'Orsay. The loyal guests take breakfast in the courtyard of this former British Embassy, where the Treaty of Paris ending the American Revolution was signed, and where Hemingway once lodged (in room 14 on 20 December 1921 – see p187). Duplex suite 51 at the top has a beamed ceiling and room 12 a four-poster bed. Breakfast is included.

HÔTEL ST-GERMAIN DES PRÉS
Map p112   Hotel €€€
☎ 01 43 26 00 19; www.hotel-paris-saint-germain.com; 36 rue Bonaparte, 6e; d €190-290, ste €325-350; ⓜ St-Germain des Prés;

With its heavy period furnishings and sensorial feast of frescoed walls, floral wallpapers and rich fabrics and tapestries, this is a hotel whose décor you either love or hate. Its location, just up from the cafés and hubbub of place St-Germain des Prés, couldn't be handier. Many guests come to lay their head where Henry Miller did (p187).

HÔTEL DES ACADÉMIES ET DES ARTS Map p108   Boutique Hotel €€€
☎ 01 43 26 66 44; www.hoteldesacadelies.com; 15 rue de la Grande Chaumiére, 6e; d €189-314; ⓜ Vavin;

Another avant-garde address inspired by 1920s Montparnasse, a five-minute walk away. This one features the distinctive signature of French street artist Jérôme Mesnager whose impish white figures back-flip up walls, scale stairs and dance above fireplaces – ride the lift to the 5th floor for the ultimate acrobatic performance.

HÔTEL VERNEUIL Map p108 Hotel €€€

☎ 01 42 60 82 14; www.hotelverneuil.com; 8 rue de Verneuil, 7e; s €148, d €178-240; M St-Germain des Prés; 🍴 💻 🛜

Footsteps from Serge Gainsbourg's former pad in the heart of gallery land, this chic little number is bourgeois Paris at its best. Cradled in a 17th-century building on a quiet street, its 26 small, individually decorated rooms (15 with air-con) are a mellow melody of low beamed ceilings, rich fabrics and soft tones of peach, taupe and pale sage green. The salon off the lobby is very much 'library in private home' and breakfast is served in a vaulted stone cellar.

HÔTEL LE PLACIDE

Map p108 Boutique Hotel €€

☎ 01 42 84 34 60; www.leplacidehotel.com; 6 rue St-Placide, 6e; d €161-390, tr €203-440; M St-Placide; 🍴 💻 🛜

Understated chic is what this strikingly elegant townhouse with white slatted-wood shutter and taupe façade just west of the Jardin du Luxembourg is all about. Oh-so-enviably cool, calm and collected, it pampers guests with just two rooms per floor, each stylishly dressed in white Moroccan leather, luxurious linens and a designer touch of chrome. Right up to the minute, it is one of the first Parisian hotels to blog (at www.ruesaintplacide.com) and tweet @ Mariegarabedian.

L'APOSTROPHE Map p108 Boutique Hotel €€

☎ 01 56 54 31 31; www.apostrophe-hotel.com; 3 rue de Chevreuse, 6e; d €150-350; M Vavin; 🍴 💻 🛜

A street work-of-art with its stencilled façade featuring the shadowy grey imprint of a leafy tree by French artist Catherine Feff, this art hotel is style. Its 16 themed rooms, each dramatically different in décor, pay homage to the written word: spray-painted graffiti tags cover one wall of room U (for 'urbain'), which has a ceiling shaped like a skateboard ramp, while room P (for 'Paris parody') sits in the clouds overlooking Paris' rooftops. Clever design features like double sets of imprinted curtains (one for day, one for night) or the 'bar table' on wheels that slots over the bed top off the design-driven ensemble.

HÔTEL DES MARRONNIERS

Map p112 Hotel €€

☎ 01 43 25 30 60; www.hotel-marronniers.com; 21 rue Jacob, 6e; s €135, d €175-190, tr €220, q €260; M St-Germain des Prés; 🍴 💻 🛜

At the end of a small courtyard 30m from the main street, this 37-room hotel has a delightful conservatory leading on to a magical garden – a true oasis in the heart of St-Germain. From the 3rd floor up, rooms ending in 1, 2 or 3 look on to the garden; the rooms on the two uppermost floors – the 5th and the 6th – have pretty views over the courtyard and the roofs of central Paris.

HÔTEL AVIATIC Map p108 Hotel €€

☎ 01 53 63 25 50; www.aviatic.fr; 105 rue de Vaugirard, 6e; d €165-285, tr €265-330; M Montparnasse–Bienvenüe; 🍴 💻 🛜

This 43-room hotel with charming, almost Laura Ashley–style décor and a delightful canopied art deco entrance has been around since 1856, so it must be doing something right. The tiny 'winter garden' is a breath of fresh air (literally). Some rooms face the street and a quieter courtyard. For more space choose a 'superior' or 'deluxe' room.

HÔTEL LA SAINTE-BEUVE

Map p108 Hotel €€

☎ 01 45 48 20 07; www.parishotelcharme.com; 9 rue Ste-Beuve, 6e; d €159-365, ste €389-445; M Notre Dame des Champs; 🍴 💻 🛜

'Home away from home' is the motto of this 22-room hôtel-maison southwest of the Jardin du Luxembourg. And indeed, its relaxed breakfast area with newspapers to read over coffee and wooden floor spilling into the lounge with a fireplace is the height of cosiness. Rooms are a riot of colour: take your pick from fuchsia-pink stylishly mixed with lime green and taupe, or racing green wed with oyster grey and burgundy. The hotel takes its name from eponymous former resident, literary critic Charles Augustin Sainte-Beuve (1804–69).

HÔTEL MUGUET Map p108 Hotel €€

☎ 01 47 05 05 93; www.hotelmuguet.com; 11 rue Chevert, 7e; s/d/tr €110/145/195; M La Tour Maubourg; 🍴 💻 🛜

This hotel, strategically placed between Invalides and the Eiffel Tower, is a great family choice thanks to its functional décor and generous-sized triples with armchair-bed to convert separate lounge area into a kids' bedroom. From the 4th floor on, the Eiffel Tower starts to sneak into view, climaxing with room 62 and its fabulous full-frontal panorama. Several rooms stare at the equally arresting Église du Dôme (p111). Back down on ground level, a trio of rooms opens onto a delightful courtyard garden.

CADRAN HÔTEL Map p108   Boutique Hotel €€

☎ 01 40 62 67 00; www.paris-hotel-cadran.com; 10 rue du Champ de Mars, 7e; d €144-225, ste €163-228; Ⓜ École Militaire; ✖ ▣ ☎

An address for gourmets, this concept hotel seduces guests with a designer tick-tock clock theme and a bold open-plan reception spilling into a rather irresistible Bar à Chocolat (Chocolate Bar). Admire, taste and buy Christophe Roussel's colourful seasonal-flavoured *macarons* and chocolates (www.roussel-chocolatier.com), then retire to one of 41 futuristic rooms with all the mod cons. If bold colour is not your thing, go for one on the white-and-beige 2nd floor; the 3rd is orange and the pink 4th is *très fille* (very girly).

HÔTEL JARDIN LE BRÉA

Map p108   Hotel €€

☎ 01 43 25 44 41; www.jardinlebrea-paris-hotel.com; 14 rue Bréa, 6e; s €111-196, d €132-222, tr €163-228; Ⓜ Notre Dame des Champs; ✖ ▣ ☎

Deception of a name aside – the Bréa has no *jardin* (garden) – this three-star hotel on the fringe of Montparnasse is the epitome of good value. Its 23 rooms are an oasis of colour, sporting striking English Designers Guild fabrics, wallpapers and upholstery. Dramatic blacks and fuchsia pinks dress the 3rd floor; softer lilacs, beiges and gold the 2nd. Reception is arranged around a glass-topped interior courtyard and breakfast is served in the atmospheric basement – an old gold stone vaulted cellar.

HÔTEL DE VARENNE Map p108   Hotel €€

☎ 01 45 51 45 55; www.hoteldevarenne.com; 44 rue de Bourgogne, 7e; d €129-280; Ⓜ Varenne; ✖ ▣

Very refined, very classic and very quiet, this hotel tucked at the end of a courtyard garden has something of a country feel to it. Most of the two dozen rooms spread over four floors look into the courtyard and a very sizable choice is room 22. The Musée Rodin is within spitting distance.

MAYET HÔTEL Map p108   Boutique Hotel €€

☎ 01 47 83 21 35; www.mayet.com; 3 rue Mayet, 6e; s €100, d €130-150, tr €170; Ⓜ Duroc; ▣

Light-hearted and loads of fun, this 23-room boutique hotel with drippy murals and a penchant for oversized clocks and primary colours has good-sized rooms and bathrooms, most with tubs. It offers excellent value and free breakfast too.

HÔTEL LINDBERGH Map p112   Hotel €€

☎ 01 45 48 35 53; www.hotellindbergh.com; 5 rue Chomel, 7e; d €126-160, tr €180, q €190; Ⓜ Sèvres–Babylone; ▣ ☎

We still haven't figured out why this *hôtel de charme* is totally kitted out in Charles Lindbergh photos and memorabilia or named after him, but somehow it all works. The 26 guestrooms are done up in shades of chocolate and red, with silk fabric on the walls and rush matting on the floors. We like the room-number plates on the doors with little Paris landmarks, the ample-sized bathrooms and the very friendly staff.

HÔTEL LE CLÉMENT Map p112   Hotel €€

☎ 01 43 26 53 60; www.clement-moliere-paris-hotel.com; 6 rue Clément, 6e; d €126-148, tr €165; Ⓜ St-Germain des Prés; ✖ ▣

Excellent value for the style and tranquillity it offers, the Clément has 28 stylish rooms, some of which overlook the Marché St-Germain (eg room 100). Note, though, that the rooms on the very top floor have sloping ceilings. The people who run the hotel clearly know what they're doing; it's been in the same family for over a century.

HÔTEL DU GLOBE

Map p112   Boutique Hotel €€

☎ 01 43 26 35 50; www.hotel-du-globe.fr; 15 rue des Quatre Vents, 6e; d €125-170; Ⓜ Odéon; ▣

This eclectic caravanserai has 14 small but nicely decorated rooms just south of the blvd St-Germain. Some rooms are tiny and there is no lift (but four floors to ascend via a very narrow staircase). Still, we're suckers for armour – there are at least two full sets here – and canopy beds (go for room 43).

HÔTEL DE SÈVRES Map p108   Hotel €€

☎ 01 45 48 84 07; www.hoteldesevres.com; 22 rue de l'Abbé Grégoire, 6e; s €99-135, d €115-180, tr €175-215; Ⓜ St-Placide; ▣ ♿

Rich autumnal browns and aubergines caress this 31-room townhouse – think dark wood floors and gilt-framed mirrors. Rooms are carpeted and decently sized, and some have a balcony peeping onto a quiet street or courtyard. Best up is the library area in reception that makes guests feel at home the second they walk in the door, and the state-of-the-art basement spa guests can loll in from 3pm daily.

HÔTEL DANEMARK
Map p108   Boutique Hotel €€

☎ 01 43 26 93 78; www.hoteldanemark.com; 21 rue Vavin, 6e; d €110-178; Ⓜ Vavin; 🔀 🖥

This positively scrumptious boutique hotel southwest of the Jardin du Luxembourg has 15 very tastefully furnished rooms and eclectic contemporary décor contrasting with ancient stone walls. Public areas such as the reception and its corner rooms are full of vibrantly coloured furniture and objects that match and contrast. The bedrooms are well soundproofed and of a generous size (minimum 20 sq metres) for a boutique hotel in central Paris, and all have bathtubs. Book online to get the best rates.

HÔTEL DES 2 CONTINENTS
Map p112   Hotel €€

☎ 01 43 26 72 46; www.hoteldes2continents.com; 25 rue Jacob, 6e; d €110-165, tr €180-230; Ⓜ St-Germain des Prés; 🔀 🖥 🛜

The 'Two Continents Hotel' – the name pays homage to the Treaty of Paris having been signed at the nearby Hôtel d'Angleterre (p334) – is a very pleasant establishment with 41 spacious rooms in a quiet street. The mural in the beamed breakfast room, viewed through parted drapes, is an early morning eye-opener. About half of the rooms are air-conditioned.

HÔTEL DU DRAGON
Map p112   Hotel €€

☎ 01 45 48 51 05; www.hoteldudragon.com; 36 rue du Dragon, 6e; s/d €108/128; Ⓜ St-Germain des Prés or St-Sulpice; 🖥 🛜

There's no lift at this five-storey hotel, just a rickety-looking old wooden staircase that leads to the 28 brightly coloured rooms. The bedside lamps are on the low-budget side and we could live without the faux-fur bed coverings, but the bathrooms are large and well maintained. The piano lounge and tiny back patio are just made for relaxing.

HÔTEL DU LYS
Map p112   Hotel €€

☎ 01 43 26 97 57; www.hoteldulys.com; 23 rue Serpente, 6e; s €100, d €105-120, tr €140; Ⓜ Odéon

Located in a 17th-century hôtel particulier, this 22-room midrange hotel has been in the same family for six decades. We love the beamed ceiling and the chinoiserie wallpaper in the lobby; rooms to go for include the blue-toned room 13 with its striped ceiling and two windows, or the darker (but more atmospheric) room 14 in terracotta and with rustic old furniture. Unusually, rates include breakfast.

GRAND HÔTEL LÉVÊQUE
Map p108   Hotel €€

☎ 01 47 05 49 15; www.hotel-leveque.com; 29 rue Cler, 7e; s €67-74, d €97-122, tr €137-144; Ⓜ École Militaire; 🔀 🛜

This partially renovated 50-room hotel is recommended less for its charms than its bon rapport qualité prix (good value for money) and an excellent location overlooking rue Cler and its market (p222). Choose any room ending in 1, 2 or 3, all of which have two windows overlooking the market. For those travellers seeking silence, your best bet is one of the rooms facing the courtyard but they're darker and smaller (eg room 10). Singles here are minuscule.

HÔTEL DU CHAMP-DE-MARS
Map p108   Hotel €

☎ 01 45 51 52 30; www.hotelduchampde mars.com; 7 rue du Champ de Mars, 7e; s/d/tr €91/98/128; Ⓜ École Militaire; 🖥 🛜

This charming 25-room hotel is on everyone's wish list so book a good month or two in advance if you want to wake up in the shadow of the Eiffel Tower. The attractive shop-front entrance leads into a colourful lobby done up in yellow and charcoal. Rooms on the lower floors can be downright cupboardlike, though; go up higher (in floors and price) and you might earn a glimpse of Mademoiselle Eiffel herself.

HÔTEL ST-ANDRÉ DES ARTS
Map p112   Hotel €

☎ 01 43 26 96 16; 66 rue St-André des Arts, 6e; s/d/tr/q €73/93/117/129; Ⓜ Odéon

Located on a lively, restaurant-lined thoroughfare, this 31-room hotel is an excellent choice if you're looking for reasonably priced but stylish accommodation in the centre of the action. The rooms are not particularly spectacular, but the public areas are very evocative of *vieux Paris* (old Paris), with their beamed ceilings, ancient stone walls and mock-Gothic chairs. Room rates include breakfast.

HÔTEL DE NESLE Map p112 Hotel €
☎ 01 43 54 62 41; www.hoteldenesleparis.com; 7 rue de Nesle, 6e; s €55-65, d €75-100; Ⓜ Odéon or Mabillon
The Nesle, a relaxed, colourfully decorated hotel in a quiet street west of place St-Michel, is such a fun place to stay. Most of its 20 rooms are painted with brightly coloured naive murals inspired by French literature. But its greatest asset is the huge (by Parisian standards) garden – a back yard really – accessible from the 1st floor, with pathways, trellis and even a small fountain. For a garden-facing room choose room 12.

EIFFEL TOWER & 16E
Not surprisingly, these two very chic neighbourhoods are somewhat short on budget and midrange accommodation options.

HÔTEL SEZZ Map p118 Boutique Hotel €€€
☎ 01 56 75 26 26; www.hotelsezz.com; 6 av Frémiet, 16e; s €285-340, d & tw €335-470, ste €450-1800; Ⓜ Passy;
Punning on the number of the posh arrondissement – 16 (*seize* in French) – in which it finds itself, this boutique bonanza is heavy on design (think Christophe Pillet), technology and *l'esprit zen* (Zen spirit). The 27 rooms, more than half of which are suites, are spacious and done up in reds and blacks, and lots of glass. There's a hammam, Jacuzzi and massage room, and the bar specialises in Champagne. Each guest has their own personal assistant during their stay.

MON HÔTEL Map p118 Hotel €€€
☎ 01 45 02 76 76; www.monhotel.fr; 1-5 rue d'Argentine, 16e; d €299-590; Ⓜ Argentine;
The Mac of the Paris hotel world, Mon Hôtel is a sleek boutique property located just behind the Arc de Triomphe. The vision here is contemporary design, and the 37 rooms feature unusual touches like

alcantara walls (a kind of synthetic suede) and, of course, cool ring-shaped iPod docks. Added luxuries like Compagnie de Provence bath products and a massage and sauna room make this one of the nicer choices near the Champs-Élysées.

GENTLE GOURMET
Map118 Bed and Breakfast €€
☎ 01 45 00 46 55; www.gentlegourmetbandb.com; 21 rue Duret, 16e; s €130, d €155; Ⓜ Argentine;
A vegan bed and breakfast, the Gentle Gourmet is definitely a unique concept in Paris. In addition to getting a comfortable room in an apartment building, there are loads of other extras, including vegan dinners (reservations essential) and tours of the kitchen gardens of France. There are only a few beds available, however, so you'll need to book well in advance.

CHAMPS-ÉLYSÉES & GRANDS BOULEVARDS
Like the 1er, the Champs-Élysées is home to deluxe palace hotels and global chains, though there are options here with more personality. Heading east the choices increase; the area between the Grands Boulevards and Pigalle is a beautiful neighbourhood and, being less touristy than the Champs-Élysées, a great place to immerse yourself in the city's charms and day-to-day life.

HÔTEL DE CRILLON Map p126 Hotel €€€
☎ 01 44 71 15 00; www.crillon.com; 10 place de la Concorde, 8e; s €750, d €750-930, ste from €1200; Ⓜ Concorde;
This colonnaded 200-year-old 'jewel in the heart of Paris', whose sparkling public areas (including *Les Ambassadeurs* restaurant, with new chef Christopher Hache at the helm) are sumptuously decorated with chandeliers, original sculptures, gilt mouldings, tapestries and inlaid furniture, is the epitome of French luxury. The 147 spacious rooms are fitted out with king-sized beds and floor-to-ceiling marble bathrooms with separate shower and bath. And Hôtel de Crillon is not just a pretty face; in 1778 the treaty in which France recognised the independence of the new USA was signed here by Louis XVI and Benjamin Franklin.

HIDDEN HOTEL Map p126 · Hotel €€€

☎ 01 40 55 03 57; www.hidden-hotel.com;
28 rue de l'Arc de Triomphe, 17e; s €245, d €285-485; Ⓜ Charles de Gaulle–Étoile; ⚄ 🖳 🛜

The Hidden is one of the Champs-Élysées' best secrets: an ecofriendly boutique hotel, it's serene, stylish and reasonably spacious, and it even sports green credentials. The earth-coloured tones are the result of natural pigments (there's no paint), and all rooms feature handmade wooden furniture, stone basins for sinks, and linen curtains surrounding Coco-mat beds. The Emotion rooms, which have a terrace, are among the most popular. Need we say that the breakfast is almost 100% organic?

HÔTEL AMARANTE Map p126 · Hotel €€€

☎ 01 53 89 77 59; www.hotelbeaumanoir.com;
6 rue de l'Arcade, 8e; s, d & tw €200-220, ste €250-280; Ⓜ Madeleine; ⚄ 🖳 🛜

Among the cosier hotels in the 8e, the Amarante has traditional-style rooms, with exposed rafters, wooden furniture and oak panelling, and it has a prime location just around the corner from place Madeleine. There's a small fitness room downstairs, and there are also decent discounts in the off season when you book online. Note that wi-fi access here costs an additional €17, though there is a computer in the sitting room.

HÔTEL AMOUR Map p126 · Hotel €€

☎ 01 48 78 31 80; www.hotelamourparis.fr; 8 rue Navarin, 9e; s €100, d €150-280; Ⓜ St-Georges or Pigalle; 🛜

Planning a romantic escapade to Paris? Say no more. One of the 'in' hotels of the moment, the inimitable black-clad Amour (formerly a love hotel by the hour) features original design and artwork in each of the rooms and is very much worthy of the hype – you won't find a more stylish place to lay your head in Paris at these prices. Of course, you have to be willing to forgo television (there isn't any) – but who needs TV when you're in love?

HÔTEL JOYCE Map p126 · Hotel €€

☎ 01 55 07 00 01; www.astotel.com; 29 rue La Bruyère, 9e; s, d & tw €150-236, ste €399; Ⓜ St-Georges; ⚄ 🖳 🛜

The Joyce is a new boutique hotel that's located in a lovely residential area in between Montmartre and l'Opéra. It's got all

top picks

HISTORIC HOTELS

- **Hôtel de Crillon** An 18th-century landmark, the Crillon is the epitome of French luxury.
- **Hôtel Langlois** For a real taste of belle époque Paris.
- **Hôtel Caron de Beaumarchais** (p344) Sleep in the past in a boutique hotel done up like an 18th-century *hôtel particulier*.
- **Hôtel St-Merry** (p329) Awaken the goth in you with a night in what was once part of a medieval church.
- **Hôtel St-Louis Marais** (p345) 'Get thee to a nunnery' could be the rallying cry for this boutique hotel converted from a 17th-century convent.

the modern design touches (iPod docks, a sky-lit breakfast room fitted out with old Range Rover seats) and even makes some ecofriendly claims – it relies on 50% renewable energy and uses organic products when available. Rates vary with the season; discounts are often available online.

HÔTEL LANGLOIS Map p126 · Hotel €€

☎ 01 48 74 78 24; www.hotel-langlois.com; 63 rue St-Lazare, 9e; s €110-120, d & tw €140-150, ste €190; Ⓜ Trinité; ⚄ 🖳 🛜

If you're looking for a piece of belle époque Paris, the Langlois won't let you down. Built in 1870, this 27-room hotel has retained its charm, from the tiny caged elevator to sandstone fireplaces in many rooms (sadly decommissioned) as well as original bathroom fixtures and tiles. Room 64 has wonderful views of the rooftops of Montmartre.

HÔTEL DE SÈZE Map p126 · Hotel €€

☎ 01 47 42 69 12; www.hoteldeseze.com; 16 rue de Sèze, 9e; s €120-150, d & tw €130-150, tr €160; Ⓜ Madeleine; ⚄ 🛜

On no account to be confused with its *almost* namesake, the posh Hôtel Sezz (p338) in the 16e, this simple but stylish establishment is excellent value mostly for its location – it's so close to the place de la Madeleine you'll wake up smelling the coffee from Fauchon (p203). For a real treat, ask for the double with Jacuzzi. Wi-fi access is an extra €5.

HÔTEL ALISON Map p126   Hotel €€

☎ 01 42 65 54 00; www.hotelalison.com; 21 rue de Surène, 8e; s €86-98, d €120-194, tr €192; Ⓜ Madeleine; ✷ 💻 📶

This excellent-value 34-room midrange hotel, just west of place de la Madeleine, attracts with the bold colours of its carpets and furnishings and modern art in the lobby. Prices depend on whether rooms have bath or shower and the view. Double room 37 (€120), for example, looks on to rue Surène, while room 31 (€174) overlooks a leafy patio.

HÔTEL PELETIER HAUSSMANN OPÉRA Map p126   Hotel €€

☎ 01 42 46 79 53; www.peletieropera.com; 15 rue Le Peletier, 9e; s €90, d €100; Ⓜ Richelieu–Drouot; 💻 📶

This is a pleasant 26-room hotel just off blvd Haussmann and close to the big department stores. Attractive packages are available at the weekend, depending on the season.

HÔTEL CHOPIN Map p126   Hotel €€

☎ 01 47 70 58 10; www.hotelchopin.fr; 46 passage Jouffroy & 10 blvd Montmartre, 9e; s €68-84, d €92-106, tr €125; Ⓜ Grands Boulevards; 📶

Dating back to 1846, the Chopin is down one of Paris' most delightful 19th-century *passages couverts* (covered shopping arcades) and a great deal for its location right off the Grands Boulevards (entrance at 10 blvd Montmartre). The sprawling 36-room hotel may be a little faded, but it's still enormously evocative of the belle époque. Wi-fi is available only in the lobby.

HÔTEL MONTE CARLO Map p126   Hotel €

☎ 01 47 70 36 75; www.hotelmontecarlo.fr; 44 rue du Faubourg Montmartre, 9e; s €55-105, d & tw €69-129, tr €119-149; Ⓜ Le Peletier; 📶

A unique budget hotel, the Monte Carlo is a steal, with colourful, personalized rooms and a great neighbourhood location. The owners go the extra mile and even provide a partly organic breakfast. The cheaper rooms come without bathroom or shower, but overall it outclasses many of the other choices in its price range. Rates vary with the season.

WOODSTOCK HOSTEL Map p126   Hostel €

☎ 01 48 78 87 76; www.woodstock.fr; 48 rue Rodier, 9e; per person dm/d Oct-Mar €19/22, Apr-Sep €25/28; Ⓜ Anvers; 💻 📶

This hostel is just down the hill from raucous place Pigalle in a quiet residential quarter. Dorm beds are in rooms sleeping four to six people in bunk beds, and each room has washbasin only; showers and toilets are off the corridor. Rooms are shut from 11am to 3pm, and the (enforced) curfew is at 2am. The eat-in kitchen, situated down the steps from the patio, has everything.

MONTMARTRE, PIGALLE & 17E

Montmartre, encompassing the 18e and the northern part of the 9e, is one of the most charming neighbourhoods in Paris and a good place to base yourself in. There is a lot of variety here, from boutique to bohemian and *hôtels particuliers* (private mansions) to hostels. Many of the hotels here have views of some kind – whether of the streets of Montmartre and Sacré Coeur or the Paris skyline stretching away to the south – and top-floor availability is a good factor to take into account when choosing your room.

To the west is the 17e arrondissement, which has a sprinkling of charming budget and midrange hotels but is less central.

HÔTEL PARTICULIER MONTMARTRE

Map p134   Boutique Hotel €€€

☎ 01 53 41 81 40; http://hotel-particulier -montmartre.com; 23 av Junot, 18e; ste €390-590; Ⓜ Lamarck–Caulaincourt; ✷ 📶

An 18th-century mansion hidden down a private alleyway in Montmartre, this jewel sparkles from every angle. Much more than an exclusive hotel, it's the equivalent of staying in a modern art collector's personal residence, with rotating exhibitions from around the world, five imaginative suites designed by top French artists (Philippe Mayaux, Natacha Lesueur), and a lush garden landscaped by Louis Benech of Jardin des Tuileries fame. Non-guests can stop by for evening cocktails (🕓 5pm-midnight); reservations required.

KUBE HÔTEL Map p134   Boutique Hotel €€€

☎ 01 42 05 20 00; www.muranoresort.com; 1-5 passage Ruelle, 18e; s €250, d €300-400, ste €500-750; Ⓜ La Chapelle; ✷ 💻 📶

The easternmost edge of the 18e, virtually the lap of Gare du Nord, is the last place in Paris you'd expect to find an über-trendy boutique hotel, but this 41-room hostelry manages to pull it off. The theme here is, of course, three dimensional square – from the glassed-in reception box in the entrance courtyard to the cube-shaped furnishings in the 41 guestrooms to the ice in the cocktails at the celebrated Ice Kube (p285) bar. The offspring of the stylish Murano Urban Resort, the Kube might have been less open-handed with the florescent reds and *faux* fur, but if that's what it takes to get guests to trek all the way to La Chapelle, so be it.

TERRASS HÔTEL Map p134 Hotel €€€
☎ 01 46 06 72 85; www.terrass-hotel.com; 12 rue Joseph de Maistre, 18e; s & d €280-340, ste €385-415; Ⓜ Blanche; ✖ 💻 🛜
This very sedate, stylish hotel at the southeastern corner of the Montmartre Cemetery and due east of the Butte de Montmartre (Montmartre Hill) has 92 spacious and well-designed rooms and suites, an excellent restaurant and bar, and quite simply the best views in town. For the ultimate Parisian experience, choose double room 608 for stunning views of the Eiffel Tower and Panthéon or room 802, which boasts its own private terrace. Some of the rooms on floors 4, 5 and 6 were designed by Kenzo.

HÔTEL DES ARTS Map p134 Hotel €€
☎ 01 46 06 30 52; www.arts-hotel-paris.com; 5 rue Tholozé, 18e; s €95, d & tw €140-165; Ⓜ Abbesses or Blanche; 💻 🛜
The Hôtel des Arts is a friendly, attractive 50-room hotel, convenient to both place Pigalle and Montmartre. It has comfortable midrange rooms done up in a traditional style (lots of floral motifs); consider spending an extra €25 for the superior rooms, which have nicer views and are a tad larger. Just up the street is the old-style windmill Moulin de la Galette – how's that for location?

NEW ORIENT HÔTEL Map p136 Hotel €€
☎ 01 45 22 21 64; www.hotelneworient.com; 16 rue de Constantinople, 8e; s €95-115, d €115-125, tw €125-155, tr & q €165; Ⓜ Europe; ✖ 💻 🛜
This delightful place is situated in a neighbourhood of the 8e north of Gare St-Lazare that seems to have only shops that sell musical instruments and/or sheet music. It has a lot of personality, especially in the public areas. The 30 guestrooms are not as nice, though several have Second Empire furnishings and decorative busts. Some,

including twin room 7 and double room 8, even have little balconies.

HÔTEL REGYN'S MONTMARTRE
Map p134 Hotel €€
☎ 01 42 54 45 21; www.hotel-regyns-paris.com; 18 place des Abbesses, 18e; s €79-99, d & tw €91-120; Ⓜ Abbesses; 💻 🛜
This 22-room hotel is a good choice if you want to stay in old Montmartre and not break the bank. It's just opposite the Abbesses metro station, which happens to have one of the best preserved art nouveau entrance canopies designed by Hector Guimard (see p103), and outside the hotel is a lovely old plane tree. Some of the rooms have views out over Paris. Wi-fi costs extra.

ERMITAGE HÔTEL Map p134 Hotel €€
☎ 01 42 64 79 22; www.ermitagesacrecoeur.fr; 24 rue Lamarck, 18e; s €82-85, d €96-100, tr €120, q €145; Ⓜ Lamarck–Caulaincourt; 💻
Located in a 19th-century townhouse, the family-run Ermitage is a quaint 12-room bed and breakfast in the shadow of Sacré Cœur. The traditional-style rooms are simple but attractive, with floral-patterned fabric on the walls and antique furnishings that convey a yesteryear charm. Like many hotels in this area, the upper floors have better views.

HÔTEL AURORE MONTMARTRE
Map p136 Hotel €€
☎ 01 48 74 85 56; www.montmartre-hotel-paris.com; 76 rue de Clichy, 9e; s €65-90, d €70-110, tr €99-140; Ⓜ Place de Clichy; 💻 🛜
The lobby and the lift may both be pint-sized and Montmartre ain't exactly one street over, but some of the 24 rooms of this hotel between place de Clichy and the Gare St-Lazare have balconies (eg room 54) overlooking the street; it is also renovated regularly. And the price is certainly right for the location.

HÔTEL ELDORADO Map p136 Hotel €
☎ 01 45 22 35 21; www.eldoradohotel.fr; 18 rue des Dames, 17e; s €35-60, d & tw €70-80, tr €80-90; Ⓜ Place de Clichy; 🛜
This bohemian place is one of Paris' greatest finds: a welcoming, reasonably well-run place with 23 colourfully decorated and (often) ethnically themed rooms in a main building on a quiet street and in an annexe with a private garden at the back. We love rooms 1 and 2 in the garden annexe; the

choicest rooms in the main building are Nos 16 and 17 with their own terraces leading out into the garden. Cheaper-category singles have washbasin only. The hotel's excellent Bistro des Dames (p246) is a bonus.

HOTEL CAULAINCOURT SQUARE

Map p134   Hotel, Hostel €

☎ 01 46 06 46 06; www.caulaincourt.com; 2 square Caulaincourt, 18e; dm €25, s €50-60, d & tw €63-76, tr €89; Ⓜ Lamarck–Caulaincourt; 🖳 🛜
This budget hotel, which also has dorm rooms, is perched on the backside of Montmartre, beyond the tourist hoopla in a real Parisian neighbourhood. The rooms are in decent condition, with parquet floors and a funky interior design, though there is no lift; beware if you have a lot of luggage.

HÔTEL BONSÉJOUR MONTMARTRE

Map p134   Hotel €

☎ 01 42 54 22 53; www.hotel-bonsejour-montmartre.fr; 11 rue Burq, 18e; s €33-69, d €56-69; Ⓜ Abbesses; 🖳
At the top of a quiet street in Montmartre, this is a perennial budget favourite. It's a simple place to stay – no lift or parquet floors – but welcoming, comfortable and very clean. Some rooms (eg Nos 14, 23, 33, 43 and 53) have little balconies attached – these are the ones to go for – and at least one room (No 55) offers a fleeting glimpse of Sacré Cœur. Communal showers cost €2.

LE VILLAGE HOSTEL Map p134   Hostel €

☎ 01 42 64 22 02; www.villagehostel.fr; 20 rue d'Orsel, 18e; per person dm/d/tr €28-38, d €70-90, tr €96-115, q €112-140; Ⓜ Anvers; 🖳 🛜
A fine 25-room hostel with beamed ceilings, a lovely outside terrace and views of Sacré Cœur. Dormitory beds are in rooms for four to six people and all have shower and toilet. Kitchen facilities are available, and there's a popular bar too. Rooms are closed between 11am and 4pm for cleaning, but there is no curfew. Internet access is available for €1/3.50 for 15/60 minutes.

PLUG-INN HOSTEL Map p134   Hostel €

☎ 01 42 58 42 58; www.plug-inn.fr; 7 rue Aristide Bruant, 18e; dm €20-30, d €60-80, tr €90; Ⓜ Abbesses or Blanche; 🖳 🛜
This new hostel has several things going for it, the first of which is its central Montmartre location. The four- to five-person dorms all have their own showers, there's a kitchen, free breakfast and the staff are

top picks

BUDGET HOTELS

- Hôtel Croix de Malte (p346) This well-tended place en route to Ménilmontant is incredible value for its location and amenities.
- Hôtel de la Paix (p350) A clever mix of new and second-hand giving this budget hotel real shabby-chic appeal.
- Hôtel de Lille (p329) It's nothing really to write home about but the Lille is clean, welcoming and right by the Louvre.
- Hôtel du Nord (p343) Flea-market antiques set the scene at this cosy address near Canal St-Martin.
- Hôtel Henri IV (p330) Its location overlooking a lovely square on the Île de la Cité makes this cheapie worth its weight in gold.
- Hôtel Monte Carlo (p340) Personable owners, colourful style and a great neighbourhood location.
- Hôtel Le Cosy (p349) Stylish rooms south of Nation – it might be away from the centre, but the price is right.
- Port Royal Hôtel (p330) A refreshingly affordable oasis of simplicity and warmth on the Latin Quarter's southernmost fringe.

even friendly (a rarity among Parisian hostels). There's a lockout during the day but no curfew; internet access and wi-fi are free of charge.

GARE DU NORD & CANAL ST-MARTIN

The areas immediately surrounding the Gare du Nord and Gare de l'Est are somewhat run-down with little to recommend, unless you're catching an early train to London or want to crash immediately upon arrival. More atmospheric is place de la République, a great neighbourhood that is also convenient for nightlife, and the Canal St-Martin, which has a few quirky hotels and hostels strung out along its banks.

HÔTEL LA VIEILLE FRANCE

Map p140   Hotel €€

☎ 01 45 26 42 37; www.hotel-vieille-france.com; 151 rue La Fayette, 10e; s €51, d €95-110, tr €130; Ⓜ Gare du Nord; 🖳
Conveniently located around the corner from the Gare du Nord, the Vieille France

is an acceptable choice if you're in need of a hotel near the station. The doubles were recently renovated and are in OK shape; stay away from the singles.

RÉPUBLIQUE HÔTEL
Map p140   Hotel €€

☎ 01 42 39 19 03; www.republiquehotel.com; 31 rue Albert Thomas, 10e; s/d/tr/q €75/88/108/159; Ⓜ République; ⊚

This hip spot is heavy on the pop art (Warhol-style silkscreens, full-door portrait of Madonna, unicolour garden gnomes in the breakfast room). While the UK paraphernalia might be a little overboard – the Union Jack and the Beatles turn up an awful lot – you simply cannot fault the inexpensive rates and fantastic location just off place République.

HÔTEL GARDEN ST-MARTIN
Map p140   Hotel €€

☎ 01 42 40 17 72; www.hotel-gardensaintmartin -paris.com; 35 rue Yves Toudic, 10e; s €72, d & tw €87, tr €108; Ⓜ Jacques Bonsergent; ⊚

A basic 32-room hotel, this place is superbly located in the heart of the Canal St-Martin district. Rooms are unspectacular but clean; it's a good fallback option if the other hotels in the area are full.

HÔTEL DU NORD
Map p140   Hotel €

☎ 01 42 01 66 00; www.hoteldunord-leparivelo. com; 47 rue Albert Thomas, 10e; s & d €69, tw €82, quad €105; Ⓜ République; ⊚

Not to be confused with the restaurant of the same name (p249), the Hôtel du Nord is a cosy place with 23 personalised rooms decorated with flea-market antiques. Beyond the bric-a-brac charm, its most winning attribute is a prized location near place République. As an added plus, they also lend bikes to their guests.

SIBOUR HÔTEL   Map p140   Hotel €

☎ 01 46 07 20 74; www.hotel-sibour.com, in French; 4 rue Sibour, 10e; s €40-60, d €45-68, tr/q €80/110; Ⓜ Gare de l'Est; ⊚

This friendly place has 45 well-kept rooms, including some that are a bit old-fashioned (the cheapest singles and doubles) and have washbasins only. Communal showers cost €3. Some of the rooms look down on pretty Église de St-Laurent. We love the trompe l'œil mural in the breakfast room.

ST CHRISTOPHER'S INN   Map p140   Hostel €

☎ 01 40 34 34 40; www.st-christophers.co.uk; 68-74 quai de la Seine, 19e; per person dm €15-38, d from €35; Ⓜ Riquet or Jaurès (from Gare du Nord); ▱ ⊚

Opened in 2008, this is certainly one of the best, biggest (300 beds) and most up-to-date hostels in Paris. It features a modern design, three types of dorms (10-bed, 8-bed, 6-bed) as well as doubles with or without bathrooms. Other perks include a canal-side café, free wi-fi (somewhat temperamental) and breakfast, an internet café (€2 per 30min), a female-only floor, and a bar. There is no kitchen. Prices vary considerably depending on the season, so you'll have to check their website for an accurate quote.

MARAIS & MÉNILMONTANT

The Marais and to the northeast Ménilmontant make up the liveliest area of the Right Bank and their top-end hostels are among the city's finest. Despite massive gentrification of the *quartiers* in recent years, there are also some less expensive hotels left and the choice of lower-priced one- and two-star hotels remains excellent.

HÔTEL LES JARDINS DU MARAIS
Map p148   Hotel €€€

☎ 01 40 21 20 00; www.lesjardinsdumarais.com; 74 rue Amelot, 11e; r €350-455, ste from €600; Ⓜ Chemin Vert; ⊠ ⊚ ⓺

You'd never know you were in Paris after walking through the door of this 263-room hotel housed in nine separate buildings designed by Gustave Eiffel and surrounding an enormous courtyard of cobblestones and gardens. Rooms have an Art Deco feel – lots of blacks, whites, purples and straight lines – and the outlets are always bursting at the seams. It's a delight but way too big to call itself a boutique hotel.

HÔTEL DU PETIT MOULIN
Map p152   Boutique Hotel €€€

☎ 01 42 74 10 10; www.hoteldupetitmoulin. com; 29-31 rue du Poitou, 3e; r €190-290, ste €350; Ⓜ Filles du Calvaire; ⊠ ⊚ ⓺

This scrumptious boutique hotel (OK, we're impressed that it was a bakery at the time of Henri IV) was designed from top to bottom by Christian Lacroix and features 17 completely different rooms. You can choose from medieval and rococo Marais sporting exposed beams and dressed in toile de Jouy wallpaper, to more modern surroundings with contemporary murals and heart-shaped mirrors just this side of kitsch. 'The Little Mill' is still one of our favourite hostelries in the Marais.

LE GÉNÉRAL HÔTEL
Map p148   Boutique Hotel €€€

☎ 01 47 00 41 57; www.legeneralhotel.com; 5-7 rue Rampon, 11e; s €155-175, d €190-220, tr €220-250, ste €280-310; Ⓜ République; 🖥 🛜 ♿

This hotel is white on the outside and a bonbon box of cherry and chocolate tones within. The décor at 'The General' is fresh and fun, and the 47 rooms are beautifully furnished. The cheery bar off the lobby is memorable – the gumdrops are a nice touch – and the amenities include a small but well-equipped fitness centre and sauna.

AUSTIN'S ARTS ET MÉTIERS HÔTEL
Map p148   Hotel €€

☎ 01 42 77 17 61; www.hotelaustins.com; 6 rue Montgolfier, 3e; s/d €114/158; Ⓜ Arts et Métiers; 🖥 🛜

This three-star hotel southwest of place de la République and facing the Musée des Arts et Métiers (p147) stands out primarily for its warm welcome and excellent service. The 29 rooms are minimally furnished but attractively done up in yellows, blues and reds. The brighter rooms face the street, while the larger ones overlook the inner courtyard. Choose room 12 if, like us, you appreciate a bathroom with a window.

CASTEX HÔTEL Map p148   Hotel €€

☎ 01 42 72 31 52; www.castexhotel.com; 5 rue Castex, 4e; s/d €125/155, ste €220; Ⓜ Bastille; 🖥 🛜

Equidistant from the Bastille and the Marais, the 30-room Castex has been modernised but manages to retain some of its 17th-century elements, including a vaulted stone cellar used as a breakfast room, terracotta tiles on the floor and toile de Jouy wallpaper. Try to get one of the independent rooms (1 and 2) off the lovely patio; No 3 is a two-room suite or family room.

HÔTEL DU VIEUX SAULE
Map p148   Hotel €€

☎ 01 42 72 01 14; www.hotelvieuxsaule.com; 6 rue de Picardie, 3e; s €120, d €150-180, tr €180-220; Ⓜ Filles du Calvaire; 🖥 🛜

This flower-bedecked 28-room hostelry in the northern Marais is something of a find because of its slightly off-the-beaten-track location. The hotel has a small sauna and there is a tranquil little garden on full display behind glass off the lobby. Breakfast is served in the 16th-century vaulted cellar.

HÔTEL BASTILLE DE LAUNAY
Map p148   Hotel €€

☎ 01 47 00 88 11; www.bastilledelaunay-hotel -paris.com; 42 rue Amelot, 11e; s €110, d €140-160; Ⓜ Chemin Vert; 🛜

Under new and very enthusiastic management, this hotel with 36 rooms in two buildings separated by a small courtyard is in the process of shaking off the old and bringing in the new; the large double-glazed windows and judicious use of mirrors creates a bright and very quiet environment just down the steps from busy blvd Beaumarchais. The hotel offers especially good value due to its central location just paces from place de la Bastille.

HÔTEL DE LA BRETONNERIE
Map p152   Hotel €€

☎ 01 48 87 77 63; www.bretonnerie.com; 22 rue Ste-Croix de la Bretonnerie, 4e; s & d €135-165, tr & q €190, ste €190-215; Ⓜ Hôtel de Ville; 🛜

This is a very charming three-star hotel in the heart of the Marais nightlife area dating from the 17th century. The décor of each of the 29 rooms and suites is unique, and some rooms have four-poster and canopy beds. Three suites on two levels are huge. It's a distant cousin of the much-loved Hôtel Chopin (p340) in the delightful passage Jouffroy.

HÔTEL CARON DE BEAUMARCHAIS
Map p152   Boutique Hotel €€

☎ 01 42 72 34 12; www.carondebeaumarchais. com; 12 rue Vieille du Temple, 4e; r €130-185; Ⓜ St-Paul; 🖥 🛜

Decorated like an 18th-century private house contemporary with Beaumarchais, who wrote Le Mariage de Figaro (The Marriage of Figaro) at No 47 on this street, this award-winning themed hotel has to be seen to be believed. The small, museum-quality lobby, with its prized 18th-century pianoforte, gaming tables, chandeliers and original Beaumarchais manuscripts, sets the tone of the place. The 19 rooms aren't huge but are positively dripping with brocade, furniture decorated with tracery, and ormolu-framed mirrors. An experience like few others.

GRAND HÔTEL MALHER Map p152   Hotel €€
☎ 01 42 72 60 92; www.grandhotelmalher.com; 5 rue Malher, 4e; s €100-125, d €120-145, tr €175-190; Ⓜ St-Paul; 🛜 ♿
This welcoming establishment run by the same family for three generations has nicely appointed rooms and a small but pretty courtyard at the back. The hotel's 31 bedrooms are a decent size, and the bathrooms are modern and relatively large; most are equipped with a bath and a few with a shower. Rooms 1 and 2 give on to the courtyard.

HÔTEL ST-LOUIS MARAIS
Map p148   Hotel €€
☎ 01 48 87 87 04; www.saintlouismarais.com; 1 rue Charles V, 4e; s €99, d & tw €115-140, tr €150, ste €160; Ⓜ Sully–Morland; 🛜
This especially charming hotel built within a converted 17th-century convent is more Bastille than Marais, but still within easy walking distance of the latter. Wooden beams, terracotta tiles and heavy brocade drapes tend to darken the 19 renovated rooms, but certainly add to the atmosphere. Be aware that this four-floor hotel has no lift. Wi-fi costs €5.

HÔTEL SAINTONGE MARAIS
Map p152   Hotel €€
☎ 01 42 77 91 13; www.hotelmarais.com; 16 rue de Saintonge, 3e; s/d €105/115, ste €175; Ⓜ Filles du Calvaire; 🛜 ♿
This renovated 23-room hotel, with exposed beams, vaulted cellar and period furniture, is really more Oberkampf/République than the Marais. But with the Musée Picasso practically next door, let's not quibble. You'll get much better value for money here than in the more central parts of the Marais, or at the Saintonge's show-off sister property, the Hôtel St-Merry (p329). Wi-fi costs €3.

HÔTEL BEAUMARCHAIS
Map p148   Boutique Hotel €€
☎ 01 53 36 86 86; www.hotelbeaumarchais.com; 3 rue Oberkampf, 11e; s €75-90, d €110-130, tr €170-190; Ⓜ Filles du Calvaire; 🎲 🛜
This brighter-than-bright 31-room boutique hotel, with its emphasis on sunbursts and bold primary colours, is just this side of kitsch; have a look at the rainbow of keys peeking out from the cubby hole. But it certainly makes for a different Paris experience. In addition, there are monthly art exhibitions and guests are invited to the *vernissage* (opening night). The rooms are bright and of a decent size.

HÔTEL DE NICE Map p152   Hotel €€
☎ 01 42 78 55 29; www.hoteldenice.com; 42bis rue de Rivoli, 4e; s €80-95, d €110-120, tr €135-145; Ⓜ Hôtel de Ville; 🛜
This is an especially warm, family-run place with 23 comfortable rooms. Some have balconies high above busy rue de Rivoli. Every square inch of wall space is used to display old prints, and public areas and bedrooms are full of Second Empire–style furniture, Oriental carpets and lamps with fringed shades.

HÔTEL DU 7E ART Map p148   Hotel €€
☎ 01 44 54 85 00; www.paris-hotel-7art.com; 20 rue St-Paul, 4e; s €75-150, d & tw €95-150; Ⓜ St-Paul; 🛜
This themed hotel on the south side of rue St-Antoine is a fun place for film buffs – *le septième art* (the seventh art) is what the French call cinema – and boasts a B&W-movie theme throughout, right down to the tiled floors and the bathrooms. The 23 rooms over five floors – there is no lift – are sizeable and quite different from one another. A lone single with just a washbasin is €75. Go for room 41 or 42 on the 4th floor; they both have windows facing in two directions.

HÔTEL LYON MULHOUSE
Map p148   Hotel €€
☎ 01 47 00 91 50; www.1-hotel-paris.com; 8 blvd Beaumarchais, 11e; s €72-90, d €94-110, tr €130; Ⓜ Bastille; 🎲 🛜
This former post house, from where carriages would set out for Lyon and Mulhouse, has been a hotel since the 1920s. The 40 rooms, though not particularly special, are comfortable, quiet and of a good size; opt for room 12 with a door leading to a courtyard. Place de la Bastille is just around the corner.

HÔTEL JEANNE D'ARC
Map p152   Hotel €€
☎ 01 48 87 62 11; www.hoteljeannedarc.com; 3 rue de Jarente, 4e; s €62-90, d & tw €90-116, tr €146, q €160; Ⓜ St-Paul; 🛜 ♿
This cosy 35-room hotel near lovely place du Marché Ste-Catherine is a great little

base for your peregrinations among the museums, bars and restaurants of the Marais, and almost has a country feel to it. About the only thing wrong with this place is that everyone knows about it, so you'll have to book well in advance. Check out the fantastic mirror in the breakfast room.

HÔTEL DU SÉJOUR BEAUBOURG

Map p148   Hotel €€

☎ 01 48 87 40 36; www.hoteldusejour.com; 36 rue du Grenier St-Lazare, 3e; s €78-95, d €90-97; Ⓜ Rambuteau; 🛜

This bright and cheerful 20-room property offers a warm welcome and excellent value just minutes from the Centre Pompidou. Rooms, at the top of a wooden staircase (no lift), are simple but some have got a recent refit and cherry seems to be the colour of choice. Double-glazing keeps the din out on the street where it belongs.

HÔTEL DE LA PLACE DES VOSGES

Map p152   Hotel €€

☎ 01 42 72 60 46; www.hotelplacedesvosges. com; 12 rue de Birague, 4e; s & d €90-95, ste €150; Ⓜ St-Paul; 🛜

This superbly situated 17-room hotel is an oasis of tranquillity due south of sublime place des Vosges. The public areas are impressive and the rooms warm and cosy. A tiny lift serves the 1st to 4th floors but it's stairs only from the ground floor and to the 5th floor. A boon to families is the suite on the top floor with choice views that can accommodate up to four people comfortably.

HÔTEL SÉVIGNÉ Map p152   Hotel €€

☎ 01 42 72 76 17; www.le-sevigne.com; 2 rue Malher, 4e; s €66, d & tw €84-95, tr €113; Ⓜ St-Paul; 🔀 🛜

In the heart of the Marais this hotel, named after the celebrated 17th-century writer the Marquise de Sévigné (whose letters give us such a wonderful insight into the Paris of her day), is excellent value for its location and price. The hotel's 29 rooms, spread over six floors and accessible by lift, are basic but comfortably furnished.

HÔTEL PRATIC Map p152   Hotel €€

☎ 01 48 87 80 47; www.hotelpratic.com; 9 rue d'Ormesson, 4e; s €75-105, d €81-121, tr €129-145; Ⓜ St-Paul; 🛜

This 23-room hotel, which is opposite the delightful place du Marché Ste-Catherine, has period features and décor – exposed

beams, gilt frames, half-timbered or stone walls – that is almost too much. Rooms, dispersed over six floors, are rather pricey for what you get, though there are frequent promotions on their website. There's no lift.

GARDEN HÔTEL Map p148   Hostel €

☎ 01 40 00 57 93; www.garden-hotel-paris.com; 1 rue du Général Blaise, 11e; s €65-100, d € 75-100, tr €85-135; Ⓜ St-Ambroise; 🛜

If you're looking for peace and quiet but want to be within easy walking distance of both Bastille and Ménilmontant, choose this hotel in a belle époque building with 42 rooms overlooking a large leafy square. There are five types of rooms – all with en suite bathroom and WC and all of a relatively decent size. And we've always been suckers for a glass art deco entranceway.

GRAND HÔTEL DU LOIRET

Map p152   Hotel €

☎ 01 48 87 77 00; www.hotel-loiret.fr; 8 rue des Mauvais Garçons, 4e; s €50-80, d €70-90, tr/q €110; Ⓜ Hôtel de Ville or St-Paul; 🖳

This 27-room budget hotel in the heart of gay Marais is very popular with young male travellers, not just because it is within easy walking distance of just about everything after dark, but because it sits on the 'Street of the Bad Boys'. A few of the singles have neither private shower nor bath nor toilet but share facilities off the corridors. Those rooms are a steal at €50. Internet access costs extra here.

HÔTEL DE NEVERS Map p148   Hotel €

☎ 01 47 00 56 18; www.hoteldenevers.com; 53 rue de Malte, 11e; s/d/tr/q €62/69/93/103; Ⓜ Oberkampf; 🛜

This 36-room budget hotel around the corner from place de la République and within easy walking distance of the nightlife of Ménilmontant is a family affair and offers excellent value. Hyperallergenics may think twice about staying here, though: there are three cats on hand to greet you. All rooms now have WC, showers and TVs.

HÔTEL CROIX DE MALTE Map p148   Hotel €

☎ 01 48 05 09 36; www.hotelcroixdemalte-paris. com; 5 rue de Malte, 11e; s €60-90, d €65-97; Ⓜ Oberkampf; 🛜

This cheery hotel will have you thinking you're in the tropics, not Paris. The breakfast room just off the lobby is bathed in light and looks out onto a tiny glassed-in courtyard with greenery and a giant jungle mural; Walasse Ting prints of jungles and parrots complete the picture. The 36 rooms are in two little buildings, only one of which has a lift.

HÔTEL DE LA HERSE D'OR
Map p148   Hotel €

☎ 01 48 87 84 09; www.hotel-herse-dor.com; 20 rue St-Antoine, 4e; basic s €49-59, d €59-76, with shower d €69-89, tr €99-110; Ⓜ Bastille; 🖥
This friendly place east of place de la Bastille has 35 serviceable rooms off a long stone corridor lined with mirrors. It's very basic and cheap; the lower-priced rooms have washbasins only. Though there's free wi-fi, those without laptops can check their emails at an internet terminal in the lobby for €1 for 10 minutes. And, in case you wondered, *herse* in French is not 'hearse' but 'portcullis'. So let's call it the 'Golden Gate Hotel'.

HÔTEL RIVOLI Map p152   Hotel €
☎ 01 42 72 08 41; 44 rue de Rivoli & 2 rue des Mauvais Garçons, 4e; s €35-55, d €44-55, tr €70; Ⓜ Hôtel de Ville
Long a Lonely Planet favourite, the Rivoli is forever cheap and cheery, with 20 basic, somewhat noisy rooms. The cheaper singles and doubles have washbasins only, but use of the shower room in the hallway is free. Annoyingly – given that it is in the heart of the Marais nightlife area – the front door is locked from 2am to 7am. Reception is on the 1st floor.

MAISON INTERNATIONALE DE LA JEUNESSE ET DES ÉTUDIANTS
Map p152   Hostel €

MIJE; ☎ 01 42 74 23 45; www.mije.com; per person dm €30, s/d/tr €49/36/32; 🖥
The MIJE runs three hostels in attractively renovated 17th- and 18th-century *hôtels particuliers* in the heart of the Marais, and it's difficult to think of a better budget deal in Paris. Costs are the same for all three hostels, and include single-sex, shower-equipped dorms with four to 10 beds per room as well as singles, twins and triples. Rooms are closed from noon to 3pm, and curfew is from 1am to 7am (though you can gain entrance if you let the guard know in advance). The maximum stay is seven nights. Individuals can make reservations at any of the three MIJE hostels listed via their website or telephoning; reception will hold you a bed till noon. During summer

and other busy periods, there may not be space after mid-morning. There's an annual membership fee of €2.50.

MIJE Le Fourcy (Map p152; 6 rue de Fourcy, 4e; Ⓜ St-Paul), with 200 beds, is the largest of the three. There's a cheap eatery here called Le Restaurant, which offers a three-course fixed-price *menu* including a drink for €10.50.

MIJE Le Fauconnier (Map p148; 11 rue du Fauconnier, 4e; Ⓜ St-Paul or Pont Marie) has 125 beds and is two blocks south of MIJE Le Fourcy.

MIJE Maubuisson (Map p152; 12 rue des Barres, 4e; Ⓜ Hôtel de Ville or Pont Marie) – the pick of the three – is half a block south of the *mairie* (town hall) of the 4e and has 99 beds.

AUBERGE DE JEUNESSE JULES FERRY
Map p148   Hostel €

☎ 01 43 57 55 60; www.fuaj.fr; 8 blvd Jules Ferry, 11e; per person dm & d €23; Ⓜ République or Goncourt; 🖳 🖥
This official hostel three blocks east of place de la République is somewhat institutional and the rooms could use a refit, but the atmosphere is fairly relaxed. The 99 beds are in two- to six-person rooms, which are locked between 10.30am and 2pm for housekeeping, but there is no curfew. You'll have to pay an extra €2.90 per night if you don't have an HI card or equivalent (€11/16 for those under/over 26). Internet access here costs €1 for 10 minutes.

BASTILLE & GARE DE LYON

East of place de la Bastille, the relatively un-touristy 11e is generally made up of unpretentious working-class areas and is a good way to see the 'real' Paris up close. Two-star comfort there is less expensive than in the Marais. At the same time the development of Bercy Village, with its selection of restaurants and bars, and the arrival of the Météor metro line (No 14) has done much to resuscitate the 12e. The neighbourhood around Gare de Lyon has a few budget hotels and an independent hostel.

BLC DESIGN HOTEL
Map p158   Boutique Hotel €€€

☎ 01 40 09 60 16; www.blcdesign-hotel-paris.com; 4 rue Richard Lenoir, 11e; s €95-180, d €180-230; Ⓜ Charonne; 🖳 🛜 ♿
Cobbled from what was a very ordinary one-star hotel, this 'symphony in white'

has raised the bar on hotel standards east of the Bastille. Its 29 rooms, as comfortable as they are 'Zen' stylish, are spread over six floors and we love the intimate little bar in the lobby. More rock star than royal, maybe, but they're on a roll.

HÔTEL CANDIDE Map p158   Hotel €€

☎ 01 43 79 02 33; www.new-hotel.com; 3 rue Pétion, 11e; s/d/tr €115/160/190; M Voltaire; 🖵 This 48-room hotel within easy striking distance of the Bastille and the Marais offers relatively good value and is very convenient to the Marché Bastille (p222) on blvd Richard Lenoir. It's on a very quiet street and we've always been impressed by the friendly, helpful service.

LE QUARTIER BASTILLE LE FAUBOURG Map p158   Boutique Hotel €€

☎ 01 43 70 04 04; www.lequartierhotelbf.com; 9 rue de Reuilly, 12e; s €113-168, d €133-163; M Gare de Lyon; 🖾 🛜 🕭 This warm and welcoming boutique hotel has 42 generously sized rooms with all the comforts and then some; big-screen TVs may be de rigueur these days but are apples

top picks

QUIRKY HOTELS

- L'Apostrophe (p335) Art hotel with stunning stencilled façade and unexpected room features like skateboard-ramp ceiling.
- Cadran Hôtel (p336) Clock-themed concept hotel with a sweet chocolate bar and shop to seduce gourmet guests.
- Hôtel Amour (p339) Planning a weekend fling in Paris? This former love hotel turned objet d'art mixes romance with style.
- Hôtel de Nice (p345) Charismatically kooky, this fun, family-run place is a trove of Oriental carpets, antique furniture, old prints and lamps with fringed shades.
- Hôtel du 7e Art (p345) If film is your thing, this hotel with a B&W-movie theme throughout is for you.
- Hôtel Eldorado (p341) Bohemian-style rooms with an attached garden and bistro, and, best of all, the price is right.
- Mama Shelter Philippe Starck has turned a former car park into one of the most desirable midrange addresses in eastern Paris.

on the bed and free liquorice at reception? Rooms are paired and share an internal hallway – ideal for families – and some (including No 72) have balconies. Its sister hotel, Le Quartier Bercy Square (Map p158; ☎ 01 44 87 09 09; www.lequartierhotelbs.com; 33 blvd de Reuilly, 12e; M Daumesnil) is in the same arrondissement about 1.5km to the south.

MAMA SHELTER Map p158   Hotel €€

☎ 01 43 48 47 40; www.mamashelter.com; 109 rue de Bagnolet, 20e; s €89-99, d €99-109, ste €299-399; M Alexandre Dumas or Gambetta; 🖾 🛜 🕭 Was Mick Jagger thinking of this place opposite La Flèche d'Or (p300) when he lipped 'If I don't get some shelter/I'm gonna fade away'? Coaxed into its zany new incarnation by designer Philippe Starck, this former car park southeast of Cimetière du Père Lachaise boasts 170 super comfortable (though smallish) rooms, trademark Starck details like a chocolate and fuchsia colour scheme, rough concrete walls and bons mots ('sweet nothings', for lack of a better translation) illuminated on the carpets. We love the open terrace on the 7th floor, the fabulous candle-lit pizzeria and the iMac in every room. Only drawback: Mama Shelter is a hike to the nearest metro stop.

HÔTEL DAVAL Map p158   Hotel €€

☎ 01 47 00 51 23; www.hoteldaval.com; 21 rue Daval, 11e; s €81, d €89-98, tr/q €109/127; M Bastille; 🖾 🛜 Always a favourite, this 23-room property is a very central option if you're looking for almost budget accommodation just off place de la Bastille. What's more, a refit has brought it well into the 21st century. Rooms and bathrooms are on the small side and if you're looking for some peace and quiet choose a back room (eg room 13).

HÔTEL DU PRINTEMPS
Map p158   Hotel €

☎ 01 43 43 62 31; www.hotel-paris-printemps. com; 80 blvd de Picpus, 12e; s €68-85, d & tw €76-105, tr € 98-120; M Picpus; 🛜 It may not be in the centre of the action, but the 38-room fresh as 'Spring Hotel' offers excellent value for its standard and location just steps from place de la Nation. What's more, there's an in-house bar open day and night. Some singles have showers but share a toilet, though that will have changed by the time you read this. All doubles have everything.

HÔTEL LES SANS CULOTTES

Map p158   Hotel €

☎ 0 877 952 230, 01 48 05 42 92; www.lessans culottesfr.com; 27 rue de Lappe, 11e; s/d from €60/75; Ⓜ Bastille

The nine rooms of this hotel above a nice little bistro (p266) of the same name are on the small side but are clean, tidy and decorated in bright colours and floral patterns. Best of all, the place is very central to restaurants and nightlife of the Bastille. Be warned that there is no lift here, though.

HÔTEL LE COSY Map p158   Hotel €

☎ 01 43 43 10 02; www.hotel-cosy.com; 50 av de St-Mandé, 12e; s €45-65, d €55-110; Ⓜ Picpus; ✂ 🛜

This slightly eccentric budget hotel immediately southeast of place de la Nation oozes charm. The 28 rooms, though basic (the cheapest singles and doubles have WC and washbasins only), are all decorated in warm pastels and have hardwood floors. If you're feeling flush, choose one of four air-conditioned 'VIP' double rooms in the courtyard annexe, especially room 3 or 4 on the 1st floor. There's a decent café–restaurant under the same name next door.

HOSTEL BLUE PLANET Map p158   Hostel €

☎ 01 43 42 06 18; www.hostelblueplanet.com; 5 rue Hector Malot, 12e; dm €25; Ⓜ Gare de Lyon; 🖳

This 43-room hostel is very close to Gare de Lyon – convenient if you're heading south or west at the crack of dawn or arriving in the wee hours. Dorm beds are in rooms for two to four people and the hostel closes between 11am and 3pm. There's no curfew. Internet access costs €3/6 for 30/60 minutes.

PLACE D'ITALIE & CHINATOWN

The 13e is where you'll find the Bibliothèque Nationale de France, as well as the *péniches* (barges) on the Seine fitted out with music clubs and restaurants. The southern chunk of this Left Bank arrondissement is a happy hunting ground for budget hotels.

HÔTEL LA DEMEURE Map p164   Hotel €€€

☎ 01 43 37 81 25; www.hotellademeureparis.com; 51 blvd St-Marcel, 13e; s/d €165/202; Ⓜ Les Gobelins; ✂ 🖳 🛜

This elegant little number at the bottom of the 5e is the domain of a charming father–son team (a former professional lawyer and a doctor, no less) who speak perfect English and are always at hand. Warm red and orange tones lend a real 'clubby' feel to public areas; wraparound balconies add extra appeal to corner rooms; and then there's those extra little touches – an iPod dock in every room, wine glasses for guests who like to BYO, art to buy on the walls…

HÔTEL LA MANUFACTURE

Map p164   Boutique Hotel €€

☎ 01 45 35 45 25; www.hotel-la-manufacture. com; 8 rue Philippe de Champagne, 13e; d €120-230; Ⓜ Place d'Italie; ✂ 🖳 🛜

The graceful, minimalist La Manufacture is located on the fringe of the Latin Quarter. The 57 individually decorated rooms adhere to clean lines and sport very bold plumage. Rooms on the top (7th) floor are the most spacious and coveted; room 71 boasts a view of the Panthéon while room 74 glimpses the Eiffel Tower. The lobby bar is a delight.

OOPS Map p164   Hostel €

☎ 01 47 07 47 00; www.oops-paris.com; 50 av des Gobelins, 13e; dm €28-35; Ⓜ Gobelins; 🖳 🛜

It might be discretely wedged between café terraces and shop fronts but once inside there is nothing discrete about this address aka 'Paris' first design hostel'. A lurid candyfloss-pink lift scales its six floors, each spotlessly clean and painted a different bold colour. Doubles (which can be booked in advance) are well sized and stylishly modern dorms max out at four to six beds, making it a superb choice for families. Breakfast is a particularly generous affair and, in keeping with that true spirit, hostel guests must vacate their room between 11am and 5pm. Reserve online.

MONTPARNASSE & 15E

With excellent links to both airports (p384) this is an easy – and affordable – area to plump for. East of Gare Montparnasse in the 14e, two- and three-star places stud rue Vandamme and rue de la Gaîté, though the latter is rife with sex shops and peep shows. The designer collection of boutique hotels around the Vavin metro station in the neighbouring 7e (p333) is as handy for Montparnasse as St-Germain.

Looking west, the 15e offers some decent accommodation options and a couple of hostels, well known among backpackers and budget travellers.

HÔTEL DELAMBRE Map p168 Hotel €€
☎ 01 43 20 66 31; www.delambre-paris-hotel. com; 35 rue Delambre, 14e; s €90, d €140-160; Ⓜ Montparnasse–Bienvenüe; ❌ ▯ 🛜 ♿
This very attractive 30-room hotel just east of Gare Montparnasse takes wrought iron as a theme and uses it both in functional pieces (bed frames, lamps, shelving) and decorative items throughout. Room 7 has its own little terrace while rooms 1 and 2 look onto a small private courtyard. The writer André Breton (1896–1966) lived here in the 1920s.

LA MAISON Map p168 Boutique Hotel €€
☎ 01 45 42 11 39; www.lamaisonmontparnasse. com; 53 rue de Gergovie, 14e; s/d/tr Mon-Thu €110/130/140, Fri-Sun €89/109/119; Ⓜ Pernety; ❌ ▯ 🛜
New kid on the block with seductive prices to match, the House goes all out to recreate home. And it does a sterling job. Enjoy homemade cakes and jams for breakfast in the stylish, open-plan kitchen–lounge or around pea-green tables in the loveliest little courtyard garden – reason alone to stay here. The dazzling, candy-striped staircase carpet leading to its 36 rooms (there's a box-sized lift too) might not be to everyone's taste, but the rooms are: think a designer mix of bold pinks, violets and soft neutral tones.

HÔTEL CARLADEZ CAMBRONNE
Map p168 Hotel €€
☎ 01 47 34 07 12; www.hotelcarladez.com; 3 place du Général Beuret, 15e; s/d/tr/q €92/95/167/180; Ⓜ Vaugirard; ▯ 🛜
This small, very dynamic hotel sits aplomb on a quintessential neighbourhood square, bench-clad beneath trees in the middle and framed with a couple of cafés with busy pavement terraces. Inside, 28 comfortable rooms are furnished in an attractive, unassuming manner and room No 11 opens directly onto a tiny courtyard with a table for two. Rent coffee- and tea-making facilities from reception (€6 for the duration of

your stay) and make yourself at home. Mid-July to mid-August and over Christmas low season rates – about €10 less – kick in.

HÔTEL DE LA PAIX
Map p168 Boutique Hotel €€
☎ 01 43 20 35 82; www.paris-montparnasse -hotel.com; 225 blvd Raspail, 14e; d €93-165; Ⓜ Montparnasse–Bienvenüe; ❌ ▯ 🛜 ♿
Stunningly good value, this recently re-styled hotel stacked on seven floors of a 1970s building (the façade still needs to be renovated) is a real charmer. A hip mix of industrial workshop and côte maison (home-like), its 39 rooms are light, modern and have at least one vintage feature in each – old pegs to hang coats on, old-fashioned school desk, wooden-slat house shutters recycled as bed head. Cheaper rooms are simply smaller than dearer ones. Oh, and the circular contraption in the reception lounge used to clock factory workers in and out…

HÔTEL AMIRAL FONDARY
Map p168 Hotel €€
☎ 01 45 75 14 75; www.amiral-fondary.com, in French; 30 rue Fondary, 15e; s €74-109, d €85-109; Ⓜ Av Émile Zola; ❌ ▯ 🛜
This reasonably priced hotel in the far-flung (but well served by metro) 15e is an excellent choice for the price. The 20 rooms are modest but well maintained; choose one looking onto the pretty (and very leafy) little courtyard that is such a delight in the warm weather.

CELTIC HÔTEL Map p168 Hotel €
☎ 01 43 20 93 53; hotelceltic@wanadoo.fr; 15 rue d'Odessa, 14e; s €49-55, d €74-95; Ⓜ Edgar Quinet; 🛜
A cheapie of the old school, this 29-room hotel is an old-fashioned place with a small lift and an up-to-date reception area with new furniture. The cheaper singles are pretty bare and even the en suite doubles and triples are not exactly tout confort (with all the mod cons), but Gare Montparnasse is only 200m away.

HÔTEL DE BLOIS Map p168 Hotel €
☎ 01 45 40 99 48; www.hoteldeblois.com; 5 rue des Plantes, 14e; s €55-80, d €60-89; Ⓜ Mouton-Duvernet; ▯ 🛜
This 25-room establishment south of Gare Montparnasse, just off big-street av du Maine, is a very cheery, affordable one-star

address – tatty from the outside, well renovated inside. Stylish rooms are stacked on five floors (no lift) and are smallish but modern; the cheapest have a shower or bath but share a toilet. Breakfast around one large shared table is rather like breakfasting at home. Wi-fi costs €3/5 per hour/five hours (free for stays of three days or more).

PETIT PALACE HÔTEL Map p168   Hotel €
☎ 01 43 22 05 25; www.paris-hotel-petit-palace. com; 131 av du Maine, 14e; d €60-85, tr €99; Ⓜ Gaîté; 💻

A palace in the conventional sense it is not; an excellent-value two-star hotel run by the same family since the 1950s it is. Strung on a main boulevard beaded with locally loved cafés and bistros, this hotel has 41 smallish but spotless rooms, several of which sleep three or four comfortably, making it a solid family choice. Look for the rather austere marble-clad facade cheered up with geraniums in the window. Wi-fi costs €4.50 per hour and parking is €11 per day.

ALOHA HOSTEL Map p168   Hostel €
☎ 01 42 73 03 03; www.aloha.fr; 1 rue Borromée, 15e; per person dm/d €25/28 incl breakfast; Ⓜ Volontaires; 💻 📶

A line-up of flags flutter outside this laid-back crash pad with a rainbow of colours as paint job (love the bright violet staircase) and opera music adding a touch of funk to the hybrid reception–lounge. Dorms have four to eight beds and the cream of the crop is its rooms for two (which cannot be reserved in advance). Rooms are locked from 11am to 5pm, curfew is at 2am, kitchen facilities are available and reception lends guests umbrellas and hairdryers.

EXCURSIONS

Paris is encircled by the Île de France (literally 'Island of France'), the romantically named 12,000-sq-km area around Paris. It is shaped by five rivers and Seine tributaries: the Epte in the northwest, the Aisne (northeast), the Eure (southwest), the Yonne (southeast) and the Marne (east). From this relatively small area the kingdom of France began to expand beginning around 1100.

Today the region's excellent rail and road links with the French capital and its exceptional sights – châteaux, cathedrals, towns that hosted and inspired Impressionist painters, theme parks – make it especially popular with day-trippers from Paris. The many woodland areas around the city, including the forests of Fontainebleau and Chantilly, offer unlimited outdoor activities within easy striking distance of the capital.

Information & Tours

The official Paris Île de France (www.nouveau-paris-ile -de-france.fr) website is a treasure trove of information on the area, and you can gem up on exactly where you're going with IGN's *Île de France* (1:250,000; €5.70) or its larger scale *Paris et Ses Environs* (1:100,000; €4.30).

If you're pressed for time or don't want to do it alone, hop on an air-conditioned coach:

Cityrama (Map p72; ☎ 01 44 55 60 00; www.paris cityrama.com; 2 rue des Pyramides, 1er; Ⓜ Tuileries) Half-day trips to Versailles (€54 to €74) or Chartres (€63); day trips combining the State Apartments at Versailles with Chartres (€110), with Fontainebleau (€115) or with Giverny (€145).

Paris Vision (Map p72; ☎ 01 42 60 30 01; www.paris vision.com; 214 rue de Rivoli, 1er; Ⓜ Tuileries) Half-day trips to Versailles/Giverny (€67/70), or a full day to both Giverny and Versailles (€145). Many more including Fontainebleau, Barbizon and Vaux-le-Vicomte (€147), Disneyland (from €81) and Parc Astérix (€62).

CHÂTEAUX

The Île de France counts some of the nation's most extravagant châteaux, in particular Versailles, whose opulence and extravagances both inside and out were partially what spurred the revolutionary mob to storm the Bastille in July 1789. The fabled château at Fontaine-bleau (p362) is one of the most important Renaissance palaces in France while the nearby (and lesser-known) Vaux-le-Vicomte (p366) was designed by the same architect who was responsible for Versailles. Those who shun crowds should consider art-rich Chantilly (p366) with its heavenly stables, gardens and woodlands.

CATHEDRALS

The area also claims some of the nation's most beautiful – and ambitious – cathedrals. Senlis (p370) near Chantilly has a magnificent Gothic cathedral said to have inspired elements of the mother of all basilicas, the cathedral at Chartres (p370). The latter, with its breathtaking stained glass and intricately carved stone portals, is one of Western architecture's greatest achievements and unmissable. As for blind ambition nothing compares with the cathedral at Beauvais (p375), which attempted to reach too high before its time and partially collapsed.

ART TOWNS

Art lovers – but especially aficionados of Impressionism – will be inspired by Giverny (p376), with Monet's pink-and-green house and flower-filled garden. Strangely moving is Auvers-sur-Oise (p377), the place where Van Gogh painted like mad for two months before dying in the bedroom of a cheap inn from a self-inflicted bullet wound.

VERSAILLES

Seven hundred rooms, 67 staircases, 352 chimneys, 2153 windows, 6300 paintings, 2100 sculptures and statues, 15,000 engravings, 5000 decorative art objects and furnishings, more than five million château visitors annually: no wonder visiting France's most famous, grandest palace can be overwhelming. Six days a week (the château is shut Monday) tourist madness consumes the prosperous, leafy and bourgeois suburb of Versailles (population 84,225), political capital and seat of the royal court from 1682 until 1789, when Revolutionary mobs massacred the palace guard and

dragged Louis XVI and Marie-Antoinette back to Paris to eventually lop off their heads.

It was during the reign of the Sun King Louis XIV (1643–1715) that Château de Versailles (☎ 01 30 83 78 00; www.châteauversailles.fr; palace ticket adult/EU citizen under 26yr & everyone under 18yr €15/free, from 3pm €10/free, Passeport sold until 3pm adult/EU citizen under 26yr & everyone under 18yr €20/free Wed-Fri & €25/free Tue, Sat & Sun Apr-Oct, €18/free Nov-Mar; ☉ 9am-6.30pm Tue-Sun Apr-Oct, 9am-5.30pm Tue-Sun Nov-Mar) was built. The basic palace ticket and more elaborate Passeport both include an English-language audioguide and allow visitors to freely visit the King's and Queen's State Apartments, chapel, the Dauphin's Apartments and various galleries. The Passeport additionally gets you into the Grand and Petit Trianons and, in high season, the Hameau de la Reine and the Grandes Eaux Musicales fountain displays.

Intended to house his court of 6000 people, the sheer scale and decor of Versailles reflected not only the absolute power of the French monarchy but also Louis XIV's taste for profligate luxury and appetite for self-glorification. He hired four talented men to take on the gargantuan task: architect Louis Le Vau; Jules Hardouin-Mansart, who took over from Le Vau in the mid-1670s; painter and interior designer Charles Le Brun; and landscape designer André Le Nôtre, under whom entire hills were flattened, marshes drained and forests moved to create the seemingly endless gardens, ponds and fountains for which Versailles is so well known. It has been on Unesco's World Heritage list since 1979.

The vast château complex – get a folding map from the tourist office – divides into four main sections: the 580m-long palace building with its innumerable wings, bedchambers, halls, and state apartments; the vast gardens, canals and pools to the west of the palace; two

DAY TRIP PLANNER

In true French fashion, even the biggest of sights shut one day a week. Note the following when planning your excursion(s):

- Monday – Château de Versailles (p356), Auvers-sur-Oise's Van Gogh sights (p377) and Monet's house in Giverny (p376) are all shut.
- Tuesday – Château de Fontainebleau (p362), Château de Chantilly (p366) and Château d'Auvers (p378) are all shut.
- Wednesday – Château de Vaux-le-Vicomte (p366) is closed from September to June.

smaller palaces known as the Grand Trianon and the Petit Trianon to the northwest; and the Hameau de la Reine (Queen's Hamlet) north of the Petit Trianon. Few alterations have been made to the château since its construction, bar most of the interior furnishings disappearing during the Revolution and many of the rooms being rebuilt by Louis-Philippe (r 1830–48), who opened part of the château to the public in 1837. The current €400 million restoration program is the most ambitious yet and until it's completed in 2020 a part of the palace is likely to be clad in scaffolding when you visit. Families with babies and young children should note that pushchairs (prams), even folded, are not allowed inside the palace; they must be left at Entrée A.

Luxurious, ostentatious appointments – frescoes, marble, gilt and woodcarvings, with themes and symbols drawn from Greek and Roman mythology – ooze from every last moulding, cornice, ceiling and door in the palace's Grands Appartements du Roi et de la Reine (King's and Queen's State Apartments). But the opulence peaks in its shimmering and sparkling Galerie des Glaces (Hall of Mirrors). This 75m-long ballroom with 17 giant mirrors on one side and an equal number of windows on the other has to be seen to be believed.

History and/or art buffs keen to delve deeper into life at court, music, the private apartments of Louis XV and Louis XI and so on can sign up for an informative lecture tour (☎ 01 30 83 78 00; adult with/without palace ticket, Passeport or ticket to the Domaine de Marie-Antoinette €7.50/14.50, under 18yr €5.50; ☉ 9am-3.15pm Tue-Sun), some in English, at the main ticket office.

The Hall of Mirrors peeps over part of the palace gardens & park (admission free except Tue, Sat & Sun Apr-Oct during the Grandes Eaux Musicales; ☉ gardens 8.30am-8.30pm Apr-Oct, 8am-6pm Nov-Mar, park 7am-7pm Apr-Oct, 8am-6pm Nov-Mar), laid out in the formal French style between 1661 and 1700. Famed for their geometrically aligned terraces, flowerbeds, tree-lined paths, ponds and fountains, they are studded with 400 marble, bronze and lead statues sculpted by the most talented sculptors of the period – winter visitors won't get to see them, as these are covered at this time of year. Meandering, sheltered paths snake through the more pastoral English-style Jardins du Petit Trianon.

The gardens' largest fountains are the 17th-century Bassin de Neptune (Neptune's Fountain), a dazzling mirage of 99 spouting fountains 300m north of the palace, and the Bassin d'Apollon (Apollo's Fountain), built in 1668 at the eastern end of the Grand Canal. The straight side of the Bassin de Neptune abuts a small, round pond graced by a winged dragon. Emerging from the water in the centre of the Bassin d'Apollon is Apollo's chariot, pulled by rearing horses. A truly magical, must-experience are the Grandes Eaux Musicales (adult/6-18yr/under 6yr €8/6/free; 11am-noon & 3.30-5.30pm Tue, Sat & Sun Apr-Sep) and Grandes Eaux Nocturnes (adult/6-18yr/under 6yr €21/17/free; 9-11.30pm Sat mid-Jun–Aug) fountain displays set to the sweet tones of baroque and classical composers throughout the grounds in summer. The grand finale of these fabulous fountain dances to soul-stirring classical music sees the Bassin de Neptune flow for 10 minutes from 5.20pm. Set the soul stirring still further with the fountains' fabulous summertime performances at night! Brilliantly lit, it is a performance to remember. Reserve tickets in advance at the Billeterie Spectacle (☎ 01 30 83 78 89; www.châteauversailles-spectacles.fr; place d'Armes; 10am-6pm Tue-Sun Apr-Sep) in front of the château or on the same day directly at garden entrances.

The Grand Canal, 1.6km long and 62m wide, is oriented to reflect the setting sun and is traversed by the 1km-long Petit Canal, thus forming a cross-shaped body of water with a perimeter of more than 5.5km. Louis XIV used to hold boating parties here. In summer you can paddle around the Grand Canal in four-person rowing boats; the dock is at the canal's eastern end. The Orangerie, built below the Parterre du Midi (a flowerbed) on the southwestern side of the palace, houses exotic plants in winter.

In the middle of the vast 90-hectare park, about 1.5km northwest of the main palace, is the Domaine de Marie-Antoinette (Marie-Antoinette's Estate; adult/adult after 4pm/EU citizen under 26yr & everyone under 18yr €10/6/free Apr-Oct, adult/EU citizen under 26yr & everyone under 18yr €6/free Nov-Mar; noon-6.30pm Apr-Oct, noon-5.30pm Nov-Mar). High-season tickets cover admission to the Grand and Petit Trianon, the Hameau de la Reine, Marie-Antoinette's dairy, theatre, English garden and so on; low-season tickets only cover the Grand Trianon, Petit Trianon and gardens. The pink-colonnaded Grand Trianon was built in 1687 for Louis XIV and his family as a place of escape from the rigid etiquette of the court. Napoleon I had it renovated in the Empire style. The ochre-coloured Petit Trianon, dating to the 1760s, was redecorated in 1867 by consort of Napoleon III, Empress Eugénie, who added Louis XVI-style furnishings. A little further north on the estate is the Hameau de la Reine, a mock village of

top picks

TO MAKE VERSAILLES VISITS MORE PLEASANT

- To avoid disappointment, resign yourself to queuing for everything, be it tickets for the château and getting into it (two vastly different things), renting an electric car or using the public toilets.
- It can't be stressed enough: buy your château ticket in advance of stepping foot in Versailles – online (www.chateauversailles.fr) or from a branch of FNAC (p294).
- Should you arrive in Versailles ticket-less, bulldoze straight to the tourist office to buy a Passeport. It will save you time.
- By noon both queues spiral out of control: visit the palace first thing in the morning or after 4pm; avoid Tuesday and Sunday, its busiest days.
- Don't miss the show! Tickets for the Grandes Eaux Musicales and Grandes Eaux Nocturnes can be like gold dust in high season. Gem up on what's on and reserve your seat by telephone or online (☎ 01 30 83 78 89; www.chateauversaillesspectacles.fr). Advance reservations are even more imperative for Bartabas' masterful equestrian displays.

thatched cottages constructed from 1775 to 1784 for the amusement of Marie-Antoinette, who played milkmaid here.

Given the park is so vast the only way to see it all is to hire a four-person electric car (☎ 01 39 66 97 66; www.astel-loisirs.com; per hr €30; drivers must be over 23yr and show their driving licence); hop aboard the train shuttle (☎ 01 39 54 22 00; www.train-versailles.com; adult/11-18yr €6.50/5), which stops at the Petit Trianon, Grand Trianon and Grand Canal; or rent a bike (☎ 01 39 66 97 66; www.astel-loisirs.com; per hr €6.50, half-day €15) from the kiosk at the eastern end of the Grand Canal or northwest of the Bassin de Neptune.

The attractive town of Versailles, crisscrossed by wide boulevards, is another Louis XIV creation. In the late 17th century the three wide thoroughfares that fan out eastwards from place d'Armes in front of the château – av de St-Cloud, av de Paris and av de Sceaux – were separated by two vast stable blocks. Versailles' celebrated school of architecture and restoration workshops fill the Petites Écuries (Little Stables) today; but it is to the Grandes Écuries (Big Stables) – stage for the prestigious Académie du Spectacle Équestre (Academy

lonelyplanet.com

VERSAILLES

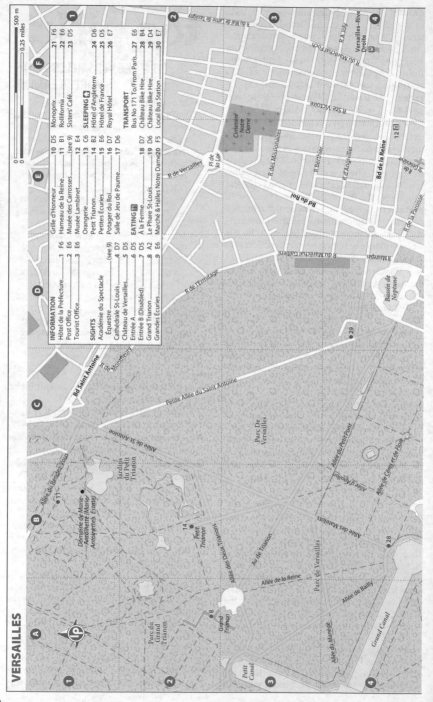

INFORMATION	
Hôtel de la Préfecture...................1	F6
Post Office...................................2	E6
Tourist Office...............................3	E6

SIGHTS	
Académie du Spectacle	
Équestre...............................(see 9)	
Cathédrale St-Louis.....................4	D7
Château de Versailles..................5	D5
Entrée A....................................6	D5
Entrée B (Disabled).....................7	D5
Grand Trianon............................8	A2
Grandes Écuries..........................9	E6

Grille d'Honneur.........................10	D5
Hameau de la Reine.....................11	B1
Musée des Carrosses................(see 9)	
Musée Lambinet..........................12	E4
Orangerie..................................13	C6
Petit Trianon..............................14	B2
Petites Écuries............................15	E6
Potager du Roi............................16	D7
Salle de Jeu de Paume..................17	D6

SLEEPING	
Hôtel d'Angleterre.......................24	D6
Hôtel de France...........................25	D5
Royal Hôtel.................................26	E7

EATING	
A la Ferme..................................18	D7
Le Phare St-Louis.........................19	D6
Marché & Halles Notre Dame.........20	E6

Monoprix...................................21	F6
Rolliforna...................................22	E6
Sisters' Café...............................23	D5

TRANSPORT	
Bus No 171 To/From Paris.............27	E6
Château Bike Hire........................28	B4
Château Bike Hire........................29	D4
Local Bus Station.........................30	E7

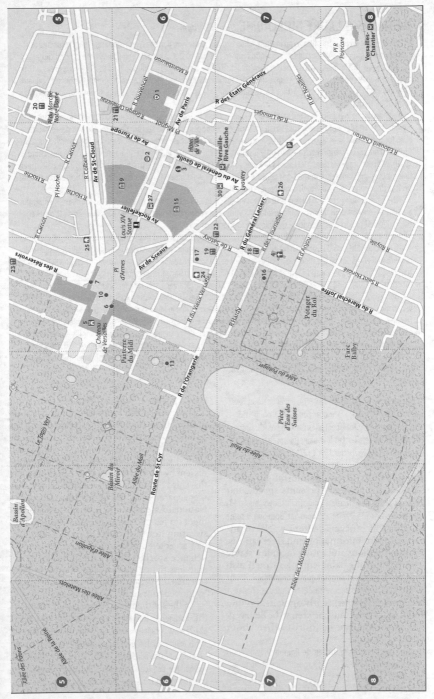

BARTABAS & LAURE GUILLAUME *Nicola Williams*

The press might well portray him as an impulsive bad boy but in the ring Bartabas – passionate, highly respected horse trainer, choreographer and film director of world renown – is the master of his own exquisitely orchestrated ceremony.

'Bartabas is the founder, artistic director and teacher of the academy. His philosophy is to develop a great artistic direction in all its forms in each rider, to give that rider sufficient autonomy to train, care and respect the horses,' explains academy equerry and teaching assistant Laure Guillaume. 'He is the heart of the academy – nothing is undertaken without his support.'

Each day in the red-brick vaulted stables at Versailles (built in 1693 to house King Louis XIV's 600 horses), some 15 equerries of Bartabas' Academy of Equestrian Art (Académie du Spectacle Équestre) are put through their paces. Students train for three years in song, dance, artistic fencing and *kyudo* (Japanese archery) before becoming an *écuyer titulaire* (qualified rider) – of which there are currently just five. Indeed, in the chandelier-lit ring during Les Matinales, Laure (b 1970), with the academy since 1991, looks like she's stepped right out of an equestrian painting. Wearing a pale-green riding jacket with ornately trimmed cuff beneath a dark-green wool cape with fur collar, this poised horsewoman with perfect chignon and enviably high cheekbones cuts a dashing figure.

'The hardest thing at the academy is to go from a course in riding to singing, then *kyudo* – it requires an enormous amount of concentration, but you quickly adapt,' Laure says, adding that riders work six days a week, with weekends being devoted to Bartabas' signature spellbinding *spectacles* (shows).

Most of the 40 mounts – Pas de Deux, Treize et Trois, Kimono, Nord and Dalí to name a few – are of the same chalk-coloured, blue-eyed Lusitanian breed kept by Louis XIV. The stubbier zebra-styled horses who gallop dramatically towards audiences during the morning training sessions to the sound of baroque music are Argentine Criollos – the hardy traditional mount of the South American cowboy and polo player. Champagne is a short stocky Quarter Horse, Edwin a thoroughbred Arab, and the six in the well-bred cavalry named after solar system planets are Sorayas.

'Horses are selected according to their race, colour and aptitudes: Lusitanians are excellent in dressage, and Criollos, very handy and fast, are used for artistic fencing', explains Laure. 'Certain horses are also selected *sur un coup de cœur* (on love at first sight)', she adds. For riders, the academy must be more than just a school or a job: 'Riders are recruited on equestrian ability, which must be very high, and also for their desire to make the academy their life's philosophy.'

Bartabas was first noticed during his teens in the late 1970s at Avignon's fringe theatre festival, Off. He went on to form his own equestrian theatre, aptly called Zingaro ('gitan' or 'gypsy' in Italian), and established the academy at Versailles in 2003 to both safeguard and promote his art.

of Equestrian Arts; ☎ 01 39 02 07 14, advance ticket reservations 0 892 681 891; www.acadequestre.fr, online tickets http://acadequestre.fnacspectacles.com, in French; Grandes Écuries, 1 av Rockefeller; Les Matinales (morning training sessions) adult/13-18yr/under 13yr €12/10/6.50; ☺ 11.15am Sat & Sun and some Thu) – that the crowds dash. In addition to its 45-minute morning training sessions, the academy presents spectacular Reprises Musicales (musical equestrian shows; adult/13-18yr/under 13yr €25/22/16; ☺ 6pm Sat, 3pm Sun & some Thu), for which tickets sell out weeks in advance; call for information and reservations. Training sessions and shows include a stable visit. Within the same complex you'll also find the Musée des Carrosses (Carriage Museum; ☎ 01 30 83 78 00; www.châteauversailles.fr; Grandes Écuries, 1 av Rockefeller; ☺ varies), with opulent moving conveyances that must be seen to be believed. Ask at the château or tourist office about opening times.

Nearby, the Salle du Jeu de Paume (Royal Tennis Court Room; ☎ 01 39 24 88 88; 1 rue du Jeu de Paume; admission €8; ☺ guided tour 3pm Sat) was built in 1686 and played a pivotal role in the Revolution a

century later. It was in Versailles that Louis XVI convened the États-Généraux made up of more than 1000 deputies representing the nobility, clergy and the so-called Third Estate (ie the middle classes) in May 1789 in a bid to deal with national debt and to moderate dissent by reforming the tax system. But when the Third Estate's reps were denied entry, they met separately on the tennis court, formed a National Assembly and took the famous Serment du Jeu de Paume (Tennis Court Oath), swearing not to dissolve it until Louis XVI had accepted a new constitution. This act of defiance sparked demonstrations of support and, less than a month later, a mob in Paris stormed the prison at Bastille. It can be visited by guided tour only.

To the south, behind a stone wall, slumbers the Potager du Roi (King's Kitchen Garden; ☎ 01 39 24 62 62; www.potager-du-roi.fr, in French; 10 rue du Maréchal Joffre; adult weekday/weekend €4.50/6.50, 12-18yr €3, under 12yr free Apr-Oct, admission all Nov-Mar €3; ☺ 10am-6pm Tue-Sun Apr-Oct, 10am-6pm Tue & Thu, 10am-1pm Sat Nov & Dec, 10am-1pm Tue & Thu Jan-Mar), laid out on nine hectares of land in the late 17th century to meet the enormous catering requirements of the court. It retains its original patch divisions and many old apple and pear orchards, producing 70 tonnes of vegetables and fruit a year.

In the same *quartier*, one of Versailles' prettiest, is the neoclassical Cathédrale St-Louis (☎ 01 39 50 40 65; 4 place St-Louis; ⏱ 8.30am-noon & 2-7.45pm), a harmonious if austere work built between 1743 and 1754, and made a cathedral in 1802. It is known for its 3636-pipe Cliquot organ and is decorated with some interesting paintings and stained-glass panels. To the northeast of the château just around the corner from the Versailles–Rive Droite train station, and housed in a lovely 18th-century residence, the Musée Lambinet (Lambinet Museum; ☎ 01 39 50 30 32; www.musee-lambinet.fr; 54 blvd de la Reine; adult/child €5.50/2.50, last Sun of the month free; ⏱ 2-6pm Tue, Thu, Sat & Sun, 1-6pm Wed, 2-5pm Fri) displays 18th-century furnishings (ceramics, sculpture, paintings and furniture) and objects connected with the history of Versailles, including the all-important Revolutionary period.

INFORMATION

Post Office (av de Paris)

Tourist Office (☎ 01 39 24 88 88; www.versailles-tourisme.com; 2bis av de Paris; ⏱ 10am-6pm Mon, 9am-7pm Tue-Sun Apr-Sep, 11am-5pm Sun & Mon, 9am-6pm Tue-Sat Oct-Mar) Sells the Passeport to Château de Versailles, a detailed visitor's guide (small €8.50, large €15) and also an IGN walking map of the area (€10.20).

EATING

Rue de Satory is lined with restaurants serving cuisine from everywhere, Indian, Chinese, Lebanese, Tunisian and Japanese included.

À la Ferme (☎ 01 39 53 10 81; www.alaferme-versailles.com; 3 rue du Maréchal Joffre; starters/mains €6.50/14, menus €17.90 & €22.50; ⏱ lunch & dinner to 11pm Wed-Sun) Cow-hide banquettes and rustic garlands strung from old wood beams add a country air to 'At the Farm', temple to grilled meats and cuisine from southwest France.

Sisters' Café (☎ 01 30 21 21 22; 15 rue des Réservoirs; menus €15.20-20.80; ⏱ lunch & dinner to 11pm Mon-Sat, noon-11pm Sun) Another break with French tradition, this relaxed 1950s-style American diner serves up club sandwiches, chicken fajitas, spinach salads and great weekend brunches. Mustard and ketchup (tomato sauce) are table standards.

Rollifornia (☎ 01 39 50 67 61; 9 rue de Satory; dishes €13-18; ⏱ lunch & dinner to 10.30pm) The dynamic choice of Versailles' sometimes stuffy dining scene: this young funky Korean quick-eat joint with designer green-and-white interior and the grooviest stainless-steel cutlery in the Île de France cooks up California rolls stuffed with imaginative combos. Good choice of vegetarian dishes.

Le Phare St-Louis (☎ 01 39 53 40 12; 33 rue du Vieux Versailles; menus €11-18; ⏱ lunch & dinner to 11pm) This cosy Breton place heaves. Pick from 15 savoury galettes (buckwheat pancakes; €3.60 to €9.80) and 40-odd different sweet crêpes (€3.60 to €7.10), including the Vieux Versailles (€5.60) topped with redcurrant jelly, pear and ice cream then set ablaze with Grand Marnier.

Self-Catering

Marché & Halles Notre Dame (place du Marché Notre Dame; ⏱ inside 7am-1pm & 3.30-7.30pm Tue-Sat, 7.30am-1pm Sun, outside 7.30am-2pm Tue, Fri & Sun) Indoor and outdoor food market.

Monoprix (9 rue Georges Clemenceau; 8.30am-9.30pm Mon-Sat)

TRANSPORT: VERSAILLES

Distance from Paris 28km

Direction Southwest

Travel time 30 to 35 minutes by RER/train

Bus 171 (€1.60 or 1 metro/bus ticket) from the Pont de Sèvres (15e) metro station to place d'Armes every six to nine minutes 5am (5.30am/6.30am Saturday/Sunday) to 1am.

Car A13 from Porte d'Auteuil, exit 'Versailles Château'

RER train Fastest way: the RER line C5 (€2.95) from Paris' Left Bank RER stations to Versailles–Rive Gauche station is 700m southeast of the château; trains run every 15 minutes until shortly before midnight. Less convenient: RER line C8 (€2.95) stops at Versailles-Chantiers station, a 1.3km walk from the château.

SNCF train From Paris' Gare St-Lazare (€3.70) SNCF operates 70-odd trains a day to Versailles–Rive Droite, 1.2km from the château. Versailles-Chantiers is likewise served by half-hourly SNCF trains daily from Gare Montparnasse (€2.95); trains on this line continue to Chartres (€11.50, 35 to 60 minutes).

Taxi Book a taxi in Versailles on ☎ 01 39 50 50 00 (www.taxis-abeille.com).

SLEEPING

Hôtel de France (☎ 01 30 83 92 23; www.hotelfrance -versailles.com; 5 rue Colbert; s & d €141, tr €174, ste €236; 🖳) If you're going to stay in this regal town, you may as well go the whole hog and plump for a canopied bed and floral bedspread in a three-star 18th-century townhouse. It's old, old-fashioned and across from the château, with 23 rooms.

Hôtel d'Angleterre (☎ 01 39 51 43 50; www.hotel -angleterre-versailles.com; 2bis rue de Fontenay; s €75-88, d €88-95, ste €120) On a quiet street away from the château mayhem sits this good-value 17-room hotel – look for the burnt-copper canopy and the lovely floral tiles above the entrance. The cheapest rooms only have a shower; rooms 15, 19 and 23 are family friendly.

Royal Hôtel (☎ 01 39 50 67 31; www.royalhotelversailles. com; 23 rue Royale; s € 65, d €65-95, tr & q €120; 🖳) In the delightful St-Louis neighbourhood, this 35-room hotel displays character and a fondness for patterned wallpaper. The smallish rooms mix bulk furnishings with old-fashioned touches and there are self-catering studios (€85 per night) for keen cooks. Laundry costs €3.50.

FONTAINEBLEAU

The smart town of Fontainebleau (population 21,800) grew up around its elegant Renaissance château, one of France's largest royal residences, surrounded by the beautiful Forêt de Fontainebleau (p364). The château is less crowded and pressured than Versailles and its forest – rich in walking, cycling, rock climbing, horse-riding opportunities and game – is as big a playground as it was in the 16th century.

The town's lifeblood is the international graduate business school Insead (www.insead.edu), which brings in some 2000 students a year and seals Fontainebleau's reputation as a nice respectable middle-class place to be – for the French and expats alike. The town has an Anglican church, its own Wednesday-morning English-language school and a dynamic pick of swish cafés, bars and cultural happenings. No wonder so many work in Paris but choose to live in this safe, healthy living space oozing, as many a local will tell you, 'a certain Swiss ambience'. It's twinned with the leafy (and well-heeled) London borough of Richmond.

Château de Fontainebleau (☎ 01 60 71 50 60; www. musee-château-fontainebleau.fr, in French; place Général de Gaulle; adult/18-25yr/EU citizen under 26yr & everyone under 18yr €8/6/free, 1st Sun of the month free for everyone; 🕙 9.30am-6pm Wed-Mon Apr-Sep, 9.30am-5pm Wed-Mon Oct-Mar), with its 1900 rooms, is one of France's most beautifully decorated and furnished châteaux. Walls and ceilings are richly coated with wood panelling, gilt carvings, frescoes, tapestries and paintings. The parquet floors are of the finest woods, the fireplaces are decorated with exceptional carvings, and many of the pieces of furniture are originals dating back to the Renaissance. An informative 1½-hour audioguide (included in the entrance fee) leads visitors around the main areas of the palace, whose list of former tenants or visitors is like a who's who of French royalty. Those who can't get enough will want to take one (or even both) of two daily **guided tours** (☎ 01 60 71 50 60; adult/18-25 yr €12.50/11; 1¼ hours) to the château's Musée Napoléon 1er (10.15am) and the Petits Appartements (2.30pm). Sign up for both tours (€19/16) and you get into the main part of the château for free. You can access the **château gardens & courtyards** (🕙 9am-7pm May-Sep, 9am-6pm Mar, Apr & Oct, 9am-5pm Nov-Feb) for free. The **park** is open 24 hours.

The first château on this site was built in the early 12th century and enlarged by Louis IX a century later. Only a single medieval tower survived the energetic Renaissance-style reconstruction undertaken by François I (r 1515–47), whose superb artisans, many of them brought over from Italy, blended Italian and French styles to create what is known as the First School of Fontainebleau. The *Mona Lisa* once hung here amid other fine artworks of the royal collection.

During the latter half of the 16th century, the château was further enlarged by Henri II (r 1547–59), Catherine de Médici and Henri IV (r 1589–1610), whose Flemish and French artists created the Second School of Fontainebleau. Even Louis XIV got in on the act: it was he who hired Le Nôtre to redesign the gardens.

Fontainebleau, which was not damaged during the Revolution (though its furniture was stolen or destroyed), was beloved and much restored by Napoleon Bonaparte. Napoleon III was another frequent visitor. During WWII the château was turned into a German headquarters. After it was liberated by US General George Patton in 1944, part of the complex served as Allied and then NATO headquarters from 1945 to 1965.

Visits take in the **State Apartments** (Grands Appartements), which embrace several outstanding rooms, including the Second-Empire salon and Musée Chinois de l'Impératice Eugénie (Chi-

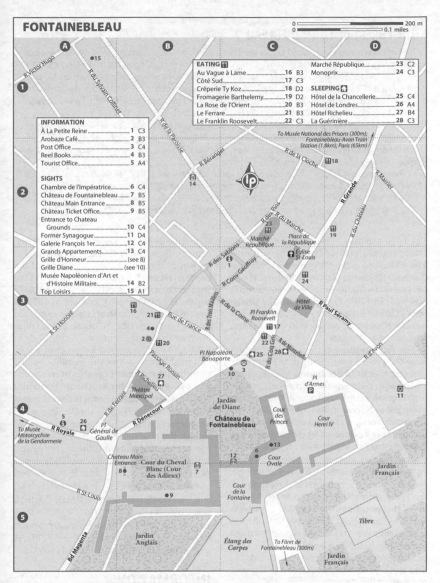

FONTAINEBLEAU

0 — 200 m
0 — 0.1 miles

INFORMATION
À La Petite Reine	**1** C3
Arobaze Café	**2** B3
Post Office	**3** C4
Reel Books	**4** B3
Tourist Office	**5** A4

SIGHTS
Chambre de l'Impératrice	**6** C4
Château de Fontainebleau	**7** B5
Château Main Entrance	**8** B5
Château Ticket Office	**9** B5
Entrance to Chateau Grounds	**10** C4
Former Synagogue	**11** D4
Galerie François 1er	**12** C4
Grands Appartements	**13** C4
Grille d'Honneur	(see 8)
Grille Diane	(see 10)
Musée Napoléonien d'Art et d'Histoire Militaire	**14** B2
Top Loisirs	**15** A1

EATING
Au Vague à Lame	**16** B3
Côté Sud	**17** C3
Crêperie Ty Koz	**18** D2
Fromagerie Barthelemy	**19** D2
La Rose de l'Orient	**20** B3
Le Ferrare	**21** B3
Le Franklin Roosevelt	**22** C3
Marché République	**23** C2
Monoprix	**24** C3

SLEEPING
Hôtel de la Chancellerie	**25** C4
Hôtel de Londres	**26** A4
Hôtel Richelieu	**27** B4
La Guérinière	**28** C3

nese Museum of Empress Eugénie), a set of four drawing rooms created in 1863 for the oriental art and curios collected by Napoleon III's wife. Louis XV wed Marie Leczinska in 1725 and the future Napoleon III was christened in 1810 in the spectacular **Chapelle de la Trinité** (Trinity Chapel), with ornamentation dating from the first half of the 17th century. The **Galerie François 1er** (François I Gallery), a jewel of Renaissance architecture, was deco-

rated from 1533 to 1540 by Il Rosso, a Florentine follower of Michelangelo. In the wood panelling, François I's monogram appears repeatedly, along with his emblem, a dragonlike salamander.

The **Salle de Bal** (Ballroom), a 30m-long room dating from the mid-16th century that was also used for receptions and banquets, is renowned for its mythological frescoes, marquetry floor and Italian-inspired coffered ceiling.

THE FOREST OF FONTAINEBLEAU

The Forêt de Fontainebleau, a 20,000-hectare wood surrounding the town, is among the region's loveliest. National walking trails GR1 and GR11 are excellent for jogging, walking, cycling and horse riding, and for climbers the forest is a veritable paradise. Rock-climbing enthusiasts have long come to its sandstone ridges, rich in cliffs and overhangs, to hone their skills before setting off for the Alps. There are different grades marked by colours, with white representing easy climbs (suitable for children) and black representing climbs up and over death-defying boulders. The website Bleau (http://bleau.info) has stacks of information on climbing in the forest.

To give it a go, contact Top Loisirs (☎ 01 60 74 08 50; www.toploisirs.fr, in French; 16 rue du Sylvain Collinet) about equipment hire and instruction. Two gorges worth visiting are the Gorges d'Apremont, 7km northwest near Barbizon, and the Gorges de Franchard, a few kilometres south of Gorges d'Apremont. The tourist office sells *Fontainebleau Climbs: The Finest Bouldering and Circuits* (€25).

The area is covered by IGN's 1:25,000 scale *Forêt de Fontainebleau* map (No 2417OT; €10.40). The tourist office sells the *Guide des Sentiers de Promenades dans le Massif Forestier de Fontainebleau* (€12), whose maps and French text cover 19 forest walks, and *À Pied en Famille – Autour de Fontainebleau* (€8.30), which maps 18 family walks, 2.5km to 5km long. It also stocks a two-hour French-language DVD called *La Forêt de Fontainebleau* (€14.90).

The large windows afford views of the Cour Ovale (Oval Courtyard) and the gardens. The gilded bed in the 17th- and 18th-century Chambre de l'Impératrice (Empress' Bedroom) was never used by Marie-Antoinette, for whom it was built in 1787. The gilding in the Salle du Trône (Throne Room), the royal bedroom before the Napoleonic period, is in three shades: gold, green and yellow.

The Petits Appartements (Small Apartments) were the private apartments of the emperor and empress; the Musée Napoléon 1er (Napoleon I Museum) contains uniforms, hats, coats, ornamental swords and knick-knacks that belonged to Napoleon and his relatives. True aficionados can get a second dose of him at the town's Musée Napoléonien d'Art et d'Histoire Militaire (Napoleonic Museum of Art & Military History; ☎ 01 60 74 64 89; 88 rue St-Honoré; adult/under 12yr €4/free; museum 2-5.30pm Tue-Sat, garden 10am-6pm or 7pm Tue-Sat), six rooms of military uniforms and weapons in the 19th-century Villa Lavaurs in town.

As successive monarchs added their own wings to the château, five irregularly shaped courtyards were created. The oldest and most interesting is the Cour Ovale, no longer oval but U-shaped due to Henri IV's construction work. It incorporates the keep, the sole remnant of the medieval château. The largest courtyard is the Cour du Cheval Blanc (Courtyard of the White Horse), from where you enter the château. Napoleon, about to be exiled to Elba in 1814, bid farewell to his guards from the magnificent 17th-century double-horseshoe staircase here. For that reason the courtyard is also called the Cour des Adieux (Farewell Courtyard).

On the northern side of the château is the Jardin de Diane, a formal garden created by Catherine de Médici. Le Nôtre's formal, 17th-century Jardin Français (French Garden), also known as the Grand Parterre, is east of the Cour de la Fontaine (Fountain Courtyard) and the Étang des Carpes (Carp Pond). The informal Jardin Anglais (English Garden), laid out in 1812, is west of the pond. The Grand Canal was excavated in 1609 and predates the canals at Versailles by more than half a century.

Should you be around longer than a day, you might catch one of the monthly guided visits the tourist office organises of an eclectic trio of lesser-known attractions: Fontaine-bleau's Musée National des Prisons (National Museum of Prisons; ☎ 01 60 74 99 99; adult/6-12yr €8/6.50; guided tour 3pm last Fri of month), a gruesome portrait of French prisons from the 17th century to the present in a magnificent 19th-century prison with 30 cells; its Musée Motocycliste de la Gendarmerie (Police Motorcycle Museum; ☎ 01 60 74 99 99; Camp Guymener; adult/6-12yr €8/6.50; guided tour quarterly); and the Centre Sportif d'Équitation Militaire (Sporting & Military Horseriding Centre; (☎ 01 60 74 99 99; allée Maintenon; adult/6-12yr €8/6.50; guided tour 10am last Wed of month), where mounted French army officers and 50 military horses are trained each year.

INFORMATION

À La Petite Reine (☎ 01 60 74 57 57; 32 rue des Sablons; hire per hr/day/week €5/15/55; 9am-7.30pm Tue-Sat, 9am-6pm Sun) Bike hire for adults and kids; a helmet or a child's seat each cost €3.

Arobaze Café (☎ 01 60 72 24 52; www.arobazecafe.eu, in French; 5 rue de Ferrare; per hr €3; 10am-10pm Mon-Sat, 2-8pm Sun) Internet café with 30 machines.

Post Office (2 rue de la Chancellerie)

Reelbooks (☎ 01 64 22 85 85; 9 rue de Ferrare; ◷ 11am-7pm Tue-Sat) English bookshop with new and secondhand titles, and a great noticeboard crammed with ads aimed at the large local Anglophone community.

Tourist Office (☎ 01 60 74 99 99; www.fontainebleau -tourisme.com; 4 rue Royale; ◷ 10am-6pm Mon-Sat, 10am-12.30pm & 3-5pm Sun May-Oct, 10am-6pm Mon-Sat, 10am-1pm Sun Nov-Apr) A converted petrol station west of the château. It sells loads of walking guides and maps; takes prepaid bookings for visits to the National Prison Museum, Police Motorcycle Museum and Sporting and Military Horseriding Centre; and has a half-dozen bikes for hire (€5/15/19 per hour/half-day/24 hours); reserve bikes in advance.

EATING

There are lovely café terraces on which to soak up the sun across from the château on place Napoléon Bonaparte, behind the old-fashioned merry-go-round, and there are a couple of drinking options on rue de la Corne. Rue de Montebello tours the world with Indian, Lebanese and other international cuisine.

Côté Sud (☎ 01 64 22 00 33; 1 rue de Montebello; starters €10-18, mains €18-24, menus €23-29; lunch & dinner daily) Our new favourite eatery, this sunny restaurant with dishes that have a southern accent, such as *daube de sanglier* (wild boar stew) and *salade landoise* (an enormous salad of fresh and cooked vegetables, goose liver and *gésiers confits*, or preserved gizzards), offers one of the warmest welcomes in town. Bring your appetite.

Le Franklin Roosevelt (☎ 01 64 22 28 73; 20 rue Grande; starters €6-13, mains €15.50-22; ◷ 10am-1am Mon-Sat) If the Fontainebleau regular is not in Le Ferrare, it's a dead cert you'll find him here. Another great brasserie, with wooden panelling, red banquette seating and oodles of atmosphere, the Franklin keeps weekday punters happy with a good-value *salades composées* (salads of fresh and cooked vegetables with meat or fish; €10).

Au Vague à Lame (☎ 01 60 72 10 32; 39 rue de France; lunch menus €12 & €16, dinner menus €25; ◷ lunch Tue-Sun, dinner to midnight Tue-Sat) This cheerful café-restaurant with a nautical theme is the place for Breton specialities as well as mussels and fresh oysters.

Le Ferrare (☎ 01 60 72 37 04; 23 rue de France; starters €5-9.50, mains €11.50-16, menus €10.90-12.50; ◷ 7.30am-4pm Mon, 7.30am-10.30pm Tue-Thu, 7.30am-1am Fri & Sat) If you want to know where locals lunch, pile into this quintessential bar/brasserie with typical fare and a blackboard full of Auvergne specialities. The *plat du jour* (daily special) is a snip at €8.80.

Crêperie Ty Koz (☎ 01 64 22 00 55; 18 rue de la Cloche; crêpes & galettes €3.60-9.80, 1L carafe cider €10.50; ◷ lunch & dinner to 10pm or 10.30pm Tue-Sun) Tucked away in an attractive courtyard, this Breton hidey-hole cooks up sweet crêpes and savoury galettes whipped up with traditional black wheat. Order a regular *simple* or double-thickness *pourleth* and wash it down with some traditional Val de Rance cider.

La Rose de l'Orient (☎ 01 60 72 66 49; 20 rue de Ferrare; meze per piece €1-3, sandwiches €4, grills €7.50; ◷ 10am-9pm Tue-Sat) This Lebanese eatery and *traiteur* (caterer) is an ideal spot for a fast and cheap lunch courtesy of two sisters, one of whom cooked for diplomats in Paris before launching into business alone. Five plastic tables inside or take away a meze-and-pita-bread picnic.

Self-Catering

Fromagerie Barthelemy (☎ 01 64 22 21 64; 92 rue Grande; ◷ 8.30am-12.30pm & 3.30-7.30pm Mon, Wed, Thu & Sat, 8am-12.30pm & 3.30-7.30pm Tue & Fri, 8.30am-1pm Sun) One of Île de France's finest cheese shops.

Marché République (rue des Pins; ◷ 8am-2pm Tue, Fri & Sun) Outdoor food market.

Monoprix (58 rue Grande; ◷ 8.45am-7.45pm Mon-Sat, 9am-1pm Sun)

TRANSPORT: FONTAINEBLEAU

Distance from Paris 69km

Direction Southeast

Travel time 35 to 60 minutes by SNCF train

Bus Line A links the train station with the château (€1.70), 2km southwest, every 10 minutes from 5.30am to 10.30pm (9.30pm Saturday, 11.30pm Sunday). The last train back to Paris leaves Fontainebleau just before midnight daily.

Car A6 from Porte d'Orléans, direction Lyon, exit 'Fontainebleau'.

SNCF train Up to 40 daily SNCF commuter trains link Paris' Gare de Lyon with Fontainebleau-Avon station (€7.90).

Taxi Book a taxi in Fontainebleau on ☎ 06 21 76 68 10.

SLEEPING

Hôtel de Londres (☎ 01 64 22 20 21; www.hoteldelondres. com; 1 place Général de Gaulle; s €90-155, d €100-170, ste from €180; 🖵) Classy, cosy and beautifully kept, the 16-room 'Hotel London' is charmingly furnished in warm reds and royal blues and has been in the same family for 80-odd years. The priciest rooms (eg room 5) have balconies with dreamy château view.

La Guérinière (☎ 06 13 50 50 37; balestier.gerard@wa nadoo.fr; 10 rue de Montebello; d incl breakfast €60, extra bed €20; 🖵) This charming B&B provides some of the best-value accommodation in town. Owner Monsieur Balestier speaks English and has five rooms, each named after a different flower and dressed in white linens and period wooden furniture. Bright and sunny *Clématite* (clematis) is particularly charming.

Hôtel Richelieu (☎ 01 64 22 26 46; www.bacchus-rich elieu.com; 4 rue Richelieu; s & d €50-80, tr €85; 🖵) Clean and welcoming, this rabbit warren of a 17-room hotel just north of the château is part of the Logis group, always a sign of quality, especially in this category. Cheaper rooms have shower and WC only and some (eg room 103) look the château directly in the face. The attached Bacchus restaurant and wine bar has a stellar reputation.

Hôtel de la Chancellerie (01 64 22 21 70; hotel.chancel -lerie@orange.fr; 1 rue de la Chancellerie; s €40-50, d €50-60) The Ritz it ain't, but if you're on a tight budget you could do worse than staying at this hotel opposite the post office with 25 old-fashioned but comfortable and spotless rooms.

VAUX-LE-VICOMTE

Privately owned **Château de Vaux-le-Vicomte** (☎ 01 64 14 41 90; www.vaux-le-vicomte.com; adult/student & child 6-16yr €14/11, candlelight visit €17/15, family ticket €44, audioguide €2; ☼ 10am-6pm Thu-Tue mid-Mar–June & Sep-early Nov, 10am-6pm daily Jul & Aug, candlelight visits 8pm-midnight Sat May-early Oct) and its magnificent French-styled gardens, 20km north of Fontainebleau, were designed and built as a precursor to Versailles by Le Brun, Le Vau and Le Nôtre between 1656 and 1661.

Unfortunately, Vaux-le-Vicomte's beauty turned out to be the undoing of its owner, Nicolas Fouquet, Louis XIV's minister of finance. Louis, seething with jealousy that he had been upstaged at the château's official opening, had Fouquet thrown into prison, where he died in 1680.

TRANSPORT: VAUX-LE-VICOMTE

Distance from Paris 61km

Direction Southeast

Travel time An hour by car or by RER and taxi.

Car A6 from Paris and then A5 (direction Melun and exit 'St-Germain Laxis'); from Fontainebleau N6 and N36.

RER train Line D2 from Paris (€7.25) to Melun, 6km southwest of the château, then taxi (€15 to €20) or Châteaubus shuttle four to six times daily Saturday and Sunday early April to early November (€3.50 each way).

Taxi For a local taxi ring ☎ 01 64 52 51 50.

Today visitors swoon over the beautifully furnished château interior, including its fabulous dome. In the vaulted cellars an exhibition looks at Le Nôtre's landscaping of the formal gardens, where there are elaborate fountain displays (☼ 3-6pm 2nd & last Sat of month mid-Mar–Oct) in season. The collection of 18th- and 19th-century carriages in the château stables, included in the château visit, forms the Musée des Équipages (Carriage Museum). At weekends and school holidays, rent prince, princess or musketeer costumes for the kids (aged four to 12) to prance around in. Fun seasonal events include Easter-egg hunts.

CHANTILLY

Whatever you do, don't come Tuesday, when Chantilly's beautiful château and its grand stables fit for a king are closed.

Situated some 50km north of Paris, this elegant old town (population 11,000) is small, select and spoiled. Its château sits in a sea of parkland, gardens, lakes and forest packed with walking opportunities; its race track is one of those prestigious hat-and-frock addresses in Europe; and that deliciously sweetened thick *crème* called Chantilly was created here. Given its large and lively English community (the town has its own Anglican church, vicar, tearoom, cricket club etc), it's thoroughly apt that Chantilly is twinned with the horse-racing town of Epsom in Surrey.

Château de Chantilly (☎ 03 44 27 31 80; www.château dechantilly.com; château & park adult/student/under 18yr €12/10/free, park €6/5/free; ☼ château 10am-6pm Wed-Mon Apr-Oct, 10am-5pm Wed-Mon Nov-Mar, park 10am-8pm Wed-Mon Apr-Oct, 10.30am-6pm Wed-Mon Nov-Mar), left in a shambles after the Revolution, is of interest mainly because of its beautiful gardens and collection of superb paintings. It consists of two attached buildings, entered through the same vestibule. Admission includes unlimited strolling around the château's vast gardens and a visit of the château interior, richly adorned with paintings (look out for the Delacroix, Ingres and Poussin), 16th-century stained glass, porcelain, lace and tapestries.

The **Petit Château** was built around 1560 for Anne de Montmorency (1493–1567), who served six French kings as *connétable* (high constable), diplomat and soldier, and died while fighting Protestants during the Counter-Reformation. The highlight of a visit is the **Cabinet des Livres** in the **Appartements des Princes** (Princes' Suites), a repository of 700 manuscripts and over 30,000 volumes, including a Gutenberg Bible and a facsimile of the *Très Riches Heures du Duc de Berry,* an illuminated manuscript dating from the 15th century that illustrates the calendar year for both the peasantry and the nobility. The **chapel**, to the left as you walk into the vestibule, has woodwork and stained-glass windows dating from the mid-16th century and was assembled by the duke of Aumale in 1882.

The attached Renaissance-style **Grand Château**, completely demolished during the Revolution, was rebuilt by the duke of Aumale, son of King Louis-Philippe, from 1875 to 1885. It forms the **Musée Condé**, a series of unremarkable 19th-century rooms adorned with paintings and sculptures haphazardly arranged according to the whims of the duke – he donated the château to the Institut de France on the condition the exhibits were not reorganised and would be open to the public. The most remarkable works, hidden in the **Sanctuaire**, include paintings by Filippino Lippi, Jean Fouquet and Raphael, though the authenticity of the last is disputed.

The château's long-neglected but now shipshape **gardens** were once among France's most spectacular. The formal **Jardin Français** (French Garden), whose flowerbeds, lakes and Grand Canal were laid out by Le Nôtre in the mid-17th century, is northeast of the main building. To the west, the 'wilder' **Jardin Anglais** (English Garden) was begun in 1817. East of the Jardin Français is the rustic **Jardin Anglo-Chinois** (Anglo-Chinese Garden), created in the 1770s. Its foliage and silted-up waterways surround the **Hameau**, a mock village dating from 1774 whose mill and half-timbered buildings inspired the Hameau de la Reine at Versailles.

The château's **Grandes Écuries** (Grand Stables), built between 1719 and 1740 to house 240 horses and over 400 hounds, are next to Chantilly's famous **Hippodrome** (Racecourse), inaugurated in 1834. Today the stables house the **Musée Vivant du Cheval** (☎ 03 44 27 31 80; www.museevivantducheval.fr; Grandes Écuries, rue du Connétable; adult/student/4-17yr €10/8.50/8; ☼ 10am-5pm Wed-Mon Apr-Oct, 2-6pm Wed-Mon Nov-Mar), whose 30 pampered and spoiled equines live in luxurious wooden stalls built by Louis-Henri de Bourbon, the seventh Prince de Condé, who was convinced he would be reincarnated as a horse (hence the extraordinary grandeur). Displays, which were under renovation at the time of research, cover everything from riding equipment to horse toys to portraits, drawings and sculptures of famous nags. The last tickets for the museum are sold one hour before it closes.

Every visitor, big and small, will be mesmerised by the one-hour **Chevaux en Fête Animation Équestre** (Horses on Holiday Show; 2.30pm Wed-Mon), a Chantilly must-do included in the admission price. Even more magical and highly sought-after are the handful of **equestrian shows** performed in the stables year-round; tickets are like gold dust and can be reserved online. A **Pass Domaine** (adult/student/4-17yr €19/17/8) allows entry to the château and the Grandes Écuries, including the show.

Less in demand but equally entertaining are the plays and theatrical pieces staged during July and August in the open-air **Theatre de la Faisanderie** (www.theatredelafaisanderie.com) of the **Potager des Princes** (☎ 03 44 57 39 66; www.potagerdesprinces. com; 17 rue de la Faisanderie; adult/under 18yr €7.50/6.50; ☼ 2-7pm Wed-Mon Apr-Oct), which is part of the château's parkland. Arrive before 5.30pm, when the last tickets of the day are sold. Hidden behind an old stone wall, these lovely little-known gardens embrace a watery and romantic **Jardin Fantastique** crossed with bridges and grottoes; an exotic **Jardin Japonais**, a flower-filled **Verger** (vegetable garden), several Italianate waterfalls, a 19th-century rose garden and puppet theatre (shows Wednesday, Saturday and Sunday). The rabbit obstacle-course races held in the **Lapinodrome** – a rabbit village with church, town hall etc – will raise a smile, be it one of amusement or sheer disbelief.

South of the château is the 6300-hectare **Forêt de Chantilly** (Chantilly Forest), once a royal hunting estate and now crisscrossed by a variety of walking and riding trails. In some areas, straight paths laid out centuries ago meet at multi-angled *carrefours* (crossroads). Long-

CHANTILLY

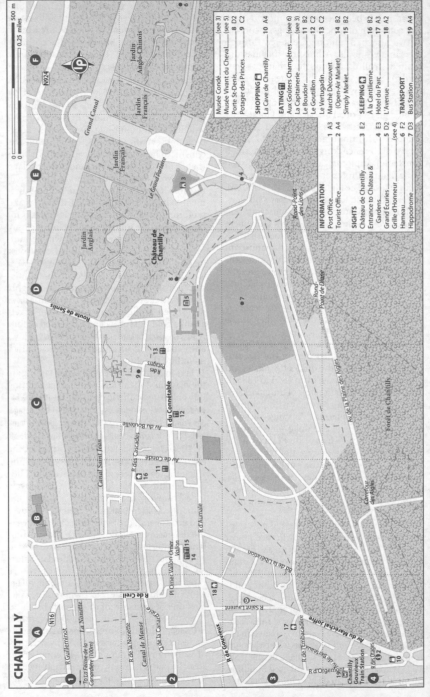

INFORMATION	
Post Office.................................	1 A3
Tourist Office.............................	2 A4

SIGHTS	
Château de Chantilly.................	3 E2
Entrance to Château &	
Gardens.................................	4 E3
Grand Écuries...........................	5 D2
Grille d'Honneur.......................	(see 4)
Hameau....................................	6 F2
Hippodrome..............................	7 D3

Musée Condé...........................	(see 3)
Musée Vivant du Cheval...........	(see 5)
Porte St-Denis.........................	8 D2
Potager des Princes..................	9 C2

SHOPPING ⌂	
La Cave de Chantilly.................	10 A4

EATING ⌂	
Aux Goûters Champêtres...........	(see 6)
La Capitainerie.........................	(see 3)
Le Boudoir...............................	11 B2
Le Goutillon.............................	12 C2
Le Vertugadin..........................	13 C2
Marché Découvert	
(Open-Air Market)................	14 B2
Simply Market..........................	15 B2

SLEEPING ⌂	
À la Cantilienne........................	16 B2
Hôtel du Parc...........................	17 A3
L'Avenue..................................	18 A2

TRANSPORT	
Bus Station...............................	19 A4

CHÂTEAU DE WHIPPED CREAM

Like every other self-respecting French château three centuries ago, the palace at Chantilly had its own *hameau* (hamlet), complete with *laitier* (dairy) where the lady of the household and her guests could play at being milkmaids. But the cows at Chantilly's dairy took their job rather more seriously than their fellow bovine actors at other faux dairies, and news of the *crème Chantilly* (sweetened whipped cream) served at the hamlet's teas became the talk of aristocratic 18th-century Europe. Indeed even the future Habsburg Emperor Joseph II visited this *'temple de marbre'* (marble temple), as he called it, clandestinely to taste the stuff in 1777. Sample it in any café or restaurant in town.

distance trails that pass through the Forêt de Chantilly include the GR11, which links the château with Senlis 10km northeast, an attractive medieval town of winding cobblestone streets, Gallo-Roman ramparts and towers and a lovely cathedral; the GR1, which goes from Luzarches (famed for its cathedral, parts of which date from the 12th century) to Ermenonville; and the GR12, which goes northeast from four lakes known as the Étangs de Commelles, to the Forêt d'Halatte.

The tourist office sells IGN's indispensable walking map *Forêts de Chantilly, d'Halatte and d'Ermenonville* (No 2412OT; 1:25,000; €9.70) and has information on walks and mountain-bike trails in the forest.

INFORMATION

Post Office (26 av du Maréchal Joffre)

Tourist Office (☎ 03 44 67 37 37; www.chantilly-tourisme.com; 60 av du Maréchal Joffre; ☒ 9.30am-12.30pm & 1.30-5.30pm Mon-Sat, 10am-1pm Sun May-Sep, 9.30am-12.30pm & 1.30-5.30pm Mon-Sat Oct-Apr) Ample information on Chantilly, including accommodation lists and three *promenades* leaflets outlining walks through town, along Chantilly's two canals and around the pristine racecourse.

EATING

Aux Goûters Champêtres (☎ 03 44 57 46 21; Le Hameau, Château de Chantilly; lunch menus €19.50-41.50; ☒ noon-6pm Wed-Mon Mar-Nov) A wonderful spot for a summery lunch in the sun, this fine restaurant sits in the windmill of the park's *hameau* (hamlet). Its chief claim to fame is its *crème Chantilly*, which of course was invented on site.

Le Goutillon (☎ 03 44 58 01 00; 61 rue du Connétable; starters €8-18, mains €18-32, menus €15-25; ☒ lunch & dinner to 11pm daily) With its red-and-white checked tablecloths, simple wooden tables and classic bistro fare, Le Goutillon is a cosy, very friendly French affair much loved by local expats. It's as much wine bar as munch place.

Le Vertugadin (☎ 03 44 57 03 19; www.restaurantlevertugadin.fr; 44 rue du Connétable; starters €12.50-42, mains

€15.50-38, menus €28; ☒ lunch daily, dinner to 11pm Mon-Sat) Old-style and elegant, this ode to regional cuisine – think meat, game and terrines accompanied by sweet onion chutney – fills a white-shuttered townhouse. A warming fire roars in the hearth in winter, and summer welcomes diners to its walled garden.

La Capitainerie (☎ 03 44 57 15 89; www.restaurantfp-chantilly.com; Château de Chantilly; lunch menus €15-31; ☒ lunch Wed-Mon) Enviably nestled beneath the vaulted stone ceiling of the château kitchens, La Capitainerie captures history's grandeur and romance. Fare is traditional and includes *crème Chantilly* at every opportunity. Its weekend *formule buffet à volonté* (help-yourself buffet deal; €24) allows unlimited starters and a *plat du jour* or the latter plus unlimited desserts. The lot costs €31.

Le Boudoir (☎ 03 44 55 44 49; 100 rue du Connétable; lunch menus €7.50-16; ☒ 11am-6pm Mon, 10am-7pm Tue-Sat, 11am-7pm Sun) This relaxed *salon de thé* (tearoom) with sofas to lounge on and magazines to read is the place to sample *crème Chantilly* in all its decadence: go for one of several hot chocolate types topped with the lashings of the stuff such as the *chococcino* (a cream-topped mix of coffee and chocolate). Le Boudoir also serves perfect light lunches – salads, savoury tarts and gourmet savoury platters.

TRANSPORT: CHANTILLY

Distance from Paris 50km

Direction North

Travel time 25 minutes by train

Car By motorway, Autoroute du Nord (A1/E19), exit No 7 'Survilliers-Chantilly'; by national road, N1 then N16 from Porte de la Chapelle/St-Denis.

SNCF train Paris' Gare du Nord is linked to Chantilly-Gouvieux station (€7.40) by SNCF trains, departing almost hourly between 6.30am and 10.30pm.

Taxi For a local taxi in Chantilly ring ☎ 06 07 19 99 93.

Self-Catering

Simply Market (5 place Omer Vallon; ☾ 8.30am-8.30pm Mon-Fri, 8.30am-8pm Sat, 9am-12.45pm Sun)

La Cave de Chantilly (69 av du Maréchal Joffre; ☾ 10am-12.15pm & 2-6.15pm Tue-Sat) Good wine selection.

Marché Decouvert (open-air market; place Omer Vallon; ☾ 8.30am-12.30pm Wed & Sat)

SLEEPING

Hôtel du Parc (☎ 03 44 58 20 00; www.hotel-parc-chantilly.com; 36 av du Maréchal Joffre; s €103-123, d €133-183, q 163-323; ☐ ☖) This 57-room, architecturally uninspiring place is part of the Best Western chain so you can expect a relatively high standard of service. The rooms have everything you need but are bland; the cheaper rooms face busy av du Maréchal Joffre.

La Ferme de la Canardière (☎ 03 44 62 00 96, 06 20 96 43 89; www.fermecanardiere.com, in French; 20 rue du Viaduc; s/d incl breakfast €130/150; ☒) Delicately embroidered cushions, country-style furnishings and a colour scheme of soft creams and beiges cast a romantic air over the country home of Sabine and Thierry – everything one would hope for in a French B&B. In summer allow plenty of time for breakfast on the terrace before plunging into the pool for a quick dip.

À la Cantilienne (☎ 03 44 57 89 49, 06 50 92 62 37; www.chantilly-chambres-dhotes.fr, in French; 15 rue des Cascades; d €120-150, extra bed €30; ☐) A five-minute stroll from the high wall of the princes' kitchen garden sits this delightful B&B, the family home of Monsieur and Madame Vergne-Hyttenhove atop a grassy hillock. Its two spacious rooms both peep out onto the pretty garden out back.

L'Avenue (☎ 03 44 57 02 55; www.hotel-avenue-chantilly.com; 3 av du Maréchal Joffre; s/d/tr €55/68/78, ste from €100; ☐ ☖) Smack dab in the section of town above a popular café-restaurant, the aptly named Avenue is an excellent, almost budget choice for this pricey town. The 10 rooms, done up in varying shades of browns and beiges, have hardwood floors and are of a good size.

SENLIS

Just 10km northeast of Chantilly, Senlis (population 21,000) is an attractive medieval town of winding cobblestone streets, Gallo-Roman ramparts and towers. It was a royal seat from the time of Clovis in the 5th and 6th centuries to Henri IV (r 1589–1610) and contains four

small but well-formed **museums** (adult/student/under 16yr €2/1/free) devoted to subjects as diverse as art and archaeology, local history, hunting and the French cavalry in North Africa.

The Gothic **Cathédrale de Notre Dame** (place du Parvis Notre Dame; ☾ 8am-6pm) was built between 1150 and 1191. The cathedral is unusually bright, but the stained glass, though original, is unexceptional. The magnificent carved-stone **Grand Portal** (1176), on the western side facing place du Parvis Notre Dame, has statues and a central relief relating to the life of the Virgin Mary. It is believed to have been the inspiration for the portal at the cathedral in Chartres.

INFORMATION

Tourist Office (☎ 03 44 53 06 40; www.senlis-tourisme.fr; place du Parvis Notre Dame; ☾ 10am-12.30pm & 2-6.15pm Mon-Sat, 10.30am-1pm & 2-6.15pm Sun Mar-Oct, 10am-12.30pm & 2-5pm Mon-Sat, 10.30am-12.30pm & 2-5pm Sun Nov-Feb) Just opposite (west of) the cathedral.

CHARTRES

Step off the train in Chartres (population 45,600) and the two very different spires – one Gothic, the other Romanesque – of its magnificent 13th-century cathedral instantly beckon.

Rising from rich farmland to dominate this charming medieval town, Chartres' **Cathédrale Notre Dame** (☎ 02 37 21 22 07, 02 37 21 75 02; www.diocese -chartres.com; place de la Cathédrale; ☼ 8.30am-7.30pm, to 10pm Tue, Fri & Sun Jun-Aug, Sunday mass 9.15am, 11am & 6pm or 6.30pm) is a must-see. Its brilliant-blue stained glass and collection of relics, including the Sainte Voile (Holy Veil) said to have been worn by the Virgin Mary when she gave birth to Jesus, have lured pilgrims since the Middle Ages. Up until 4pm daily, the shop below the North Tower inside the cathedral rents informative, 25-/45-/70-minute English-language audioguide headsets costing €3.20/4.20/6.20 – you'll need to leave your passport or other ID as a deposit. Guided **tours in English** (☎ 02 37 28 15 58; millerchartres@aol.com; tour €10; ☼ noon & 2.45pm Mon-Sat Apr-Oct) with the incomparable 'Maître de Chartres' (Master of Chartres) Malcolm Miller depart from the shop as do **tours in French** (adult/10 to 18 years, student & senior €6.20/4.20; ☼ 10.30am Tue-Sat & 3pm daily Apr-Oct, 2.30pm daily Nov-Mar) year-round.

One of the crowning architectural achievements of Western civilisation, this 130m-long cathedral was built in the Gothic style during the early 13th century to replace a Romanesque cathedral devastated by fire in 1194. Construction took only 30 years, resulting in a high degree of architectural unity. It is France's best-preserved medieval cathedral, having been spared postmedieval modifications, the ravages of war and the Reign of Terror.

Its three entrances all have superbly ornamented triple **portals**, but the western **Portail Royal** is the only one that predates the fire. Carved between 1145 and 1155, its superb statuary, whose features are elongated in the Romanesque style, represents the glory of Christ in the centre, and the Nativity and Ascension to the right and left, respectively. The structure's other main Romanesque feature is the 105m-high **Clocher Vieux** (Old Bell Tower or South Tower), begun in the 1140s. It is the tallest Romanesque steeple still standing.

A visit to the 112m-high **Clocher Neuf** (New Bell Tower or North Tower; adult/18-25yr/under 18yr €7/4.50/ free, admission free on 1st Sun of some months; ☼ 9.30am-12.30pm & 2-6pm Mon-Sat, 2-6pm Sun May-Aug, 9.30am-12.30pm & 2-5pm Mon-Sat, 2-5pm Sun Sep-Apr) is worth the ticket price and steep climb up the spiral stairway (350 steps). Access is just behind the cathedral bookshop. A 70m-high platform on the flamboyant Gothic spire, built from 1507 to 1513 by Jehan de Beauce after an earlier

wooden spire burned down, affords superb views of the three-tiered flying buttresses and the 19th-century copper roof, turned green by verdigris.

Extraordinary are the cathedral's 172 stained-glass windows, mostly 13th-century originals, covering 2.6 sq km and forming one of Europe's most important medieval stained-glass collections. The three most important, dating to 1150, cast a magical light over the west entrance, below the rose window. Survivors of the 1194 fire, they are renowned for the depth and intensity of their blue tones, famously called 'Chartres blue'. To see more stained glass close up, nip into the **Centre International du Vitrail** (International Stained-Glass Centre; ☎ 02 37 21 65 72; www.centre-vitrail.org; 5 rue du Cardinal Pie; adult/16-18yr/under 15yr €4/3/free; ☼ 9.30am-12.30pm & 1.30-6pm Mon-Fri, 10am-12.30pm & 2.30-6pm Sat, 2.30-6pm Sun), in a half-timbered former granary.

The cathedral's 110m-long **crypt** (guided tour adult/7-18yr €2.70/2.10; ☼ tours 11am Mon-Sat & 2.15pm, 3.15pm, 4.30pm & 5.15pm daily late Jun-late Sep, 11am Mon-Sat & 2.15pm, 3.15pm & 4.30pm daily Apr-late Jun & late Sep-Oct, 11am Mon-Sat & 4.15pm Nov-Mar), a tombless Romanesque structure built in 1024 around a 9th-century predecessor, is the largest crypt in France. Guided tours in French (with written English translation) lasting 30 minutes are available year-round. Guided tours of the crypt from April to October depart from **La Crypte** (☎ 02 37 21 56 33; 18 Cloître Notre Dame; ☼ Apr-Oct), the cathedral-run souvenir shop to the southeast. From November to March, tours depart from the gift shop inside the cathedral under the North Tower.

The most venerated object in the cathedral is the **Sainte Voile** (Holy Veil) relic, originally part of the imperial treasury of Constantinople but offered to Charlemagne by the Empress Irene when the Holy Roman Emperor proposed marriage to her in 802. It has been in Chartres since 876, when Charles the Bald presented it to the town. It is contained in a cathedral-shaped reliquary and is displayed in a side chapel at the end of the north aisle behind the choir.

Chartres' **Musée des Beaux-Arts** (Fine Arts Museum; ☎ 02 37 90 45 80; 29 Cloître Notre Dame; adult/student/under 18yr €3.10/1.60/free, with temporary exhibition €5.10/2.60/ free; ☼ 10am-noon & 2-6pm Mon & Wed-Sat, 2-6pm Sun May-Oct, 10am-noon & 2-5pm Mon & Wed-Sat, 2-5pm Sun Nov-Apr), accessed via the gate next to the cathedral's north portal, is in the former Palais Épiscopal (Bishop's Palace), built in the 17th and 18th centuries. Its collections include

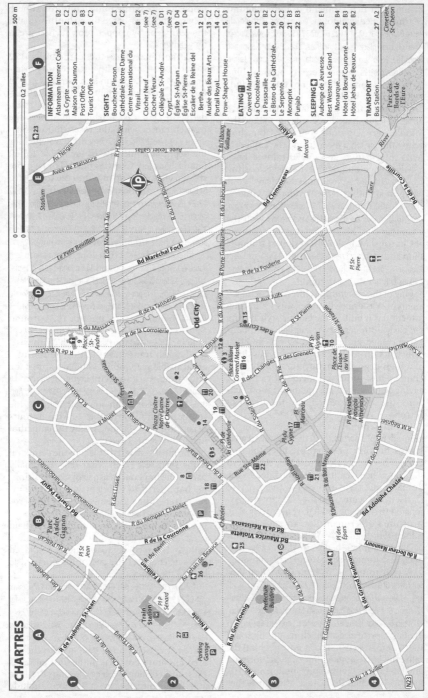

CHARTRES

INFORMATION	
Atlanteam Internet Café	1 B2
La Crypte	2 C2
Maison du Saumon	3 C3
Post Office	4 B3
Tourist Office	5 C2

SIGHTS	
Boucherie Pinson	6 C3
Cathédrale Notre Dame	7 C2
Centre International du Vitrail	8 B2
Clocher Neuf	(see 7)
Clocher Vieux	(see 7)
Collégiale St-André	9 D1
Crypt	(see 2)
Église St-Aignan	10 D4
Église St-Pierre	11 D4
Escalier de la Reine del Berthe	12 D2
Musée des Beaux Arts	13 C2
Portail Royal	14 C2
Prow-Shaped House	15 D3

EATING	
Covered Market	16 C3
La Chocolaterie	17 C2
La Passacaille	18 B2
Le Bistro de la Cathédrale	19 C2
Le Serpente	20 C2
Monoprix	21 B3
Punjab	22 B3

SLEEPING	
Auberge de Jeunesse	23 E1
Best Western Le Grand Monarque	24 B4
Hôtel du Bœuf Couronné	25 B3
Hôtel Jehan de Beauce	26 B2

TRANSPORT	
Bus Station	27 A2

SAVED BY RED TAPE

Anyone who has tried to live or work legally in France will know that bureaucracy *à la française* is at best perfect material for a comedy sketch, and at worst a recipe for madness. Yet were it not for administrative bumbling, the magnificent cathedral at Chartres would probably have been destroyed during the French Revolution.

While antireligious fervour was reaching fever pitch in 1791, the Revolutionaries decided that the cathedral deserved something more radical than mere desecration: demolition. The question was how to accomplish that. To find an answer, they appointed a committee, whose admirably thorough members deliberated for four or five years. By that time the Revolution's fury had been spent, and – to history's great fortune – the plan was shelved.

16th-century enamels of the Apostles made for François I, paintings from the 16th to 19th centuries and polychromatic wooden sculptures from the Middle Ages.

Chartres' carefully preserved old town is northeast and east of the cathedral along the narrow western channel of the Eure River, spanned by a number of footbridges. From rue Cardinal Pie, staircases called *tertres* and streets such as Tertre St-Nicolas and rue Chantault, the latter lined with medieval houses (No 29 is the oldest house in Chartres), lead down to the 12th-century Collégiale St-André, a Romanesque church that closed in 1791 and was damaged in the early 19th century and again during WWII. It is now an exhibition centre.

Along the river's eastern bank, rue de la Tannerie and its extension rue de la Foulerie are lined with flower gardens, millraces and the restored remnants of riverside trades: wash houses, tanneries and the like. Rue aux Juifs (Street of the Jews) on the western bank has been extensively renovated. Half a block down the hill there's a riverside promenade. Up the hill, rue des Écuyers has many structures dating from around the 16th century, including a half-timbered, prow-shaped house at No 26 with its upper section supported by beams. At No 35 is the Escalier de la Reine Berthe (Queen Bertha's Staircase), a towerlike covered stairwell that dates back to the early 16th century.

There are some lovely half-timbered houses north of here on rue du Bourg and to the west on rue de la Poissonnerie; look for the magnificent 16th-century Maison du Saumon (Salmon House) at Nos 8 to 10, with its carved consoles of the eponymous salmon, the Archangel Gabriel and Mary and Archangel Michael slaying the dragon. It now houses a branch of the tourist office and a multimedia exhibition on Chartres and its history.

From place St-Pierre you get a good view of the flying buttresses holding up the 12th- and 13th-century Église St-Pierre. Once part of a Benedictine monastery founded in the 7th century, it was outside the city walls and thus vulnerable to attack; the fortresslike, pre-Romanesque bell tower attached to it was used as a refuge by monks, and dates from around 1000. The fine, brightly coloured clerestory windows in the nave, choir and apse date from the early 14th century.

To the northwest on place St-Aignan, Église St-Aignan is interesting for its wooden barrel-vault roof (1625), arcaded nave and painted interior of faded blue and gold floral motifs (c 1870). The stained glass and the Renaissance Chapelle de St-Michel date from the 16th and 17th centuries.

Le Petit Chart' Train (☎ 02 37 25 88 50; www.promotrain.fr/gbcircuit.htm; adult day/night €6/6.50, child €3; ⏰ 10.30am-7pm Apr-Oct), Chartres' electric tourist train, covers the main sights in 35 minutes; it departs from in front of the tourist office.

INFORMATION

Atlanteam (☎ 02 37 36 62 15; 13bis rue Jehan de Beauce; €1/2/3.60 per 15/30/60min; ⏰ 11.30am-10pm Mon-Fri, 11.30am midnight Sat, 2-7pm Sun) Internet café with 35 terminals.

Post Office (3 blvd Maurice Violette)

Tourist Office (☎ 02 37 18 26 26; www.chartres-tourisme.com; place de la Cathédrale; ⏰ 9am-7pm Mon-Sat,

TRANSPORT: CHARTRES

Distance from Paris 91km

Direction Southwest

Travel time 55 to 70 minutes by train

Car A6 from Paris' Porte d'Orléans (direction Bordeaux-Nantes), then A10 and A11 (direction Nantes), exit 'Chartres'.

SNCF train Almost three-dozen SNCF trains a day (20 on Sunday) link Paris' Gare Montparnasse (€13.60) with Chartres, all of which pass through Versailles-Chantiers (€11.50, 45 to 60 minutes). The last train back to Paris leaves Chartres just after 10.30pm Sunday to Friday and at 8.40pm on Saturday.

Taxi For a local taxi ring ☎ 02 37 36 00 00.

9.30am-5.30pm Sun Apr-Sep, 9am-6pm Mon-Sat, 9.30am-5pm Sun Oct-Mar) Rents 1½-hour English-language audioguide tours (€5.50/8.50 for one/two) of the medieval city as well as binoculars (€2), fabulous for seeing details of the cathedral close up. There's now a branch with an exhibition on Chartres' history in the historic Maison du Saumon (8-10 rue de la Poissonnerie; 9am-1pm & 2-6pm Mon-Fri, 10am-1pm & 4-6pm Sat).

EATING

Le Bistro de la Cathédrale (☎ 02 37 36 59 60; 1 Cloître Notre Dame; starters €6.50-15, mains €12.50-25, menus €21-22; lunch & dinner to 10.30pm closed Tue-Thu & Sep-Easter Sun) Our favourite in the shadow of the cathedral, this stylish wine bar is the place for a long lazy lunch over a glass or three of wine. Tasty morsels to soak it up are chalked on the boards inside and out.

Le Serpente (☎ 02 37 21 68 81; 2 Cloître Notre Dame; starters €7.60-14.90, mains €15.90-21.50; 10am-11pm) Its location slap-bang opposite the cathedral ensures this brasserie and *salon de thé* is always full. The cuisine is traditional and its chef also constructs some well-filled sandwiches (€3.90 to €5.90) and meal-sized salads (€12.60).

La Passacaille (☎ 02 37 21 52 10; 30 rue Ste-Même; starters €3.90-9.60, mains €8.90-14.20, menu €15.90; lunch & dinner to 10.30pm Thu-Tue) This welcoming Italian place has particularly good pizzas (€ 8.10 to € 10.50) and fresh pasta (€8.90 to €9.90).

Punjab (☎ 02 37 21 31 36; 13 rue Ste-Même; starters € 3-6, mains €4-9.50; lunch & dinner to 10.30pm) If like us you need a fix of curry and/or biryani even in the midst of medieval Gothic splendour, head for this cheap and cheerful Pakistani eatery southwest of the cathedral. No alcohol served.

La Chocolaterie (☎ 02 37 21 86 92; 14 place du Cygne; 8am-7.30pm Tue-Sat, 10am-7.30pm Mon & Sun) Revel instead in local life at this bar-cum-chocolate-shop overlooking the open-air flower market (Tuesday, Thursday and Saturday) in place du Cygne. Its coloured macaroons – flavoured with orange, apricot, pistachio, peanut, pineapple and so on – are to die for, as are its sweet homemade crêpes, brownies and tiny madeleine sponge cakes.

Self-Catering

Covered Market (place Billard; 7am-1pm Wed & Sat)

Monoprix (21 rue Noël Ballay & 10 rue du Bois Merrain; 9am-7.30pm Mon-Sat) Department store with supermarket.

SLEEPING

Best Western Le Grand Monarque (☎ 02 37 18 15 15; www.bw-grand-monarque.com; 22 place des Épars; s €107-185, d €127-175, tr €185, ste €215-255;) With its teal-blue shutters piercing a facade dating to 1779, lovely stained-glass ceiling and treasure trove of period furnishings, old B&W photos and knick-knacks, the Grand Monarch, recently renovated from top to tail, is a historical gem and very central.

THE BUTCHER OF CHARTRES *Nicola Williams*

There's nothing sinister about the butcher of Chartres. Pinson, the medieval town's oldest *boucherie*, tucked behind cherry-red and chocolate ironwork at 4 rue du Soleil d'Or, is all about good, honest, old-fashioned charm.

The shop has been in business since 1892, and Roland Pinson has wielded the proprietor's knife with precision since 1958. He might well be in his late 70s, but it's clear from the ferocious passion with which he discusses his cuts that he is here to stay.

'It's my life', he says with a wry smile, as if it could possibly be anything but. A historic relic, this butcher's shop is a blast from the past. There is no cash register (just a paper ledger), no digital scales, no meat behind glass or hiding the nasty bits in a back room (fat trimmed from Pinson's legendary *entrecôte* and other joints are popped in a wooden drawer). Hunks of meat hang on hooks above a long wooden chopping block, used so long it's U-shaped. White marble clads all four walls bar one in which a 1930s refrigerated larder – the nearest thing to modernity – is embedded. The patterned mosaic floor is original.

Customers, fiercely loyal, have grown up with this shop. Each is greeted first by Madame Pinson, well wrapped in winter coat, hat and scarf (there doesn't appear to be any heating in the shop) – kiss, kiss, one on each cheek – followed by Monsieur Pinson between chops. He wears a shirt and tie underneath his bloodied apron and service is endearingly slow.

'Do you have any calf kidneys today Roland?' 'No, only lamb.' It's not all about attentive personal service. As EU regulations (to which this butcher's shop, being a protected historical monument, appears immune) are fast seeing certain meat cuts disappear, this butcher of Chartres is one of France's last bastions of *une bouffe d'autrefois* (cuisine of yesteryear).

Hôtel Châtelet (☎ 02 37 21 78 00; www.hotelchatelet.com; 6-8 av Jehan de Beauce; s €92-118, d €129-154; ☐ ☕) This 48-room new kid on the block, with its flashing light-trick of a facade and enormous fireplace in the lobby, is a welcome addition to Chartres' hospitality industry. The most expensive rooms on the 2nd and 3rd floors face the garden and cathedral.

Hôtel Jehan de Beauce (☎ 02 37 21 01 41; www.accommodation-chartres.com; 19 av Jehan de Beauce; s €58-72, d €66-72, tr €81, q €89; ☐) If you're looking for budget accommodation this hotel has 46 clean, but very spartan rooms. The cheaper ones face the street and (sometimes) the cathedral. Reception (and the lift) is on the 1st floor.

Hôtel du Bœuf Couronné (☎ 02 37 18 06 06; leboeuf couronne@hotmail.com; 15 place Châtelet; s/d with shower €50/59, s/d with bath €65/72; ☐) The red-curtained entrance lends a vaguely theatrical air to this two-star Logis guesthouse in the centre of everything. Its summertime terrace restaurant cooks up cathedral-view dining and the Dickens music bar is right next door.

Auberge de Jeunesse (☎ 02 37 34 27 64; www.auberge-jeunesse-chartres.com; 23 av Neigre; dm incl breakfast €13.70; reception ☙ 3-10pm) An easy 1.5km stroll northeast from the train station via blvd Charles Péguy and blvd Jean Jaurès or, from the train station, a trip aboard bus 2 (direction La Mouffle) to the Béthouart stop brings you to Chartres' well-run hostel. Rates include breakfast with cathedral view, but sheets are €2.20.

BEAUVAIS

This friendly town's soaring cathedral, whose 48m-high choir has the highest Gothic vaults ever built, and its pair of fine museums make Beauvais (population 50,900) a great 80km day trip from Paris.

Beauvais' unfinished **Cathédrale St-Pierre** (☎ 03 44 48 11 60; www.cathedrale-beauvais.fr; rue St-Pierre; ☙ 9am-12.15pm & 2-6.15pm Apr-Jun, Sep & Oct, 9am-6.15pm Jul & Aug, 9am-12.15pm & 2-5.30 Nov-Mar) is to church architecture what the Venus de Milo is to sculpture: a fantastically beautiful work with certain key extremities missing – in this case, the nave. When the town's Carolingian cathedral was partly destroyed by fire in 1225, a series of ambitious local bishops and noblemen decided that its replacement should surpass anything ever built. Unfortunately, their soaring and richly adorned creation surpassed not only its rivals but the limits of the technology of the time, and in 1272 and again

in 1284 the 48m-high vaults collapsed. Inside, at the end of the north transept, the oldest chiming clock in the world (1303) sounds out the hour. Next to it, the **astronomical clock** (adult/16-25yr/6-15yr €4/2.50/1),built in 1868 and set to solar time (and thus more than 50 minutes behind Central European Time), begins a 25-minute sound and light show at 10.40am, 11.40am, 2.40pm, 3.40pm and 4.40pm daily.

The outstanding **Musée Départemental de l'Oise** (Oise Departmental Museum; ☎ 03 44 11 43 83; www.oise.fr; 1 rue du Musée; admission free; ☙ 10am-noon & 2-6pm Wed-Mon, no midday closure in Jul & Aug) is housed in the former bishops' palace with its distinctive round bastions just west of the cathedral. It has sections dedicated to archaeology, medieval wood carvings, French and Italian paintings (including a number of gruesome 16th-century works depicting decapitations), ceramics and art nouveau. Highlights include the *Dieu Guerrier Gaulois de St-Maur*, a slender and aristocratic-looking Celtic warrior made of hammered sheet brass in the 1st century AD; the early-17th-century funerary monument of nobleman Charles de Fresnoy; and a wonderfully complete, late-19th-century art nouveau dining room.

To the east of the cathedral, the **Galerie Nationale de la Tapisserie** (National Tapestry Gallery; ☎ 03 44 15 39 10; www.monum.fr; 22 rue St-Pierre; admission free; ☙ 10.30am-5.30pm Tue-Sun), built in 1976 on the still visible buttresses of a 3rd-century Gallo-Roman wall, has a stunning permanent collection of Flemish,

TRANSPORT: BEAUVAIS

Distance from Paris 80km

Direction North

Travel time 55 to 70 minutes by train

Bus Local bus 12 (€0.90; 8 daily Mon-Sat) and a private *navette* (shuttle; €4; eight daily) link the train station with the airport. For information on getting from the airport directly to Paris, see p385).

Car N1 from Paris' Porte de la Chapelle, then the A1 to the A16 and exit 14 ('Beauvais – Centre').

SNCF train Some two-dozen trains (half that number on Sunday) link Beauvais' train station 1.2km southeast of the cathedral with Paris' Gare du Nord (€12.40, 75 minutes) The last train back to Paris leaves Beauvais just after 8pm (9pm on Sunday).

Taxi For a local taxi in Beauvais ring ☎ 02 37 36 00 00.

Gobelins, Arbusson and Beauvais tapestries dating from the 15th century to the present day and mounts several temporary exhibits each year.

INFORMATION

Tourist Office (☎ 03 44 15 30 30 www.beauvaistour isme.fr; 1 Rue Beauregard; ⏰ 9.30am-12.30pm & 1.30-6.30pm Mon-Sat year-round, 10am-5pm Sun Apr-Oct). Diagonally opposite Galerie Nationale de la Tapisserie.

EATING

Les Vents d'Anges (☎ 03 44 15 00 08; www.lesventsdanges. com; 3 rue de Étamine; starters €8-14, mains €15-23, menus €15.50-18; ⏰ lunch & dinner Tue-Sat) A straw poll among local people suggests that this restaurant in the shadow of the Église de St-Étienne (Church of St Stephen) about 150m south of the tourist office is the best in town. It serves traditional but inventive French cuisine and its own wines in bright, upbeat surroundings.

Le Palais Bleu (☎ 02 44 45 06 52; 75 rue St-Pierre; starters €7.50, mains €13.50, menus €19.50-25.50; lunch Thu-Tue, dinner Thu-Mon) It's not cheap but this stylish eatery just opposite the cathedral, that looks more like a stylish farmhouse than the 'Blue Palace' that its name describes, is *the* place in Beauvais to sample *la cuisine picarde* (Picardy cuisine). Go for *flamiche* (leek and egg savoury tart), *ficelle picarde* (ham and mushroom crêpe) or the inventive *tiramisu* with bacon and *crème de chorizo* (cream of chorizo sausage).

Taverne Karlbrau (☎ 03 44 06 32 72; www.lesrelais d'alsace.com; 16 rue Pierre Jacoby; starters €6.50-15.80, mains €12.90-22.50, menus €10.90-19.90; lunch & dinner to 11pm daily) *Choucroute garnie* (sauerkraut with assorted meats), oysters on the half-shell and a skylit dome in the centre – it's Central Casting Alsatian-style in Picardy. But the welcome is warm, the location central and the *menus* more than affordable.

Self-Catering

Marché Plus (4 rue Pierre Jacoby; ⏰ 7am-9pm Mon-Sat, 9am-1pm Sun) Large central supermarket.

SLEEPING

Chenal Hôtel (☎ 03 44 06 04 60; www.chenalhotel.fr; 63 blvd du Général de Gaulle; s & d €99-149; 🖥) If early morning transport links are a concern – be it a plane, the train or a shuttle bus into Paris – this unmiss-

able three-star with blue awnings and 29 rooms opposite the railway station on av de la République is just the ticket. And with the Bulldog café-pub on the ground floor attracting every English-speaking man, woman and German shepherd within barking distance, you might never get to bed.

Hôtel du Palais (☎ 03 44 45 12 58; www.hoteldupalais beauvais.com; 9 rue St-Nicolas; s & d €48, tr €60; 🖥) Simple but stylish (we love the brightly painted walls with floral stencils and the big old-fashioned wooden staircase), the 14-room 'Palace' finds itself in one of the more interesting *quartiers* (neighbourhoods) of Beauvais, west of the cathedral with the odd half-timbered house peeking out from among the concrete.

Hôtel du Cygne (☎ 03 44 48 68 40; www.contact-hotel. com; 24 rue Carnot; s €45-59, d & tw €48-73, tr €66-84, q €89; 🖥) It's a simple but very central affair, the Swan, with 20 rooms spread over three liftless floors. The cheaper rooms share the WC but every room at least has a shower, making it an excellent budget selection.

GIVERNY

The prized drawcard of this tiny village (population 525), northwest of Paris en route to Rouen, is the **Maison de Claude Monet** (House of Claude Monet; ☎ 02 32 51 28 21; www.fondation-monet.com; 84 rue Claude Monet; adult/student/7-11yr/under 7yr €6/4.50/3.50/ free; ⏰ 9.30am-6pm daily Apr-Oct), the home and flower-filled garden of one of the leading Impressionist painters and his family from 1883 to 1926. Here Monet painted some of his most famous series of works, including *Décorations des Nymphéas* (Water Lilies). Unfortunately, the hectare of land that Monet owned here has become two distinct areas, cut by the Chemin du Roy, a small railway line that has been converted into the D5 road.

The northern area of the property is **Clos Normand**, where Monet's famous pastel pink-and-green house and the **Atelier des Nymphéas** (Water Lilies Studio) stand. These days the studio is the entrance hall, adorned with precise reproductions of his works and ringing with cash-register bells from the busy gift shop. Outside are the symmetrically laid-out gardens. Visiting the house and gardens is a treat in any season. From early to late spring, daffodils, tulips, rhododendrons, wisteria and irises appear, followed by poppies and lilies. By June, nasturtiums, roses and sweet peas are in blossom. Around September, there are dahlias, sunflowers and hollyhocks.

TRANSPORT: GIVERNY

Distance from Paris 74km

Direction Northwest

Travel time 45 minutes by train to Vernon, then 20 minutes by bus or bicycle

Car Route A13 from Paris' Port de St-Cloud (direction Rouen), exit No 14 to route N15 (direction Vernon, Giverny & Bonnières).

SNCF train From Paris' Gare St-Lazare there are two early-morning SNCF trains to Vernon (€12.50, 1¼ hours), from where seasonal shuttle buses (€4 return; ☼ Apr-Oct) continue from the station to Giverny, 7km to the southeast. Miles more fun is to hire a bike for €12 a day from the café facing the station, Bar-Restaurant du Chemin de Fer (☎ 02 32 21 16 01; 1 pl de la Gare; ☼ 6.30am-11pm); take your passport as a deposit. Cyclo News (☎ 02 32 21 24 08; 7 cours du Marché aux Chevaux; ☼ 8:30am-7.30pm Tue-Sat), about 800m from the Vernon train station, rents bikes for the same amount. Between 5pm and 9pm there's roughly one train an hour back to Paris.

From the Clos Normand's far corner a foot tunnel leads under the D5 to the Jardin d'Eau (Water Garden). Having bought this piece of land in 1895 after his reputation had been established (and his bank account had swelled), Monet dug a pool, planted water lilies and constructed the famous Japanese bridge, since rebuilt. Draped with purple wisteria, the bridge blends into the asymmetrical foreground and background, creating the intimate atmosphere for which the 'Painter of Light' was famous.

About 100m northwest of the Maison de Claude Monet is the Musée des Impressionismes Giverny (Giverny Museum of Impressionisms; ☎ 02 32 51 94 65; http://giverny.org/museums/Impressionism/guide; 99 rue Claude Monet; adult/student & 12-18yr/7-12yr/under 7 yr €6.50/4.50/3/free, free to all 1st Sun of month; ☼ 10am-6pm daily Apr-Oct) until 2009 known as the Musée d'Art Américain (American Art Museum), which focused on a fine collection of works by American Impressionist painters who flocked to France in the late 19th and early 20th centuries. The name of the new museum suggests that that all aspects of the Impressionist movement, both home-grown and abroad, and the influence they exerted on later artists would be covered. And, gratefully, Giverny is finally expected to get what it has lacked until now – a collection of Monet's original works drawn from various state-run museums in France.

INFORMATION

Vernon Tourist Office (☎ 02 32 51 39 60; http://giverny.org; 36 rue Carnot; ☼ 9am-noon & 2.30-6.30pm Mon-Sat, 10am-noon Sun May-Oct, 10am-noon & 2-5pm Tue-Sat Nov-Apr) The closest tourist office is in Vernon, 7km northwest of Giverny, and the transport springboard for the village.

EATING & SLEEPING

Many Giverny restaurants and hotels are only open in season.

Auberge du Vieux Moulin (☎ 02 32 51 46 15; www.vieuxmoulingiverny.com; 21 rue de la Falaise; salads €12, lunch menus €15-18, dinner menus €24-35; ☼ lunch daily, dinner to 10pm Fri & Sat Apr-Oct, lunch Fri-Sun Nov-Mar) The lovely little 'Old Mill Inn', a couple of hundred metres east of the Maison de Claude Monet, is an excellent place for lunch and has a lovely terrace.

Hôtel La Musardière (☎ 02 32 21 03 18; www.lamusardiere.fr; 123 rue Claude Monet; s €76, d & tw €81-93, tr €116-125, q €136; ☐) This two-star 10-room hotel dating back to 1880 and evocatively called the 'Idler' is set amid a lovely garden less than 100m northeast of the Maison de Claude Monet. Dining in its summer restaurant (*menus €26 and €36*) is a pleasure.

AUVERS-SUR-OISE

On 20 May 1890 the painter Vincent Van Gogh left a mental asylum in Provence and moved to this small village (population 6940) 35km north of Paris. He came here to reacquaint himself with the light with which he was so familiar in his native Holland, and to be closer to his friend and benefactor Dr Paul Ferdinand Gachet (1828–1909), whose house, the Maison du Docteur Gachet (☎ 01 30 36 81 27; 78 rue du Docteur Gachet; adult/18-25yr/under 18yr €4/3.50/free; ☼ 10.30am-6.30pm Wed-Sun Apr-Oct), can be visited. He set to work immediately, producing at least one painting or sketch every day until his death on 29 July, two months after his arrival.

Today Auvers-sur-Oise is predominantly a shrine to Van Gogh. Foremost is the Maison de Van Gogh (☎ 01 30 36 60 60; www.maisondevangogh.fr; place de la Mairie; adult/12-18yr/under 12yr €5/3/free; 10am-6pm Tue-Sun Mar-early Nov), actually the Auberge Ravoux, where the artist stayed during his 70 days here. Bar the seasonal restaurant on the ground floor, for the most part it's empty. However, there's an excellent video on Van Gogh's life and work, and the bedroom in which he fatally wounded himself is strangely moving. Enter from place rue de la Sansonne. There's an imposing **statue of Van Gogh** by the Russian-born sculptor Ossip Zadkine (1890–1967) in the park to the east.

Above the tourist office in the delightful Manoir des Colombières is the small **Musée Daubigny** (01 30 36 80 20; rue de la Sansonne; adult/student/under 18yr €4/2/free; 2-6pm Wed-Fri, 10.30am-12.30pm & 2-6pm Sat & Sun Apr-Oct, 2-6pm Wed-Fri, 10.30am-12.30pm & 2-5pm Sat & Sun Nov & mid-Jan–Mar), named after the artist Charles-François Daubigny (1818–78), who began the practice of painting *en plein air* (outside), pre-empting the Impressionists. It puts on temporary exhibitions related to art but not always Impressionism or Daubigny's work. To learn more about the forays and frolics of Daubigny, his friends and pupils, head a couple of hundred metres northwest to the **Maison-Atelier de Daubigny** (01 34 48 03 03; 61 rue Daubigny; adult/under 12yr €5.50/free; 2-6.30pm Thu-Sun Easter–mid-Jul & mid-Aug–early Nov), his house and studio. He decorated the walls of his studio from top to bottom with help from painters Camille Corot (1796–1875) and Honoré Daumier (1808–79), and the result is stunning.

To the southwest is the sprawling 17th-century **Château d'Auvers** (01 34 48 48 48; www.chateau-auvers.fr; rue de Léry; adult/student & 6-18yr/family

€12/7.90/28.90; 10.30am-6pm Tue-Sun Apr-Sep, 10.30am-4.30pm Tue-Sun Oct–mid-Dec & mid-Jan–Mar), whose enormously informative and very entertaining interactive audiovisual presentation on Van Gogh and other artists who found their way to Auvers is essential for anyone wanting to truly immerse themselves in Impressionism and the era. You won't soon forget the train journey through an orgy of Impressionist flowers or the re-enacted café and *spectacle* (show). Get in the mood with a visit to the **Musée de l'Absinthe** (01 30 36 83 26; 44 rue Callé; adult/student & 15-17yr/under 15yr €4.50/3.80/free; 1.30-6pm Wed-Fri, 11am-6pm Sat & Sun mid-Jun–mid-Sep, 11am-6pm Sat & Sun mid-Sep–Nov & Mar–mid-Jun) to discover the history of the liqueur that possibly contributed to Van Gogh's downfall.

Finally, there's the **Église Notre Dame** (rue Daubigny; 9.30am-6pm), subject of Van Gogh's painting *L'Église d'Auvers* (1890), and the **cemetery** (Chemin des Vallées) where he and his brother Théo are buried. Look for their plots halfway along the west wall.

Note that apart from the château and the less-than-enthralling Musée Daubigny, all sights are shut in winter.

INFORMATION

Post Office (place de la Mairie)

Tourist Office (01 30 36 10 06; www-auvers-sur-oise.com, in French; rue de la Sansonne; 9.30am-12.30pm & 2-6pm Tue-Sun Apr-Oct, 9.30am-12.30pm & 2-5pm Tue-Fri, to 5.30pm Sat & Sun Nov-Mar) Ask for its excellent free brochure, *Parcours des Peintres de la Vallée de l'Oise*, which maps out the spots where Van Gogh, Daubigny and others

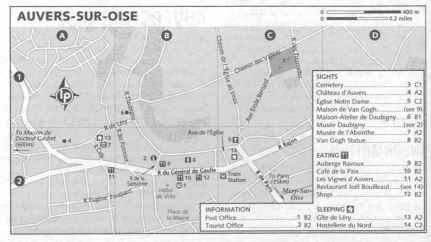

AUVERS-SUR-OISE

SIGHTS	
Cemetery	3 C1
Château d'Auvers	4 A2
Église Notre Dame	5 C2
Maison de Van Gogh	(see 9)
Maison-Atelier de Daubigny	6 B1
Musée Daubigny	(see 2)
Musée de l'Absinthe	7 A2
Van Gogh Statue	8 B2

EATING	
Auberge Ravoux	9 B2
Café de la Paix	10 B2
Les Vignes d'Auvers	11 B2
Restaurant Joël Bouilleaut	(see 14)
Shopi	12 B2

INFORMATION	
Post Office	1 B2
Tourist Office	2 B2

SLEEPING	
Gîte de Léry	13 A2
Hostellerie du Nord	14 C2

ABSINTHE: SPIRIT OF THE AGE

It was the marijuana of the 1960s, the cocaine of the '80s…But until it became the drink of choice among artists, artistes and the underclasses (and thus gained in notoriety), absinthe had been a bourgeois favourite, sipped quietly and innocuously in cafés around the land. It was only when the creative world discovered the wormwood-based liqueur and its hallucinogenic qualities that it took off, and everyone from Verlaine, Rimbaud, Oscar Wilde, Manet, Degas, Toulouse-Lautrec and, of course, Van Gogh wrote about it, painted it and/or drank it. Whether or not it was the *fée verte* (green fairy), as absinthe was known during the Belle Époque, that pushed Van Gogh over the edge is not known; some say he was so poor he couldn't even afford this relatively cheap libation and instead sometimes ate paint containing lead, which may have driven him mad. More than anything else, the easy availability and low cost of the spirit led to widespread alcoholism and in 1915, having just entered into war against Germany and its allies, France found it prudent to ban the drink altogether. In 1998 a much watered-down version of absinthe became legal again in France and the EU. Try it for just under €4 a 2cL shot at Auvers' Café de la Paix.

painted. The office sells the Pass'auvers allowing entry to nine/four attractions for €36/20 throughout the season. It runs guided Van Gogh–themed tours (€5.50) around the village, departing at 3pm on Sunday mid-March to October and there's a 12-minute video (€1) on the village and Van Gogh in French and English in a room just off the office.

EATING

Restaurant Joël Boilleaut (☎ 01 30 36 70 74; 6 rue du Général de Gaulle; menus €49-79; ☺ lunch Tue-Fri & Sun, dinner Tue-Sat Sun) Attached to the Hostellerie du Nord, the racing-green canopied entrance sets the tone for Auvers' fine-dining restaurant, presided over by the eponymous master chef Boilleaut. It is best in summer when tables spill into the walled garden with a view of *that* church.

Auberge Ravoux (☎ 01 30 36 60 60; www.maisondevangogh.fr; 52 rue du Général de Gaulle; menus €29-38; ☺ lunch Wed-Sun, dinner to 9.30pm Fri & Sat early Mar-Nov) What could be a more appropriate way to celebrate the life of Vincent Van Gogh than by having lunch or dinner in the house in which he died? Auberge Ravoux has been a *café d'artistes* (artists' café) since 1876, so it predates Van Gogh's fateful sojourn by more than a dozen years. Reservations essential.

Café de la Paix (☎ 01 30 36 73 23; 11 rue du Général de Gaulle; starters €3/50-8, mains €8.50-12.50, lunch menus €15 & €21; ☺ 7am-3pm Mon, 7am-8.30pm Wed-Sun) Across the road from Auberge Ravoux, locals pile into the 1950s village cinema, now a café-restaurant with stage and wooden floor where art is shown and monthly jazz concerts take place. Food covers the whole gamut, from *bistrot*-style dishes to grills. It occasionally opens on weekend evenings in the height of summer.

Les Vignes d'Auvers (☎ 01 34 48 43 73; rue du Général de Gaulle; lunch menu €15; ☺ 7am-7pm Mon, Thu & Fri, 7.30am-3pm Tue, 8am-7pm Sat & Sun) An excellent place for weekday lunch just south of the Musée de l'Absinthe, the 'Vines of Auvers' serves traditional cuisine in an intimate dining room seating just 30 people.

Shopi Market (rue du Général de Gaulle; ☺ 7am-8pm Mon-Sat, 8am-12.45pm Sun) Central, well-stocked supermarket.

SLEEPING

Gîte de Léry (☎ 01 30 36 86 08; http://gitedelery.free.fr; 17 rue de Léry; apt one/two-night weekend €158/198, week €350-395) This picture-postcard inn housed in

TRANSPORT: AUVERS-SUR-OISE

Distance from Paris 35km

Direction North

Travel time 60 to 70 minutes by train, bus or RER/bus

Car Route A15 from Paris' Porte de Clignancourt, exit 7 to route N184 (direction Beauvais), exit 'Méry-sur-Oise' to D928.

RER train Line A3 from Gare de Lyon or Châtelet–Les Halles (€5.05) to Cergy Préfecture station, then Val d'Oise bus 95-07 (destination Butry) to place de la Mairie. The last bus (☎ 01 34 25 30 81) back to Paris leaves Auvers just before 8pm weekdays (and about 6.45pm weekends).

SNCF train Suburban train from Gare du Nord or Gare St-Lazare to Pontoise or Persan Beaumont then a connecting train to Auvers-sur-Oise (total cost: €5.50); the last train to Paris leaves just after 9pm weekdays (10.45pm weekends). From April to October, SNCF runs a direct train (30 minutes) at weekends departing from Gare du Nord at 9.56am and leaving Auvers at 6.18pm.

a 19th-century farmhouse sleeps five in two bedrooms and boasts an enclosed 550-sq-metre garden. It's around the corner from the Musée de l'Absinthe and less than 100m from the château.

Hostellerie du Nord (☎ 01 30 36 70 74; www.hostel leriedunord.fr; 6 rue du Général de Gaulle; d €99-129, ste €189; ✗ ⌨) The 17th-century townhouse in which this eight-room inn slumbers was one of France's first post offices. Each room evokes a different artist: Van Gogh with its sloping ceiling faces the church the artist so famously painted; Forrière showcases flowery watercolours for sale by the local artist; and Ferré – the only room to have a terrace – is for sculpture lovers.

DISNEYLAND RESORT PARIS

It took almost €4.6 billion and five years of backbreaking work to turn the beet fields east of the capital into Europe's first Disney theme park, which opened amid much fanfare and controversy in 1992. Rocky start now a million moons away, what started out as Euro-Disney sees visitors (mostly families) pour into the park to scare themselves silly in the blood-curdling Tower of Terror, dance in a High School Musical, dive with Nemo, hit 70km/h in a Space Mountain rocket, shake Winnie the Pooh's paw and share a fiesta of other magical moments with Mickey and his Disney mates. And the kids can't seem to get enough. As its marketing bumph boasts, at Disneyland 'the party never stops'.

One-day admission fees at **Disneyland Resort Paris** (☎ 01 60 30 60 53, www.disneylandparis.com; adult/3-11yr €52/44; ☺ Disneyland Park 10am-8pm Mon-Fri, 9am-8pm Sat & Sun early May–mid-Jun & Sep-Mar, 9am-11pm early Jul-Aug; Walt Disney Studios Park 9am-7pm late Jun–early Sep, 10am-7pm Mon-Fri & 9am-7pm Sat & Sun early Sep-late Jun) include unlimited access to all rides and activities in *either* Disneyland Park or Walt Disney Studios Park. Those who opt for the latter can enter Disneyland Park three hours before it closes. Multiple-day passes are also available: a one-day pass (adult/child €65/57) allows entry to both parks for a day and its multiday equivalents (two days €111/94, three days €138/117) allow you to enter and leave both parks as often as you like over non-consecutive days used within one year. Some shows and activities, such as a meal with Disney characters (from €22/15 per adult/child) or the 1½-hour Buffalo Bill's Wild West Dinner Show (from €58/44), cost extra. Admission fees change season to season and a multitude of special offers and accommodation/transport packages are always available.

Anyone who abhors long queues, go elsewhere: waiting times here are hideous and can make it hard going for those with younger children in tow. Buy your tickets at tourist offices or train stations in Paris beforehand to avoid at least one queue (for tickets); once in, reserve your time slot on the busiest rides using FastPass, the park's ride reservation system (limited to one reservation at a time).

Disneyland comprises three areas plus a golf course: **Disney Village**, with its hotels, shops, restaurants and clubs; **Disneyland Park**, with its five theme parks; and **Walt Disney Studios Park**, which brings film, animation and TV production to life, most recently in the walking, talking, life-sized shape of alien puppy Stitch and the dimly lit rollercoaster ride, Crush's Coaster. Fans of the film *Cars* will love the Cars Race Rally. RER and TGV train stations separate the first two, and the studio's neighbour Disneyland Park. Moving walkways whisk visitors to the sights from the far-flung car park.

Disneyland Park's *pays* (lands) include **Main Street USA**, a spotless avenue just inside the main entrance reminiscent of Norman Rockwell's idealised small-town America circa 1900; **Frontierland**, a re-creation of the 'rugged, untamed American West' with the legendary Big Thunder Mountain ride (minimum height for entry: 1.02m); and **Adventureland**, which evokes the Arabian Nights, the wilds of Africa and other exotic lands portrayed in Disney films, including that of the *Pirates of the Caribbean*; the spiralling 360-degree roller coaster, Indiana Jones and the Temple of Peril,

---

TRANSPORT: DISNEYLAND RESORT PARIS

Distance from Paris 32km

Direction East

Travel time 35 to 40 minutes by RER train

Car Route A4 from Porte de Bercy, direction Metz-Nancy, exit No 14.

RER train Line A4 to Marne-la-Vallée/Chessy, Disneyland's RER station, from central Paris (€6.55). Trains run every 15 minutes or so, with the last train back to Paris just after midnight.

is the biggie here (minimum height: 1.40m). Pinocchio, Snow White and other fairy-tale characters come to life in Fantasyland, while Discoveryland is the spot for high-tech attractions and massive-queue rides such as Space Mountain: Mission 2 (minimum height: 1.32m), Star Tours and the *Toy Story 2*–inspired Buzz Lightyear Laser Blast, apparently still the hottest thing since sliced bread.

Before hot-footing it to Disney, devote a good hour on its website planning your day – which rides, shows, characters etc you really want to see.

EATING & SLEEPING

No picnics are allowed at Disneyland Paris, but there are ample themed restaurants to pick from. Options include Buzz Lightyear's Pizza Planet (Discoveryland), Planet Hollywood or the *Happy Days*–inspired Annette's Diner (Disney Village), the meaty Silver Spur Steakhouse or Mexican Fuente del Oro (Frontierland) and the sea-faring Blue Lagoon for future pirates or African-themed Hakuna Matata (Adventureland). Most have *menus* and meal coupons for adults/children (€24/10) are available. Opening hours vary. To avoid another queue, pick your place online and reserve a table in advance (☎ 01 60 30 40 50).

The resort's seven own American-themed hotels (central booking ☎ 01 60 30 60 30) and a handful of others are linked by free shuttle bus to the parks. Rates vary hugely, peaking in July and August and around Christmas; on Friday and Saturday nights and during holiday periods April to October; and on Saturday night mid-February to March. The cheapest rates are Sunday to Thursday January to mid-February, mid-May to June, September, and November to mid-December.

Advertised rates are for packages of from one to four nights and include breakfast and park admission. Lucky hotel guests are often entitled on designated days to two 'Magic hours' in Disneyland Park when the park is closed to regular punters. Consider Disney's Hotel New York for Big Apple 1930s art deco, its Newport Bay Club for a well-heeled nautical theme, Hotel Cheyenne for Wild West Hollywood, and Santa Fe for Tex-Mex. Otherwise, try the prince or the pauper of the sleeping scene:

Disneyland Hôtel (d 1-night package from €281; ☒) The flagship of Disneyland Resort Paris accommodation, this 496-room Victorian palace stares in all its majesty at Sleeping Beauty's 43m-tall castle.

Disney's Davy Crockett Ranch (d 1-night package from €128) As 'relaxing' as you're gonna get at Disney, this trapper's village is not bad. Imagine 535 log cabins planted in a 57 hectare-large wood with limited self-catering facilities (fridge, microwave). Cabins sleep up to six.

PARC ASTÉRIX

Just beyond Roissy Charles de Gaulle airport, this seasonal theme park splits into five 'worlds': Gaul, the Roman Empire, Ancient Greece, the Kings and Across Time. Rides are numerous, invariably hair-raising and as much a hit with kids as the various shows, spectacles and devilishly Gaullist pranks throughout the day.

INFORMATION

Parc Astérix (☎ 0 826 301 040; www.parcasterix. fr; adult/3-11yr/under 3yr €39/29/free, parking €8; ☽ 10am-6pm Apr, 10am-7pm Wed-Sun May-early Jun, 10am-7pm early Jun-Aug, 10am-7pm Wed, Sat & Sun Sep-early Oct) The park stays open to10.30pm on some Saturdays in July and August; see website for more info.

TRANSPORT

Few roads *don't* lead to Paris, one of the most visited destinations on earth. Practically every major airline flies though it, and most European train tracks and bus routes cross it.

As for getting around – easy! The metro system is vast, efficient and spans every pocket of Paris. Buses are more scenic but can be slowed by traffic, while getting to know the many different routes is an art in itself.

For those who prefer a spot of fresher air in their lungs or who simply want to make getting from A to B a historical and aesthetic feast in itself, walking and in-line skating are serious options. With city sights spread across a distance no greater than 10km, the major places of interest are pleasurably walkable. That is, of course, if Paris' innovative, highly praised communal bicycle scheme, Vélib' (p384), doesn't tempt you into some footloose and fancy-free pedal-powered action.

Book flights, tours and train tickets online at www.lonelyplanet.com/travel_services.

AIR

Most international airlines fly through Paris; for flight, route and carrier info contact Aéroports de Paris (☎ 39 50, from abroad +33 1 70 36 39 50; www.aeroportsdeparis.fr).

Airports

Paris is served by Aéroport d'Orly and Aéroport Roissy Charles de Gaulle, both well linked by public transport to central Paris. More of a trek is Aéroport de Beauvais, which handles charter and some budget carriers, including Ryanair (www.ryanair.com) and Wizz Air (www.wizzair.com).

ONLINE TICKET RESOURCES

No great deal to be struck going straight to the airline website? See what these online airline ticketing resources throw up:

- Anyway (www.anyway.fr, in French)
- Bargain Holidays (www.bargainholidays.com)
- Cheap Flights (www.cheapflights.co.uk)
- ebookers (www.ebookers.com)
- Go Voyages (www.govoyages.com, in French)
- Last Minute (www.lastminute.com)
- Opodo (www.opodo.com)
- Skyscanner (www.skyscanner.net)
- Travelocity (www.travelocity.com)
- Voyages SNCF (www.voyages-sncf.com, in French)

ORLY

The older, smaller of Paris' two major airports, Aéroport d'Orly (ORY; Map p355; ☎ 39 50, from abroad +33 1 70 32 93 50; www.aeroportsdeparis.fr), is 19km south of the city. Its two terminals, Orly Ouest (Orly West) and Orly Sud (Orly South), are linked by a shuttle bus service that continues to/from the airport car parks and RER C station Pont de Rungis-Aéroport d'Orly (see the boxed text, p384); the Orlyval automatic metro links both terminals with the RER B station Antony (see boxed text, p385).

See the following section for info on getting from Orly to Roissy Charles de Gaulle (or vice versa).

ROISSY CHARLES DE GAULLE

Aéroport Roissy Charles de Gaulle (CDG; Map p355; ☎ 39 50, from abroad +33 1 70 36 39 50; www.aeroportsdeparis.fr), 28km northeast of central Paris in the suburb of Roissy, has three *aérogares* (terminals) – aptly numbered 1, 2 and 3 – and two train stations served by commuter trains on RER line B3: Aéroport Charles de Gaulle 1 (CDG1), which serves terminals 1 and 3, and the sleek Aéroport Charles de Gaulle 2 (CDG2) for terminals 2A to 2G. A shuttle bus links the terminals with the train stations.

To get between Charles de Gaulle and Orly, take the RER line B3 (direction Massy Palaiseau or St-Rémy-les-Chevreuse) to the Antony stop then pick up the Orlyval automatic metro (total fare adult/child 4-9yr €17.60/10.50) or hop aboard the Air France shuttle bus 3 (adult/child 2-11yr €19/9.50; 6.30am-10.30pm) linking the two airports. Both journeys take an hour, as does a taxi (about €50 to €65).

BEAUVAIS
Charter companies and budget airlines land/take off at Aéroport Paris-Beauvais (BVA; ☎ 0 892 682 066; www.aeroportbeauvais.com), 75km north of central Paris.

BICYCLE
Two-wheeling has never been so good in the city of romance thanks to Vélib' (a crunching of *vélo*, meaning bike, and *liberté*, meaning freedom), a self-service bike scheme whereby you pick up a pearly-grey bike for peanuts from one roadside Vélib' docking station, pedal wherever you're going, and park it right outside at another.

A runaway success since its launch in 2007, Vélib' (☎ 01 30 79 79 30; www.velib.paris.fr; day/week/year subscription €1/5/29, bike hire 1st/2nd/3rd & each additional half-hr free/€2/4) has revolutionised how Parisians get around. Its almost 1500 *stations Vélib'* across the city – one every 300m – sport 20-odd bike stands a head (at the last count there were 23,300 bicycles in all flitting around Paris and the suburbs) and are accessible around the clock. iPhone launched a Vélib' application in mid-2010.

To get a bike, you need a Vélib' account: One- and seven-day subscriptions can be purchased at the terminals found at docking stations with a major credit card provided it has a

GETTING INTO TOWN FROM THE AIRPORT
Getting into town is straightforward and inexpensive thanks to a fleet of public-transport options, listed under airport headings. Bus drivers sell tickets. Children under four travel free and those between four and nine (inclusive) pay half-price on most of the services listed here; exceptions are noted.

Pricier, door-to-door alternatives include taxi (€35 to €50 between central Paris and Orly, €45 to €60 to/from Charles de Gaulle, €140 to €180 to/from Beauvais; see p389 for taxi telephone numbers); or a private minibus shuttle such as Allô Shuttle (☎ 01 41 10 98 11; www.alloshuttle.com), Paris Airports Service (☎ 01 55 98 10 80; www.parisairportservice.com) or PariShuttle (☎ 01 53 39 18 18; www.parishuttle.com). Count on around from €20/30 per one/two people (from €40 between 8pm and 6am) for Orly or Charles de Gaulle and from €140 for one to four people to/from Beauvais. Book in advance and allow ample time for other pick-ups and drop-offs.

Aéroport d'Orly
Unless noted otherwise, these options to/from Orly call at both terminals.

Air France bus 1 (☎ 0 892 350 820; http://videocdn.airfrance.com/cars-airfrance; adult single/return €11.50/18.50; 6.15am-11.150pm from Orly, 6am-11.30pm from Invalides) This *navette* (shuttle bus) runs every 30 minutes to/from the eastern side of Gare Montparnasse (Map p168; 35 minutes) and Aérogare des Invalides (Map p108; 35 minutes) in the 7e. Children aged two to 11 pay half-price.

Noctilien bus 31 (☎ 32 46; www.noctilien.fr; adult €6.40 or 4 metro tickets; 12.30am-5.30pm) Part of the RATP's night service, Noctilien bus 31 links Gare de Lyon (Map p158), Gare d'Austerlitz (Map p158) and place d'Italie (Map p164) with Orly-Sud. It runs every hour and journey time is 45 minutes to an hour.

Orlybus (☎ 32 46; www.ratp.fr; adult €6.40; 6am-11.20pm from Orly, 5.35am-11.05pm from Paris) This bus runs every 15 to 20 minutes between both terminals and metro Denfert-Rochereau (Map p168; 20 to 30 minutes) in the 14e, making several stops in the eastern 14e en route.

Orlyval (☎ 32 46; www.ratp.fr; adult €9.85; 6am-11pm) From either terminal take the Orlyval automatic rail (€7.60) to the RER B station Antony, then RER B4 north (€2.25; 35 to 40 minutes to Châtelet, every four to 12 minutes). Orlyval tickets are valid for the subsequent RER and metro journey.

RATP bus 183 (☎ 32 46; www.ratp.fr; adult €1.60 or 1 metro/bus ticket; 6am-9.40pm from Orly, 5.35am-8.35pm from Porte de Choisy) The cheapest means of getting to/from Orly Sud, this slow public bus links the South Terminal with metro Porte de Choisy (Map p164; one hour), on the southern edge of the 13e, every 30 minutes. Another metro ticket gets you into central Paris.

RATP bus 285 (☎ 32 46; www.ratp.fr; adult €6.40 or 4 metro tickets; 5.05am-midnight from Orly, 5am-12.40am from Paris) Formerly known as Jetbus, the 285 runs every 10 to 30 minutes to/from metro Villejuif Louis Aragon (55 minutes), a bit south of the 13e on the city's southern fringe, from where a metro/bus ticket gets you into town.

microchip (be warned North Americans). As a deposit you'll need to pre-authorise a *caution* (deposit or guarantee) of €150, which is debited if your bike is not returned or is reported as stolen. If the station you want to return your bike to is full, swipe your card across the multilingual terminal to get 15 minutes for free to find another station. Bikes are geared to cyclists aged 14 and over, and are fitted with gears, antitheft lock with key, reflective strips and front/rear lights. Bring your own helmet though!

Note that bicycles are not allowed on buses or the metro except on line 1 on Sunday and public holidays until 4.30pm. You can, however, take your bicycle to the suburbs on RER lines before 6.30am, between 9am and 4.30pm and after 7pm on weekdays, and all day at the weekend and on public holidays. More-lenient rules apply to SNCF commuter services. Contact SNCF (p390) for details.

For more information on cycling in Paris, and a list of rental outlets where you can rent two wheels for longer periods of time, see p312. Guided bicycle tours are listed on p400.

BOAT

For pleasure cruises on the Seine, Canal St-Martin and Canal de l'Ourcq, see p401.

For a more flexible, hop-on-and-off approach, sail with Batobus (☎ 0 825 050 101; www.batobus.com; adult 1-/2-/3-day pass €13/17/20, student €9/12/14, child 2-16yr €7/9/10; ☒ 10am-9.30pm late May–Aug, 10am-7pm Sep–early Nov & mid-Mar–late May, 10.30am-4.30pm mid-Nov–early Jan & early Feb–mid-Mar,

RER C & shuttle (☎ 32 46; www.ratp.fr; adult €6.20; ☒ 5am-11.30pm) From the airport, hop aboard the airport shuttle bus (every 15 to 30 minutes) to the RER station Pont de Rungis-Aéroport d'Orly, then RER C2 train to Paris' Gare d'Austerlitz (50 minutes). Coming from Paris, be sure to get the shuttle at Pont de Rungis that goes to the correct terminal. This service as formerly known as Orlyrail.

Aéroport Roissy Charles de Gaulle

Air France bus 2 (☎ 0 892 350 820; http://videocdn.airfrance.com/cars-airfrance; adult single/return €15/24; ☒ 5.45am-11pm) Links the airport every 30 minutes with the Arc de Triomphe outside 1 av Carnot, 17e (Map p126; 45 minutes) and Porte Maillot metro station (17e) on line 1 (Map p134; 35 to 50 minutes). Children aged two to 11 pay half-price.

Air France bus 4 (☎ 0 892 350 820; http://videocdn.airfrance.com/cars-airfrance; adult single/return €16.50/27; ☒ 7am-9pm from CDG, 6.30am-9.30pm from Paris) Links the airport every 30 minutes with Gare de Lyon (Map p158; 50 minutes) and Gare Montparnasse (Map p168; 55 minutes). Children aged two to 11 pay half-price.

Noctilien bus 140 & 143 (☎ 32 46; www.noctilien.fr; adult €4.80 or 3 metro tickets; ☒ 12.30am-5.30pm) Part of the RATP night service, Noctilien bus 140 from Gare de l'Est and 143 from Gare de l'Est and Gare du Nord go to Roissy-Charles de Gaulle hourly.

RATP bus 350 (☎ 32 46; www.ratp.fr; adult €4.80 or 3 metro tickets; ☒ 5.30am-11pm) Links Aérogares 1 and 2 with Gare de l'Est (Map p140; one hour, every 30 minutes) and Gare du Nord.

RATP bus 351 (☎ 32 46; www.ratp.fr; adult €4.80 or 3 metro tickets; ☒ 5.30am-11pm) Links the eastern side of place de la Nation (Map p158) with Roissy-Charles de Gaulle (50 minutes, every 30 minutes).

RER B (☎ 32 46; www.ratp.fr; adult €8.50; ☒ 5.20am-midnight) Though this line was under extensive renovation at the time of research, with replacement buses on duty, RER line B3 usually links CDG1 and CDG2 with the city (30 minutes; every 10 to 15 minutes).

Roissybus (☎ 32 46; www.ratp.fr; adult €9.10; ☒ 5.30am-11pm) Direct public bus linking several points at both terminals with Opéra (corner of rue Scribe and rue Auber) in the 9e (Map p126; 45 to 60 minutes, every 15 minutes).

Aéroport Paris-Beauvais

Navette Officielle (Official Shuttle Bus; ☎ 0 892 682 064, airport 0 892 682 066; 1 way €14) Leaves Parking Pershing (Map p134), west of the Palais des Congrès de Paris, 3¼ hours before flight departures (board 15 minutes before) and leaves the airport 20 minutes after arrivals, dropping passengers south of the Palais des Congrès on place de la Porte Maillot (Map p134). Journey time is one to 1¼ hours and tickets can be purchased at the sales point just outside the terminal and from a kiosk in the car park. You no longer have to produce a plane ticket in order to board the bus.

closed early Jan–early Feb). Its fleet of glassed-in trimarans dock at eight small piers along the Seine and tickets are sold at each stop as well as tourist offices. For those keen to combine boat with bus, its Paris à la Carte deal allows two/three consecutive days of unlimited travel on Batobus boats and L'Open Tour buses (p401) for €41/44 (child€20/20). Boats depart every 15 to 30 minutes from various stops:

Champs-Élysées (Map p126; Port des Champs-Élysées, 8e; Ⓜ Champs-Élysées–Clemenceau)

Eiffel Tower (Map p118; Port de la Bourdonnais, 7e; Ⓜ Champ de Mars–Tour Eiffel)

Hôtel de Ville (Map p152; quai de l'Hôtel de Ville, 4e; Ⓜ Hôtel de Ville)

Jardin des Plantes (Map p100; quai St-Bernard, 5e; Ⓜ Jussieu)

Musée d'Orsay (Map p108; quai de Solférino, 7e; Ⓜ Musée d'Orsay)

Musée du Louvre (Map p76; quai du Louvre, 1er; Ⓜ Palais Royal–Musée du Louvre)

Notre Dame (Map p100; quai de Montebello, 5e; Ⓜ St-Michel)

St-Germain des Prés (Map p108; quai Malaquais, 6e; Ⓜ St-Germain des Prés)

BUS
Local Buses

Paris' bus system, operated by RATP (see p388), runs from 5.30am to 8.30pm Monday to Saturday; after that, certain *service en soirée* (evening service) lines continue until between midnight and 12.30am. Services are drastically reduced on Sunday and public holidays, when buses run from 7am to 8.30pm. Among useful evening routes – distinct from the Noctilien overnight services described here – are route 26 between the Gare St-Lazare and Nation via Gare du Nord; route 38 linking Gare du Nord, Gare de l'Est, Châtelet and Porte d'Orléans via blvd St-Michel; route 92 from Gare Montparnasse to place Charles de Gaulle via Alma Marceau; and route 95 between Porte de Montmartre and Porte de Vanves via Opéra and St-Germain. The same fares and conditions apply on evening routes as on regular daytime services.

Night Buses

Night buses pick up after the last metro (around 1.15am Sunday to Thursday, 2.15am

Friday and Saturday). Buses depart hourly from 12.30am to 5.30pm. The RATP runs 47 night bus lines known as **Noctilien** (www.noctilien.fr), including direct or semidirect services out to the suburbs. The services pass through the main *gares* (train stations) and cross the major axes of the city before leading out to the suburbs. Many go through Châtelet: rue de Rivoli, blvd Sébastopol and av Victoria (Map p76, which is a central hub for night buses). Look for navy-blue N or Noctilien signs at bus stops. There are two circular lines within Paris (the N01 and N02) that link four main train stations – St-Lazare, Gare de l'Est, Gare de Lyon and Gare Montparnasse – as well as popular nightlife areas (Bastille, Champs-Elysées, Pigalle, St-Germain).

The buses are equipped with security surveillance systems linked to local police, and RATP staff members are posted at major points to help passengers. Do remain alert, however, and watch your bags and pockets – especially on weekends when the post-drinking crowd circulates.

Noctilien services are included on your Mobilis or Paris Visite (p389) pass for the zones in which you are travelling. Otherwise you pay a certain number of standard €1.60 metro/bus tickets, depending on the length of your journey. The driver can sell you a ticket for €1.70 and will explain how many you need to get to your destination.

Tickets & Fares

Normal bus rides embracing one or two bus zones cost one metro/bus ticket; longer rides require two or even three tickets. Transfers to other buses – but not the metro – are allowed on the same ticket as long as the change takes place 1½ hours between the first and last validation. This does not apply to Noctilien services.

Whatever kind of single-journey ticket you have, you must *oblitérer* (cancel) it in the *composteur* (cancelling machine) next to the driver. If you have a Mobilis or Paris Visite (p389) pass, flash it at the driver when you board. Do *not* cancel the magnetic coupon that accompanies your pass.

Long-Distance Buses

Eurolines (Map p100; ☎ 0 892 899 091, from abroad +33 1 41 86 24 21; www.eurolines.fr; 55 rue St-Jacques, 5e; ⏰ 9.30am-6.30pm Mon-Fri, 10am-1pm & 2-5pm Sat; Ⓜ Cluny-La Sorbonne), an association of national and private bus companies in some 30 countries that links Paris with points all over Western and Central Europe, Scandinavia and Morocco, can organise ticket reservations and sales. The **Gare Routière Internationale de Paris-Galliéni** (Map p68; ☎ 0 892 899 091; 28 av du Général de Gaulle; 🕑 6am-11pm; Ⓜ Galliéni), the city's international bus terminal, is in the eastern suburb of Bagnolet.

CAR & MOTORCYCLE

While driving in Paris is nerve-wracking, it's not impossible – except for the faint-hearted or indecisive. The fastest way to get across the city is usually via the blvd Périphérique (Map p68), the ring road that encircles the city.

Hire

You can get a small car (eg a Renault Twingo or Opel Corsa) for one day for as low as €45, including 100km and insurance. Most of the larger companies have offices throughout Paris and at airports and main train stations, including **Gare de Nord** (Map p140; Ⓜ Gare de Nord). Several are represented at **Aérogare des Invalides** (Map p108; Ⓜ Invalides) in the 7e.

Avis (☎ 0 821 230 760; www.avis.fr, in French)

Budget (☎ 0 825 003 564; www.budget.fr, in French)

Europcar (☎ 0 825 358 358; www.europcar.fr, in French)

Hertz (☎ 0 825 889 265; www.hertz.fr)

Sixt (☎ 0 820 007 498; www.sixt.fr, in French)

Smaller agencies often offer more-reasonable rates and have several branches throughout Paris. Find a complete list in the Yellow Pages (www.pagesjaunes.fr, in French) under 'Location d'Automobiles: Tourisme et Utilitaires'.

ADA (☎ 0 825 169 169; www.ada.fr, in French) has a dozen branches in Paris including 8e arrondissement (Map p126; ☎ 01 42 93 65 13; 72 rue de Rome, 8e; Ⓜ Rome) and 11e arrondissement (Map p148; ☎ 01 48 06 58 13; 34 av de la République, 11e; Ⓜ Parmentier).

Rent a Car Système (☎ 0 891 700 200; www.rentacar.fr, in French) has 14 outlets in Paris, including Bercy (Map p158; ☎ 01 43 45 98 99; 79 rue de Bercy, 12e; Ⓜ Bercy) and 16e arrondissement (Map p118; ☎ 01 42 88 40 04; 84 av de Versailles, 16e; Ⓜ Mirabeau).

A godsend for those who need a car for just a couple of couple of hours or half a day is the self-service pay-as-you-go scheme **Connect by Hertz** (☎ 0 800 450 400; www.connectbyhertz.com), a carbon-copy of the popular Streetcar service in London. After registering and pay-

ing the €120 annual membership, you locate via the internet the closest available vehicle to where you are staying, unlock the car with your membership card, release the key with a PIN and drive on. Prices start at €4/32 an hour/day, with each kilometre €0.35. Rates include all insurance and petrol.

At the time of writing the Mairie de Paris announce plans to create a network by late 2011 of electrical rental cars called Autolib' (www.paris.fr) – not unlike its namesake Vélib' (p384). Details were sketchy but would involve 3000 vehicles available at 1000 locations, 700 of which would be in central Paris.

If you've got the urge to look like you've just stepped into (or out of) a black-and-white French film from the 1950s, a motor scooter will fit the bill perfectly.

Freescoot (p312) Rents 50cc scooters per day/24 hours/weekend/week from €30/35/75/145, and 125cc scooters for €45/55/110/245. Prices include third-party insurance as well as helmets, locks, raingear and gloves. To rent a 50/125cc scooter you must be at least 21/23 and leave a credit card deposit of €1300/1600.

Left Bank Scooters (☎ 06 82 70 13 82; www.leftbankscooters.com; 🕑 8am-8pm) Run by a young Australian-British couple, this outfit rents spanking-new (they are replaced every 6000km) pastel-coloured Vespa XLV 50cc scooters for 24 hours at between €70 and €80 and 125cc scooters for €80 to €90, including insurance, helmet and wet-weather gear. They'll deliver to and pick up from your hotel and can arrange tours (from €130) as far as Versailles. Renters must be at least 30 years old and hold a motorcycle license. Credit-card deposit is €1000.

Parking

In most parts of Paris, street parking costs €1.50 to €3 an hour from 9am to 7pm Monday to Saturday and is limited to a maximum of two hours. Parking meters do not accept coins but require a Paris Carte, available at any *tabac* (tobacconist) for €10 to €30. The machine will issue you a ticket for the allotted time, which should be placed on the dashboard behind the windscreen. Municipal public car parks, of which there are more than 200 in Paris, charge between €2 and €3.50 an hour or €20 to €25 per 24 hours. Most open 24 hours.

Parking attendants dispense fines ranging from €11 to €35, depending on the offence and its gravity, with great abandon. To pay a fine, buy a *timbre amende* (fine stamp) for the amount written on the ticket from any *tabac* (tobacconist), stick a stamp on the preaddressed coupon and put it in a postbox.

METRO & RER NETWORKS

Paris' underground network, run by RATP (Régie Autonome des Transports Parisians), consists of two separate but linked systems: the Métropolitain, aka the *métro*, with 16 lines (including the now independent 3b and 7b) and 300 stations (with 384 stops); and the RER (Réseau Express Régional), a network of suburban lines (designated A to E and then numbered) that pass through the city centre. When giving the names of stations in this book, the term 'metro' is used to cover both the Métropolitain and the RER system within Paris proper.

Information

For information on the metro, RER and bus systems, contact RATP (☎ 32 46; www.ratp.fr; ☉ 7am-9pm Mon-Fri, 9am-5pm Sat & Sun). Metro maps of various sizes and degrees of detail are available for free at metro ticket windows; several can also be downloaded for free from the RATP website.

Metro

Metro lines have a terminus at each end; the name of the line depends on which direction you are travelling. To simplify matters further, on maps and plans each line has a different colour and number (from 1 to 14, plus 3b and 7b).

Signs in metro and RER stations indicate the way to the correct platform for your line. The *direction* signs on each platform indicate the terminus. On lines that split into several branches (such as lines 7 and 13), the terminus of each train is indicated on the cars with backlit panels, and on the electronic signs on each platform giving the number of minutes until the next and subsequent train.

Signs marked *correspondance* (transfer or change) show how to reach connecting trains. At stations with many intersecting lines, like Châtelet and Montparnasse Bienvenüe, walking from one train to the next can take a very long time.

Different station exits are indicated by white-on-blue *sortie* (exit) signs. You can get your bearings by checking the *plan du quartier* (neighbourhood maps) posted at exits.

Each line has its own schedule, but trains usually start at around 5.30am, with the last train beginning its run between 12.35am and 1.15am (2.15am on Friday and Saturday).

RER

The RER is faster than the metro but the stops are much farther apart. Some attractions, particularly those on the Left Bank (eg the Musée d'Orsay, Eiffel Tower and Panthéon), can be reached far more conveniently by the RER than by the metro.

RER lines are known by an alphanumeric combination – the letter (A to E) refers to the line, the number to the spur it will follow somewhere out in the suburbs. As a rule of thumb, even-numbered RER lines head for Paris' southern or eastern suburbs, while odd-numbered ones go north or west. Stations served are usually indicated on electronic destination boards above the platform.

Tickets & Fares

The same RATP tickets are valid on the metro, the RER (for travel within the city limits), buses, trams and the Montmartre funicular. A ticket – white in colour and called *Le Ticket t+* – costs €1.60 (half-price for children aged four to nine years) if bought individually and

CLIMATE CHANGE & TRAVEL

Every form of transport that relies on carbon-based fuel generates CO_2, the main cause of human-induced climate change. Modern travel is dependent on aeroplanes and while they might use less fuel per kilometre per person than most cars, they travel much greater distances. It's not just CO_2 emissions from aircraft that are the problem. The altitude at which aircraft emit gases (including CO_2) and particles contributes significantly to their total climate change impact. The Intergovernmental Panel on Climate Change believes aviation is responsible for 4.9% of climate change – double the effect of its CO_2 emissions alone.

Lonely Planet regards travel as a global benefit. We encourage the use of more climate-friendly travel modes where possible and, together with other concerned partners across many industries, we support the carbon offset scheme run by ClimateCare. Websites such as climatecare.org use 'carbon calculators' that allow people to offset the greenhouse gases they are responsible for with contributions to portfolios of climate-friendly initiatives throughout the developing world. Lonely Planet offsets the carbon footprint of all staff and author travel.

€11.60 for adults for a *carnet* (book) of 10 (NB: half-price carnets are both available for children). Tickets are sold at all metro stations; ticket windows and vending machines accept most credit cards.

One ticket lets you travel between any two metro stations (no return journeys) for a period of 1½ hours, no matter how many transfers are required. You can also use it on the RER for travel within zone 1, which encompasses all of central Paris. A single ticket can be used to transfer between buses, but not to transfer from the metro to bus or vice-versa. Transfers are not allowed on Noctilien buses.

Always keep your ticket until you exit from your station; you may be stopped by a *contrôleur* (ticket inspector) and will have to pay a fine (€25 to €50 on the spot or €47 to €72 within two months) if you don't have a valid ticket.

TRAVEL PASSE

If you're staying in Paris longer than a few days, the cheapest and easiest way to use public transport in Paris is to get a combined travel pass that allows unlimited travel on the metro, RER and buses for a week, a month or even a year. You can get passes for travel in two to six zones but, unless you'll be using the suburban commuter lines extensively, the basic ticket valid for zones 1 and 2 should be sufficient.

Navigo (www.navigo.fr, in French), like London's Oyster or Hong Kong's Octopus cards, is a system that provides you with a refillable weekly, monthly or yearly unlimited pass that you can recharge at machines in most metro stations; to pass through the station barrier swipe the card across the electronic panel as you go through the turnstiles. Standard Navigo passes, available to anyone with an address in Île de France, are free but take up to three weeks to be issued; ask at the ticket counter for a form or visit the Navigo website. Otherwise pay €5 for a Nagivo Découverte (Navigo Discovery) card, which is issued on the spot but (unlike the standard Navigo pass) not replaceable if lost or stolen. Both passes require a passport photo and can be recharged for periods of one week or more.

A weekly ticket (*coupon hebdomadaire*) pass costs €17.20 for zones 1 and 2 and is valid from Monday to Sunday. It can be purchased from the previous Friday until Thursday; from the next day weekly tickets are available for the following week only. Even if you're in Paris for three or four days, it may work out cheaper than buying carnets and will certainly cost less than buying a daily Mobilis or Paris Visite pass. The monthly ticket (*coupon mensuel*; €56.60 for zones 1 and 2) begins on the first day of each calendar month; you can buy one from the 20th of the preceding month. Both are sold in metro and RER stations from 6.30am to 10pm and at some bus terminals.

TOURIST PASSES

The Mobilis and Paris Visite passes are valid on the metro, RER, SNCF's suburban lines, buses, night buses, trams and Montmartre funicular railway. No photo is needed, but write your card number on the ticket. Passes are sold at larger metro and RER stations, SNCF offices in Paris, and the airports.

The Mobilis card coupon allows unlimited travel for one day in two/three/four/five/six zones and costs €5.90/7.90/9.80/13.20/16.70. Buy it at any metro, RER or SNCF station in the Paris region. Depending on how many times you plan to hop on/off the metro in a day, a *carnet* might work out cheaper.

Paris Visite allows unlimited travel (including to/from airports) as well as discounted entry to certain museums and other discounts and bonuses. Passes are valid for either three or six zones. The zone 1 to 3 pass costs €8.80/14.40/19.60/28.30 for one/two/three/five days. Children aged four to 11 years pay half-price.

TAXI

The *prise en charge* (flagfall) is €2.20. Within the city limits, it costs €0.89 per kilometre for travel between 10am and 5pm Monday to Saturday (*Tarif A*; white light on taxi roof and meter). At night (5pm to 10am), on Sunday from 7am to midnight, and in the inner suburbs the rate is €1.14 per km (*Tarif B*; orange light). Travel in the outer suburbs is at *Tarif C*, €1.33 per kilometre (blue light). There's a €2.95 surcharge for taking a fourth passenger, but drivers often refuse for insurance reasons. The first piece of baggage is free; additional pieces over 5kg cost €1 extra. When tipping, round up to the nearest €1 or so.

Flagging down one of Paris' 16,600-odd licensed taxis can be difficult, particularly after 1am. Some 'freelance' (illegal) taxis nip around town but are not organised (like minicabs are in London) and offer no guarantee on price or safety.

To order a taxi, call Paris' central taxi switchboard (☎ 01 45 30 30 30, passengers with reduced mobility

01 47 39 00 91; 🕓 24hr) or reserve online with **Alpha Taxis** (☎ 01 45 85 85 85; www.alphataxis.com, in French), **Taxis Bleus** (☎ 01 49 36 29 48, 0 891 701 010; www.taxis-bleus.com, in French) or **Taxis G7** (☎ 01 47 39 47 39; www.taxisg7.fr, in French).

TRAIN

Suburban

The RER and the commuter lines of the SNCF (Société' Nationale des Chemins de Fer; ☎ 0 891 362 020; www.transilien.com) serve suburban destinations outside the city limits (ie zones 2 to 6) in the Île de France. Purchase your ticket *before* you board the train or you won't be able to get out of the station when you arrive. You are not allowed to pay the additional fare when you get there.

If you are issued with a full-sized SNCF ticket for travel to the suburbs, validate it in one of the time-stamp pillars *before* you board the train. You may also be given a *contremarque magnétique* (magnetic ticket) to get through any metro-/RER-type turnstiles on the way to/from the platform. If you are travelling on a Mobilis or Paris Visite (p389) pass, do *not* punch the magnetic coupon in one of the time-stamp machines. Most but not all RER/SNCF tickets purchased in the suburbs for travel to the city allow you to continue your journey by metro. For some destinations, tickets can be purchased at any metro ticket window; for others you have to go to an RER station on the line you need to buy a ticket.

Mainline & International

Thanks to very fast TGV (*train à grande vitesse*) trains, of which the French are inordinately proud, many of the most exciting and scenic cities in provincial France are all within a few hours of the capital from one of six major train stations, each with its own metro station: Gare d'Austerlitz (13e), Gare de l'Est (10e), Gare de Lyon (12e), Gare du Nord (10e), Gare Montparnasse (15e) and Gare St-Lazare (8e). Each station handles passenger traffic to different parts of France and Europe. Information for SNCF mainline services (☎ 36 35, 0 892 353 535; www.voyages-sncf.com) is available by phone or internet.

The super-speedy Eurostar (☎ 0 892 353 539; in UK 0 8432 186 186; www.eurostar.com) links Gare du Nord with London's St-Pancras International train station in a just over two hours and not much longer with dozens of other regional stations in the UK; through-ticketing to/from Paris and regional stations throughout the UK is now possible. Gare du Nord is likewise the point of departure/terminus for Thalys (☎ 36 35, 0 892 353 536; www.thalys.com) trains to Brussels, Amsterdam and Cologne.

Mainline stations in Paris have left-luggage offices and/or *consignes* (lockers). They cost €4/7/9.50 per 48 hours for a small/medium/large bag, then €5 per day per item. Most left-luggage offices and lockers open from around 6.15am to 11.15pm.

TRAM & FUNICULAR

Paris has three tram lines run by the RATP, although the majority of visitors are unlikely to use any of them. T1 links the northern suburb of St-Denis (metro line 13) with Noisy le Sec on RER line E2 via metro La Courneuve 8 Mai 1945 on metro line 7 and Bobigny Pablo Picasso on metro line 5; T2 runs south along the Seine from La Défense to metro Porte de Versailles on metro line 12; and the ever-expanding T3 currently traces a 7.9km-long curve around the southern edge of Paris from Pont du Gariglian (15e), through Porte de Versailles (where it links with the T2 and metro line 12), Porte d'Orléans, Porte d'Italie and up to Porte d'Ivry on metro line 7. Normal metro tickets and passes remain valid here and function in the same way as on the buses. Buy tickets at automatic machines at each tram stop.

One form of transport that most travellers will use is the Funiculaire de Montmartre (Montmartre funicular), which whisks visitors up the southern slope of Butte de Montmartre from square Willette (Ⓜ Anvers on line 2) to Sacré Cœur.

TRANSPORT TRAIN

DIRECTORY

BUSINESS HOURS

Small businesses are open daily, except Sunday and sometimes Monday. Hours are usually 9am or 10am to 6.30pm or 7pm, often with a midday break from 1pm to 2pm or 2.30pm. Shops that are open on Monday usually get started late (eg at 11.30am).

Banks usually open from 8am or 9am to between 11.30am and 1pm, and then from 1.30pm or 2pm to 4.30pm or 5pm, Monday to Friday or Tuesday to Saturday. Exchange services may end 30 minutes before closing time.

Most post offices open 8am to 7pm weekdays and 8am or 9am till noon on Saturday.

Supermarkets open Monday to Saturday from 8.30am or 9am to 8pm, though a few now open on Sunday morning as well. Small food shops are mostly closed on Sunday and often Monday too, so Saturday afternoon may be your last chance to stock up on certain types of food (eg cheese) until Tuesday.

Restaurants keep the most convoluted hours of any business in Paris; for details see p219.

Most museums are closed one day a week, usually Monday or Tuesday. Some museums have a weekly *nocturne* in which they remain open until as late as 10pm, including the Louvre (Wednesday and Friday) and the Musée d'Orsay (Thursday).

CHILDREN

Paris is extraordinarily kid-friendly and we're not talking Disneyland: children are welcome participants in many aspects of social life in France, including visiting museums and eating out. If you're on a family trip, you'll find no shortage of things to do, from playing tag around Daniel Buren's black-and-white columns at Palais Royal (p78), laughing with puppets in the Jardin du Luxembourg (p106), sailing down the Seine (p401) or resting little legs with a city sightseeing tour via one of its two above-ground metro lines (2 and 6).

Many midrange restaurants are fairly casual when it comes to dining with children. Some wait staff may make a face but they won't stop you from splitting one dish between two kids, and other diners are not going to frown disapprovingly if your three-year-old can't sit still

for more than 15 minutes. However, very few places will offer crayons or games, so make sure you come prepared. Some restaurants serve a *menu enfant* (set children's menu), usually for children under 12, though starters or the savoury crêpes served in brasseries are usually more imaginative (hamburger patties – without the bun – and fries get tiresome after two days). *Cafétérias* (p218) are a good place to bring kids for quick, inexpensive meals, as are French chain restaurants (p219). When the weather is nice, picnics by the Seine or in a park are probably the easiest (and often a very delicious) option.

For information on finding accommodation, see p326.

Note that you cannot buy a *carnet* (book of 10) of children's metro tickets. They have to be purchased individually.

Information

Check the *What's On* directory on www.parisinfo.com for a list of current exhibitions, workshops, performances and seasonal amusement parks (eg the Ferris wheel at place de la Concorde) for children. *Pariscope* and *L'Officiel des Spectacles* (p294) both have decent 'Enfants' sections covering the week's performances and circuses for kids. The newspaper *Libération* (p40) produces a bimonthly supplement *Paris Mômes* (www.parismomes.fr, in French). It is sometimes translated into English, but don't count on it. For those who read French the twice-monthly freebie *Bubble Mag* (www.bubblemag.fr) has plenty of information on what to do with kids.

Lonely Planet's *Travel with Children* includes useful advice for travelling parents. The Michelin Green Guide *Paris Enfants* is an excellent resource even for those who don't speak French as there are lots of listings.

Sights & Activities

Many museums organise educational, fun-packed *ateliers enfants* (kids' workshops) for children aged four or six and upwards. Sessions cost €3 to €10, last one to three hours, and must be booked in advance; some are in English. Favourites include hands-on art workshops at Les Arts Décoratifs (p74),

Musée de la Halle St-Pierre (p135), Musée d'Orsay (p107), Palais de Tokyo (p120), Centre Pompidou (p78) and **Musée en Herbe** (Map p72; ☎ 01 40 67 97 66; www.musee-en-herbe.com, in French; 21 rue Herold, 1e; workshop €10; ☻ 10am-7pm; Ⓜ Les Halles); money- and medal-making at the Musée de la Monnaie de Paris (p107); meeting marine life at the Centre de la Mer (p104); learning about animals through activities and film at the Musée National d'Histoire Naturelle (p99); and calligraphy, Arab music and mosaics workshops at the Institut du Monde Arabe (p99).

Building an Eiffel Tower, Parisian church or entire village from thousands of miniature wooden planks is what kids do at the innovative **Centre Kapla** (Map p158; ☎ 01 43 56 13 38; www.kapla.com/centre_kapla.php; 27 rue de Montreuil, 11e; session €10; ☻ 10.30am-6pm Wed & Sat, daily during school holidays; Ⓜ Faidherbe-Chaligny). It runs three 1½-hour building sessions daily; book in advance.

Around Paris, the mesmerising equestrian displays and stable visits at Versailles (p354) and Chantilly (p366) make magical half-day trips; the Disney (p380) and Astérix theme parks (p381) require at least a full day.

Playgrounds are easy to find; useful ones include **Port de Plaisance de Paris-Arsenal** (Map p158; 4e; Ⓜ Bastille), **Jardin du Luxembourg** (Map p108; 6e; Ⓜ Luxembourg) and **Square Suzanne Buisson** (Map p138; Montmartre, 18e; Ⓜ Abbesses). The **Jardin des Tuileries** (Map p72; 1e; Ⓜ Concorde), near the Louvre, has kid's activities on Wednesday, Saturday and Sunday, and a summer amusement park. The best playground in the Paris area is in the **Parc Floral** (off Map p158; www.parcfloraldeparis.com; rte du Champ de Manoeuvre, Bois de Vincennes; free except Wed, Sat & Sun June-Sep adult/under 7 yr €5/free; ☻ 9.30am-8pm; Ⓜ Château de Vincennes), a perfect picnic spot with outdoor jazz concerts, puppet shows and giant climbing webs, 30m-high slides and a zip line, among other attractions. In summer, Paris Plages (p19) is an excellent spot for kids of all ages, though it can get crowded.

See the Neighbourhoods chapter for details on the following suggestions:

Aquarium Tropical (p162) Aquarium (€15 to €23 for a family of four).

CinéAqua (p120) Aquarium (€64 for a family of four).

Cité de la Musique (p143) Saturday-morning educational concerts, music discovery workshops, concerts and shows for children.

Cité des Sciences et de l'Industrie (p142) Hands-on science exhibits for kids aged two and up, plus two special-effects cinemas and a planetarium.

Eiffel Tower (p116) Need we say more?

Jardin d'Acclimation (p122) Great amusement park for kids with puppet shows, boat rides, a small water park, art exhibits for kids and sometimes special movies.

Ménagerie du Jardin des Plantes (p98) Small zoo near the Musée National d'Histoire Naturelle.

Musée de la Magie (p151) Magic shows.

Musée National d'Histoire Naturelle (p99) Many of the world's animals (mounted by taxidermists) and dinosaur skeletons in two separate buildings.

Palais de la Découverte (p129) Hands-on science exhibits.

Parc Zoologique de Paris (p161) Zoo.

Babysitting

L'Officiel des Spectacles (p294) lists *gardes d'enfants* (babysitters) available in Paris.

Au Paradis des Petits (☎ 01 43 65 58 58; per hr from €7.20, subscription €10) English services limited.

Baby Sitting Services (☎ 01 46 21 33 16; per hr from €7, 10hr or 1 day €65, subscription €12.90) English spoken.

Étudiants de l'Institut Catholique (Map p108; ☎ 01 44 39 60 24; 21 rue d'Assas, 6e; per hr from €8, plus €2 for each session; Ⓜ Rennes) Some English; closed during school holidays.

Fondation Claude Pompidou (☎ 01 40 13 75 00) Specialises in looking after children with disabilities.

CLIMATE

The Paris basin lies midway between coastal Brittany and mountainous Alsace and is affected by both climates. The Île de France region, of which Paris is the centre, records among the lowest annual precipitation (about 640mm) in the nation, but rainfall is erratic; you're just as likely to be caught in a heavy spring shower or an autumn downpour as in a sudden summer cloudburst. Paris' average

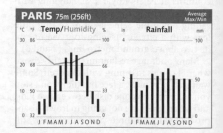

yearly temperature is just under 12°C (2°C in January, 19°C in July), but the mercury sometimes drops below zero in winter and can climb into the 30s in the middle of summer.

Check the Météo France website (www. meteofrance.com, in French) for a reliable three-day forecast. The national forecast can be heard on ☎ 0 899 701 234 in French or ☎ 0 899 701 111 in one of 11 different languages. Call charges for either number are €1.35 then €0.35 per minute.

COURSES
Cooking
What better place to discover the secrets of *la cuisine française* than in Paris, the capital of gastronomy? Courses are available at different levels and durations, and the cost of tuition varies widely. One of the most popular – and affordable – courses for beginners is the Les Coulisses du Chef Cours de Cuisine Olivier Berté (Map p72; ☎ 01 40 26 14 00; www.coursdecuisineparis.com; 2nd fl, 7 rue Paul Lelong, 2e; Ⓜ Bourse), which offers three-hour courses (adult/child €100/30) at 10.30am from Wednesday to Saturday with an additional class from 6pm to 9pm on Friday. 'Carnets' of five/20 courses cost €440/1500. Children's classes (ages seven and up) are on Wednesday at 3pm.

Much more expensive are the Paris Cooking Classes with Patricia Wells (www.patriciawells.com; US$5000) led by the incomparable American food critic and author at her cooking studio in rue Jacob, 6e. The class runs from Monday to Friday, is limited to seven participants and includes market visits, tastings, local transport and daily lunch. See also the boxed text on p208.

A new private class is run by Eye Prefer Paris (www.eyepreferparistours.com; €185; Ⓨ Wed-Sun). Courses last 4½ hours and focus on French cuisine with influences from Southeast Asia, the Middle East and Africa.

Other cooking schools in Paris include the following:

Coin-Cuisine (Map p168; ☎ 01 45 79 01 40; www.coin-cuisine.fr, in French; 110 rue du Théatre, 15e; Ⓜ Av Émile Zola) Courses of various themes and levels lasting from one to four hours (€18 to €85).

Cook'n with Class (Map p138; ☎ 01 42 55 70 59; www.cooknwithclass.com; 21 rue Custine, 18e; Ⓜ Château Rouge) Morning/evening/pastry classes available for €160/160/100.

École Le Cordon Bleu (Map p168; ☎ 01 53 68 22 50; www.cordonbleu.edu; 8 rue Léon Delhomme, 15e;

Ⓜ Vaugirard or Convention) Dating back to 1895, the Cordon Bleu school has professional courses as well as one-day themed workshops (€170) on topics like terrines and pastries, and two- (€299) and four-day (€869) courses on sauces and the secrets of bread making.

École Ritz Escoffier (Map p72; ☎ 01 43 16 30 50; www.ritzescoffier.com; 15 place Vendôme, 1er; Ⓜ Concorde) This prestigious cooking school is based in what is arguably Paris' finest hotel (though you also enter from 38 rue Cambon, 1er). A four-hour Saturday themed workshop (petits fours, truffles, carving fruit and vegetables, pairing food and wine etc) costs €140.

La Cuisine Paris (Map p100; ☎ 01 40 51 78 18; www.lacuisineparis.com; 89 bd St-Michel, 5e; Ⓜ Luxembourg) The love child of American banker Jane and French management consultant Olivier, this courtyard cooking school has two kitchens and a band of expert chefs running themed workshops (€65, two hours) in English or French. Monthly programme available online.

L'Atelier des Chefs (www.atelierdeschefs.fr; Ⓨ Mon-Sat) Variety of cooking classes lasting from 30 minutes to four hours and covering all levels. The good news: they're not for tourists. The bad news: they're in French only. Six locations in Paris; classes from €15.

Language
All manner of French-language courses, lasting from two weeks to a full academic year, are available in Paris, and many places begin new courses every month or so.

Alliance Française (Map p108; ☎ 01 42 84 90 00; www.alliancefr.org; 101 bd Raspail, 6e; Ⓨ 8.30am-7pm Mon & Tue, 8.30am-6pm Wed-Fri; Ⓜ St-Placide) French courses (minimum two weeks) for all levels begin every two weeks; registration (€57) takes place five days before. *Intensif* courses meet for four hours a day five days a week, start at 9am and 1.30pm, and cost from €420/736 for two weeks/one month; *extensif* courses involve three hours of class for three days a week, start at the same two times and cost from €184/348.

Cours de Langue et Civilisation Françaises de la Sorbonne (Map p100; ☎ 01 44 10 77 00; www.ccfs-sorbonne.fr; 46, rue Saint-Jacques, 5e; Ⓨ 10am-noon & 2-4pm Mon-Fri; Ⓜ Cluny La Sorbonne or Maubert–Mutualité) The Sorbonne's prestigious French Language and Civilisation Course has courses for all levels. A four-week summer course starts at €560, while 20 hours a week of lectures and tutorials costs €1380 per semester. Instructors take a very academic (though solid) approach to language teaching.

Eurocentres (Map p112; ☎ 01 40 46 72 00; www.eurocentres.com; 13 passage Dauphine, 6e; Ⓨ 8.15am-6pm Mon-Fri; Ⓜ Odéon) Intensive courses lasting from two to

12 weeks with eight participants cost from €624 to €3216. New courses begin every two, three or four weeks.

Inlingua (Map p108; ☎ 01 45 51 46 60; www.inlingua -paris.com; 109 rue de l'Université, 7e; ⏰ 7.30am-8.30pm Mon-Fri, 9am-1.30pm Sat; Ⓜ Invalides) Individual and group lessons for all levels, from 'first contacts' through to that linguistic state we all aspire to, 'full control'. It has four centres in Paris, including in La Défense and Versailles. French lessons for kids too.

Institut Parisien de Langue et de Civilisation Françaises (Map p126; ☎ 01 40 56 09 53; www.institut-parisien. com; 5 rue du Helder, 9e; ⏰ 8.30am-5pm Mon-Fri; Ⓜ Opéra) Flexible courses with a maximum of 10 students per class cost €154/228/302/375 for 10/15/20/25 hours a week plus an enrolment fee of €40.

Langue Onze (Map p148; ☎ 01 43 38 22 87; www. langueonzeparis.com; 10 rue Gambey, 11e; ⏰ 10am-6pm Mon-Fri; Ⓜ Parmentier) Well-received independent language school with two-/four-week intensive courses of four hours' instruction a day for €410/695; evening classes (four hours a week) start at €190 for four weeks. Classes have a maximum of nine students.

CUSTOMS REGULATIONS

Duty-free shopping within the EU was abolished in 1999; you cannot, for example, buy tax-free goods in, say, France and take them to the UK. However, you can still enter an EU country with duty-free items from countries *outside* the EU (eg Australia, the USA) where the usual allowances apply: 200 cigarettes, 50 cigars or 250g of loose tobacco; 2L of still wine and 1L of spirits; 50g of perfume and 250cc of eau de toilette.

Do not confuse these with *duty-paid* items (including alcohol and tobacco) bought at normal shops in another EU country (eg Spain or Germany) and brought into France, where certain goods might be more expensive. Here allowances are generous: 800 cigarettes, 200 cigars, 400 small cigars or 1kg of loose tobacco; and 10L of spirits (more than 22% alcohol by volume), 20L of fortified wine or aperitif, 90L of wine or 110L of beer.

DISCOUNT CARDS

European citizens under 26 get free entry to national museums and monuments, so *don't* buy museum passes if you qualify. Additionally, museums, the national rail service SNCF (Société Nationale des Chemins de Fer), ferry companies and other institutions give discounts to those aged under 26 (ie holders of the International Youth Travel

Card, IYTC – including non-Europeans), students with an International Student Identity Card (ISIC; age limits may apply) and seniors (usually those aged over 60). Look for the words *tarif réduit* (reduced rate) or *demi-tarif* (half-price) and then ask if you qualify. Those under 18 years of age get an even wider range of discounts (often getting in for free). Some 22 museums are free on the first Sunday of every month, though not necessarily year-round. For specifics, see p84.

The Paris Museum Pass (www.parismuseumpass.fr; 2/4/6 days €32/48/64) is valid for entry to some 38 venues in Paris – including the Louvre, Centre Pompidou, Musée d'Orsay and the Arc de Triomphe – but not the Eiffel Tower. Outside the city limits but still within the Île de France region, it will get you into another 22 places, including the Basilique de St-Denis (p173) and parts of the châteaux at Versailles (p354) and Fontainebleau (p362). One of the best features of the Pass is that you can bypass the long admission queues at major attractions. But be warned, the pass is valid for a certain number of days, not hours, so if you activate a two-day pass late Friday afternoon, for instance, you will only be able to use it for a full day on Saturday. Also keep in mind that most museums are closed on either Monday or Tuesday. The pass is conveniently available online as well as at participating museums, tourist desks at the airports, branches of the Paris Convention & Visitors Bureau (p406), Fnac outlets (p294), RATP (Régie Autonome des Transports Parisians) information desks and major metro stations.

ELECTRICITY

France runs on 220V at 50Hz AC. Plugs are the standard European type with two round pins. French outlets often have an earth (ground) pin in which case you may have to have a French adapter to use a two-pin European plug. The best place for adapters and other electrical goods is the Bazar de l'Hôtel de Ville (p206) department store near Hôtel de Ville, or any branch of the electronics chain Darty (☎ 0 821 082 082, per min €0.21; www. darty.com, in French; ⏰ 10am-7.30pm Mon-Sat), which has a République branch (Map p148; 1 av de la République, 11e; Ⓜ République) and a Ternes branch (Map p126; 8 av des Ternes, 17e; Ⓜ Ternes). Some Monoprix supermarkets also have a limited selection of adapters.

EMBASSIES

It's important to realise what your own embassy – the embassy of the country of which you are a citizen – can and cannot do to help you if you're in trouble. In general, it won't be much help if the trouble you're in is even remotely your own fault. Remember that you are bound by French law while visiting Paris. Your embassy will not be sympathetic if you commit a crime locally, even if such actions are legal in your own country.

In genuine emergencies you might get some assistance, but only if other channels have been exhausted. For example, if you need to get home urgently, a free ticket home is exceedingly unlikely – the embassy would expect you to have insurance. If all your money and documents are stolen, it might assist with getting a new passport, but a loan for onward travel is usually out of the question.

The following is a list of selected embassies and consulates in Paris. For a more complete list, consult the Pages Jaunes (Yellow Pages; www.pagesjaunes.fr, in French) under 'Ambassades et Consulats' or the website of the tourist office (www.parisinfo.com).

Australia (Map p168; ☎ 01 40 59 33 00; www.france. embassy.gov.au; 4 rue Jean Rey, 15e; Ⓜ Bir Hakeim)

Belgium (Map p126; ☎ 01 44 09 39 39; www.diplomatie. be/paris; 9 rue de Tilsitt, 17e; Ⓜ Charles de Gaulle-Étoile)

Canada (Map p126; ☎ 01 44 43 29 00; www.amb-canada.fr; 35 av Montaigne, 8e; Ⓜ Franklin D Roosevelt)

Germany consulate (Map p118; ☎ 01 53 83 46 40; 28 rue Marbeau, 16e; Ⓜ Porte Maillot); embassy (Map p126; ☎ 01 53 83 45 00; www.paris.diplo.de; 13 av Franklin D Roosevelt, 8e; Ⓜ Franklin D Roosevelt)

Ireland (Map p118; ☎ 01 44 17 67 00; www.embassy ofireland.fr; 4 rue Rude, 16e; Ⓜ Argentine)

Italy (Map p108; ☎ 01 49 54 03 00; www.ambparigi. esteri.it; 47-51 rue de Varenne, 7e; Ⓜ Rue du Bac)

Japan (Map p136; ☎ 01 48 88 62 00; www.fr.emb-japan. go.jp; 7 av Hoche, 8e; Ⓜ Courcelles)

Netherlands (Map p108; ☎ 01 40 62 33 00; www.amb -pays-bas.fr; 7 rue Eblé, 7e; Ⓜ St-François Xavier)

New Zealand (Map p118; ☎ 01 45 01 43 43; www. nzembassy.com/france; 7ter rue Léonard de Vinci, 16e; Ⓜ Victor Hugo)

South Africa (Map p108; ☎ 01 53 59 23 23; www. afriquesud.net; 59 quai d'Orsay, 7e; Ⓜ Invalides)

Spain (Map p126; ☎ 01 44 43 18 00; www.maec.es; 22 av Marceau, 8e; Ⓜ Alma–Marceau)

Switzerland (Map p108; ☎ 01 49 55 67 00; www.eda. admin.ch/paris; 142 rue de Grenelle, 7e; Ⓜ Varenne)

UK consulate (Map p126; ☎ 0 892 230 175; 18bis rue d'Anjou, 8e; Ⓜ Concorde); embassy (Map p126; ☎ 01 44 51 31 00; http://ukinfrance.fco.gov.uk; 35 rue du Faubourg St-Honoré, 8e; Ⓜ Concorde)

USA consulate (Map p72; ☎ 0 810 264 626; 18 av Gabriel, 8e; Ⓜ Concorde); embassy (Map p126; ☎ 01 43 12 22 22; http://france.usembassy.gov; 2 av Gabriel, 8e; Ⓜ Concorde)

EMERGENCY

The following numbers are to be dialled in an emergency. See p398 for hospitals with 24-hour accident and emergency departments.

Ambulance (SAMU; ☎ 15)

EU-wide emergency hotline (☎ 112)

Fire brigade (☎ 18)

Police (☎ 17)

Rape crisis hotline (Viols Femmes Informations; ☎ 0 800 059 595; ⏱ 10am-7pm Mon-Fri)

SOS Helpline (☎ 01 46 21 46 46; ⏱ in English 3-11pm)

SOS Médecins (☎ 01 47 07 77 77, 24hr house calls 3624; www.sosmedecins-france.fr, in French)

Urgences Médicales de Paris (Paris Medical Emergencies; ☎ 01 53 94 94 94; www.ump.fr, in French)

Lost Property

All objects found anywhere in Paris – except those picked up on trains or in train stations – are brought to the city's Bureau des Objets Trouvés (Lost Property Office; ☎ 0 821 002 525, per min €0.12; www. prefecture-police-paris.interieur.gouv.fr/demarches/article/ service_objets_trouves.htm, in French; 36 rue des Morillons, 15e; ⏱ 8.30am-5pm Mon-Thu, 8.30am-4.30pm Fri; Ⓜ Convention), which is run by the Préfecture de Police. Since telephone enquiries are impossible, the only way to find out if a lost item has been located is to go there and fill in the forms in person.

Items lost on the metro are held by station agents (☎ 3246; ⏱ 7am-9pm Mon-Fri, 9am-5pm Sat & Sun) before being sent to the Bureau des Objets Trouvés. Anything found on trains or in stations is taken to the lost-property office (usually attached to the left-luggage office) of the relevant station. Phone enquiries (in French) are possible:

Gare d'Austerlitz (☎ 01 53 60 71 98)

Gare de l'Est (☎ 01 40 18 88 73)

Gare de Lyon (☎ 01 53 33 67 22)

Gare du Nord (☎ 01 55 31 58 40)

Gare Montparnasse (☎ 01 40 48 14 24)

Gare St-Lazare (☎ 01 53 42 05 57)

HOLIDAYS

There is at least one public holiday a month in France and, in some years, up to four in May alone. Be aware, though, that unlike in the USA or UK, where public holidays usually fall on (or are shifted to) a Monday, in France a *jour férié* (public holiday) is celebrated strictly on the day on which it falls. Thus if May Day falls on a Saturday or Sunday, no provision is made for an extra day off.

The following holidays are observed in Paris:

New Year's Day (Jour de l'An) 1 January

Easter Sunday & Monday (Pâques & Lundi de Pâques) Late March/April

May Day (Fête du Travail) 1 May

Victory in Europe Day (Victoire 1945) 8 May

Ascension Thursday (L'Ascension) May (celebrated on the 40th day after Easter)

Pentecost/Whit Sunday & Whit Monday (Pentecôte & Lundi de Pentecôte) Mid-May to mid-June (seventh Sunday and Monday after Easter)

Bastille Day/National Day (Fête Nationale) 14 July

Assumption Day (L'Assomption) 15 August

All Saints' Day (La Toussaint) 1 November

Armistice Day/Remembrance Day (Le Onze Novembre) 11 November

Christmas (Noël) 25 December

INTERNET ACCESS

Wi-fi is widely available at midrange and top-end hotels in Paris, and almost everyone (except very expensive hotels and a lot of hostels) offers it as a free service. You'll also find it available at some 260 public hotspots, located in parks, train stations, tourist offices, libraries and other city buildings (look for a network with 'gratuit' in the name). The public wi-fi scheme is limited, however (in some spots no more than 20 minutes); you're better off looking for a local café (the symbol 🛜 in this book indicates wi-fi is available) or a major chain.

If you don't have a laptop or wi-fi access, don't fret: Paris is awash with internet cafés, and you'll probably find at least one in your im-

mediate neighbourhood. Expect to pay about €4 for one hour; some places have non-French keyboards available if you ask. Cafés offering free access are not as common as in London or New York. For a list of free-access wi-fi cafés in Paris, visit www.cafes-wifi.com (in French).

Among the most convenient:

Cyber Cube (Map p168; ☎ 01 56 80 08 08; www.cyber cube.fr; 9 rue d'Odessa, 14e; per 15/30min €1/2, per 5/10hr €30/40; 🕑 10am-10pm Mon-Fri, noon-10pm Sat & Sun; Ⓜ Montparnasse–Bienvenüe) One of three branches; expensive but convenient to Gare Montparnasse.

Cyber Latin (Map p108; ☎ 01 42 22 89 35; 35bis rue de Fleurus, 6e; per 15/30/60min €1.25/2.25/4, per 5/10/20hr €17/34/56; 🕑 9.30am-7.30pm Mon-Fri, 11.30am-7.30pm Sat; Ⓜ St-Placide) Just west of the Jardin du Luxembourg.

Cyber Squ@re (Map p148; ☎ 01 48 87 82 36; www.cybersquare-paris.com; 1 place de la République, 3e; per 5/15/30/60min €0.76/2.29/3.81/6.10, per 10/20hr €45.73/76.22; 🕑 10am-8pm Mon-Sat; Ⓜ République) This small but convivial place on two levels is entered from passage Vendôme.

Hitel (Map p140; 147 rue La Fayette, 10e; per 15/30/60min €1/1.50/2; 🕑 9am-midnight; Ⓜ Gare du Nord) Just around the corner from the Gare du Nord. Also sells French SIM cards.

Internet Café (Map p138; ☎ 01 42 59 64 14; place des Abbesses, 18e; per 10/60min €1/4; 🕑 9am-7.45pm Mon-Fri, 10am-7pm Sat & Sun; Ⓜ Abbesses) In the heart of Montmartre.

Milk (Map p100; ☎ 01 43 54 55 55; www.milklub.com; 17 rue Soufflot, 5e; per 15/30/60min €1.99/2.99/3.99; 🕑 24hr; Ⓜ Luxembourg) One of seven locations; there's also a big Les Halles branch (Map p76; ☎ 01 40 13 06 51; 31 bd de Sébastopol, 1er; 🕑 24hr; Ⓜ Les Halles) open round the clock.

Phon'net (Map p158; 74 rue de Charonne, 11e; per hr €2; 🕑 10am-midnight; Ⓜ Charonne or Ledru Rollin)

Taxiphone Internet (Map p138; ☎ 01 42 59 64 14; 2 rue de la Vieuville, 18e; per 5/10/20/30/60min €0.50/1/2/3/4, per 5hr €10; 🕑 9am-7.30pm Mon-Sat; Ⓜ Abbesses) One of the few internet cafés in high-rent Montmartre.

Web 46 (Map p152; ☎ 01 40 27 02 89; 46 rue du Roi de Sicile, 4e; per 15/30/60min €2.50/4/7, per 5hr €29; 🕑 9.30am-10.30pm Mon-Fri, 9.30am-9pm Sat, 11am-10.30pm Sun; Ⓜ St-Paul) Pleasant, well-run café in the heart of the Marais.

Zeidnet (Map p100; ☎ 01 44 07 20 15; www.zeidnet.com; 18 rue de la Bûcherie, 5e; per 10/30/60min €1/2.50/4; 🕑 10.30am-11pm; Ⓜ Maubert–Mutualité; 🛜) Small and personal, handy to Notre Dame.

LAUNDRY

There's a *laverie libre-service* (self-service laundrette) around every corner in Paris; your hotel or hostel can point you to one in the neighbourhood. Machines usually cost €3.50 to €4.50 for a small load (around 6kg) and €5.50 to €8 for a larger one (about 10kg). Drying costs €1 for 10 to 12 minutes. Some laundrettes have self-service *nettoyage à sec* (dry-cleaning) machines.

You usually pay at a *monnayeur central* (central control box) – not the machine itself – and push a button that corresponds to the number of the washer or dryer you wish to operate. Some machines don't take notes; come prepared with change for the *séchoirs* (dryers) as well as the *lessive* (laundry powder) and *javel* (bleach) dispensers.

The control boxes are sometimes programmed to deactivate the machines 30 minutes to an hour before closing time.

LEGAL MATTERS
Drink Driving

As elsewhere in the EU, the laws in France are very tough when it comes to drinking and driving, and for many years the slogan has been: '*Boire ou conduire, il faut choisir*' (roughly – to make it rhyme in English too – 'To drive or to booze, you have to choose'). The acceptable blood-alcohol limit is 0.05%, and drivers exceeding that amount but still under 0.08% (the limit in the UK and Ireland) face a fine of €135; over 0.08% and it could cost you €4500 (or a maximum of two years in jail). Licences can also be immediately suspended. If you cause an accident while driving under the influence, the fine could be increased to €30,000. And if you cause serious bodily harm or commit involuntary manslaughter, you face 10 years in jail and a fine of up to €150,000.

Police

Thanks to the Napoleonic Code on which the French legal system is based, the police can search anyone they want to at any time – whether or not there is probable cause.

France has two separate police forces. The Police Nationale, under the command of departmental prefects (and, in Paris, the Préfet de Police), includes the Police de l'Air et des Frontières (PAF; the border police). The Gendarmerie Nationale, a paramilitary force under the control of the Ministry of Defence, handles airports, borders and so on. During times of crisis (eg a wave of terrorist attacks), the army may be called in to patrol public places.

The American concept of neighbourhood cops walking their beat or the British bobby giving directions does not exist whatsoever in France; police here are to maintain order, not mingle and smile. If asked a direct question, a French policeman or policewoman will be correct and helpful but not much more; assisting tourists is not part of their job description. If the police stop you for any reason, be polite and remain calm. They have wide powers of search and seizure and, if they take a dislike to you, they may choose to use them all. Be aware that the police can, without any particular reason, decide to examine your passport, visa, *carte de séjour* (residence permit) and so on. (You are expected to have photo ID on you at all times.) Do *not* challenge them.

French police are very strict about security. Do not leave baggage unattended; they are quite serious when they say that suspicious objects will be summarily blown up. Your bags will be inspected and you will have to pass through security gates not only at airports but also at many public buildings (including certain museums and galleries) throughout the city. If asked to open your bag or backpack for inspection, do so willingly – it's for your (and everyone's) safety ultimately.

MAPS

The most ubiquitous (and user-friendly) pocket-sized street atlas available is L'Indispensable's *Paris Practique par Arrondissement* (€4.90) – newer versions also include Vélib' stations – though the similar *Paris Utile* (€4.50) from Blay Foldex has its supporters. More detailed is Michelin's *Paris Poche Plan* (No 50; €2.20). All of these are usually available from newsstands and the Institut Géographique National bookstore **Espace IGN** (Map p126; ☎ 01 43 98 80 00; www.ign.fr; 107 rue La Boétie, 8e; ☼ noon-6.30pm Mon, 11am-7pm Tue-Fri, 11am-6.30pm Sat; Ⓜ Franklin D Roosevelt), which also sells walking maps, city plans, compasses, satellite images, historic maps and guidebooks. See also http://maps.google.fr and www.mappy.com for reliable interactive maps.

MEDICAL SERVICES

If you are not an EU citizen, it is imperative that you organise some travel insurance before your departure. EU passport holders have access to the French social security system, which can reimburse up to 70% of medical costs.

Hospitals

There are some 50 *assistance publique* (public health service) hospitals in Paris. If you need an ambulance, call ☎ 15; the EU-wide emergency number (with English speakers) is ☎ 112. For emergency treatment, call Urgences Médicales de Paris (☎ 01 53 94 94 94) or SOS Médecins (☎ 01 47 07 77 77, 3624). Both offer 24-hour house calls costing between €35 and €90 depending on the time of day and whether you have French social security.

Hospitals in Paris include the following:

American Hospital in Paris (☎ 01 46 41 25 25; www.american-hospital.org; 63 bd Victor Hugo, 92200 Neuilly-sur-Seine; Ⓜ Pont de Levallois Bécon) Private hospital offering emergency 24-hour medical and dental care.

Hertford British Hospital (☎ 01 46 39 22 22; www.ihfb.org; 3 rue Barbès, 92300 Levallois-Perret; Ⓜ Anatole France) A less expensive private English-speaking option than the American Hospital.

Hôpital Hôtel Dieu (Map p82; ☎ 01 42 34 82 34; www.aphp.fr, in French; 1 place du Parvis Notre Dame, 4e; Ⓜ Cité) One of the city's main government-run public hospitals (Assistance Publique Hôpitaux de Paris); after 8pm use the emergency entrance on rue de la Cité.

Dental Clinics

For emergency dental care contact either of the following:

Hôpital de la Pitié-Salpêtrière (Map p164; ☎ 01 42 16 00 00; rue Bruant, 13e; Ⓨ 6am-10.30pm; Ⓜ Chevaleret) The only dental hospital with extended hours. After 5.30pm use the emergency entrance at 83 bd de l'Hôpital, 13e (metro St-Marcel).

SOS Dentaire (Map p164; ☎ 01 43 36 36 00; 87 bd de Port Royal, 13e; Ⓨ 8-11pm Mon-Fri, 9.45am-11pm Sat & Sun; Ⓜ Port Royal) A private dental office that offers services when most dentists are off duty.

Pharmacies

Pharmacies with extended hours:

Pharmacie Bader (Map p112; ☎ 01 43 26 92 66; 12 bd St-Michel, 5e; Ⓨ 9am-9pm; Ⓜ St-Michel)

Pharmacie de la Mairie (Map p152; ☎ 01 42 78 53 58; 9 rue des Archives, 4e; Ⓨ 9am-8pm; Ⓜ Hôtel de Ville)

Pharmacie des Champs (Map p126; ☎ 01 45 62 02 41; Galerie des Champs, 84 av des Champs-Élysées, 8e; Ⓨ 24hr; Ⓜ George V)

Pharmacie des Halles (Map p76; ☎ 01 42 72 03 23; 10 bd de Sébastopol, 4e; Ⓨ 9am-midnight Mon-Sat, 9am-10pm Sun; Ⓜ Châtelet)

Pharmacie Européenne (Map p136; ☎ 01 48 74 65 18; 6 place de Clichy, 9e; Ⓨ 24hr; Ⓜ Place de Clichy)

MONEY

France is among the 16 member-states of the EU that have adopted the euro (abbreviated € and pronounced *eu*-roh in French) as its national currency. One euro is divided into 100 cents (*centimes* in French). There are seven euro notes in different colours and sizes; they come in denominations of €5, €10, €20, €50, €100, €200 and €500. The designs on the recto (generic windows or portals) and verso (imaginary bridges, map of the EU), exactly the same in all 16 countries, symbolise openness and cooperation.

The eight coins in circulation are in denominations of €1 and €2, and one, two, five, 10, 20 and 50 cents. The 'head' side of the coin, on which the denomination is shown, is identical throughout the euro zone; the 'tail' side is specific to each member-state, though euro coins can be used wherever euros are accepted. In France the €1 (silver centre with brassy ring) and €2 (brassy centre with silver ring) coins portray the tree of liberty; the 10, 20 and 50 cent coins (all brass) have *la Semeuse* (the Sower), a recurring theme in the history of the French franc; and the one, two and five cent coins (all copper) portray Marianne, the symbol of the French Republic.

Exchange rates are given in the Quick Reference section on the inside front cover of this book. The latest rates are available on websites such as www.oanda.com and www.xe.com. For a broader view of the local economy and costs in Paris, see p21.

ATMs

You'll find an ATM, which is known here as a DAB (*distributeur automatique de billets*) or *point d'argent*, linked to the Cirrus, Maestro, Visa or MasterCard networks, virtually on every corner. Most French banks don't charge transaction fees to use their ATMs; however, check with your own bank before you go to know if and how much you will be charged for international cash withdrawals. Unless you have particularly high transaction fees, ATMs are usually the best and easiest way to deal with currency exchange.

Changing Money

In general, cash is not a very good way to carry money. Not only can it be stolen, but in France it doesn't usually offer the best exchange rates. What's more, in recent years ATMs and the euro have virtually wiped out *bureaux de change*, and even centrally located banks rarely offer exchange services these days.

That said, some banks, post offices and *bureaux de change* pay up to 2.5% or more for travellers cheques, more than making up for the 1% commission usually charged when buying the cheques in the first place.

Post offices that have a Banque Postale can offer the best exchange rates, and they accept banknotes (commission €4.50) in various currencies as well as travellers cheques issued by Amex (no commission) or Visa (1.5%, minimum €4.50).

Commercial banks usually charge a similar amount per foreign-currency transaction. For example, BNP Paribas charges €5.95 for cash, while Société Générale takes €5.40 (or €11.40 if you don't bank with them). The rates charged on travellers cheques vary, but neither BNP Paribas nor Société Générale charge a fee to change travellers cheques in euros.

In Paris, *bureaux de change* are usually more efficient, open longer hours and give better rates than most banks. It's best to familiarise yourself with the rates offered by the post office and compare them with those on offer at *bureaux de change*, which are not generally allowed to charge commissions. *Bureaux de change* charge anything between 6% and 13% plus €3 or €4 on cash transactions, and 6% to just under 10% (plus €3) to change travellers cheques.

Among some of the better *bureaux de change* are the following:

Best Change (Map p76; ☎ 01 42 21 46 05; 21 rue du Roule, 1er; ☒ 9.30am-7.30pm Mon-Sat; Ⓜ Louvre Rivoli) Three blocks southwest of Forum des Halles.

CCO (Map p126; ☎ 01 47 42 20 96; 9 rue Scribe, 9e; ☒ 9am-6pm Mon-Fri, 9.30am-5pm Sat; Ⓜ Opéra)

European Exchange Office (Map p138; ☎ 01 42 52 67 19; 6 rue Yvonne Le Tac, 18e; ☒ 10am-noon & 2-6pm Mon-Sat; Ⓜ Abbesses) A few steps from the Abbesses metro station.

Kanoo (Map p126; ☎ 01 53 30 99 00; 11 rue Scribe, 9e; ☒ 9am-6.30pm Mon-Sat; Ⓜ Auber or Opéra)

Le Change du Louvre (Map p76; ☎ 01 42 97 27 28; 151 rue St-Honoré, 1er; ☒ 10am-6pm Mon-Fri; Ⓜ Palais Royal–Musée du Louvre) This moneychanger is on the northern side of Le Louvre des Antiquaires (p75).

Multi Change (Map p112; ☎ 01 42 22 41 00; 180 bd St-Germain, 6e; ☒ 9.30am-6.30pm Mon-Sat; Ⓜ St-Germain des Prés) West of Église St-Germain des Prés.

Société Touristique de Services (Map p108; ☎ 01 43 54 76 55; 2 place St-Michel, 6e; ☒ 9am-8pm Mon-Fri, 10am-8pm Sat; Ⓜ St-Michel) A *bureau de change* in the heart of the Latin Quarter.

Credit Cards

In Paris, Visa/Carte Bleue is the most widely accepted credit card, followed by MasterCard (Eurocard). Amex cards can be useful at more upmarket establishments. In general, all three cards can be used to pay for train travel and restaurant meals and for cash advances. Note that France uses a smartcard with an embedded microchip and PIN. North Americans will thus not be able to use their credit cards at automated machines (such as at a metro station), though in most cases an attendant will be nearby who can swipe your card for you.

When you get a cash advance on your Visa or MasterCard account, your issuer charges a transaction fee, which can be high; check with your card issuer before leaving home. Some banks charge a commission of 4% (minimum around €6) for a cash advance, though BNP Paribas does it for free (however, your own bank will probably charge a commission) to a maximum of €1000. American Express takes a 5% commission on cash advances on Visa cards.

Call the following numbers if your card is lost or stolen. It may be impossible to get a lost Visa or MasterCard reissued until you get home, so two different credit cards are generally safer than just one.

Amex (☎ 01 47 77 72 00)

Diners Club (☎ 0 820 820 536)

MasterCard/Eurocard (☎ 0 800 901 387, 01 45 16 65 65)

Visa/Carte Bleue (☎ 0 892 705 705, 0 800 901 179)

Travellers Cheques

The most flexible travellers cheques are issued by American Express (in US dollars or euros) and Visa, as they can be changed at many post offices. If your Amex travellers cheques are lost or stolen while you are in Paris, call ☎ 01 47 77 72 00 (24-hour).

NEWSPAPERS & MAGAZINES

Among English-language newspapers widely available in Paris are the *International Herald Tribune*, the *Guardian* and the more compact *Guardian Weekly*, the *Financial Times*, the *Times of London* and the *USA Today*. English-language news weeklies that are widely available include *Newsweek, Time* and the *Economist*. For information about the French-language press, see p40.

The Paris-based *Fusac* (*France USA Contacts*), a freebie issued every two weeks and still going strong after two decades, consists of hundreds of classified ads. To place one yourself, contact Fusac (☎ 01 56 53 54 54; www.fusac.fr). It is distributed free at Paris' English-language bookshops, pubs and the American Church in Paris (Map p108; ☎ 01 40 62 05 00; www.acparis.org; 65 quai d'Orsay, 7e; ☼ reception 9am-noon & 1-10pm Mon-Sat, 2-7.30pm Sun; Ⓜ Pont de l'Alma or Invalides), which functions as a community centre for English speakers and is an excellent source of information on au-pair work, short-term accommodation etc. For classified ads, also check http://paris.craigslist.org.

ORGANISED TOURS

In addition to the open-topped hop-on/hop-off bus tours prevalent everywhere (p401), some excellent bike, boat and walking tours are available too. Worth investigating are community tours led by local volunteers (p402), which are an excellent way to get beyond the trodden tourist path.

Although it's not exactly a tour, Paris Story (Map p126; ☎ 01 42 66 62 06; www.paris-story.com; 11bis rue Scribe, 9e; adult/student & 6-17yr/family €10/6/26, under 6yr free; ☼ 10am-6pm; Ⓜ Auber or Opéra) offers a one-hour audiovisual romp through Paris' 2000-year history on the hour, with headset commentary in 14 languages; an interactive model of Paris called Paris Miniature; and Paris Experience, a gallery of five themed video clips.

Air

Hot-air balloon Ballon Air de Paris (Map p168; ☎ 01 44 26 20 00; www.ballondeparis.com, in French; Parc André Citroën, 2 rue de la Montagne de la Fage, 15e; adult/12-17yr/3-11yr €10/9/5, Sat & Sun €12/10/6, under 3yr free; ☼ 9am-5.30pm or 9.30pm Mon-Fri (seasonal); Ⓜ Balard), in the Parc André Citroën in southwestern Paris, lifts you 150m off the ground and offers fabulous views of Paris and the Seine. Don't expect to get very far though; the helium-filled balloon remains firmly tethered to the ground. Be sure to call in advance as the balloon does not ascend in windy conditions.

A company called iXAir (Map p168; ☎ 01 30 08 80 80; www.ixair.com, in French; 4 av de la Porte de Sèvres, 15e; Ⓜ Porte de Sèvres) at the Héliport de Paris next to the Aquaboulevard in the 15e offers limited circuits by helicopter over the city lasting between 30 and 60 minutes for €138 to €239. You should book well ahead; some tours only run the first weekend of the month.

Bicycle

Fat Tire Bike Tours (Map p168; ☎ 01 56 58 10 54; www.fattirebiketours.com; 24 rue Edgar Faure, 15e; ☼ office 9am-6pm; Ⓜ La Motte-Picquet Grenelle) offers daytime bike tours of the city (adult/student €28/26; four hours), starting at 11am daily from mid-February to early January, with an additional departure at 3pm from April to October. Night bicycle tours depart at 7pm from April to October and 6pm (not always daily) in the low season. Other tours go to Versailles, Monet's garden in Giverny and the Normandy beaches.

Participants generally meet opposite the Eiffel Tower's South Pillar at the start of the Champ de Mars; just look for the yellow signs. Costs include the bicycle and, if necessary, rain gear. Reserve in advance.

The same company runs City Segway Tours (www.citysegwaytours.com), which feature the self-balancing 'Human Transporter'. Segway tours (€80) last four hours and depart at 9.30am from mid-February to early January, with an extra tour at 2pm from March to November. You must book these tours in advance.

Bike About Tours (Map p148; ☎ 06 18 80 84 92; www.bikeabouttours.com; 4 Rue Lobau, 4e; ☼ office 10am-7pm; Ⓜ Hôtel de Ville) is another expat-run tour group, offering 3.5-hour daytime tours (adult/student €30/28). Tours begin at 10pm and run from mid-February to November, with an extra 3pm tour from mid-May to September. They leave from in front of Notre Dame; reservations are recommended. Private family and group tours are also available.

Bike tours from cycle shop Gepetto & Vélos (Map p100; ☎ 01 43 54 19 95; www.gepetto-et-velos.com, in French; 59 rue du Cardinal Lemoine, 5e; tours €25; ☼ 9am-1pm & 2-7.30pm Tue-Sat, 10am-1pm & 2-7pm Sun; Ⓜ Cardinal Lemoine) last four hours and include a guide, bicycle and insurance. You'll need a minimum of eight people for the tour to go though.

Paris à Vélo, C'est Sympa! (Map p148; ☎ 01 48 87 60 01; www.parisvelosympa.com, in French; 22 rue Alphonse Baudin, 11e; ☯ 9.30am-1pm & 2-6pm Mon, Wed & Fri, 9am-1pm & 2-7pm Sat & Sun Apr-Oct, 9.30am-1pm & 2-5.30pm Mon, Wed & Fri, 9am-1pm & 2-6pm Sat & Sun Nov-Mar; Ⓜ St-Sébastien Froissart) is an association that offers five different three-hour bike tours (adult/12 to 26 years/under 12 years €34/28/18). Prices include bicycles and insurance. There are no tours on Tuesday or Thursday, except for large groups.

Boat

A boat cruise – whether along 'the lifeline of Paris' (the Seine) or the rejuvenated canals to the northeast – is the most relaxing way to watch the city glide by. If it's your first time in Paris, a cruise down the Seine is also a good way to get a quick introduction to the city's main monuments. See p385 for details on the hop-on/hop-off boat service, the Batobus.

CANAL CRUISES

Canauxrama (Map p140 & Map p148; ☎ 01 42 39 15 00; www.canauxrama.com; Bassin de la Villette, 13 quai de la Loire, 19e; adult/student & senior/4-12yr €15/11/8; ☯ Mon-Fri Mar-Nov, call in winter; Ⓜ Jaurès) has barges that run from the Bastille to Parc de la Villette along the Canal St-Martin and Canal de l'Ourcq. Departures are at 9.45am and 2.30pm or 2.45pm from the Bastille and Parc de la Villette. Note that the boat goes at a very leisurely pace (2½ hours total) as it passes through four double locks. There is also an underground section (with an art installation).

Paris Canal Croisières (Map p140; ☎ 01 42 40 96 97; www.pariscanal.com; Bassin de la Villette, 19-21 quai de la Loire, 19e; adult/senior & 12-25yr/4-11yr €17/14/10; ☯ late Mar–mid-Nov; Ⓜ Jaurès or Musée d'Orsay) has 2½-hour cruises starting near the Musée d'Orsay (quai Anatole France) at 9.30am, and departing from Parc de la Villette for the return trip at 2.30pm.

RIVER CRUISES

On the Right Bank just east of Pont de l'Alma, **Bateaux-Mouches** (Map p126; ☎ 01 42 25 96 10; www.bateauxmouches.com; Port de la Conférence, 8e; adult/senior & 4-12yr €10/5; ☯ mid-Mar–mid-Nov; Ⓜ Alma Marceau) runs nine 1000-seat glassed-in tour boats, the largest on the Seine and a favourite with tour groups. Cruises (70 minutes) run regularly from 10.15am to 11pm April to September

and 13 times a day between 11am and 9pm the rest of the year. Commentary is in French and English.

From its base northwest of the Eiffel Tower, **Bateaux Parisiens** (Map p118; ☎ 01 76 64 14 45; www.bateauxparisiens.com; Port de la Bourdonnais, 7e; adult/3-11yr €11/5; ☯ every 30min 10am-10.30pm Apr-Sep, hourly 10am-10pm Oct-Mar; Ⓜ Pont de l'Alma) runs smaller boats that do one-hour river circuits with recorded commentary in 13 different languages.

La Marina de Paris (Map p108; ☎ 01 43 43 40 30; www.marinadeparis.com; port de Solferino, quai Anatole France, 7e; Ⓜ Musée d'Orsay) offers lunch cruises at 12.15pm (€53; Friday to Sunday) and dinner cruises at 6.30pm (€48; daily) and 9pm (€78; daily). They last about 2¼ hours, and a menu for children under 12 (€40) is available at all meals.

Vedettes du Pont Neuf (Map p82; ☎ 01 46 33 98 38; www.vedettesdupontneuf.fr; square du Vert Galant, 1er; adult/4-12yr €12/6; Ⓜ Pont Neuf), whose centrally located dock is at the far western tip of the Île de la Cité in the 1er, has one-hour boat excursions year-round. Cruises run (almost) half-hourly from 10.30am to 10.30pm from mid-March to November, and less regularly from 10.30am to 10pm the rest of the year.

Bus

L'Open Tour (Map p126; ☎ 01 42 66 56 56; www.pariscityrama.com; 13 rue Auber, 9e; adult/4-11yr 1 day €29/15, 2 consecutive days €32/15; Ⓜ Havre Caumartin or Opéra) runs open-deck buses along four circuits (central Paris, Montmartre–Grands Boulevards, Bastille–Bercy and Montparnasse–St-Germain) daily year-round. You can jump on and off at main sites, which makes these buses very convenient for whirlwind tours of the city. On the 'Grand Tour' of central Paris, which has some 20 stops on both sides of the river between Notre Dame and the Eiffel Tower, buses depart every 10 to 15 minutes from 9.30am to 6pm April to October and every 25 to 30 minutes from 9.30am to 5.30pm November to March. Holders of the Paris Visite card (p389) pay €25 for a one-day pass. Buy tickets from the driver. For €40 (€19 for children aged 4 to 11), you can buy a two-day bus-Batobus (hop-on/hop-off boat) combo ticket.

Another hop-on/hop-off bus tour is available through **Les Cars Rouges** (☎ 01 53 95 39 53; www.carsrouges.fr; 2 days adult/4-12yr €24/12). The red double-decker buses run to nine major sites around Paris, from roughly 10am to 8.30pm. In total, the tours last two hours and 15 minutes, and various audio guides can be downloaded as mp3s from their website. Buy tickets online or at your hotel.

Cityrama (Map p72; ☎ 01 44 55 60 00; www.pariscityrama.com; 2 rue des Pyramides, 1er; adult/4-11yr €22/11; ⏰ tours 10am, 11.30am & 2.30pm; Ⓜ Tuileries), which owns L'Open Tour, also runs some 10 other Paris tours, including 1½-hour general city tours, which are accompanied by taped commentaries in 16 languages.

In season, the RATP's **Balabus** (☎ 3246; www.ratp.fr; €1.70 or 1 metro/bus ticket; ⏰ departures 12.30-8pm from La Défense, 1.30pm from Gare de Lyon Sun Apr-Sep), designed for tourists, follows a 50-minute route to/from Gare de Lyon (Map p158) and La Défense (Map p175), passing many of central Paris' most famous sights.

Walking

The following organisations offer walking tours that make for a great way to get beneath the skin of the city and discover how Parisians really live. If your French is up to it, you can also look at either *Pariscope* or *Officiel des Spectacles* (p294), which list a number of themed walks each week under the heading 'Conférences' or 'Visites Conférences'.

Ça Se Visite (☎ 01 43 57 59 50; www.ca-se-visite.fr, in French; €12) Meet local artists and craftspeople on resident-led 'urban discovery tours' of the northeast arrondissements (10e, 11e, 18e, 19e, 20e). Reserve ahead for tours in English.

Context Paris (☎ 01 72 81 36 35; www.contexttravel.com; €44-80) Small group walks led by specialists on various subjects.

Enjoy Your Paris (www.enjoyourparis.com) This community organises walks, activities, concerts etc. You have to become a member to participate.

Eye Prefer Paris (www.eyepreferparistours.com; 3 people €195) New Yorker turned Parisian leads offbeat tours of the city. Cooking classes also available.

Paris Go (☎ 01 53 30 74 40; www.parisgo.fr; €20) Two-hour thematic tours followed by drinks in a local café or bar. Reserve ahead for English-language tours.

Paris Greeter (www.parisiendunjour.fr; by donation) See Paris through local eyes with these two- to three-hour city tours. Volunteers lead groups (maximum six people) to their favourite spots in the city. Minimum two weeks' advance notice needed.

Paris Passé, Présent (☎ 01 42 58 95 99; http://paris passepresent.free.fr, in French; €10) French-language walks throughout the week.

Paris Walks (☎ 01 48 09 21 40; www.paris-walks.com; adult/15-21yr/under 15yr €12/10/8) Long established and highly rated by our readers, Paris Walks offers thematic tours (fashion, chocolate, the French Revolution) in English.

PLACES OF WORSHIP

The following places offer services in English. For a more comprehensive list of churches and other places of worship, check the Pages Jaunes (Yellow Pages; www.pagesjaunes.fr, in French) or the website of the tourist office (http://en.parisinfo.com/guide-paris/worship). Catholics can attend a French Mass; there is only one regular English-language Mass in Paris.

Adath Shalom Synagogue (Map p168; ☎ 01 45 67 97 96; www.adathshalom.org, in French; 8 rue George Bernard Shaw, 15e; Ⓜ Dupleix) Conservative Jewish.

American Cathedral in Paris (Map p126; ☎ 01 53 23 84 00; www.americancathedral.org; 23 av George V, 8e; Ⓜ Alma Marceau) Protestant.

American Church in Paris (Map p108; ☎ 01 40 62 05 00; www.acparis.org; 65 quai d'Orsay, 7e; Ⓜ Invalides) Nondenominational Protestant.

Church of Jesus Christ of the Latter Day Saints (Map p140; ☎ 01 42 45 29 29; 64-66 rue de Romainville, 19e; Ⓜ Porte des Lilas) Mormon.

First Church of Christ Scientist (Map p168; ☎ 01 47 07 26 60; 36 bd St-Jacques, 14e; Ⓜ St-Jacques) Christian Scientist.

Mosquée de Paris (Map p100; ☎ 01 45 35 97 33; www.mosquee-de-paris.org, in French; 2bis place du Puits de l'Ermite, 5e; Ⓜ Censier Daubenton or Place Monge) Muslim.

Sri Manikar Vinayakar Alayam Temple (Map p138; ☎ 01 40 34 21 89; www.templeganesh.fr; 72 rue Philippe de Girard, 18e; Ⓜ Marx Dormoy) Hindu.

POST

Most post offices *(bureaux de poste)* in Paris are open from 8am to 7pm weekdays and 8am or 9am till noon on Saturday. *Tabacs* (tobacconists) usually sell postage stamps.

The main post office (Map p72; www.laposte.fr, in French; 52 rue du Louvre, 1er; ⏰ 24hr; Ⓜ Sentier or Les Halles), five blocks north of the eastern end of the Musée du Louvre, is open round the clock, but only for basic services such as sending letters and picking up poste restante mail (window 11; €0.54 per letter). Other services, including currency exchange, are available only during regular opening hours. Be prepared for long queues. Poste restante mail not specifically addressed to a particular post office branch will be delivered here. There is a one-hour closure from 6.20am to 7.20am Monday to Saturday and from 6am to 7am on Sunday.

Each arrondissement has its own five-digit postcode, formed by prefixing the number of the arrondissement with '750' or '7500' (eg 75001 for the 1er arrondissement, 75019 for the 19e). The only exception is the 16e, which has two postcodes: 75016 and 75116. All mail to addresses in France *must* include the postcode. Cedex *(Courrier d'Entreprise à Distribution Exceptionelle)* simply means that mail sent to that address is collected at the post office rather than delivered to the door.

Domestic letters weighing up to 20/50g cost €0.56/0.90. Postcards and letters up to 20/50g sent within the EU cost €0.70/1.30 and €0.85/1.70 to the rest of the world.

RADIO

You can pick up a mixture of the BBC World Service and BBC for Europe in Paris on 648 kHz AM. However, for those with access to a computer, it's probably easiest to listen via the web. The BBC iPlayer has a variety of live programmes available through www.bbc.co.uk; likewise, the US National Public Radio (NPR) also broadcasts all their programmes online at www.npr.org. For a French perspective on the news, check out Radio France Internationale's (RFI) hourly newscasts in English at www.english.rfi.fr.

The following are some of the more popular French-language radio stations:

FIP (105.1MHz FM; www.radiofrance.fr) Eclectic mix of musical genres, with some news and cultural info.

France Info (105.5 MHz FM; www.france-info.com) A 24-hour all-news station.

France Inter (87.8 MHz FM; www.radiofrance.fr) France's main public radio station, specialising in news, various one-hour programmes (discussion of social issues, politics, food, arts criticism etc) and some music.

Radio Classique (101.1 MHz FM; www.radioclassique.fr) Classical.

Radio FG (98.2 MHz FM; www.radiofg.com) The station for house, techno, garage, trance, club news and gigs.

Radio Nova (101.5 MHz FM; www.novaplanet.com) Mix of world, hip-hop, electronic and alternative rock.

TSF (89.9 MHz FM; www.tsfjazz.com) Jazz.

RELOCATING

If you're considering moving to Paris and you are not a citizen of the EU, you must have both a *carte de séjour* (residence permit; p407) and an *autorisation de travail* (work permit; p409). Neither is easy to come by.

For practical information on living and working in Paris and France in general, pick up a copy of *Live and Work in France* by Victoria Pybus; *Living, Studying, and Working in France* by Saskia Reilly, or *Living and Working in France: A Survival Handbook* by David Hampshire.

The fortnightly *Fusac* (p400) is an excellent source for job-seekers.

SAFETY

In general, Paris is a safe city and random street assaults are rare. The so-called Ville Lumière (City of Light) is generally well lit, and there's no reason not to use the metro until it stops running at some time between 12.30am and just past 1am. As you'll notice, women *do* travel alone on the metro late at night in most areas, though not all who do so report feeling 100% comfortable.

Metro stations that are best avoided late at night include Châtelet–Les Halles and its seemingly endless corridors, Château Rouge in Montmartre, Gare du Nord, Strasbourg St-Denis, Réaumur Sébastopol and Montparnasse Bienvenüe. *Bornes d'alarme* (alarm boxes) are located in the centre of each metro/RER platform and in some station corridors.

Nonviolent crime such as pickpocketing and thefts from handbags and packs is a problem wherever there are crowds, especially packs of tourists. Places to be particularly careful include Montmartre (especially around Sacré Cœur); Pigalle; the areas around Forum des Halles and the Centre Pompidou; the Latin Quarter (especially the rectangle bounded by rue St-Jacques, bd St-Germain, bd St-Michel and quai St-Michel); below the Eiffel Tower; and anywhere on the metro during rush hour (particularly on line 4 and the western part of line 1). Take the usual precautions: don't carry more money than you need, and keep your credit cards, passport and other documents in a concealed pouch, a hotel safe or a safe-deposit box.

Vigipirate is a security plan devised by the Paris city council to combat terrorism. Both citizens and visitors are asked to report any abandoned luggage or package at all times. When the full Vigipirate scheme is put into action, public litter bins are sealed, left-luggage services in train stations and at airports are unavailable, checks at the entrances to public buildings and tourist sites are increased, and cloakrooms and lockers in museums and at monuments are closed.

TAXES & REFUNDS

France's value-added tax (VAT) is known as TVA *(taxe sur la valeur ajoutée)* and is 19.6% on most goods except medicine and books, for which it's 5.5%. Prices that include TVA are often marked TTC *(toutes taxes comprises; literally 'all taxes included')*.

If you're not an EU resident, you can get a TVA refund provided that: you're aged over 15; you'll be spending less than six months in France; you purchase goods worth at least €175 at a single shop on the same day (not more than 10 of the same item); the goods fit into your luggage; you are taking the goods out of France within three months after purchase; and the shop offers *vente en détaxe* (duty-free sales).

Present a passport at the time of purchase and ask for a *bordereau de vente à l'exportation* (export sales invoice) to be signed by the retailer and yourself. Most shops will refund less than the full amount (about 14%) to which you are entitled, in order to cover the time and expense involved in the refund procedure.

As you leave France or another EU country, have all three pages of the *bordereau* validated by the country's customs officials at the airport or at the border. Customs officials will take one sheet and hand you two. You must post one copy (the pink one) back to the shop and retain the other (green) sheet for your records in case there is any dispute. Once the shop where you made your purchase receives its stamped copy, it will send you a *virement* (fund transfer) in the form you have requested. Be prepared for a wait of up to three months.

If you're flying out of Orly or Roissy Charles de Gaulle, certain shops can arrange for you to receive your refund as you're leaving the country though you must complete the steps outlined above. You must make such arrangements at the time of purchase.

For more information contact the customs information centre (☎ 0 811 204 444; www.douane.minefi. gouv.fr; ⏲ 8.30am-6pm Mon-Fri).

TELEPHONE

There are no area codes in France – you always dial the 10-digit number. Telephone numbers in Paris always start with ☎ 01, unless the number is provided by an internet service provider (ISP), in which case it begins with ☎ 09. Mobile phones throughout France commence with either ☎ 06 or 07. France's country code is ☎ 33.

The domestic *service des renseignements* (directory enquiries or assistance) is now offered by over a dozen operators on six-digit numbers starting with ☎ 118 (France Télécom, for example, uses ☎ 118 712, Pages Jaunes uses ☎ 118 008). For a complete listing in French consult www.allo118.com. Expect to pay a minimum €1 per request. If you can read basic French, directory enquiries are best done via the Yellow Pages (www.pagesjaunes.fr; click on Pages Blanches for the White Pages), which will provide more information, including maps, for free. From a mobile phone, use the site http://mobile.pagesjaunes.fr.

Note that while numbers beginning with ☎ 0 800, 0 804, 0 805 and 0 809 are toll-free in France, other numbers beginning with '8' are not. For example (this list is by no means comprehensive), a number starting with ☎ 0 810 or 0 811 is charged at local rates (€0.078, then €0.028), one beginning with ☎ 0 820 or 0 821 costs €0.12 per minute, and if the prefix numbers are ☎ 0 890 it costs €0.15. The ubiquitous ☎ 0 892 numbers are billed at an expensive €0.45 per minute whenever you call. Numbers starting with ☎ 0 899 cost €1.35 per connection, then €0.34 per minute. Numbers beginning with ☎ 0 897 cost a flat €0.60 per call.

Most four-digit numbers starting with ☎ 10, 30 or 31 are free of charge.

To call abroad from Paris, dial France's international access code (☎ 00), the country code, the area code (usually without the initial '0', if there is one) and the local number. International Direct Dial (IDD) calls to almost anywhere in the world can be placed from public telephones. The international reduced rate applies from 7pm to 8am weekdays and all day at the weekend.

For international directory enquiries, dial ☎ 3212. Note that the cost for this service is €3 per call.

Mobile Phones

You can use your smartphone or mobile phone *(portable)* in France provided it is

GSM (the standard in Europe which is becoming increasingly common elsewhere) and tri-band or quad-band. It is a good idea to ensure it is 'unlocked', which means you can use another service provider while abroad. If you meet the requirements, you can check with your service provider about using it in France, but beware of calls being routed internationally, which can make a 'local' call very expensive indeed.

Rather than staying on your home network, it is usually more convenient to buy a local SIM card from a French provider such as Orange/France Telecom (☎ 1014, outside France +33 1 41 43 79 40; www.orange.fr, in French), which will give you a local phone number. A SIM card with €5 calling time (nine minutes) plus a €5 recharge card costs €15. Throw a phone into the deal and it costs €29. The company www.callineurope.com offers mobile phone packages for travellers to France and Europe.

For more time, buy a prepaid Mobicarte recharge card (€5 to €100) from *tabacs* (tobacconists), mobile phone outlets, supermarkets etc. Mobicartes from €25 upward offer extra talk time (€5 bonus for €25, €10 bonus for €35 etc). The biggest outlet is La Boutique Orange (Map p126; 16 place de la Madeleine, 8e; ☷ 10am-7pm Mon-Sat; Ⓜ Madeleine). Other major service providers include SFR (http://international-travellers.sfr.fr) and Bouygues (www.bouyguestelecom.fr).

Phonecards

Although mobile phones and Skype (www.skype.com) may have killed off the need for public phones, they do still exist. In France they are all phonecard-operated, but in an emergency you can use your credit card to call. All public phones can receive both domestic and international calls. If you want someone to call you back, just give them France's country code and the 10-digit number, usually written after the words 'Ici le…' or 'No d'appel' on the tariff sheet or on a little sign inside the phone box. Remind them to drop the '0' from the initial '01' of the number. When there's an incoming call, the words 'décrochez – appel arrive' (pick up receiver – incoming call) will appear in the LCD window.

Public telephones in Paris usually require a *télécarte* (phonecard; €7.50/15 for 50/120 calling units), which can be purchased at post offices, *tabacs*, supermarkets, SNCF ticket windows, metro stations and anywhere you see a blue sticker reading 'télécarte en vente ici' (phonecard for sale here).

You can buy prepaid phonecards in France such as Allomundo (www.allomundo.com, in French) that are up to 60% cheaper for calling abroad than the standard *télécarte*. They're usually available in denominations of up to €15 from *tabacs*, newsagents, phone shops and other sales points, especially in ethnic areas such as rue du Faubourg St-Denis (10e), Chinatown (13e) and Belleville (19e and 20e). In general they're valid for two months, but the ones offering the most minutes for the least euros can expire in just a week.

TIME

France uses the 24-hour clock in most cases, with the hours usually separated from the minutes by a lower-case 'h'. Thus, 15h30 is 3.30pm, 00h30 is 12.30am and so on.

France is on Central European Time, which is one hour ahead of (ie later than) GMT. During daylight-saving time, which runs from the last Sunday in March to the last Sunday in October, France is two hours ahead of GMT.

Without taking daylight-saving time into account, when it's noon in Paris it's 11pm in Auckland, 11am in London, 6am in New York, 3am in San Francisco and 9pm in Sydney.

TIPPING

French law requires that restaurant, café and hotel bills include a service charge (usually between 12% and 15%); for more information on tipping at restaurants and cafés, see p220. Taxi drivers expect small tips of between 5% and 10% of the fare, though the usual procedure is to round up to the nearest €1 regardless of the fare.

TOILETS

Public toilets in Paris are signposted *toilettes* or *WC*. The tan-coloured, self-cleaning cylindrical toilets you see on Parisian pavements are open 24 hours and are free of charge, though, of course, they never seem to be around when you need them. Look for the words *libre* ('available'; green-coloured) or *occupé* ('occupied'; red-coloured).

Café owners do not appreciate you using their facilities if you are not a paying customer; however, if you have young children they may make an exception (ask first!). When desperate, try a major department store or even a big hotel (fast-food chains often require door codes which are printed on a receipt). The best strategy is to remember to use the toilets before you leave any monument or museum. There are free public toilets in front of Notre Dame cathedral, near the Arc de Triomphe, east down the steps at Sacré Cœur, at the northwestern entrance to the Jardins des Tuileries and in some metro stations. Check out the wonderful art-nouveau public toilets, built in 1905, below place de la Madeleine, 8e (Map p126). In older cafés and bars, you may find a *toilette à la turque* (Turkish-style toilet), which is what the French call a squat toilet.

TOURIST INFORMATION

The main branch of the Paris Convention & Visitors Bureau (Office de Tourisme et de Congrès de Paris; Map p72; www.parisinfo.com; 25-27 rue des Pyramides, 1er; ☿ 9am-7pm Jun-Oct, 10am-7pm Mon-Sat & 11am-7pm Sun Nov-May; Ⓜ Pyramides) is about 500m northwest of the Louvre.

The bureau maintains a handful of centres elsewhere in Paris, most of which are listed here (telephone numbers and websites are the same as for the main office). There are also information desks at Charles de Gaulle airport, where you can pick up maps and brochures. For details of the area around Paris, check out Paris Île de France (www.nouveau-paris-ile-de-france.fr).

Anvers (Map p138; opposite 72 bd Rochechouart, 18e; ☿ 10am-6pm, closed Christmas Day, New Year's Day & May Day; Ⓜ Anvers)

Gare de l'Est (Map p140; place du 11 Novembre 1918, 10e; ☿ 8am-7pm Mon-Sat, closed Christmas Day, New Year's Day & May Day; Ⓜ Gare de l'Est) In the arrivals hall for TGV trains.

Gare de Lyon (Map p158; Hall d'Arrivée, 20 bd Diderot, 12e; ☿ 8am-6pm Mon-Sat; Ⓜ Gare de Lyon) In the arrivals hall for mainline trains.

Gare du Nord (Map p140; 18 rue de Dunkerque, 10e; ☿ 8am-6pm, closed Christmas Day, New Year's Day & May Day; Ⓜ Gare du Nord) Under the glass roof of the Île de France departure and arrival area at the eastern end of the station.

Syndicate d'Initiative de Montmartre (Map p138; ☎ 01 42 62 21 21; 21 place du Tertre, 18e; ☿ 10am-7pm; Ⓜ Abbesses) This locally run tourist office and shop is in Montmartre's most picturesque square and open year-round. It sells maps of Montmartre and organizes tours in July and August.

Information offices beyond central Paris include those at La Défense and St-Denis:

Espace Info-Défense (Map p175; ☎ 01 47 74 84 24; www.ladefense.fr, in French; 15 place de la Défense; ☿ 10am-6pm Sun-Fri, 10am-7pm Sat; Ⓜ La Défense–Grande Arche) La Défense's tourist office has reams of free information, including the useful *Discover La Défense* brochure and details on cultural activities.

Office de Tourisme de St-Denis Plaine Commune (Map p174; ☎ 01 55 87 08 70; www.saint-denis-tourisme.com, in French; 1 rue de la République; ☿ 9.30am-1pm & 2-6pm Mon-Sat, 10am-2pm Sun Oct-Mar, 9.30am-1pm & 2-6pm Mon-Sat, 10am-1pm & 2-4pm Sun Apr-Sep; Ⓜ Basilique de St-Denis) This helpful tourist office is 100m west of the basilica.

Blogs

If there's one country in Europe where blogging is a national pastime (so *that's* what they do outside their 35-hour work week!), it's France. The blogosphere is the underbelly of what French people are thinking right now, with everyone and everything from streets and metro stops to bands, bars and the president having their own blog. Two great blog rolls worth looking at for other blog ideas are Meg Zimbeck (http://megzimbeck.com) and Paris By Appointment Only (www.parisbao.com).

For clubbing, music and nightlife links see p294. For anything on politics, fashion, gossip and bags more in the capital (in English), try any of the following:

Adrian Moore (http://adrianmoore.blogspot.com) George V concierge by day, 'bad boy' food blogger when away.

Chocolate & Zucchini (http://chocolateandzucchini.com) Food-driven blog by a 30-year-old foodie called Clotilde from Montmartre.

Girls' Guide to Paris (www.girlsguidetoparis.com) Restaurants, spas, fashion, art and culture – and not just for girls.

My Little Paris (www.mylittleparis.com) A team of five Parisians in search of secret boutiques, inventive restaurants, hidden treasures and latest trends.

Paris by Mouth (www.parisbymouth.com) L(a)unched in mid-2010, this superb food and restaurant website is *le dernier cri* (the latest thing) in Paris.

Paris Daily Photo (www.parisdailyphoto.com) An image a day with detailed commentary from friendly Parisian Eric Tenin in the 9e arrondissement.

Paris Kitchen (www.thepariskitchen.com) Great blog on dining out in Paris – which also a happens to run the Paris Supper Club (p262).

Paris Wise (www.pariswise.com) New kid in town Christopher brings a lot more on architecture, art and history to the Parisian party.

Petite Brigitte (http://petitebrigitte.com) 'Inside Paris: Gossip, News, Fashion' with a savvy Parisian gal in St-Germain des Prés.

Secrets of Paris (www.secretsofparis.com) Great resource from Paris-based American travel writer Heather Stimmler-Hall, full of venue recommendations and lots of great bar/nightlife info.

TRAVELLERS WITH DISABILITIES

Paris is an ancient city and therefore not particularly well equipped for *les handicapés* (disabled people): kerb ramps are few and far between, older public facilities and bottom-end hotels usually lack lifts, and the metro, dating back more than a century, is mostly inaccessible for those in a wheelchair (*fauteuil roulant*). But efforts are being made and early in the new millennium the tourist office launched its 'Tourisme & Handicap' initiative in which museums, cultural attractions, hotels and restaurants that provided access or special assistance or facilities for those with physical, mental, visual and/or hearing disabilities would display a special logo at their entrances. For a list of the places qualifying, visit the tourist office's website (www.parisinfo.com) and click on 'Practical Paris'.

Information & Organisations

The SNCF has made many of its train carriages more accessible to people with disabilities. A traveller in a wheelchair can travel in both the TGV (*train à grande vitesse*; high-speed train) and in the 1st-class carriage with a 2nd-class ticket on mainline trains provided they make a reservation by phone or at a train station at least a few hours before departure. Details are available in the SNCF booklet *Le Mémento du Voyageur Handicapé* (Handicapped Traveller Summary) available at all train stations. For advice on planning your journey from station to station, contact the SNCF service Accès Plus (☎ 0 890 640 650; www.accessibilite.sncf.com, in French).

For information on accessibility on all forms of public transport in the Paris region, get a copy of the *Guide Practique à l'Usage des Personnes à Mobilité Réduite* (Practical Usage Guide for People with Reduced Mobility) from the Syndicate des Transports d'Île de France (☎ 0 810 646 464; www.stif-idf.fr). Its Info Mobi (www.infomobi.com, in French) is especially useful.

For information about what cultural venues in Paris are accessible to people with dis-

abilities, visit the website of Accès Culture (www.accesculture.org, in French).

Access in Paris, a 245-page guide to the French capital for the disabled, is available online from Access Project (www.accessinparis.org; 39 Bradley Gardens, West Ealing, London W13 8HE, UK).

The following organisations can provide information to disabled travellers:

Association des Paralysées de France (APF; ☎ 01 40 78 69 00; www.apf.asso.fr, in French; 17 bd Blanqui, 75013 Paris) Brochures on wheelchair access and accommodation throughout France, including Paris.

Groupement pour l'Insertion des Personnes Handicapées Physiques (GIHP; ☎ 01 43 95 66 36; www.gihpnational.org, in French; 32 rue de Paradis, 75010 Paris) Provides special vehicles outfitted for people in wheelchairs for use within the city.

Mobile en Ville (☎ 09 52 29 60 51; www.mobile-en-ville.asso.fr, in French; 8 rue des Mariniers, 75014 Paris) Association set up in 1998 by students and researchers with the aim of making independent travel within the city easier for people in wheelchairs.

VISAS

There are no entry requirements for nationals of EU countries. Citizens of Australia, the USA, Canada and New Zealand do not need visas to visit France for up to three months. Except for people from a handful of other European countries (including Switzerland), everyone, including citizens of South Africa, needs a so-called Schengen Visa, named after the Schengen Agreement that has abolished passport controls among 22 EU countries and has also been ratified by the non-EU governments of Iceland, Norway and Switzerland. A visa for any of these countries should be valid throughout the Schengen area, but it pays to double-check with the embassy or consulate of each country you intend to visit.

Visa fees depend on the current exchange rate, but transit and the various types of short-stay (up to 90 days) visas all cost €60, while a long-stay visa allowing stays of more than 90 days costs €99. You will need: your passport (valid for a period of three months beyond the date of your departure from France); a return ticket; proof of sufficient funds to support yourself; proof of prearranged accommodation; recent passport-sized photo; and the visa fee in cash payable in local currency. Check www.france.diplomatie.fr for the latest visa regulations and the closest French embassy to your current residence.

If all the forms are in order, your visa will usually be issued on the spot. You can also apply for a French visa after arriving in Europe – the fee is the same, but you may not have to produce a return ticket. If you enter France overland, your visa may not be checked at the border, but major problems can arise if the authorities discover that you don't have one later on (for example, at the airport as you leave the country).

Titre de Séjour

If you are issued a long-stay visa valid for six months or longer, you should apply for a *titre de séjour* (residence permit; also called a *carte de séjour*) after arrival in France. Students should *first* check with their school about the proper procedure. The website of the Préfecture de Police also has instructions for all possible situations: check www.prefecturedepolice.interieur.gouv.fr, then select Vos démarches/Ressortissants étrangers (the instructions are in French, though an English pdf is available for students by clicking on 'Médiathèque' on the page given above).

Those holding a passport from one of 31 European countries and seeking to take up residence in France no longer need to acquire a *titre de séjour;* their passport or national ID card is sufficient. Check the website given above to see which countries are included.

Foreigners with non-European passports should check the website of the Préfecture de Police or call ☎ 01 58 80 80 58.

Long-Stay & Student Visas

If you would like to work, study or stay in France for longer than three months, apply to the French embassy or consulate nearest to you for the appropriate *long séjour* (long-stay) visa. For details of au pair visas, which must be arranged *before* you leave home (unless you're an EU resident), see p410.

Unless you hold an EU passport or are married to a French national, it's extremely difficult to get a visa that will allow you to work in France. For any sort of long-stay visa, begin the paperwork in your home country several months before you plan to leave. Applications usually cannot be made in a third country nor can tourist visas be turned into student visas after you arrive in France. People with student visas can apply for permission to work part-time; enquire at your place of study.

Visa Extensions

Tourist visas *cannot* be extended except in emergencies (such as medical problems). If you have an urgent problem, you should call the Service Étranger (Foreigner Service) at the Préfecture de Police (☎ 01 58 80 80 58, 0 891 012 222) for guidance.

If you don't need a visa to visit France, you'll almost certainly qualify for another automatic three-month stay if you take the train to, say, Geneva or Brussels and then re-enter France. The fewer recent French entry stamps you have in your passport, the easier this is likely to be.

If you needed a visa the first time round, one way to extend your stay is to go to a French consulate in a neighbouring country and apply for another one there.

WOMEN TRAVELLERS

In 1923 French women obtained the right to – wait for it – open their own mail. The right to vote didn't come until 1945 during De Gaulle's short-lived postwar government, and a woman still needed her husband's permission to open a bank account or get a passport until 1964. It was in such an environment that Simone de Beauvoir wrote *Le Deuxième Sexe* (The Second Sex) in 1949.

Younger French women are quite outspoken and emancipated but self-confidence has yet to translate into equality in the workplace, where women are often passed over for senior and management positions in favour of their male colleagues. Women attract more unwanted attention than men, but female travellers need not walk around Paris in fear: people are rarely assaulted on the street. However, the French seem to have given relatively little thought to sexual harassment *(harcèlement sexuel)*, and many men still think that to stare suavely at a passing woman is to pay her a compliment.

Information & Organisations

France's women's movement flourished as in other countries in the late 1960s and early '70s, but by the mid-80s had become moribund. For reasons that have more to do with French society than anything else, few women's groups function as the kind of supportive social institutions that exist in English-speaking countries.

La Maison des Femmes de Paris (Map p158; ☎ 01 43 43 41 13; http://maisondesfemmes.free.fr, in French; 163 rue de Charenton, 12e; ⏰ office 11am-7pm Mon, Thu & Fri, 9am-

5pm Tue & Wed; **M** Reuilly Diderot) is a meeting place for women of all ages and nationalities, with events, workshops and exhibitions scheduled throughout the week.

A useful resource is the website of Paris Woman (www.pariswoman.com), which deals with news, issues and events affecting expat women in Paris.

France's national rape crisis hotline (☎ 0 800 059 595; ⏱ 10am-7pm Mon-Fri) can be reached toll-free from any telephone, without using a phonecard. It's run by a group called Collectif Féministe contre le Viol (CFCV; Feminist Collective Against Rape; www. cfcv.asso.fr, in French).

In an emergency, you can always call the police (☎ 17). Medical, psychological and legal services are available to people referred by the police at the Service Médico-Judiciaire (☎ 01 42 34 86 78; ⏱ 24hr) of the Hôtel Dieu (p398).

WORK

To work legally in France you need a *titre de séjour* (p408). Getting one is almost impossible if you aren't a citizen of the EU, unless you are a full-time student. Also, non-EU nationals cannot work legally unless they obtain an *autorisation de travail* (work permit) before arriving in France. This is no easy matter, as a prospective employer has to convince the authorities that there is no French person – or other EU national, for that matter – who can do the job being offered to you.

In addition to the fortnightly *Fusac* (p400), an excellent source for job-seekers, and http://paris.cragislist.org, the following agencies might be of some assistance.

Agence Nationale pour l'Emploi (ANPE; National Employment Agency; www.anpe.fr, in French), France's national employment service, has lists of job openings and branches throughout the city.

Centres d'Information et de Documentation Jeunesse (CIDJ; Youth Information & Documentation Centres; www.cidj. com, in French) offices have information on housing, professional training and educational options, and noticeboards with work possibilities. Its Paris headquarters (Map p168; ☎ 01 44 49 12 00, 0 825 090 630; 101 quai Branly, 15e; ⏱ 10am-6pm Mon-Wed & Fri, 1-6pm Thu, 9.30am-1pm Sat; **M** Champ de Mars–Tour Eiffel) is a short distance southwest of the Eiffel Tower.

Doing Business

If you are going to Paris on business, it's a good idea to contact one of the main commercial offices or your embassy's trade office in Paris before you leave home, to establish contacts and make appointments. These include the following:

American Chamber of Commerce (Map p126; ☎ 01 56 43 45 67; www.amchamfrance.org; 1st fl, 156 bd Haussmann, 75008 Paris; **M** Miromesnil)

Australian Trade Commission (Map p168; ☎ 01 40 59 34 63; www.austrade.gov.au; 4 rue Jean Rey, 75015 Paris; **M** Bir Hakeim)

Canadian Government Department of Commercial & Economic Affairs (Map p126; ☎ 01 44 43 29 00; www.amb-canada.fr; 35-37 av Montaigne, 75008 Paris; **M** Franklin D Roosevelt)

Chambre de Commerce et d'Industrie de Paris (CCIP; Map p76; ☎ 01 55 65 40 03, 0 820 012 112; www.ccip.fr, in French; Bourse de Commerce, 2 rue de Viarmes, 75001 Paris; **M** Les Halles)

France-Canada Chamber of Commerce (Map p108; ☎ 01 43 59 32 38; www.ccfc-france-canada.com, in French; 5 rue Constantine, 75007 Paris; **M** Invalides)

Franco-British Chamber of Commerce & Industry (Map p126; ☎ 01 53 30 81 30; www.francobritishchamber.com; 3rd fl, 31 rue Boissy d'Anglas, 75008 Paris; **M** Madeleine)

Irish Embassy Trade Office (Map p118; ☎ 01 44 17 67 04; www.embassyofirelandparis.com; 4 rue Rude, 75016 Paris; **M** Argentine)

New Zealand Embassy Trade Office (Map p118; ☎ 01 45 01 43 10; www.nzembassy.com/france; 7ter rue Léonard de Vinci, 75116 Paris; **M** Victor Hugo)

UK Embassy Trade Office (Map p126; ☎ 01 44 51 34 56; www.amb-grandebretagne.fr; 35 rue du Faubourg St-Honoré, 75008 Paris; **M** Concorde)

USA Embassy Trade Office (Map p126; ☎ 01 43 12 70 83; www.buyusa.gov/france/en; NEO Building, 14 bd Haussmann, 75009 Paris)

If you are looking to set up a business in France and need a temporary office or secretarial assistance, contact the following:

Copy-Top (www.copytop.com, in French; ⏱ 9am-7pm) This chain is useful for photocopying, printing etc, and has 26 outlets in central Paris, including a Bastille branch (Map p148; ☎ 01 48 05 80 84; 87 bd Voltaire, 11e; **M** Voltaire) and a Montparnasse branch (Map p168; ☎ 01 42 22 80 58; 52 bd du Montparnasse, 15e; **M** Montparnasse–Bienvenüe).

NewWorks (www.newworks.net, in French; ⏱ 9am-7pm) This *service bureau* chain can supply most of your office and secretarial needs and serve as your temporary office too. There are four outlets, including the Champs-Élysées branch (Map p126; ☎ 01 72 74 24 54; 10 rue du Colisée, 8e; **M** Franklin D Roosevelt).

Volunteering

Under what's called the au pair system, single people aged 18 to 27 can live with a French family and receive lodging, full board and some pocket money in exchange for taking care of the kids, babysitting, doing light housework and perhaps teaching English to the children. Most families prefer young women, but some positions are also available for men. Many families want au pairs who are native English speakers; knowing at least some French may be a prerequisite. For practical information, pick up the recently updated *Au Pair and Nanny's Guide to Working Abroad* by Susan Griffith and Sharon Legg and visit the website of the International Au Pair Association (www.iapa.org).

By law, au pairs must have one full day off a week. Some families may provide metro passes. The family must also pay for French social security, which covers about 70% of medical expenses (get supplementary insurance if you are not an EU citizen).

Residents of the EU can easily arrange for an au pair job after their arrival in France. Non-EU nationals who decide to look for au pair work after having entered the country cannot do so legally and won't be covered by the protections usually provided under French law.

Check the bulletin boards at the American Church (p400) and the classifieds in *Fusac* (p400) for job ads. In the latter, you'll find au pair work listed under 'Childcare'.

LANGUAGE

Whatever you may have heard about the French people and their reputation for arrogance when it comes to foreigners on their beat who don't speak their language, you'll find any attempt to communicate in French will be much appreciated. What is usually perceived as

arrogance is often just a subtle objection to the assumption by many travellers that they should be able to speak English anywhere, in any situation, and be understood. You can easily avoid the problem by approaching people and addressing them in French. Even if the only sentence you can muster is *Pardon, madame/monsieur, parlez-vous anglais?* (Excuse me, madam/sir, do you speak English?), you're sure to be more warmly received than if you stick blindly to English.

If you want to learn more French than we've included here, pick up a copy of Lonely Planet's comprehensive and user-friendly *French* phrasebook. Lonely Planet iPhone phrasebooks are available through the Apple App store.

Be Polite

Politeness pays dividends in Parisian daily life and the easiest way to make a good impression on Parisian merchants is always to say *Bonjour Monsieur/Madame/Mademoiselle* when you enter a shop, and *Merci Monsieur/Madame/Mademoiselle, au revoir* when you leave. *Monsieur* means 'sir' and can be used with any adult male. *Madame* is used where 'Mrs' or 'Ma'am' would apply in English. Officially, *Mademoiselle* (Miss) relates to unmarried women, but it's much more common to use *Madame*, unless of course you know the person's marital status! Similarly, if you want help or need to interrupt someone, approach them with *Excusez-moi, Monsieur/Madame/Mademoiselle*.

SOCIAL
Meeting People

Hello.
Bonjour./Salut. (polite/informal)
Goodbye.
Au revoir./Salut. (polite/informal)
Please.
S'il vous plaît.
Thank you (very much).
Merci (beaucoup).
Yes./No.
Oui./Non.
Do you speak English?
Parlez-vous anglais?
Do you understand (me)?
Est-ce que vous (me) comprenez?
Yes, I understand.
Oui, je comprends.

No, I don't understand.
Non, je ne comprends pas.

Could you please …?
Pourriez-vous …, s'il vous plaît?
  repeat that   répéter
  speak more   parler plus lentement
    slowly
  write it down   l'écrire

Going Out

What's on …?
Qu'est-ce qu'on joue …?
  locally   dans le coin
  this weekend   ce week-end
  today   aujourd'hui
  tonight   ce soir

Where are the …?
Où sont les …?
  clubs   clubs/boîtes
  gay venues   boîtes gaies
  places to eat   restaurants
  pubs   pubs

Is there a local entertainment guide?
Y a-t-il un programme des spectacles?
Where is the toilet?
Où sont les toilettes?

PRACTICAL
Question Words

Who?   Qui?
Which?   Quel/Quelle? (m/f)
When?   Quand?

Where?	Où?
How?	Comment?
How much?	Combien?
How many …?	Combien de …?

Numbers & Amounts

0	zéro
1	un
2	deux
3	trois
4	quatre
5	cinq
6	six
7	sept
8	huit
9	neuf
10	dix
11	onze
12	douze
13	treize
14	quatorze
15	quinze
16	seize
17	dix-sept
18	dix-huit
19	dix-neuf
20	vingt
21	vingt et un
22	vingt-deux
30	trente
40	quarante
50	cinquante
60	soixante
70	soixante-dix
80	quatre-vingts
90	quatre-vingt-dix
100	cent
1000	mille

Days

Monday	lundi
Tuesday	mardi
Wednesday	mercredi
Thursday	jeudi
Friday	vendredi
Saturday	samedi
Sunday	dimanche

Banking

I'd like to …
Je voudrais …
cash a cheque	encaisser un chèque
change money	changer de l'argent
change travellers cheques	changer des chèques de voyage

Where's the nearest …?
Où est … le plus prochain?
| ATM | le guichet automatique |
| foreign exchange office | le bureau de change |

Post

Where is the post office?
Où est le bureau de poste?

I want to send a …
Je voudrais envoyer …
letter	une lettre
parcel	un colis
postcard	une carte postale

I want to buy …
Je voudrais acheter …
an aerogram	un aérogramme
an envelope	une enveloppe
a stamp	un timbre

Phones & Mobiles

I want to buy a phone card.
Je voudrais acheter une carte téléphonique.
I want to make a call (to Australia/to Rome).
Je veux téléphoner (en Australie/à Rome).
I want to make a reverse-charge/collect call.
Je veux téléphoner avec préavis en PCV.
    ('PCV' is pronounced 'pay say vay')

Where can I find a/an …?
Où est-ce que je peux trouver …?
I'd like a/an …
Je voudrais …
adaptor plug	une prise multiple
charger for my phone	un chargeur pour mon portable
mobile/cell phone for hire	louer un portable
prepaid mobile/ cell phone	un portable pré-payé
SIM card for your network	une carte SIM pour le réseau

Internet

Where's the local internet cafe?
Où est le cybercafé du coin?

I'd like to …
Je voudrais …
| check my email | consulter mon courrier électronique |
| get online | me connecter à l'internet |

Transport

What time does the … leave?
À quelle heure part …?

bus	le bus
ferry	le bateau
plane	l'avion
train	le train

What time's the … bus?
Le … bus passe à quelle heure?

first	premier
last	dernier
next	prochain

Are you free? (taxi)
Vous êtes libre?
Please put the meter on.
Mettez le compteur, s'il vous plaît.
How much is it to …?
C'est combien pour aller à …?
Please take me to (this address).
Conduisez-moi à (cette adresse), s'il vous plaît.

FOOD

breakfast	le petit déjeuner
lunch	le déjeuner
dinner	le dîner
snack	un casse-croûte
eat	manger
drink	boire

Can you recommend a …
Est-ce que vous pouvez me conseiller un …

bar/pub	bar/pub
cafe	café
restaurant	un restaurant

A table for two, please.
Une table pour deux, s'il vous plaît.
Is service/cover charge included in the bill?
Le service est compris?
Do you have a menu in English?
Est-ce que vous avez la carte en anglais?
I'd like the set menu.
Je prends le menu.
I'd like the dish of the day.
Je voudrais avoir le plat du jour.
I'm a vegetarian.
Je suis végétarien/végétarienne. (m/f)
May I see the wine list?
Puis-je voir la carte des vins, s'il vous plaît?
I'd like a glass of red/white wine.
Je voudrais un verre de vin rouge/blanc, s'il vous plaît.

Cheers!
Santé! (pronounced 'son-tay')
The bill, please.
La note, s'il vous plaît.

I don't eat …
Je ne mange pas de …

meat	viande
fish	poisson
seafood	fruits de mer

For more information on food and dining out, see p214.

Food Glossary

MEAT, CHICKEN & POULTRY

agneau	lamb
bœuf	beef
brochette	kebab (on skewer)
canard	duck
charcuterie	cooked or prepared meats
côte	chop of pork, lamb or mutton
cuisses de grenouilles	frogs' legs
dinde	turkey
escargot	snail
foie	liver
foie gras de canard	duck liver pâté
jambon	ham
lapin	rabbit
lard	bacon
porc	pork
poulet	chicken
rognons	kidneys
saucisson	large sausage
veau	veal
viande	meat
volaille	poultry

ORDERING A STEAK

bleu	nearly raw
saignant	very rare (lit: 'bleeding')
à point	medium rare but still pink
bien cuit	lit: 'well cooked', but more like medium rare

FISH & SEAFOOD

anchois	anchovy
anguille	eel
calmar	squid
chaudrée	fish stew
coquille St-Jacques	scallop
crabe	crab
crevette grise	shrimp

crevette rose	prawn
fruits de mer	seafood
huître	oyster
langouste	crayfish
moules	mussels
poisson	fish
saumon	salmon
thon	tuna
truite	trout

VEGETABLES

ail	garlic
asperge	asparagus
betterave	beetroot
carotte	carrot
céleri	celery
champignon	mushroom
chou	cabbage
citrouille	pumpkin
concombre	cucumber
courgette	courgette (zucchini)
échalotte	shallot
épinards	spinach
haricots	beans
haricots verts	French (string) beans
laitue	lettuce
légumes	vegetables
lentilles	lentils
maïs	sweetcorn
oignon	onion
petit pois	peas
poireau	leek
poivron rouge/vert	red/green pepper
pomme de terre	potato
riz	rice
salade	salad or lettuce
tomate	tomato

FRUIT & NUTS

abricot	apricot
arachide	peanut
banane	banana
cacahuète	peanut
cassis	blackcurrant
cerise	cherry
citron	lemon
fraise	strawberry
framboise	raspberry
marron	chestnut
melon	melon
noisette	hazelnut
orange	orange
pamplemousse	grapefruit
pêche	peach
poire	pear
pomme	apple
prune	plum
raisin	grape

BASICS

beurre	butter
chocolat	chocolate
confiture	jam
crème fraîche	cream (naturally thickened)
farine	flour
huile	oil
miel	honey
œuf	egg
poivre	pepper
sel	salt
sucre	sugar
vinaigre	vinegar

DRINKS

au lait	with milk
avec sucre	with sugar
bière	beer
café	coffee
eau	water
eau minérale	mineral water
lait	milk
jus d'orange	orange juice
thé	tea
vin rouge/blanc	red/white wine

EMERGENCIES

It's an emergency!
C'est urgent!
Could you please help me/us?
Este-ce que vous pourriez m'aider/nous aider, s'il vous plaît?
Call the police/a doctor/an ambulance!
Appelez la police/un médecin/une ambulance!
Where's the police station?
Où est le commissariat (de police)?

HEALTH

Where's the nearest ...?
Où est ... le/la plus prochain/e? (m/f)

chemist (night)	la pharmacie (de nuit)
dentist	le dentiste
doctor	le médecin
hospital	l'hôpital (m)

I need a doctor (who speaks English).
J'ai besoin d'un médecin (qui parle anglais).

I have (a) ...
J'ai ...

diarrhoea	la diarrhée
fever	de la fièvre
headache	mal à la tête
pain	une douleur

GLOSSARY

(m) indicates masculine gender, (f) feminine gender, (pl) plural and (adj) adjective

accueil (m) – reception (eg at a hotel)

adjoint (m) – deputy mayor

alimentation générale (f) – grocery store

ancien régime (m) – 'old order'; France under the monarchy before the Revolution

apéritif (m) – a drink taken before dinner

arrondissement (m) – one of 20 administrative divisions in Paris; abbreviated on street signs as 1er (1st arrondissement), 2e or 2ème (2nd) etc

auberge (de jeunesse) (f) – (youth) hostel

avenue (f) – avenue (abbreviated av)

banlieues (f pl) – suburbs

belle époque (f) – 'beautiful age'; era of elegance and gaiety characterising fashionable Parisian life roughly from 1870 to 1914

bière à la pression (f) – draught/draft beer

bière (f) – beer

bière blonde (f) – lager

billet (m) – ticket

billeterie (f) – ticket office or window

biologique or bio (adj) – organic

boucherie (f) – butcher

boulangerie (f) – bakery

boules (f pl) – a game played with heavy metal balls on a sandy pitch; also called *pétanque*

brasserie (f) – 'brewery'; a restaurant that usually serves food all day long

brioche (f) – small roll or cake, sometimes made with nuts, currants or candied fruits

bureau de change (m) – currency exchange bureau

bureau des objets trouvés (m) – lost and found bureau, lost property office

cacher (adj) – kosher

café du quartier (m) – neighbourhood café

carnet (m) – a book of (usually) 10 bus, tram, metro or other tickets sold at a reduced rate

carrefour (m) – crossroads, intersection

carte (f) – card; menu; map

carte de séjour (f) – residence permit

cave (f) – (wine) cellar

chai (m) – wine storehouse

chambre (f) – room

chambre d'hôte (f) – private room, usually bed and breakfast

chanson française (f) – 'French song'; traditional musical genre where lyrics are paramount

chansonnier (m) – cabaret singer

charcuterie (f) – a variety of meat products that are cured, smoked or processed, including sausages, hams, pâtés and rillettes; shop selling these products

cimetière (m) – cemetery

consigne (f) – left luggage office

consigne manuelle (f) – left-luggage locker

correspondance (f) – linking tunnel or walkway, eg in the metro; rail or bus connection

cour (f) – courtyard

DAB (m) – distributeur automatique de billets; ATM

défendu – prohibited

dégustation (f) – tasting, sampling

demi (m) – half; 330mL glass of beer

département (m) – administrative division of France

dessert (m) – dessert

digestif (m) – 'digestive'; a drink served after a meal

eau (f) – water

eau-de-vie (f) – 'water of life'; any of a number of brandies made from fruits, berries or nuts

église (f) – church

embarcadère (m) – pier, jetty

entrée (f) – entrance; first course or starter

épicerie (f) – small grocery store

escalier (m) – stairway

espace (m) – space; outlet

exposition universelle (f) – world exhibition

fête (f) – festival; holiday

ficelle (f) – string; a thinner, crustier 200g version of the baguette not unlike a very thick breadstick

fin de siècle (adj) – 'end of the century'; characteristic of the last years of the 19th century and generally used to indicate decadence

forêt (f) – forest

formule (f) – similar to a *menu* but allows choice of whichever two of three courses you want (eg starter and main course or main course and dessert)

fromagerie (f) – cheese shop

funiculaire (m) – funicular railway

galerie (f) – gallery; covered shopping arcade (also called *passage*)

galette (f) – a pancake or flat pastry, with a variety of (usually savoury) fillings; see also *crêpe*

gare or gare SNCF (f) – railway station

gare routière (f) – bus station

gendarmerie (f) – police station; police force

grand magasin (m) – department store

grand projet (m) – huge, public edifice erected by a government or politician generally in a bid to immortalise themselves

Grands Boulevards (m pl) – 'Great Boulevards'; the eight contiguous broad thoroughfares that stretch from place de la Madeleine eastwards to the place de la République

halles (f pl) – covered food market

hameau (m) – hamlet

hammam (m) – steam room, Turkish bath

haute couture (f) – literally 'high sewing'; the creations of leading designers

haute cuisine (f) – 'high cuisine'; classic French cooking style typified by elaborately prepared multicourse meals

hors service – out of order
hôtel de ville (m) – city or town hall
hôtel particulier (m) – private mansion

interdit – prohibited
intra-muros – 'within the walls' (Latin); refers to central Paris

jardin (m) – garden
jardin botanique (m) – botanical garden
jeux d'eau (m pl) – fountain displays

kir (m) – white wine sweetened with a blackcurrant (or other) liqueur

laverie (f) – laundrette
laverie libre-service (f) – self-service laundrette
libre-service – self-service
lycée (m) – secondary school

mairie (f) – city or town hall
maison de la presse (f) – newsagent
marché (m) – market
marché aux puces (m) – flea market
marché couvert (m) – covered market
marché découvert (m) – open-air market
menu (m) – fixed-price meal with two or more courses; see *formule*
musée (m) – museum
musette (f) – accordion music

navette (f) – shuttle bus, train or boat
nocturne (f) – late night opening at a museum, department store etc

orangerie (f) – conservatory for growing citrus fruit

pain (m) – bread
palais de justice (m) – law courts
parc (m) – park
parvis (m) – square in front of a church or public building
passage (couvert) (m) – covered shopping arcade (also called *galerie*)
pastis (m) – an aniseed-flavoured aperitif mixed with water
pâté (m) – potted meat; a thickish paste, often of pork, cooked in a ceramic dish and served cold (similar to terrine)
pâtisserie (f) – cakes and pastries; shop selling these products
pelouse (f) – lawn
pétanque (f) – see *boules*
pied-noir (m) – 'black foot'; French colonial born in Algeria
place (f) – square or plaza
plan (m) – city map
plan du quartier (m) – map of nearby streets (hung on the wall near metro exits)
plat du jour (m) – daily special in a restaurant
point d'argent (m) – ATM
poissonnerie (f) – fishmonger, fish shop

pont (m) – bridge
port (m) – harbour, port
port de plaisance (m) – boat harbour or marina
porte (f) – door; gate in a city wall
poste (f) – post office
pourboire (m) – tip
préfecture (f) – prefecture; capital city of a *département*
produits biologique – organic food

quai (m) – quay
quartier (m) – quarter, district, neighbourhood

raï – a type of Algerian popular music
RATP – Régie Autonome des Transports Parisiens; Paris' public transport system
RER – Réseau Express Regional; Paris' suburban train network
résidence (f) – residence; hotel usually intended for long-term stays
rillettes (f pl) – shredded potted meat or fish
rive (f) – bank of a river
rond point (m) – roundabout
rue (f) – street or road

salle (f) – hall; room
salon de thé (m) – tearoom
séance (f) – performance or screening (film)
service des urgences (f) – casualty ward, emergency room
SNCF – Société Nationale de Chemins de Fer; France's national railway organisation
soldes (m pl) – sale, the sales
sonnette (f) – doorbell
sono mondiale (f) – world music
sortie (f) – exit
spectacle (m) – performance, play or theatrical show
square (m) – public garden
syndicat d'initiative (m) – tourist office

tabac (m) – tobacconist (which also sells bus tickets, phonecards etc)
tarif réduit (m) – reduced price (for students, seniors, children etc)
tartine (f) – a slice of bread with any topping or garnish
taxe de séjour (f) – municipal tourist tax
télécarte (f) – phonecard
TGV – train à grande vitesse; high-speed train
tour (f) – tower
tous les jours – every day (eg on timetables)
traiteur (m) – caterer, delicatessen

Vélib' (m) – communal bicycle rental scheme in Paris
vélo (m) – bicycle
version française or v.f. (m) – literally 'French version', a film dubbed in French
version originale or v.o. – literally 'original version', a nondubbed film in its original language with French subtitles
vin de table (m) – table wine
voie (f) – way; railway platform

BEHIND THE SCENES

THIS BOOK

This is the 8th edition of Paris, written by Steve Fallon, Nicola Williams and Chris Pitts. The 1st edition was researched and written by Daniel Robinson and Tony Wheeler. The 2nd, 3rd, 4th and 5th editions were updated by Steve Fallon. The 6th edition was updated by Steve Fallon and Annabel Hart and the 7th by Steve Fallon and Nicola Williams. This guidebook was commissioned in Lonely Planet's London office, and produced by the following:

Commissioning Editors Paula Hardy, Jo Potts

Coordinating Editors Laura Crawford, Chris Girdler

Coordinating Cartographers Anita Banh, Jennifer Johnston

Coordinating Layout Designer Jane Hart

Managing Editors Sasha Baskett, Annelies Mertens

Managing Cartographers Shahara Ahmed, Amanda Sierp, Julie Sheridan, Herman So

Managing Layout Designer Indra Kilfoyle

Assisting Editors Cathryn Game, Justin Flynn, Alison Ridgway, Martine Power, Angela Tinson, Branislava Vladisavljevic

Assisting Cartographers Valeska Cañas, Jolyon Philcox, Peter Shields, Xavier di Toro

Cover Research Pepi Bluck, lonelyplanetimages.com

Internal Image Research Aude Vauconsant, lonelyplanetimages.com

Thanks to Ryan Evans, Carol Jackson, Liz Heynes, Lisa Knights, Adrian Persoglia, Navin Sushil, Lyahna Spencer, Raphael Richards, Naomi Parker, Rebecca Skinner, Celia Wood

Cover photographs Detail of the Arc de Triomphe, Mattes RenA/Photolibrary (top); The Grande Pyramide at the Musée du Louvre entrance, John Lawrence/Getty (bottom).

© Pyramide du Louvre, arch. I.M. Pei, musée du Louvre

Internal photographs
All images are copyright of the photographer unless otherwise indicated. Many of the images in this guide are available for licensing from Lonely Planet Images: www.lonelyplanetimages.com.

THANKS
STEVE FALLON

A number of people helped me in the updating of my sections of *Paris* but first and foremost stands resident Brenda Turnnidge, whose knowledge of all things Parisian never ceases to amaze. Thanks, too, to Zahia Hafs, Olivier Cirendini, Caroline Guillemot, Daniel Meyers, Patricia Ribault and Chew Terrière for assistance, ideas, hospitality and/or a few laughs during what was a very cold, very snowy, very dark winter in the City of Light. And *merci bien* to my co-authors, Chris Pitts and in particular 'first-generation professional' Nicola Williams, both for tips and discoveries and for keeping to deadlines and word counts. Bravo. As always, I'd like to dedicate my share of *Paris* to my partner Michael Rothschild, a veritable walking *Larousse Gastronomique*.

CHRIS PITTS

First off, thanks to my family – American and French alike – for personally testing or recommending many of the places that made it into this guide. Thanks as well to friends, neighbours and colleagues in Paris who made their own

---

THE LONELY PLANET STORY

Fresh from an epic journey across Europe, Asia and Australia in 1972, Tony and Maureen Wheeler sat at their kitchen table stapling together notes. The first Lonely Planet guidebook, *Across Asia on the Cheap*, was born.

Travellers snapped up the guides. Inspired by their success, the Wheelers began publishing books to Southeast Asia, India and beyond. Demand was prodigious, and the Wheelers expanded the business rapidly to keep up. Over the years, Lonely Planet extended its coverage to every country and into the virtual world via lonelyplanet.com and the Thorn Tree message board.

As Lonely Planet became a globally loved brand, Tony and Maureen received several offers for the company. But it wasn't until 2007 that they found a partner whom they trusted to remain true to the company's principles of travelling widely, treading lightly and giving sustainably. In October of that year, BBC Worldwide acquired a 75% share in the company, pledging to uphold Lonely Planet's commitment to independent travel, trustworthy advice and editorial independence.

Today, Lonely Planet has offices in Melbourne, London and Oakland, with over 500 staff members and 300 authors. Tony and Maureen are still actively involved with Lonely Planet. They're travelling more often than ever, and they're devoting their spare time to charitable projects. And the company is still driven by the philosophy of *Across Asia on the Cheap*: 'All you've got to do is decide to go and the hardest part is over. So go!'

SEND US YOUR FEEDBACK

We love to hear from travellers – your comments keep us on our toes and help make our books better. Our well-travelled team reads every word on what you loved or loathed about this book. Although we cannot reply individually to postal submissions, we always guarantee that your feedback goes straight to the appropriate authors, in time for the next edition. Each person who sends us information is thanked in the next edition and the most useful submissions are rewarded with a free book.

To send us your updates – and find out about Lonely Planet events, newsletters and travel news – visit our award-winning website: lonelyplanet.com/contact.

Note: We may edit, reproduce and incorporate your comments in Lonely Planet products such as guidebooks, websites and digital products, so let us know if you don't want your comments reproduced or your name acknowledged. For a copy of our privacy policy visit lonelyplanet.com/privacy.

suggestions, and to co-authors Steve and Nicola for their excellent recommendations and insights. Most of all, thanks to Elliot, Céleste and Perrine for sharing the ups and downs and magical moments of everyday life in our home city.

NICOLA WILLIAMS

As always my chunk of *Paris* would not have been nearly as inspired without the insider wisdom of the very many, very busy Parisians I chatted with during my capital stay: internet entrepreneur Tariq Krim (www.jolicloud. com); Patricia Wells (www.patriciawells.com); Romée de Goriainoff (Experimental Cocktail Club); Jane Bertch (www. lacuisineparis.com); Laure Chouillou; Sophie Maisonnier *(un grand merci* for the best-ever scoop on Left Bank eating, drinking and dancing); and Alain Moreau. My coordinating author and font of Paris knowledge, Steve Fallon, was super-heroic to work with as usual. And then there's Matthias Luefkens, my treasure of a travel-mad husband who

explored Paris with three kids under 10 while I worked, and flagged not once. My chunk of this book is dedicated to them: Niko (8), Mischa (6) and Princess Kaya (4 months).

OUR READERS

Many thanks to the travellers who used the last edition and wrote to us with helpful hints, useful advice and interesting anecdotes:

Badong Abesamis, Paul Beach, Gero Berkemeier, Élisabeth Boileau, Andrew England, Shaina Fay, Richard Fung, James Green, Samia Guitoun, James Gurd, Roger Hart, Maria Holm, Ansh Jain, Alexia Kulterer, David Leaney, Sebastien Lochen, Sophie Masson, Nicolle McLeod, Joel Montague, Peter Orban, Niccolò Petrilli, Brian Phillips, Virginia Rosen, Andrew Rush, Patrick Sanders, Stefanie Schout, Alexander Slack, Suzie Sloan, Michael Stavy, John Van Bavel, Rebecca Wiles, Joann Woods

Notes

INDEX

See also separate
indexes for:

Arts	p423
Drinking	p424
Eating	p424
Gay & Lesbian Paris	p427
Nightlife	p427
Shopping	p428
Sights	p428
Sleeping	p430
Sports & Activities	p431
Top Picks	p431

13e arrondissement,
see Place d'Italie &
Chinatown
15e arrondissement,
see Montparnasse & 15e
16e arrondissement,
see Eiffel Tower & 16e
area
17e arrondissement,
see Montmartre, Pigalle
& 17e

A
absinthe 379
accommodation 324-51,
see also Sleeping *subindex*
Bastille & Gare de Lyon
347-9
Champs-Élysées &
Grands Boulevards
338-40
Eiffel Tower area &
16e 338
Gare du Nord & Canal
St-Martin 342-3
Île St-Louis & Île de la
Cité 330
Latin Quarter 330-3
Louvre & Les Halles
328-9
Marais & Ménilmontant
343-7

000 map pages
000 photographs

Montmartre, Pigalle &
17e 340-2
Montparnasse & 15e
349-51
Place d'Italie &
Chinatown 349
St-Germain & Invalides
333-8
activities 309-16, *see
also* Sports & Activities
subindex
aerial tours 400
air travel 383-4
airports 383-4
apartments 324-5, 326-7,
see also Sleeping *subindex*
Arc de Triomphe 124-5, **93**
architecture 55-62
arts 45-55, 293, *see
also* Arts *subindex*
ATMs 398-9
Auvers-sur-Oise 377-80
Av des Champs-Élysées 125

B
B&Bs 325-6, *see also*
Sleeping *subindex*
babysitters 392
bakeries 215
ballet 55
bars, *see* Drinking *subindex*
Basilique de St-Denis 173-4
Basilique du Sacré Cœur
132-3, **11**, **94**
Bastille & Gare de Lyon
156-62, **158-9**
accommodation 347-9
drinking 289-90
food 261-2
shopping 210-12
Bastille Day 19
bathrooms 405-6
Baudelaire, Charles 46-7
Beauvais 375-6
Belle, David 315
bicycle travel, *see* cycling
bistros 217, *see also* Eating
subindex
blogs 406-7
boat travel 385-6
tours 401
Bois de Boulogne 122

Bois de Vincennes 161
books 45-8
architecture 59
fiction 46
general nonfiction 46
history 40
bookshops, *see* Shopping
subindex
boules 313-14
bowling 313-14
brasseries 217, *see also* Eating *subindex*
bread 215
bureaux de change 399
bus travel 386-7
tours 401-2
business hours 192, 219-
20, 391, *see also inside
front cover*

C
cabaret 295-6
cafés 217-18, *see also* Eating, Drinking *subindexes*
Camus, Albert 48
Canal St-Martin 139, **140-1**
car travel 387
Catacombes 167, 170
Cathédrale de Notre Dame
de Paris 81, 83, **10**
Cathédrale Notre Dame
(Chartres) 371
cell phones 404-5
cemeteries, *see* Sights
subindex
Centre Pompidou 78-9, **10**
Cézanne, Paul 50
Champs-Élysées & Grands
Boulevards 124-31,
126-7
accommodation 338-40
drinking 283
food 240-4
shopping 201-3
chansons françaises 52,
304-5
Chantilly 366-70, **368**
charcuterie 216
Chartres 370-5, **372**
Château de Chantilly 366-7
Château de Fontainebleau
362

Château de Vaux-le-
Vicomte 366
Château de Versailles
356, **11**
cheese 215-16
children, travel with 391-2
accommodation 326
highlights 18
Chinatown, *see* Place
d'Italie & Chinatown
Chirac, Jacques 36-7
churches 402, *see also*
Sights *subindex*
cinema 53-4, 305-6
cinemas, *see* Arts *subindex*
Clichy & Gare St-Lazare
132-8, **136-7**
climate 16, 392-3
climate change 388
Clos Montmartre 179, **95**
clothes, *see* Shopping *index*
clubbing 296-9, *see also*
Nightlife *subindex*
comedy 299
consulates 395
costs 21
accommodation 327-8
discount cards 394
food 220
courses 393-4
credit cards 399
crêperies 218, *see also*
Eating *subindex*
Cubism 50
customs regulations
394
cycling 311-13
hire 312-13
self-service 384-5
Tour de France 19, 316
tours 400-1

D
Da Vinci Code, the 106
Dalí, Salvador 50, 135
dance 55, 305, *see also* Arts
subindex
dangers 403-4
de Beauvoir, Simone 43, 48
de Gaulle, Charles 33-4
Degas, Edgar 50
Deneuve, Catherine 43

disabilities, travellers with 407
discounts 295, 394
Disneyland Resort Paris 380-1
Domaine de Marie-Antoinette 357
drinking 276-92, 318-20, *see also* Drinking *subindex*
driving 387
Duchamp, Marcel 50
Dumas, Alexandre 46

E
Église St-Germain des Prés 105-6, **91**
Église St-Sulpice 106, **91**
Eiffel Tower 116-17, **2**
Eiffel Tower area & 16e 116-23, **118-19**
  accommodation 338
  food 238-40
electricity 394
embassies 395
emergencies 395, *see also inside front cover*
environmental issues 38-9
etiquette 214
Eurodisney 380-1
events 17-21
exchange rates, *see inside front cover*

F
fashion 41-3, *see also* Shopping *index*
  festivals 17
  haute-couture 41, 203
  vintage 211
Faubourg St-Germain 111
Faure-Brac, Philippe 241
Fauvism 50
festivals 17-21
film 53-4, 305-6
flats 324-5, 326-7
Flaubert, Gustave 46-7
Fontainebleau 362-6, **363**
food 214-74, **6-7**, *see also* Eating, Shopping *subindexes*
  bread 215
  business hours 219-20
  charcuterie 216
  cheese 215-16

cooking courses 393
costs 220
etiquette 214
markets 222
regional specialities 216-17
self-catering 220-1
street food 217
university canteens 219
vegetarian & vegan travellers 218, 264
venues 217-18, 219
football 315-16
Forêt de Fontainebleau 364
Foucan, Sébastien 315
freerunning 315
French Open 18, 316
French Revolution 28-9

G
Gainsbourg, Serge 52, 111
galleries, *see* Sights *subindex*
gardens, *see* Sights *subindex*
Gare de Lyon, *see* Bastille & Gare de Lyon
Gare du Nord & Canal St-Martin 139-44, **140-1**
  accommodation 342-3
  drinking 285-6
  eating 248-52
  shopping 204-5
Gare Montparnasse 170-1
Gaucheron, Eric 331
Gauguin, Paul 50
gay travellers 318-21, *see also* Gay & Lesbian *subindex*
Giverny 376-7
government 39-40
Grand Palais 129
Grande Arche de la Défense 177
Grande Pyramide 71, **5**
Grands Boulevards, *see* Champs-Élysées & Grands Boulevards
Guillaume, Bartabas 360
gyms 311

H
hammams 310-11
Harry's New York Bar 277
Haussmann, Baron Georges-Eugène 35

haute-couture 41, 203
Haynes, Jim 273
health spas 310-11
Hippodrome d'Auteuil 316
history 23-37
  belle époque 32
  books 40
  Carolingians 24
  contemporary 35-7
  Dreyfus Affair 32
  Fifth Republic 34-5
  Fourth Republic 34
  French Revolution 28-9
  Middle Ages 24-5
  Occupation 33-4
  Paris Commune 31
  Reformation 26-7
  Reign of Terror 29
  Renaissance 25-6
  Resistance 33-4
  Second Empire 31
  Third Republic 31
  WWI 32-3
  WWII 33-4
holidays 16, 396
homestays 325-6
horse racing 316
hospitals 398
hostels 325, *see also* Sleeping *subindex*
Hôtel de Ville 145-6
Hôtel des Invalides 111, 113-14
Hôtel du Nord 143
hotels 325, *see also* Sleeping *subindex*
Hugo, Victor 46

I
ice skating 313
Île de la Cité 81-97, 330, **82**
Île St-Louis 97, **82**
  accommodation 330
  food 226-7
  shopping 196-7
Impressionism 50
in-line skating 313
internet access 396
internet resources 21
  accommodation 324
  blogs 406-7
  flights 383
  gay & lesbian 321
Invalides, *see* St-Germain & Invalides

Islands, the, *see* Île de la Cite, Île St-Louis
itineraries 66-7, 125, 157, 172

J
Jardin des Plantes 98-9
Jardin des Tuileries 75-6, **86**
Jardin du Luxembourg 106-7, **90**
Jardin du Palais Royal 78
Joan of Arc 25
jogging 313

K
Kerouac, Jack 47, 187
Krim, Tariq 307

L
La Défense 175-7, **175**
  food 272-3
language 43-4, 411-16
  courses 393-4
Latin Quarter 98-104, 227-31, **101-2**
  accommodation 330-3
  drinking 279-80
  food 227
  shopping 197-8
  walking tour 187-9, **188**
laundry services 397
left luggage 390
legal matters 397
Les Halles, *see* Louvre & Les Halles
lesbian travellers 317, 318-21, *see also* Gay & Lesbian *subindex*
literature 45-8
live music 299-305
lost property 395-6
Louis XIV 27
Louis XVI 28-9
Louvre & Les Halles 70-80, **72-3**, **76**
  accommodation 328-9
  drinking 276-9
  food 221-6
  gay & lesbian 319
  shopping 192-6
Louvre Museum 70-1, 74

M
magazines 400
Manet, Édouard 50
maps 397

Marais & Ménilmontant 145-55, **148-9**
  accommodation 343-7
  drinking 286-9
  food 252-61
  gay & lesbian 319-20
  shopping 205-10
  walking tour 184-7, **185**
markets 222, *see also* Eating, Shopping, Sights *subindexes*
measures, *see inside front cover*
medical services 398
memorials, *see* Sights *subindex*
Ménilmontant, *see* Marais & Ménilmontant
metric conversions, *see inside front cover*
metro stations 103, **11**
metro travel 388
mobile phones 404-5
Molière 55
Mona Lisa 75
Monet, Claude 50, 77, 117
money 398-400
Montmartre, Pigalle & 17e 132-8, **134**
  accommodation 340-2
  drinking 284-5
  food 244-8
  shopping 203-4
  walking tour 178-80, **179**
Montparnasse & 15e 167-72, **168-9**
  accommodation 349-51
  food 270-2
  shopping 212
monuments, *see* Sights *subindex*
Mosquée de Paris 99
motorcycle travel 387
Moulin Rouge 295, **94**
Musée de l'Orangerie 77, **4**
Musée d'Orsay 107, 110, **5**
Musée du Louvre 70-1, 74
Musée Rodin 111, **5**
museums 51, 151, *see also* Sights *subindex*
music 51-3, 299-305

N
Napoleon, Bonaparte 29-30
newspapers 40, 400

nightlife 294-308, *see also* Nightlife *subindex*
Notre Dame 81-3, **10**

O
Odéon, *see* St-Germain & Invalides
opera 306-7
Opéra de Paris Bastille 157, **96**

P
Palais de Chaillot 117, 120
Palais Garnier 125, 128-9, **92**
Panthéon 99, 101, **8**
Parc Astérix 381
Parc de la Villette 139, 142
parkour 315
parks, *see* Sights *subindex*
pâtisseries 235, *see also* Eating *subindex*
Piaf, Édith 42, 304
Pigalle, *see* Montmartre, Pigalle & 17e
Place des Vosges 146, **87**
Place d'Italie & Chinatown 163-6, **164-5**
  accommodation 349
  food 268-70
  planning 16-22, 66-7
Pletzl 145, **152-3**
police 397
politics 39-40
Pont Neuf 97
postal services 402-3
Proust, Marcel 42, 47
pubs, *see* Drinking *subindex*

R
radio 40-1, 403
Reign of Terror 29
relocations 403
RER 388
responsible travel 21-2
restaurants 218, 219, *see also* Eating *subindex*
Right Bank Area **76**
river cruises 401
Rodin, Auguste 43, 111
Rousseau, Jean-Jacques 46
rugby 316

S
Sacré Cœur 132-3, **11**, **94**
safe travel 403-4
Salle du Jeu de Paume 360

Sarkozy, Nicolas 37
Sartre, Jean-Paul 43, 48
sculpture 51
Seine, the 130, **12**
Senlis 370
serviced apartments 324-5, *see also* Sleeping *subindex*
shopping 191-212, **8-9**, *see also* Shopping *subindex*
skating 313
spas 310, 311
sports 163, 309-16, *see also* Sports & Activities *subindex*
St-Denis 173-5, **174**
  food 274
St-Germain & Invalides 105-15, **108-9**
  accommodation 333-8
  drinking 281-3
  food 231-8
  shopping 198-201
street food 217
sustainable travel 21-2
swimming 314-15

T
taxes 192, 404
taxis 389-90
tearooms, *see* Drinking, Eating *subindexes*
telephone services 404-5
tennis 315, 316
theatre 55, 307-8, *see also* Arts *subindex*
time 405
tipping 220, 405
toilets 405-6
Tour de France 19, 316
tourist information 406-7
tours 400-2
  walking tours 178-89, 402
train travel 390
tram travel 390
travellers cheques 399-400
TV 41

U
university canteens 219

V
vacations 16, 396
Van Gogh, Vincent 50
Vaux-le-Vicomte 366
vegetarian & vegan travellers 218, 264, *see also* Eating *subindex*

Versailles 354-62, **358-9**
Villon, François 45
vintage clothes 211
visas 407-8
visual arts 48-51
Voltaire 42, 46
volunteering 410

W
walking tours 178-89, 402
weather 16, 392-3
weights, *see inside front cover*
wi-fi 396
wine bars, *see* Drinking, Eating *subindexes*
wine-tasting 278
women travellers 408-9
work 409-10

Y
yoga 315

Z
Zola, Émile 47

ARTS

CINEMAS

Cinéma des Cinéastes 305
Cinémathèque Française 305
La Pagode 305-6
Le Champo 306
MK2 Bibliothèque 306
UGC Ciné Cité la Défense 306

CLASSICAL MUSIC

Conservatoire National Supérieur de Musique et de Danse 301
Lucinaire 301
Salle Pleyel 301
Théâtre du Châtelet 301

COMEDY

Comédie Française 307-8
Point Virgule 299

DANCE

Le Regard du Cygne 305
Théâtre de la Ville 305

OPERA

Opéra Comique 307
Opéra de Paris Bastille 306
Palais Garnier 306, **92**

THEATRE

Comédie Française 307-8

DRINKING

BARS

3W Kafé 319
Au Petit Fer à Cheval 286
Au P'tit Garage 286
Au Rendez-Vous des Amis 284
Café Baroc 287
Café Charbon 287
Café Chéri(e) 285
Café La Fusée 277
Café La Palette 282
Chez Prune 285
Curio Parlor Cocktail Club 279
Delaville Café 285
Eagle Paris 319
Félicie 291
Iguana Café 289
La Caravane 286
La Chaise au Plafond 286
La Champmeslé 319
La Fourmi 284
La Liberté 289
La Perle 287
La Sardine 285-6
L'Alimentation Générale 287
L'Atmosphère 286
Le Café Noir 276
Le Cochon à l'Oreille 277
Le Cœur Fou 276-7
Le Cox 319
Le Crocodile 280
Le Jemmapes 285
Le Palais Bleu 376
Le Piano Vache 280
Le Pick-Clops 287
Le Quetzal 319
Le Sancerre 284
Le Tambour 277
Le Troisième Lieu 319
Le Vieux Chêne 280
Le Zéro de Conduite 281

000 map pages
000 photographs

Les Étages 287
Les Etages St-Germain 281, **9**
Les Funambules 289
Les Jacasses 319
Les Marronniers 320
Les Vents d'Anges 376
Les Vignes d'Auvers 379
L'Imprévu 277
L'Interface 320
Little Café 320
L'Urgence Bar 281
Lush Bar 284
Olympic Café 284
Open Café 320
Pop In 287
Prescription Cocktail Club 281
Sanz Sans 289
Sputnik 290
Taverne Henri IV 279
Troll Café 289
Wolf Bar 319

CAFÉS

Au Chat Noir 287
Au Général La Fayette 283
Au Rendez-Vous des Amis 284
Au Sauvignon 283
Café Baroc 287
Café Charbon 287
Café Chéri(e) 285
Café de Flore 281
Café de la Paix 379
Café Delmas 280
Café des Phares 287
Café du Musée Rodin 281
Café La Fusée 277
Café La Palette 282
Café Le Basile 281-2
Café Suédois 287-8
Café Thoumieux 282
Cave La Bourgogne 280
Chào Bà Café 284
Chez Prune 285
Delaville Café 285
Félicie 291
La Sardine 285-6
L'Apparement Café 288
L'Atmosphère 286
L'Autre Café 288
Le Café des Initiés 277
Le Cochon à l'Oreille 277
Le Pick-Clops 287
Le Progrès 284
Le Pure Café 289-90

Le Select 291
Le Tambour 277
Le Verre à Pied 280
Le Wepler 285
Les Deux Magots 282, **90**
Les Marronniers 320
Little Café 320
O P'tit Douai 284-5
Open Café 320
Pause Café 290
Troll Café 289

COCKTAIL BARS

Alcazar 282
Andy Walhoo 288
Buddha Bar 283
Cubana Café 291
Curio Parlor Cocktail Club 279
Harry's New York Bar 277-8
Ice Kube 285
Le China 290
Le Fumoir 278
Le Rosebud 291-2

PUBS

Café Oz 278
Cricketer 283
Frog & British Library 290-1
Le 10 282
Le Pub St-Hilaire 280
Le Violon Dingue 280
Lizard Lounge 288
O'Sullivan's 283
Pure Malt 288
Quiet Man 288
Stolly's Stone Bar 288

TEAROOMS

À Priori Thé 279
Angélina 279
Kilàli 282
La Charlotte en Île 279
Le Loir dans la Théière 288-9

WINE BARS

Au Limonaire 283
Au Sauvignon 283
Bar à Vins du Cinéma des Cinéastes 285
Cave la Bourgogne 280
Chai 33 290
Comptoir des Cannettes 283

La Cave de l'Os à Moëlle 292
La Tartine 289
Le Baron Rouge 290
Le Bistrot du Peintre 290
Le Café du Passage 290
Tandem 29

EATING

AFGHAN

Kootchi 230

AFRICAN

À La Banane Ivoirienne 266
Le Mono 247
Le Petit Dakar 257
Le Porokhane 259
Nouveau Paris-Dakar 242-3
Waly Fay 266

ALSATIAN

Chez Jenny 255
Mon Vieil Ami 226
Taverne Karlbrau 376

AMERICAN

Breakfast in America 260
Bugsy's 243
Joe Allen 224

ARGENTINIAN

Unico 262

AUVERGNE

L'Ambassade d'Auvergne 256

BASQUE

Au Bascou 254
Chez Gladines 269
La Plancha 267

BERBER

À La Grande Bleue 247

BISTROS

Au Goût Dujour 272
Bistrot Les Papilles 227
Bistrot Les Sans Culottes 266
Bistrot Paul Bert 264
Chartier 243
Chez Allard 233

Chez Janou 255
Chez Nénesse 254-5
Chez Paul 265
Chez René 228
Hôtel Amour 243
Jadis 270-1
L'Agrume 227-8
L'Arbre à Cannelle 225
L'Ardoise 223
L'Avant Goût 268-9
Le Baratin 253-4
Le Bistro de la Cathédrale 374
Le Chateaubriand 252
Le Clown Bar 256
Le Comptoir du Relais 233, **90**
Le Hangar 255
Le Mouton Noir 264
Le Petit Marché 254
Le Petit Pontoise 228
Le Pré Verre 229
Le Trumilou 257-8
L'Encrier 266
L'Épi d'Or 224
Les Galopins 265-6
Les Troubadours 225
L'Os à Moëlle 271
Willi's Wine Bar 223

BRASSERIES
Au Pied de Cochon 223-4
Bofinger 253
Brasserie Lipp 234
Brasserie Thoumieux 233
La Closerie des Lilas 270
La Coupole 270
L'Arbuci 234
Le Comptoir du Panthéon 230
Le Petit Zinc 233, **91**
Le Train Bleu 261
Le Vaudeville 224
Les Fous de l'Île 226
Les Grandes Marches 264
Terminus Nord 249

BRAZILIAN
Porta da Selva 225

BRETON
Breizh Café 259
Crêperie Bretonne Fleurie de l'Épouse du Marin 267
Le Phare St-Louis 361
Marche ou Crêpe 260

CAFÉS
À La Renaissance 265
Au Bon Coin 247-8
Bert's 239
Café de l'Industrie 266-7
Café Hugo 258
La Tête de Goinfre 247
Le Bastringue 251
Le Comptoir du Panthéon 230
Le Coquelicot 248
Le Flore en l'Île 227
Le Viaduc Café 265
Les Éditeurs 233-4
Patati Patata 267
Sisters' Café 361

CAMBODIAN
Le Cambodge 251

CHEESE
Fil 'O' Fromage 269

CHINESE
Happy Nouilles 260
La Chine Masséna 269
La Fleuve de Chine 269
Les Pâtes Vivantes 243
New Nioullaville 259
Tai Yien 260

CORSICAN
L'Alivi 254
Le Temple 254
Paris Main d'Or 265

CREOLE
Waly Fay 266

CRÊPES
Crêperie Pen-Ty 248
Marche ou Crêpe 260

CUBAN
El Paladar 257

DELICATESSENS
Breakfast in America 260
Da Rosa 236

FRENCH
58 Tour Eiffel 239
À la Cloche d'Or 244
À la Ferme 361

À la Renaissance 265
Au Bascou 254
Au Bon Coin 247-8
Au Goût Dujour 272
Au Pied de Cochon 223-4
Au Pied de Fouet 237
Au Trou Normand 258
Au Vieux Chêne 263
Auberge du Vieux Moulin 377
Auberge Nicolas Flamel 254
Auberge Ravoux 379
Aux Deux Canards 249
Aux Lyonnais 223
Aux Négociants 247
Aux Vins des Pyrénées 256
Bistrot de l'Oulette 252-3
Bistro des Dames 246
Bistrot du Sommelier 240
Bistrot Les Papilles 227
Bistrot Les Sans Culottes 266
Bistrot Paul Bert 264
Bofinger 253
Bouillon Racine 234, **89**
Brasserie Lipp 234
Brasserie Thoumieux 233
Breizh Café 259
Café Beaubourg 224
Café Burq 245
Café Constant 234
Café de L'Industrie 266-7
Café Hugo 258
Café Marly 223, **9**, **86**
Casa Olympe 241
Charlot, Roi des Coquillages 244
Chartier 243
Chez Allard 233
Chez Gladines 269
Chez Jacky 268
Chez Janou 255
Chez Jenny 255
Chez La Vieille 223
Chez Léna et Mimille 228-9
Chez Michel 249
Chez Nathalie 268
Chez Nénesse 254-5
Chez Papa 250
Chez Paul (11e) 265
Chez Paul (13e) 268
Chez Plumeau 245
Chez Ramulaud 263
Chez René 228
Chez Toinette 244
Comme Cochons 263

Comptoir de la Gastronomie 224
Crèmerie Restaurant Polidor 235-6
Crêperie Bretonne Fleurie de l'Épouse du Marin 267
Cul de Poule 246
Derrière 253
Drouant 221
Fil 'O' Fromage 269
Firmin le Barbier 239
Georget (Robert et Louise) 258
Hôtel du Nord 249
Jadis 270-1
Jambo 250
Jean 240
La Cabane à Huîtres 272
La Cagouille 271
La Cantine de Quentin 250
La Closerie des Lilas 270
La Coupole 270
La Gazzetta 262
La Marine 249-50
La Mascotte 244
La Muse Vin 263
La Partie de Campagne 267
La Salle à Manger 230
La Serpente 374
La Table des Gourmets 226
La Tête de Goinfre 247
La Tour d'Argent 227
L'Agrume 227-8
L'Alivi 254
L'Ambassade d'Auvergne 256
L'Aoc 228
L'Arbre à Cannelle 225
L'Arbuci 234
l'Ardoise 223
L'Astrance 238
L'Avant Goût 268-9
Le Baba Bourgeois 229
Le Baratin 253
Le Bastringue 251
Le Boudoir 241
Le Café Qui Parle 245
Le Chansonnier 250
Le Chateaubriand 252
Le Chéri-Bibi 245
Le Clown Bar 256
Le Comptoir du Relais 233
Le Coupe-Chou 228
Le Cristal de Sel 271-2
Le Cristal Room 238
Le Dôme 270
Le Dôme Bastille 253

Le Dôme du Marais 255
Le Flore en l'Île 227
Le Gai Moulin 318
Le Grand Colbert 223
Le Grand Véfour 221
Le Hangar 255
Le Hide 242
Le Mâchon d'Henri 236
Le Maquis 245
Le Miroir 244-5
Le Mouton Noir 264
Le Parc aux Cerfs 271
Le Persil Fleur 242
Le Petit Mâchon 223
Le Petit Marché 254
Le Petit Pontoise 228
Le Petit Rétro 239
Le Petit Zinc 233
Le Pré Verre 229
Le Refuge des Fondus 247
Le Relais Gascon 247
Le Repaire de Cartouche 253
Le Réveil du Xe 250
Le Roi du Pot au Feu 242
Le Salon d'Hélène 231
Le Square Trousseau 264
Le Tastevin 226
Le Temple 254
Le Temps des Cérises 269
Le Tire Bouchon 257
Le Train Bleu 261
Le Trumilou 257-8
Le Vaudeville 224
Le Véro Dodat 225
Le Verre Volé 250
Le Villaret 253
L'Ébauchoir 263
L'Écailler du Bistrot 262
L'Encrier 266
L'Entrepôt 272
L'Épi d'Or 224
Les Cocottes 234
Les Domaines Qui Montent 265
Les Éditeurs 233-4
Les Fous de l'Île 226
Les Galopins 265-6
Les Grandes Marches 264
Les Ombres 238
Les Pipos 229
Les Troubadours 225
L'Office 249
L'Os à Moëlle 271

000 map pages
000 photographs

L'Oulette 261
Makoto Aoki 241-2
Marche ou Crêpe 260
Moissonier 229
Mon Vieil Ami 226
Pain, Vin, Fromage 318
Paris Main d'Or 265
Restaurant Joël Boilleaut 379
Roger La Grenouille 236
Sensing 232
Terminus Nord 249
Willi's Wine Bar 223

FUSION
Café de l'Esplanade 232
KGB 232
L'Ave Maria 258
Market 240-1
Spoon 240
Toyo 232
Ze Kitchen Galerie 232-3

HUNGARIAN
Au Petit Budapest 246

ICE CREAM
Amorino 237-8
Berthillon 227, **88**
Pozzetto 260

INDIAN
Dishny 251
Krishna Bhavan 252
Passage Brady 251

INDONESIAN
Djakarta Bali 224

INTERNATIONAL
Café Beaubourg 224
Café de l'Homme 238
Curieux Spaghetti 257
L'Atelier de Joël Robuchon 231-2
Le Viaduc Café 265
Patati Patata 267
Restaurant du Palais Royal 221
Scoop 225

ITALIAN
Bistro Florentin 256
Casa Bini 232
Fiori 272

Il Duca 246
La Maffiosa di Termoli 248
La Passacaille 374
Le Cherche Midi 236
L'Enoteca 254
L'Épicerie 247
Les Amis de Messina 262-3
Les Cailloux 268
Michelangelo 245
Sardegna a Tavola 261-2
Swann et Vincent 266

JAPANESE
Chez Hanafousa 234
Higuma 226
Kaï 221
Kunitoraya 225
La Maison des Frigos 269-70
Ta Sushi 226
Taeko 259-60

JEWISH
Chez Marianne 259
La Boule Rouge 242
L'As de Felafel 260
Les Ailes 242

KOREAN
Chez Heang 267
Maison Marais 256-7
Rollifornia 361

LYONNAIS
Aux Lyonnais 223
Le Petit Mâchon 223
Moissonier 229

MARKETS
Marché Bastille 222
Marché Belleville 222
Marché Biologique Batignolles 222
Marché Biologique Brancusi 222
Marché Couvert Beauvau 222
Marché Couvert des Enfants Rouges 222
Marché Couvert St-Quentin 222
Marché Grenelle 222
Marché Maubert 222
Marché Monge 222
Marché Président Wilson 222

Marché Raspail 222
Marché St-Charles 222
Rue Cler 222
Rue Montorgueil 222
Rue Mouffetard 222

MEXICAN
La Perla 259

MOROCCAN
404 256
Mansouria 264

NORTH AFRICAN
404 256
À la Grande Bleue 247
La Mosquée de Paris 228
Le Souk 265
Mansouria 264
Merguez Factory 261

ORGANIC
Bioart 268
Jardin des Voluptés 251
Le Jardin des Pâtes 230
Supernature 243

OYSTER BARS
Huîterie Regis 236
La Cabane à Huîtres 272

PAKISTANI
Passage Brady 251
Punjab 374

PANASIAN
Asianwok 259

PÂTISSERIES
Boulangerie Bruno Solques 235
Boulangerie-Pâtisserie Stéphane Secco 235
Dalloyau 235
Gérard Mulot 235
La Chocolaterie 374
La Fougasse 235
La Pâtisserie des Rêves 235
Ladurée 235
Le Nôtre 235
Sacha Finkelsztajn 235
Stohrer 235

INDEX

PIZZERIAS
Fiori 272
La Briciola 260-1
La Maffiosa di Termoli 248
Pink Flamingo 251

ROMANIAN
Athanor 263

RUSSIAN
La Cantine Russe 239
La Gaieté Cosaque 246

SANDWICH BARS
Cojean 243
Cosi 237
Cuisine de Bar 237
La Grande Épicerie 236
Lina's 267

SARDINIAN
Sardegna a Tavola 261-2

SAVOIE
Le Refuge des Fondus 247

SEAFOOD
Charlot, Roi des Coquil-
    lages 244
Fish la Boissonnerie 236
La Cagouille 271
La Mascotte 244
Le Dôme 270
Le Dôme Bastille 253
L'Écailler du Bistrot 262

SENEGALESE
Le Petit Dakar 257
Le Porokhane 259
Nouveau Paris-Dakar 242-3

SOUTH AMERICAN
Machu Picchu 230
Porta da Selva 225
Unico 262

SOUTHWEST FRENCH
Bistrot de l'Oulette 252-3
Chez Papa 250
Le J'Go 242
Le Relais Gascon 247
L'Oulette 261

SPANISH
Agua Limón 266
Bellota Bellota 233
Caffé Boboli 257
La Paella 249
La Plancha 267
Les Caves St-Gilles 257

TEAROOMS
Aux Cérises de Lutèce 231
Chez Les Filles 237
La Jacobine 237
Mamie Gâteaux 237
Matteo et Paola 233
The Tea Caddy 230

THAI
Baan Boran 225
Isaan 248
Khun Akorn 263-4
Krung Thep 258
Madame Shawn 250
Mai Thai 256
Reuan Thai 258-9
Sawadee 271
Thai Classic 226
Villa Papillon 318

TIBETAN
Khatag 226
Tashi Delek 231

TOGOLESE
Le Mono 247

TURKISH
Istanbul 251

VEGETARIAN
Au Grain de Folie 248
Bob's Juice Bar 252
Grand Appétit 260
Joy in Food 248
Krishna Bhavan 252
Le Potager du Marais 255-6
Le Puits de Légumes 230
Paris Hanoi 267
Saveurs Végét'halles 225
Soya Cantine Bio 258
Supernature 243

VIETNAMESE
Dong Huong 260
Kim Anh 272
Le Foyer du Vietnam 231

WINE BARS
La Muse Vin 263
Le Réveil du Xe 250
Le Verre Volé 250
Les Domaines Qui Montent
    265
Les Pipos 229

WOK
La Grande Épicerie 236-7

GAY & LESBIAN PARIS
CLUBBING
Le Duplex 320
Le Tango 320
Raidd Bar 320

DRINKING
3W Kafé 319
Eagle Paris 319
La Champmeslé 319
Le Cox 319
Le Quetzal 319
Le Troisième Lieu 319
Les Jacasses 319
Les Marronniers 320
L'Interface 320
Little Café 320
Open Café 320
Wolf Bar 319

EATING
Le Gai Moulin 318
Pain, Vin, Fromage 318
Villa Papillon 318

HOTELS
Hôtel Central Marais 320

SHOPPING
Les Mots à la Bouche 318

NIGHTLIFE
CABARET
Crazy Horse 295
Le Lido de Paris 296
Moulin Rouge 295, **94**

CHANSONS
Au Lapin Agile 304
Le Vieux Belleville 304
Les Trois Baudets 305

CLUBBING
Folie's Pigalle 296
La Dame de Canton 296
La Scène Bastille 296
Le Balajo 296
Le Batofar 297
Le Divan du Monde 297
Le Djoon 297
Le Duplex 320
Le Nouveau Casino 297
Le Redlight 297
Le Rex Club 297
Le Tango 320
Le Wagg 298
Les Bains Douches 298
Peniche el Alamein
    298
Queen 298
Raidd Bar 320
Regine's 298
Showcase 298
Social Club 299

JAZZ & BLUES
Café Universel 301
Caveau de la Huchette
    301-2
Le Baiser Salé 302
Le Petit Journal St-Michel
    302
New Morning 302
Sunset/Sunside 302

ROCK, POP & INDIE
Alhambra 299
La Cigale 299-300
La Flèche d'Or 300
Le Bataclan 300
Le Motel 300
L'Élysée-Montmartre
    300
Les Disquaires 300
L'Olympia 300
Point Éphemère 300

WORLD MUSIC
Barrio Latino 302
Cabaret Sauvage 302
Cité de la Musique 302-3
Dancing la Coupole 303
La Chapelle des Lombards
    303
La Favela Chic 303
La Java 303
L'Attirail 303

L'Entrepôt 303
Satellit Café 303-4

SHOPPING
ART & ANTIQUES
Hapart 198
Hôtel Drouot 201
Ivoire 198

BOOKS & COMICS
Abbey Bookshop 197
Album (5e) 197
Album (12e) 210
Brentano's 193
I Love My Blender 205
Les Mots à la Bouche 318
Librairie de l'Hôtel de Sully 205
Librairie Gourmande 193
Librairie Le Moniteur 198
Librairie Ulysse 196
Red Wheelbarrow Bookstore 205
Shakespeare & Company 197, **89**
Taschen 198
Tea & Tattered Pages 198
Village Voice 198
Virgin Megastore 203
WH Smith 193

CLOTHING & ACCESSORIES
Abou d'Abi Bazar 206
Agnès B Femme 193
Alexandra Sojfer 199
Alternatives 206
André 193
Antoine 193-4
Antoine et Lili 204
APC 206
Barbara Bui 194
Bazar Éthic 204-5
Bonpoint 194
Colette 194
Ekivok 194
Eres 202
Erotokritos 206
Galerie François Rénier 199
Isabel Marant 210
Kabuki Femme 194

000 map pages
000 photographs

Kenzo 194
Kiliwatch 195
La Citadelle 204
L'Éclaireur 206
L'Habilleur 206
Lin et Cie 199
Liza Korn 205
Maje 205
Maria Luisa Femme 195
Marithé & François Girbaud 195
Première Pression Provence 210
Shine 207
Sic Amor 207
Sobral 196
Surface to Air 207

COSMETICS & PERFUME
Fragonard 205
Guerlain 202
L'Arbre à Beurre 212
L'Artisan Parfumeur 205
Séphora 202
Shu Uemura 198

DEPARTMENT STORES
Bazar de l'Hôtel de Ville 206
Galeries Lafayette 202, **88**
Le Bon Marché 199, **8**
Le Printemps 202
Merci 206
Tati 204

FLEA MARKETS
Marché aux Puces d'Aligre 210
Marché aux Puces de la Porte de Vanves 212
Marché aux Puces de St-Ouen 212

FOOD & DRINK
À l'Olivier 207
Cacao et Chocolat 199
Cave St-Sulpice 200
Chemins de Bretagne 210
Ets Lion 204
Fromagerie Alléosse 202
Hédiard 202
Huilerie J Leblanc et Fils 200
Julien Caviste 207
La Dernière Goutte 200

La Maison du Miel 203
La Petite Scierie 196
Lafayette Gourmet 202
L'Arbre à Beurre 212
Lavinia 195
Le Palais des Thés 207
Le Repaire de Bacchus 207
Legrand Filles & Fils 195
Les Caves Augé 203
Mariage Frères 207
Pâtisserie Sadaharu Aoki 200
Pierre Hermé 200
Place de la Madeleine 203
Produits des Monastères 207-8
Vert d'Absinthe 208

FOOD MARKETS
Marché Couvert des Enfants Rouges 222
Marché Maubert 222
Marché Monge 222
Rue Montorgueil 222

GAMES & HOBBIES
Album (5e) 197
Album (12e) 210
Au Plat d'Étain 200
Au Vieux Campeur 197
Boutique Obut 208
La Boutique du Créateur de Jeux 197
La Maison de l'Astronomie 208
La Maison de Poupée 200
La Maison du Cerf-Volant 210
Magie 197
Mini Paris 212
Play Factory 197-8
Puzzle Michèle Wilson 209
Rouge et Noir 200
Tumbleweed 210

GIFTS & SOUVENIRS
Atelier d'Autrefois 208
Boîtes à Musique Anna Joliet 195
Canicrèche 195
CSAO Boutique & Gallery 209
La Boutique des Inventions 209

La Charrue et les Étoiles 209
La Maison du Cerf-Volant 210
L'Agenda Moderne 209
L'Écritoire 196
Mélodies Graphiques 209

HOME & GARDEN
A Simon 196
Antoine et Lili 204
Astier de Villatte 196
Bains Plus 209
Bazar Éthic 204-5
Deyrolle 200
E Dehillerin 196
Fermob 212
Flamant Home Interiors 201
Kindal 204
La Maison du Hamac 209
Les Beaux Draps de Jeanine Cros 201
Vitra 212

JAPANESE
Kaï 221

MUSIC
Virgin Megastore 203

SHOPPING CENTRES
Carrousel du Louvre 193

TOYS
Bonton Bazar 201
Clair de Rêve 196-7
Le Petit Bazar 212
L'Ours du Marais 209
Tumbleweed 210

SIGHTS
AMUSEMENT PARKS
Disneyland Resort Paris 380
Parc Astérix 381

AQUARIUMS
Aquarium Tropical 162
Centre de la Mer 104
Cinéaqua 120

INDEX

CATHEDRALS & CHURCHES

Basilique de St-Denis 173-4
Basilique du Sacré Cœur 132-3, **11**, **94**
Cathédrale de Notre Dame de Paris 81, 83, **10**
Cathédrale St-Pierre 375
Chapelle Expiatoire 130
Chapelle Notre Dame de la Medaille Miraculeuse 106
Église de Ste-Marie Madeleine 129
Église Notre Dame de la Pentecôte 177
Église Notre Dame de l'Espérance 157
Église St-Étienne du Mont 104
Église St-Eustache 79
Église St-Germain des Prés 105-6, **91**
Église St-Germain L'Auxerrois 75
Église St-Sulpice 106, **91**

CEMETERIES

Cimetière de Montmartre 133, **95**
Cimetière du Montparnasse 170
Cimetière du Père Lachaise 155

CHÂTEAUX

Château de Chantilly 366-7
Château de Fontainebleau 362
Château de Vaux-le-Vicomte 366
Château de Versailles 356, **11**

CULTURAL CENTRES

Docks en Seine 166

EXHIBITION CENTRES

Cité des Sciences et de l'Industrie 142-3

FACTORIES

Manufacture des Gobelins 166

GALLERIES

Centre Pompidou 78-9, **10**
Fondation Cartier pour l'Art Contemporain 171
Fondation Dubuffet 107
Galerie-Musée Baccarat 121
Galeries Nationale 129
Grand Palais 129
Jeu de Paume 77
Le 104 144
Les Frigos 166
Louis Vuitton Espace Culturel 130-1
Maison Rouge 160
Musée de la Halle St-Pierre 135
Musée de l'Orangerie 77, **4**

MARKETS

Marché aux Fleurs 97

MEMORIALS

Flame of Liberty Memorial 122
Mémorial de la Shoah 151
Mémorial des Martyrs de la Déportation 97
Wall for Peace Memorial 117

MONUMENTS

Colonne de Juillet 156-7
La Conciergerie 83

MOSQUES

Mosquée de Paris 99

MUSEUMS

Bibliothèque Nationale de France 163
Cité de l'Architecture et du Patrimoine 117, 120
Cité Nationale de l'Histoire de l'Immigration 161-2
Dalí Espace Montmartre 135
Galerie-Musée Baccarat 121
Institut du Monde Arabe 99, **89**
La Pinacothèque 129
Louvre Museum 70-1, 74
Maison Européenne de la Photographie 151
Musée Atelier Zadkine 107
Musée Bourdelle 171-2
Musée Carnavalet 146
Musée Cernuschi 138
Musée Cognacq-Jay 147
Musée Dapper 121
Musée d'Art et d'Histoire 174-5
Musée d'Art et d'Histoire du Judaïsme 147, 150
Musée d'Art Moderne de la Ville de Paris 120
Musée Daubigny 378
Musée de la Chasse et de la Nature 147
Musée de la Contrefaçon 123
Musée de la Défense 177
Musée de la Franc-Maçonnerie 131
Musée de la Halle St-Pierre 135
Musée de la Magie 151, 154
Musée de la Marine 120
Musée de la Mode et du Textile 74-5
Musée de la Monnaie de Paris 107
Musée de la Poste 172
Musée de la Poupée 150
Musée de la Publicité 74
Musée de la Vie Romantique 133
Musée de l'Assistance Publique-Hôpitaux de Paris 104
Musée de l'Érotisme 135, 138
Musée de l'Éventail 144
Musée de l'Homme 120
Musée de l'Orangerie 77, **4**
Musée de Montmartre 133, 135
Musée Départemental de l'Oise 375
Musée des Arts Décoratifs 74
Musée des Arts et Métiers 147
Musée des Arts Forains 161
Musée des Égouts de Paris 115
Musée des Impressionnismes Giverny 377
Musée d'Orsay 107, 110, **5**
Musée du Fumeur 157
Musée du Louvre 70, 71-4
Musée du Montparnasse 172
Musée du Parfum 130
Musée du Quai Branly 117, **10**
Musée du Stylo et de l'Écriture 123
Musée du Vin 121
Musée Édith Piaf 155
Musée Ernest Hébert 110
Musée Galliera de la Mode de la Ville de Paris 121, **9**
Musée Grévin 131
Musée Guimet des Arts Asiatiques 120
Musée Jacquemart-André 133
Musée Maillol-Fondation Dina Vierny 111
Musée Marmottan-Monet 117
Musée National d'Histoire Naturelle 99
Musée National du Moyen Age 104
Musée National du Sport 163
Musée National Eugène Delacroix 111
Musée National Gustave Moreau 130
Musée Nissim de Camondo 133
Musée Pasteur 172
Musée Picasso 146-7
Musée Rodin 111, **5**
Palais de la Découverte 129-30
Paris Historique 151
Petit Palais 130

NOTABLE BUILDINGS & STRUCTURES

Arc de Triomphe 124-5, **93**
Arc de Triomphe du Carrousel 75
Archives Nationales 147
Arènes de Lutèce 104
Assemblée Nationale 114
Bourse de Commerce 80
Catacombes 167, 170
Cité de la Musique 143
Crypte Archéologique 83, 85
Eiffel Tower 116-17, **2**

Fondation Pierre Bergé-
  Yves Saint Laurent 121
Gare Montparnasse 170-1
Grande Arche de la Défense
  177
Grande Pyramide 71, **5**
Hôtel de Sully 146
Hôtel de Ville 145-6
Hôtel des Invalides 111,
  113-4
Louvre des Antiquaires 75
Maison de Claude Monet
  376
Maison de Van Gogh 377
Maison du Docteur Gachet
  377
Opéra de Paris Bastille
  157, **96**
Palais Garnier 125, 128-9,
  92
Palais Royal 78, **86**
Panthéon 99, 101, **11**
Pont Neuf 97
Porte St-Denis 144
Porte St-Martin 144
Ste-Chapelle 97, **88**
Viaduc des Arts 157, 60, **96**

PALACES
Palais de Chaillot 117, 120
Palais de la Porte Dorée
  161-2
Palais de Tokyo 120, **4**

**PARKS &
GARDENS**
Jardin des Plantes 98-9
Jardin des Tuileries 75-6,
  86
Jardin du Luxembourg
  106-7, **90**
Jardin du Palais Royal 78
Parc de Belleville 154
Parc de Bercy 160-1, **96**
Parc de la Villette 139, 142
Parc des Buttes-Chaumont
  143-4
Parc du Champ de Mars 117

**SPORTING
VENUES**
Stade de France 175

000 map pages
000 photographs

SQUARES
Place de la Bastille 156-7
Place de la Concorde
  129, **92**
Place de la Madeleine 129
Place des Vosges 146, **87**
Place du Tertre 133, **95**
Place Georges Pompidou
  79
Place Vendôme 77-8

TOWERS
Eiffel Tower 116-17, **2**
Tour Jean Sans Peur 80
Tour Montparnasse 171
Tour St-Jacques 80
Tours de Notre Dame 83

SLEEPING
B&BS
Alcôve & Agapes 326
B&B Paris 326
Fleurs de Soleil 326
Gentle Gourmet 338
Good Morning Paris 326

**BOUTIQUE
HOTELS**
BLC Design Hotel 347-8
Cadran Hôtel 336
Hôtel Beaumarchais 345
Hôtel Caron de
  Beaumarchais 344-5
Hôtel Danemark 337
Hôtel de la Paix 350
Hôtel des Académies et des
  Arts 334-5
Hôtel du Globe 336
Hôtel du Petit Moulin 343-4
Hôtel La Manufacture 349
Hôtel Le Placide 335
Hôtel Particulier
  Montmartre 340
Hôtel Sezz 338
Kube Hôtel 340-1
La Maison 350
La Villa 334
L'Apostrophe 335
Le Général Hôtel 344
Le Quartier Bastille Le
  Faubourg 348
Le Six 333
L'Hôtel 334
Mayet Hôtel 336
Select Hôtel 331

HOSTELS
Aloha Hostel 351
Auberge de Jeunesse
  (Chartres) 375
Auberge de Jeunesse Jules
  Ferry 347
BVJ Paris-Louvre 329
BVJ Paris-Quartier Latin
  329
Garden Hôtel 346
Hostel Blue Planet 349
Hotel Caulaincourt Square
  342
Le Village Hostel 342
Maison Internationale de la
  Jeunesse et des
  Étudiants 347
Oops 349
Plug-Inn Hostel 342
St Christopher's Inn 343
Woodstock Hostel 340
Young & Happy Hostel
  333

HOTELS
Austin's Arts et Métiers
  Hôtel 344
Best Western Le Grand
  Monarque 374
Castex Hôtel 344
Celtic Hôtel 350
Chenal Hôtel 376
Ermitage Hôtel 341
Familia Hôtel 332
Grand Hôtel de
  Champaigne 328
Grand Hôtel du Loiret 346
Grand Hôtel Lévèque 337
Grand Hôtel Malher 345
Hidden Hotel 339
Hostellerie du Nord 380
Hôtel Alison 340
Hôtel Amarante 339
Hôtel Amiral Fondary 350
Hôtel Amour 339
Hôtel Aurore Montmartre
  341
Hôtel Aviatic 335
Hôtel Bastille de Launay
  344
Hôtel Bonséjour
  Montmartre 342
Hôtel Britannique 328
Hôtel Candide 348
Hôtel Carladez Cambronne
  350

Hotel Caulaincourt Square
  342
Hôtel Central Marais 320
Hôtel Châtelet 375
Hôtel Chopin 340
Hôtel Croix de Malte 346-7
Hôtel d'Angleterre (Paris)
  334
Hôtel d'Angleterre
  (Versailles) 362
Hôtel Daval 348
Hôtel de Blois 350-1
Hôtel de Crillon 338
Hôtel de France 362
Hôtel de la Bretonnerie 344
Hôtel de la Herse d'Or 347
Hôtel de la Place des
  Vosges 346
Hôtel de l'Abbaye Saint
  Germain 334
Hôtel de Lille 329
Hôtel de Lutèce 330
Hôtel de Nesle 338
Hôtel de Nevers 346
Hôtel de Nice 345
Hôtel de Notre Dame
  Maître Albert 330-1
Hôtel de Sèvres 336-7
Hôtel de Sèze 339
Hôtel de Varenne 336
Hôtel de l'Espérance 332
Hôtel Delambre 350
Hôtel des 2 Continents 337
Hôtel des Arts 341
Hôtel des Grandes Écoles
  332
Hôtel des Marronniers
  335
Hôtel du 7e Art 345
Hôtel du Boeuf Couronné
  375
Hôtel du Champ-de-Mars
  337
Hôtel du Collège de France
  332
Hôtel du Cygne 376
Hôtel du Dragon 337
Hôtel du Levant 332
Hôtel du Lys 337
Hôtel du Nord 343
Hôtel du Palais 376
Hôtel du Printemps 348-9
Hôtel du Séjour Beaubourg
  346
Hôtel du Vieux Saule 344
Hôtel Eldorado 341-2
Hôtel Esmeralda 332

Hôtel Favart 329
Hôtel Garden St-Martin 343
Hôtel Henri IV 330
Hôtel Henri IV Rive Gauche 330
Hôtel Jardin le Bréa 336
Hôtel Jeanne d'Arc 345-6
Hôtel Jehan de Beauce 375
Hôtel Joyce 339
Hôtel La Demeure 349
Hôtel La Musardière 377
Hôtel La Sainte-Beuve 335
Hôtel La Vieille France 342-3
Hôtel Langlois 339
Hôtel Le Clément 336
Hôtel Le Clos Médicis 334
Hôtel Le Cosy 349
Hôtel Les Jardins du Marais 343
Hôtel Les Sans Culottes 349
Hôtel Lindbergh 336
Hôtel Lyon Mulhouse 345
Hôtel Meurice 328
Hôtel Minerve 331
Hôtel Monte Carlo 340
Hôtel Muguet 335-6
Hôtel Peletier Haussmann Opéra 340
Hôtel Pratic 346
Hôtel Regyn's Montmartre 341
Hôtel Relais St-Germain 333-4
Hôtel Résidence Henri IV 330
Hôtel Ritz Paris 328
Hôtel Rivoli 347
Hôtel Saintonge Marais 345
Hôtel Sévigné 346
Hôtel St-André des Arts 337-8
Hôtel St-Christophe 332
Hôtel St-Germain des Prés 334
Hôtel St-Jacques 331
Hôtel St-Louis 330
Hôtel St-Louis Marais 345
Hôtel St-Merry 329
Hôtel Thérèse 328
Hôtel Tiquetonne 329
Hôtel Verneuil 335

Hôtel Vivienne 329
Le Relais du Louvre 329
Mama Shelter 348
Mon Hôtel 338
New Orient Hôtel 341
Petit Palace Hôtel 351
Port Royal Hôtel 332-3
Relais Christine 333
République Hôtel 343
Royal Hôtel 362
Sibour Hôtel 343
Terrass Hôtel 341

PENSIONS
Pension Les Marronniers 327
Résidence Cardinal 327
Résidence des Palais 327

SERVICED APARTMENTS
Adagio City Aparthotel 325
Adagio Montmartre City Aparthotel 325
Apart'hotels Citadines 325
Résidence Le St-Germain 325

SPORTS & ACTIVITIES
BOWLING
Bowling Mouffetard 314
Le Bowling 314

CYCLING
Au Point Vélo Hollandais 313
Fat Tire Bike Tours 312
Freescoot 312-13
Gepetto & Vélos 312
Paris à Vélo, C'est Sympa! 312
Vélo Cito 312

GYMS
Club Med Gym 311
Espace St-Louis 311
Vit'halles Beaubourg 311

HAMMAMS
Hammam de la Mosquée de Paris 310
Hammam Medina 311
Les Bains du Marais 310-11

HORSE RACING
Hippodrome d'Auteuil 316

SKATING
Nomades 313
Patinoire de la Bibliothèque François Mitterand 313
Patinoire de l'Hôtel de Ville 313
Patinoire de Montparnasse 313
Patinoire Pailleron 313
Patinoire Sonja Henie 313

SPAS
Espace Joïya 310
Harnn & Thann 310
Spa Nuxe 311

SWIMMING
Forest Hill Aquaboulevard 314
Piscine de la Butte Aux Cailles 314
Piscine Joséphine Baker 314
Piscine Keller 314
Piscine Pontoise 314-15
Piscine Roger Le Gall 315

TOP PICKS
accommodation options 323
activities 309
art & sculpture museums 51
art to buy 199
arts, the 293
Asian restaurants 269
bakeries 215
bar-hopping 279
Bastille & Gare de Lyon 156
beyond Central Paris
books about architecture 59
books about history 40
books about Paris & the French 46

bookshops 196
boutique hotels 333
brunch options 271
budget hotels 342
café terraces 286
CDs 52
Champs-Élysées & Grands Boulevards 124
children, travelling with 18, 121
clubs 297
cocktails 282
dining with a view 246
drinking options 275
eating options 213
films set in Paris 54
first-timers to Paris 19
food on a budget 239
food streets 229
food to take home 201
free shows 295
Eiffel Tower area & 16e 116
Gare du Nord & Canal St-Martin 139
gay & lesbian Paris 317
gift ideas 195
historic hotels 339
Islands, the 81
late-night bites 255
Latin Quarter, the 98
live music bars 303
Louvre & Les Halles 70
Marais & Ménilmontant 145
Montmartre, Pigalle & 17e 132
Montparnasse & 15e 167
neighbourhoods 63
nightlife 293
parks & gardens 38
quirky events 20
quirky hotels 348
shopping streets 204
shopping strips 193
shopping tips 194
shops 191
sports 309
St-Germain & Invalides 105
tearooms 291
vegetarian & vegan restaurants 264
Versailles tips 357

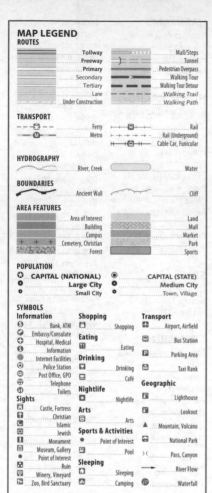

MAP LEGEND

ROUTES

Tollway	Mall/Steps
Freeway	Tunnel
Primary	Pedestrian Overpass
Secondary	Walking Tour
Tertiary	Walking Tour Detour
Lane	Walking Trail
Under Construction	Walking Path

TRANSPORT

Ferry	Rail
Metro	Rail (Underground)
	Cable Car, Funicular

HYDROGRAPHY

River, Creek	Water

BOUNDARIES

Ancient Wall	Cliff

AREA FEATURES

Area of Interest	Land
Building	Mall
Campus	Market
Cemetery, Christian	Park
Forest	Sports

POPULATION

○ CAPITAL (NATIONAL)	◉ CAPITAL (STATE)
● Large City	◎ Medium City
● Small City	○ Town, Village

SYMBOLS

Information
- Bank, ATM
- Embassy/Consulate
- Hospital, Medical
- Information
- Internet Facilities
- Police Station
- Post Office, GPO
- Telephone
- Toilets

Sights
- Castle, Fortress
- Christian
- Islamic
- Jewish
- Monument
- Museum, Gallery
- Point of Interest
- Ruin
- Winery, Vineyard
- Zoo, Bird Sanctuary

Shopping
- Shopping

Eating
- Eating

Drinking
- Drinking
- Café

Nightlife
- Nightlife

Arts
- Arts

Sports & Activities
- Point of Interest
- Pool

Sleeping
- Sleeping
- Camping

Transport
- Airport, Airfield
- Bus Station
- Parking Area
- Taxi Rank

Geographic
- Lighthouse
- Lookout
- Mountain, Volcano
- National Park
- Pass, Canyon
- River Flow
- Waterfall

Published by Lonely Planet Publications Pty Ltd
ABN 36 005 607 983

Australia (Head Office)
Locked Bag 1, Footscray, Victoria 3011,
☎03 8379 8000, fax 03 8379 8111,
talk2us@lonelyplanet.com.au

USA 150 Linden St, Oakland, CA 94607,
☎510 250 6400, toll free 800 275 8555,
fax 510 893 8572, info@lonelyplanet.com

UK 2nd fl, 186 City Rd, London, EC1V 2NT,
☎020 7106 2100, fax 020 7106 2101,
go@lonelyplanet.co.uk

Printed by Toppan Security Printing Pte. Ltd.
Printed in Singapore

MIX
Paper from
responsible sources
FSC™ C021741
www.fsc.org